The Legal Environment of Business

The Legal Environment of Business

SECOND EDITION

Douglas Whitman
University of Kansas

John William Gergacz
University of Kansas

Originally called
*The Legal and Social
Environment of Business*

RANDOM HOUSE
BUSINESS DIVISION
NEW YORK

To
Doyle Collins Whitman and Anna Mary Whitman;
John W. Gergacz and Ann K. Gergacz,
our parents,
and to Joan M. Gergacz

Second Edition

9876543

Copyright © 1985, 1988 by Random House, Inc.

Library of Congress Cataloging-in-Publication Data

Whitman, Douglas.
  The legal environment of business.

  Rev. ed. of: The legal and social environment of business. 1st ed. c1985.
  Includes bibliographies and index.
  1. Industrial laws and legislation—United States.
2. Trade regulation—United States. 3. Commercial law—United States. I. Gergacz, John William.
II. Whitman, Douglas. Legal and social environment of business. III. Title.
KF1600.W47 1988   346.73'07   87-16273
ISBN 0-394-36623-9   347.3067

Manufactured in the United States

Cover design: Katherine Urban

Preface

The Legal Environment of Business, Second Edition, integrates the teaching of law into the business school curriculum. For too long business law and legal environment courses have been limited to summarizing an enormous number of legal rules without providing the connection between the principles underlying those rules and *business*. The structure of those courses and texts has been more suited to review for a bar exam than for preparing the student for a professional career in business. Yet the law plays a very important role in providing an understanding of the business system and decision making.

Thus, when a student successfully completes the legal environment of business course, the law should be viewed as far more than an unconnected series of rules. The law should, in fact, be seen as providing the foundation for the operation of the economy and an executive's activities as a part of this economy. *The Legal Environment of Business* provides the student with this perspective and understanding. It also provides the background for further courses in business law, either elective or required, that can focus more precisely on other substantive areas (for example, business organizations, contracts, or commercial law). However, without "the big picture" that is provided by this text, such courses can be no more than an unconnected rehash of law school and not appropriate for future business executives, who will be hiring lawyers and who have very special legal educational needs.

Legal studies should be an exciting and dynamic experience, and we believe that this book preserves the excitement and tension that accompany great legal issues. Because tomorrow's business executives undoubtedly will be affected by such issues, today's business students should understand the scope and complexity of legal issues. To that end we have written the second edition of *The Legal Environment of Business*.

CHAPTER HIGHLIGHTS

To provide the necessary overview of the place of law in the world of business, *The Legal Environment of Business* divides the study of law into six general parts. Parts I and II serve as an introduction to the law and the legal system and are designed to provide some structural background to the balance of the material. The future business manager should appreciate the complexities of the legal system, which have a major effect on modern business decisions and on the economy. To help the student understand these complexities, Chapters 1–7 present the system's structure and its actors—judges, lawyers, and legislators—all of whom have as much to do with the law affecting business as do the legal rules developed throughout the text.

Part III focuses on the legal foundations of American business and is designed to illustrate the fundamental nature of law to all other areas of study in the business school. Those areas presume a system of property where rights are established, protected, and owned; they presume a system of contract law under which private transfers of those rights occur; they presume a system of tort law whereby costs imposed (injuries in tort) on innocent parties by business will be borne by that business. The chapters in this part do not dwell on every legal rule associated with those topics, although basic principles are discussed. Instead, the primary emphasis in Chapters 8–10 is on the development and purposes of the topics and the changes or trends that are occurring in them.

Part IV focuses on the legal aspects of the firm and its regulation. This section has two purposes: first, to provide the student with an understanding of the various ways the law permits businesses to be organized and the legal implications of being a part of a certain legal organizational structure (Chapter 11); second, to provide the student with a study in how law acts to regulate organizational power in the capital markets (federal securities law, Chapter 12) and in the competitive environment (antitrust, Chapters 13–15). Additional materials highlight regulation through the criminal process (Chapter 16) and through nonlegal means, such as ethics (Chapter 17). Chapter 17, "Ethics and Business: Extra-Legal Controls on Business and Business Decision Making," presents a unique analytical method for reviewing business problems in a socially responsible manner and amply fulfills the AACSB requirements in this important area.

Part V focuses on the law's regulation of certain types of business activity from liability for the products it sells (Chapter 18), to liability of business to consumers (Chapter 19), to its relationship with its employees (Chapters 20–22) to its effect on the natural environment (Chapter 23). These chapters are illustrative of the explosion of government controls of business that have arisen in the last twenty-five years.

Part VI focuses on international regulation of business activity and is designed to expand the student's legal horizon to match the world in which business must operate. All business today is affected by international competition and international markets for its goods. Consequently, business is also affected by international law; Chapter 24 provides an introduction to this complex area. We urge the student to seek elective courses that can more fully develop the legal environment of international business activity.

FEATURES OF THE SECOND EDITION

Considerable thought was given to the most important legal topics for people in business today. All of the chapters were revised extensively to ensure that this text deals with these issues and is up to date. In order to have the most complete coverage, we decided to include separate chapters on business organizations, federal securities law, products liability, consumer law, and international law. Furthermore, certain new topics were added to the current chapters, such as alternative dispute resolution and the RICO Act.

The second edition expands the number of end-of-chapter review questions. We have attempted to write questions that are genuine *review* questions. All of the end-of-chapter problems can be answered by any student who has read the material. Using these questions is an excellent way to illustrate many of the important points brought out in each chapter.

We also added several "boxes" to each chapter. These boxes are drawn from current business events and relate to the information discussed in the chapters.

A great deal of time was spent selecting case material for this text. We have chosen what we consider to be the most interesting, readable, and pertinent cases—both classic and more recent—to illustrate the various points of law. They have been edited to a manageable length, but in such a way that the language, context, tone, and meaning of the original case are retained. To enhance readability, cases are clearly distinguished from text material and introduced by the fact of the case in a section separate from a judge's opinion.

A list of cases and an extensive glossary of key legal terms are included. In addition, the appendixes afford the student easy access to the following important information: the Constitution; Warranty Provisions of the Uniform Commercial Code and Unconscionability; Restatement of Torts, Second; National Labor Relations Act; the Sherman Act; and the Clayton Act.

We have prepared an instructor's resource package that contains a wealth of source material. Both the Instructor's Manual and the Test Bank were written entirely by us. For the student, a Study Guide has been prepared by Susan E. Grady, University of Massachusetts, Amherst.

ACKNOWLEDGMENTS

Many individuals helped us prepare *The Legal Environment of Business*. We would like to acknowledge the work of our research assistants who ably performed the many tasks we assigned to them. A special note of appreciation should go to Traci Hicks and Ron Powell for their first-rate work throughout the preparation of this second edition.

We are also grateful to the following reviewers who generously offered numerous suggestions that improved the manuscript in each successive draft: Anita Cava, University of Miami; Benson Diamond, Suffolk University; Mary Jane Dundas, Arizona State University; James Hill, Central Michigan University; Clay Hipp, Clemson University; Michael E. Howard, University of Iowa; Nancy Reeves Mansfield, Georgia State University; Margaret M. Noteman, University of North Carolina at Greensboro; Mark M. Phelps, University of Oregon; Kent Royalty, St. Mary's University, San Antonio, Texas; Linda B. Samuels, George Mason University; and Wayne Wells, St. Cloud State University.

Finally, we would like to thank our colleagues at Random House for assisting us in the preparation of the second edition. Their counsel and encouragement tempered some of the more difficult tasks that we faced: Susan Badger, acquisitions editor; Dan Alpert, developmental editor; Holly Gordon, project editor; Lisa Mitchell, assistant editor; and June Smith, executive editor of the business division.

Douglas Whitman
John William Gergacz

Contents in Brief

Contents in Detail

List of Legal Cases

PART I

Introduction to Law and Business

 Introduction to the Law and the Legal Environment of Business

Law in Business and Society
Recurring Themes in the Study of the American Legal Environment of Business
Historical and Social Movements and the Development of Law: From Slavery to Employment Discrimination
The Law and Its Efforts to Control Concentrations of Power
The Law As a Means of Adjusting Claims of Rights

The study of law is the study of a people, a civilization, as it has existed and as it currently exists. As a discipline, the law embodies the history, values, and culture of a society. It is a series of concepts and rules that shifts to meet social changes. The productive activity of a society—its business practice—is one of the major facets of this study. The legal environment of business, therefore, involves the legal system, its principal actors, and the major substantive rules of law that influence economic activity.

Legal rules and institutions exist and have evolved throughout American history. Thus, the reader of this text will find numerous references to historical developments that led to today's legal rules. Trends in the legal environment will also be explored; that is, how today's social issues and culture interact to reshape the configuration of current legal doctrine. Tomorrow's business executive must be aware of the changeable nature of the legal environment and the forces that lead to that change.

But law is neither magical nor mysterious. It is merely rules of conduct and relationships that are formally recognized by a government. These rules, however, are not necessarily just, nor are they necessarily designed for the good of the people. Law existed in ancient Greece, in Elizabethan England, and in Nazi Germany. In each of those societies there was a body of rules called law that regulated conduct and relationships among people. The existence of law does not ensure that a just society will also exist. As Grant Gilmore, the prominent legal scholar, wrote, "The better the society, the less law there will be. In Heaven there will be no law, and the lion will lie down with the lamb. The values of an unjust society will reflect themselves in an unjust law. The worse the society, the more law there will be. In Hell there will be nothing but law, and due process will be meticulously observed."[1]

LAW IN BUSINESS AND SOCIETY

Law and business are inextricably intertwined. Business is the organization of capital and labor to produce a product or service with every aspect of that organization regulated by law. Buying and selling, employment practices, and even the nature of the business organization itself are examples of business activity controlled by law. Therefore, any business decision has a legal component, and the prudent business manager should take care to consider it.

However, it is folly to presume that the business manager will be an authority on law, able to evaluate the legal rules and determine their influence on the problem at hand. Such a task is best left to lawyers. Business managers instead must understand law in the general sense. They must appreciate the nature of the legal environment in which their businesses operate. The law, as distinguished from legal rules, needs to be understood as managers understand other people—what motivates them, angers them, pleases them—without becoming authorities in anthropology, sociology, or psychology.

Limits of Law

A law cannot make a person just, sober, or ethical. It cannot make people love their neighbors, nor can it make a business prosper. Many desirable goals cannot be achieved through law. Other social institutions—the family, church, and community—have major roles to play in the makeup of society.

Law provides minimum rules of conduct that society will sanction. Those rules must possess several general characteristics to be effective: predictability, flexibility, and reasonable application and coverage. If any of the characteristics is missing, then often the rule will have an inconsequential effect without excessive law enforcement efforts. In a free society, such an occurrence is intolerable.

Predictability. One must be able to predict with some accuracy the legal effect of future conduct. Otherwise no activity would ever be legally safe. However, predictability does not necessarily mean certainty. That snow will fall in Vermont during December and that the Chicago Cubs will not win the pennant are predictions of future events that are reasonably assured to occur. However, warm New England Decembers have happened.

Similarly, when a corporation sells its redesigned personal computer, hires new employees, or raises additional capital, legal issues arise. These common business activities would be impossible to complete if executives could not rely on a body of law for predictable resolutions, even though absolute certainty is impossible. Thus, those governed by a legal rule must be able to anticipate its application.

Flexibility. Most law was developed by people who are no longer alive. Those lawmakers had few of the experiences of modern society. Many never saw an automobile or an airplane. Many never watched television or used computers. Yet the rules of law (for example, the United States Constitution) are applicable and relevant to new situations that have occurred in modern life. They can grow and develop to reflect changes in society around them. So, while an effective law in our system must have a predictable outcome in its application, it must also be flexible enough to meet changing conditions.

Reasonable Application and Coverage. Law must be reasonable both in its application and in its subject. In order to have reasonable application, those affected by the law must have the opportunity to know its requirements. This concept is contained in the due process guarantee in the Constitution and is meant to prevent secret laws from being applied. However, it does not mean that a person who does not know what the law is at a given time need not be concerned with its application. The old maxim, "Ignorance of the law is no excuse," does have applicability. No one, lawyer or nonlawyer, knows all the law. What the requirement means is that all people will have access to the laws and to legal advisors to assist them in conforming their conduct to existing standards.

An example of a legal system without the protection of reasonable application was described in *The Trial* by Franz Kafka. In the novel, K awoke one morning to find that he was placed under arrest for a crime that he did not know he had committed. In fact he never knew what law he had allegedly violated. He was to be tried in a court that had no known procedures, and he had no known way of defending himself. The novel offers a frightening example of a system of laws that is not reasonable in its application.

The subject of the law's regulation must also be reasonable. Our system presumes that people will voluntarily obey the laws because laws that reflect the norms of society will be considered reasonable and will readily be obeyed by most people. However, laws that a large number of people find to be unreasonable will soon become unenforceable. The best example of this phenomenon in this country was Prohibition in the 1920s. The temperance movement was not strong enough to convince Americans to voluntarily stop drinking. So its leaders, through lobbying and political pressure, had the law forbid people to drink liquor. The result was over a decade of growth of organized crime as criminals happily supplied illegal liquor. People's respect for the rule of law was seriously harmed, and corruption was common. Ironically, people did not drink less. Unless we are willing to change our form of government, unreasonable or unpopular laws will not be effective in our society.

RECURRING THEMES IN THE STUDY OF THE AMERICAN LEGAL ENVIRONMENT OF BUSINESS

Rules of law, the workings of institutions, current legal issues, and past conflicts raise and restate over and over what might be characterized as *themes*. Beethoven used the four-note theme that opened his Fifth Symphony as a pattern around which the masterpiece was woven. Similarly, the rules and current disputes in today's legal environment of business are woven around three themes to be discussed in the balance of the chapter and illustrated by materials in this text.

First, the development of legal rules and institutions is closely associated with historical and social movements. For example, an understanding of such complex regulatory areas as antitrust and labor relations is enhanced by an appreciation of the historical movements that led to their creation. As an introduction to this theme, a focused study of the civil rights movement will be made in this chapter. In Chapter 22, current manifestations of this movement will be explored under the topic of employment discrimination.

A second recurring theme is that the law seeks to control concentrations of power. The risk the law tries to avoid is that those who have power will abuse it to the detriment of others. At first, the concern was concentration of power in government. A study of the constitutional structure of this country is a study of the decision to diffuse the massive power any government will have. Recently, concern has developed about concentrations of power in private hands, in corporations, which are beyond the diffusion of power commands of the Constitution. Therefore, the law will also be seen throughout this text as a means of limiting concentrations and abuses of corporate power.

The final theme in the legal environment of American business involves the concept of legal rights. The law recognizes and adjusts claims of individual rights within a society. At times, important rights conflict and the law must act to balance them. Yet the suggestion that individual rights may be controlled raises the problem of that control's causing a lack of such rights in practice. The tension in the law between protecting individual rights and allowing some control over their exercise is one of the recurring American legal problems.

HISTORICAL AND SOCIAL MOVEMENTS AND THE DEVELOPMENT OF LAW: FROM SLAVERY TO EMPLOYMENT DISCRIMINATION

The study of black Americans' struggle for equality under the law illustrates the effect of historical and cultural attitudes on the law. The Constitution was, in part, a product of compromise between the interests of Northerners and Southerners. The Constitution as originally drafted permitted slavery and the importation of slaves. Slaves were considered to be capital assets of their owners. Slaves were property, and many pre–Civil War cases concern various aspects of buying, selling, and transferring the legal rights to a slave from one person to another.

Although a bloody civil war was necessary to resolve the question of slavery, it did not provide equal rights for black Americans. People may have disagreed on the issue of slavery in the mid-nineteenth century, but they did not disagree on the issue of integration and equality between the races. The Northern states were not a mecca of racial harmony, and the law reflected this. The case of *Roberts* v. *City of Boston* (1849) is an example of Northern attitudes toward blacks before the Civil War. In that case, a suit was filed on behalf of a five-year-old black girl who was required to attend a public school devoted to the exclusive instruction of black children. This school was at a greater distance from her home than another public school limited to white children. The case was based upon a Massachusetts statute that provided that damages might be recovered by any child who was unlawfully excluded from public school instruction. The court held that the school laws of Massachusetts provided that the local school committee had the power to make operating decisions regarding public schools, and there was nothing inherently illegal in creating a dual public school system, one for black students and one for white students.

After the Civil War, the Thirteenth, Fourteenth, and Fifteenth Amendments, called the **Civil War Amendments,** were added to the Constitution. They were designed to forever abolish slavery and to treat the races equally in the eyes of the law. However, the legal interpretations of those amendments were consistent with the mores of the day rather than with an abstract notion of equal or civil rights.

In 1896, the United States Supreme Court decided *Plessy* v. *Ferguson*. That case involved a claim that a Louisiana statute, which required railway companies to carry white and black passengers in separate coaches, violated the Fourteenth Amendment. Justice Brown, writing for the Court, denied that claim by translating mores into the rule of law.

> The object of the amendment was undoubtedly to enforce the absolute equality of the two races before the law, but in the nature of things it could not have been intended to abolish distinctions based upon color, or to enforce social, as distinguished from political equality, or a commingling of the two races upon terms unsatisfactory to either. Laws permitting, and even requiring, their separation in places where they are liable to be brought into contact do not necessarily imply the inferiority of either race to the other.
>
> We consider the underlying fallacy of the plaintiff's argument to consist in the assumption that the enforced separation of the two races stamps the colored race with a badge of inferiority.
>
> The argument assumes that social prejudices may be overcome by legislation, and that equal rights cannot be secured to the negro except by an enforced commingling of the two races. We cannot accept this proposition. If the two races are to meet upon terms of social equality, it must be the result of natural affinities, a mutual appreciation of each other's merits and a voluntary consent of individuals. Legislation is powerless to eradicate racial instincts or to abolish distinctions based upon physical differences, and the attempt to do so can only result in accentuating the difficulties of the present situation. If the civil and political rights of both races be equal one cannot be inferior to the other civilly or politically. If one race be inferior to the other socially, the Constitution of the United States cannot put them upon the same plane.

"Separate but equal" as a constitutional doctrine survived for nearly sixty years after the *Plessy* v. *Ferguson* case. Separate schools, segregated eating facilities, segregated rest rooms, separate drinking fountains, and black- or white-only businesses were common. The post–World War II civil rights movement's demand for an end to racial segregation was given a legal boost in 1954 by *Brown* v. *Board of Education*. In that case the plaintiffs were black children who challenged a Kansas statute that permitted cities to maintain separate school facilities for blacks and whites. The district court found that segregation in public education had a detrimental effect upon black children, but denied relief on the ground that the school facilities were substantially equal. The United States Supreme Court, in an opinion by Chief Justice Warren, reversed, holding that "separate but equal" had no place in public education. Note how the Court used social norms to reach its conclusion in much the same way as the Court in *Plessy*.

In approaching this problem, we cannot turn the clock back to 1868 when the Amendment was adopted, or even to 1896 when *Plessy* v. *Ferguson* was written. We must consider public education in the light of its full development and its present place in American life throughout the Nation. Only in this way can it be determined if segregation in public schools deprives these plaintiffs of the equal protection of the laws.

Today, education is perhaps the most important function of state and local governments. Today it is a principal instrument in awakening the child to cultural values, in preparing him for later professional training, and in helping him to adjust normally to his environment. In these days, it is doubtful that any child may reasonably be expected to succeed in life if he is denied the opportunity of an education. Such an opportunity, where the state has undertaken to provide it, is a right which must be made available to all on equal terms.

We come then to the question presented: Does segregation of children in public schools solely on the basis of race, even though the physical facilities and other "tangible" factors may be equal, deprive the children of the minority group of equal educational opportunities? We believe that it does.

To separate black children from others of similar age and qualifications solely because of their race generates a feeling of inferiority as to their status in the community that may affect their hearts and minds in a way unlikely ever to be undone. Whatever may have been the extent of psychological knowledge at the time of *Plessy* v. *Ferguson*, this finding is amply supported by modern authority. Any language in *Plessy* v. *Ferguson* contrary to this finding is rejected.

Brown v. *Board of Education* was the first major legal development implementing the goals of the civil rights movement. Thereafter, legally imposed racial segregation fell. In 1964, the Congress enacted a historic bill with profound and wide-ranging implications. The Civil Rights Act of 1964 set in motion newly created federal rules designed to ensure fair and equal treatment for all persons in public accommodations, housing, and employment, regardless of race, sex, religion, color, or national origin. Today the struggle continues. Issues of preferential treatment for minorities, racial quotas, and the economic plight of the black family carry forward the debate over integrating black people into the mainstream of American life.

THE LAW AND ITS EFFORTS TO CONTROL
CONCENTRATIONS OF POWER

The study of law is the study of attempts to limit exploitation by the powerful. Chronicles of this exploitation can be found in innumerable novels. Philosophers as diverse as John Locke and Karl Marx were concerned about the abuse of power caused by the concentration of property in the king (government) or in the capitalist (business). American legal history is replete with examples of laws being enacted to curb activities of the powerful. A prime example is the United States Constitution.

Having freed themselves from a British government they regarded as tyrannical, the early leaders of this country established a government with limited powers and divided the important functions of government among three distinct branches. This diffusion of power reflected their concern that an all-powerful central government could easily abuse its authority.

However, concentrations of power are not limited to the government. New concentrations of power arose in the late nineteenth century as very large corporations developed. Before the Industrial Revolution, most businesses produced products sold by the maker directly to the purchaser. With the growth of mass production techniques tied to improved systems of delivering goods, many businesses grew larger. After several decades, buyers found themselves separated by great distances from sellers. The buyers dealt with retailers or wholesalers rather than the manufacturer.

Interest groups urged that controls be enacted over the concentration of power in the hands of private business. This led to the adoption of the antitrust laws, which are covered in Chapters 13, 14, and 15 of this text. The labor union movement, discussed in Chapters 20 and 21, rose out of conflicts between workers and big business. The consumer movement grew from consumer complaints over the relationship between business and the public.

The following case is an example of the law being asked to regulate an abuse of power. Drug testing is one of the most volatile issues facing business today. Drug

COMPUTER SURVEILLANCE BY THE GOVERNMENT

Computerized libraries are estimated to hold over 3.5 billion records on individuals. Thus, by simply matching social security numbers, the government would have the ability to comb those files and put together detailed dossiers on various individuals. For example, a welfare agency might seek to match its clients with earnings records on file with the Social Security Administration as a way to detect fraudulent welfare claims. Currently, the Drug Enforcement Agency is using computer generated information to prepare profiles of potential illegal drug sellers.

Constitutional and privacy concerns have been expressed about the existence of a huge national data base where sup-posedly confidential information is used by the government. Furthermore, the accuracy of the information in the various data bases is also of concern. The Commerce Department recently matched its employment records with a data base containing those who were collecting unemployment compensation to determine if any of its twenty-two thousand employees were included. The computer noted ninety-eight matches, however when the accuracy of the computer survey was checked, only ten employees were found to have wrongfully collected unemployment compensation. Thus, large numbers of innocent people may be subject to investigation and unwarranted suspicion.

abuse in the workplace is a major problem for employers, yet employees are concerned about indiscriminate testing that treats them more like race horses than human beings. Note that the concern of the court is with the arbitrary use of power by the local government-employer over the police officers and fire fighters. The government-employer's conduct is governed by the Constitution, which the court used to suggest a balance that restricts the power of the employer to make unilateral testing decisions. Similar constitutional provisions do not generally apply to private employers.

City of Palm Bay v. Bauman
Florida Court of Appeal
475 So.2d 1322 (1985)

The City of Palm Bay appeals a final judgment permanently enjoining it from requiring its police officers and fire fighters to give urine specimens at random and unspecified times for the purpose of determining the presence of controlled substances, unless probable cause exists to believe the employee has been using a controlled substance, or except during regularly scheduled periodic physical examinations.

In February 1984, the city manager ordered all fire fighters and police officers to submit to urine testing. In fact, Chief Green was told by the city manager to advise the employees that if they did not consent to the testing, they would be terminated. This lawsuit arose from that policy.

Orfinger, Judge

A citizen has a reasonable expectation of privacy in the discharge and disposition of his urine. At the same time, police officers and fire fighters, because of the nature of their jobs, must reasonably expect their employer to have, and to demonstrate, legitimate concern that their ability to discharge their job responsibilities is not compromised by the use of controlled substances.

The City has the right to adopt a policy which prohibits police officers and fire fighters from using controlled substances at any time while they are so employed, whether such use is on or off the job. The nature of a police officer's or fire fighter's duties involves so much potential danger to both the employee and to the general public as to give the city legitimate concern that these employees not be users of controlled substances.

The question is whether the city's testing plan, considered in the light of its scope, nature, incidence and effect, is unreasonable when the immediate end sought is weighed against the private right affected. Palm Bay's "policy" does not articulate any standards for its implementation and no separate written standards have been promulgated. Reasonable suspicion plays no part—the testing is to be all encompassing. The Chief of Police has received no information, and has no independent knowledge, that any member of the Palm Bay Police Department has used marijuana. The incidence of known marijuana use among fire fighters is less than six (6) people. While not suggesting that this figure is insignificant, it is hardly a legal springboard for the trip the City now seeks to take. Without a scintilla of suspicion directed toward them, many dedicated fire fighters and police officers are told, in effect, to submit to such testing and prove themselves innocent, or suffer disciplinary action. When the immediate end sought is weighed against the private right affected, the proposed search and seizure is constitutionally unreasonable.

The decision of the trial court is affirmed with the following modification. Other courts which have considered this and analogous issues have held that the "reasonable suspicion standard" (something less than probable cause) is the basis upon which this type of search can be justified. The "reasonable suspicion" test requires that to justify this intrusion, officials must point to specific objective facts and rational inferences that they are entitled to draw from these facts in the light of their experience. It is a suspicion which has some factual foundation in the surrounding circumstances observed by the officer, when those situations are interpreted in light of the officer's knowledge.

THE LAW AS A MEANS OF ADJUSTING CLAIMS OF RIGHTS

Sources of Rights

"You cannot do that to me. I have my **rights**." People who make this assertion usually mean that some injustice, sometimes perceived only by them, has been done, and they believe that it should not be allowed. However, in order to know what is meant by "my rights," the nature and source of the injustice must be understood. Similarly, in order to understand the concept of legal rights, the injustice from which those rights arose should be explored. Sometimes, the injustice arose through the activities of the government, and rights were found that protected the individual from the power of the government. The Bill of Rights in the United States Constitution provides for various protections of an individual from the power and activities of the government. These protections were deemed necessary because of experiences under British rule before independence.

However, injustice may arise from the acts of other individuals or private business rather than by the government. These injustices, too, give rise to the creation of rights. These rights involve the regulation of individual, private conduct, either through legislation or through judicial decision. One example of such regulation is the Equal Pay Act, which makes it illegal for an employer to pay women and men differently for the same job. The injustice that preceded the creation of this statutory right was sexually discriminatory wage rates that existed in private industry.

The study of legal rights, however, cannot be limited to constitutional or statutory provisions. Courts, too, may be seen as a source of legal rights. For example, the Supreme Court created the constitutional right of privacy through judicial decision. Furthermore, legal philosophers argue that rights exist independent of any formal government recognition, since all persons have certain natural rights by virtue of being human. The concept of natural rights is very old. It was advanced by Aristotle, by the drafters of the Declaration of Independence, and more recently by the Carter administration's human rights foreign policy. Calls for natural rights or human rights occur when individual freedom is lacking. Totalitarian regimes that jail or kill dissenters, prohibit or discourage religious worship, or arrest people without charge and punish them without trial give rise to the assertion that there are natural or human rights of which no government may deprive its people.

But constitutions, statutes, court decisions, and philosophical ideas are not the sources of our rights. At most, they are their outward manifestations. Constitutions, statutes, and judicial decisions are only words. The concept of natural rights is a philosophical idea. Yet these mere words and ideas represent the real source of our rights—us. Quite simply, we have certain rights in this country because we as a nation want to have them. When we no longer believe in those rights, the law that recognizes them can easily be ignored. Clarence Darrow, the noted trial lawyer, once stated, "It is all right to preserve freedom in constitutions, but when the spirit of freedom has fled from the hearts of the people, then its matter is easily sacrificed under law."[2]

In order to understand this idea, it is helpful to look into early American history. We can review nineteenth-century cases, such as *Bradwell* v. *State* (Chapter 22), with twentieth-century eyes and see a couple of important things. First, as that case noted, certain rights will not exist if our society will not recognize them. Today, no state could prohibit a woman from becoming a lawyer solely because she was a woman. We can say that she would have the right to pursue her chosen profession. However, as noted in *Bradwell*, this was not the case in 1872. Second, as we change as a society our rights will change to reflect our new values. The status of women in America has changed vastly since 1872. The law and our rights reflect that change.

Limitations on Rights

In a complex and crowded nation, an individual's rights may well involve impositions on other people. For instance, if you have the right to distribute handbills outlining your disagreement with the current administration, then others are subjected to your standing on the street corner waving the handbills as they pass by. If a newspaper has the right of freedom of the press, then a politician arrested for drunk driving will be embarrassed if named on the front page. Even rights that are most zealously protected, like freedom of speech, are not without restriction. You may have the right to give a speech for your favorite political candidate. But you do not have the right to give that speech at 2:00 A.M. outside your professor's bedroom window. Both you and your professor have certain rights: you, to give a political speech; your professor, to be able to sleep undisturbed by loud speeches. If a dispute between you and your professor arises, a court may be called upon to determine the conflict of rights. The court will weigh and balance various factors, including the importance of both your rights to society, and render a decision.

Rights are not absolute because we all possess them, and frequently rights in a complex society will clash. Therefore, all rights are subject to some limitation. Because of such limitation, troubling questions are raised concerning the extent of freedom. We tend to agree with the concept of rights if we agree with the person asserting them against limitations. The works of Shakespeare, the Bible, and the poetry of Carl Sandburg are protected from government censorship without protest by the First Amendment. However, J. D. Salinger's *Catcher in the Rye* and Studs Terkel's *Working* have been subjected to attempts by pressure groups to obtain government censorship.

The fact that our rights are not absolute raises a danger that the limits placed upon them will lead to the loss of those rights in practice. This is the central difficulty courts face in deciding disputes concerning the rights of criminals, obscenity cases, land use regulation, and other matters that call upon them to review limits imposed on rights of the people. Totalitarian governments frequently have constitutions that provide many of the same freedoms that exist in the United States. Yet it is clear that their citizens have no such rights in practice.

The following cases illustrate the conflict of rights. The first case, *Wexler* v. *Greenberg*, involves the conflict between the right of an individual to work and earn a living and the right of the individual's former employer to protect business secrets. The second case, *Regina* v. *Dudley and Stephens*, contains a clash of the most basic rights of any civilized society—the right of an individual to survival and the right of society to prohibit the killing of its members.

Wexler v. Greenberg

Supreme Court of Pennsylvania
160 A.2d 430 (1960)

Buckingham Wax Company is engaged in the manufacture, compounding, and blending of sanitation and maintenance chemicals. In March 1949 Greenberg, a qualified chemist in the sanitation and maintenance field, entered the employ of Buckingham as its chief chemist and continued there until August 28, 1957. In the performance of his duties, Greenberg analyzed and duplicated competitors' products and then used the resulting information to develop various new formulas.

Brite Products Co., Inc., did most of their purchasing from Buckingham; and from August 1956 until August 20, 1957, the date of Brite's last order, Brite exclusively purchased Buckingham's manufactured products. These products were in turn distributed by Brite to its customers, mostly industrial users, marked with labels that identified the products as products of Brite. Brite's purchases of sanitation and maintenance products from Buckingham amounted annually to approximately thirty-five thousand dollars.

Dickler, president of Brite, met Greenberg in 1952 as a result of his business transactions with Buckingham, and had contact with Greenberg over the years in connection with the special products that were being made by Buckingham for Brite. In June 1957 Greenberg first approached Dickler in reference to employment, and negotiations began for Greenberg to associate himself with Brite. An agreement between them was reached whereby Greenberg became a director, the treasurer, and chief chemist of Brite and, as a further consideration, received 25 percent of Brite's outstanding and issued capital stock. In August 1957 Greenberg left Buckingham and went to work for Brite.

Before Greenberg's association with Brite, the corporation's business consisted solely of selling a complete line of maintenance and sanitation chemicals, including liquid soap cleaners, wax base cleaners, disinfectants, and floor finishes. Upon Greenberg's arrival, however, the corporation purchased equipment and machinery and, under the guidance and supervision of Greenberg, embarked on a full-scale program for the manufacture of a cleaner, floor finish, and disinfectant, products previously purchased from Buckingham. The formulas in issue in this litigation are the formulas for each of these respective products.

Colten, Justice

The formulas had been developed by Greenberg himself, while in the pursuit of his duties as Buckingham's chief chemist, or under Greenberg's direct supervision. We are thus faced with the problem of determining the extent to which a former employer, without the aid of any express covenant, can restrict his ex-employee, a highly skilled chemist, in the uses to which this employee can put his knowledge of formulas and methods he himself developed during the course of his former employment because this employer claims these same formulas, as against the rest of the world, as his trade secrets.

In this era of electronic, chemical, missile and atomic development, many skilled technicians and expert employees are currently in the process of developing potential trade secrets. Competition for personnel of this caliber is exceptionally keen, and the interchange of employment is commonplace. We must therefore be particularly mindful of any effect our decision in this case might have in disrupting this pattern of employee mobility, both in view of possible restraints upon an individual in the pursuit of his livelihood and the harm to the public in general in forestalling, to any extent widespread technological advances.

The burden the appellees must thus meet brings to the fore a problem of accommodating competing policies in our law; the right of a businessman to be protected against unfair competition stemming from the usurpation of his trade secrets and the right of an individual to the unhampered pursuit of the occupations and livelihoods for which he is best suited. There are cogent socio-economic arguments in favor of either position. Society as a whole greatly benefits from technological improvements. Without some means of post-employment protection to assure that valuable developments or improvements are exclusively those of the employer, the business-

man could not afford to subsidize research or improve current methods. In addition, it must be recognized that modern economic growth and development has pushed the business venture beyond the size of the one-man firm, forcing the businessman to a much greater degree to entrust confidential business information relating to technological development to appropriate employees. While recognizing the utility in the dispersion of responsibilities in larger firms, the optimum amount of "entrusting" will not occur unless the risk of loss to the businessman through a breach of trust can be held to a minimum.

On the other hand, any form of post-employment restraint reduces the economic mobility of employees and limits their personal freedom to pursue a preferred course of livelihood. The employee's bargaining position is weakened because he is potentially shackled by the acquisition of alleged trade secrets; and thus, paradoxically, he is restrained, because of his increased expertise, from advancing further in the industry in which he is most productive. Moreover, as previously mentioned, society suffers because competition is diminished by slackening the dissemination of ideas, processes and methods.

There is nothing in the record to indicate that the formulas in issue were specific projects of great concern and concentration by Buckingham; instead it appears they were merely the result of Greenberg's routine work of changing and modifying formulas derived from competitors. Since there was no experimentation or research, the developments by change and modification were fruits of Greenberg's own skill as a chemist without any appreciable assistance by way of information or great expense or supervision by Buckingham, outside of the normal expenses of his job. Nor can we find anything that would indicate to Greenberg that these particular results were the goal which

Buckingham expected him to find for its exclusive use.

Accordingly, we hold that appellant Greenberg has violated no trust or confidential relationship in disclosing or using formulas which he developed or were developed subject to his supervision. Rather, we hold that this information forms part of the technical knowledge and skill he has acquired by virtue of his employment with Buckingham and which he has an unqualified privilege to use.

Regina v. Dudley and Stephens
Queen's Bench Division (England)
14 Q.B.D. 273 (1884)

Indictment for the murder of Richard Parker on the high seas within the jurisdiction of the Admiralty.

On July 5, 1884, the prisoners, Thomas Dudley and Edward Stephens, and Brooks, all able-bodied English seamen, and the deceased, an English boy, between seventeen and eighteen years of age, were cast away in a storm on the high seas 1600 miles from the Cape of Good Hope, and were compelled to put into an open boat. In this boat they had no supply of water and no supply of food, except two 1 lb. tins of turnips. For three days they had nothing else to subsist upon. On the fourth day they caught a small turtle, upon which they subsisted for a few days. This was the only food they had up to the twentieth day when the act now in question was committed. On the twelfth day the remains of the turtle were entirely consumed, and for the next eight days they had nothing to eat. They had no fresh water, except such rain as they from time to time caught in their oilskin capes. The boat was drifting on the ocean, and was probably more than 1000 miles away from land. On the eighteenth day, when they had been seven days without food and five without water, the prisoners spoke to Brooks as to what should be done if no succour came. They suggested that someone should be sacrificed to save the rest. Brooks dissented, and the boy, to whom they were understood to refer, was not consulted.

On the 24th of July, the day before the act now in question, the prisoner Dudley proposed to Stephens and Brooks that lots should now be cast who should be put to death to save the rest. Brooks refused to consent, and it was not put to the boy, and in point of fact there was no drawing of lots. On that day the prisoners spoke of their having families, and suggested it would be better to kill the boy that their lives should be saved, and Dudley proposed that if there was no vessel in sight by the morrow morning the boy should be killed.

The next day, the 25th of July, no vessel appearing, Dudley told Brooks that he had better go and have a sleep, and made signs to Stephens and Brooks that the boy had better be killed. The prisoner Stephens agreed to the act, but Brooks dissented from it. The boy was then lying at the bottom of the boat quite helpless, and extremely weakened by famine and by drinking sea water, and unable to make any resistance, nor did he ever assent to his being killed. The prisoner Dudley offered a prayer asking forgiveness for them and that their souls might be saved. Dudley, with the assent of Stephens, went to the boy, and telling him that his time was come, put a knife into his throat and killed him then and there. The three men fed upon the body and blood of the boy for four days. On the fourth day after the act had been committed the boat was picked up by a passing vessel, and the prisoners were rescued, still alive, but in the lowest state of prostration. They were carried to the port of Falmouth, and committed for trial at Exeter. If the men had not fed upon the body of the boy they would probably not have survived to be picked up and rescued, but would within the four days have died of famine. The boy, being in a much weaker condition, was likely to have died before them.

At the time of the act in question there was no sail in sight, nor any reasonable prospect of relief. Under these circumstances there appeared to the prisoners every probability that unless they then fed or very soon fed upon the boy or one of themselves they would die of starvation. There was no appreciable chance of saving life except by killing someone for the others to eat. Assuming any necessity to kill anybody, there was no greater necessity for killing the boy than any of the other three men.

[You write the opinion. How should these rights be balanced?]

SUMMARY   Law is not separate from the culture, history, and times in which it exists. The study of law is not limited to learning legal rules. Understanding the legal environment of business, therefore, requires a broad understanding of the people and basic trends that influence the relationship between law and business.

Three such trends or themes may be identified: first, that historical and social movements affect the development of law. A brief history of the attitude of the law toward equal rights for black Americans chronicled the historical movements that led to today's civil rights laws. A second recurring theme is the efforts of the law to control concentrations and abuses of power, whether it be in the hands of government or private business. Finally, the law may be seen as a mechanism for adjusting claims of conflicting rights. These themes will surface time and again throughout the remaining chapters of this book. More importantly, they influence the legal environment in which the business manager operates.

REVIEW QUESTIONS

1. Define the following terms:
   a. Civil War Amendments
   b. Separate but equal
   c. Rights

2. Why does the law act to control or limit the concentration of power and its exercise? Is there a paradox inherent in this control?

3. Why are there no absolute rights?

4. Is there a danger in limitations that the law places on the exercise of rights?

5. Discuss the themes that recur in the law. Give examples other than those mentioned in the text.

6. What characteristics must law possess in order for it to be effective in our system?

7. Discuss the historical and social trends which led to the development of civil rights laws.

8. Which is more dangerous to individual freedom, the concentration of power in government or the concentration of power in private business?

9. You are an executive of the ABC Corporation, a very large multinational firm. One afternoon you are reviewing the terms of a deal that one of your subordinates has negotiated with XYZ, Inc., a small distribution company. The agreement provides that if XYZ does not sell a certain quota of ABC products, it will pay ABC a penalty of ten times the cost of those products. Without discussing applicable legal rules, would you expect a potential problem to arise with such a clause? If so, give reasons.

10. Smith is a highly trained engineer who is in charge of computer design changes at High Tech, Inc. He has been instrumental in developing numerous features of the corporation's line of computers and is currently involved in its secret work involving artificial intelligence. AI, Inc., a competitor of High Tech, lures Smith from High Tech in order to organize its newly formed artificial intelligence

division. Smith eagerly accepts the new position, and High Tech is upset that he has left. Without discussing applicable legal rules, what are the concerns of Smith and High Tech that could be central to a suit filed by High Tech against Smith?

11. You have been assigned to Hong Kong by your company to head its Far East division. You are in charge of operations in Taiwan, Korea, and Malaysia. Discuss the sources of differences in law between those areas and the United States, without focusing on legal rules. How might you begin to understand, or at least appreciate, those differences?

12. Jones is marketing manager for Sellit, Inc. She supervises fifteen sales representatives. Jones is an avid professional football fan and each year plans an outing with the representatives as a way to build "team spirit." Carson, one of the sales representatives, dislikes professional football. He believes it is overcommercialized and panders to primitive violent instincts. One year he mentioned casually to Jones that he would prefer a different type of group outing, noting his lack of interest in football. Jones listened but thereafter began to regularly criticize Carson's work. Finally, she fired him. Previously, Carson had been one of the top sales representatives. Without discussion of applicable legal rules, discuss any legal problems that might arise.

NOTES

[1] G. Gilmore, *The Ages of American Law* (New Haven: Yale University Press, 1977), pp. 110–111.

[2] A. Weinberg (ed.), *Attorney for the Damned* (New York: Simon & Schuster, 1977), p. 57.

PART II

The American Legal System

CHAPTER 2

Introduction to Courts

Structure of the Court System
Personnel in the Judicial System

Courts are institutions designed for settling disputes. They are the units of government concerned with the administration of justice. At times individuals, businesses, and the government disagree over the application of various laws in society or seek to use the law as a means of controlling the behavior of others. A function of the court is to settle those disputes. However, courts do much more than decide who was at fault for an accident, whether an accused person actually stole the goods, or whether a marriage should be dissolved. In the course of deciding these and other questions, courts make law. Judicial lawmaking is not the same as lawmaking by a legislature, yet it has the same effect.

Judicial lawmaking may be divided into three categories. First, there is the creation of a body of law, called common law, arising solely from judicial decisions. These decisions give an indication of probable future court rulings to other parties with similar problems. The parties rely on the courts following their past decisions or giving them precedential effect. Such areas of law as contracts and torts emphasize this type of judicial lawmaking.

A second type of judicial lawmaking occurs when a court interprets a statute. For example, the Uniform Commercial Code, a statute regulating personal property transactions, provides that buyers and sellers are to act in a commercially reasonable manner. But what precisely does the term *commercially reasonable* mean? A particular buyer and seller may have differing opinions, resulting in a dispute that finds its way into court. In the process of settling that dispute, the court must interpret the term *commercially reasonable*. By interpreting the term, the court makes law through its decision in the case. Thereafter, other buyers and sellers will have the advice of that particular case to assist them in understanding the statute requiring commercially reasonable conduct.

The third type of judicial lawmaking occurs through the interpretation of the Constitution. This is a special type of lawmaking simply because of the profound effect constitutional rulings may have. This type of judicial lawmaking is frequently controversial. The argument that judges should not make law or impose their views of policy in cases usually arises in situations of constitutional lawmaking. This criticism is not peculiarly modern, but has been made throughout American history.

Although courts do their work within the limited context of settling particular disputes between parties, at the same time they have a much greater effect on the law. The next three chapters discuss important facets of the judicial branch. This chapter provides an introduction to the courts, focusing on important actors in the judicial process and some issues that affect their roles, while Chapter 3 is a very practical discussion of civil litigation. Chapter 4 provides the theoretical background for understanding various aspects of the judicial process and judicial dispute settling.

STRUCTURE OF THE COURT SYSTEM

A very general description of the court systems in the United States will provide a foundation for understanding how courts operate. This discussion will describe courts from two different perspectives: first by their jurisdiction (federal or state courts), and second by their function (trial or appellate courts).

The Federal and State Systems

There are two jurisdictional groups of courts in this country: federal courts and state courts. There is one federal court system in the United States, while each state (and the District of Columbia) has its own court system. Discussion of judges, courts, or judicial lawmaking in fact requires generalization about many different and separate court systems.

Federal Courts. The federal court system has three major levels of courts (see Figure 2.1). The first level is the federal district courts. There are the trial courts of the federal system. In these courts, juries are impaneled, witnesses are heard, and verdicts are rendered. Federal district courts are generally confined to all or part of one state,

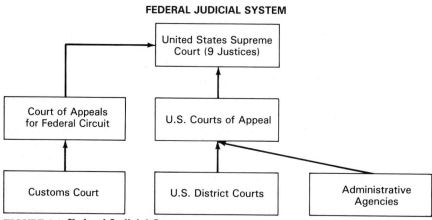

FIGURE 2.1 Federal Judicial System

the number of districts within that state depending upon the population. For example, there are two federal districts in the state of Indiana, the northern federal district and the southern federal district. Delaware has one federal district, while California has four. In addition to the district courts at the first level of the federal system, there are also some specialized federal courts that are designed to hear cases arising under one major area of law. For example, federal bankruptcy courts hear cases arising under bankruptcy law. The federal tax court is empowered to hear cases concerning federal taxation. If a taxpayer disputes the amount of tax the IRS claims is due, the taxpayer may appeal through the IRS and then seek relief in the tax court. Alternatively, the taxpayer may pay the amount in dispute and pursue relief through the federal district court.

Federal courts are limited in the types of disputes that they can decide. The limitation is called jurisdiction. Unless there is a question of federal law in the case (statutory or constitutional) or the parties are from different states and have more than ten thousand dollars in dispute, the matter cannot be heard in a federal court. For example, the law concerning the proper formalities to follow in order to incorporate a business is governed by state law. Each state has its own statute concerning the proper procedure to follow in order to be recognized as a **corporation** doing business within that particular state. There are no federal rules governing the incorporation procedure. Therefore, a dispute involving whether a corporation was properly formed in a given state will not be heard in federal court. Instead the dispute will be settled by the courts of that particular state. However, if the parties in the dispute are from Alabama and Florida and the amount in dispute is ten thousand dollars, then the case may be heard in federal court.

Within the federal court system there is a hierarchy of courts; that is, certain courts have control over other courts. The federal district courts are grouped geographically in circuits. For example, the seventh circuit contains the federal district courts in Indiana, Illinois, and Wisconsin. The second circuit contains the federal district courts in New York, Vermont, and Connecticut. There are thirteen federal judicial circuits in the United States; eleven contain the district courts from various states. A separate circuit exists for Washington, D.C. There is also a court of appeals for the Federal Circuit. Each circuit has one court of appeals. The Seventh Circuit Court of Appeals is located in Chicago. The Second Circuit Court of Appeals is located in New York City. The court of appeals is an appellate court. It does not hear witnesses or preside over trials. Its function is to decide questions that are appealed to it by parties who are dissatisfied with the decision of a district court.

The ruling of a court of appeals is binding **precedent** for all the federal district courts within that circuit. If another similar case arises in one of the district courts, a prior decision of the court of appeals on the relevant point of law is binding. However, a decision of a court of appeals is not binding outside its circuit. For example, recently some state legislatures have enacted statutes providing state tax benefits for residents who send their children to private schools. These statutes have been challenged in federal district court by others who contend that the statute violates the First Amendment of the United States Constitution in that it impermissibly entangles the government with religion. These people contend that most of the private schools are church-operated. One federal court of appeals struck down such a statute as unconstitutional. Thereafter, any state enacting such a statute within the geographical boundaries of that circuit would virtually be assured that it would be declared unconstitutional. However, in another circuit, the federal court of appeals found a similar statute to be constitutional. Thereafter, other states within the circuit that enacted this statute could be virtually assured that it would be upheld as constitutional. Thus, although there is one federal court system, its organization into separate jurisdictions may well lead to results that are not consistent from circuit to circuit.

Of course, there is one more level of the federal court hierarchy—the United States Supreme Court. It, too, is an appellate court, although on rare occasions it may exercise original jurisdiction—that is, hear a dispute without the requirement that it first be decided by a lower level court. The United States Supreme Court is the highest court to which an appeal may be taken. It is located in Washington, D.C., and has nine judges, called justices, who together, generally, decide its cases.

Appeals may be taken to the United States Supreme Court from a number of sources. A party displeased with the decision of a federal circuit court of appeals may seek to have that case reviewed by the Supreme Court. Even if the case did not go through the federal court system, it may be appealed to the Supreme Court in some circumstances. For example, after a case has gone through the state court system and the state supreme court has ruled on the matter, a final appeal may be made to the United States Supreme Court, provided that there is a federal question in the case. Even though the Supreme Court is the highest court in the land, it too is limited in the cases it may hear by the concept of jurisdiction.

State Courts. The federal court system is complemented by the judicial systems of each of the states (see Figure 2.2). These state court systems may differ, making a single, complete description of their structure impractical. Some states do not have an intermediate court of appeals. Those who object to a decision reached at trial appeal directly to the state supreme court. Some states, especially those with large cities, have different divisions of trial level courts. There may be a criminal division that handles the trial of criminal cases, or a probate division that handles matters dealing with wills and estates, or a family law division that handles divorce and related matters. Furthermore, many states have special courts at a level lower than that of the trial court. These courts are generally limited to very minor disputes, such as minor traffic offenses or disputes involving only a few hundred dollars. Often these courts act more like informal arbitrators, with more relaxed rules of evidence and no jury trials. In fact, in some of these courts the appearance of lawyers for the parties is prohibited. A party who wants to appeal from such a lower level court usually may obtain a trial de novo (a total retrial) in the regular trial courts of that state.

The organization of the courts within a state is very similar to the federal court organization, with trial level and appellate level courts. The trial level courts may hear the cases that arise in their particular area of the state. For example, assume the state of X has two counties, Jefferson County and Jackson County. Each county has its own trial court. A case arising in Jackson County will be heard by the court in Jackson County. The Jefferson County court would not be the proper one to hear the dispute. In states that have more than one intermediate appellate court (like the courts of appeals in the federal court system) the same organizational concepts and

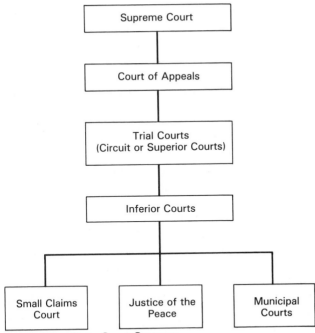

FIGURE 2.2 State Court Systems

issues arise. However, there is one important difference between the state court system and the federal court system. As already stated, a federal court must have jurisdiction to hear a case; that is, there must be a federal law issue involved in the dispute (statutory or constitutional) or the parties to the dispute must be from different states. However, state courts may hear disputes concerning federal law as well as disputes concerning the law of that particular state. But there is still one jurisdictional limitation on the state courts. Just as the federal courts of the United States do not hear disputes arising in Canada (those are for the courts of Canada), the courts of one state do not hear disputes arising in another. Geographical boundaries are important in the structure and organization of court systems.

In the previous section, we described courts by their jurisdiction, as state or federal courts. Courts may also be described by function, as trial or appellate courts. Although procedures in one jurisdiction's trial or appellate courts may differ from those in another, the basic function of the courts would be similar.

Trial and Appellate Courts

Trial Courts. The **trial court** is the first place the judicial system considers the disputes of parties. The trial court listens to the evidence and renders a verdict or judgment based upon that evidence. Trials may be heard by a jury or only by a judge. A trial heard only by a judge is called a **bench trial.** Contrary to popular belief, most trials are bench trials.

The following example illustrates the basic features of the trial function of courts. Mary Smith took her automobile to XYZ, Inc., auto repair shop for a tune-up. When she returned for the car, she noticed that the paint was badly scratched on the trunk and sides of the car. Smith claimed that the car was in perfect condition when she brought it to XYZ. XYZ claimed that the scratches were already there. Since the parties were not able to agree concerning the damaged vehicle, Smith hired an attorney who filed a suit against XYZ for one thousand dollars in damage to her car. XYZ also retained an attorney to represent their interests in the lawsuit.

At the trial, witnesses were called and examined under oath. Smith and a couple of acquaintances testified that the car was in perfect condition prior to the day of the tune-up. XYZ employees testified that the car was scratched when they first saw it. Exhibits were shown at the trial. One was a drawing showing the relationship between the location of the scratches and sharp objects in the tune-up area. In major cases, films and scale models may be developed to help the attorney present the case.

At the trial level, the facts of the matter are determined and the relevant law is applied, resulting in a verdict. In the process of reaching a verdict, what actually happened in the events under dispute will have to be decided. This is frequently a difficult task, because witnesses will often offer conflicting versions of the same event. The trier (either a jury or a judge) must decide which of the witnesses is to be believed and which of the witnesses' testimony can be discounted. However, the verdict itself does not include a summary of the facts of the case. Most often a simple decision in the matter will be reached (e.g., the jury finds for the plaintiff, Mary Smith, or the jury finds for the defendant, XYZ). Occasionally, a jury will be required to render a special verdict. A special verdict requires the jury to answer a number of questions concerning the major issues in the case. The jury, therefore, must make a special finding on each material issue in the case. However, the jury does not draft a summary of the facts of the case.

Most disputes go no further than the trial court stage. In fact, very few of the cases that are filed actually result in a trial. Trials are expensive and time-consuming. Usually, the parties must pay their own attorneys' fees. Therefore, there are substantial incentives for the parties to settle the matter out of court. These incentives also inhibit people from pursuing valid legal claims. The Smith-XYZ example is illustrative of this point. The costs to each party to litigate the matter would probably exceed the amount of money (one thousand dollars) in dispute. It is unlikely that they would pursue their dispute through trial.

Appellate Courts. Sometimes a litigant wants to have another judicial review after the trial stage, usually because that party was dissatisfied with the verdict. The party may then file an appeal with the **appellate court** designated to hear such an appeal. An appellate court does not conduct a new trial. It hears no direct evidence in the case. Instead the appellate court reviews the entire record of the case in order to determine whether any errors were made during the trial. The record includes copies of all the pleadings and documents filed in the case, all the exhibits entered as evidence in the case, and a transcript of all the testimony during the trial itself. Both parties in the case also file **briefs.** The briefs are written arguments to the court concerning the points the parties want the court to consider. The party seeking the appellate review (called the **appellant**) will point out the errors in the application of law made by the trial judge and argue that the verdict should be overturned because of those errors. The opposing party (called the **appellee**) will usually argue that no errors were made at trial or that they were minor errors that would have no effect on the outcome of the case. The appellee will argue that the appellate court should simply affirm the decision reached at trial.

In addition to the briefs, sometimes the parties also present an oral argument to the court. Appellate oral argument does not involve the questioning of witnesses or the presentation of evidence. Instead, the attorneys are given a certain period of time to argue their position before the court. Frequently the appellate court justices will interrupt the attorney to ask questions concerning the case, the applicable law, and the attorney's basic argument. Later, the appellate court will render a decision with an opinion discussing the reasons for its decision. These opinions are usually published and are available in all law libraries. Sometimes a justice may agree with the appellate court's decision, but disagree with the reasoning of the court. That justice may then file a separate opinion in the case, called a **concurring opinion.** However, appellate court justices do not always agree concerning the outcome of a particular case. In that event, a separate opinion, called a **dissenting opinion,** may be filed outlining the reasons for the disagreement.

An appellate court's role is considered to be the correction of errors of law made by the trial court judge, not the making of factual determinations. These errors of law may involve various rulings made by the judge concerning evidence during the course of the case, or they may involve the judge's instructions on the law to the jury.

Although appellate courts are said to consider questions of law rather than questions of fact, it is sometimes rather difficult to determine exactly when questions are legal and when instead they are factual. Some people suggest that if a question is (or should be) decided by a judge, then that question is one of law; if not, then it is a question of fact. Clearly, this argument begs the question. Yet is shows that often appellate courts, in making decisions, base them on a reading of the facts that may not be at all consistent with the interpretation of the facts that led to the verdict in the trial court.

PERSONNEL IN THE JUDICIAL SYSTEM

The judicial system is made up of a variety of different people, each of whom has a role to play in the administration of justice. Two of the most important members of the judicial system, the judge and the lawyer, will be the focus of this section.

The Judge

There are several different types of judges: state court and federal court judges, judges who handle trials, and judges who handle appeals. Some judges hear only one type of legal matter. For example, there are tax court judges who decide only questions dealing with federal taxation, and in some states there are criminal court judges who hear only criminal cases. Although there are differences among the types of work judges do, there are enough similarities to observe some major characteristics of the judiciary.

Function of a Judge in General. Judges decide cases and make law—at the same time. Of course, some cases are relatively routine, involving issues and kinds of facts that have been ruled upon numerous times in the past. In such cases, the case-deciding function of the judge is paramount. For example, assume a judge is hearing a simple traffic violation case. The defendant is accused of driving through a stop sign. However, the defendant contends that a full stop was made. The only witness for the state is the arresting police officer. The only witness for the defense is the defendant. In the hundreds of similar cases preceding this one, the judge has found the stop-sign runner guilty even though the testimony at trial conflicted, the fine being thirty-five dollars. If the same result occurs in the present case, the most evident thing done by the judge is the finding of guilt—the settling of a dispute between the state and a driver. Yet, in a sense, law was being made at the same time. First, it continues to be the legal rule in that judge's court that defendants in a stop-sign-running case will have to produce more evidence than their own testimony in order to prevail, in light of conflicting testimony by a police officer. This is the law as to the particular judge's consideration of the evidence. Second, the thirty-five-dollar fine has been imposed so often as to almost become administrative in nature. You ran a stop sign, you pay thirty-five dollars in this judge's court.

However, take the same basic facts with a different result and the judicial lawmaking function becomes dominant. Assume, in the same case, that the judge refused to find the defendant guilty of running the stop sign because the state had not proved its case "beyond a reasonable doubt," the standard necessary for a conviction. The only evidence was the word of the police officer against the word of the defendant, and there was no indication that the defendant was a habitual liar or somehow untrustworthy in giving testimony (except for an interest in not being convicted and having to pay a thirty-five-dollar fine). In this case, too, a dispute was settled between the state and an allegedly errant driver. However, a potentially important new law was made. In the future, the state will have to do much more than produce a police officer in order to convict stop-sign runners. More evidence will be necessary. The state may have to change its law-enforcement procedures: perhaps assign two police officers to each traffic detail, perhaps film certain intersections (assuming there are no constitutional problems), perhaps seek a witness who may have been strolling by during the incident in question. Clearly, the new evidence rule in this minor traffic matter would make a change in law-enforcement procedures. If the alternatives were too expensive, fewer stop-sign-running cases would be brought before the courts.

The lawmaking done by courts is confined to the particular disputes that come before them. Courts do not have the ability to seek out problems in the law that need correction or clarification and simply draft a new rule. In fact, federal courts and the courts of most states are prohibited from giving advice on the law or on the constitutionality of a proposed law to other branches of government. Such advice is called an **advisory opinion.** A few states do permit this practice, but it is not often used.

As the preceding examples illustrate, judicial decision making can have a broader effect than simply rendering a judgment directly relating to the parties in a case. The decision often indicates to others how they should act in order to prevail in the courtroom. In one example, the investigative practices of the state may have to change.

Judicial Activism. Judicial decision making often involves reviewing the activities of other branches of governments. Historically, courts would either find the activity inconsistent with the Constitution (unconstitutional) or uphold the action. In effect the decision would be a yes or no type of judgment. The court would use its reviewing power to set limits concerning what other branches of government could do. Today, however, judges frequently find themselves going well beyond merely setting limits on the activities of other units of government. Judges today may require that certain specific action be taken by the government in order to cure a constitutionally defective practice. For example, a lawsuit may be brought by an inmate of a prison contending that the conditions of the prison are so poor as to violate his constitutional rights. A court, in finding that the prison indeed violates prisoner rights, may fashion a remedy that involves the court in day-to-day prison decisions.

Finney v. Arkansas Board of Corrections
United States Eighth Circuit Court of Appeals
505 F.2d 194 (1974)

A class action suit was brought by inmates at the Cummins Prison Farm and the Tucker Intermediate Reformatory. They assert that the manner in which Arkansas is operating its prison system violates the United States Constitution. The Eighth Circuit Court of Appeals agreed.

Lay, Circuit Judge

This court recognizes the difficult issues the district court has passed upon since the commencement of this litigation in 1969. We are nevertheless compelled to find on the basis of the overall record that there exists a continuing failure by the correctional authorities to provide a constitutional and in some respects, even a humane environment within their institutions. We find major constitutional deficiencies particularly at Cummins in housing, lack of medical care, infliction of physical and mental brutality and torture upon individual prisoners, racial discrimination, abuses of solitary confinement, continuing use of trusty guards, abuse of mail regulations, arbitrary work classifications, arbitrary disciplinary procedures, inadequate distribution of food and clothing, and total lack of rehabilitative programs. We are therefore convinced that present prison conditions, now after almost five years require the retention of federal jurisdication and the granting of further relief.

We do not consider it too great a burden on the Board of Correction and prison officials to require them to make an evidentiary showing in the district court. If, as urged, there is now constitutional compliance, it should be fairly simple for respondents to demonstrate it to the district court. Once the district court is convinced that constitutional standards, as we defined them, have been met, it may terminate its jurisdiction of the case. We recognize that the sooner the district court may discharge its jurisdiction of the case, the better it is for everyone.

It is difficult to see how relief can be afforded in cases such as this without an expanded role for the courts. In a sense, this type of extraordinary relief has always been available to the courts. In contract disputes, the traditional damage award to the party injured by a breach of contract is money damages. If X agrees to sell Y a textbook for twenty dollars, a contract will be said to exist between X and Y. If, however, on the agreed day of sale, X instead sells the book to Z for twenty-two dollars, X has breached the contract. Y rushes to the bookstore and purchases the needed book for twenty-five dollars. Y has been injured by the contract breach in the sum of five dollars. That would be the usual money damage relief granted by the court. However, if the book were a one-of-a-kind masterpiece and X refused to sell it to Y as agreed, money damages would probably not be sufficient. In that event, a court might require that X perform the contract as agreed, that is, impose on X a duty to act in a certain way to provide full relief to the other party. This is called the doctrine of specific performance in contract. The specific action required by the courts today in such cases as the preceding prison example is similar.

Expansive judicial decisions—decisions in whose implementation the court has a part—are the source of the current criticism of judges and courts as being too activist. The use of such decisions in constitutional disputes is a major extension of judicial decisions into areas that had usually called for political decisions: decisions based on trade offs made by the other branches of government. Many people contend that a judge has no expertise in making specific decisions concerning the operation of a prison system or the structure and operation of a school system. Another frequent complaint is that such decisions are most often made by federal court judges who are appointed for life with no direct accountability to the general public who would be affected by their decisions. Traditional court action, such as ordering remedies like specific performance, merely affected parties to the lawsuit. Many of the activist decisions today, however, affect the general public, since often tax money must either be raised or shifted to pay for the court-imposed remedy. Yet the taxpayers have no way to influence that spending decision, since it was mandated by a court in response to a lawsuit.

Other people claim that such judicial activity is necessary in today's complex legal world. Government does many more things for (and to) people today than in the past. Furthermore, today more individual rights are recognized in the law, and people are demanding that those rights be protected. Equal rights under law for people irrespective of race, sex, national origin, or a number of other factors is a very recent development in the law. Segregated public schools were declared unconstitutional only approximately thirty years ago. In addition, certain groups, such as prisoners, welfare recipients, and mental patients, have also been found to have basic rights in relation to government activity aimed at them. For a court to say no to government action today may not be enough, especially when the problem is government inaction. When a prison system is so underfunded as to cause unreasonable overcrowding or when school boards do not act to dismantle the vestiges of a once racially segregated school system, a more intrusive remedy may be needed to correct the wrong. Judges may require government to act to fulfill the minimum requirements set out by a statute or by the Constitution. Lack of certain governmental activity may be just as harmful to individual rights as too intrusive activity. However, each type of problem may require a different type of judicial solution.

One effect of such judicial activism is to, in a sense, shift some very difficult political decisions from the legislature, where the voters have an influence, to the judiciary (especially the federal courts), where the judges are not accountable to the electorate. For example, politicians may call for harsher penalties and longer jail terms for a wide variety of criminal offenders. However, the same politicians may refrain from making the extremely tough budgetary decisions to go along with their anticrime position, namely, funding for more prison facilities to house the additional inmates. This would require either additional taxes or a switch of funds from an already existing program. Neither of these alternatives would be popular. So the politicians may simply enact popular, strict criminal laws that soon begin to increase the prison population. After a time, conditions become so crowded that a lawsuit is brought by a prisoner and a judge is asked to solve an essentially political question. The only way to solve the problem is to require certain government action, either building additional facilities or releasing prisoners before they have finished serving their time. The judge then catches the political heat. One may not agree with certain activist judicial decisions, but one should realize that such decisions are a product of the increasing role of government in our lives coupled with the greater recognition of individual rights. The legal and political systems have become very complex, often leading to litigation involving not only disputes between parties but also grievances against entire institutions.

Selection of Judges. Given the importance of the judge and the potential broad effect of judicial decision making, it is important that judges be carefully selected. This section will briefly review the two general methods of putting individuals on the bench, the election of candidates and the appointment of candidates. Federal judges are appointed by the president with the advice and consent of the Senate, as provided in the Constitution. They serve for life, with impeachment as the means for removal. Impeachment is very rarely used. Since federal judges are appointed rather than elected, the focus of this section will be on state court judges. However, a few of the issues concerning appointment of the state court judiciary may also be applicable to federal judges.

Some states elect their judges in the same manner as any other official. The political parties nominate candidates to fill the judicial positions. The judge is then chosen by the voters in the general election. The elected judge serves a term like other elected officials and is then subject to renomination and election at the next general election. Some people contend that election of judges is consistent with our form of government in that it assures that the judicial branch will be held accountable to and be a reflection of the demands of the citizens. Popular control of judges may be seen as highly desirable. Since a judge, like any public official, exercises a great deal of power and control, the people should have a part in selecting the individuals who serve as judges.

However, others argue that the election of judges risks placing individuals on the bench who are not especially qualified. Candidates for judgeships may be selected in part based on their politics and party loyalty rather than on their judicial qualifications. This political litmus test may be more important than objective criteria in selecting the candidates for the job.

Furthermore, how are voters to determine the most suitable candidates for the judgeships? Much of a judge's work involves only a few members of a community and is not especially newsworthy. Studies have suggested that voters often have little knowledge about candidates for judgeships. If this is so, the argument that the election process makes judges accountable to the public is weakened. Instead it makes judges accountable to the political party that nominates them. Voters may be expected to show an interest in a judicial election if the candidate for election was involved in a highly controversial matter. The result may be that a judge exercises less independent decision making. The very nature of politics, with campaign contributions, campaign slogans, and advertising, raises problems about the independence of the various judicial candidates.

Yet these elected judges do have a limited term in office and can be removed by the voters. Political parties may use politics as a selection factor, yet the political leaders should be interested in competent candidates, since each candidate reflects and has an effect on the party ticket as a whole. Mistakes made in the election of judges are more easily corrected than mistakes made in the appointment process.

However, the problems inherent in the election of judges, as well as the appearance of political influence on judicial candidates, have led a number of states to move away from the election of judges toward an appointive system, often called the **Missouri plan.** The Missouri plan involves a governor-appointed panel including a judge, lawyers, and lay members, who recommend suitable candidates for judicial appointment by the governor. Periodically the appointed judges' names appear on a ballot where voters may vote on whether or not to retain the judges for an additional term. This is not a contest between candidates, but a yes-or-no decision by the voters. This plan removes political parties from the process yet retains periodic voter approval. However, given the general lack of voter knowledge about judges, the removal of poor judges from the bench by this process is unlikely.

Although proponents of this plan contend that it removes the selection of judges from the harmful and partisan effects of the political arena, others argue that it merely changes the type of politics involved. Instead of traditional political party influence, those who seek judgeships are subject to private political infighting between the organized bar and the governor. The governor could be expected to appoint members of the nominating panel and to select judges with compatible political views. Therefore a judicial candidate may seek political favor from powerful persons in the state in order to be nominated by the panel or selected by the governor. It is as if political activity by candidates for a judicial post somehow becomes untainted when it occurs outside of the traditional political system. Another major criticism of the Missouri plan is that the judges who are selected are not necessarily representative of the community at large. Some people contend that the makeup of the selection committees does not reflect the varied interests of the public in general. A political party must develop sensitivity to the community in order to have its members elected to office, but no such pressures exist on the selection committee. The selected judges may be better in terms of objective judicial criteria, however, they may not reflect the makeup of the community.

The selection of individuals to judgeships is a very important task. Methods of selection are designed to find the best candidates as well as make them accountable without sacrificing their independent judgment on the cases that come before them. The plans just discussed have elevated fine people to the bench. Yet these plans are not without problems.

Independence and Accountability of Judges. The discussion of judges so far raises two conflicting points. A judge should be independent of influence but at the same time should be somehow accountable to the public. Judges should not be beholden to certain individuals for their positions. In virtually all court cases, there will be a winner and a loser, and one of the parties will leave the courthouse with an adverse decision. This fact of judicial decision making does not make the judge popular with fifty percent of the litigants. It is in the interest of the community and the law, however, that judicial decisions be based upon the law and facts relevant to the dispute, not on the identity of the parties before the court. A judge who is independent of extraneous pressure is an important factor in achieving justice in the courtroom.

Independence of the judiciary is important in assuring that the judge makes decisions based upon the law and the facts in dispute. However, this independence cannot be absolute. To have no control on the work of judges would be as dangerous to justice as it would be to have judges who were controlled by others.

Two major factors act as controls on the judiciary. These factors temper the independence given to the judiciary and help prevent that independence from being abused. One factor is that of peer and community pressure. The other factor is the possibility of removal from the bench for misconduct.

Although, ideally, judges will be insulated from various influences on their decision making in particular cases, they also want to do a competent job as measured by others. A competent job for a judge is not tied to "who wins" in a given suit. Instead it is a combination of things that make up the notion of a good judge. Briefly, these things include skill in understanding and applying the law to a given set of facts, being fair and even-handed in decision making, and judicial temperament. Judges err, sometimes by making a simple mistake in applying the law. More often, as will be shown in later chapters, the law in question is subject to varied interpretations in a particular case. In these instances, courts of appeal will act to reverse the decision of a judge, showing in their opinion exactly where the judge erred. These opinions are published and form a record of mistakes made by judges in their work. Judges who regularly err feel the pressure of lawyers on their reputation as a judge. Law reviews, publications that comment on legal issues and judicial decisions, are another source of peer pressure. It is one thing to have an article published that criticizes a judge's work on a philosophical or political level; it is quite another to have the article point out a judge's misapplication of the law in reaching a certain decision. A judge's reputation and constant scrutiny by other courts, by attorneys, by the law reviews, and by newspapers work to control the behavior of a judge.

The same peer pressure affects the competence of the judge on two other levels. Since judicial decisions are not secret, judges who are inconsistent in their decision making or who are not even-handed in their treatment of litigants before them are also subject to criticism. A good judge not only works hard in conscientiously applying the legal rules to a given case but also is fair in that certain people are not favored (or disfavored).

A third factor in the makeup of a competent judge is an intangible factor called judicial temperament. Judicial temperament includes such things as tolerance, patience, and understanding of the parties in litigation. It means looking at the case at hand and not being influenced by the lifestyle of the litigants, as well as showing respect to those people who appear in court. Often, people involved in a lawsuit are very tense and behave in a manner unlike their normal conduct. Judges must have a feeling for the pressures on the litigants in the course of a trial.

However, sometimes peer and public pressures are not enough to discourage abuse of judicial independence (judicial immunity from lawsuit) by a judge. It would be unwise to provide the necessary independence for the judiciary and then rely solely on the conscience of the individual judge and the peer pressure of colleagues

---

IMPROPER REMARKS BY A JUDGE

In open court during a hearing on a settlement agreement, before trial or any evidentiary hearing, Federal District Court Judge Miles W. Lord made the following remarks to the firm's president, vice president, and general counsel, who were present in court that day. In the agreement, the A. H. Robins Company, the manufacturer of the Dalkon Shield intrauterine contraceptive device, agreed to pay $4.6 million in a products liability suit. Excerpts of his remarks follow:

Today as you sit here attempting once more to extricate yourselves from the legal consequences of your acts, none of you has faced up to the fact that more than nine thousand women claim they gave up part of their womanhood so that your company might prosper. . . .

If one poor young man were, without authority or consent, to inflict such damage upon one woman, he would be jailed for a good portion of the rest of his life. Yet your company, without warning to women, invaded their bodies by the millions and caused them injuries by the thousands. And when the time came for these women to make their claims against your company, you attacked their characters. You inquired into their sexual practices and

into the identity of their sex partners. You ruined families and reputations and careers in order to intimidate those who would raise their voices against you. You introduced issues that had no relationship to the fact that you had planted in the bodies of these women instruments of death, of mutilation, of disease.

Mr. Robins, Mr. Forest, Dr. Lunsford: You have not been rehabilitated. Under your direction, your company has continued to allow women, tens of thousands of them, to wear this device—a deadly depth charge in their wombs, ready to explode at any time. . . . You have taken the bottom line as your guiding beacon and the low road as your route. That is corporate irresponsibility at its meanest. . . .

What corporate officials could learn a lesson from this? The only lesson they might learn is that it pays to delay compensating victims and to intimidate, harass, and shame the injured parties.

The United States Court of Appeals for the Eighth Circuit criticized Judge Lord for his verbal reprimand of the Robins' executives. It ruled he had deprived the officials of notice and an opportunity for a hearing.

to ensure that no abuse of that independence occurs. Using voters as a check, either through elective judgeships or by having appointed judges subject to voter removal, will not really act as a control mechanism. This will be a check on unpopular decisions rather than a check on the abuse of judicial independence. Judges who exclude evidence from a trial based on the current state of Fourth Amendment law may face harsh public condemnation and potential loss of their judicial positions, especially if a case involves a noteworthy criminal. Yet the legal decision may be correct. The result may be to discourage judges from making legally correct but unpopular decisions, or to encourage judicial gamesmanship—delaying the release of such decisions until after election day. In any event, independence is sacrificed, but control is not really enhanced. A more powerful form of control is the existence of a judicial code of conduct coupled with procedures for removal of misbehaving judges from the bench.

It is impossible to remove all abuses of judicial independence. Some judges may be intoxicated with their power in the courtroom, and attorneys, witnesses, and the parties in litigation may be uncomfortable appearing before such judges. But it must be remembered that there is a trade off. More weight being placed on judicial independence will necessarily mean less weight being placed on judicial control. A judicial system that values independent decision making requires this trade off.

The following is an example of a case in which the judge clearly abused his power.

Aetna Life Insurance Co. v. Lavoie et al.
United States Supreme Court
106 S.Ct. 1580 (1986)

Aetna Life Insurance refused to pay the full amount of a hospital bill. The insured brought suit in an Alabama state court for Aetna's alleged bad-faith refusal to pay a valid claim. The jury ruled for the insured. On appeal, the Alabama Supreme Court affirmed the jury verdict in an opinion written by Justice Embry. It was later learned that Justice Embry had two cases pending against insurance companies at the time he wrote the opinion in question which alleged bad-faith failure to pay claims. Aetna filed a motion challenging Justice Embry's participation in the case. The Alabama Supreme Court denied this motion. Aetna appealed to the United States Supreme Court which ruled that Justice Embry should not have participated in the case.

Chief Justice Burger

It certainly violates the Fourteenth Amendment to subject a person's liberty to the judgment of a court the judge of which has a direct, personal, substantial, pecuniary interest in reaching a conclusion against him in his case.

More than 30 years ago Justice Black, speaking for the Court, reached a similar conclusion and recognized that under the Due Process Clause no judge "can be a judge in his own case or be permitted to try cases where he has an interest in the outcome."

Justice Embry's opinion for the Alabama Supreme Court had the clear and immediate effect of enhancing both the legal status and the settlement value of his own case. When Justice Embry made the judgment, he acted as a judge in his own case. His interest was direct, personal, substantial and pecuniary.

We conclude that Justice Embry's participation in this case violated Aetna's due process rights. We make clear that we are not required to decide whether in fact Justice Embry was influ-

enced, but only whether sitting on the case then before the Supreme Court of Alabama would offer a possible temptation to the average judge to lead him to not to hold the balance nice, clear and true. The Due Process Clause may sometimes bar trial by judges who have no actual bias and who would do their very best to weight the scales of justice equally between contending parties. But to perform its high function in the best way, justice must satisfy the appearance of justice.

Because of Justice Embry's leading role in the decision under review, we conclude that the appearance of justice will best be served by vacating the decision and remanding for further proceedings.

Lawyers

The following section will examine another important actor in the legal system—the attorney. Three topics will be examined under this section. First, the function of an attorney in representing a client; second, the attorney's relationship with a client, focusing on the concept of the attorney-client privilege; and finally, the age-old question, "How can an attorney represent a guilty client?"

Function of Lawyers. Contrary to popular belief, most lawyers never appear in court. Their work in representing clients involves a variety of tasks often called **preventive law.** Preventive law involves advising clients on a variety of matters so that the clients minimize the chance of having legal problems. Just as plenty of exercise and a proper diet are techniques of preventive medicine, properly drafted legal documents and legal analysis of proposed business activities are elements of preventive law. In advising their clients, these lawyers seek to predict the outcome of legal matters before the issue arises. In order to make this determination, the lawyer studies past judicial decisions. The work of the court, therefore, is very important to these noncourtroom lawyers.

Trial lawyers, on the other hand, play a larger role as actors in the judicial process. The court system in the United States is operated as an adversary process. The adversary process is based upon the idea that the truth will emerge and justice will ultimately be done if each side in a dispute presents its case to an impartial hearing officer (the judge or the jury, depending on the case). The adversary nature of the proceedings involves being able to attack and test the arguments, evidence, and proof of the opposing party throughout the proceeding. Attorneys play a key role in this process because they represent the competing sides in a conflict and, through their courtroom skills, attack and test the case of the opposing party.

Although attorney courtroom strategy, tactics, and flair may make impressive

HIRING THE RIGHT LAWYER

Margaret Mitchell, the author of *Gone With the Wind*, sold her book to Macmillan. Prior to the time of publication, the company clearly realized her book would be a best seller. Macmillan retained an agent to convince a movie studio to make a film based on Mitchell's book. After a period of time, the agent succeeded in eliciting an offer of fifty thousand dollars for the book. Macmillan forwarded the contract to Mitchell for her signature.

Mitchell's father and brother were attorneys in Atlanta, primarily engaged in patent law. They reviewed the contract for her and suggested changes in it. Among other things, Mitchell was concerned about a clause in the contract related to libel suits. She also wanted final script approval of the film. Mitchell, her brother, attorneys for Macmillan, and attorneys for the film studio met to iron out the differences in the contract which Mitchell eventually signed.

Mitchell became very unhappy soon after signing because she learned from a friend that movie studios make a great deal of money from such matters as licensing. Nothing about this was ever discussed at the meeting with the attorneys, mainly because her brother was not familiar with negotiating movie rights. While a person should review a contract before signing it, preferably with an attorney, this example suggests that a person should hire an attorney familiar with the specific issues dealt with in the contract. Although Mitchell received fifty thousand dollars for the movie rights and did get the changes in the contract with respect to liability that she desired, one could argue that she might have gotten a better deal had her attorney had some experience in negotiating this type of contract.

reading, the most successful advocates win on the basis of thorough and exhaustive preparation of the case. Trial skills are important during actual courtroom confrontation, but the key to success is hard work and preparation of the case. This includes studying the applicable law and gathering evidence and data needed to bolster the client's argument.

Attorney-Client Relationship. The attorney's first and utmost duty is to the client. An attorney owes the client a fiduciary duty that is a duty of highest care, trust, loyalty, and good faith in the exercise of the representation of that client. Clients do not often understand the law and the procedures necessary for the protection of their interests. By necessity, the client places trust in the attorney. Although the lawyer is ethically bound to zealously represent the client, there are limits to that representation, for the attorney also owes a duty to the courts and to the legal system. The lawyer is considered an officer of the court, and may not lie or misrepresent to the courts, fabricate evidence, or encourage the client to lie.

The following case discusses the ethical dilemma that confronts an attorney who must zealously represent his client but at the same time prevent frauds upon the court.

Nix v. Whiteside

United States Supreme Court
106 S.Ct. 988 (1986)

Whiteside was accused of murder. While consulting with his attorney, Gary Robinson, prior to trial he indicated that he thought he saw a gun in the hands of the deceased. Shortly before trial, while conferring with his attorney, he changed his story. He stated that "in Howard Cook's case there was a gun. If I don't say I saw a gun I'm dead." His attorney believed this to be perjury and told Whiteside he would not allow him to perjure himself in court. As a result of this, Whiteside did not testify to this effect at trial. Whiteside was thereafter convicted. He brought this appeal based on the theory that he had been denied effective assistance of counsel and of his right to present a defense by his attorney's refusal to allow him to testify as he had proposed. The Supreme Court found that Whiteside's constitutional rights had not been violated.

Chief Justice Burger

We granted certiorari to decide whether the Sixth Amendment right of a criminal defendant to assistance of counsel is violated when an attorney refuses to cooperate with the defendant in presenting perjured testimony at his trial.

In *Strickland* v. *Washington,* we held that to obtain relief by way of federal habeas corpus on a claim of a deprivation of effective assistance of counsel under the Sixth Amendment, the movant must establish both serious attorney error and prejudice. To show such error, it must be established that the assistance rendered by counsel was constitutionally deficient in that "counsel made errors so serious that counsel was not functioning as 'counsel' guaranteed the defendant by the Sixth Amendment." To show prejudice, it must be established that the claimed lapses in counsel's performance rendered the trial unfair so as to "undermine confidence in the outcome" of the trial.

Whether Robinson's conduct is seen as a successful attempt to dissuade his client from committing the crime of perjury, or whether seen as a "threat" to withdraw from representation and disclose the illegal scheme, Robinson's representation of Whiteside falls well within accepted standards of professional conduct and the range of reasonable professional conduct acceptable under *Strickland.*

Robinson's admonitions to his client can in no sense be said to have forced respondent into an *impermissible* choice between his right to counsel and his right to testify as he proposed for there was no *permissible* choice to testify falsely. For defense counsel to take steps to persuade a criminal defendant to testify truthfully, or to withdraw, deprives the defendant of neither his right to counsel nor the right to testify truthfully.

We hold that, as a matter of law, counsel's conduct complained of here cannot establish the prejudice required for relief under the second strand of the *Strickland* inquiry. Although a defendant need not establish that the attorney's deficient performance more likely than not altered the outcome in order to establish prejudice under *Strickland,* a defendant must show "that there is a reasonable probability that, but for counsel's unprofessional errors, the result of the proceeding would have been different." According to *Strickland,* "[a] reasonable probability is a probability sufficient to undermine confidence in the outcome." The *Strickland* Court noted that the "benchmark" of an ineffective assistance claim is the fairness of the adversary proceeding, and that in judging prejudice and the likelihood of a different outcome, "[a] defendant has no entitlement to the luck of a lawless decisionmaker."

Whether he was persuaded or compelled to desist from perjury, Whiteside has no valid claim that confidence in the result of his trial has been diminished by his desisting from the contemplated perjury. Even if we were to assume that the jury might have believed his perjury, it does not follow that Whiteside was prejudiced.

The adversary system, in order to operate effectively, requires that the lawyer strongly represent the client's interests within the guidelines and the framework of that system. This does not mean that all decisions reached through the adversary system are correct decisions. What it does mean is that the attorney has acted consistently with what we consider to be the fairest and most efficient way for discovering the truth in a dispute.

While it is true that an attorney presents a client's case in court, he is not retained to act as an arbiter of the relative merits of the case. That is the function of the trier of facts—the judge or the jury, if a jury is employed at trial. The lawyer's function is to array the facts in such a fashion that it will convince the trier of facts that his or her position is correct. The trier of facts is to base its decision on the evidence presented during the trial, not on the arguments of counsel which are presented as a mere aid to the trier of facts.

For this purpose it is irrelevant whether the lawyer believes or disbelieves the absolute merit of the client's claim. The lawyer's personal opinion with respect to which party should prevail at trial is therefore irrelevant. This point is discussed in the next case.

United States v. Young
United States Supreme Court
105 S.Ct. 1038 (1985)

Young was tried in a criminal case for participating in a scheme to deceive Apco Oil Corporation. At the close of the case, the defense counsel attacked the prosecutor and accused him of not believing Young was guilty of attempting to defraud Apco. The prosecutor did not object at that time, but in his closing remarks stated his personal opinion that he believed Young was guilty. This violated professional rules of conduct which prohibit an attorney from stating his personal opinion as to the justness of a case, the truth or falsity of any testimony or evidence, or the guilt or innocence of an accused. Federal rules of criminal procedure permit a court, in the event an attorney fails to make a timely objection to improper conduct by the opposing attorney, to reverse a decision, if the actions of the attorney in question were "plain error." The court of appeals reversed Young's conviction—holding the prosecutor's statements constituted plain error. The Supreme Court reversed the court of appeals.

Chief Justice Burger

The principal issue to be resolved is not whether the prosecutor's response to defense counsel's misconduct was appropriate, but whether it was "plain error" that a reviewing court could act on absent a timely objection.

A criminal conviction is not to be lightly overturned on the basis of a prosecutor's comments standing alone, for the statements or conduct must be viewed in context; only by so doing can it be determined whether the prosecutor's conduct affected the fairness of the trial. To help resolve this problem, courts have invoked what is sometimes called the "invited response" or "invited reply" rule.

In order to make an appropriate assessment of whether a response was invited, the reviewing court must not only weigh the impact of the prosecutor's remarks, but must also take into account defense counsel's opening salvo. Thus the import of the evaluation has been that if the prosecutor's remarks were "invited," and did no more than respond substantially in order to "right the scale," such comments would not warrant reversing a conviction.

As we suggested earlier, the dispositive issue under the holdings of this Court is not whether the prosecutor's remarks amounted to error, but whether they rose to the level of "plain error" when he responded to defense counsel. In this setting and on this record the prosecutor's response—although error—was not "plain error" warranting the court to overlook the absence of any objection by the defense.

Another matter related to the attorney-client relationship is the **attorney-client privilege.** Attorney-client privilege provides that a client's confidential discussions with an attorney remain confidential. The purpose of the privilege is to encourage client disclosure of all the facts to the lawyer, even those harmful to the client. An attorney cannot adequately represent a client unless all the facts (both favorable and unfavorable) about the matter are known. The information is needed so the attorney can prepare the client's case.

Attorney-client privilege has existed for a long time in the law. Some writers date it to Roman times, when advocates were barred from testifying against their clients. Other writers date it to the reign of Elizabeth I of England. At that time the privilege was not based upon the rationale of protection of client's interests but instead was based upon the honor of the lawyer. Trial lawyers were considered gentlemen and it was a point of honor with gentlemen to keep their confidences. Today, as already shown, the privilege belongs to the client and exists as a matter of law to further the goals of the adversary system rather than for the protection of the attorney's honor.

Of course, at times the existence of the privilege may cause an injustice to occur. A wrongdoer may be set free. A person who breaches a contract may not be held liable. The end result of the privilege is evidence that may be central to the case, if it is privileged, may not be used in court. A case therefore may proceed with incomplete information. For example, assume George confides in an attorney, after being arrested for theft, that he did indeed steal the car. George refuses to say anything to the police. At trial he is acquitted. George did not testify, and because of the attorney-client privilege, the attorney could not reveal the client's confession. Was justice served in that particular case? The truth was withheld from the adversary system by the attorney-client privilege doctrine. Yet the possibility of this type of result (which is rare) must be balanced against the overall good the attorney-client privilege is seeking.

Clients, even with the existence of the privilege and of an ethical bar to attorneys discussing client confidences with others, are reluctant to confide in their attorneys. Often an important task of the attorney is to gain the trust of the client in order to obtain full information. Few people are eager to confess an error, whether it is a crime they committed or the fact that they were not attentive as they were driving down the street prior to an accident.

Clients, when discussing very personal and sometimes emotional facts, may try to rationalize their conduct. The privilege is a tool to reassure clients that no court will use their attorneys to bring evidence against them. The privilege therefore serves a crucial function in the administration of justice in our legal system. Without it attorneys would have little hope of gaining the confidence or a truthful statement of the facts from their clients. Consequently, the adversary system would not work properly. The case would be argued and prepared based upon false or incomplete facts. (In the law, small factual differences often will cause a change in the way a case is handled by an attorney and perhaps even affect which legal rules are applicable.) The expected result is that clients will most likely not receive a fair trial. Injustice to clients and to the system that relies on the clash in the courtroom in the search for truth would result. The concept of attorney-client privilege is an ideal strongly protected by the courts since it furthers the search for truth and justice through the operation of our adversary system.

How Can an Attorney Represent a Guilty Person? One of the most persistent questions asked of attorneys, and one that troubles a great number of people, is: How can an attorney represent a guilty person? A related question is: How can an attorney, in good conscience, seek to have evidence thrown out of court, resulting in a criminal's being set free to prey on other victims? These difficult questions have been responded to in a variety of ways. Some have argued that an attorney cannot let personal considerations overcome professional obligations to the legal system, which provides that accused parties shall have the right to counsel to represent their interests in court. Others have contended that the attorney's role in the adversary system is to zealously represent clients. The decision-making role rests with the judge or the jury and is not a part of the role given to the lawyer in the judicial system. Samuel Johnson once said: "An argument which does not convince yourself, may convince the Judge to whom you urge it; and if it does convince him, why, then, Sir, you are wrong, and he is right. It is his business to judge, and you are not to be confident in your own opinion that a cause is bad, but to say all you can for your client, and then hear the Judge's opinion."[1]

Such arguments focus on the lawyer's responsibility to the legal system and the lawyer's role in the legal system. The question is still not answered and the inquirer is left to ask, "What kind of system is this, which encourages attorneys to use all the devices of the law to set free a guilty person?"

It is possible to respond adequately to that question, since it is much like asking, "Do you still kick your dog?" The inquirer presupposes an unsatisfactory response due to a lack of insight into the nature of the adversary system. Therefore, a response to the question of how an attorney can represent a guilty person must be rather involved. First, the term *guilty person* has two meanings. One of them is the everyday usage of that term, covering actual and, in a sense, moral guilt. Did the accused commit the act? Did the defendant steal the car? Did the corporation dump waste in the river? This concept of guilt or innocence focuses solely on the actions of the wrongdoer. It is the way the term *guilt* is used by the questioner.

However, the legal system's concept of guilt is much broader. In the legal system, guilt means that the state has proven its case beyond a reasonable doubt and may punish the wrongdoer. Legal guilt is a prerequisite for an individual's loss of liberty under our system of government. *Guilt* is a shorthand term for this occurrence and includes many more considerations than simply whether the accused did or did not commit the act, although that is a major factor.

Guilt describes the amount of proof (beyond a reasonable doubt) which must be provided by the state before a person can be punished by the state. Thus, the person who committed a crime might be set free simply because the state could not gather enough evidence. Additionally, guilt in the legal system presumes that the state used proper procedures throughout the case. The necessity for such procedures is twofold. First, uniform procedures are necessary for evenhanded administration of justice. That is, all accused parties must be afforded the same rights and the same process before they may be punished by the state. This is important in that it prevents favoritism being built into the legal process.

A second important function of the procedures for determining legal guilt is that they operate as a safeguard for individual freedoms. The procedures are important in order to protect us, in the long run, from the power of the government. When people are forced to speak against their will in a police station, when a person's home may be invaded at any time by the police, a feeling of terror and a loss of liberty will result. Under such a system, wrongdoers would be punished, but at a very great cost to society. People would not know when the knock on the door would come for them, and when it did occur, how they would defend themselves.

Our adversary system of justice is based on the theory that justice—the goal of the system—can best be served through vigorous argument and testing in a courtroom of all aspects of the case. In the adversarial context, guilt is made up of a number of factors (such as the accused's mental state, the way evidence was obtained, whether the accused understood the consequences of cooperation with the authorities, whether the prosecutor presented enough evidence, and whether the accused did the act). Sometimes those factors clash. In order for legal guilt to be established, all factors involved in that concept must be established.

Contrary to popular notions, people who commit crimes (do the act) and face trial are usually found legally guilty. The system *does* work. The lawyer who appears to "get the criminal off" really does not do so. Instead what has happened is that in the testing of the state's evidence and procedures, flaws have been found.

The idea of an attorney representing a guilty client is more complex than the question as originally posed implies. That question usually results from a desire to see the wrongdoer brought to justice. But the process of bringing the wrongdoer to justice by establishing legal guilt calls for a broader inquiry than one that focuses merely on whether that person actually did the criminal act. At times these other factors are central to the finding of a court that an individual was guilty. The testing of these other factors is the lawyer's task, and legal guilt cannot be established until those factors are tested.

SUMMARY

Courts are major institutions in the legal environment. Courts render decisions that can have a profound effect on the operation of a firm. A general study of courts or the judicial system is therefore important. The judicial system may be reviewed either structurally—state or federal courts—or it may be reviewed by function—trial or appellate courts.

Understanding the judicial system involves more than gaining an appreciation of its form. It also requires understanding the roles of the major participants in the system, the judge and the attorney. One of the important features of the judicial role is the balance between an independent judiciary and controls on the power that independence brings. Fair decision making is hampered by a judge who is unable to assess a matter free of influence. However, given the powers of a judge, a lack of controls could also cause harm to the administration of justice.

The role of the attorney is another important element of the judicial system. An attorney's task involves zealously guarding a client's interests within the policies and goals of the adversary system. Often, questions concerning the secrecy of client communications with counsel or the representation of a "guilty" client ignore the important functions of the legal system.

REVIEW QUESTIONS

1. Define the following terms:
   a. Trial court
   b. Appellate court
   c. Missouri plan

2. What are the major characteristics of the federal judicial system? Can federal courts hear any case that arises? What are the differences and similarities between the federal court system and a state court system?

3. What is the difference between a trial court and an appellate court?

4. Briefly describe the general functions of a judge. Is it accurate to say that a judge should not make the law? What is meant by judicial lawmaking?

5. Devise a system for the selection of judges. The criteria for you to use include: highly qualified candidates, sensitivity to the community, independence of outside influence, a public voice in selecting and retaining the judge, and accountability to the general public.

6. Why does the judicial system value the independence of its judges? What would be the effect on a judicial system of greatly restricting the independence of the judiciary?

7. What is meant by the term *attorney-client privilege*? What is it designed to accomplish in the legal system?

8. Should an attorney represent a "guilty" person? What would be the effect on our legal system if attorneys did not represent people who actually committed criminal acts?

9. A woman was brought to court on a disorderly

conduct charge. Judge Yengo made certain judgments about the woman based upon his perception of people like her. He told her to shut up. He arbitrarily raised the time she had to serve in jail from 90 to 120 days solely because of a remark she made to her mother during the court proceeding. Should Judge Yengo be disciplined for misconduct in office?

10. Radiant Burners, Inc., sought to raise the attorney-client privilege in order to keep certain documents confidential. May a corporation claim the attorney-client privilege?

11. The Internal Revenue Service sued Upjohn Corporation because of questionable payments made to foreign officials in order to secure their business. Upjohn's attorneys had already conducted an intracompany investigation of the payments and the IRS asked Upjohn for the records of the investigation. Upjohn refused, citing the doctrine of attorney-client privilege. Is Upjohn correct?

12. Javor's attorney dozed off during a substantial portion of his trial. Should Javor be given a new trial?

13. Allen was arrested for a nonjailable crime. Judge Pulliam imposed bail, and when Allen was unable to meet the bail, Pulliam sent him to jail. Allen brought suit to enjoin Pulliam from jailing persons who could not meet bail. Can Judge Pulliam be prevented from engaging in this practice in the future?

14. Johns was accused of a crime. At trial, Johns did not testify, and his attorney did not present the court with jury instructions that could have included a less serious crime than Johns was accused of in this case. Johns was subsequently convicted. The reason Johns's attorney did this, he later testified, was because he felt he could not in conscience argue to the jury that Johns should be acquitted because of what Johns had previously told him. In light of the attorney's actions, should Johns be entitled to a new trial?

NOTE

[1] James Boswell, *The Life of Samuel Johnson* (1791), p. 333.

CHAPTER 3

Civil Litigation and Alternative Dispute Resolution

Civil Litigation
Trial Procedure
The Appeal

Judges perform their duties of making law and settling disputes through litigation. To understand those duties we must focus on the process of litigation, more particularly civil litigation. Civil litigation may be distinguished from criminal litigation. **Civil litigation** is all the trial work of our system that does *not* involve the violation of a **criminal law.** Most areas of the law therefore are affected by the civil litigation process: tort law, contract law, property law, and labor law are examples.

Often factors other than the rules of law are crucial to the outcome of a dispute. Yet these factors are frequently considered to be "mere technicalities." A portion of this chapter will discuss a very important factor in any trial—the jury. Much of the discussion of the jury in the context of civil litigation will also be relevant to criminal trials. The jury is one of the most important institutions in our legal system. It is the one direct day-to-day method in which persons without legal training can have an effect on our legal system.

CIVIL LITIGATION

In General

A trial is a search for truth. It is not a perfect mechanism for obtaining the truth, however. There is no process or procedure that will guarantee that the just and correct result will be obtained in all cases. As we have already discussed, in our system a trial is conducted through an adversary process—one in which each side in a dispute presents its case in the best possible light. The decision maker at the trial, either the judge or the jury, listens to the arguments presented by the parties and essentially chooses which one to accept. A trial is a competition. The parties compete by presenting their different versions of the facts and making analyses of the applicable law. For if the parties agreed upon the facts and application of the law, then there would be no dispute and no need for a trial.

This does not mean that in every trial there is one truth teller and one liar and that the function of the decision maker is to select the truth teller. "Facts" are difficult to pinpoint. Both parties may be telling the truth, yet the evidence presented at the trial may conflict. Witnesses may see the very same event differently.

The views of parties directly involved in the dispute will most likely differ, and their views may both differ from the views of a casual witness. The decision maker must decide which of the factual versions is closer to the events that actually took place. However, as will be discussed in Chapter Four on judicial reasoning and in the material on the jury that follows, the decision makers too have personality factors that influence their work in deciding the case.

The Adversary System

The **adversary system** is based on the theory that all facts will be uncovered, the truth will come out, and justice will be done if each side in a dispute presents its case in the best possible light. This not only means gathering witnesses, documents, and exhibits that bolster one view of the case, it also means exposing any weaknesses and inconsistencies in the case presented by the opposing party. Each side builds its own case and attempts to discredit the case of its opponents. In this way, the accuracy of witness observations, the evasiveness of answers to questions, and even outright lies will most likely come to light during the trial.

Alternatives to Trying a Case

From the moment a client first consults an attorney, the attorney generally considers the possibility of settling the case rather than actually litigating it. Sometimes cases are settled quite soon after an attorney is retained. In other cases, the settlement comes after the filing of the case against the defendant. Sometimes cases are not settled until the parties appear at the courthouse on the day set for the trial. The cases that go to trial are those where the parties are unable to come to an agreement that is satisfactory to all sides. This often occurs when one party makes a demand that the other party regards as unreasonable. In other cases, the law may be unclear. The parties will then litigate the case to determine what the duties of the parties are.

Lawyers try to predict the outcome of litigation, but as soon as the decision in a case is placed in the hands of a third party, the lawyer has lost all control over the outcome. Most lawyers can relate stories of how they lost cases that they thought they would win or, more likely, how they won a case that was "hopeless." Risk of the unknown encourages the parties to settle a case rather than litigate it.

Settlement. Relatively few legal disputes actually result in a trial; most are settled out of court. There are incentives for litigants to do so. The time and expense of proceeding to trial must be weighed against the advantages of immediate settlement. An injured party may want to collect money damages as soon as possible, thereby hastening an out-of-court settlement. Additionally, settlements can be structured so that payments can be made in ways other than in one lump sum (i.e., they may be spread over a number of years). This option also makes settlement attractive to the party who must pay damages.

There is often great delay in getting a case into court, another reason litigants are willing to settle rather than wait for a trial. Then, of course, there is always the risk of loss at trial.

Arbitration. Arbitration is sometimes used as a substitute for a trial and is quicker and less costly than litigation in a court. The arbitrator, the person who hears and decides the dispute, is selected by the parties. Frequently, the arbitrator is an authority in the area in which the dispute arises. Arbitration is often used in labor disputes and in construction-contract disputes. The parties, informally and at convenient times, submit their cases to an arbitrator. The arbitrator, like a judge, weighs the evidence, applies the law, and renders a decision. Arbitration is another practical alternative to the delay and expense of the court system. In addition to being quicker

---

LAWSUIT SETTLEMENT

Steve Jobs was one of the founders of Apple Computer, Inc. In June 1985, Jobs was removed from any management responsibility with the firm and later resigned in a dispute with Apple management concerning his role in his new computer business, Next, Inc. Next is an effort to bring sophisticated computer technology to the university, to create a "scholar's work station."

In September 1985, Apple sued Jobs, contending that he was using Apple research for his other company and that he was enticing key Apple personnel to join Next. Prior to this suit, five of Apple Computer's top young engineers had resigned to join Jobs's new venture. The suit was settled in early 1986. Some key provisions of the settlement barred Jobs from marketing his new scholar's computer for eighteen months and from using certain undisclosed technology in it.

Additionally, Apple Computer was given the right to inspect any newly developed computer for thirty days prior to marketing to determine if any Apple proprietary information was used. However, authorities on trade secrets noted that in other technology-use disputes the inspections have lasted for months. Jobs agreed not to hire additional Apple Computer employees for six months. Finally, the parties agreed that any further disputes over the use of technology were to be submitted to arbitration.

Both parties were pleased with the settlement. Apple Computer's general counsel noted that the corporation's goals were met, and rights were protected by the settlement. Jobs, although convinced he would win at trial, was pleased to have the emotional stress of major litigation behind him.

and cheaper than trying a case in court, arbitration has the advantage of being more informal. Furthermore, if the parties desire to keep the matter out of the public eye, arbitration can be used to keep a matter private. This is a major factor in many cases for resorting to arbitration.

Various means may be used to select an arbitrator. Sometimes as many as three arbitrators hear a case. In such situations, each party generally selects a person, then a neutral third party selects the third arbitrator. Usually, however, cases are heard before a single arbitrator. These arbitrators are often provided by the American Arbitration Association.

The arbitration is dependent on the parties' agreement to arbitrate rather than litigate the dispute through a court. If they decide to submit the dispute to binding arbitration, a court will refuse to rehear the entire matter. At most, the court will review the work of the arbitrator for errors. When the parties have signed an agreement that contains a broad arbitration clause, the courts will order the parties to arbitrate any dispute arising under or related to the agreement in the absence of clear evidence the parties did not intend to arbitrate the matter.

An example of a broad arbitration clause is as follows: "Any controversy or claim arising out of or relating to this contract, or the breach thereof, shall be settled by arbitration in accordance with the Commercial Arbitration Rules of the American Arbitration Association, and judgment upon the award rendered by the Arbitrator(s) may be entered in any Court having jurisdiction thereof." It is not necessary to include such a broad arbitration clause in a contract. The parties may limit the scope of the clause by specifying that only certain matters be arbitrated or by excluding certain kinds of disputes. However, if a contract is ambiguous, the terms of the contract will be constructed in favor of arbitrability where such construction is not obviously contrary to the intent of the parties. This point is illustrated by the following case.

Kansas City Royals Baseball Corp. v. Major League Baseball Players Assn.
United States Court of Appeals, Eighth Circuit
532 F.2d 615 (1976)

Dave McNally and Andy Messersmith, two major league baseball players, "played out their options" during the 1975 baseball season in an attempt to gain free-agent status. (McNally retired during the 1975 season, however.) The baseball owners denied Messersmith the right of free agency at the end of the 1975 baseball season because of the practice and contractual term that allowed a team to renew a player's contract on a year-to-year basis for a reasonable number of years. In practice, this tied the player to one team throughout his career unless the team decided to trade him to another team. Messersmith claimed that after he had fulfilled his contract for the 1975 season, he was able to join any other team he chose. Messersmith sought arbitration of his grievance through the arbitration panel set up by the 1973–1975 collective bargaining agreement of the Players Association and the team owners. The arbitrators, by a two-to-one vote, declared Messersmith a free agent. The baseball owners attempted, in federal court, to have the decision overturned.

Heaney, Circuit Judge

Article X of the agreement between the Major League Players Association and the team owners set forth a comprehensive procedure for the resolution of certain grievances. "Grievance" was defined as "a complaint which involves the interpretation of, or compliance with, the provision of any agreement between the Association and the Clubs or any of them, or any agreement between a Player and a Club. . . ." Certain disputes not pertinent here were excepted.

The Club Owners responded to both Messersmith-McNally grievances on October 24, 1975. Their primary contention was that the claims raised fell outside the scope of the agreed upon grievance procedures and were, therefore, not subject to the jurisdiction of the arbitration panel. They argued that Article XV of the 1973 agreement excluded disputes concerning the "core" or "heart" of the reserve system (the system which bound a player to one team) from the grievance procedures set forth in Article X.

A party may be compelled to arbitrate a grievance only if it has agreed to do so. In resolving questions of arbitrability, the courts are guided by Congress's declaration of policy that arbitration is the desirable method for settling labor disputes. Accordingly, a grievance arising under a collective bargaining agreement providing for arbitration must be deemed arbitrable "unless it may be said with positive assurance that the arbitration clause is not susceptible of an interpretation that covers the asserted dispute. Doubts should be resolved in favor of coverage."

If it is determined that the arbitrator had jurisdiction, judicial review of his award is limited to the question of whether it "draws its essence from the collective bargaining agreement." We do not sit as an appellate tribunal to review the merits of the arbitrator's decision.

We begin with the proposition that the language of Article X of the 1973 agreement is suffi-ciently broad to require arbitration of the Messersmith-McNally grievances. We think this clear because the disputes involve the interpretation of the provisions of agreements between a player or the Players Association and a club or the Club Owners. The grievances require the construction of agreements manifested in paragraphs 9(a) and 10(a) of the Uniform Player's Contract.

Although we find that the grievances are arbitrable under Article X standing alone, we cannot ignore the existence of Article XV, which provides inter alia, that the agreement "does not deal with the reserve system."

We cannot say that Article XV, on its face, constitutes a clear exclusionary provision. First, the precise thrust of the phrase "this Agreement does not deal with the reserve system" is unclear. The agreement incorporates the provision which comprise the reserve system. Also, the phrase is qualified by the words "except as adjusted or modified hereby." Second, the impact of the language "This Agreement shall in no way prejudice the position . . . of the Parties" is uncertain. Third, the "concerted action" which the parties agree to forego does not clearly include bringing grievances. Fourth, Article XV affords no basis for the Club Owners' distinction between the "core" and the periphery of the reserve system. Finally, Article X(A)(1), which declares certain disputes non-grievable, is silent as to the reserve system. We find, however, that Article XV creates an ambiguity as to whether the grievances here involved are arbitrable. Accordingly, we must look beyond the face of the agreement and determine whether the record as a whole evinces the most forceful evidence of a purpose to exclude these grievances from arbitration.

The weight of the evidence, when viewed as a whole, does not support the conclusion that Article XV was intended to preclude arbitration of any grievances otherwise arbitrable.

We hold that the arbitration panel had jurisdiction to hear and decide the Messersmith-McNally grievances, that the panel's award drew its essence from the collective bargaining agreement, and that the relief fashioned by the District Court was appropriate. Accordingly, the award of the arbitration panel must be sustained, and the District Court's judgment affirmed. In so holding, we intimate no views on the merits of the reserve system. We note, however, that Club Owners and the Players Association's representatives agree that some form of a reserve system is needed if the integrity of the game is to be preserved and if public confidence in baseball is to be maintained.

Parties may elect to arbitrate virtually any dispute. In general, federal law favors the arbitration of all disputes. This policy in favor of arbitration is expressed in the United States Arbitration Act. Many states have passed the Uniform Arbitration Act. Some issues, however, may not be submitted to an arbitrator because federal law prohibits it. In general, matters relating to federal securities laws, federal antitrust laws, and bankruptcy may not be arbitrated (subject to some exceptions). State law also sometimes prohibits the arbitration of certain matters. However, due to the preemption doctrine (discussed in Chapter 6 on Constitutional Law), state laws restricting arbitration may be overruled where interstate commerce is involved.

Disputes that occur in the United States concerning securities and antitrust laws normally may not be arbitrated. However, if an international agreement is involved, these matters can be arbitrated. This will be dealt with more thoroughly in Chapter 24.

Mediation. Another device used to try to resolve disputes is **mediation.** In an arbitration case, the arbitrator actually decides the case for the parties. In most cases, such a decision may be appealed. A mediator, on the other hand, merely tries to help the parties work out their differences. The mediator lacks the power to decide the case for the parties.

Both arbitration and mediation are commonly used in the labor-relations field. The federal government operates the Federal Mediation and Conciliation Service to help parties to a labor dispute mediate their differences.

In most cases, the parties elect to resolve their dispute through the court system rather than through use of a mediator or arbitrator.

Other Alternatives. Another method of resolving a dispute is the **minitrial.** When the parties to a case use a minitrial, they present evidence before a neutral advisor who may be a judge or other lawyer. The neutral advisor then gives the party an opinion on how he or she feels the case would be resolved in court. When the parties hear the major issues aired in a courtroom-like setting, they are more likely to see the strengths and weaknesses of their cases. This, hopefully, will encourage them to come to a settlement of their dispute. If they do not settle the matter, they can always try the case at a later date.

A slight variation of the minitrial is the **summary trial.** In a summary trial, each side presents a summary of its case before a judge or small jury. A decision is then rendered in the case. The decision may be binding on the parties if they agree that it will be binding.

There are a variety of other techniques for dispute resolution that are becoming increasingly popular as alternatives to a formal trial.

In the event the parties are unable to settle a dispute and they choose not to rely upon one of these alternatives, they must present their case before a judge or jury. A court will not, however, hear a case unless it has the power to do so, which is discussed in the next section.

Jurisdiction. The civil trial system is designed to encourage the efficient disposition of cases. Not every trial court is empowered to hear every type of case. For instance, some courts cannot hear certain cases because of the nature of the legal doctrines from which the matter arose or the amount of money in dispute in the case. Geographical rules also decide the proper court in which to bring a case. A person with a legal claim may not simply bring a case to any court in the nation. There are requirements of **jurisdiction** (concerning whether a particular court is empowered to hear the case) and venue (concerning whether an otherwise empowered court is the proper one in which to file the suit) that must first be met.

Jurisdiction refers to the *power* of a court to hear a case. A court must have jurisdiction over the *subject matter* of the case. It must also have *in personam* jurisdiction—jurisdiction over the *parties* to the case.

A court has jurisdiction over the subject matter of a case if it is the type of case the court is authorized to hear. Some state courts are courts of general jurisdiction—they can hear any case arising in the state. Other courts are courts of limited jurisdiction—they can hear only certain types of cases. For example, suppose that a judge presides over a probate court in a given state. A **probate** court handles the estates of deceased persons and guardianships. If a plaintiff filed suit in the probate court for damages arising out of an automobile accident, the probate judge would be required to dismiss the suit for lack of jurisdiction. An automobile accident case has nothing to do with the power of the court to hear probate and guardianship matters. All federal courts are courts of limited jurisdiction; that is, they have the power to hear only certain types of cases. For example, in some types of civil cases heard in federal court, the amount in controversy must be at least ten thousand dollars. In cases in which there is no federal question, only if the amount in controversy is ten thousand dollars and diversity of citizenship exists does a federal court have jurisdiction. (**Diversity of citizenship** exists when all the plaintiffs are from states other than the state of residence of any of the defendants.)

It is not sufficient for a court merely to have jurisdiction over the subject matter of the case. The court must also have in personam jurisdiction, which gives the court the power to impose liability on the person or businesses involved in the case.

In some situations, a court need only have jurisdiction over the property involved in the case—this is called *in rem* jurisdiction. A court that has jurisdiction over property involved in a case, but not over a person, may render a judgment that is binding on the property that is the subject matter of a case. If a court is unable to obtain in personam jurisdiction, but property that is the subject matter of the suit is located in the state, the court may permit the trial of a case. Any judgment may be enforced with respect to the property involved in the case. The judgment may not, however, be enforced beyond the borders of the state, because the court lacks in personam jurisdiction over the defendant. Assets owned by the defendant that are located beyond the borders of the state court exercising in rem jurisdiction may not be used to pay the judgment.

In personam jurisdiction over the person of the plaintiff is obtained by the plaintiff filing the suit. In personam jurisdiction over the defendant normally is obtained by the service of a summons and petition on the defendant. Generally, the states permit service upon anyone in the home of the defendant who is of a certain age. In certain circumstances, service of the summons and petition may be accomplished in other ways—for example, by publication.

A more serious problem arises when the defendant is not physically present within the state. For many years, the courts adhered to the belief that service could be accomplished only by personally serving the defendant while that person was physically within the borders of the state.

The following case recognizes the power of the state, in civil suits, to serve a summons and petition beyond the physical borders of the state. It should be noted that the discussion here applies only to *civil*, as opposed to criminal, suits. This case is of great importance because it permitted the state of Washington to obtain in personam jurisdiction over the International Shoe Company even though the company asserted that it never was physically present in the state. Note that the Supreme Court declares that in personam jurisdiction may, under certain circumstances, be obtained over a person or company not physically present within the borders of the state.

International Shoe Co. v. State of Washington
United States Supreme Court
326 U.S. 310 (1945)

This case deals with a dispute between International Shoe and the state of Washington. Though International Shoe's principal place of business was in St. Louis, it conducted business in other states. It was engaged in the manufacture and sale of shoes. International Shoe, the appellant in this case, had no office in Washington, made no contracts there, and maintained no merchandise there. From 1937 to 1940, it employed eleven to thirteen salesmen whose principal activities were confined to the state of Washington. The salesmen exhibited samples and solicited orders in Washington and transmitted the orders to St. Louis for acceptance or rejection.

The state of Washington brought suit against International Shoe for payments it felt International owed the Washington unemployment compensation fund. In this case, notice of the assessment for the years 1937 to 1940 was personally served upon a salesman in Washington, and a copy of the notice was mailed by registered mail to International Shoe's home office in St. Louis. International Shoe challenged the power of the courts in Washington to force it to go to Washington to defend this suit. International Shoe claimed that forcing it to defend the suit in Washington would violate the due process clause of the Fourteenth Amendment.

Chief Justice Stone

Appellant insists that its activities within the state were not sufficient to manifest its "presence" there and that in its absence the state courts were without jurisdiction, that consequently it was a denial of due process for the state to subject appellant to suit.

Historically the jurisdiction of courts to render judgment in personam is grounded on their de facto power over the defendant's person. Hence his presence within the territorial jurisdiction of a court was prerequisite to its rendition of a judgment personally binding him. But now due process requires only that in order to subject a defendant to a judgment in personam, if he be not present within the territory of the forum, he have certain minimum contacts with it such that the maintenance of the suit does not offend "traditional notions of fair play and substantial justice."

Since the corporate personality is a fiction it is clear that unlike an individual its "presence" without, as well as within, the state of its origin can be manifested only by activities carried on in its behalf by those who are authorized to act for it.

"Presence" in the state in this sense has never been doubted when the activities of the corporation there have not only been continuous and systematic, but also give rise to the liabilities sued on, even though no consent to be sued or authorization to an agent to accept service of process has been given. Conversely it has been generally recognized that the casual presence of the corporate agent or even his conduct of single or isolated items of activities in a state in the corporation's behalf are not enough to subject it to suit on causes of action unconnected with the activities there. To require the corporation in such circumstances to defend the suit away from its home or other jurisdiction where it carries on more substantial activities has been thought to lay too great

and unreasonable a burden on the corporation to comport with due process.

Whether due process is satisfied must depend upon the quality and nature of the activity in relation to the fair and orderly administration of the laws which it was the purpose of the due process clause to insure. That clause does not contemplate that a state may make binding a judgment in personam against an individual or corporate defendant with which the state has no contacts, ties, or relations.

The activities carried on in behalf of appellant in the State of Washington were neither irregular nor casual. They were systematic and continuous throughout the years in question. They resulted in a large volume of interstate business, in the course of which appellant received the benefits and protection of the laws of the state, including the right to resort to the courts for the enforcement of its rights. The obligation which is here sued upon arose out of those very activities. It is evident that these operations establish sufficient contacts or ties with the state of the forum to make it reasonable and just according to our traditional conception of fair play and substantial justice to permit the state to enforce the obligations which appellant has incurred there. Hence we cannot say that the maintenance of the present suit in the State of Washington involves an unreasonable or undue procedure.

We are likewise unable to conclude that the service of the process within the state upon an agent whose activities establish appellant's "presence" there was not sufficient notice of the suit, or that the suit was so unrelated to those activities as to make the agent an inappropriate vehicle for communicating the notice. It is enough that appellant has established such contacts with the state that the particular form of substituted service adopted there gives reasonable assurance that the notice will be actual. Nor can we say that the mailing of the notice of suit to appellant by registered mail at its home office was not reasonably calculated to apprise appellant of the suit.

Appellant having rendered itself amenable to suit upon obligations arising out of the activities of its salesmen in Washington, the state may maintain the present suit in personam to collect the tax laid upon the exercise of the privilege of employing appellant's salesmen within the state. For Washington has made one of those activities, which taken together establish appellant's "presence" there for purposes of suit, the taxable event by which the state brings appellant within the reach of its taxing power. The state thus has constitutional power to lay the tax and to subject appellant to a suit to recover it. The activities which establish its "presence" subject it alike to taxation by the state and to suit to recover the tax.

As a result of the *International Shoe* case, states have adopted what are commonly called **long-arm statutes.** These statutes permit a plaintiff to obtain service of the summons and petition beyond the physical borders of the state. However, as noted in the *International Shoe* case, a defendant may not be required to appear in court in another state if such an appearance would violate the due process clause of the United States Constitution. The due process clause requires that individuals have fair warning that a particular activity may subject them to the jurisdiction of a foreign sovereign.

Suppose that a manufacturer sells a product which injures a person in a state other than where the manufacturer is located. Is it fair to force the manufacturer to go to that state to defend a suit brought by the injured party? If a company delivers its products into the stream of commerce with the expectation that they will be purchased by consumers in the state where the injured party is located, and its product injures someone in that state, personal jurisdiction over the company may be asserted by a court in the state in which the injured party is located.

What if instead the parties have entered into a contract. Suppose that one person lives in Texas and the other person lives in California. If the California plaintiff wishes to force the Texas defendant to come to California to defend a suit, may it do so?

The fair-warning requirement of the due process clause requires that the Texas defendant purposefully establish some minimum contacts with the state of California. The defendant must have a continuing relationship with the plaintiff in California. The mere fact that a contract was entered into with an out of state party alone does not establish minimum contacts. Nor does the fact that the contract in question may specify which state law is to be applied in resolving any disputes related to the contract. A court must examine the prior negotiations and contemplated future consequences along with the terms of the contract and the parties' actual course of dealing to determine if the defendant purposefully established minimum contacts within the forum.

Assuming a court finds that the Texas defendant did purposefully establish minimum contacts with California, these contacts must then be considered in light of other factors to determine whether the assertion of personal jurisdiction is consistent with fair play and justice. Even if the defendant purposefully engaged in activities in California, jurisdiction may not be asserted unless it is consistent with fair play and substantial justice.

It should be noted that in judging minimum contacts, a court should focus on the relationship among the defendant, the forum, and the litigation.

The typical long-arm statute is designed for a situation such as an automobile accident. Suppose that Smith travels to state X from his home state, Texas. While in state X, he is involved in an automobile accident. He then returns to Texas. The resident of state X now wishes to file suit in his home state and wishes to serve the summons and petition on the defendant in Texas. Because Smith committed a tort within state X (torts are discussed in Chapter 9), the plaintiff generally is permitted to serve the summons and petition beyond the physical borders of the state.

All states have provisions that permit the courts to obtain jurisdiction over nonresident individuals and corporations. A typical statute authorizes service of process outside the state on individuals or corporations for in personam actions arising out of (1) the transaction of any business in a state, (2) the commission of a tortious act within a state, or (3) the ownership, use, or possession of real estate in the state.

The typical procedure is to file the lawsuit in the appropriate state court, sending a copy of the petition and a summons to the secretary of state. The secretary of state then sends this information to the defendant by registered mail. Although the defendant is beyond the physical borders of state X, he or she must return to state X to defend the suit.

The following case deals with a situation in which a foreign corporation was sued in the United States.

Helicopteros Nacionales de Colombia, S.A. v. Hall
United States Supreme Court
104 S.Ct. 1868 (1984)

Helicol was a Colombian Corporation with its principal place of business in Bogota, Colombia. It provided helicopter service for South American companies. Consorcio/WSH needed helicopters to move personnel and equipment in Peru. The chief executive officer of Helicol, Francisco Restrepo, flew to Houston to confer with representatives of Consorcio/WSH. The parties entered into an agreement at that time. A contract, written in Spanish, was formally signed in Peru. The contract stated that all controversies arising out of the contract would be submitted to the jurisdiction of the Peruvian courts. Consorcio/WSH was to make payments to Helicol's account with the Bank of America in New York City. During the years 1970 to 1977, Helicol purchased helicopters and parts from Bell Helicopter in Fort Worth, Texas. It also sent prospective pilots as well as management and maintenance personnel to Fort Worth for training.

Helicol has never been authorized to do business in Texas, nor has it ever had an agent for the service of process in Texas. It never operated in Texas, solicited business, or signed a contract in Texas. It had no office or establishment there.

While operating in Peru, a Helicol helicopter crashed. Four United States citizens were aboard. Representatives of the deceased filed a wrongful death suit against Helicol in state court in Texas. Helicol filed a special appearance and moved to dismiss for lack of in personam jurisdiction over it. The supreme court of Texas ruled that Helicol's contacts with the state of Texas were sufficient to allow a Texas state court to assert jurisdiction over the corporation in a cause of action not arising out of or related to the corporation's activities within the state. The Supreme Court reversed.

Justice Blackmun

The Due Process Clause of the Fourteenth Amendment operates to limit the power of a State to assert *in personam* jurisdiction over a nonresident defendant. Due process requirements are satisfied when *in personam* jurisdiction is asserted over a nonresident corporate defendant that has "certain minimum contacts with [the forum] such that the maintenance of the suit does not offend 'traditional notions of fair play and substantial justice.' " *International Shoe Co. v. Washington*.

When a controversy is related to or "arises out of" a defendant's contacts with the forum, the Court has said that a relationship among the defendant, the forum, and the litigation is the essential foundation of *in personam* jurisdiction.

Even when the cause of action does not arise out of or relate to the foreign corporation's activities in the forum State, due process is not offended by a State's subjecting the corporation to its *in personam* jurisdiction when there are sufficient contacts between the State and the foreign corporation. *Perkins v. Benquet Consolidated Mining Co.*

In *Perkins*, the Court addressed a situation in which state courts had asserted general jurisdiction over a defendant foreign corporation. During the Japanese occupation of the Philippine Islands, the president and general manager of a Philippine mining corporation maintained an office in Ohio from which he conducted activities on behalf of the company. He kept company files and held directors' meetings in the office, carried on correspondence relating to the business, distributed salary checks drawn on two active Ohio bank

accounts, engaged an Ohio bank to act as transfer agent, and supervised policies dealing with the rehabilitation of the corporation's properties in the Philippines. In short, the foreign corporation, through its president, had been carrying on in Ohio a continuous and systematic, but limited, part of its general business, and the exercise of general jurisdiction over the Philippine corporation by an Ohio court was "reasonable and just."

All parties to the present case concede that respondents' claims against Helicol did not "arise out of," and are not related to, Helicol's activities within Texas. We thus must explore the nature of Helicol's contacts with the State of Texas to determine whether they constitute the kind of continuous and systematic general business contacts the Court found to exist in *Perkins*. We hold that they do not.

It is undisputed that Helicol does not have a place of business in Texas and never has been licensed to do business in the State. Basically, Helicol's contacts with Texas consisted of sending its chief executive officer to Houston for a contract-negotiation session; accepting into its New York bank account checks drawn on a Houston bank; purchasing helicopters, equipment, and training services from Bell Helicopter for substantial sums; and sending personnel to Bell's facilities in Fort Worth for training.

The Texas Supreme Court focused on the purchases and the related training trips in finding contacts sufficient to support an assertion of jurisdiction. We do not agree with that assessment, for the Court's opinion in *Rosenberg Bros. & Co. v.*

Curtis Brown Co. makes clear that purchases and related trips, standing alone, are not a sufficient basis for a State's assertion of jurisdiction.

In accordance with *Rosenberg,* we hold that mere purchases, even if occurring at regular intervals, are not enough to warrant a State's assertion of *in personam* jurisdiction over a nonresident corporation in a cause of action not related to those purchase transactions. Nor can we conclude that the fact that Helicol sent personnel into Texas for training in connection with the purchase of helicopters and equipment in that State in any way enhanced the nature of Helicol's contacts with Texas. The training was a part of the package of goods and services purchased by Helicol from Bell Helicopter. The brief presence of Helicol employees in Texas for the purpose of attending the training sessions is no more a significant contact than were the trips to New York made by the buyer for the retail store in *Rosenberg.*

We hold that Helicol's contacts with the State of Texas were insufficient to satisfy the requirements of the Due Process Clause of the Fourteenth Amendment. Accordingly, we reverse the judgment of the Supreme Court of Texas.

Venue. Venue deals with the issue of which court is the proper court in which to bring the suit in a given state. Once a determination has been made that a suit may be brought within a given state, the plaintiff examines the venue statute to determine where in the state suit may be filed. The typical state statute specifies which courts in the state may hear a case.

For example, a state statute might permit suit to be brought in any county in which the defendant resides, or in which the plaintiff resides if the defendant is served therein, or in which the cause of action arose. Suppose that Smith was involved in an automobile accident in Johnson County. The defendant was a resident of Shawnee County—which is located in the same state as Johnson County. The plaintiff is a resident of Wyandotte County, which is also located in the same state as Johnson County. Such a statute would permit the plaintiff to bring suit in either Johnson or Shawnee County. The plaintiff could also file in Wyandotte County if the defendant is served with the summons and petition while in Wyandotte County. Suit could not, however, be brought in Saline County.

Venue statutes generally provide special rules for corporations, partnerships, and nonresidents of the state.

Petition

The statements of the respective contentions of the parties to a lawsuit are called pleadings. They are written documents filed with the court prior to trial that state the position of each party to the suit. In order to start a civil lawsuit, the plaintiff must file the first pleading, a document commonly referred to as a petition (sometimes called a complaint or a declaration), which generally the defendant responds to with a document called an answer.

The **petition** is a document filed with the court asking that the plaintiff be granted some type of relief. The petition states paragraph by paragraph the nature of the claims the plaintiff has against the defendant and the relief requested of the court. The petition thus tells the defendant what the plaintiff believes the defendant did or failed to do and what the plaintiff wants the defendant to do or cease doing.

Summons

To institute a suit, the plaintiff requests that the court serve the defendant with a **summons.** It is not a part of the pleadings, but rather is a command of the clerk of the court that the defendant answer the allegations in the petition within a designated period of time. The summons thus notifies the defendant that suit has been brought against him or her and the time period in which the defendant must reply to the petition. The summons and a copy of the petition are commonly served by the sheriff or other law-enforcement personnel on the defendant. However, in some circumstances, private service may be authorized by a court. Generally, someone, such as the sheriff, actually hands a copy of the summons and petition to the defendant. In certain circumstances, the law permits service on the defendant by a simple delivery of the summons and petition to the defendant's home, or by mail, or by publication.

Answer

In response to the plaintiff's petition, the defendant files with the court an **answer** or reply within the time designated in the summons. A copy of the answer is also sent to the plaintiff's attorney. In the answer the defendant states his or her response to the plaintiff's allegations. Quite frequently the defendant denies all or most of the matters stated in the plaintiff's petition. Any matter denied must be established by the plaintiff if the case goes to trial.

A **counterclaim** is a claim presented by a defendant against the plaintiff. Answers often contain counterclaims against the plaintiff. Some types of claims, called compulsory counterclaims, must be asserted by the defendant in his or her answer. If a counterclaim is compulsory, it must be asserted in the action or is forever barred. Other types of counterclaims are not compulsory but may be stated in the answer. These are called permissive counterclaims.

Suppose the plaintiff alleged in its petition that the defendant failed to pay for goods delivered by the plaintiff. The defendant could allege in its answer that the plaintiff failed to deliver some goods pursuant to another contract. This claim the defendant has against the plaintiff arising out of another contract is a counterclaim.

A sample petition appears in Figure 3.1. In this petition, the plaintiff claims that his landlord has wrongfully retained certain items of property owned by the defendant. The plaintiff wishes to recover the value of this property from the landlord. Figure 3.2 illustrates a typical response to such a petition. In this case, the landlord admitted renting the home for the time in question and to terminating the tenancy and reentering the home. However, the landlord denied taking possession of the tenant's property and therefore denied any liability to the tenant.

Motion to Dismiss

Attorneys seldom file suits unless they believe a recovery in the case is possible. On occasion an attorney may file suit based on a theory of recovery not recognized at that time in the jurisdiction. In response to this the defendant quite likely will file a **motion to dismiss.** In essence, what the defendant is saying is that even if everything the plaintiff says is true, the plaintiff still is not entitled to a remedy.

Following the filing of such a motion, the parties argue the motion before the judge. The judge, after listening to the arguments of the attorneys, decides whether to permit the suit to proceed. If the judge grants the motion to dismiss, the case ends (subject to the right in many cases to refile a new petition stating new factual allegations, or subject to the right to amend the petition by inserting these new allegations in the petition).

IN THE DISTRICT COURT OF DOUGLAS COUNTY, KANSAS

JOHN DOE,
                          Plaintiff,

    vs.
                                              Case No. 10011
MARY SMITH,
                          Defendant.

Proceeding Under K.S.A. Chapter 60

PETITION

COMES NOW the petitioner and states as his cause of action against the defendant.

1. From November 1, 1982 to January 7, 1983 plaintiff occupied, as defendant's tenant, defendant's house located at 140 Main, City of Lawrence, State of Kansas.

2. On January 3, 1983, Defendant terminated such tenancy by sending a written notice to the plaintiffs demanding they vacate the trailer by January 8, 1983.

3. On January 7, 1983, the defendant re-entered the home, and took possession of it and all personalty therein.

4. On that date, the following items of personalty in the home were owned solely by plaintiff: a 1982 R.C.A. color t.v. and a Pioneer stereo. The reasonable value of such property on that date was $900.00.

5. At the time defendant took possession of the home, she took possession of the plaintiff's property. Plaintiff demanded that the defendant return possession of such personalty to plaintiff, but defendant with willful disregard of plaintiff's legal right to possession of such personalty has refused and failed to surrender possession thereof to plaintiff and still refuses to do so.

6. By reason of defendant's willful conversion of such property with knowledge of plaintiff's legal right to its possession, plaintiff is entitled to compensatory damages in the amount of $900.00.

7. WHEREFORE, plaintiff prays judgment against the defendant for $900.00 compensatory damages for the loss of his personal property, for court costs, and for such other and further relief as to the court may seem just and proper.

DEMAND FOR JURY TRIAL

Plaintiff herein demands trial by jury on all issues of fact contained in plaintiff's petition.

John Doe
Attorney for plaintiff
100 Tennessee Street
Lawrence, Kansas 66044
1-913-845-0000

FIGURE 3.1 Sample Petition

IN THE DISTRICT COURT OF DOUGLAS COUNTY, KANSAS

JOHN DOE,
                              Plaintiff,
        vs.

MARY SMITH,   Case No. 10011
                              Defendant.

Proceeding Under K.S.A. Chapter 60

ANSWER

COMES NOW the defendant and for her reply states:

1. That she admits the allegations contained in paragraphs 1–3 of plaintiff's Petition.
2. That she denies each and every other allegation contained in plaintiff's Petition.

John Jones
Attorney for defendant
100 Main Street
Lawrence, Kansas 66044
1-913-100-0000

FIGURE 3.2 Sample Answer to a Petition

If the judge declines to grant the motion to dismiss, this does not mean the plaintiff wins the case. It merely means the defendant must answer the petition and proceed with the case.

Normally the defendant's counsel makes a motion to dismiss in response to the plaintiff's petition. However, a motion to dismiss may be raised at any stage of the lawsuit—including on appeal.

As the prior material indicates, motions are simply applications to the court for some type of order. The motion to dismiss is merely one type of motion that may be made during the course of a legal proceeding. Motions may be filed prior to trial and argued before a judge, made orally during a trial and decided at that time, or lodged following a trial and argued before a judge. Other motions might be made in response to a petition: for example, a motion to strike a paragraph or paragraphs from the plaintiff's petition, or a motion requesting the plaintiff make its petition more definite.

Judgment on the Pleadings

At the close of the pleadings, the plaintiff or defendant may make a motion for a **judgment on the pleadings.** Essentially, this serves the same function as a motion to dismiss, but the attorney files it after the pleadings are closed rather than in response to the petition.

Suppose the judge finds no basis for a verdict on behalf of the plaintiff, even if the allegations in the plaintiff's petition are assumed to be true. In that case, the suit may be dismissed. However, if the petition is deficient, the judge may allow the plaintiff to amend its petition if the defect can be corrected.

After the plaintiff files a petition, the defendant answers, and the parties have learned something about the facts of the case, one of the parties may believe he or she is entitled to a judgment as a matter of law. Generally, the parties have at least taken the affidavits (sworn statements) of some of the important parties to the case. In some cases, other devices, such as depositions, which are discussed later in this chapter, may have been obtained.

Motion for Summary Judgment

Thus, unlike the judgment on the pleadings, in a **motion for summary judgment** the judge considers matters outside the pleadings—such as affidavits and depositions.

Essentially, the party making a motion for summary judgment is saying that no genuine issue of material fact remains to be decided in the case, and therefore the judge should grant the motion. If any issue of material fact remains, the judge should deny the motion.

Even assuming the judge grants the motion for a summary judgment, he or she still must rule on how the law applies to the facts in question. If the judge feels the law favors the plaintiff, the judge rules for the plaintiff. If the judge decides the law requires a verdict on behalf of the defendant, he or she enters a verdict for the defendant. The critical concept here is that no trial is required because all issues of fact have been resolved. That being the case, the judge merely needs to apply the law to the facts.

One important aspect of the filings in a civil suit is a time limit imposed on the party who files. This time limit is called a **statute of limitations**. A statute of limitations sets a time period. These periods vary depending upon the type of document that is to be filed in a given lawsuit, the type of lawsuit that is originally filed, and the jurisdiction in which the case is brought. For example, if an accident occurs today, the statute of limitations may require that any lawsuit concerning such an accident be filed within two years of its occurrence. A party who waits longer than two years may find that its otherwise justifiable legal claim is denied.

Statute of Limitations

In certain instances, the statute of limitations is tolled; that is, certain acts or events cause the statute of limitations to not begin running or to stop running. For example, statutes of limitations often provide that if a person conceals himself, the statute will not run while the person is concealed, or if after the **cause of action** accrues the defendant absconds from the state, the time of absence will not be counted as any part of the period within which the action must be brought.

Discovery, in a civil case, is a process through which opposing counsel can learn, before a trial begins, the case to be presented by the other side. In general, each side must disclose the identity of its witnesses to the other. In addition, opposing sides have the opportunity to interrogate those witnesses. Documents relevant to the case are generally disclosed. Briefly, then, the discovery rules permit each side in a civil case to fully learn about the other.

Discovery

The purpose of discovery is to do away with the element of surprise in a trial and encourage settlement out of court. Once both sides are fully aware of the facts they can usually reach a negotiated resolution of the dispute.

There are a number of mechanisms for obtaining discovery in civil litigation. Although the discovery rules are designed to operate without court order, the courts do exercise a supervisory role in the process. Courts may limit discovery if they believe it too burdensome. They may impose sanctions upon a party that refuses to permit discovery. Sanctions may include ordering a party to pay the attorneys' fees of the opposing party or may even include entering a default judgment against that party.

Discovery may be obtained through the interrogation under oath of witnesses and parties to the lawsuit. This discovery technique is called **deposition.** It may be used to preserve the testimony of witnesses who will not be available at trial because of death or illness, or for some other reason. A deposition may also be used to raise questions concerning the truthfulness of a witness at the trial. Consider, for example, that a witness's deposition and trial testimony may conflict. It may also be used as a general tool for having facts revealed about the incident in question and the case of the opposition.

Other discovery tools include the submission of written questions to be answered under oath. The written questions are called **interrogatories.** Documents may also be obtained through the discovery process. Additionally, parties are encouraged to admit to certain portions of the litigation in order to reduce the number of issues to be decided at the trial. This may be accomplished through a request for admissions.

The discovery rules contain a number of techniques litigants may use to gather facts relevant to the litigation. As a result, such techniques help foster fair, fast, and inexpensive resolution of cases through settlement rather than waiting for a disposition through trial.

However, liberal discovery rules sometimes create problems. Many attorneys argue, especially in very large cases, that the discovery stage of a proceeding is the portion of the case where the most decisive "battles" are waged. These battles often involve abuse of the discovery tools, either by the party seeking information or by the party providing it. For example, the party responding to discovery requests may attempt to relinquish the minimum amount of information required to avoid court sanction. As a result, the discovering party must work extremely hard to gather the needed information. Techniques used include providing evasive or incomplete answers to requests for discovery made by the opposing party. This technique will require the discovering party to try to have the requested material supplied through further discovery or through judicial proceedings. Additionally, a responding party may delay in responding to the discovery requests or provide a very large amount of material (usually in the form of requested documents) in an unorganized manner. The discovering party will be required to spend a great deal of time and money sorting through the information.

However, not all discovery abuses may be claimed by the party to whom the discovery is aimed. The discovering party, too, can abuse the system. This can be accomplished by bombarding the other side with a huge number of discovery requests. As a result, again a great deal of time and expense will be involved in responding to discovery requests. The litigation costs increase as a result. The better-financed party may be able to coerce a settlement from the other party through abuse of the discovery system.

Though discovery can be abused, such abuses do not, of course, occur in all cases; they occur most frequently in very large, complex cases. Discovery is a portion of the system of civil litigation in which many business managers and other nonlawyers are involved.

We have seen thus far that a plaintiff must institute a suit by filing a petition, to which the defendant responds by filing an answer or a motion such as the motion to dismiss. Suits may not be arbitrarily filed against anyone in any state. The court in which suit is filed must have jurisdiction over the persons and the subject matter of the suit. Suit must be filed in a court with proper venue. Suit also must be filed within a certain period of time, specified in the statute of limitations. Once suit is underway, the discovery phase begins.

We are now ready to examine the actual steps of a civil trial. Trials begin at the conclusion of the discovery period. Great attention is devoted in this material to the function of the jury system in civil litigation—one of the great institutions of the American legal system.

TRIAL PROCEDURE

After suit has been filed and the parties have finished with discovery, if it appears the parties intend to litigate or try a case rather than settling it, the judge sets the case for a **pretrial conference.**

Pretrial Conference

Formal or Informal. At the pretrial conference, the attorneys representing all parties to the dispute meet with a judge. Quite frequently, in many parts of the country, this person is the judge who will actually preside at the trial. In the more metropolitan areas, however, one or two judges may conduct all pretrial hearings for that district.

The degree of formality of this hearing depends upon the judge. Some pretrial hearings are quite formal. Other judges may elect to keep the proceeding more casual—they may meet with opposing counsel in their chambers.

Narrowing the Issues. The primary function of the pretrial conference is to narrow and simplify the factual issues. The judge usually tries to get the parties to stipulate (agree to) as many facts as possible at this stage. By agreeing to certain facts, the parties reduce the amount of time necessary to try a case.

Once the case is set for trial and the parties have completed the pretrial conference, they may settle the case. Quite often, a case is settled on the very day it is scheduled for trial. If this does not happen, the parties appear on the scheduled date.

One of the first steps in the trial, after the parties indicate they are willing to proceed, is the selection of a jury, assuming the case is to be tried in front of a jury. The following section notes the various provisions in the United States Constitution relating to jury trials. Thereafter, the text discusses the types of juries used throughout the United States.

The Constitution provides for jury trials in several instances.

United States Constitution

Article III. Article III, Section 2 requires, excepting the case of the impeachment of the president, that the trial of the crime must be held in the state in which the crime was committed. Two other provisions of the Constitution relate to criminal trials—the Fifth and Sixth Amendments.

The Fifth Amendment. The Fifth Amendment states that "No person shall be held to answer for a capital, or otherwise infamous crime, unless on a presentment or indictment of a Grand Jury." Grand juries are discussed later in this chapter.

The Sixth Amendment. The Sixth Amendment adds to this the right, in criminal cases, to be tried in the district where the crime was committed. It also requires a speedy and public trial by an impartial jury.

The Seventh Amendment. The Seventh Amendment deals with civil trials. It provides: "In suits at common law, where the value in controversy shall exceed twenty dollars, the right of trial by jury shall be preserved, and no fact tried by a jury, shall be otherwise re-examined in any court of the United States, than according to the rules of the common law."

Take note of the fact that the Seventh Amendment merely *preserves* the right to trial in suits at common law. It does not *create* a right to trial by jury. Without going into the details of what the common law is, suffice it to say that if a matter was regarded as part of the common law at the time of the drafting of the Constitution, litigants may request a trial by jury for such issues today. If the case was not a common law matter, no right to a trial by jury exists under the United States Constitution. A right to a jury trial may exist, however, under the applicable *state* constitution.

Types of Juries

The courts chiefly use one of two types of juries, grand juries and petit juries. (There are other so-called juries, as well. Coroner's juries, which are used in many cities, determine whether a deceased person died of natural causes. A hearing is held by the coroner with the assistance of a jury.)

Grand Juries. The function of a **grand jury** is to determine whether there exists probable cause to initiate a criminal prosecution. Grand juries are used only in *criminal* cases.

The United States Constitution in the Fifth Amendment guarantees a right to a grand jury in certain instances: "No person shall be held to answer for a capital, or otherwise infamous crime, unless on a presentment or indictment of a Grand Jury."

Murder is one of the types of crimes for which the Fifth Amendment guarantees an accused person the right to a grand jury. It should be noted that the Supreme Court has decided that states are not required to use grand juries. However, some state constitutions require that a grand jury be provided in certain types of cases.

What is the purpose of the grand jury? To prevent the unjustified criminal prosecution of a person accused of a crime. Unless the grand jury hands down an **indictment,** the prosecutor may not pursue the case further. The prosecutor representing the state or federal government must convince the members of the grand jury (typically twenty-three in number) that a crime has been committed and, if the prosecutor claims a particular person committed a crime, that some evidence exists that suggests that the accused committed the crime. If the grand jury agrees with the prosecutor, it signs the indictment, referred to as a **true bill.**

Petit Juries. It is the function of the **petit jury** to hear evidence presented by witnesses at the trial, and based upon instructions given to them by the judge, to render a decision in a case. Petit juries are used in both civil and criminal cases. Unlike the grand jury, members of these juries actually function as a part of a civil or a criminal trial.

Keep in mind the function of a jury—a jury decides the *facts* of a case. It applies the law that controls in the case to whatever set of facts it finds. The judge instructs the jury on the law. Thus, when using a jury, the *judge determines the law* applicable to the case, but the *jury determines the facts.*

If the parties try the case without the assistance of a jury, the judge decides both the facts and the law.

If the parties schedule a trial before a jury, the court instructs the clerk of the court to call in on the day set for the trial a specified number of persons, called veniremen, for possible service. Typically, the court asks for two or three times the number of people needed for the trial because some will be unable, for one reason or another, to serve on the jury.

Selection of a Jury

Statutory Exemptions. Some states are very liberal in excusing people from jury service. Some state statutes excuse a large number of categories of persons, such as employees of the state, physicians, and ministers, while other states permit very few excuses. The theory in those states which exempt certain categories of persons from jury service is that some of these people will better serve society by working on their jobs. Others, state employees, for example, are excused because of their possible prejudice.

The problem for the parties to a trial, however, is to get enough people in the pool of available jurors to constitute a fair cross section of the community. When the state automatically exempts certain categories of persons, these people never even appear at the trial. They simply sign a form and return it to the clerk listing the reason for their exemption from jury service. Permitting too many people an excuse from jury duty lessens the pool of available jurors.

Exemptions by the Judge. Not only do some state statutes permit certain categories of persons to avoid even appearing as potential jurors, but judges also have considerable discretion in excusing people from serving at a trial. For example, if someone were to state that jury duty would pose a hardship, a judge would normally allow that person to be excused.

Voir Dire. After dealing with the basic matters, the judge then permits the attorneys to question the jurors about the case. This stage of the trial is called the **voir dire,** the purpose of which is to determine the qualifications of the prospective jurors to sit as triers of fact in the case and to determine whether they are subject to challenge. In some places, the judge conducts the voir dire based on questions submitted to him or her by the attorneys. The length of the voir dire is substantially up to the discretion of the judge. However, in very serious cases, judges typically allow extensive questioning of the jurors to avoid challenges of the jury on appeal.

The courts allow two types of challenges to a juror. The first is a **challenge for cause.** There is no limit to the number of challenges for cause. These are made to the court, and the court determines whether sufficient cause exists to remove the challenged venireman. The for cause challenge allows an attorney to challenge any venireman on the grounds of bias or prejudice. That is, if the attorney can show that a person is not able to make a fair and impartial decision, the attorney can request the judge to dismiss that person. If he or she can show that the venireman is either unwilling or unable to follow or decide questions, the attorney can request that person be dismissed for these reasons as well.

The other type of challenge, the **peremptory challenge,** is designed to serve the other purposes mentioned, that is, to give an attorney's client the best chance possible. This type of challenge is determined solely by the party exercising the challenge. The court may not refuse to excuse a challenged venireman nor is the party required to give any reason for the challenge when an attorney is exercising a peremptory challenge. Unlike challenges for cause, of which there can be an unlimited number, the peremptory challenge may be exercised only a limited number of times, a number usually specified by statute.

Exercising any challenges or deciding which prospective jurors to challenge is largely a matter of strategy. Some attorneys may argue that it makes no difference who serves on a jury. However, seasoned trial attorneys are quite attuned to the fact that the makeup of the jury may be critical to the outcome of a trial. Psychological studies of small-group decision making tend to support this thinking. For this reason, the voir dire is a very important stage in the trial.

In most cases, the attorneys question prospective members of the jury in great depth. They want to know as much as possible about each juror. Here is what Clarence Darrow had to say about the process of picking a jury:

> Choosing jurors is always a delicate task. The more a lawyer knows of life, human nature, psychology, and the reactions of the human emotions, the better he is equipped for the subtle selection of his so-called "twelve men, good and true." In this undertaking, everything pertaining to the prospective juror needs to be questioned and weighed: his nationality, his business, religion, politics, social standing, family ties, friends, habits of life and thought; the books and newspapers he likes and reads, and many more matters that combine to make a man; all of these qualities and experiences have left their effect on ideas, beliefs and fancies that inhabit his mind. Understanding of all this cannot be obtained too bluntly. It usually requires finesse, subtlety and guesswork. Involved in it all is the juror's method of speech, the kind of clothes he wears, the style of haircut, and, above all, his business associates, residence and origin.

Why do seasoned trial attorneys like Darrow want to know so much about the jurors? The reason is that not everyone thinks the same. Some people are quite bigoted. Others are very tight with the dollar. Still others invariably favor the plaintiff or the defendant.

What the attorneys are trying to do, to put it crudely, is to stereotype people. They hope to put each person into a category based on the attorney's life experiences and trial experiences. The attorney hopes to eliminate people adverse to his or her cause and to assemble a group of people favorably disposed to the trial strategy he or she plans to adopt.

This brings up an important point: In theory, parties to a trial are entitled to a jury composed of fair and impartial jurors. In practice, however, a trial attorney does not necessarily want fair and impartial jurors. Attorneys want people predisposed toward certain positions and ideas. The law as it operates in practice is very different from what one would gather simply by reading a few cases.

Fortunately, the Supreme Court intervenes from time to time to help assure participants in a trial that those who serve on a jury do not come to court with certain preformed opinions. For example, a person might be so biased as to base a decision of guilt or innocence on the defendant's race. The Court permits questions on the issue of bias.

Lawyers ask, or try to ask, a variety of questions concerning the jurors. Why would an attorney be concerned that members of the jury might harbor some prejudice against his or her client? The juror might vote against a minority person's position because of his or her prejudices, not because of the evidence presented at the case. Naturally, persons who refuse to decide a case based on the evidence ought to be excluded from the jury.

Racial prejudice is one of the more obvious prejudices. Every individual is a composite of attitudes, any of which might play a critical part in the juror's hearing or recollection of the evidence or in his or her attitude toward various witnesses, the judge, and the other jury members. A person's personality also influences the manner in which he or she interacts in small-group decision making—such as occurs on a jury! An attorney, usually operating on gut instinct, tries to evaluate each person as a prospective juror. The more information he or she possesses about each person, the easier this decision becomes.

Before conducting the voir dire, however, the attorney must do some initial

SELECTING A JURY

MCI Communications Corporation brought an antitrust suit against AT&T. At that trial, MCI was awarded $1.8 billion. MCI's attorneys spent a considerable amount of time preparing for every facet of this trial.

One of the factors the attorneys were interested in was the type of juror who would be of greatest use to MCI. In order to determine this information, attorneys representing MCI hired a public opinion pollster to learn about the attitudes of persons in Chicago, the place where the trial was scheduled to take place, toward big business. MCI wanted to determine the type of juror who would keep an open mind about MCI's case.

As a result of the work done by the public opinion pollster, MCI's attorneys developed a profile of the type of person they needed to get on the jury. The poll told them to select self-made people who understood competition, who were first or second generation Americans, and who were intelligent enough to understand this rather complex case. Six of the twelve jurors who eventually heard the case had college backgrounds.

Obtaining information of this nature is obviously useful to attorneys in selecting the proper group of persons to look for during the voir dire. The size of this verdict suggests that MCI's attorneys selected the jury very astutely.

investigation and preparation. The attorney must first learn about the backgrounds of all prospective jurors to determine whether he or she wishes to challenge any of them. This will also help to establish the necessary jury rapport. Some of this information can be obtained through various public sources, including the city directory, telephone directory, and other such public listings. Perhaps the best method is simply talking to people who know the juror, such as neighbors and coworkers.

Some states provide information of this type to attorneys prior to trial. In other states, attorneys must search out information about jurors prior to trial or at trial. The juror questionnaire in Figure 3.3 is a typical example of a form prospective jurors might be asked to fill out.

Having accumulated as much information as he or she desires, both prior to trial and during the voir dire, the attorney must now apply some practical psychology.

IN THE SEVENTH JUDICIAL DISTRICT COURT OF THE STATE OF KANSAS IN AND FOR THE COUNTY OF DOUGLAS
JUROR QUESTIONNAIRE

You have been selected for the privilege to serve as a juror in the District Court of Douglas County. Please carefully read and answer the questions on this form and return it immediately in the enclosed self-addressed, stamped envelope: Questionnaires *must* be returned *within five days,* whether or not you may expect to be excused from reporting. This questionnaire is for the purpose of determining your qualification for jury duty. Your answers to these questions are for Court use only and will not be made public. Your cooperation and willingness to serve as a juror is appreciated. *PLEASE PRINT OR TYPE YOUR ANSWERS.*

1. Name _____ Age _____

2. Residence Address _____ City _____ Zip _____

    Residence Phone Number _____ Work Phone Number _____

3. Years in residence in Kansas _____ In Douglas County _____

4. Former Residence _____

5. Marital Status   _____ Married   _____ Separated   _____ Widower
    (Please check)   _____ Single   _____ Divorced   _____ Widow

6. Number of children _____ Ages _____ Can care be provided? _____

7. Have you any ill dependents who require your personal and constant care? _____

    If so, give details: _____

8. Occupation _____ Employer _____

    Do you own your business? _____ Number of employees _____

9. Full name of spouse_____Occupation_____

    Employer _____ Work Address _____ Phone _____

10. If you are not now employed; give your last occupation and employer:

    _____

11. Have you ever served as a juror? _____

    Civil Case?_____When and where_____

    Criminal Case?_____When and where_____

12. Have you or any members of your immediate family been a party to any lawsuit? _____

Criminal?_____Civil?_____When and where_____

Who in your family was involved? _____

13. Have you ever been convicted of a felony? _____ For what _____

Where and when _____

14. If you believe you have a physical disability which would prevent you from serving as a juror, please state what: _____

15. Has any Court ever found you to be incompetent or incapacitated? _____

Where and when _____ If restored, give date _____

16. Are you a close friend of, or are you related to any law enforcement officer? _____

If so, please check:_____Federal_____State_____Sheriff's Office_____City Police

17. Do you drive an automobile? _____ Is transportation available? _____

If you live outside city limits, state mileage one way to city limits _____

18. Can you read, write and understand English? _____

19. Please show the extent of your formal education. (Circle highest level completed.)

Elementary or secondary school: 1 2 3 4 5 6 7 8 9 10 11 12 College: 1 2 3 4 5 6 7 +

20. Have you had any vocational or professional training? _____ If so, please state what kind and to what extent: _____

_____

21. If enrolled in a college or university, please state year and course of study:

_____

22. If you feel there is any reason you cannot serve as a juror, please state:

_____
_____
_____
_____
_____
_____
_____
_____
_____
_____
_____
_____
_____

I affirm that the answers I have given to the above questions are true and correct.

Signed:_____

Dated: _____

FIGURE 3.3 Juror Questionnaire

What strategy does the attorney hope to follow in the conduct of the case? His or her strategy should be a factor in selecting the jurors.

As far as possible, an attorney tries to eliminate persons perceived to be unfavorable through for cause objections. Basically, the attorney objects to a particular juror on the ground that the person is "incapable of sitting as a fair and impartial juror." For example, a person who flatly states he or she could not fairly decide the case because the defendant is a minority member clearly would be excused for cause. Convincing the judge to excuse prospective jurors for cause is an art and is not easily accomplished. Furthermore, such objections must be made tactfully, or an attorney will destroy his or her rapport with the jury. An important factor with respect to for cause objections is they are unlimited in number.

At the close of the questioning of the veniremen, a few people will always have managed to stay on the panel in spite of the best effort of the attorneys to exclude them for cause. Either attorney will then ask the judge to strike these people from the jury by exercising a peremptory challenge. Each attorney possesses the right to exercise only a few peremptory challenges.

Opening Statement

Following the voir dire, the attorneys present their **opening statements.** In a civil case, the plaintiff's attorney makes his or her statement first. The defendant then has the option of making an opening statement at that time or waiting until the plaintiff has finished presenting evidence. In a criminal case, the state presents its statement, then the defendant may elect to make a statement at that time or after the state finishes presenting evidence.

The purpose of the opening statement is to give the jurors a broad overview of the case. The attorney probably will introduce his or her witnesses, describe their anticipated testimony, stress certain rules of law, tell the jurors what the attorney hopes to prove, and comment upon what the other side intends to do. The attorney ought to present plausible reasons why, after hearing the evidence, the jury should find in his or her client's favor. Thus, the opening statement amounts to a broad overview of the trial to come. The jurors are fresh at this point. They listen avidly. Such information may help clarify points in the trial they might misunderstand or fail to hear. The attention span of the jurors surely is best at this point, and for that reason alone the opening statement is of critical importance.

Nothing said during the opening statements is part of the evidence. They are merely statements of what the attorneys expect the proof to be, merely outlines of the case. The decision in a case must be rendered based on the testimony of witnesses who appear at trial. Nonetheless, a good lawyer starts the jury thinking about his or her position in the case during the opening statement, and possibly even influences the jurors' thinking at this point.

Burden of Proof. One matter often discussed in the opening statement is **burden of proof.** The burden of proof is the duty of a party to substantiate an allegation or issue to avoid dismissal of that issue early in the trial or to convince the trier of facts of the truth of the claim and therefore win at trial.

In a civil case, the plaintiff has the initial burden of proof. If the plaintiff fails to establish its burden of proof, the judge dismisses the case—even if the defendant never presented any evidence at trial!

Because the plaintiff has the initial burden of proof, it must present evidence first. It must convince the judge there is sufficient evidence to meet its burden of proof. Once this is accomplished, the burden shifts to the defense to dispute the points brought up by the plaintiff. In other words, the defense automatically loses the case if it fails to meet its burden of proof.

At the close of the plaintiff's case, the defense may make a **motion.** A motion is a request to the court for an order or rule in favor of the party making the request. Motions may be made prior to or during the trial. When the defendant makes a motion to dismiss the case at the close of the prosecution's or plaintiff's case, many states refer to it as a **motion for a directed verdict.** The moving party really is saying that the other side has failed to prove all the facts necessary to establish a case. If the court grants such a motion at this point, the judge dismisses the case and discharges the jury. Such motions are routinely made at trial.

At the close of the defendant's presentation of evidence, both sides may ask the judge for a directed verdict. Again, if the judge grants such a motion, he or she enters a verdict for one party or the other.

In most cases, the case goes to the jury, which generally renders a verdict. After the jury announces its verdict, the defeated party generally makes a **motion for a judgment notwithstanding the verdict;** in other words, the defeated party is asking the judge to set the jury verdict aside because it was not supported by the evidence or the law.

Quite frequently, when counsel for one of the parties makes a motion, the judge either asks the jury to retire to the jury room or moves the proceedings to his or her chambers. All the remarks made during such a break, like those made during the rest of the trial, are recorded by the court reporter. The judge often considers whether to admit certain testimony during these breaks. If the judge decides not to admit the testimony, jurors will never hear the evidence in question. In certain cases, however, the parties record the evidence or at least some indication of the nature of the proffered evidence in case of an appeal.

Motions

Certain evidence may be admitted at trial, other evidence may not. Certain rules of evidence result in evidence being suppressed (not admitted). A good example is the rule against the admission of hearsay evidence.

Hearsay is evidence that a witness offers not from personal knowledge but rather based upon a statement made by another person. The hearsay rule applies to both oral and written statements. It is subject to a number of exceptions.

An example of the hearsay rule follows. Mr. Smith is on the stand. He has just testified that while at Al's Bar, he overheard someone say the defendant murdered Mr. Jones. This is hearsay—Mr. Smith is not testifying from his own personal knowledge but based upon a statement he heard from someone else. If this statement is offered to prove that the defendant murdered Jones, the judge will not admit it in evidence. The judge, following an objection to the statement, will order the jury to disregard the statement.

The contemporaneous-objection rule requires an *immediate* objection following the introduction of evidence. Also, the attorney could not just stand up and say "I

Rules of Evidence

object to the introduction of this evidence," but rather must give a reason for objecting—for example, stating that the evidence violates the hearsay rule.

Many other objections exist. Some of them relate to the form of a question—such as the objection that a question is "leading and suggestive." Suppose an attorney asks the witness, "Were you wearing a beard on June 12, 1983?" Such a question suggests the possible answer an attorney wants the witness to give. A question of this nature should be stated in this manner: "Tell us about your physical condition on June 12, 1983," or some similar wording that does not suggest the desired answer.

Cross Examination

If a party calls a witness to the stand and asks him or her questions, the courts refer to such questioning as the **direct examination.** When the attorney for the opposing party questions this same witness, the courts call such questioning the **cross examination.**

The purpose of the cross examination is to permit the opposite party to test what has just been stated by the witness. The attorney tries to demonstrate that the witness's memory is faulty, or that he or she was not in a position to perceive the events in question, or that the witness has not explained the facts clearly.

Closing Arguments

Following the close of the defendant's case and after the judge considers any motions made by the parties, each side presents a **closing argument.** In a civil case, the plaintiff has the option of opening. The defendant may then make concluding statements, followed by the plaintiff's response. Criminal cases operate in the same fashion, with the state making the first comments.

A closing argument really is a review of all the evidence heard during the trial. The attorneys refresh the jurors' memory of important points made during the trial. Generally, there is some theme to the closing remarks the attorney wishes to convey to the jury. Through this theme he or she tries to analyze and review the testimony. The attorneys also review the instructions of law the judge will present. They try to explain these instructions so the jurors apply the law correctly. The attorneys must attempt to explain the law because the judge generally just reads the instructions to the jurors.

Making a good closing argument is an art. It involves a combination of strategy and logic. An attorney must make the jurors think about his or her position. Sometimes overly zealous and unethical lawyers misstate the evidence to try to confuse the jurors. If the opposing counsel catches the error, he or she objects and asks the judge to admonish the attorney for misstating the evidence. Of course, poor preparation for the closing or excessive emotion may also result in an unintentional erroneous presentation of the testimony.

Quite often, the closing argument is based on pure emotion—in other words, rule for my client because he or she is a very sympathetic person. Such appeals work well with certain pitiful persons, such as a child injured by a truck owned by a large company. The attorney representing the child often tries to convince the jury to rule for the child because the child has been injured—as opposed to deciding the case based on the law and facts presented in court.

The following quotation is a classic example of an appeal to emotion, rather than the law, in the closing argument. It was delivered in the case *Burden* v. *Hornsby* in the Court of Common Pleas at Warrensburg, Missouri, September 23, 1870. This case involved a matter of principle—the death of a man's dog, Old Drum, for which he claimed fifty dollars damages. The speech was delivered by Senator George Graham Vest. During it, counsel for the defendant sensed the cause was lost. He is rumored to have whispered facetiously to his partner, "We had better get out of the courtroom with our client, else all might be hanged."

EULOGY, TO THE DOG

Gentlemen of the Jury: The best friend a man has in this world may turn against him and become his enemy. His son or daughter that he has reared with loving care may prove ungrateful. Those who are nearest and dearest to us, those whom we trust with our happiness and our good name, may become traitors to their faith. The money that a man has he may lose. It flies away from him perhaps when he needs it most. A man's reputation may be sacrificed in a moment of ill-considered action. The people who are prone to fall on their knees to do us honor when success is with us, may be the first to throw the stones of malice when failure settles its cloud upon our heads. The one absolutely unselfish friend that a man can have in this selfish world, the one that never deserts him, the one that never proves ungrateful or treacherous, is his dog.

Gentlemen of the jury, a man's dog stands by him in prosperity and in poverty, in health and in sickness. He will sleep on the cold ground where the wintry winds blow and the snow drives fierce, if only he may be near his master's side. He will kiss the hand that has no food to offer; he will lick the wounds and sores that come from encounter with the roughness of the world. He guards the sleep of his pauper master as if he were a prince. When all other friends desert, he remains. When riches take wing and reputation falls to pieces, he is as constant in his love as the sun in its journey through the heavens.

If fortune drives the master forth an outcast in the world, friendless and homeless, the faithful dog asks no higher privilege than that of his company to guard against danger, to fight against his enemies. And when the last scene of all comes, and death takes the master in its embrace and his body is laid away in the cold ground, no matter if all other friends pursue their way, there by his graveside will the noble dog be found, his head between his paws, his eyes sad but open in alert watchfulness, faithful and true even in death.

Appeals to emotion can and do work on closing—with the right jury. It may lead jurors to react emotionally as opposed to thinking about the evidence.

Instructions to the Jury

Following the closing statements of counsel, the judge instructs the members of the jury on the law. Generally, a judge merely reads the instructions to the jury. They may be long, complex, and confusing. Some states permit the jurors to have a copy of them during their deliberations. It is critical for an attorney to explain the meaning of the instructions to the jury in the closing argument. Merely hearing or reading the instructions often does little to clarify the law for the jurors.

Basically, the instructions state the facts a jury must find to arrive at a decision in the case. The instructions are arrived at as a result of suggestions by the attorneys to the judge. Sometimes a judge gives an instruction an attorney thinks misstates the law, or the judge refuses to give a requested instruction. When this happens, the losing party generally challenges on appeal the instructions given at trial. Erroneous instructions may result in a retrial.

Today, most states have suggested instructions that must be used at trial. This eliminates the need for the attorneys to write their own instructions. The attorney merely selects the instructions he or she wishes the judge to deliver at trial. If the judge consents, he reads them to the jury. The parties and the judge discuss which instructions to give out of the hearing of the jury, normally in the judge's chambers.

Jury Deliberations

The jury retires to the jury room at the close of the judge's instructions. The judge tells them to elect a foreman. As indicated earlier, attorneys often try to determine who the foreman will be because of the influential position the foreman occupies.

Jurors deliberate in secret. The deliberations may not be recorded or witnessed by nonjurors. However, jurors usually may discuss the case following the announcement of the verdict if they wish.

Formerly, all the jurors were required to agree upon a verdict. Today, the United States Supreme Court has ruled that the Constitution permits less-than-unanimous verdicts in civil or criminal cases. For example, a vote of nine jurors for the plaintiff could be sufficient for the plaintiff to win, even if three jurors think the plaintiff should lose. Whether juries must come to a unanimous verdict in civil or criminal cases is controlled by the law of the state in which the trial takes place. In the federal courts, federal rules control this issue. Thus, states may require a unanimous verdict, or they may permit less-than-unanimous verdicts.

If the jurors are unable to arrive at a verdict, the judge declares the jury a **hung jury;** that is, the jurors are said to be deadlocked or unable to reach a decision. The judge then dismisses the case. Such cases, *criminal or civil, may be retried.* However, it costs money and takes time to retry cases. If a case ends in a hung jury, the parties may just drop the case.

Judges may try to encourage the jurors to resolve a case. The judge frequently calls the jurors back to the courtroom to urge them to come to a decision. The forcefulness of this message depends upon the personality of the judge—as does the time the judge gives the jury to resolve a case. Many jurors do not realize they need not resolve a case. Some think they must stay until they arrive at a decision. For this reason, as a strategic matter, an attorney who hopes for a hung jury may find it advantageous to try to get a person on the jury who has participated before in a jury that hung. This person knows the jury need not arrive at a decision and doubtless will tell the other jurors so. This *may* result in less pressure to resolve a case and a higher likelihood it will hang.

The judge, although he or she possesses considerable discretion, may not hold the jurors forever. If the judge keeps the jury too long, the losing party may challenge the verdict on appeal.

The Verdict

When the jury reaches a decision, the jury foreman fills out the appropriate form provided by the judge. The jurors return to the courtroom, and the judge or bailiff announces the jury verdict in open court.

At this point the attorney for the losing party may ask to *poll* the jury. Each juror is then asked individually if he or she agreed with the verdict. What the attorney polling the jury hopes for is that a juror will state he or she disagreed with the verdict, but was pressured into agreeing with it. In such a case, the judge probably will declare a mistrial and refuse to accept the verdict.

Jurors may render two types of verdicts: a general verdict and a special verdict.

In a **general verdict,** the jury decides for one of the parties without any special findings of fact. A **special verdict** requires the jury to answer a number of questions concerning the major issues in the case. The jury must make a special finding on each material issue in the case. The court then applies the law to these facts.

In certain cases, the jury may arrive at a compromise verdict. The jurors may, in a case involving damages, merely add up the amount each juror feels the plaintiff deserves and divide by the number of jurors. This is called a *quotient verdict,* and it is improper. If the jury arrives at a verdict in this manner, the decision of the jury will be set aside. A decision of the jury is supposed to be a verdict of all the jurors. All jurors should agree on the same amount as damages.

Post-Trial Motions

Following the announcement of the jurors' verdict, the judge enters a verdict consistent with that verdict. However, if the judge thinks the jury arrived at a decision inconsistent with the evidence presented at trial, the judge may decline to enter the jury's verdict.

Counsel for the losing party, when the jury announces its decision, makes a motion for a judgment notwithstanding the verdict. If the court grants this motion, it enters a verdict that the court feels is consistent with the evidence, as opposed to the jury verdict.

Following the entry of the verdict, usually within thirty days after the end of the trial, counsel for the losing party may make a motion for a new trial. The attorney points out any reversible errors he or she thinks took place during the trial. If the trial judge agrees, the judge may set the verdict aside and order a new trial.

If the judge denies this motion, the attorneys and clients must either live with the verdict or appeal.

THE APPEAL

A decision to appeal generally must be made fairly quickly after the termination of the trial, for example, within thirty days. The costs associated with an appeal quite often discourage the losing party from appealing the case from the trial court to an appeals court.

Unlike the trial court, which actually hears witnesses and admits evidence, an appeals court does not perform these functions.

At the appellate level, the appeals court merely examines the record of the trial court to determine if the trial court made any reversible errors. The appeals court often hears oral arguments of the attorneys in the case. It also receives a written discussion of the case—called a **brief**—from each side, and in certain cases, from other interested parties. The court examines only that part of the transcript provided to it by the parties. It does not review the entire trial transcript. It does not hear witnesses. The appeals court generally considers only issues of law.

If it agrees with the trial court decision, the appeals court affirms the decision. If it finds an error, it may merely reverse the decision, or it may reverse and *remand* (send the case back to the trial court) for a new trial.

As a practical matter, it costs a fairly substantial sum of money to appeal. The losing party must evaluate its interest in the case and the expense of the appeal in deciding whether to continue with the case. Sometimes a party may feel the decision was in error but lack the money or the interest to pursue the case to a higher court.

SUMMARY   The American system of civil litigation is adversarial in form; that is, each party to a case is permitted the opportunity to present his or her version of the dispute. It is widely believed that this process is the best possible system to achieve a just and fair resolution of disputes. Alternatives to a trial, such as arbitration, do exist, however.

In order to institute a suit, the plaintiff must file a petition with the appropriate court. In response to the petition, the defendant files an answer with the court. Suits may not be instituted willy-nilly. A court must have the power to hear the type of dispute described in the petition. This is referred to as a court having jurisdiction over a particular type of dispute and over the parties to the suit. Only recently has the United States Supreme Court permitted state courts to obtain personal jurisdiction over persons who are not physically present within the state.

If a given case is not settled prior to trial, which is the outcome of some disputes, a party may elect to have a jury trial under certain circumstances. Attorneys to a case are permitted some control over the composition of the jury. They may ask questions of prospective jury members during the voir dire, and based on the answers received, the attorneys may disqualify certain persons from serving on the jury panel. The process of selecting a jury involves a good deal of psychological thinking on the part of attorneys.

A trial gets underway after the opening statements by the attorneys trying the case. The rules of evidence govern which and in what form statements can or cannot be admitted. Witnesses may be cross examined by the opposing side. At the conclusion of the presentation of the evidence, the attorneys present their closing arguments, the judge instructs the jury as to the applicable law, and the jury retires to deliberate the case. Once the jury verdict is announced, the losing party usually makes a motion for a new trial. If that fails, the losing party must either live with the judgment or attempt to get it reversed on appeal.

REVIEW QUESTIONS

1. Define the following terms:
   a. Petit jury
   b. Grand jury
   c. Voir dire
   d. Peremptory challenge
   e. Burden of proof
   f. Adversary system
   g. Statute of limitations
   h. Discovery
   i. Deposition

2. What is the purpose of the concepts of jurisdiction and venue in the operation of the civil

litigation system? Describe problems that might arise if those concepts were removed from the process.

3. Mary was injured in an automobile accident on August 30, 1975. The accident was caused by Tom, who negligently drove his car through a red light and struck the vehicle being driven by Mary. The statute of limitations for filing an automobile negligence lawsuit is two years. When must Mary file her lawsuit? Why does such a rule exist? If Mary files her suit after the date you gave above, are

there any additional facts that could be added to this problem to allow Mary to argue that her claim should be allowed to proceed?

4. Discuss the advantages and abuses that exist in our system of discovery. What would you suggest as possible remedies for the abuses?

5. Sally bought a bag of apples, which was to have contained one dozen. After she returned home from the store, she discovered that the bag only contained eleven apples. Sally wants to sue the store for a breach of contract. Would you advise her to file that suit? If so, why? If not, why not? Are there alternatives other than filing a lawsuit that Sally might pursue?

6. Duren was indited for murder and robbery in Missouri. The state's jury selection procedure allowed women an automatic exemption from jury duty. As a result, approximately fifteen percent of the jurors on the jury panels at trial were women. Duren's jury of twelve was chosen from a panel of forty-eight men and five women. He challenged the fairness of his trial in light of the automatic exemption of women from the jury. Is Duren entitled to a jury panel with more women?

7. Do attorneys select people for a jury solely on the basis of whether a person appears to be fair and impartial?

8. Plaintiffs instituted suit against defendants for personal injuries sustained in Oklahoma in an accident involving an automobile that had been purchased by plaintiffs in New York. The automobile was being driven through Oklahoma at the time of the accident. The defendants included the automobile retailer and its wholesaler, both New York corporations that did no business in Oklahoma. Seaway (the retailer) and World-Wide Volkswagen Corporation (the wholesaler) did not engage in any business in Oklahoma, did not ship or sell any products to or in Oklahoma, nor did they purchase advertisements in any media calcu-

lated to reach Oklahoma. World-Wide distributed automobiles and parts under a contract with Volkswagen to retail dealers in New York, New Jersey, and Connecticut. Seaway had its place of business in New York. The defendants challenged the power of the Oklahoma court to exercise in personam jurisdiction over them. Are the defendants correct that Oklahoma courts may not exercise in personam jurisdiction over them?

9. Linda Anaya challenged the jury selection in her case. She alleged that blue collar workers were underrepresented in the jury pool in violation of the Sixth Amendment. Does a jury pool of this nature violate the fair-cross-section requirement?

10. Billy Greenwood brought a suit against McDonough Power Equipment Incorporated to recover for damages sustained by Billy when his feet came in contact with the blades of a riding lawn mower manufactured by McDonough. Following a trial, the jury decided for McDonough. On appeal, Greenwood alleged that one of the jurors had not responded to a question on voir dire. The question concerned whether a member of the juror's immediate family had sustained injuries that resulted in a disability or prolonged pain and suffering. In fact, one juror's son had sustained a broken leg as a result of an exploding tire. Greenwood asked for a new trial based upon the failure of the juror to respond affirmatively to this question. Is Greenwood entitled to a new trial?

11. Burger King is a Florida corporation with its principal offices in Miami, Florida. Burger King licenses franchisees to use its trademarks and service marks. The governing contracts provide that the franchise relationship is established in Miami and governed by Florida law. The Miami headquarters sets policy and works directly with franchisees on major problems. Day-to-day contact with the franchisees is con-

ducted by a regional office that reports to the Miami headquarters.

Burger King sold John Rudzewicz, a Michigan resident, a franchise in the Detroit, Michigan, area. A dispute broke out between the parties, and Burger King filed suit in federal court in Florida based on breach of contract. Florida's long-arm statute extended jurisdiction to "any person, whether or not a citizen or resident of this state . . . who breaches a contract in this state by failing to perform acts required by the contract to be performed in this state." Rudzewicz asserted that the federal court in Florida lacked personal jurisdiction over him. Is this correct?

12. Plaintiff, Kathy Keeton, brought suit against *Hustler* magazine. Keeton was a resident of New York. *Hustler* magazine is an Ohio corporation with its principal place of business in California. *Hustler* sold around fifteen thousand copies per month in New Hampshire. Keeton filed suit in federal court in New Hampshire. She claimed that she had been libeled in five separate issues of the magazine. *Hustler* asserted that the federal court in New Hampshire should dismiss Keeton's suit because it could not assert jurisdiction over *Hustler*. *Hustler* objected to the fact that Keeton wished to recover for damages she sustained in New Hampshire and other states. Is this a valid objection? Does it make any difference that Keeton had limited contacts with New Hampshire? Does it make any difference that Keeton was not a resident of New Hampshire?

13. Plaintiff, Shirley Jones, is a resident of Florida. She brought suit against the *National Enquirer,* a Florida corporation with its principal place of business in Florida. Jones claimed she had been libeled by an article published in the *Enquirer.* Jones also brought suit against the author of the article in question, and the editor (who was also the president of the *Enquirer*) of the article. Both the author and the editor were Florida residents. Suit was filed in state court in California. The *Enquirer* did not challenge the jurisdiction of the California court—however, the author and editor argued there were not sufficient contacts between them and California to justify the assertion of personal jurisdiction over them by the California courts.

The *National Enquirer* has a circulation of around six-hundred thousand copies per week in California. The article in question impugned Jones' professional reputation. Her acting career was centered in California. Is it proper for the California state court to assert personal jurisdiction over the editor and author?

14. In a rape and murder trial, the judge permitted the press to attend only three days of a six-week voir dire. The balance of the voir dire was closed to the public. Press-Enterprise (a paper covering the trial) had moved, before the voir dire examination of prospective jurors had begun, that the voir dire be open to the public. Was it proper to prevent the press from attending the voir dire of the jury?

CHAPTER 4

 Judicial
Reasoning and
Decision Making

**The Judge As a Person: The Personality Factor
Factors in Judicial Decision Making**

The study of the methods by which judges reach decisions provides an understanding of the functioning of courts in our system, as well as an understanding of the law in general. This chapter will examine a number of important components that make up a judicial decision. One factor, the personality of the judge, is not to be found in any written judicial opinion. Yet it has an important effect on the outcome of any case. The other factors that influence how a judge makes a decision are history and custom, a balancing of the various interests involved in a particular case, deferring to other branches of government, reaching a decision that is "right" under the circumstances, applying social science studies, and the doctrine of stare decisis or the application of legal precedent. These factors are used by the judge to justify whatever decision is finally reached. As will be shown, judicial opinions may well be based on one or more of these factors' being applied to a given case.

However, no set mixture of ingredients combines to make a judicial decision. The weight of each factor may differ with each judge and with each case before a judge. Therefore, a study of the components of judicial decision making should provide a needed supplement to the legal rules that are presented throughout this text. Determining what the law is in a given situation is far more complex than simply looking up the relevant legal rules. Gaining an understanding of the nature of judicial decision making will provide the manager with a more sophisticated view of the legal environment than can be provided by a mere introduction to various legal rules.

THE JUDGE AS A PERSON: THE PERSONALITY FACTOR

A frequently heard saying about our legal system is that it is a system of laws, not of men. As with most folk wisdom—"wind from the west, fish bit the best"—there is an element of truth in it. Our system of government and the decisions of our courts are based upon established rules and procedures that apply to all parties affected by the system. For instance, the general rule that **contracts** for the sale of land must be in writing before they will be enforceable in a court of law applies to all land contracts, whether the parties are rich or poor, black or white, politically powerful or politically weak. In that sense, our system is one of laws. But it is also a system of men and women. Judges are people, not computers or mechanical devices programmed to decide cases based upon existing laws or procedures. Judges do not become any less human upon donning their black robes. As a result, the personality of the judge—who the judge is, the background of the judge, the likes and dislikes of the judge—all must be considered in determining how a particular judge will decide a particular case.

By studying a judge's personality, a major distinction between the law and legal rules becomes apparent. Legal rules, like theorems in geometry, exist in a vacuum, that is, in discussing their applicability, no mention is made of the effect of a certain person applying them to a situation. For example, the rules for applying the tort of negligence are stated as if a "correct" outcome is readily apparent to all who understand them. However, in fact, numerous "correct" outcomes can exist when different people accurately apply those rules.

Throughout this text, cases appear with both a majority opinion (the ruling in the case) and a dissenting opinion. These cases most readily illustrate the application of the personality factor in judicial decision making. In both opinions, the same legal rules are being applied. However, the personal characteristics of the individual judges caused their differing resolutions. It is this aspect of legal decision making, called here "the personality factor," that distinguishes the study of legal rules from the study of law.

However, the personality factor does not suggest that a judge is deliberately biased concerning various litigants who appear in court, or that a judge decides a case beforehand or cannot divorce personal feelings from professional efforts. A good judge attempts to keep any bias, prejudice, or personal feelings from affecting the decision in a case. As Samuel Johnson said: "If he [the judge] was such a rogue as to make up his mind upon a case without hearing it, he should not have been such a fool as to tell it."[1] Judges who let bias or prejudice influence their decisions are scofflaws: Such judges are beyond the scope of this discussion of judicial decision making and unfit for their jobs.

Judges are not unique in having their individual characteristics affect their decision making. Such characteristics as personal values, social and family background, likes and dislikes, and basic philosophy of life undoubtedly affect a person's decision to, say, become an accountant instead of a teacher. These and other characteristics are involved in legal decision making as well.

A humorous example appeared on a recent Public Broadcasting System program, imported from England, titled *Rumpole of the Bailey*. Rumpole was a crafty old barrister (trial lawyer) who had tried many cases before various judges in London for a number of years. As a result, Rumpole knew those judges and their personality quirks. In one episode, a young attorney was trying her first case before a certain elderly judge. Rumpole was representing the opposing party. Rumpole, ever the crafty advocate, told the young attorney that the judge was particularly fond of lengthy argument consisting of a great deal of citation of legal precedent. In fact, the judge became annoyed if attorneys cited cases as authority in his courtroom. He liked short arguments based upon the principle of the case at hand. As expected, the young attorney made a strong, legitimate argument on behalf of her client citing numerous cases and quoting from the opinions of the other judges, while the elderly judge seethed with annoyance. When the young attorney finished, Rumpole made a few comments, and the judge in short order found for Rumpole's client.

The viewer of that television program had no way of knowing whether justice was done in that case or whether a different argument by the young attorney would actually have changed its outcome. However, it was clear that one style of argument carried very little persuasive weight before that judge. Quite possibly, however, a different judge would have been more impressed with lengthy citation. Thus, understanding the personality quirks of the decision maker is an important component of the legal environment.

Another example further illustrates the personality factor as it influences the application of legal rules. Apply this statute to the facts that follow: "It shall be a criminal offense to willfully damage public property (including trees and vegetation) in public parks." As judge you may assess, on those who violate this statute, any combination of the following penalties:

1. *Jail*—zero to thirty days in the county jail. Judge has the option of deciding which days (for example, weekends only).

2. *Fine*—zero to five hundred dollars.

3. *Probation*—no jail or fine. However, conviction goes on criminal record and defendant must report to a probation officer for six months.

4. *Diversion*—no jail or fine. If the defendant stays out of trouble for one year, then no criminal record.

The following are two cases that come before you one day while you are performing your duties as a judge. For each case decide: (1) Did the person violate the statute? (2) What penalty should be assessed against each violator?

PROBLEM 1

Mary, age twenty-one, is a senior at college. Her father and mother are doctors. Mary plans to go to medical school. Her premed grades are 3.95/4.00. Mary belongs to the top sorority on campus. She is active in campus events. She is engaged to be married in June.

On the weekend before final exams, Mary's sorority threw its annual Christmas party. This was a traditional event. In the afternoon, the sorority hosted a Christmas party for underprivileged children. Mary was in charge of that event. In the evening, the party would become a wild celebration of the end of another semester and an outlet before final exam studies began.

When the last child left (about 5:30 P.M.) Mary and her sorority friends began to drink some wine. After the first glass, Mary was a bit giddy and ran from the house laughing and saying, "We need another Christmas tree." She drove to a local park and cut down an evergreen. However, a passing police officer stopped her and arrested her. She spent the night in jail.

The next day the local newspapers carried stories concerning Mary's arrest. She was released from jail (pending trial) but was humiliated. She could not face returning to school for finals and took incompletes in all her classes.

Mary pled guilty to the offense. The tree was worth fifty dollars. She had never even had a parking ticket before.

PROBLEM 2

Leroy, age twenty-one, dropped out of high school during his junior year. His parents are divorced and he lives on a farm with his uncle. He is currently unemployed—by choice. Leroy has had a number of jobs: grocery store clerk, farm laborer, gas station attendant. He was fired from each because of his "don't give a damn" attitude. He refuses to help work on his uncle's farm and refuses to look for another job.

Leroy is a 1950s-style hood, although he has never been in trouble with the law. He is clean shaven and has long hair, which he greases back. Leroy dresses in black, keeping his shirt front open. His pleasures consist of driving his souped-up pickup truck around town and playing pool at the local tavern.

Leroy does not attend any church nor does he participate in the community. In short, Leroy does not care about anything.

On the Saturday before Christmas, Leroy was on his way home. He was thrown out of a local tavern for insulting the owner. He was not intoxicated—he had not even finished his first beer. While driving, Leroy decided to stop by a local park. He got out of his pickup truck and chopped down an evergreen—for the heck of it. A passing police officer stopped him and arrested him. He spent the night in jail.

The next day the event was reported in the local newspapers. Leroy was released from jail (pending trial) but did not care. The evergreen was worth fifty dollars.

Make a decision in each case and compare your decisions and the reasons behind them with those given by your fellow students.

Of course, judges realize the effect of personality on their perception of legal issues, legal arguments, and the facts of a case. Therefore, the competent judge will make every attempt to separate personal feelings from a final decision. As just suggested, however, removing personal feelings from the decision-making process does not entirely erase a personality factor, just the most obvious outward manifestations of it.

Attorneys recognize the profound effect the personality factor may have upon the outcome of a particular case. At times an attorney may seek to have a particular judge removed from hearing a case. The attorney may also seek to "judge shop," that is, to file the initial complaint in the court of a judge whose personality is such as to increase the likelihood of success in the case. This does not necessarily mean that attorneys believe that the judge assigned to hear a case is biased, prejudiced, or predisposed to ruling in a certain way (although this too is a reason for an attorney to seek to have a judge removed from a case). It may well mean that the particular personality of a particular judge may be more (or less) compatible with the client, arguments, or facts to be presented in court.

Sometimes a judge may be concerned that the personality factor may bias the outcome of a pending case. In such a circumstance, the judge may decline to hear the case. This process is called **recusal.** It usually occurs when the case concerns a factual matter or a party with which the judge is so personally involved as to risk a possible conflict of interest—for example, a case upon which the judge had worked on behalf of one of the parties prior to becoming a judge, or a lawsuit against a corporation in which the judge is a shareholder. Recusal reflects two things: first, the judge's realization of the importance of the personality factor and of the possible influence of that factor on the decision; second, the importance of a recusal to the appearance of justice where a judge's personal interest may raise questions about the fairness or impartiality of a decision. When a judge's quirks or background unfairly interferes with the professional judgment needed to resolve the dispute, recusal is appropriate.

The following case, although not from a court within the United States, is an example of the personality factor becoming an issue in the litigation. The judge is responding to an attempt to have him removed from hearing a case because of his personal feelings about the crimes the defendant committed.

State of Israel v. Adolph Eichmann
District Court of Jerusalem
April 17, 1961

Adolph Eichmann was given the responsibility for the extermination of the Jews by the Nazis during World War II. He established death camps, such as Auschwitz, as the "final solution" to the Jewish "problem." After the war, Eichmann escaped from Germany and was given refuge in Argentina. In 1960, Israeli agents captured Eichmann and brought him to Israel for trial.

Landau, Presiding Judge

After reading out the indictment, Dr. Servatius—the Defence Counsel for the accused—voiced arguments regarding the invalidity of the judges sitting in this court, and regarding the lack of competence of the court to judge upon the counts in the indictment. We shall deal with the two matters in their order, and we shall reason our decision.

Regarding the invalidity of the judges: Dr. Servatius said that the accused fears that the judges will not be able in this case to be unprejudiced. The fear is not against one judge in particular, but against the three judges, being members of the Jewish nation and citizens of Israel. The counsel for the Defence says that it is to be feared that the memory of the catastrophe and the holocaust which exterminated their people—this which is the background for the counts and offences in the indictment—may influence the judges and may impair their ability to do justice. He also requested that every one of the judges examine himself, if his personal suffering or the suffering of his relatives during the years of the catastrophe invalidates him from sitting in judgment.

And this is our reply to these arguments:

The subject of the indictment is the responsibility of the accused for the acts described in the indictment. And when these acts are being clarified, it will not be difficult to safeguard the interests of the accused according to the procedure of our Criminal Code Ordinance, that everyone appearing before the court is innocent and his judgment will be declared only in accordance with the evidence brought before this court. Those who sit in judgment are professional judges, used and accustomed to weighing evidence brought before them and do their work in the public eye and the criticism of the public. Learned lawyers and counsels defend the accused. And as far as the fears of the accused regarding the background which is the background for this case, we must only repeat what has been said and what holds good in all courts: That when a court of judgment sits to judge, the judge is still a human being, flesh and blood, with feelings and senses, but he is ordered by the law to restrain those feelings and senses, because otherwise there will never be a judge fit to sit in a criminal case where the abhorrence of the judge is aroused, like treason, murder, or any other serious crime. It is true that the memory of the catastrophe and the holocaust stirs every Jew, but when this case has been brought before us, it is our duty to restrain those feelings when we sit in judgment in this case. And this duty we shall keep.

After weighing all arguments brought by the counsel for the Defence, the learned counsel for the Defence, the Court finds and each judge finds himself fit to sit in judgment.

FACTORS IN JUDICIAL DECISION MAKING

The remainder of this chapter will discuss a number of factors that judges acknowledge in making decisions. The factors to be examined are (1) history and custom (how the norms of society become a part of the law and influence the law); (2) balancing of interests (how a court will weigh the varied interests involved in the particular lawsuit in reaching its decision); (3) "doing what is right" (this factor involves the concept of natural law and notions of what may be called fundamental rights); (4) deferring to other branches of the government (a court may suggest that any change in the way it has decided a particular case is not within its province as a court); (5) use of nonlegal materials to justify the legal decision (often this involves the court's reviewing current sociological, psychological, or behavioral studies and making the conclusions of those studies a part of its justification); (6) the doctrine of stare decisis or precedent (focusing on the conflict between stability and flexibility in the law).

These factors are not used by a judge in the same manner a recipe is used by a chef. A judicial decision does not contain one part history, two parts precedent, and a dash of doing what is "right." In fact, some judicial decisions may be justified entirely by one of the factors, while others may use two or more factors in arriving at the result. No set rule exists for using or weighing them. The use of factors in justifying a decision is up to the judge.

Notice too what we are saying about the factors to be discussed in the balance of this chapter. They are used by the judge to *justify* the decision reached in a case. This once again suggests the importance of the personality factor. A judge cannot be compared to an empty slate as a case is being presented. Upon hearing the case, the judge makes an initial decision based upon the law. Then, with a decision firmly in hand, the judge uses the applicable factors to legally justify it. If the decision cannot be justified by the usual factors, then the judge will usually alter the initial decision. This is the essence of judicial decision making, which is also judicial lawmaking.

History and Custom

History (a nation's past) and custom (a nation's present habits—formed, of course, by its history) are important factors that may influence a judge's legal opinion. The law does not exist apart from the world around it. Law evolves as a result of a nation's (or within the United States, even a state's) history. Law is based on and is derived from the values of the people. It is a function of all that has affected a nation in its history. The judge may look to the history and norms of the community in formulating the decision in a case. Furthermore, the judge, as a person, is a part of that community and is a part of the history of the people.

Custom is like the historical factor, but with a much shorter time span. Frequently it concerns a type of business practice adopted by a firm or industry that has become standard. The following case is an example of a court's using custom to justify its decision.

Ghen v. Rich
Federal District Court, Massachusetts
8 Fed. 159 (1881)

In the early spring months, the easterly part of Massachusetts Bay is frequented by the species of whale known as the finback. Fishermen from Provincetown pursue them in open boats from the shore and shoot them with bomb lances fired from guns made expressly for the purpose. When killed, the whales sink at once to the bottom, but in the course of from one to three days they rise and float on the surface. Some of them are picked up by vessels and towed into Provincetown. Some float ashore at high water and are left stranded on the beach as the tide recedes. Others float out to sea and are never recovered. The person who happens to find them on the beach usually sends word to Provincetown, and the owner comes to the spot and removes the blubber. The finder usually receives a small salvage for his services. A whale swims with great swiftness, and for that reason cannot be taken by the harpoon and line. Each boat's crew engaged in the business has its peculiar mark or device on its lances, and in this way it is known by whom a whale is killed.

The libelant has been engaged in whaling for ten years past. On the morning of April 9, 1880, in Massachusetts Bay, near the end of Cape Cod, he shot and instantly killed with a bomb lance the whale in question. It sunk immediately, and on the morning of April 12, was found stranded on the beach in Brewster, within the ebb and flow of the tide, by one Ellis, seventeen miles from the spot where it was killed. Instead of sending word to Provincetown, as is customary, Ellis advertised the whale for sale at auction and sold it to the respondent, who shipped off the blubber and tried out the oil. The libelant heard of the finding of the whale on the morning of April 15, and immediately sent one of the boat's crew to the place and claimed it. Neither the respondent nor Ellis knew the whale had been killed by the libelant, but they knew or might have known, if they had wished, that it had been shot and killed with a bomb lance by some person engaged in this species of business.

Nelson, District Judge

The usage on Cape Cod, for many years, has been that the person who kills a whale in the manner and under the circumstances described, owns it, and this right has never been disputed until this case. The libelant claims title to the whale under this usage. The respondent insists that this usage is invalid. In a previous case, it was decided by Judge Sprague, that when a whale has been killed, and is anchored and left with marks of appropriation, it is the property of the captors; and if it is afterwards found, still anchored, by another ship, there is no usage or principle of law by which the property of the original captors is diverted, even though the whale may have dragged from its anchorage.

Judge Lowell, in another case, decided that a custom among whalemen in the Arctic seas, that the iron holds the whale, was reasonable and valid. In that case a boat's crew from the respondent's ship pursued and struck a whale in the Arctic ocean, and the harpoon and the line attached to it remained in the whale, but did not remain fast to the boat. A boat's crew from the libelant's ship continued the pursuit and captured the whale, and the master of the respondent's ship claimed it on the spot. It was held by the learned judge that the whale belonged to the respondents.

The usage for the first iron, whether attached to the boat or not, to hold the whale was fully established; and he added that, although local usages of a particular port ought not to be allowed to set aside the general maritime law, this objection did not apply to a custom which embraced an entire business, and had been concurred in for a long time by every one engaged in the trade.

I see no reason why the usage proved in this case is not as reasonable as that sustained in the cases cited. It has been recognized and acquiesced in for many years. It required in the first taker the only act of appropriation that is possible in the nature of the case. Unless it is sustained, this branch of industry must necessarily cease, for no person would engage in it if the fruits of his labor could be appropriated by any chance finder. It gives reasonable salvage for securing or reporting the property. That the rule works well in practice is shown by the extent of the industry which has grown up under it, and the general acquiescence of a whole community interested to dispute it. It is by no means clear that without regard to usage the common law would not reach the same result. I hold the usage to be valid, and that the property in the whale was in the libelant.

| Balance of Interests | The statue of justice, a robed, blindfolded woman holding an evenly balanced scale, is a familiar symbol of a court. This statue is a good representation of the next factor to be considered: the balancing of the various interests in the case. When a judge decides that X or Y should win a particular case, that decision may have an effect on persons other than the parties in the case. For example, some cases that the United States Supreme Court hears involve major social questions of the day (such as civil rights or abortion), and although the persons most directly interested in the case are the parties before the Court, frequently the Court's decision will have an effect on others, even though others are not technically bound by that decision. Courts, of course, are aware of this effect of some of their decisions. So are other |

interested parties. Often, those other interests will file their own written arguments with the courts, called **amicus curiae briefs.**

Thus, judges may note the competing interests at stake in a case as a means of justifying their decisions. Frequently, these balanced interests will be offered as illustrations that the decisions are consistent with some applicable legal principle. For example, in *United Steelworkers v. Weber* (1979), the United States Supreme Court used this approach to justify upholding an affirmative action plan. Numerous interests were involved: that of Brian Weber, the employee who contended he was denied a place in a training program because of his race; that of black workers who, as a class, had been denied job opportunities prior to the enactment of Title VII of the Civil Rights Act of 1964; that of the company and union, both of whom risked discrimination lawsuits from black workers if no affirmative action plan was created; and that of other white workers who would be denied certain training program class slots reserved for black workers, but for only a time.

These interests were not legal issues before the Court. The case only involved the applicability of Title VII to an affirmative action plan negotiated between an employer and a union being challenged by a white employee. However, in justifying its decision to uphold that plan, the Court suggested that it considered those other interests that would be effected. The decision, therefore, gained practical legitimacy as those groups observed that the Court took care to consider their interests.

A third factor that a court may use in justifying a decision is that the decision is right, just, or fair. This factor is called many different things. Legal philosophers call it **natural law;** that is, an overriding sense of justice or fairness that is fundamental to the law. This concept may be said to arise from God or from the rational sense of the people. The concept of natural law is based on the assumption that there is some natural or fundamental order in the universe. Natural law ideals serve as a means for a judge to test rules made by people.

Doing "What Is Right"

Courts use a number of legal doctrines in making a judicial decision based upon "what is right." The law of equity is based on principles of fairness. The Constitution contains the due process clause, which has been interpreted to mean fundamental fairness in our system of justice. Some statutes, like the Uniform Commercial Code (UCC), contain provisions that involve the court's applying in its decision making a standard of review based upon reasonableness or fairness; the common law makes the same demand. For example, one provision in the UCC gives the court the power to refuse to enforce a term of a contract if it is found to be unconscionable. Courts have defined **unconscionability** as meaning something that is grossly unfair or that shocks the conscience of the court. In addition, courts in the common law would refuse to enforce certain contracts because they conflict with public policy. For instance, a clause in a contract that provides for the removal of a finger of the breaching party will not be enforced in the courts. Note that no statute or legal doctrine explicitly tells a judge that "Contract clauses involving the removal of fingers from those who breach a contract will not be enforced in courts." In fact, the general policy in the law is to favor and enforce various contractual terms that parties to a contract have provided. Yet courts will refuse, upon grounds of public policy or unconscionability, to enforce such a contractual clause. Both those grounds are based upon a judgment of the court that such a provision in a contract is simply not right.

Determining whether a contract clause (or any other dispute before the court) involves a question of what is right is not an objective exercise. No complete list of "right" exists, nor is there a test that will produce the answer. The judge reaches such a decision on the basis of collective personal experiences and general societal norms. (Once again the personality factor can influence a decision. Who a judge is and what that judge's experiences have been may well be crucial in determining whether something is "right.")

Certain behavior or the results of certain behavior may be so unsavory as to clearly yield a conclusion that it is wrong. If society cannot agree on basic principles of right and wrong, then there is no society, no civilization, and no law. This does not mean that on all issues there is agreement concerning "what is right." Murder is wrong—it involves the killing of another human being. But is killing someone, as a soldier does, in the performance of duty, also wrong? Is the production of nuclear weapons wrong? People strongly disagree concerning such issues, but underlying that disagreement is a fundamental social norm of right and wrong conduct. This norm is what judges apply, filtered through their own personalities, when they use the "what is right" factor.

Riggs v. Palmer
New York Court of Appeals
22 N.E. 188 (1889)

On August 13, 1880, Francis B. Palmer made his last will and testament, in which he gave small legacies to his two daughters, Mrs. Riggs and Mrs. Preston, the plaintiffs in this action, and the remainder of his estate to his grandson, the defendant Elmer E. Palmer. Elmer lived with Francis Palmer as a member of his family, and at Francis Palmer's death was sixteen years old. He knew of the provisions made in his favor in the will, and that he might prevent his grandfather from revoking such provisions, which he had manifested some intention to do. To obtain the speedy enjoyment and immediate possession of his property, Elmer willfully murdered his grandfather by poisoning him. The defendant now claims the property, and the sole question for our determination is, can he have it?

Earl, Justice

The defendant says that Francis Palmer, the testator, is dead; that his will was made in due form, and has been admitted to probate; and that therefore it must have effect according to the letter of the law. It is quite true that statutes regulating the making, proof, and effect of wills and the devolution of property, if literally construed, and if their force and effect can in no way and under no circumstances be controlled or modified, give this property to the murderer. The purpose of those statutes was to enable testators to dispose of their estates to the objects of their bounty at death, and to carry into effect their final wishes legally expressed; and in considering and giving effect to them this purpose must be kept in view.

But all laws, as well as all contracts, may be controlled in their operation and effect by general, fundamental maxims of the common law. No one shall be permitted to profit by his own fraud, or to take advantage of his own wrong, or to found any claim upon his own iniquity, or to acquire property by his own crime. These maxims are dictated by public policy, have their foundation in universal law administered in all civilized countries, and have nowhere been superseded by statutes. These maxims, without any statute giving them force or operation, frequently control the effect and nullify the language of wills.

Here there was no certainty that this murderer would survive the testator, or that the testator would not change his will, and there was no certainty that he would get this property if nature was allowed to take its course. He therefore murdered the testator expressly to vest himself with an estate. Under such circumstances, what law, human or divine, will allow him to take the estate and enjoy the fruits of his crime? The will spoke and became operative at the death of the testator. The defendant caused that death, and thus by his crime made it speak and have operation. Shall it speak and operate in his favor? If he had met the testator, and taken his property by force, he would have had no title to it. Shall he acquire title by murdering him? The defendant cannot take any of this property as heir. He made himself an heir by the murder, and he seeks to take property as the fruit of his crime. He cannot vest himself with title by crime.

Deferring to Other Branches of Government

Judges are limited in what they can do by the issues brought before them and by the facts and information involved in a particular case. A court cannot conduct its own investigation, call its own witnesses or hire its own experts to study a matter before rendering a decision. Legislatures and administrative agencies, which also make law, are not as limited as a court. They can initiate investigations of issues. They may call witnesses and consult experts to assist in gathering the information that is necessary to make a legal rule. Legislatures are made up of a large number of officials who are directly accountable to the people. An administrative agency is created to provide expertise about a particular problem. The Environmental Protection Agency was created by Congress to regulate pollution and other environmental problems.

Because of the practical differences just mentioned between judges and other branches of government, courts may refuse to change the law in a case and instead defer the possibility of change to the legislature. Also, a court may decide to uphold a rule of an administrative agency in recognition of the superior expertise of that agency. A court thus recognizes its institutional limitations. Often deference to another lawmaking branch is used when the issue involved is highly controversial and perhaps may be more readily settled through the political process and its inevitable compromises rather than by judicial decision.

TVA v. Hill
United States Supreme Court
437 U.S. 153 (1978)

The Little Tennessee River originates in the mountains of northern Georgia and flows through the national forest lands of North Carolina into Tennessee, where it converges with the Big Tennessee River near Knoxville.

In this area of the Little Tennessee River, the Tennessee Valley Authority, a wholly owned public corporation of the United States, began constructing the Tellico Dam and Reservoir Project. Of particular relevance to this case is one aspect of the project, a dam that the TVA determined to place on the Little Tennessee a short distance from where the river's waters meet those of the Big Tennessee. When fully operational, the dam would impound water covering some 16,500 acres—much of which represents valuable and productive farmland—thereby converting the river's shallow, fast-flowing waters into a deep reservoir over thirty miles in length.

A discovery was made in the waters of the Little Tennessee that would profoundly affect the Tellico Project. Exploring the area around Coytee Springs, which is about seven miles from the mouth of the river, a University of Tennessee ichthyologist, Dr. David A. Etnier, found a previously unknown species of perch, the snail darter.

Until recently the finding of a new species of animal life would hardly generate a cause célèbre. This is particularly so in the case of darters, of which there are approximately 130 known species, 8 to 10 of these having been identified only in the last five years. The moving force behind the snail darter's sudden fame came some four months after its discovery, when the Congress passed the Endangered Species Act of 1973.

Chief Justice Burger

The Tellico Dam will either eradicate the known population of snail darters or destroy their critical habitat. Petitioner does not now seriously dispute this fact. In any event, under §4(a)(1) of the Act, the Secretary of the Interior is vested with exclusive authority to determine whether a species such as the snail darter is "endangered" or "threatened" and to ascertain the factors which have led to such a precarious existence. By §4(d) Congress has authorized—indeed commanded—the Secretary to "issue such regulations as he deems necessary and advisable to provide for the conservation of such species." The Secretary promulgated regulations which declared the snail darter an endangered species whose critical habitat would be destroyed by creation of the Tellico Reservoir. There is no suggestion that the Secretary exceeded his authority or abused his discretion in issuing the regulations.

It may seem curious to some that the survival of a relatively small number of three-inch fish among all the countless millions of species extant would require the permanent halting of a virtually completed dam for which Congress has expended more than $100 million. The paradox is not minimized by the fact that Congress continued to appropriate large sums of public money for the project, even after congressional Appropriations Committees were apprised of its apparent impact upon the survival of the snail darter. We conclude, however, that the explicit provisions of the Endangered Species Act require precisely that result.

Here we are urged to view the Endangered Species Act "reasonably," and hence shape a remedy "that accords with some modicum of common sense and the public weal." But is that our function? We have no expert knowledge on the subject of endangered species, much less do we have a mandate from the people to strike a balance of equities on the side of the Tellico Dam. Congress has spoken in the plainest of words, making it abundantly clear that the balance has been struck in favor of affording endangered species the highest of priorities, thereby adopting a policy which it described as "institutionalized caution."

Our individual appraisal of the wisdom or

unwisdom of a particular course consciously se-lected by the Congress is to be put aside in the process of interpreting a statute. Once the mean-ing of an enactment is discerned and its constitu-tionality determined, the judicial process comes to an end. We do not sit as a committee of review, nor are we vested with the power of veto.

In our constitutional system the commitment to the separation of powers is too fundamental for us to pre-empt congressional action by judicially decreeing what accords with "common sense and the public weal." Our Constitution vests such re-sponsibilities in the political branches.

Use of Social Science Data

A fifth factor that courts use to justify their decisions is different from the other decision-making factors. The other factors include arguments and rules created by the legal system that a court uses to bolster its conclusion in a given case. This factor involves studies performed by various social scientists—sociologists, psychologists, and the like. Studies by such people are made outside the confines of the particular case and not at the behest of the courts or a litigant. Therefore, this factor is different from the use of expert testimony given during a trial. Expert testimony by a soci-ologist or other social scientist presented at trial is used as an advocate's tool and focused specifically on the facts of the case at hand. The social science factor discussed in this section does *not* arise from testimony at trial, although the existence of the data most likely was brought to the attention of the court by one of the attorneys or witnesses in the case. The social science data that make up this factor were gathered independently of the trial, perhaps as part of a general study, perhaps long before the case at hand arose. The conclusions of the study, however, could support a decision in favor of one of the parties.

The earliest use of this factor was in a 1908 United States Supreme Court case concerning whether a state could constitutionally make it a crime for an employer to require female employees to work more than ten hours in a day. Louis D. Brandeis (who later served as a justice of the United States Supreme Court) filed a brief on behalf of the state of Oregon arguing that the law should be upheld as constitutional. His brief contained extracts from more than ninety social science studies and reports that showed that long hours of work are physically dangerous for women. The Court used this information in deciding that the state of Oregon could constitutionally limit the working hours of women. This technique for writing briefs came to be called a **Brandeis brief.**

Use of sociological studies as a factor in justifying legal decisions has been subjected to criticism. Such studies are not designed for use in an adversary pro-ceeding. Furthermore, some people contend that courts do not use such studies properly nor are judges familiar enough with social science studies in general to use them as support for certain legal propositions. Of course, what is generally accepted by social scientists at one time is not necessarily still accepted at a later time, but the rule established by the case is not generally changed by the court in a subsequent case to reflect modifications in the social science studies relied upon by the court in its original decision. Note, for example, the social science information supplied by Brandeis in the case concerning restrictive legislation for working women. Today the law generally rejects work classifications and requirements based solely on the sex of the worker.

Precedent: The Doctrine of Stare Decisis

One of the most important factors used by judges in justifying their decisions is the concept of precedent, or the doctrine of **stare decisis.** This factor embodies two competing notions. The first notion is that the law is stable; that is, because it has a firm foundation in legal history, and is built on the legal rules and decisions of the past, it must therefore be certain and predictable. The second notion is that the law is flexible, that it is not so rigid as to become antiquated. The law is able to change, to move, to be modified as circumstances and society change.

The doctrine of stare decisis means that in making a judicial decision the court applies rules made in similar cases in the past to justify a decision in a current dispute. The past cases are said to be precedents. Decisions of a higher court become what is called binding precedent for the lower courts. For example, assume that the supreme court of the state of X held that walking barefoot across a city park precluded a person from collecting damages from the city if a piece of glass injured the walker. Assume that later a very similar injury occurred and a case was brought to a trial level court in the state. That trial court is considered to be bound by the ruling of the supreme court. Under the doctrine of stare decisis, the supreme court's decision would be applied against the injured walker. If that case was then appealed to the state supreme court, the supreme court could simply cite its previous case as authority (or precedent) for the decision that the walker cannot collect damages from the city.

However, if a similar case occurred in the state adjacent to state X, the decision mentioned would not be considered precedent in that neighboring state. Of course, the courts of the other state are free to refer to that decision, but they have no obligation to consider or follow that case. In fact they could reach an opposite decision without even considering or discussing the ruling of the neighboring state's supreme court. The doctrine of stare decisis thus is limited in its application to the geographical boundaries of a certain judicial system.

Purpose, Function, and Use of Precedent. Precedent is an important feature of our legal system. It lends stability, certainty, and predictability to the legal system. Of course, in law, as in life, nothing is ever absolutely certain. In an athletic competition between a very strong team and a very weak team, it is predictable, virtually certain, that the strong team will win. However, upset victories by the very weak team are not unheard of. The situation is similar with the use of legal precedent as a provider of certainty to the legal system. Legal rules (that is what precedent becomes) are not applied to facts as if they were a mathematical formula. The other factors discussed in this chapter influence and are part of the decision and its justification as offered by the deciding judge.

Judges, however, are careful to follow precedent. They understand the importance to attorneys and people who are affected of the law's being predictable and based on past decisions. Attorneys predict what a future decision will be in order to advise clients concerning how to conform their conduct to the law and stay out of legal trouble. In fact, precedent and the importance to the legal system of certainty and predictability are so highly valued that good lawyers are usually very good predictors of future outcomes of legal disputes. Judges usually stay with tradition and will usually follow precedent in deciding cases. A judge who regularly ignores past legal decisions will be considered arbitrary and somewhat dangerous by attorneys, who, with this judge, would have no way of advising their clients concerning the status of the law or how to conform their conduct to the requirements of the law.

The following case is an example of a court that justified its decision by the doctrine of stare decisis. Note how important the values of certainty, predictability, and stability in the law are to the court in this case. The court applied past judicial decisions to the dispute at hand to justify its decision that professional baseball was exempt from the antitrust laws.

Flood v. Kuhn
United States Supreme Court
407 U.S. 258 (1971)

The petitioner, Curtis Charles Flood, born in 1938, began his major league career in 1956 when he signed a contract with the Cincinnati Reds for a salary of four thousand dollars for the season. He had no attorney or agent to advise him on that occasion. He was traded to the St. Louis Cardinals before the 1958 season. Flood rose to fame as a center fielder with the Cardinals during the years from 1958 to 1969. In those twelve seasons, he compiled a batting average of .293. He ranks among the ten major league outfielders possessing the highest lifetime fielding averages. Flood's St. Louis compensation ranged from $13,500 in 1961 to $90,000 in 1969.

At the age of thirty-one, in October 1969, Flood was traded to the Philadelphia Phillies of the National League in a multiplayer transaction. He was not consulted about the trade. He was informed by telephone and received formal notice only after the deal had been consummated. In December, he complained to the commissioner of baseball and asked that he be made a free agent and be placed at liberty to strike his own bargain with any other major league team. His request was denied.

Flood then instituted this antitrust suit in January 1970, in federal court for the Southern District of New York. The defendants (although not all were named in each cause of action) were the commissioner of baseball, the presidents of the two major leagues, and the twenty-four major league clubs. In general, the complaint charged violations of the federal antitrust laws.

Flood declined to play for Philadelphia in 1970, despite a $100 thousand salary offer, and he sat out the year. After the season was concluded, Philadelphia sold its rights to Flood to the Washington Senators. Washington and the petitioner were able to come to terms for the 1971 season at a salary of $110 thousand. Flood started the season but, apparently because he was dissatisfied with his performance, he left the Washington club on April 27, early in the campaign. He has not played baseball since then.

Judge Cooper, in a detailed opinion, held that *Federal Baseball Club* v. *National League* and *Toolson* v. *New York Yankees, Inc.* were controlling. On appeal, the Second Circuit felt "compelled to affirm." The Supreme Court granted **certiorari** in order to look once again at this troublesome and unusual situation.

Justice Blackmun

For the third time in 50 years the Court is asked specifically to rule that professional baseball's reserve system is within the reach of the federal antitrust laws.

Federal Baseball Club v. National League (1922) was a suit for treble damages instituted by a member of the Federal League (Baltimore) against the National and American Leagues and others. Mr. Justice Holmes, in speaking succinctly for a unanimous Court, said:

> "The business is giving exhibitions of baseball, which are purely state affairs. The restrictions by contract that prevented the plaintiff from getting players to break their bargains and the other conduct charged against the defendants were not an interference with commerce among the States."

Federal Baseball was cited a year later, and without disfavor, in another opinion by Mr. Justice Holmes for a unanimous Court. In the years that followed, baseball continued to be subject to intermittent antitrust attack. The courts, however, rejected these challenges on the authority of Federal Baseball.

In Toolson v. New York Yankees, Inc. (1953), Federal Baseball was cited as holding "that the business of providing public baseball games for profit between clubs of professional baseball players was not within the scope of the federal antitrust laws." . . . The emphasis in Toolson was on the determination, attributed even to Federal Baseball, that Congress had no intention to include baseball within the reach of the federal antitrust laws.

In view of all this, it seems appropiate now to say that with its reserve system enjoying exemption from the federal antitrust laws, baseball is, in a very distinct sense, an exception and an anomaly. Federal Baseball and Toolson have become an aberration confined to baseball. It is an aberration that has been with us now for half a century, one heretofore deemed fully entitled to the benefit of stare decisis, and one that has survived the Court's expanding concept of interstate commerce. It rests on a recognition and an acceptance of baseball's unique characteristics and needs.

Accordingly, we adhere once again to Federal Baseball and Toolson and to their application to professional baseball. If there is any inconsistency or illogic in all this, it is an inconsistency and illogic of long standing that is to be remedied by the Congress and not by this Court. Under these circumstances, there is merit in consistency even though some might claim that beneath that consistency is a layer of inconsistency.

And what the Court said in Federal Baseball in 1922 and what it said in Toolson in 1953, we say again here in 1972; the remedy, if any is indicated, is for congressional, and not judicial, action.

When Precedent Is Not Followed. The doctrine of stare decisis also embodies the notion that law is flexible, subject to change, and has the capacity for growth. Keeping the law stable yet flexible is one of the great functions of the doctrine of stare decisis.

Good lawyers can find precedent or cases from the past to support almost any position taken in court. One of the skills of a good lawyer is the ability to demonstrate that a precedent case supports a certain line of reasoning, yielding a result under the doctrine of stare decisis. This does not involve any trickery or misrepresentations to the court, for no two cases are exactly alike. Even though a past case may have arisen from similar facts, there are usually enough factual differences between the past case and the present case to render the precedential case distinguishable. Legal argument before the court often involves distinguishing away cases cited as having precedential effect by one's adversary while arguing that other cases deserve precedence.

Often, since different cases from the past will be offered to a court as precedent, judges will engage in distinguishing cases that in their opinion justify their decisions. Case reports are not always clear concerning the rule made by the court. Sometimes cases are read very narrowly, that is, as applying only to very similar facts. Other cases are read rather broadly; that is, they stand for a very general proposition of law, which is thereafter considered precedent in a variety of different matters. Attorneys urge such different interpretations of the same case on a court, and judges often use the reading that best suits their decision in a case in order to justify it. Precedent therefore is not as clear or so easy to establish as one might first think.

In some judicial opinions, the court makes remarks about the law that are not precisely at issue in the case. In the *Parker* v. *Foote* case in Chapter 10, the issue is whether the jury should decide whether the obstruction of sunlight was permissible, or whether such a decision at trial was rightfully made by the judge. The opinion quoted in this text, and the part of the case cited as precedent by other courts, concerns whether the right to sunlight may be obtained in this country by the mere long-term enjoyment of the sunlight. However, that discussion was not the ruling of the case, from which precedent is usually obtained. A discussion of this kind is called **dicta** and is not a part of the judge's decision in the case. Dicta are not considered to have precedential effect. However, it is not always easy to clearly predict what a court will consider dicta from a past opinion or what legal ruling will deserve precedential value. Sometimes a case is read in such a way as to give precedential effect to what are usually considered dicta in an opinion.

A court may also give an opinion on an issue in the case beyond that which is necessary for its decision. This may be the judge's opinion of the ramifications of the ruling on a closely related issue. It too is considered dicta and is not the rule of the case that has precedential value. However, as we have stated, a court may use such language from an opinion as precedent supporting its decision in another case. One of the best-known instances of such dicta was Justice Stone's footnote number 4 in *United States* v. *Carolene Products Co.* (1938). The Supreme Court at that time was, after enormous pressure, beginning to uphold various legislative controls of economic activity enacted by Congress as part of Roosevelt's New Deal. The footnote in *Carolene Products* suggested that the Court might continue very strict constitutional review of legislative attempts to regulate liberty rights even though they were loosening their review standard for legislation that regulated property rights. That footnote, which was merely an opinion about the Court's standard of constitutional review for certain legislative restrictions, was the starting point for the development today of the distinction between property rights and liberty rights treatment by the courts.

Thus, the nature of judicial decision making and the opinion that justifies a decision may cause difficulty in determining exactly what the precedent is in a given case. Since cases may be interpreted in different ways, their precedential effect may also be different, depending upon the court that uses that case.

Sometimes, although rarely, courts will choose not to follow clear legal precedent. In such situations the existing legal rule is usually outdated, and a need for change in the law is quite evident. Sometimes following the long-established legal precedent will yield an injustice or keep a legal rule when the purposes and reasons for the rule no longer exist. However, the ultimate goal of the law is justice, and a court may not blindly abide by the legal decisions of the past if an injustice will be perpetrated in the present. The temptation to ignore precedent in order to achieve justice must be balanced with the importance of stability and certainty in the law. This struggle in the law between stability and flexibility is most clearly embodied in the doctrine of stare decisis. The following case is an example of a court's disregarding long-standing precedent and changing a legal rule that it believes is no longer fair or just.

Flagiello v. Pennsylvania Hospital

Supreme Court of Pennsylvania

208 A.2d 193 (1965)

Mrs. Mary C. Flagiello was injured in the Pennsylvania Hospital in Philadelphia. It is enough to say that she avers that through the negligence of two employees of the hospital, she fell, sustaining in the fall a fracture to her right ankle. She and her husband, Thomas Flagiello, brought an action in trespass against the hospital and the two employees alleged to have been immediately responsible for the accident. The defendant hospital answered that it was an eleemosynary institution engaged in charitable enterprise and, therefore, not responsible in damage to the plaintiffs.

Musmanno, Justice

In the early days of public accommodation for the ill and the maimed, charity was exercised in its pure and pristine sense. Many good men and women, liberal in purse and generous in soul, set up houses to heal the poor and homeless victims of disease and injury. They made no charge for this care. The benefactors felt themselves richly rewarded in the knowledge that they were befriending humanity. Charity in the biblical sense prevailed.

Whatever the law may have been regarding charitable institutions in the past, it does not meet the conditions of today. Charitable enterprises are no longer housed in ramshackly wooden structures. They are not mere storm shelters to succor the traveler and temporarily refuge those stricken in a common disaster. Hospitals today are growing into mighty edifices in brick, stone, glass and marble. Many of them maintain large staffs, they use the best equipment that science can devise, they utilize the most modern methods in devoting themselves to the noblest purpose of man, that of

helping one's stricken brother. But they do all this on a business basis, submitting invoices for services rendered—and properly so.

And if a hospital functions as a business institution, by charging and receiving money for what it offers, it must be a business establishment also in meeting obligations it incurs in running that establishment. One of those inescapable obligations is that it must exercise a proper degree of care for its patients, and, to the extent that it fails in that care, it should be liable in damages as any other commercial firm would be liable. If a hospital employee negligently leaves a sponge in the abdominal cavity of a paying patient, why should the hospital be freed from liability, any more than a restaurant owner should escape responsibility for the damage inflicted by a waitress who negligently overturns a tray of hot dishes on a guest?

A person may recover damages if he is injured, as the result of negligence, in a hotel, theater, street car, store, skating rink, natatorium, bowling alley, train or ship, yet he cannot recover if he is hurt in the place where accidents are considered most unlikely to occur—in a hospital, where one goes to be cured of an already existing infirmity and not to be saddled with additional woe and torment. This is indeed the paradox of paradoxes. It has no logic, reason, and, least of all, justice, to support it. And still more paradoxical is the argument that, by refusing recovery to the victim of a hospital's own negligence, one somehow is serving charity!

If there was any justification for the charitable immunity doctrine when it was first announced, it has lost that justification today. Each court which has upheld the immunity rule has relied for its authority on a previous decision or decisions, scarcely ever placing the subject for study on the table of self-asserting justice. No attempt is ever made by the advocates of the immunity doctrine to justify in moral law and fair dealing a doctrine which deprives an injured person of a forum guaranteed to all others.

Nor is it to be feared that with the imposition of liability for torts, accidents in the hospitals will disproportionately increase. It would be a voodoo prediction that with the lifting of the immunity doctrine, hospital patients would leap out of beds to break legs, scar themselves with X-ray machines, rip off bandages, smash plaster of Paris casts, and ingest wrong medicines, in order to further disable themselves and thus collect money damages. No sane person would prefer money to a sane and healthy body, free of pain, agony and torment.

Stare decisis channels the law. It erects lighthouses and flys the signals of safety. The ships of jurisprudence must follow that well-defined channel which, over the years, has been proved to be secure and trustworthy. But it would not comport with wisdom to insist that, should shoals rise in a heretofore safe course and rocks emerge to encumber the passage, the ship should nonetheless pursue the original course, merely because it presented no hazard in the past. The principle of stare decisis does not demand that we follow precedents which shipwreck justice.

Stare decisis is not an iron mold into which every utterance by a Court—regardless of circumstances, parties, economic barometer and sociological climate—must be poured, and, where, like wet concrete, it must acquire an unyielding rigidity which nothing later can change.

The history of law through the ages records numerous inequities pronounced by courts because the society of the day sanctioned them. Reason revolts, humanity shudders, and justice recoils before much of what was done in the past under the name of law. Yet, we are urged to retain a forbidding incongruity in the law simply because it is old. That kind of reasoning would have retained prosecution for witchcraft, imprisonment for debt and hanging for minor offenses which today are hardly regarded misdemeanors.

A rule that has become insolvent has no place in the active market of current enterprise. When a rule offends against reason, when it is at odds with every precept of natural justice, and when it cannot be defended on its own merits, but has to depend alone on a discredited genealogy, courts not only possess the inherent power to repudiate, but, indeed, it is required, by the very nature of judicial function, to abolish such a rule.

Of course, the precedents here recalled do not justify a light and casual treatment of the doctrine of stare decisis but they proclaim unequivocally that where justice demands, reason dictates, equality enjoins and fair play decrees a change in judge-made law, courts will not lack in determination to establish that change.

SUMMARY

It is important to understand the nature of the decision-making process in order to appreciate the complexity and difficulty of predicting what a legal result will be in any case. The factors that compose the judicial decision-making process may clash, thereby yielding the sometimes logically conflicting rulings in certain cases. Law is not a logically based, mathematically precise instrument. It is a means of civilizing a society whose goal is justice.

Seven factors involved in the judicial reasoning and decision-making process may be identified. One is unacknowledged in judicial opinions but, nevertheless, is central to understanding law. It is the personality factor. The decisions made by any particular judge are a function of that judge's personality. Six other factors appear as acknowledged justifications for the judicial decision reached in a case. These factors reflect important policies in the law. At times one or more of these factors may conflict if applied to a given case. The first of these factors is history and custom (how the practices and norms of a society are reflected in its laws and in the judicial decisions rendered in its courts). A balancing of the interests involved in the case is the second factor. This involves the recognition that at times not only do each of the parties in a court dispute have interests to be considered, but so also do others who are not directly affected by the case. Their interest focuses on the possible precedential effect given to that case by other courts. A third factor is doing "what is right." This involves an ideal of the law—to render fair and just results in decisions made in the courts. It may be used by a court to modify an existing legal rule in order that an unjust result not occur. A fourth factor is deferring to other branches of government. A fifth factor is the use by courts of social science data to lend support to their decisions and conclusions in a case. The final factor is one of the most important: the concept of stare decisis or legal precedent. This notion embodies the conflicting values of stability and flexibility in the law.

REVIEW QUESTIONS

1. Define the following terms:
   a. Stare decisis
   b. Natural law
   c. History
   d. Custom
   e. Precedent
   f. Brandeis brief
   g. Recusal

2. What are the six factors (leaving the personality factor out of consideration) identified in this chapter as components of a judicial decision?

3. For each of the six factors discuss the following: (a) What the factor attempts to accomplish in the law. (b) Advantages involved in each factor; what in each factor is good for the legal system and its goal of justice?

4. The case, *TVA* v. *Hill,* was used to illustrate the "deferring-to-other-branches" factor. Render a decision in that case using the "balance-of-interests" factor.

5. Justices of the United States Supreme Court place their assets in a **blind trust.** A blind trust is a legal device where a person is appointed to invest the property of the justice. However, the nature of those investments is kept secret. Why is this done? Assuming that there are no dishonest justices, why is this necessary?

6. In 1967, State University had restricted hours for its women students. All women students were required to live in campus housing and could not be out later than midnight. Based upon some or all of the factors raised in this chapter, what justifications could be made by a decision maker either for refusing to abolish such a rule or for abolishing the rule?

7. Discuss the doctrine of stare decisis and the effect of precedent on the legal system. Give an example of a case in which precedent should be followed and a case in which precedent should not be followed.

8. Brewing, Inc., is a beer manufacturing corporation. It agreed to supply the Dew Drop Inn with five barrels of beer per month. A barrel is defined by statute as containing 31 gallons. After a few months, the Inn noticed that they seemed to be receiving less than 31 gallon barrels. Upon checking, they learned that the barrels ranged from 31 gallons to 29.7 gallons. As barrels in the beer industry age, they hold less and less liquid because the hoops that hold the barrel together must be driven closer to the center in order to keep them tight. Over time, this reduces the size of the barrel. The Dew Drop Inn sues Brewing. What might the corporation argue in defense?

9. You are an executive with the XYZ Corporation. The corporation has been sued by a disgruntled supplier. Counsel has informed you that five cases that discuss the issue in the lawsuit have been found in your jurisdiction. All five cases support the position of the supplier. How might you expect the issue to be resolved?

10. Given the facts in number 9, under what circumstances would you expect the opposite outcome?

11. Jenkins is very liberal politically. She supports increased government regulation of large corporations and has participated in numerous causes, such as the pro-choice movement, gay rights, and nuclear freeze activities. She is a top-flight attorney and legal scholar and is considered one of the most well-qualified judicial candidates in the country. Would you anticipate her being nominated for a federal judgeship by a very conservative president? Give reasons.

12. Grace and Sam Stamos are an elderly couple who recently moved to the United States from Greece. They understand only a little English. Richards visited them at home in order to sell them a freezer. At first they were not interested, since they did not have a great deal of money. However, Richards discussed the matter with them for ten hours that day. Finally, they agreed to purchase a freezer and signed a fifteen page contract. The contract was written in English, with complex legal terminology, and was in very small print. No one explained the terms of the contract to the Stamoses. One provision provided that if they were late making a payment on the freezer, all their other property could be taken by the seller and sold to pay their debt. The freezer was worth three hundred dollars. The contract required a thirty-dollars-per-month payment for five years.

Without discussing applicable legal rules, if the seller attempts to enforce the contract against the Stamoses and a court rules in their favor, how might the court justify its decision?

NOTE

[1] James Boswell, *The Life of Samuel Johnson* (1791), p. 958.

CHAPTER 5

The Legislature, Legislation, and the Executive Branch

A Comparison of Lawmaking by the Courts and the Legislature
The Legislature and Lawmakers
Statutory Construction
The Executive Branch

This chapter contains introductory and background information on the legislative branch of government and an overview of the executive branch. The discussion of the legislature will first focus on an overview of various issues surrounding the legislature and the legislative process. Thereafter, an analysis of judicial construction and interpretation of statutes will be presented.

A COMPARISON OF LAWMAKING BY THE COURTS AND THE LEGISLATURE

Context in Which the Lawmaking Occurs

Judicial Case-by-Case Approach. Courts make laws on a case-by-case basis. Judge-made law is the decision in a particular case. However, a judge is not a roving "do-gooder" sitting on the bench and resolving all society's problems. For example, if no cases arise involving tort law, then there can be no judge-made tort law. Even if a particular judge is convinced that a doctrine of tort law should be modified because it causes gross injustice, that judge may not simply declare such a legal rule to be henceforth changed. The legal rule can only be changed within the context of a dispute brought before the court. Furthermore, in making law on a case-by-case basis, courts have no power to independently investigate the facts and gather information that may be helpful in rendering a decision. Courts generally are limited to the facts presented to them by the parties at trial. However, simply because judicial lawmaking must occur within a case, its effect is not therefore narrow. Courts have announced very broad principles while deciding particular cases.

Legislative Approach. A legislature's lawmaking ability is not institutionally confined in that its lawmaking is not limited to cases people bring. In fact, a legislature is not the proper forum for the settlement of individual disputes. Legislation is limited only by the Constitution. For example, a problem or general issue may exist that interests only certain legislators. The legislature has mechanisms—committees, subcommittees, and special investigatory panels—to study that issue. In studying the issue, legislators may call witnesses representing a broad spectrum of opinion. Witnesses may be required to appear and answer questions posed by the legislators. In addition, legislative staff and investigators may seek data and prepare reports. The purpose of the investigation is to provide the legislature with information—facts from which to draw in its decision whether to enact a statute. Additionally, the information gathered assists the legislature in drafting the statute so as to take into account its full range of effects.

Since information and facts are needed by the legislature to properly draft a statute, legislators have broad authority to order pertinent studies, to hold hearings, to call witnesses, and even to require certain witnesses to testify. Some legislative investigations have been highly publicized and very noteworthy. In the early 1950s, Senator Joseph McCarthy of Wisconsin conducted investigations of possible communist infiltration of and influence on various segments of American life. In the early 1960s, Senator John L. McClellan led a committee that investigated organized crime in the United States. These hearings enabled the American people to witness the spectacle of alleged mobsters refusing to answer questions posed by the legislators on the grounds that those questions violated their constitutional rights. In the 1970s, the Watergate investigation by a Senate committee led by Senator Sam Ervin uncovered corruption in the Nixon White House that led to the only resignation of a president in American history.

These examples are legislative investigations that have become almost a part of American folklore. The stated purpose of these investigations was to provide background information to the legislature concerning a particular problem. The investigating committee would then ideally be in a position to recommend legislation regulating the area from which the problem or issue arose.

Although the power of the legislature to investigate is very broad, it is not without limit. Individuals are protected from governmental activity by various provisions of the Constitution. For example, the Fifth Amendment provides the right to refuse to answer incriminating questions.

The doctrine of stare decisis is a very important factor in judicial lawmaking. Courts seek to apply past decisions to current disputes in order to promote stability and certainty in the law. Judges are therefore reluctant to ignore the effect of past cases on present disputes. Consider, however, the legislature's ability to make new law to meet present needs, without being doctrinally bound to the law as it had previously

Relationship to the Past of Any Newly Made Law

existed. Broad investigative powers give the legislature the ability to thoroughly study the effect of a new approach to a problem before enacting any legislation.

When courts defer to the legislature it is often because a new approach is needed, and the legislature is institutionally designed to provide that new approach without being confined by past work in the area. The New Mexico Solar Rights Act is an example of a bold enactment by a legislature seeking to resolve a troubling problem— protecting the access to sunlight that is necessary to power a solar energy collector. Before the enactment of this statute, the only law in New Mexico that provided for such access was the common law, embodied in the *Parker* v. *Foote* and *Fontainebleau* v. *Forty-Five Twenty-Five* cases (discussed in Chapter 10), which represented, in summary, that solar access could only be protected if the solar energy user purchased the needed access rights from adjoining landowners. The New Mexico statute provided that solar rights could be obtained by the first person to use a path of sunlight to power a solar energy collector. In short, the first solar use established a legal right for continued use of the sunlight. The New Mexico legislature did not limit its lawmaking to a step-by-step progression as courts usually do under the doctrine of stare decisis. Instead, the Solar Rights Act outlined a radical change in the relevant law.

Although the legislature does not operate under a doctrine similar to stare decisis, it too seeks to avoid being labeled arbitrary in its work. Therefore, the legislature is considerate and ever mindful of the policies behind the doctrine of stare decisis when devising a new statute. In a sense, legislators are like architects who rehabilitate an old office building. The interior is transformed, its function and use completely different than originally intended. Yet the outside appearance of the building remains the same. A legislature often performs much the same feat when enacting a statute.

The legislator is more confident of the success of a particular statute if it is similar to a statute that already exists. For example, although the New Mexico solar rights statute is a completely new approach for protecting solar access, it is firmly built on an existing body of law, including rules of civil procedure that provide mechanisms for the enforcement of legal rights; rules that govern eminent domain or the power of the government to take private property for public use; and rules that govern the transfer and use of property rights, including those which are created by the statute in favor of the solar energy user.

Additionally, the solar rights statute is modeled after New Mexico's water allocation law, which has had years of use and numerous judicial constructions of its terms. In fact, many of the terms used in the solar rights statute are identical to the terms in the water law—"prior appropriation" and "beneficial use," for example. These terms have developed a special meaning in water law. The New Mexico legislature expected a similar meaning to exist in their new use as a part of the solar energy access scheme. Furthermore, the entire procedure for acquiring a legal right to solar access is similar to the procedure for acquiring a legal right to use water in New Mexico.

Legislatures may also look to the experiences of other states in determining the type of statute to enact regulating a certain area. A legislature will use another state's statute as a model for the one it is enacting. Perhaps upon study, the legislature may make a refinement in the statutory language to repair weaknesses that have surfaced. Perhaps the refinements will reflect some differences between the states. In any event, the legislature uses existing law and existing statutes as guides and models for what is to be newly enacted. In this way, legislation is built on the past while maintaining a new and unique identity.

THE LEGISLATURE AND LAWMAKERS

Historical Development of Legislation

Legislation as a general means of regulating conduct in this country is only about one hundred years old. Before the end of the nineteenth century, most of the law in the United States was common law. Such bodies of law as torts, commercial contracts, and negotiable paper were a function of long-time judicial lawmaking, first in England and then in the United States. For the most part, statutes enacted before the late nineteenth century were used to fill in "gaps" in various areas of common law or to change a judicially created common law doctrine.

The nature of common law is that it is a body of cases that acts as precedent for deciding disputes. Its rules were created on an ad hoc basis, determined by the type of disputes before the courts. The common law as a whole, therefore, could not be modified or changed. Near the end of the nineteenth century, a movement in American law for codification of the common law was begun. This would enable a legislature to clear away confusion existing because of conflicting precedents and to pass one act governing a given area. The first area to receive attention was the area of civil procedure—the mechanical rules of bringing a case and proceeding with it through a court of law.

Later, committees worked to draft uniform laws to be proposed in the state legislatures. These uniform statutes were drafted on the basis of the common law in a given area. For example, one such law was called the Uniform Sales Act and was based on the judicial decisions in the area of sales of goods transactions. This common law was in part based on the old law merchant developed in Europe in the Middle Ages by merchants settling their disputes at fairs. The Uniform Sales Act was an attempt to give some form and structure to this area of law. The Uniform Sales Act and other uniform acts were proposed and enacted by various state legislatures. The Uniform Sales Act has been replaced by another uniform law—the Uniform Commercial Code.

Today much of the law has been codified. Such major areas of law as commercial law, partnership, corporations, limited partnership, wills, and trusts have been put in statutory form. Additionally, state legislatures and Congress have been drafting statutes for new areas of legal coverage, such as civil rights, the environment, health and safety in the workplace, and consumer problems.

Functions of Legislators

Although Congress as an institution seems to have image problems, political scientists have found, curiously, that the same attitude does not necessarily attach itself to one's own congressman. It is as though the problems with Congress are caused by someone else's representative. These impressions of the legislative branch are more than just curiosities. They tend to reflect the wide range of tasks performed by a representative as well as the nature of a legislature as a lawmaking branch.

Lawmaking Function. A congressman (and a state legislator, although this discussion will be limited to Congress) serves a number of functions. One of them is that of lawmaker. The statutes just mentioned and discussed elsewhere in this text are examples of the end product of this legislative function. This function is, of course, also the most visible. If Congress enacts a statute we may praise it or condemn it, depending upon how that statute affects us. However, more criticism comes from the seeming inability of the Congress to pass *any* statute that concerns a problem affecting the voters. For example, when the economy is faltering, the most that usually occurs in Congress is debate, delay, and perhaps a watered-down compromise bill—never "decisive action." People complain when Congress takes a recess while national problems are not yet solved. When it returns, the problems are still there, but no action ever seems forthcoming. Much of the hostile reaction toward Congress comes from this perceived flaw—inactivity and indecision in the face of problems. Yet the very source of the criticism of Congress is also the nature of its strength.

The power of Congress is dispersed rather than centralized, as it is in the case of the president (or governor) in the executive branch and the judge in the judicial branch. As an institution Congress represents the factions and interests that surround any issue in this country. Therefore, Congress is unable to decisively act upon an issue until a consensus has been reached.

One may yearn for a decisive, powerful, and efficient legislative branch to spew forth statutes to meet the problems of the day. Yet strong, decisive leadership may well not be responsive to legitimate interests involved in an issue. Ultimately, in a system of government based on a philosophy of limited governmental power and voluntary compliance with the law, the present concept of Congress is the best mechanism for producing effective legislation.

Overseer Function. A second function of the congressman is that of overseer of other areas of government, primarily the bureaucracy and the executive branch. The investigative function of the legislature allows the congressman to review the activities of various other governmental units and to enact legislation based upon abuses found in the course of that investigation. Congressional limitations on the power of the CIA and on the president's war-making power were an outgrowth of the Watergate and Vietnam era investigations.

Ombudsman Function. A final general function of the congressman is constituent service. In a sense, a congressman serves as an ombudsman for voters who become frustrated in dealing with the maze of bureaucracy. This service function is an important element in keeping the voter at home satisfied and enhancing the image of the individual legislator.

Furthermore, a congressman, by virtue of being elected from a specific district, often has very localized interests rather than a broad, national outlook. The congressman therefore must balance home district needs with those of the military and other national subsidies. Legislators who regularly sacrifice the needs of their districts will not usually be the ones who are returned to Congress in the next election.

The Legislative Process

A statute is merely a group of words that expresses the legislature's ideas concerning a certain policy. Most of the materials in this text, for example antitrust or environmental law, are based on statutes. However, the legislature does not act alone. The executive branch often wields great influence in the legislative policy debate. Courts and administrative agencies must implement the statute by applying it to specific situations.

Thus, legislation may be described as the cornerstone of the governmental process. It is a fundamental element of the legal environment of business since the outcome of legislative policy ideas (statutes) can materially affect business activity. For example, in 1964, Congress enacted the Civil Rights Act which, in part, prohibited certain types of employment discrimination. Thereafter, business personnel practices changed since applicants and employees could not be treated differently based on race or sex. Subsequently, through administrative agency activity (Equal Employment Opportunity Commission) and court decisions, the statute was applied to issues of comparable worth, affirmative action, and sexual harassment. None of those issues was directly addressed in the statute, but each relates to the general nondiscriminatory policy that it represents.

The process of enacting a law generally operates the same at the federal or state level. Figure 5.1 shows the path of a bill from its preparation through its passage by the legislature and presentment to the governor. Note the multitude of steps that the legislative idea must take in order to become law. Note too the diversions a bill might take in the process.

However, the steps in the legislative process only illustrate the procedure for enacting a statute. The substance of the statute itself is what is of concern to business. How (or whether) Congress decides to regulate acid rain is of greater concern than the path the bill followed through the House and Senate. That statute will reflect numerous compromises, deals, bargains, and political pressures that arise throughout the process and may bear only slight resemblance to the bill that was initially proposed. The process is not very tidy. Since the legislature is a political body, its actions are influenced by practical political considerations.

Statutes, in a sense, may be viewed as political documents. The campaigns and candidates that are chosen on election day will be those enacting legislation that can greatly affect personal or business behavior. That point, of course, is obvious, but statutes are sometimes treated as if they were handed down by some Higher Authority instead of being the creations of politicians. In practice, the final bill may be passed as much because of political influence (campaign contributions, endorsements, or logrolling) as because of its merits.

Therefore, business maintains a presence during the legislative process. Primarily this is done through lobbyists or with campaign contributions to certain legislators. Business requires access to the legislature so that its interests are considered during the bargaining that occurs in order for a bill to be passed.

The legislator's role in the statutory process is primarily political, to translate certain policy ideas into a bill that can garner enough votes to pass. Frequently, the legislator never reads the bill before voting, although the committee report may be consulted. That legislator's vote may be based on directions from party leadership, public opinion, advice of an aide who has studied the bill, or the arguments made by a lobbyist. In fact, the bill itself is most often drafted by aides or lobbyists and not by any individual legislator.

Thus, the most effective efforts to influence law occur during the legislative process. One of the most common means is through campaign contributions. These contributions are designed to influence the legislator or to reinforce a legislator's

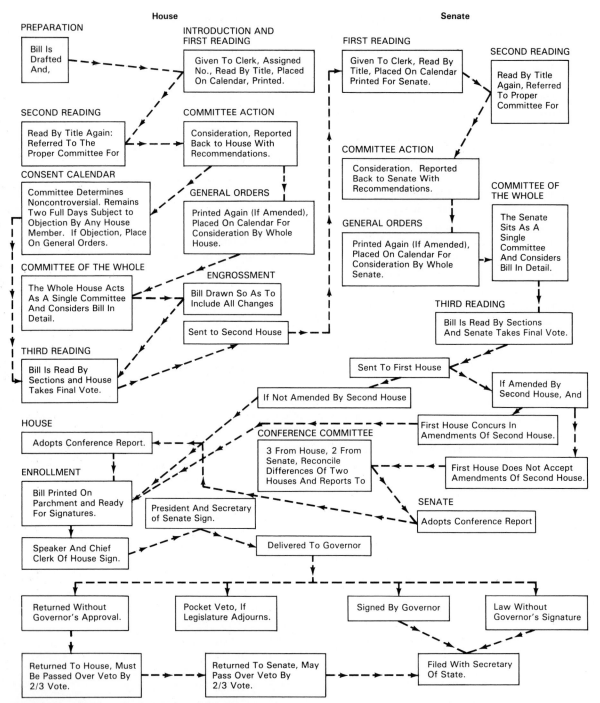

FIGURE 5.1 Course of a Bill Through the Kansas Legislature A bill may originate in either the house of representatives or the senate. The chart shows the course of a bill introduced into the house. The procedure for a bill introduced into the senate would be the same by changing "house" to "senate," and other words appropriately.

voting record that has been beneficial to the donor. Common types of contributions are those made to members of a certain key committee that oversees bills that directly effect the business of the donor. These donations are made usually without regard to the political leanings of the legislator or whether the legislator needs the funds to wage an electoral campaign against a tough opponent. Frequently, newly elected legislators will receive contributions from donors who did not support them during the election. These funds are not necessarily from businesses and individuals in the legislator's district. Instead, they are from those who are interested in the outcome of certain legislative policy debates.

Donors hope that the contributions will at least provide access to the legislator. Given the legislator's limited time, such access would permit the donor to make arguments and provide information that might be persuasive in the legislator's ultimate actions on the issue.

The political arena is a vital component of the legal environment of business. Once a statute is enacted, the role of the legislature ceases (except to possibly modify the statute at some point in the future). The courts are then charged with interpreting the statutory language. As will be noted in the next section, the courts use various methods in applying a statute, none of which includes the private interests of the parties.

STATUTORY CONSTRUCTION

As soon as a statute is enacted, people begin conforming to its terms and conditions. One of the important functions of preventive law is assisting people in modifying their behavior in order to stay within the confines of newly enacted legislation. However, disputes may arise concerning the meaning of a particular statute or statutory provision. Legislatures do not give indications concerning their meaning other than what was originally conveyed by the statute in question. They do not sit as bodies to clarify portions of their statutes that may cause eventual interpretation problems. This job falls to the courts.

The process of understanding the meaning of statutes not only involves reading the words drafted by the legislature, but also involves reading judges' opinions. Courts play a major role in interpreting the work of the legislature. A court and the legislature work together in the area of legislative lawmaking in order to produce an understandable standard of conduct for people to follow.

Not all statutes, of course, become subject to judicial scrutiny. Some statutes or parts thereof are abundantly clear. For instance, a statute that prohibits driving on an expressway faster than fifty-five miles per hour is clear: No difficulty arises in interpreting the amount of speed that will create a violation. A person arrested for driving sixty miles per hour cannot argue that the statute should be construed to allow sixty miles per hour within its terms. Judges in interpreting statutes simply do not have the right to do whatever they like in a case. Even if the judge believes that a fifty-five-miles-per-hour limitation is foolish or unwise, that judge may not simply ignore the statutory command. In fact, in cases brought before courts under such a statute this notion is clear and accepted; no one will argue that the court should substitute its own miles-per-hour standard for that imposed by the legislature.

Not all statutes are as clear and straightforward as the speed limit example.

Perhaps the terms of a statute, when confronted by the facts in a case, seem unclear or outdated. Perhaps applying the statute to such facts creates a great injustice or actually defeats the purpose of the statute. Perhaps technology has changed in such a way that the wrong the statute sought to correct is being done in a way not contemplated by the exact words of the statute. If so, then a court will be called upon to interpret the statute—make law along with the legislature—concerning the application of the statute to particular facts.

The need for judicial construction of legislation may be shown by a hypothetical statute enacted in 1876. The statute says "that it is unlawful to walk across or drive a vehicle across a public flower garden." Apply those words to the following facts. Does the conduct violate the statute?

1. A person runs across a public flower garden.

2. In 1881, a person drives a horse and buggy across a public flower garden.

3. A doctor, while strolling in the park, sees a child fall from a tree and become seriously injured in the middle of a public flower garden. The doctor walks across the garden to administer aid to the child.

4. In 1987, a person drives a car across a public flower garden.

As shown by the example, proper application of the words of the legislature is not always clear. This portion of the chapter will discuss the construction and interpretation of statutes by a court. After an introduction to statutory construction, three general interpretative techniques will be discussed: first, the use of legislative history; second, interpreting the words of the statute themselves; and finally, the construction of a statute based upon its purpose.

Statutory Construction in General

The study of English literature often involves interpreting poems and novels on a variety of levels. The investigation into the "true" meaning (or meanings) of those literary works is very similar to what a court must do in order to interpret a statute. The writer and legislator put their ideas into words. The English professor and the judge will then be called upon to interpret or construe those words. The same word may have multiple meanings and may have to be interpreted differently depending upon the way it is being used. Pick up any standard dictionary. You will notice that such commonly used words as *front*, *fence*, and *frog* have very different meanings depending upon the context in which they are being used. Language itself is vague. Interpretation is needed in order to understand what the writer has meant.

A single literary work may have a number of meanings depending upon which style of interpretation is being applied to the work. Herman Melville's *Moby Dick* is considered by some scholars to be the greatest of all American novels; however, they disagree about its meaning. In one interpretation, only the words of the book will be considered, and it is read as an adventure story about the sea and whaling. Another method of interpretation requires a study of the life of the author, the influences on his life, and the historical events taking place during the writing of the novel. These factors will be used to gain an understanding of what Melville was attempting to say in *Moby Dick*—other than simply relating a story about the sea. A third method of interpretation will review the work apart from its author and attempt to extract from the book some basic principles or theories, which may not have even formally existed at the time it was written, but which the scholars contend are contained within the novel itself.

Note that the very same novel, the same group of words, can have vastly different meanings to scholars of literature, depending upon the technique used to interpret the work. The question is not what Herman Melville intended when he wrote the novel. First of all, Melville is dead and cannot be of assistance in interpreting his work. All that we have are the words that he left us, and the question instead is, "What does the book mean?" Perhaps Melville had nothing specific in mind when he wrote the book, except to earn a few dollars. Perhaps he actually intended the novel to be able to be read in a number of ways—in a sense, purposely made its meaning vague and ambiguous.

Literary interpretation is similar to statutory interpretation. Judges and English professors deal with words. The legislator, like the writer, seeks to convey certain ideas by use of words. However, sometimes disputes arise when people attempt to understand or apply those words.

Technical Statutes. Sources of statutory ambiguity that call for judicial interpretation may be divided into three categories. First, the nature of the area of statutory regulation may be so technical and difficult as to cause questions concerning the meaning and applicability of the statutory language to particular facts. Examples of such ambiguity may be found in such statutes as the federal securities laws and the tax laws. Courts may be asked to determine if a complex business arrangement would indeed be considered a security within the provisions of the securities act. Orange groves in Florida and beauty products have been found by courts to be securities, because the promoters were actually selling investment interests rather than those products.

Sources of Statutory Ambiguity

Nature of Language. A second source of ambiguity in statutes may be the language of the statute itself. In the example of the flower garden statute earlier in this section, the nature of the term *vehicle* had changed between the time when the statute was enacted (1876) and the time when an individual drove an automobile across the flower garden. In 1876, use of the term *vehicle* could not have been meant to include technology that did not even exist. Yet the mischief which the statute sought to control—damaged flowers—would occur to an even greater extent with an automobile. The job of a court would be to interpret the 1876 statute to determine if it should encompass the automobile violation.

Deliberate Vagueness. A third source of ambiguity in statutes is the deliberate creation of vagueness by the legislature when drafting the statute. A statute may purposely be worded imprecisely to garner enough votes to pass it. Or several legislators may interpret a provision in a statute differently. The vague provision in a statute may enable enough legislators to vote in favor of the bill, yet determining what the terms of the statute actually meant would fall to the courts.

A statute may be kept deliberately ambiguous to discourage those subject to its regulation from loophole finding—staying within the terms of the statute, but violating its spirit. The Uniform Commercial Code contains many examples of this type of vagueness. Many of its provisions contain the requirement of reasonable or commercially reasonable conduct. Nowhere does the legislator or drafter of that statute precisely outline the type of conduct that will meet the reasonableness test. Undoubtedly, if a series of clear guidelines were presented for reasonable conduct, someone could conform to those guidelines but under particular facts of a case exercise unreasonable conduct. Courts are given the leeway to interpret *reasonableness* in the statute, and people are notified to exercise caution at least in sharp business practices.

A final reason for deliberate legislative ambiguity in a statute is that the circumstances which the statute is created to regulate are so varied that more particularized language may be impossible to insert in the statute. For example, Section 2-205 of the Uniform Commercial Code provides that a "firm offer," unless otherwise stated, will remain open for acceptance for a commercially reasonable time not to exceed three months. A "firm offer" to sell a crate of just-picked strawberries and a "firm offer" to sell a crate of books may be the same thing legally, but the facts of each situation make the length of time such an offer could remain open very different. That is, as strawberries will rot, a commercially reasonable time will be much shorter for them than for a crate of books.

Courts often must work with legislatures in statutory lawmaking. The task of the court is to give meaning to a statute as it applies to specific facts. Although courts frequently claim that they are searching for the legislative intent, no such inquiry is possible. Courts do not have at their disposal the means to read the minds and determine the mental state of the legislature when it enacted a particular statute that the court is construing. Instead the courts apply judicially created doctrines to try to determine what the words of the statute mean. Interpreting a statute is, in the end, an act of human judgment by the court, much like the human judgments that make up any judicial decision.

The following three sections will outline the most basic techniques used by judges in interpreting legislation. These techniques are an inquiry into the legislative history, use of the words of the statute, and inquiry into the purpose of the statute—what it was meant to accomplish. Although the interpretative techniques do give the judge some leeway in deciding how to construe a particular statute, the judge may not simply rewrite the statute.

Legislative History

In order to attempt to determine the meaning of a statute, a court may consult a body of documentation called the **legislative history.** Legislative history consists of reports, studies, speeches, statements, committee findings, and similar materials that were created at the time the statute was drafted. These documents are consulted to determine the legislature's purpose in enacting a statute. The English language is not so precise an instrument as to always convey ideas clearly. Sometimes in order to understand a statement, a reader must consult additional source material. The judge, in consulting legislative history, acts in much the same way. By doing research into the deliberations of the legislature in enacting the statute, the judge may be able to better understand its meaning.

Use of legislative history, although a solid research technique, has been criticized. It assumes that there is only one meaning for the statute and that if the judge searches hard enough in the background documents that one meaning will appear. Statutory construction involves judicial interpretation, and a statute, like a piece of literature, may be interpreted in different ways by different readers.

More practically, actually finding the legislative purpose through a review of the statutory history may be very difficult. How can the study of the statements of a few legislators and the reports of a committee or two enable a judge to determine that the legislature as a whole passed the statute with a certain purpose in mind? Maybe the deciding vote was cast because of political pressure or as part of an agreement that delivered legislative support on a wholly different issue. Some writers argue that use of legislative history by a court may encourage a legislator to create a historical record of a particular interpretation of an act, which in fact is not the one most fellow legislators would have agreed upon.

Use of historical materials by a judge in a case involves judgment, as does use of historical materials by a scholar writing about, say, the presidency of Thomas Jefferson. Which "historical" material should be considered reliable and which unreliable? If the documents clash, how are the inconsistencies to be resolved? How much documentation is enough to allow one to safely make a conclusion concerning the historical background? Use of legislative history might not produce a clear answer.

The following case is an example of the use of legislative history. *United Steelworkers* v. *Weber* (1979) upheld a voluntary affirmative action plan that was challenged as a violation of Title VII of the Civil Rights Act of 1964. Such a claim was commonly called "reverse discrimination." The excerpt that follows, from the dissenting opinion of Justice Rehnquist, uses legislative history to bolster the argument that the Civil Rights Act does not allow race-conscious employment practices that favor black workers. Note his use of materials from the debates in Congress in the mid-1960s when the Civil Rights Act was passed. The majority of the Court did not agree with this historical analysis.

United Steelworkers of America v. Weber

United States Supreme Court
443 U.S. 193 (1979)

Justice Rehnquist (dissenting)

By a tour de force reminiscent not of jurists such as Hale, Holmes, and Hughes, but of escape artists such as Houdini, the Court eludes "uncontradicted" legislative history in concluding that employers are, after all, permitted to consider race in making employment decisions. It may be that one or more of the principal sponsors of Title VII would have preferred to see a provision allowing preferential treatment of minorities written into the bill. But a reading of the legislative debates concerning Title VII, in which proponents and opponents alike uniformly denounced discrimination in favor of, as well as discrimination against, Negroes, demonstrates clearly that any legislator harboring an unspoken desire for such a provision could not possibly have succeeded in enacting it into law.

When H.R. 7152, the bill that ultimately became the Civil Rights Act of 1964, reached the House floor, the opening speech in support of its passage was delivered by Representative Celler, Chairman of the House Judiciary Committee and the Congressman responsible for introducing the legislation. A portion of that speech responded to criticism "seriously misrepresent[ing] what the bill would do and grossly distort[ing] its effects:

> "[T]he charge has been made that the Equal Employment Opportunity Commission to be established by Title VII of the bill would have the power to prevent a business from employing and promoting the people it wished, and that a 'Federal inspector' could then order the hiring and promotion only of employees of certain races or religious groups. This description of the bill is entirely wrong. . . .
>
> "Even [a] court could not order that any preference be given to any particular race, religion or other group, but would be limited to ordering an end of discrimination. The statement that a Federal inspector could order the employment and promotion only of members of a specific racial or religious group is therefore patently erroneous.
>
> "It is likewise not true that the Equal Employment Opportunity Commission would have power to rectify existing 'racial or religious imbalance' in employment by requiring the hiring of certain people without regard to their qualifications simply because they are of a given race or religion. Only actual discrimination could be stopped." 110 Cong. Rec. 1518 (1964).

In the opening speech of the formal Senate debate on the bill, Senator Humphrey addressed the main concern of Title VII's opponents, advising that not only does Title VII not require use of racial quotas, it does not permit their use. "The truth," stated the floor leader of the bill, "is that this title forbids discriminating against anyone on account of race. This is the simple and complete truth about Title VII." 110 Cong. Rec. 6549 (1964).

At the close of his speech, Senator Humphrey returned briefly to the subject of employment quotas: "It is claimed that the bill would require racial quotas for all hiring, when in fact it provides that race shall not be a basis for making personnel decisions."

A few days later the Senate's attention focused exclusively on Title VII, as Senators Clark and Case rose to discuss H.R. 7152. Of particular relevance to the instant litigation were their observations regarding seniority rights. As if directing their comments at Brian Weber, [the plaintiff in this case] the Senators said:

> "Title VII would have no effect on established seniority rights. Its effect is prospective and not retrospective. Thus, for example, if a business has been discriminating in the past and as a result has an all-white working force, when the title comes into effect the employer's obligation would be simply to fill future vacancies on a nondiscriminatory basis. He would not be obliged—or indeed permitted—to fire whites in order to hire Negroes, or to prefer Negroes for future vacancies, or, once Negroes are hired, to give them special seniority rights at the expense of the white workers hired earlier."

Thus, with virtual clairvoyance the Senate's leading supporters of Title VII anticipated precisely the circumstances of this case and advised their colleagues that the type of minority preference employed by Kaiser would violate Title VII's ban on racial discrimination.

Kaiser instituted an admissions quota preferring blacks over whites, thus confirming that the fears of Title VII's opponents were well founded. Today Title VII, adopted to allay those fears, is invoked by the Court to uphold imposition of a racial quota under the very circumstances that the section was intended to prevent.

Construing the Meaning of the Words Themselves

In addition to the review of the proceedings surrounding the enactment of a particular statute (its legislative history), courts have adopted doctrines that assist them in interpreting the words of the statute themselves. Three general word interpretation techniques will be discussed: plain meaning, ejusdem generis, and reference to other parts of the same statute.

Plain Meaning Doctrine. The **plain meaning doctrine** is the most straightforward of statutory interpretation techniques. The court will look solely to the ordinary and usual meaning of the words of the statute in order to determine what the statute says. In a sense, this technique is akin to reading *Moby Dick* as a whale-hunting adventure story. The court will construe the statute based upon its words. Frequently, judicial opinions that use this technique refer to normally accepted usage or simply cite a dictionary definition of the terms. The following case is an example of the Court's using the plain meaning doctrine in applying and construing a particular statute.

Diamond v. Chakrabarty
United States Supreme Court
447 U.S. 303 (1980)

In 1972, Chakrabarty, a microbiologist, filed a patent application, assigned to the General Electric Co. The application asserted thirty-six claims related to Chakrabarty's invention of a bacterium. This human-made, genetically engineered bacterium is capable of breaking down multiple components of crude oil. Because of this property, which is possessed by no naturally occurring bacteria, Chakrabarty's invention is believed to have significant value for the treatment of oil spills.

Chakrabarty's patent claims were of three types: first, process claims for the method of producing the bacteria; second, claims for an inoculum comprised of a carrier material floating on water, such as straw, and the new bacteria; and third, claims to the bacteria themselves. The patent examiner allowed the claims falling into the first two categories, but rejected claims for the bacteria. His decision rested on two grounds: (1) microorganisms are "products of nature" and (2) as living things, they are not patentable subject matter under 35 U.S.C. § 101.

Chakrabarty appealed the rejection of these claims to the Patent Office Board of Appeals, and the Board affirmed the examiner. The Board concluded that § 101 was not intended to cover living things such as these laboratory created microorganisms.

Chief Justice Burger

The Constitution grants Congress broad power to legislate to "promote the Progress of Science and useful Arts, by securing for limited Times to Authors and Inventors the exclusive Right to their respective Writings and Discoveries." The authority of Congress is exercised in the hope that the productive effort thereby fostered will have a positive effect on society through the introduction of new products and processes of manufacture into the economy, and the emanations by way of increased employment and better lives for our citizens.

The question before us in this case is a narrow one of statutory interpretation requiring us to construe 35 U.S.C. § 101, which provides:

Whoever invents or discovers any new and useful process, machine, manufacture, or composition of matter, or any new and useful improvement thereof, may obtain a patent therefor, subject to the conditions and requirements of this title.

Specifically we must determine whether respondent's micro-organism constitutes a "manufacture" or "composition of matter" within the meaning of the statute.

In cases of statutory construction we begin, of course, with the language of the statute. And "unless otherwise defined, words will be interpreted as taking their ordinary, contemporary, common meaning." We have also cautioned that courts should not read into the patent laws limitations and conditions which the legislature has not expressed.

Guided by these canons of construction, this Court has read the term "manufacture" in § 101 in accordance with its dictionary definition to mean the production of articles for use from raw or prepared materials by giving to these materials new forms, qualities, properties, or combinations, whether by hand-labor or by machinery. Similarly, "composition of matter" has been construed consistent with its common usage to include all compositions of two or more substances and all composite articles, whether they be the results of chemical union, or of mechanical mixture, or whether they be gases, fluids, powders or solids. In choosing such expansive terms as "manufacture" and "composition of matter," modified by the comprehensive "any," Congress plainly contemplated that the patent laws would be given wide scope. This is not to suggest that § 101 has no limits or that it embraces every discovery. The laws of nature, physical phenomena, and abstract ideas have been held not patentable.

Judged in this light, respondent's micro-organism plainly qualifies as patentable subject matter. His claim is not to a hitherto unknown natural phenomenon, but to a nonnaturally occurring manufacture of composition of matter—a product of human ingenuity "having a distinctive name, character [and] use."

It is, of course, correct that Congress, not the courts, must define the limits of patentability; but it is equally true that once Congress has spoken it is "the province and duty of the judicial department to say what the law is." Congress has performed its constitutional role in defining patentable subject matter in § 101; we perform ours in construing the language Congress has employed. In so doing, our obligation is to take statutes as we find them, guided, if ambiguity appears, by the legislative history and statutory purpose. Here, we perceive no ambiguity. The subject-matter provisions of the patent law have been cast in broad terms to fulfill the constitutional and statutory goal of promoting "the Progress of Science and the useful Arts." Broad general language is not necessarily ambiguous when congressional objectives require broad terms.

Ejusdem Generis Doctrine. The **ejusdem generis doctrine** refers to a technique of interpretation in certain types of statutes. Sometimes a catchall phrase is inserted in a statute after a series of specific words. The doctrine provides that the general phrase shall be interpreted to include words of the same kind as those used in the series of words before it. For example, suppose a legislature has redrafted the flower garden trespass statute discussed earlier in this section. The statute now prohibits going across the flower garden by "car, bicycle, motorcycle, van, truck, bus, or other vehicle." If someone drives a moped across the flower garden, the court would have to determine whether the statute would include moped within its terms even though the word *moped* appears nowhere in the statute. Under the doctrine of ejusdem generis, it might be expected that the court could read the general term *other vehicle* to include a moped, since it is of the same type as the vehicles specifically listed in the statute.

Referring to Other Parts of the Statute. Often we may be unsure of the precise meaning of a word in a book we are reading. Frequently, the meaning of a word can be gleaned by reference to the accompanying subject matter. Courts sometimes use the same style of interpretation when construing language in a statute. Sometimes statutes are quite lengthy and contain a number of separate provisions all aimed at regulating a certain area. If a word or phrase in a particular section of the statute is not clear, there may be some dispute as to the particular meaning of that word or phrase in a given case. Sometimes a court will read the unclear portion of the statute together with, and with reference to, the rest of the statute. In that way, the word or phrase is interpreted as it relates to the legislative enactment as a whole. The word is read within the statutory context in which it is being used.

Someone may observe the letter of a certain law but violate its spirit. What that generally means is that the behavior of the person in question is consistent with a literal reading of the words of a statute. However, a statute or a rule is not merely a set of words. It exists for a reason and was enacted to further a goal of the legislature. The expression means that the behavior is contrary to legislative purpose, even though it is technically correct given the meaning of the words of the statute. In such a case, a court may interpret the statute consistent with its purpose rather than with the plain meaning of its words.

The Spirit or Purpose of the Statute

Return to the garden trespassing statute, discussed earlier in this section, for an example. The statute prohibited individuals from walking across a public flower garden. If a person ran across the garden, would the statute apply? Clearly, the aim of the statute was to prevent people from trampling flowers in the public park. Yet the plain meaning of the word *walk* does not include the act of running. In this sense, the behavior of the runner was within the letter of the law but not within the spirit. A court may well hold that running too is prohibited by the statute. The court would be applying the statute to specific incidents as they arise consistent with the purpose and aim of the statute.

As previously noted, sometimes events occur after the passage of an act that could not have occurred to the legislators as they were drafting the statute. Perhaps mores have changed. Perhaps new technology has been developed. Either of those instances might give rise to a situation not specifically covered by the terms of the statute but clearly covered by its spirit. In the example of the flower garden statute, the act as passed in 1876 prohibited vehicles from crushing the flowers. Suppose that in 1987 an automobile is driven across the flower garden. Clearly, under a legislative history test, the statute could not be applied to automobiles, since they did not exist at the time of the enactment and perhaps were not even considered except in the imaginations of inventors. Yet given the act's purpose, it should include the prohibition of automobile use. A court may well apply the purpose of the statute to the facts of the case and extend its applicability to automobiles.

Statutes, through such interpretation, can remain vital and useful in the ever-changing world. A legislator could not hope to consider all the factors a statute should cover. Courts, working with the legislature and writing opinions consistent with the aim of the statute, expand or contract its coverage to meet the needs and demands of modern society.

The following case is an example of the purpose of a statute being used to interpret it in a certain situation.

Lennon v. Immigration and Naturalization Service
United States Court of Appeals, Second Circuit
527 F.2d 187 (1975)

On October 18, 1968, detectives from the Scotland Yard drug squad conducted a warrantless search of John Lennon's apartment at 34 Montague Square, London. There, the officers found one-half ounce of hashish inside a binocular case and thereupon placed Lennon under arrest. Lennon pleaded guilty to possession of cannabis resin in Marylebone Magistrate's Court on November 28, 1968; he was fined £150.

On August 13, 1971, Lennon and his wife, Yoko Ono, arrived in New York. They had come to this country to seek custody of Mrs. Lennon's daughter by a former marriage to an American citizen.

The Immigration and Nationality Act§ 212(a) lists thirty-one classes of "excludable aliens" who are ineligible for permanent residence. Among those excludable is "any alien who has been convicted of a violation of any law or regulation relating to the illicit possession of marihuana." Since John Lennon's conviction appeared to render him excludable, the Immigration and Naturalization Service (INS) specifically waived excludability. The Lennons were then given temporary visas valid until September 24, 1971; the INS later extended the expiration date to February 29, 1972.

The day after Lennon's visa expired, March 1, Sol Marks, the New York District Director of the INS, notified the Lennons by letter that, if they did not leave the country by March 15, deportation proceedings would be instituted. On March 3, Lennon and his wife filed third preference petitions. In response to these applications, the INS instituted deportation proceedings three days later.

In March, April, and May, 1972, deportation hearings were held before Immigration Judge Fieldsteel. The immigration judge filed his decision on March 23, 1973. Since Yoko Ono had obtained permanent resident status in 1964, he granted her application. But, because he believed that John Lennon was an excludable alien, the immigration judge denied his application and ordered him deported.

Kaufman, Chief Judge

We have come a long way from the days when fear and prejudice toward alien races were the guiding forces behind our immigration laws. The Chinese exclusion acts of the 1880's and the "barred zone" created by the 1917 Immigration Act have, thankfully, been removed from the statute books and relegated to the historical treatises. Nevertheless, the power of Congress to exclude or deport natives of other countries remains virtually unfettered. In the vast majority of deportation cases, the fate of the alien must therefore hinge upon narrow issues of statutory construction. To this rule, the appeal of John Lennon, an internationally known "rock" musician, presents no exception. We are, in this case, called upon to decide whether Lennon's 1968 British conviction for possession of cannabis resin renders him, as the Board of Immigration Appeals believed, an excludable alien under § 212(a)(23) of the Immigration and Nationality Act (INA), which applies to those convicted of illicit possession of marihuana. We hold that Lennon's conviction does not fall within the ambit of this section.

The immigration judge and the Board of Immigration Appeals believed that Lennon's 1968 conviction made him excludable under this section. We are of the view that it did not. We base this result upon our conclusion that Lennon was convicted under a law which in effect makes guilty knowledge irrelevant and such a law does not render the convicted alien excludable.

The language of the British statute under which Lennon was convicted is deceptively simple: "A person shall not be in possession of a drug unless . . . authorized. . . ." But around this concise provision, judicial interpretation has created a scholastic maze as complex and baffling as the Labyrinth at Knossos in ancient Crete. However, we conclude, from analyzing British law as it existed in 1968, that Lennon was convicted under a statute which made guilty knowledge irrelevant. Under British law a person found with tablets which he reasonably believed were aspirin would be convicted if the tablets proved to contain heroin. And a man given a sealed package filled with heroin would, if he had had any opportunity to open the parcel, suffer the same fate—even if he firmly believed the package contained perfume.

Any analysis of § 212(a)(23) of the Immigration and Nationality Act must find its starting point in the statute's plain language. That language provides compelling evidence of a knowledge requirement, for it renders excludable "any alien who has been convicted of a violation of . . . any law or regulation relating to the illicit possession of marihuana."

This unambiguous wording is bolstered by the settled doctrine that deportation statutes must be construed in favor of the alien. Furthermore, deportation is not, of course, a penal sanction. But in severity it surpasses all but the most Draconian criminal penalties. We therefore cannot deem wholly irrelevant the long unbroken tradition of the criminal law that harsh sanctions should not be imposed where moral culpability is lacking.

We are now called upon to decide whether the exclusion of convictions for possession obtained under laws imposing absolute liability would significantly impede the enforcement or undermine the purpose of the Immigration and Nationality Act. If we find that it does not, then we cannot, in the light of these firmly established precepts of statutory construction, conclude that Congress intended to include such convictions within the ambit of § 212(a)(23).

The general purpose of § 212(a)(23) is, of course, to bar undesirable aliens from our shores. There is also, we note, some indication that Congress, in enacting § 212(a)(23), was far more concerned with the trafficker of drugs than with the possessor. We do not believe that our holding will subvert these Congressional ends. Virtually every undesirable alien covered by the drug conviction provision would also be barred by other sections of the statute. Moreover, addicts are barred. Finally, our holding will not, of course, give any comfort to those convicted in the United States of drug violations.

Given, in sum, the minimal gain in effective enforcement, we cannot imagine that Congress would impose the harsh consequences of an excludable alien classification upon a person convicted under a foreign law that made guilty knowledge irrelevant.

Before closing with the traditional words of disposition, we feel it appropriate to express our faith that the result we have reached in this case not only is consistent with the language and purpose of the narrow statutory provision we construe, but also furthers the intent of the immigration laws in a far broader sense. The excludable aliens statute is but an exception, albeit necessary, to the traditional tolerance of a nation founded and built by immigrants. If, in our two hundred years of independence, we have in some measure realized our ideals, it is in large part because we have always found a place for those committed to the spirit of liberty and willing to help implement it. Lennon's four-year battle to remain in our country is testimony to his faith in this American dream.

Accordingly, the denial of Lennon's application for adjustment of status and the order of deportation are vacated and the case remanded for reconsideration in accordance with the views expressed in this opinion.

Mulligan, Circuit Judge (dissenting)

That statute would exclude any alien who has been convicted of a violation of any law or regulation relating to the illicit possession of narcotic drugs or marihuana. Since the statute applies to any alien it makes no difference whether he be John Lennon, John Doe or Johann Sebastian Bach.

The undisputed fact however is that Lennon did plead guilty to the possession of cannabis resin, and while this may have been convenient or expedient because of his wife's pregnancy and his disinclination to have her testify in court, it is elementary that we cannot go behind the plea.

The majority here concludes that the Congress was more concerned with trafficking in drugs than in possession and their opinion does not cover the trafficker who obviously is fully aware of the nature of the business he is pursuing. The

statute however bars the possesser as well as the trafficker. If there were no users there would be no trafficking. It must also be emphasized that the vast majority of those who are arrested with illicit drugs in their homes or on their persons are users who are fully aware of their presence and their properties. It is the unusual case where contraband such as this is surreptitiously planted in one's reticule or blue jeans pocket. Yet by disregarding convictions under the British statute or any other foreign counterpart, the majority would admit to the United States those who knowingly possessed any illicit drugs. This holding seems to me to conflict with INA § 212(a)(23) which plainly bars those who have been convicted of a violation. Lennon's guilty plea here puts him within the statute.

THE EXECUTIVE BRANCH

Although throughout this chapter the executive branch of government will be referred to as the presidency, that branch includes many officials besides the president (see Figure 5.2). The executive branch also contains a number of agencies, called executive agencies, which carry out many different functions—such agencies as the Department of Agriculture, the Department of Commerce, the State Department on the federal level, and the office of the prosecutor and the police department on the state or local level. The discussions in the next chapter concerning administrative agencies would be generally applicable to executive agencies as well.

Normally, one thinks of the executive branch as being primarily responsible for carrying out statutes enacted by the legislature and orders of the courts. However, the work of the executive branch is much broader.

Relationship of the Executive with Other Branches of Government. The three branches of government act to check and balance one another's powers, so that no

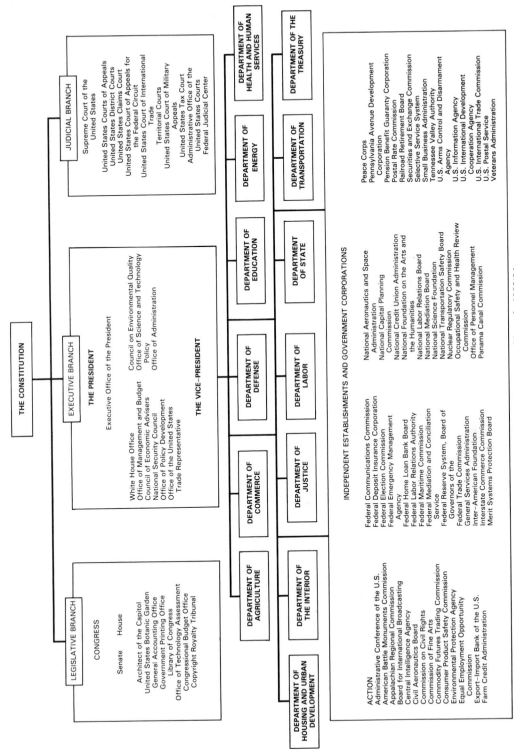

FIGURE 5.2 *Source:* Office of the Federal Register, *The United States Government Manual, 1983/84* (Washington, D.C.: U.S. Government Printing Office, 1983), p. 810.

one branch or individual acquires too much power. Both the Congress and the courts act as checks on the president and are at the same time dependent on the president in the carrying out of their governmental functions. The Congress is largely dependent on the executive branch for the implementation of the laws it enacts. A president who vigorously supports certain legislation will most likely vigorously enforce the congressional policy. However, a president who does not agree with a statute may well frustrate the purposes of the enacted law by having a weak enforcement program.

The Congress, however, does have leverage over the executive and can certainly frustrate the plans and policies of a president. The ultimate control by Congress is the power to impeach and remove the president from office. However, other congressional powers act more regularly as checks on the power of the executive branch. Congress has control over the appropriation of federal funds, and may either underfund or refuse to fund an executive's key programs. Congress also has the power to refuse to consent to certain presidential appointments. Thus Congress can frustrate the plans of the executive by refusing to appoint certain individuals to executive positions. Lastly, the Congress has the ability to shape legislative programs. Although most program initiatives come from the executive, the final form of the program is the province of the Congress.

The judicial branch may also act to check the power of the executive. Judges do not seize property, keep people in jail, or make sure a school is integrated on a day-to-day basis. A judge may order that any of those things occur, but the judge does not execute those orders. Their implementation is left to the executive branch of government. However, at the same time that the court relies on the executive, the court also has the power to set the limits of the executive's power. This function of the judiciary will be seen in a number of forthcoming cases.

Lawmaking Powers of the Executive

Although, classically, the duties of the executive branch of government are considered to be limited to the carrying out or enforcement of law, that is not its only function. The executive branch is actively involved in making the law as well. The lawmaking powers of the president may be divided into three groups: first, the general power to draft rules called executive orders; second, the ability to make law through the carrying out of general executive duties; and third, the ability to make law by virtue of policy initiation.

Executive Orders. The president has the power to issue **executive orders,** which can have the same force and effect as statutes enacted by the Congress or regulations enacted by an administrative agency. Often these orders are merely housekeeping rules—setting government job categories at certain salary levels, authorizing the creation of boards or committees to coordinate compliance with a statute. However, executive orders may have a much greater effect. Executive orders have controlled wages and prices, set curfews and made energy policy.

One of the most noteworthy executive orders was President Lyndon Johnson's 1965 executive order requiring affirmative action in hiring by contractors who did business with the federal government. This was an important and far-reaching rule in that it, in effect, regulated business practices of a large number of firms throughout the United States. Johnson's executive order went far beyond any existing policy or law of the government at that time to remedy racial discrimination.

The president, however, does not have unlimited power and authority to create law through executive order. That power is limited by the Constitution and by congressional legislation. For example, the president would not have the authority to make an executive order prohibiting federal courts from applying the antitrust laws. Although a president may support such a limitation, the Constitution confers that power solely on the Congress. Additionally, executive orders must be drafted within the confines of the express or implied powers set by the Congress for the president to make such an order. A president does not have the ability to draft executive orders to fit any situation that may come to mind. The order must not conflict with limits set by the Congress or the Constitution.

Therefore the executive's lawmaking power is far more limited than that of the legislature or even that of the courts. The law may be made only pursuant to authority granted by the Constitution or by Congress to draft executive orders covering certain topics. When a dispute arises, it is the duty of the courts to determine whether the executive order was properly made and therefore effective.

To illustrate, President Harry Truman ordered the steel mills seized during the Korean War because of a labor dispute. Truman argued that he had this power both under constitutional authority and as implied by a number of war-related congressional statutes. Article 2, Section 3 of the Constitution requires that the president "take care that the laws be faithfully executed." Truman contended that his executive order calling for seizure of the mills was necessary to execute wartime legislation concerning material procurement and wage and price stability. Truman lost. The United States Supreme Court found neither congressional nor Constitutional support for Truman's action. Justice Black, writing for the Court, noted: "The President's order does not direct that a congressional policy be executed in a manner prescribed by Congress—it directs that a presidential policy be executed in a manner prescribed by the President. . . . The Constitution does not subject this lawmaking power of Congress to presidential or military supervision or control."

Lawmaking through Action. The president also makes law by virtue of various actions taken in his role as the executive. This type of lawmaking does not involve the drafting of any rules or regulations. Instead, through judgment and policy choices, the executive makes law in determining how to enforce it. This type of lawmaking may arise either directly from the exercise of powers granted the executive by the Constitution, or from the exercise of judgment by the executive in carrying out the duty to faithfully execute the laws of Congress.

Under the Constitution, the president has certain powers with respect to law made by the legislature and by the judiciary. The president has the right to veto any bill passed by the Congress. The possibility of a veto will often move the Congress to draft legislation compatible with the goals of the president. In this way, through this constitutional power, the president is closely involved with the creation of legislation.

The president has similar constitutional power over decision making by the federal courts. Federal judges are appointed by the president (with the advice and consent of the Senate). As a practical matter, the overwhelming majority of judges appointed by the president are confirmed by the Senate. Therefore, over time, a president has the ability to appoint judges with certain political and social philosophies. (Remember the discussion of the factor of the judge's personality in Chapter 4). A president may be able to influence the law for years after leaving office by appointing certain individuals to the federal bench.

The decision-making function of a court may also be affected by constitutional powers given to the president to pardon a person from criminal acts that may have been committed or commute a sentence imposed by a court. By pardoning an individual from alleged crimes, the president removes the judiciary from adjudicating the guilt of that individual. By commuting a sentence imposed by a court, the president overrides a judgment of the court that is designed to render such decisions.

The executive may also make law through the exercise of judgment while carrying out the law. On a local level, for example, on some highways, motorists may safely travel in excess of sixty miles per hour without worrying about being ticketed by the police, even though the maximum speed limit is fifty-five miles per hour. Judgment by the executive concerning how to deploy its traffic control resources has effectively changed the speed limit in that locale. In some communities, the prosecutor will not file drug charges against someone arrested for possessing a small amount of marihuana for personal use. Laws against the possession of marihuana may be on the books, but in practice they are used by that prosecutor to regulate dealers. Users, if arrested at all, are charged with a much lesser crime. By discretion and use of judgment, the executive in the carrying out of the laws has, in effect, made law in day-to-day practice.

Therefore, the personality of the executive, like the personality of the judge, is important in the law. The law at any given time is a function of the actions and decisions of the legislative, judicial, and executive branches of government as well as the working of relevant administrative agencies. To understand the legal environment, a general appreciation of the interaction of these various governmental units is needed.

Lawmaking through Policy. The president has another effect on the law, by virtue of the policy-making function of the office. Legislation is generally initiated by the executive branch. The president presents the Congress with a legislative package, often with drafts of bills included in the package. Congress works through that package in its task of enacting legislation. This is a powerful lawmaking tool for the executive, who sets the lawmaking priority for the Congress and then has the ability to lobby and pressure various lawmakers to get that package enacted. This key aspect of the power of the president did not always exist. In the latter part of the nineteenth century, the president was more of an administrator, and the power for initiating legislation, as well as enacting it, rested with the Congress. The shift of the legislation-initiating power began in this century and was fully developed during the Roosevelt administration with the flurry of legislative proposals sent to Congress to combat the Great Depression.

Limits on Executive Lawmaking Power. The limits on the lawmaking power of the president are generally based upon unwritten rules, past practice, and basic political accommodation between the various branches of government. Limits are not explicitly set until the president goes beyond what could generally be considered to be proper boundaries of executive power. The national experiences with the Vietnam War and with the revelations of Watergate served to move the Congress to legislate limits on certain lawmaking powers of the president where in the past only unwritten rules existed. In the end, however, the people will act or demand that action be taken to curb executive abuses. A recent example demonstrates this point.

Although the Constitution gives Congress the power to declare war, the president, as commander-in-chief of the armed forces, committed troops to a number of areas (the Caribbean, North Africa to fight the Barbary pirates) throughout American history without a formal congressional declaration of war. However, none of those actions was on as large a scale as the conflict in Vietnam, nor did these actions last as long. During the Vietnam War, Congress never acted to formally declare war. As a result, after the war, Congress sought to limit the unwritten power of the president alone to make war through the enactment of the War Powers Act.

General Issues Involving the Executive Branch

The limits of the power of the executive branch are only rarely adjudicated by the courts. Such issues necessarily involve a test of our form of government. Although a court may well limit the power of the executive, who is to enforce that limitation? Courts may use public opinion and the prestige of their position, but in the end the executive must voluntarily accept the limits imposed by the courts. Any other decision by the executive may well lead to the loss of our system of government.

As a result, courts do not generally confront the executive branch on the limitation of its powers. Frequently courts will simply refuse to decide a challenge to executive action, holding it a political, not a judicial, issue. In the end, most questions of executive authority are solved through the give and take of the political arena.

Political Questions. As suggested earlier, courts will at times refuse to review the extent of the power exercised by a president. As a practical matter, any limitation placed on that power while it is being exercised could cause the gravest of constitutional crises. After all, both the president and the courts are sworn to uphold the Constitution. Furthermore, as suggested in Chapter 6, on the Constitution, the meaning of the various terms of the Constitution is certainly subject to diverse good-faith interpretations.

A court, therefore, may refuse to even hear a challenge to an action taken by the president, claiming that such an action is a political question or that the issue is not **justiciable.** This means that the issue presented to the court is not one that is in its power to decide. Other forums in the government or the ballot box may be more appropriate for resolving the conflict. A recent example was the issues raised concerning the constitutionality of the Vietnam War. Cases were brought while the war was being fought. Congress had never declared war, which was fought pursuant to executive order and a resolution passed by the Congress called the Tonkin Gulf Resolution. However, Congress continually funded the war effort. The following case is from a lower court where the issue was raised.

Orlando and Berk v. Laird

United States Court of Appeals, Second Circuit

443 F.2d 1039 (1971)

This case consolidates two actions by servicemen to challenge the constitutional sufficiency of the authority of the executive branch to wage war in Vietnam. The servicemen, in separate actions in June 1970, sought to enjoin the secretary of defense, the secretary of the army, and the commanding officers, who signed their deployment orders, from enforcing them. The plaintiffs contended that these executive officers exceeded their constitutional authority by ordering them to participate in a war not properly authorized by Congress.

Anderson, Circuit Judge

The Government takes the position that the suits concern a nonjusticiable political question; that the military action in South Vietnam was authorized by Congress in the "Joint Resolution to Promote the Maintenance of Internal Peace and Security in Southeast Asia" (the Tonkin Gulf Resolution) considered in connection with the Seato Treaty; and that the military action was authorized and ratified by congressional appropriations expressly designated for use in support of the military operations in Vietnam.

Although appellant-servicemen do not contend that Congress can exercise its war-declaring power only through a formal declaration, they argue that congressional authorization cannot, as a matter of law, be inferred from military appropriations that does not contain an express and explicit authorization for the making of war by the President. Putting aside for a moment the explicit authorization of the Tonkin Gulf Resolution, we disagree with appellants' interpretation of the declaration clause for neither the language nor the purpose underlying that provision prohibits an inference of the fact of authorization from such legislative action as we have in this instance. The framers' intent to vest the war power in Congress is in no way defeated by permitting an inference of authorization from legislative action furnishing the manpower and materials of war for the protracted military operation in southeast Asia.

The choice, for example, between an explicit declaration on the one hand and a resolution and war-implementing legislation, on the other, as the medium for expression of congressional consent involves "the exercise of a discretion demonstrably committed to the . . . legislature," and therefore, invokes the political question doctrine.

Such a choice involves an important area of decision making in which, through mutual influence and reciprocal action between the President and the Congress, policies governing the relationship between this country and other parts of the world are formulated in the best interests of the United States. If there can be nothing more than minor military operations conducted under any circumstances, short of an express and explicit declaration of war by Congress, then extended military operations could not be conducted even though both the Congress and the President were agreed that they were necessary and were also agreed that a formal declaration of war would place the nation in a posture in its international relations which would be against its best interests. For the judicial branch to enunciate and enforce such a standard would be not only extremely unwise but also would constitute a deep invasion of the political question domain. What has been said and done by both the President and the Congress in their collaborative conduct of the military operations in Vietnam implies a consensus on the advisability of not making a formal declaration of war because it would be contrary to the interests of the United States to do so. The making of a policy decision of that kind is clearly within the constitutional domain of those two branches and is just as clearly not within the competency or power of the judiciary.

Foreign Policy. Courts will similarly usually refuse to review the decisions of the president in the area of international relations. This is a recognition of the power of the president and a recognition of the expertise of the executive branch to conduct foreign affairs. The following case is an example of this judicial deferral to executive foreign-policy decision making. It concerns the agreement between the United States and Iran that freed the hostages from the embassy in Teheran.

Chas. T. Main Int'l. v. Khuzestan Water and Power Authority

United States Court of Appeals, First Circuit

651 F.2d 800 (1981)

The plaintiff, an engineering firm, brought an action to recover payment for services rendered in connection with Iranian electrification projects. After the Iranian hostage release agreement, the plaintiff brought a second action against the United States, seeking a declaration that the executive agreement with Iran and the implementing executive orders and regulations were in excess of the President's authority. This appeal represents a consolidation of these cases.

Campbell, Circuit Judge

On January 19, 1981, Iran released the hostages pursuant to an agreement with the United States, embodied in two Declarations of the Government of the Democratic and Popular Republic of Algeria. The agreement states that it is "the purpose of both parties . . . to terminate all litigation as between the Government of each party and the nationals of the other, and to bring about the settlement and termination of all such claims through binding arbitration." In furtherance of this goal, the agreement calls for the establishment of an Iran–United States Claims Tribunal (Tribunal), which will, with certain exceptions, arbitrate any such claims not settled within six months of the date of agreement; awards of the Tribunal will be "final and binding" and "enforceable . . . in the courts of any nation in accordance with its laws."

On January 19, 1981, President Carter issued a series of executive orders implementing the terms of the agreement with Iran. In pertinent part, these orders revoked all licenses permitting persons to exercise "any right, power or privilege" with regard to Iranian funds, securities or deposits, "nullified" all non-Iranian interests in such assets acquired subsequent to the November 14, 1979, blocking order, and required those holding blocked Iranian assets to transfer them to the Federal Reserve bank of New York, "to be held or transferred as directed by the Secretary of the Treasury." On February 24, 1981, President Reagan "ratified" the January 19 orders; he also ordered "suspended" all "claims which may be presented to the [Tribunal]" and provided that they "shall have no legal effect in any action now pending in any court of the United States."

International agreements settling claims by nationals of one state against the government of another "are established international practice reflecting traditional international theory." In numerous instances, dating back to the earliest days of this country's history, the President, often acting without the advice or consent of the Senate, has agreed to extinguish claims of United States nationals against foreign governments, in return for lump sum payments or the establishment of arbitration procedures.

It is not difficult to understand why it has become generally accepted that the President possesses power, at least in times of crisis in our international relations, to settle the claims of United States nationals against a foreign government. The matter becomes particularly clear if, as Justice Jackson maintained in his *Youngstown* concurrence, "any actual test" of the President's constitutional powers, especially in the foreign relations field, "is likely to depend on the imperatives of events and contemporary imponderables rather than on abstract theories of law." This case well illustrates the imperative need to preserve a presidential flexibility sufficient to diffuse an international crisis, in order to prevent the crisis from escalating or even leading to war. As the Supreme Court has consistently recognized, it is the President who is charged with responsibility as the United States representative and negotiator in the international arena. The authority to remove impediments to the peaceful resolution of international disputes is an authority necessary to meet the responsibilities of presidential office, and, in the words of the Supreme Court, a "modest implied" attribute of presidential power.

We need not and do not hold that the executive possesses plenary power to settle claims, even as against foreign governmental entities. It may be that much of this area is within that "zone of twilight in which [the President] and Congress may have concurrent authority." The sheer magnitude of such a power, considered against the background of the diversity and complexity of modern international trade, cautions against any broader construction of authority than is necessary. Here, however, the President has acted to resolve what was indisputably a major crisis in the foreign relations of this country. His settlement of the claims of Main and others was not an isolated event but a necessary incident to the resolution of a dispute between our nation and another. Whatever may be the reach of the executive power under circumstances that implicate less squarely the conduct of foreign relations, the executive power extends so far as to permit the accord reached here.

We hold, therefore, that the President had authority to settle Main's claims against the Iranian defendants, by providing for their submission to binding arbitration. This being the case, we need not decide whether the President went too far in purporting to "order" the "suspension" of litigation relating to the claims. The claims having been settled, they are no longer cognizable in the courts, except insofar as permitted by the settlement's terms.

SUMMARY   The legislative and executive branches of government have a major effect on the legal environment of business. Although the legislature is usually considered to be the lawmaking branch of government, the executive branch is also involved in crafting legal rules that may affect business. Therefore, understanding these branches of government and their relationship with the judicial branch is very important.

Various issues surrounding the legislative and executive branches illustrate their importance in the legal environment. For example, issues of legislative immunity and executive privilege show that the lawmaking and governing goals of our system may clash with basic-rights protections available to individuals. Furthermore, other issues, such as how legislative representation is to be determined and the extent of presidential power, illustrate the power of judicial review of fundamental issues involving other branches of government.

The major area where the judiciary works together with other branches of government is statutory construction. Various techniques are used by the courts to give meaning to a piece of legislation that is confronted by modern-day problems. Courts and legislatures work together in the area being regulated by legislation to create standards of conduct for individuals and businesses.

REVIEW QUESTIONS

1. Define the following terms:
   a. Plain meaning doctrine
   b. Ejusdem generis
   c. Executive order

2. Use statutory interpretation techniques to discuss how the statute involved in the following problem should be interpreted. Make sure you can identify the technique urged on the court by each party in the dispute.

   Glen filed a lawsuit against the United States government. He represents a class of plaintiffs who are terminally ill with cancer and would like to use the drug Laetrile as part of their treatment. The United States government would not permit the interstate shipment and sale of Laetrile, since it was not approved by the secretary of the Department of Health, Education, and Welfare pursuant to the Food, Drug, and Cosmetic Act. The act will not permit the distribution of any new drug without such approval. The act defines a "new drug" as "any drug not generally recognized, among experts qualified by scientific training and experience to evaluate the safety and effectiveness of drugs, as safe and effective for use under the conditions prescribed, recommended or suggested in the labeling."

   Scientific experts have determined that Laetrile is not generally recognized as safe and effective as a treatment for cancer, since no adequate studies exist that demonstrate the drug's safety or effectiveness. Remarks made in Congress at the time of the act's passage show that the lawmakers were concerned about drugs being placed on the market before adequate testing was done, the danger being the harm that their use

   could cause to the people. Furthermore, the Congress was concerned about fraudulent cures being offered as drugs to people who were ill. However, terminally ill patients might be distinguished from the general population because there is no cure leading to recovery from their disease.

3. Use statutory interpretation techniques to discuss how the statute involved in the following problem should be interpreted. Make sure you can identify the technique urged on the court by each party in the dispute.

   A jury returned a verdict for Baker against Jacobs. Immediately thereafter, Baker treated the jury to cigars at a local hotel as a gesture of appreciation. Upon learning of this, Jacobs sought to have a court set aside the verdict rendered by the jury. He relied on the following statute: "If a party obtaining a verdict in his favor shall, during the term of the court in which such a verdict is obtained, give to any of the jurors in the case, knowing him to be such, any victuals or drink, or procure the same to be done, by way of treat, either before or after such verdict, on proof thereof being made the verdict shall be set aside and a new trial granted."

4. Congress enacted general statutes concerning the importance of wage and price stability in this country. They specifically prohibited the president from ordering wage and price controls. However, the president has the power to enter into contracts on behalf of the government to carry out the appropriation of funds

decisions made by Congress. Assume that the president drafts an executive order requiring all companies that do business with the government to freeze their prices and wages on pain of losing future government contracts if they do not comply. Is that executive order within the power of the president to make?

5. Compare lawmaking by the legislature with lawmaking by judicial decision.

6. Discuss the techniques of statutory construction.

7. Discuss the lawmaking powers existing in the executive branch of government.

8. What is the purpose of judicial use of legislative history when construing a statute? Discuss its advantages and disadvantages.

9. You are an executive with the XYZ Corporation. The corporation is involved in the landscaping business. A major part of its business is supplying plants and seeds. A statute reads as follows: "No flower, vegetable, bush or other plant may be imported into the United States without approval from the USDA." You learn that a unique variety of tree, available only in Japan, is available for your corporation to import into the United States. However, the delay and cost in obtaining approval for importing the special trees would make them too expensive to import. Must the corporation ob-

tain approval before importing the trees? Give reasons.

10. Why do courts often defer political questions and foreign policy issues to the discretion of the executive branch?

11. A statute reads as follows: "No business may keep a large, vicious dog on its premises." The statute was enacted after several small children were attacked by guard dogs that broke loose from the businesses they were protecting. During consideration of the bill, several representatives filed reports showing similar incidents throughout the country. Many argued that innocent citizens, especially children, should not have to fear attack from beasts. A few noted that alarm systems, if properly installed, would adequately protect any business.

    You own a small business that has been robbed several times. After reading the statute just referred to, you buy a mountain lion to keep at your business to deter burglars. Are you in violation of the statute? Give reasons.

12. Does business have more influence in lawmaking by the legislature or in lawmaking by the courts? Explain.

13. Compare the process of enacting a statute by the legislature with the techniques used by courts to interpret that statute. Do those techniques reflect the reality of the legislative process?

CHAPTER 6

The Constitution and Business

The United States Constitution
Judicial Review
Structure and Organization of the Government
Federal Power to Regulate Business
State Power to Regulate Business
Limitations on Governmental Power
The First Amendment and Business

A study of the Constitution of the United States, its amendments, and its judicial interpretations embodies the history of this country. This chapter presents a discussion of the Constitution as a means of providing an appreciation for that document and its place in the American legal environment.

The first section of the chapter is a general overview of the Constitution and the role of the judicial branch of government in constitutional lawmaking. A general discussion of judicial construction of the Constitution will be analyzed. Note the importance of the judicial branch in developing Constitutional law. The chapter then discusses the structure and organization of the government.

The major focus of this chapter concerns the power of the government to regulate business. We first address the question: To what extent may the federal government regulate business? As will be evident from the material in the chapter, the federal government has enormous power to control the activities of business. The primary source of federal power, the commerce clause, has been interpreted as a very broad grant of power to Congress. We then move to the power of state governments to regulate business. Their power comes from what is known as the police power. It permits the states to place extensive controls over business.

In the last part of this chapter, we address various limits on the powers of both the federal and state governments to regulate business. The drafters of the United States Constitution placed certain constitutional limits on the power of federal and state governments to keep them from unfairly dealing with people.

THE UNITED STATES CONSTITUTION

Carefully read the Constitution (see Appendix A of this text). Note its two major functions. First, it sets forth the basic structure of the government. Not only is this organizational material contained in the articles of the Constitution, but also many of the amendments pertain to governmental organization (for example, the Twenty-second Amendment, limitation on the number of terms a president may serve, and the Twenty-fifth Amendment, presidential succession). The second major function of the Constitution is to provide for individual rights. Most often the provisions in the Bill of Rights (the first ten amendments) are cited as performing this function. However, individual freedoms, such as the right to trial by jury in a criminal case (Article III, Section 2), are also provided in the articles of the Constitution and in other amendments, for example, the "Civil War Amendments" (the Thirteenth, Fourteenth, and Fifteenth Amendments) which were the constitutional basis for the legal battle for civil rights.

JUDICIAL REVIEW

The words used in the Constitution of the United States are imprecise. They are general terms that can be applied differently in various situations. The provisions of the Fourteenth Amendment concerning due process and equal protection of the laws are certainly not clear. As a result, courts are asked to resolve disputes concerning the application of those principles to actions of other branches of government, especially the legislature. A court will review a statute or governmental activity to determine whether it violates various constitutional guarantees. If the statute or activity is not consistent with the Constitution, then the court will declare it to be unconstitutional and void. This power of the court is called **judicial review.**

The power of judicial review is not contained in the Constitution. Article III of the Constitution created the judicial branch of government. Neither that article nor any act of Congress granted the judiciary the power to declare a statute unconstitutional, to, in effect, review the activities of the other branches of government. This power was assumed by the judiciary in a famous 1803 Supreme Court decision in *Marbury* v. *Madison*. The decision was written by Chief Justice John Marshall, and its implications continue to give rise to legal arguments concerning the role of the judiciary in our system of government.

Marshall argued the duty of a judge is to decide what the law is in a given case, that is, the judge must interpret the law and apply it to the facts. Sometimes there is more than one applicable law, and the judge must choose which to apply. At times, the conflicting laws involve a statute and a provision of the Constitution. In that event, since the Constitution is the supreme law of the land, and since a judge is required by oath to uphold and support the Constitution, the judge has a duty to resolve the conflict in favor of the higher law: the Constitution. A law that conflicts with the Constitution is given no effect—it is declared unconstitutional.

As a doctrine, judicial review is an accepted practice today. The courts do occasionally declare laws to be unconstitutional, although that is a rare occurrence. There is no constitutional check on this judicial power, short of impeachment. However, the judiciary as an institution has unwritten rules concerning the use of the power of judicial review. When it is used, the courts generally follow three guidelines. First, they will not decide a constitutional issue raised in a case unless it is absolutely essential in making a decision. As a result, courts shy away from making holdings based upon the Constitution. If a decision in a case can be reached by deciding nonconstitutional issues, the court will decide the case on the basis of those issues.

A second general rule of judicial review is to interpret a statute that conflicts with the Constitution in such a manner as to make it consistent with the Constitution. A court will not declare an entire statute unconstitutional if there is a way to interpret all or part of the statute within constitutional standards. The court thereby reflects legislative policy choices.

A third rule followed by courts in exercising judicial review is to make any constitutional ruling as restrictive as possible. Under this guideline, a court will not make general or broad pronouncements concerning constitutional rulemaking. Problems that are not immediately before the court will not be considered. In this way, the courts work to minimize their power over the workings of the legislature.

The general rules for judiciary review are not always followed. Some people argue that the judiciary, especially the Supreme Court, acts as a superlegislature, imposing personal preferences on judicial decisions and interpretations of the Constitution. Others argue that the drafters of the Constitution purposely created a broadly interpretive document, leaving it to individual courts to provide more specific meanings in settling of disputes. Nevertheless, rulings by the United States Supreme Court concerning the Constitution are the supreme law of the land.

STRUCTURE AND ORGANIZATION OF THE GOVERNMENT

The United States Constitution created the organizational structure of the federal government and also set forth the structural relationship between the federal and state governments. This structure is called federalism and has been a source of debate in this country throughout its history.

Separation of Powers

The Constitution created three separate branches of the federal government to carry out its basic functions: Article I of the Constitution created the legislative branch; Article II created the executive branch; and Article III created the judicial branch. Each branch has been provided certain powers, which, when combined, empower a government. The legislative branch was given the power to make laws and to control the funds of the government; the executive was granted general administrative power to carry out the laws passed by Congress; and the judicial branch was created to decide controversies arising under the laws of the United States. The branches of government seem to have very separate and distinct functions. However the work of the branches overlaps.

The principle of **separation of powers** was crafted into the Constitution to ensure that the main functions of government—adjudicating, legislating, and executing the laws—did not combine. Such a combination of powers, it was feared, would give rise to a tyrannical form of government. However, the three branches were not set apart as autonomous units. Instead a system of checks and balances was created to minimize the risk of the accumulation of power in a single branch.

The Constitution thus provides for a set of checks and balances on each branch of government so that no one branch can become too powerful.

Exactly what power does the federal government have to regulate the activities of business? This point is discussed in the next section.

FEDERAL POWER TO REGULATE BUSINESS

The **commerce clause** is of great significance with respect to the power of the federal government to regulate business. This clause appears in the United States Constitution in Article I, Section 8, Subsection 3. It reads as follows: Congress shall have the power "To regulate Commerce with foreign Nations, and among the several States, and with the Indian Tribes." The commerce clause serves not only as a source of congressional power to regulate commerce, but also as a limitation on the power of the states to enact legislation that regulates commerce.

This clause gives Congress three areas over which it can regulate commerce—that involving the Indian tribes, commerce with foreign nations, and commerce among the states. We will leave the matter of trade with the Indian tribes to another course. The latter two areas are very important to business.

Foreign Commerce

Throughout the history of the United States, there has never been any question that the federal government has the exclusive right to regulate foreign commerce and that this power extends to all aspects of foreign trade. Chief Justice Marshall in 1824 so held in *Gibbons* v. *Ogden*. The states and local governments therefore may not interfere in any way with foreign trade. Suppose that a city wished to bar the importation of goods from Russia. If it passed an ordinance to this effect, such an ordinance would be struck down by a court as beyond the power of the city. The commerce clause reserves the power to pass such legislation exclusively to the federal government.

Commerce among the States

Most legislation passed by Congress related to business must be within Congress's power under the commerce clause in order for a court to uphold the legislation. This clause is a major source of congressional power, although by no means the only source of power. For example, some legislation has been held to be within the power of Congress to pass based upon its taxing power. The commerce clause, however, is the most significant source of congressional power. As interpreted today, this clause grants enormous power to the federal government.

The United States Supreme Court, in examining this grant of power to Congress, initially adhered to one interpretation of the clause. In the classic case, *Gibbons* v. *Ogden* (1824), the Court took a very broad view of the meaning of this phrase. The Court regarded "commerce" as activity that concerns or affects more than one state. This was the "commerce" that constitutionally could be regulated by Congress.

A New York statute gave Ogden a monopoly to run a steamboat on a New York river. The federal government enacted a statute awarding Gibbons the right to operate a steamboat on the same waterway. Ogden initially obtained an injunction prohibiting Gibbons from operating his steamboat on the waterway. The Supreme Court decided, in light of the federal statute, that the grant given to Ogden by New York must fall. The commerce clause gave Congress the power to regulate this activity. Article VI of the Constitution (the supremacy clause) provides that the Constitution, laws, and treaties of the United States "shall be the supreme law of the land." As the New York statute conflicted with a statute lawfully enacted by Congress pursuant to the commerce clause, the United States law prevailed because of the supremacy clause.

As time passed, the Court moved away from the interpretation expressed in *Gibbons v. Ogden*. The Court chose to interpret the clause more restrictively, essentially saying that the commerce clause dealt with physical, interstate movement. This made it more difficult for Congress to lawfully pass regulations involving purely local acts.

During this period, state legislatures passed innumerable statutes dealing with commercial activities. In the absence of federal legislation, the Court interpreted the clause in such a way as to uphold this legislation. Such an interpretation worked well until Congress began to regulate business activity. Sustaining federal legislation while adhering to a narrow interpretation of the commerce clause posed significant problems for the Court. The Court adopted various interpretations of the clause in order to sustain some federal business regulatory legislation.

In the early 1900s, the Court decided that various federal statutes were enacted beyond the power of Congress to regulate commerce. For example, in 1918, in *Hammer v. Dagenhart*, the court refused to sustain an act dealing with goods manufactured by firms employing children. The Court held that manufacturing was not commerce and was therefore beyond the power of Congress to regulate.

In the 1930s, the United States found itself in the midst of the Great Depression. Franklin D. Roosevelt assumed the office of the presidency in 1933. He immediately proposed statutes, which were enacted by Congress as part of the New Deal, that were aimed at pulling the United States out of the Depression. The Supreme Court held that much of the New Deal legislation was outside Congress's commercial clause power. For example, in *Schechter Poultry* (1935), the Court ruled that Congress lacked the power to regulate the chicken processing industry under the commerce clause. The Court also refused to uphold federal legislation dealing with prices, working hours, and wages.

These cases caused a major confrontation between President Roosevelt and the Court. In the wake of the controversy over Roosevelt's proposal to change the composition of the United States Supreme Court by increasing its membership, the Supreme Court reversed its long-held interpretation of the commerce clause. In *N.L.R.B. v. Jones of Laughlin Steel Corp.* (1937), it laid to rest the idea that Congress cannot reach intrastate activities.

> Although activities may be intrastate in character when considered separately, if they have such a close and substantial relation to interstate commerce that their control is essential or appropriate to protect that commerce from burdens and obstructions, Congress cannot be denied the power to exercise that control.

In a later case, *Wickard v. Filburn* (1942), the Court examined a federal marketing quota concerning the amount of wheat a farmer could grow. The farmer planted 23 acres of wheat in violation of the order to plant only 11.9 acres. The farmer argued that his activity was purely local and therefore could not be regulated by Congress. Nonetheless, the Court upheld the federal legislation. Furthermore, it held the government may regulate something that is *not* commerce, if it could have a substantial effect on commerce in a cumulative sense. That is, if the action of all farmers, taken as a group, will affect commerce, Congress may regulate the activity in question.

Today, the power of Congress to regulate both intrastate and interstate commerce of private enterprises remains inviolable. Congress possesses the power to pass a wide array of legislation regulating private businesses through the powers granted to it by the commerce clause of the United States Constitution as interpreted by the Supreme Court.

The following is a famous case in which the Supreme Court upheld the provisions of the Civil Rights Act of 1964. It illustrates the approach of today's Supreme Court with respect to the scope of the federal government's power to regulate business activities.

Katzenbach v. McClung
United States Supreme Court
379 U.S. 294 (1964)

Ollie McClung had operated Ollie's Barbeque in Birmingham, Alabama, since 1927. Ollie's was located eleven blocks from the nearest interstate highway, somewhat farther from the nearest railroad or bus terminal, and six miles from the airport. Two-thirds of Ollie's thirty-six employees were blacks, but the restaurant had from its beginning refused to serve blacks in its dining room. Approximately forty-six percent of the food served by Ollie's was shipped from outside Alabama.

Title II of the Civil Rights Act of 1964 prohibits racial discrimination by a restaurant if it serves or offers to serve interstate travelers or if a substantial portion of the food it serves has moved in interstate commerce. Ollie's continued to refuse service to blacks after the passage of the act. When the Justice Department sought to enforce the act against similar restaurants, McClung sought a declaratory judgment in the federal district court that the act would interfere with his business and property rights. He demonstrated that the restaurant would lose a substantial portion of its business if forced to serve blacks.

The district court held that: (1) The food shipped to Ollie's from out of state ceased to be in commerce when it reached its destination, and the serving of it became a wholly intrastate activity; (2) Congress may not make a presumptive finding that any particular restaurant activities affect interstate commerce; and (3) Ollie's would be deprived of its property rights without due process of law in violation of the Fifth Amendment.

The government appealed the decision to the United States Supreme Court.

Justice Clark

The record is replete with testimony of the burdens placed on interstate commerce by racial discrimination in restaurants. A comparison of per capita spending by Blacks in restaurants, theaters, and like establishments indicated less spending, after discounting income differences, in areas where discrimination is widely practiced. This condition, which was especially aggravated in the South, was attributed in the testimony of the Under Secretary of Commerce to racial segregation. In addition, the Attorney General testified that this type of discrimination imposed "an artificial restriction on the market" and interfered with the flow of merchandise.

Moreover there was an impressive array of testimony that discrimination in restaurants had a direct and highly restrictive effect upon interstate travel by Blacks. This resulted, it was said, because discriminatory practices prevent Blacks from buying prepared food served on the premises while on a trip, except in isolated and unkempt restaurants and under most unsatisfactory and often unpleasant conditions. This obviously discourages travel and obstructs interstate commerce for one can hardly travel without eating. Likewise, it was said, that discrimination deterred professional, as well as skilled, people from moving into areas where such practices occurred and thereby caused industry to be reluctant to establish there.

We believe that this testimony afforded ample basis for the conclusion that established restaurants in such areas sold less interstate goods because of the discrimination, that interstate travel was obstructed directly by it, that business in general suffered and that many new businesses refrained from establishing there as a result of it. Hence the District Court was in error in concluding that there was no connection between discrimination and the movement of interstate commerce. The court's conclusion that such a connection is outside "common experience" flies in the face of stubborn fact.

It goes without saying that, viewed in isolation, the volume of food purchased by Ollie's Barbecue from sources supplied from out of state was insignificant when compared with the total foodstuffs moving in commerce. But, as our late Brother Jackson said for the Court in *Wickard v. Filburn*:

"That appellee's own contribution to the demand for wheat may be trivial by itself is not enough to remove him from the scope of federal regulation where, as here, his contribution, taken together with that of many others similarly situated, is far from trivial."

Congress has determined for itself that refusals of services to Blacks have imposed burdens both upon the interstate flow of food and upon the movement of products generally. Of course, the mere fact that Congress has said when particular activity shall be deemed to affect commerce does not preclude further examination by this Court. But where we find that the legislators, in light of the facts and testimony before them, have a rational basis for finding a chosen regulatory scheme necessary to the protection of commerce, our investigation is at an end.

Confronted as we are with the facts laid before Congress, we must conclude that it has a rational basis for finding that racial discrimination in restaurants had a direct and adverse effect on the free flow of interstate commerce. Insofar as the sections of the Act here relevant are concerned Congress prohibited discrimination only in those establishments having a close tie to interstate commerce, i.e., those, like the McClungs', serving food that has come from out of the State. We think in so doing that Congress acted well within its power to protect and foster commerce in extending the coverage of Title II only to those restaurants offering to serve interstate travelers or serving food, a substantial portion of which has moved in interstate commerce.

The power of Congress in this field is broad and sweeping; where it keeps within its sphere and violates no express constitutional limitation it has been the rule of this Court, going back almost to the founding days of the Republic, not to interfere. The Civil Rights Act of 1964, as here applied, we find to be plainly appropriate in the resolution of what the Congress found to be a national commercial problem of the first magnitude. We find it in no violation of any express limitations of the Constitution and we therefore declare it valid.

To determine if an exercise of congressional power under the commerce clause is valid, the courts go through the following analysis. First, if there is any rational basis for a congressional finding that an activity affects interstate commerce, a court must defer to this finding. In the *Katzenbach* case, the Court noted the extensive information in the record that supported the conclusion that racial discrimination in restaurants affects interstate commerce. Consequently, it deferred to the congressional finding that discrimination affects interstate commerce. Secondly, the courts examine whether the means chosen by Congress are reasonably adapted to the end permitted by the Constitution. If a court finds Congress acted rationally in adopting a particular regulatory scheme, it must uphold the legislation.

Congress may regulate even an activity that is purely intrastate in character where the activity, combined with like conduct by others similarly situated, affects commerce among the states or with foreign nations. Thus, even if a particular restaurant engaged in purely intrastate sales, Congress still may regulate its activities if, when combined with conduct by other restaurants, such activity affects commerce among the states or with foreign nations.

In light of this test, it would appear that, as a practical matter, there is no real limit today on the power of the federal government to regulate business.

It is not only the federal government that may regulate business, state governments may do so also. In the next section we address this power of state governments.

STATE POWER TO REGULATE BUSINESS

The power of the states to regulate is referred to as the police power of the states. The states reserved this power when they banded together to form the United States. The states in turn have delegated some of their power to regulate to local governments.

The power of the states to regulate is not without limitation. As noted earlier, the commerce clause is not only a source of congressional power to regulate commerce, it also is a limitation on the power of the states to enact legislation that regulates commerce.

If a state passes legislation that is local in character, it may still be held to be unconstitutional under certain circumstances. Some areas of regulation are deemed to be areas in which only the federal government can regulate. These are areas where uniformity on a nationwide basis is essential. A famous example of this involved an attempt by the state of Arizona to limit the length of passenger trains to fourteen cars and the length of freight trains to seventy cars. The United States Supreme Court in *Southern Pacific R.R.* v. *Arizona* ruled that even though Congress had not passed any legislation pertaining to the length of trains, Arizona could not limit the length of trains passing through the state of Arizona. The Court reasoned that if train length were to be regulated at all, then national uniformity would be necessary and could be prescribed only by Congress.

A second area in which states may not regulate commerce is those situations where Congress has preempted an area. By **preemption** the courts mean that Congress has completely occupied a field. Sometimes Congress will expressly state in an act that it intends to preempt the field. However, if congressional legislation is extensive in a particular area, the courts may find that Congress has preempted the area by implication. A good example of this can be found in *City of Burbank* v. *Lockheed Air Terminal, Inc.* That case dealt with an ordinance passed by the city of Burbank, California, which attempted to prohibit aircraft from taking off between the hours of 11:00 P.M. and 7:00 A.M. After examining the extensive federal regulation of this area, the Court concluded that even though Congress never expressly preempted this area, it had preempted the area by implication. Such a decision makes sense in light of the chaos that would be created if every town could create its own rules relating to aircraft takeoffs and landings.

Businesses are subject to a great deal of regulation by the states. In particular, the insurance, banking, and savings-and-loan industries are heavily regulated by the states. Likewise, most regulations relating to professional conduct have been passed by the state governments.

The following case involves the issue of whether the federal government's extensive regulation of the field of nuclear energy precludes a state court from rendering a **punitive damage** award.

Silkwood v. Kerr-McGee Corporation
United States Supreme Court
104 S.Ct. 615 (1984)

Karen Silkwood was a laboratory analyst for Kerr-McGee at a plant engaged in fabricating plutonium fuel pins for use as reactor fuel in nuclear power plants. She was contaminated by plutonium from the Kerr-McGee plant. Thereafter she was killed in an unrelated automobile accident. Her father brought suit based on common law tort principles under Oklahoma law to recover for the contamination injuries to Karen's person and property. The jury awarded Silkwood actual damages of $505 thousand and punitive damages of $10 million. Kerr-McGee argued that federal law precluded an award of punitive damages. The Tenth Circuit agreed, but the United States Supreme Court reversed, holding federal law did not preclude an award of punitive damages.

Justice White

This case requires us to determine whether a state authorized award of punitive damages arising out of the escape of plutonium from a federally-licensed nuclear facility is preempted either because it falls within that forbidden field or because it conflicts with some other aspect of the Atomic Energy Act.

As we recently observed in *Pacific Gas & Electric Co.* v. *State Energy Resources Conserva-* *tion & Development Comm'n*, state law can be preempted in either of two general ways. If Congress evidences an intent to occupy a given field, any state law falling within that field is preempted. If Congress has not entirely displaced state regulation over the matter in question, state law is still preempted to the extent it actually conflicts with federal law, that is, when it is impossible to comply with both state and federal law, or where the state law stands as an obstacle to the accomplishment of the full purposes and objectives of Congress.

Although the Price-Anderson Act does not apply to the present situation, the discussion preceding its enactment and subsequent amendment indicates that Congress assumed that persons injured by nuclear accidents were free to utilize existing state tort law remedies.

No doubt there is a tension between the conclusion that safety regulation is the exclusive concern of the federal law and the conclusion that a state may nevertheless award damages based on its own law of liability. But as we understand what was done over the years in the legislation concerning nuclear energy, Congress intended to stand by both concepts and to tolerate whatever tension there was between them. We can do no less. It may be that the award of damages based on the state law of negligence or strict liability is regulatory in the sense that a nuclear plant will be threatened with damages liability if it does not conform to state standards, but that regulatory consequence was something that Congress was quite willing to accept.

We do not suggest that there could never be an instance in which the federal law would preempt the recovery of damages based on state law. But insofar as damages for radiation injuries are concerned, preemption should not be judged on the basis that the federal government has so completely occupied the field of safety that state remedies are foreclosed but on whether there is an irreconcilable conflict between the federal and state standards or whether the imposition of a state standard in a damages action would frustrate the objectives of the federal law. We perceive no such conflict or frustration in the circumstances of this case.

We conclude that the award of punitive damages in this case is not preempted by federal law.

Assuming Congress has not preempted a field and it is not one deemed to be an area in which only Congress can pass regulations, then a state, pursuant to its police power, may pass legislation that regulates business. However, there still are some limitations on state power. For example, a state law may not be in irreconcilable conflict with a federal law. In the event of such an irreconcilable conflict, the supremacy clause of the United States Constitution requires that the state law be struck down. Furthermore, a state law must not discriminate in favor of intrastate commerce. States cannot pass legislation that favors local businesspersons at the expense of out-of-state businesses. It should also be noted that a state law must not place an undue burden on interstate commerce.

The following case discusses the issue of discrimination against interstate commerce by a state government.

Maine v. Taylor
United States Supreme Court
106 S.Ct.2440 (1986)

The state of Maine by statute prohibited the importation of live baitfish into Maine. The golden shiner, a species of minnow, is commonly used as live bait in sport fishing. Robert Taylor, who operated a bait business in Maine, arranged to have

158,000 live golden shiners delivered to him outside the state. He was arrested for violating the Lacey Act which makes it a federal crime to import fish in violation of any state law. Taylor argued the indictment should be dismissed because Maine's import ban unconstitutionally burdens interstate commerce and therefore could not form the basis for a federal prosecution under the Lacey Act. The district court found Maine's statute to be constitutional and convicted Taylor. The court of appeals reversed his conviction. The Supreme Court reversed the court of appeals. It held Maine's statute to be constitutional.

Justice Blackmun

The Commerce Clause of the Constitution grants Congress the power "[t]o regulate Commerce with foreign Nations, and among the several States, and with the Indian Tribes." Although the Clause thus speaks in terms of powers bestowed upon Congress, the Court long has recognized that it also limits the power of the States to erect barriers against interstate trade. Maine's statute restricts interstate trade in the most direct manner possible, blocking all inward shipments of live baitfish at the State's border. Still, as both the District Court and the Court of Appeals recognized, this fact alone does not render the law unconstitutional. The limitation imposed by the Commerce Clause on state regulatory power is by no means absolute, and the States retain authority under their general police powers to regulate matters of "legitimate local concern," even though interstate commerce may be affected.

In determining whether a State has overstepped its role in regulating interstate commerce, this Court has distinguished between state statutes that burden interstate transactions only incidentally, and those that affirmatively discriminate against such transactions. While statutes in the first group violate the Commerce Clause only if the burdens they impose on interstate trade are clearly excessive in relation to the putative local benefits, statutes in the second group are subject to more demanding scrutiny. The Court explained in *Hughes v. Oklahoma* that once a state law is shown to discriminate against interstate commerce "either on its face or in practical effect," the burden falls on the State to demonstrate both that the

statute "serves a legitimate local purpose," and that this purpose could not be served as well by available nondiscriminatory means.

Maine's ban on the importation of live baitfish is constitutional only if it satisfies the requirements ordinarily applied under *Hughes v. Oklahoma* to local regulation that discriminates against interstate trade: the statute must serve a legitimate local purpose, and the purpose must be one that cannot be served as well by available nondiscriminatory means.

The District Court found after an evidentiary hearing that both parts of the *Hughes* test were satisfied.

After reviewing the expert testimony presented to the magistrate we cannot say that the District Court clearly erred in finding that substantial scientific uncertainty surrounds the effect that baitfish parasites and non-native species could have on Maine's fisheries. Moreover, we agree with the District Court that Maine has a legitimate interest in guarding against imperfectly understood environmental risks, despite the possibility that they may ultimately prove to be negligible.

Nor do we think that much doubt is cast on the legitimacy of Maine's purposes by what the Court of Appeals took to be signs of protectionist intent. Shielding in-state industries from out-of-state competition is almost never a legitimate local purpose, and state laws that amount to "simple economic protectionism" consequently have been subject to a virtually *per se* rule of invalidity. But there is little reason in this case to believe that the legitimate justifications the State has put forward for its statute are merely a sham or a *"post hoc rationalization."*

The Commerce Clause significantly limits the ability of States and localities to regulate or otherwise burden the flow of interstate commerce, but it does not elevate free trade above all other values. As long as a State does not needlessly obstruct interstate trade or attempt to place itself in a position of economic isolation, it retains broad regulatory authority to protect the health and safety of its citizens and the integrity of its natural resources. The evidence in this case amply supports the District Court's findings that Maine's ban on the importation of live baitfish serves legitimate local purposes that could not adequately be served by available nondiscriminatory alternatives. This is not a case of arbitrary discrimination against interstate commerce; the record suggests that Maine has legitimate reasons, apart from their origin, to treat [out-of-state baitfish] differently. The judgment of the Court of Appeals setting aside appellee's conviction is therefore reversed.

LIMITATIONS ON GOVERNMENTAL POWER

The drafters of the United States Constitution realized that governmental power could be abused. Consequently, they placed some limits on the exercise of governmental power in the Constitution. In particular, they were concerned about the intrusion of the government on the rights supposedly retained by the people at the time the United States government was formed.

State Action Requirement

The Constitution of the United States provides protection for individual rights. As originally drafted, the Constitution did not contain many protections of individual freedoms. Some of our most cherished rights were added by amendment (for example, freedom of speech, freedom from unreasonable search). The articles in the original document did contain a few basic provisions protecting individual rights, but many of the states during the ratification process were concerned that additional rights' protections were not explicitly contained in the document.

The concern for individual rights was genuine, and arose from recent experiences. When the country was under British rule, troops were placed in homes without permission, and searches were made without warrants. However, the British government was not the only source of rights violations. Some of the states under the Articles of Confederation also abused individual rights. Certain state legislatures passed bills of attainder, sentencing certain individuals to death without the benefit of a jury trial. At least one state levied a tax that was so burdensome to newspapers as to severely limit freedom of the press.

The drafters of the constitutional rights guarantees were concerned with abuse by government, not abuse by various individuals. The actions of the British colonial government and the governments of the states under the Articles of Confederation gave rise to practical concern by many leaders in the late eighteenth century that individual rights had to be expressly protected from abuse by the government. This is the foundation of an important idea behind the protection of constitutional rights: the concept of "state action." Purely private and individual activity is not covered by the Bill of Rights. It is against the government and the power of the government, with its attendant danger to the freedoms of all, that the individual is protected by the Bill of Rights. For example, it is not constitutionally prohibited for an individual to refuse to invite a classmate to a party solely because that person wrote poetry. It may not be a decision one would approve, but it does not violate the Constitution. However, the government may not pass a statute prohibiting poets from attending parties. The statute would be stricken as having a "chilling effect" on First Amendment freedoms.

The following case is an example of the complex concept of state action arising under the Fourteenth Amendment. The concept has been interpreted very broadly to cover a large number of seemingly private activities that have some connection with a branch of the government. Note, however, that private, individual behavior may be controlled by legislation enacted under constitutional provisions that do not contain "state action" requirements (for example, the commerce clause, under which various antidiscrimination statutes have been applied to private activity in the workplace).

Moose Lodge No. 107 v. Irvis
United States Supreme Court
407 U.S. 163 (1972)

Irvis, a black (hereafter appellee), was refused service by appellant Moose Lodge, a local branch of the national fraternal organization located in Harrisburg, Pennsylvania. Appellee claimed that because the Pennsylvania liquor board had issued appellant Moose Lodge a private club license that authorized the sale of alcoholic beverages on its premises, the refusal of service to him was state action for the purposes of the Equal Protection Clause of the Fourteenth Amendment. He named both the Moose Lodge and the Pennsylvania Liquor Authority as defendants, seeking injunctive relief that would have required the defendant liquor board to revoke the Moose Lodge's license so long as it continued its discriminatory practices.

A three-judge district court, convened at appellee's request, upheld his contention on the merits and entered a decree declaring invalid the liquor license issued to the Moose Lodge "as long as it follows a policy of racial discrimination in its membership or operating policies or practices." Moose Lodge 107 appealed from the decree.

Justice Rehnquist

In 1883, this Court in The Civil Rights Cases set forth the essential dichotomy between discriminatory action by the State, which is prohibited by the Equal Protection Clause, and private conduct, "however discriminatory or wrongful," against which that clause "erects no shield."

While the principle is easily stated, the question of whether particular discriminatory conduct is private, on the one hand, or amounts to "state action," on the other hand, frequently admits of no easy answer. Only by sifting facts and weighing circumstances can the nonobvious involvement of the State in private conduct be attributed its true significance.

The Court has never held, of course, that discrimination by an otherwise private entity would be violative of the Equal Protection Clause if the private entity receives any sort of benefit or service at all from the State, or if it is subject to state regulation in any degree whatever. Since state-furnished services include such necessities of life as electricity, water, and police and fire protection, such a holding would utterly emasculate the distinction between private as distinguished from state conduct set forth in The Civil Rights Cases and adhered to in subsequent decisions.

The Moose Lodge building is located on land owned by it, not by any public authority. Far from apparently holding itself out as a place of public accommodation, Moose Lodge quite ostentatiously proclaims the fact that it is not open to the public at large. Nor is it located and operated in such surroundings that although private in name, it discharges a function or performs a service that would otherwise in all likelihood be performed by the State. In short Moose Lodge is a private social club in a private building.

The Pennsylvania Liquor Control Board plays absolutely no part in establishing or enforcing the membership or guest policies of the club that it licenses to serve liquor. There is no suggestion in this record that Pennsylvania law, either as written or as applied, discriminates against minority groups either in their right to apply for club licenses themselves or in their right to purchase and be served liquor in places of public accommodation. The only effect that the state licensing of Moose Lodge to serve liquor can be said to have on the right of any other Pennsylvanian to buy or be served liquor on premises other than those of Moose Lodge is that for some purposes club licenses are counted in the maximum number of licenses that may be issued in a given municipality.

The limited effect of the prohibition against obtaining additional club licenses when the maximum number of retail licenses allotted to a municipality has been issued, when considered together with the availability of liquor from hotel, restaurant, and retail licensees, falls far short of conferring upon club licensees a monopoly in the dispensing of liquor in any given municipality or in the State as a whole. We therefore hold that the operation of the regulatory scheme enforced by the Pennsylvania Liquor Control Board does not sufficiently implicate the State in the discriminatory guest policies of Moose Lodge so as to make the latter "state action" within the ambit of the Equal Protection Clause of the Fourteenth Amendment.

Justice Douglas (dissenting)

Liquor licenses in Pennsylvania, unlike driver's licenses, or marriage licenses, are not freely available to those who meet racially neutral qualifications. There is a complex quota system. The Harrisburg quota, where Moose Lodge No. 107 is located, has been full for many years. No more club licenses may be issued in that city.

This state-enforced scarcity of licenses restricts the ability of blacks to obtain liquor, for liquor is commercially available only at private clubs for a significant portion of each week. Access by blacks to places that serve liquor is further limited by the fact that the state quota is filled. A group desiring to form a nondiscriminatory club which would serve blacks must purchase a license held by an existing club, which can exact a monopoly price for the transfer. The availability of such a license is speculative at best, however, for, as Moose Lodge itself concedes, without a liquor license a fraternal organization would be hard pressed to survive.

Thus, the State of Pennsylvania is putting the weight of its liquor license, concededly a valued and important adjunct to a private club, behind racial discrimination.

As the first Justice Harlan, dissenting in the

Civil Rights Cases, said:

"No State, nor the officers of any State, nor any corporation or individual wielding power under State authority for the public benefit or the public convenience, can, consistently . . . with the freedom es-

tablished by the fundamental law . . . discriminate against freemen or citizens, in those rights, because of their race."

The regulation governing this liquor license has in it that precise infirmity.

There are constitutional protections for individual rights other than those contained in the first ten amendments. These protections can be found, for the most part, in the "Civil War Amendments" (the Thirteenth, Fourteenth, and Fifteenth Amendments), which were enacted between 1865 and 1870. These amendments provided the constitutional foundations for the revolution in civil rights law and criminal procedure that has occurred in this country in the last thirty years. Of those amendments, the most influential is the Fourteenth Amendment with its "due process" and "equal protection" clauses.

Due Process Clause

Section 1 of the Fourteenth Amendment provides that no state shall "deprive any person of life, liberty, or property, without due process of law." A similar provision applicable to the federal government is contained in the Fifth Amendment. Although this phrase has a nice ring to it, what does it mean? What is the liberty and property of an individual that the state may not take away without **due process**? Furthermore, what exactly is "due process"—that is, what procedures must a state provide before it can deprive a person of life, liberty, or property? These questions have been raised and litigated in countless cases. Quite frankly, there is no clear answer.

What has occurred in this area of constitutional law is a large amount of judicial lawmaking concerning the applicability of the amendment language. For example, note the precise choice of words in the Bill of Rights. It is worded in such a way as to limit the power of *Congress* as that power applies to individuals. It does not mention state governments. Until rather recently, the Bill of Rights did not apply to the states. Many states had bills of rights in their own constitutions, but they were not necessarily construed in the same manner as the Bill of Rights in the United States Constitution. However, by use of the Fourteenth Amendment's due process clause, most of the rights guaranteed to the individual by the Bill of Rights have been held by the courts to be applicable to the states—as being liberty or property which is protected from arbitrary state as well as federal government interference.

At one time the United States Supreme Court required the federal and state governments not only to adopt and follow fair procedures, it also required the provisions of any rule enforced by the governments to be fair and reasonable. This latter method of analysis under the due process clause is called substantive (as opposed to procedural) due process. Substantive due process requires that the provisions of a governmental rule be fair and reasonable.

To illustrate how the Supreme Court applied the doctrine of substantive due process at one time, consider the concept of freedom of contract. In the 1800s, the Supreme Court regarded freedom of contract as a liberty protected by the term *due process*. The Supreme Court reviewed any legislation that was alleged to be an interference with the freedom of the parties to a contract to voluntarily enter an agreement. The Supreme Court decided whether the law in question interfered with the parties' freedom to contract in an unreasonable manner. The *Lochner* case, which appears in Chapter 8, is an example of a case in which the United States Supreme Court struck down a piece of state legislation because the Court viewed the state legislation as an unconstitutional deprivation of the parties' right to freely contract. The substantive due process doctrine made it very difficult for the federal or state governments to pass any legislation that regulated the economy. During the 1930s, the Supreme Court finally rejected the substantive due process doctrine once and for all, at least as it applied to economic legislation. This enabled the federal and state governments to pass much of the legislation now on the books that regulates how business is conducted. Today, the Court no longer reviews the wisdom of economic regulations passed by the government.

To a limited extent, however, through its power to interpret the meaning of the phrase *liberty* in the due process clause, the Court still engages in a form of substantive due process analysis in certain cases involving social, as opposed to economic, questions. For example, the Court has found that the Constitution guarantees people a right to privacy. It used this concept to strike down state laws that prohibit abortions.

Today, however, due process analysis is for the most part a guarantee of procedural protection against unfair or intrusive governmental behavior. It does not refer to what the government may *do* to people; it concerns itself with *how* the government may do it. Due process is a general term that stipulates that government owes duties of fairness in its treatment of individuals.

A few general principles of due process must be observed before a person is deprived of life, liberty, or property. One principle is that the affected individuals must have notice of the government activity being taken against them. This allows the individuals to prepare a defense or challenge to the government's activity. It eliminates the horror of being subjected to governmental processes without knowing the basis for the action.

A second principle involves various components of a fair hearing. Merely knowing the basis of the government's action would be valueless if the individual could not effectively challenge that action. A fair hearing involves a neutral, unbiased decision maker who renders a judgment on the evidence presented at the hearing. This is an important factor in that it requires the government to justify its activities to the decision maker. It also provides a forum in which the individual may raise a defense. Additional factors include the rights to present evidence and to test the evidence of the government at the hearing.

The following case is an example of the due process clause—depriving a person of property without due process of law. Note that the clothesline ordinance was specifically directed toward the defendants. Note, also, that the court upheld the ordinance. The dissenting opinion makes interesting points about the extent of the power of government.

People v. Stover
Court of Appeals of New York
191 N.E.2d 272 (1963)

The defendants, Mr. and Mrs. Stover, residents of the city of Rye since 1940, live in a two-and-one-half-story, one-family dwelling, located in a pleasant, built-up residential district. A clothesline, filled with old clothes and rags, made its first appearance in the Stovers' front yard in 1956 as a form of "peaceful protest" against the high taxes imposed by the city. And, during each of the five succeeding years, the defendants added another clothesline to mark their continued displeasure with the taxes. In 1961, therefore, six lines, from which there hung tattered clothing, old uniforms, underwear, rags, and scarecrows, were strung across the Stovers' yard—three from the porch across the front yard to trees along Forest Avenue and three from the porch across the side yard to trees along Rye Beach Avenue.

In August of 1961, the city enacted an ordinance prohibiting the erection and maintenance of clotheslines or other devices for hanging clothes or other fabrics in a front or side yard abutting a street. However, the ordinance provides for the issuance of a permit for the use of such clotheslines if there is "a practical difficulty or unnecessary hardship in drying clothes elsewhere on the premises" and grants a right of appeal to the applicant if a permit is denied.

Following enactment of the ordinance, Mrs. Stover applied for a permit to maintain clotheslines in her yard. Her application was denied because, she was advised, she had sufficient other property available for hanging clothes, and she was directed to remove the clotheslines in the yards abutting the streets. The clotheslines were not removed. The city thereupon charged the defendants with violating the ordinance. They were tried and convicted and their judgments of conviction have been affirmed by the County Court of Westchester County. The defendant, Webster Stover, urges that the ordinance, as it has been applied to him and his wife, is unconstitutional as a deprivation of property without due process.

Fuld, Judge

It is a fair inference that adoption of the ordinance before us was prompted by the conduct and action of the defendants but we deem it clear that, if the law would otherwise be held constitutional, it will not be stricken as discriminatory or invalid because of its motivation. Our problem, therefore, is to determine whether the law exceeds the police power vested in a city on the ground that it was enacted without regard to considerations of public health, safety and welfare.

It is our opinion that the ordinance may be sustained as an attempt to preserve the residential appearance of the city and its property values by banning, insofar as practicable, unsightly clotheslines from yards abutting a public street. In other words, the statute, though based on what may be termed aesthetic considerations, proscribes conduct which offends sensibilities and tends to debase the community and reduce real estate values.

We have recognized the governmental interest in preserving the appearance of the community by holding that, whether or not aesthetic considerations are in and of themselves sufficient to support an exercise of the police power, they may be taken into account by the legislative body in enacting laws which are also designed to promote health and safety.

Once it be conceded that aesthetics is a valid subject of legislative concern, the conclusion seems inescapable that reasonable legislation designed to promote that end is a valid and permissible exercise of the police power. Consequently, whether such a statute or ordinance should be voided should depend upon whether the restriction was "an arbitrary and irrational method of achieving an attractive, efficiently functioning, prosperous community—and not upon whether the objectives were primarily aesthetic."

Cases may undoubtedly arise, as we observed above, in which the legislative body goes too far in the name of aesthetics but the present, quite

clearly, is not one of them. The ordinance before us is in large sense regulatory rather than prohibitory. It causes no undue hardship to any property owner, for it expressly provides for the issuance of a permit for clotheslines in front and side yards in cases where there is practical difficulty or unnecessary hardship in drying clothes elsewhere on the premises. Moreover, the ordinance imposes no arbitrary or capricious standard of beauty or conformity upon the community. It simply proscribes conduct which is unnecessarily offensive to the visual sensibilities of the average person. It is settled that conduct which is similarly offensive to the senses of hearing and smell may be a valid subject of regulation under the police power and we perceive no basis for a different result merely because the sense of sight is involved.

Van Voorhs, Judge (dissenting)

This ordinance is unrelated to the public safety, health, morals or welfare except insofar as it compels conformity to what the neighbors like to look at. In our age of conformity it is still not possible for all to be exactly alike, nor is it the instinct of our law to compel uniformity wherever diversity may offend the sensibilities of those who cast the largest numbers of votes in municipal elections. The right to be different has its place in this country. The United States has drawn strength from differences among its people in taste, experience, temperament, ideas, and ambitions as well as from differences in race, national or religious background. Even where the use of property is bizarre, unsuitable or obstreperous it is not to be curtailed in the absence of overriding reasons of public policy. The security and repose which come from

protection of the right to be different in matters of aesthetics, taste, thought, expression and within limits in conduct are not to be cast aside without violating constitutional privileges and immunities. This is not merely a matter of legislative policy, at whatever level. In my view, this pertains to individual rights protected by the Constitution.

Unless clotheslines create traffic or health hazards, it seems to me that they should not be interfered with by law in suburban or rural areas. More important than this, however, does it seem that extensions of categories of local legislation for purely aesthetic purposes should be defined and limited, and, if they are to be enlarged, it should not be under reasoning which sets no ascertainable bounds to what can be done or attempted under this power.

| Equal Protection Clause | Section 1 of the Fourteenth Amendment also provides that no state shall "deny to any person within its jurisdiction the equal protection of the laws." As with due process, it is not quite clear what this section of the amendment means. Its meaning has changed during the one hundred plus years since its adoption. As noted in Chapter 1, the language did not always prohibit legislated segregation of the races. |

Such an interpretation is a recent phenomenon. In fact, the use of the equal protection clause to attack government-imposed discrimination based on a host of individual characteristics (such as race, sex, wealth, alienage) is also a rather recent development.

The **equal protection clause** does not prohibit the law from treating different groups of people differently. What it does is to require that the state show that such differential treatment serves an interest of the state. The Supreme Court, in interpreting the clause, employs a sliding scale of interests that the government must demonstrate are furthered by the classification. Certain governmental classifications are examined by the Court under a *strict scrutiny* test. This test requires governmental classifications to be closely related to the furtherance of a governmental purpose and that no less discriminatory alternative means of achieving the government's aims be available. For example, racial classifications are considered by the Court to be "suspect," and to require the strictest standard of judicial review. Any legislation that treats people differently on the basis of race does not meet the equal protection standard, unless the government can show that it had a compelling interest in making that classification, which could not be served in any other way. This is a very difficult standard to meet.

The minimum review standard, generally applicable to regulation of business, is whether the legislature had some reasonable basis for the classification. This is referred to as the *rational basis test*. Governmental classifications must have a rational relationship to the achievement of a valid governmental objective. In general, the courts tend to defer to the legislature's judgment, as is illustrated by the following case.

Minnesota v. Clover Leaf Creamery Company
United States Supreme Court
449 U.S. 456 (1981)

The Minnesota legislature enacted a statute that banned the retail sale of milk in plastic, nonreturnable, nonrefillable containers. The act permitted the sale of milk in other nonreturnable, nonrefillable containers, such as paperboard milk containers. This legislation was necessary, as indicated in the statute, because this packaging "represents solid waste management problems for the state, promotes energy waste and depletes natural resources."

The Clover Leaf Creamery Company, a dairy that sold milk in plastic, nonreturnable containers, challenged this law. The company argued, among other things, that the act violated the equal protection clause of the United States Constitution.

The trial court and the Minnesota Supreme Court agreed that the act violated the equal protection clause of the United States Constitution. The United States Supreme Court reversed. It held that the equal protection clause had not been violated.

Justice Brennan

The parties agree that the standard of review applicable to this case under the Equal Protection Clause is the familiar "rational basis" test. Moreover, they agree that the purposes of the Act cited by the legislature—promoting resource conservation, easing solid waste disposal problems, and conserving energy—are legitimate state purposes. Thus, the controversy in this case centers on the narrow issue whether the legislative classification between plastic and nonplastic nonreturnable milk containers is rationally related to achievement of the statutory purposes.

States are not required to convince the courts of the correctness of their legislative judgments. Rather, those challenging the legislative judgment must convince the court that the legislative facts on which the classification is apparently based could not reasonably be conceived to be true by the governmental decisionmaker.

Although parties challenging legislation under the Equal Protection Clause may introduce evidence supporting their claim that it is irrational, they cannot prevail so long as it is evident from all the considerations presented to the legislature, and those of which we may take judicial notice, that the question is at least debatable. Where there is evidence before the legislature reasonably supporting the classification, litigants may not procure invalidation of the legislation merely be tendering evidence that the legislature was mistaken.

Among the reasons identified by the State why the classification between plastic and nonplastic returnables is rationally related to the articulated statutory purposes, the State argues that the elimination of the popular plastic milk jug will encourage the use of environmentally superior containers. There is no serious doubt that the plastic containers consume energy resources and require solid waste disposal, nor that refillable bottles and plastic pouches are environmentally superior. Citing evidence that the plastic jug is the most popular, and the gallon paperboard carton the most cumbersome and least well regarded package in the industry, the State argues that the ban on plastic nonreturnables will buy time during which environmentally preferable alternatives may be further developed and promoted.

We find the State's approach fully supportable under our precedents. This Court has made it clear that a legislature need not strike at all evils at the same time or in the same way and that a legislature may implement its program step-by-step, adopting regulations that only partially ameliorate a perceived evil and deferring complete elimination of the evil to future regulations. The Equal Protection Clause does not deny the State of Minnesota the authority to ban one type of milk container conceded to cause environmental problems, merely because another type, already established in the market, is permitted to continue in use. Whether in fact the Act will promote more environmentally desirable milk packaging is not the question: The Equal Protection Clause is satisfied by our conclusion that the Minnesota Legislature could rationally have decided that the ban on the plastic nonreturnable milk jugs might foster greater use of environmentally desirable alternatives.

In between the strict scrutiny test as it is applied to race and the rational basis test as it is applied to business, there are a number of different standards of review, depending upon the type of classification. For example, discrimination based upon sex, the right to travel, and the right of access to justice have different standards of equal protection review.

The following case is an example of the Court's analyzing a piece of legislation that classified people on the basis of sex.

Craig v. Boren

United States Supreme Court
429 U.S. 190 (1976)

The interaction of two sections of an Oklahoma statute prohibits the sale of "non-intoxicating" 3.2 percent beer to males under the age of twenty-one and to females under the age of eighteen. The question to be decided is whether such a gender-based differential constitutes a denial to males eighteen to twenty years of age of the equal protection of the laws in violation of the Fourteenth Amendment.

Justice Brennan

After the Court of Appeals for the Tenth Circuit held in 1972, on the authority of *Reed v. Reed* that the age distinction was unconstitutional for purposes of establishing criminal responsibility as adults the Oklahoma Legislature fixed age 18 as applicable to both males and females. In 1972, 18 also was established as the age of majority for males and females in civil matters except that sections 241 and 245 of the 3.2% beer statute were simultaneously codified to create an exception to the gender-free rule.

Analysis may appropriately begin with the reminder that *Reed* emphasized that statutory classifications that distinguish between males and females are "subject to scrutiny under the Equal Protection Clause." To withstand constitutional challenge, previous cases establish that classifications by gender must serve important governmental objectives and must be substantially related to achievement of those objectives.

Clearly, the protection of public health and safety represents an important function of state and local governments. However, appellees' statistics in our view cannot support the conclusion that the gender-based distinction closely serves to achieve that objective and therefore the distinction cannot under *Reed* withstand equal protection challenge.

The appellees introduced a variety of statistical surveys showing differences between young male and female drinking problems.

Even were this statistical evidence accepted as accurate, it nevertheless offers only a weak answer to the equal protection question presented here. The most focused and relevant of the statistical surveys, arrests of 18–20-year-olds for alcohol-related driving offenses, exemplifies the ultimate unpersuasiveness of this evidentiary record. Viewed in terms of the correlation between sex and the actual activity that Oklahoma seeks to regulate—driving while under the influence of alcohol—the statistics broadly establish that .18% of females and 2% of males in that age group were arrested for that offense. While such a disparity is not trivial in a statistical sense, it hardly can form the basis for employment of a gender line as a classifying device. Certainly if maleness is to serve as a proxy for drinking and driving, a correlation of 2% must be considered an unduly tenuous "fit." Indeed, prior cases have consistently rejected the use of sex as a decision-making factor even though the statutes in question certainly rested on far more predictive empirical relationships than this.

Moreover, the statistics exhibit a variety of other shortcomings that seriously impugn their value to equal protection analysis. Setting aside the obvious methodological problems, the surveys do not adequately justify the salient features of Oklahoma's gender-based traffic-safety law. None purports to measure the use and dangerousness of 3.2% beer as opposed to alcohol generally, a detail that is of particular importance since, in light of its low alcohol level, Oklahoma apparently considers the 3.2% beverage to be "nonintoxicating." Moreover, many of the studies, while graphically documenting the unfortunate increase in driving while under the influence of alcohol, make no effort to relate their findings to age-sex differentials as involved here. Indeed, the only survey that explicitly centered its attention upon young drivers and their use of beer—albeit apparently not of the diluted 3.2% variety—reached results that hardly can be viewed as impressive in justifying either a gender or age classification.

There is no reason to belabor this line of analysis. It is unrealistic to expect either members of the judiciary or state officials to be well versed in the rigors of experimental or statistical technique. But this merely illustrates that proving broad sociological propositions by statistics is a dubious business, and one that inevitably is in tension with the normative philosophy that underlies the Equal Protection Clause. Suffice to say that the showing offered by the appellees does not satisfy us that sex represents a legitimate, accurate proxy for the regulation of drinking and driving. In fact, when it is further recognized that Oklahoma's statute prohibits only the selling of 3.2% beer to young males and not their drinking the beverage once acquired (even after purchase by their 18–20-year-old female companions), the relationship between gender and traffic safety becomes far too tenuous to satisfy *Reed's* requirement that the gender-based difference be substantially related to achievement of the statutory objective.

We hold, therefore, that under *Reed,* Oklahoma's 3.2% beer statute invidiously discriminates against males 18–20 years of age.

The government is also limited in its power to restrict the freedom of speech by people as is discussed in the following material.

THE FIRST AMENDMENT AND BUSINESS

The first amendment to the United States constitution reads as follows: "Congress shall make no law respecting an establishment of religion, or prohibiting the free exercise thereof; or abridging the freedom of speech, or of the press, or the right of the people peaceably to assemble, and to petition the government for a redress of grievances."

This section of the chapter concerns that portion of the First Amendment which governs freedom of speech, with an emphasis on business. Freedom of speech is one of the most important guarantees in the Constitution. The free exchange of information helps ensure the preservation of democracy. The drafters of the Constitution believed that through the free and open exchange of ideas the truth, sooner or later, would be exposed. Once the citizens know the truth, they are able to make more intelligent decisions.

What Is "Freedom of Speech"?

Many rules have been found in the First Amendment that a person could not find by looking at the literal language of the amendment. What is speech? Is slander speech? Is threatening another person speech? Are pornographic statements speech? Are agreements to fix prices speech? If so, how can Congress regulate or prohibit such speech? The Constitution, after all, says Congress may pass *no* law. It does not say Congress may restrict pornography, or threats to other people, or slander.

To obtain a *workable* reading of the First Amendment, the justices read certain things into the language of the Constitution that a literal reading would not permit. This is true not only of the First Amendment, but of the rest of the Constitution, treaties, statutes, contracts, and so on. The ability to "interpret" the law gives judges considerable discretion to determine what the law is. By the same token, the more imprecise and vague the language used in a document, the more open to varying interpretations it is.

Instead of using extremely precise terms, the drafters of the United States Constitution elected in many places to use phrases that left the courts considerable discretion in interpreting the Constitution. The drafters hoped to create a document that would last this country for many generations. By drafting the Constitution in imprecise terms in certain places, they created a flexible Constitution that could be reinterpreted according to the needs of the times.

Nowhere is this flexible approach more obvious than in the area of freedom of speech. One could interpret this language, by reading it literally, as prohibiting any form of restriction on pure speech whatsoever. Former Supreme Court Justices Black and Douglas probably came closest to adopting such an interpretation. Other justices sitting on the Supreme Court have been more inclined to permit restrictions on speech. For example, Justice Holmes once wrote that a person does not have the right to yell "fire" in a crowded theater. In other cases, the justices characterized the activity discussed in the case as more than speech, and therefore beyond the scope of the First Amendment.

The core of the First Amendment clearly is the protection of freedom of political expression. To the extent that speech involves something other than political ex-

---

FREE SPEECH

On July 9, 1986, the Attorney General's Commission on Pornography released its final draft of a report. The report asserted that pornography probably leads to sexual violence. The report identified pornography as "sexually explicit" material "intended primarily for the purpose of sexual arousal." The report urged that sexually explicit materials be proscribed. It also found that organized crime plays a large part in the pornography industry.

This report contradicted the findings of the 1970 President's Commission on Obscenity and Pornography, which had found pornography does not pose a danger to the public.

About the same time as the release of the 1986 report, a number of special interest groups began to object to the sale of what they regarded as pornographic literature by convenience stores. These groups picketed convenience stores owned by the Southland Corporation—7-Eleven stores. These stores publicly displayed such magazines as *Playboy* on their magazine display rack.

Interestingly, this report as well as the protests by various interest groups, resulted in the removal of *Playboy* from the Southland Corporation's stores. This happened in spite of the provision in the United States Constitution that guarantees the public the right of free speech and a free press. Of course, one should bear in mind that the actions of the Southland Corporation are private actions, not the actions of the government. The United States Constitution does not protect the public from restrictions on free speech by private parties.

pression, the Court has been more willing to permit state regulation of such peripheral areas. One example is the area of commercial speech, or speech by business. Do corporations have the same First Amendment rights as human beings? Are corporate advertisements "speech" as protected by the First Amendment?

Business and Free Speech

The Supreme Court, in *First National Bank of Boston* v. *Bellotti*, in 1978, clarified the issue of whether corporations, as well as private citizens, may exercise the right of free speech.

First National Bank of Boston v. Bellotti
United States Supreme Court
435 U.S. 765 (1978)

A Massachusetts statute prohibited corporations from making contributions or expenditures "for the purpose of . . . influencing or affecting the vote on any question submitted to the voters, other than one materially affecting any of the property, business or assets of the corporation." It specifically prohibited such contributions or expenditures on votes relating to taxation. The statute provided for penalties of fines and imprisonment. Appellants, the bank, wanted to spend money to publicize their views on a proposed constitutional amendment relating to a graduated income tax. They sought to have the law declared unconstitutional. The Supreme Court of Massachusetts upheld this act. The United States Supreme Court ruled the statute violated the Constitution.

Justice Powell

The referendum issue that appellants wish to address falls squarely within the First Amendment. In appellants' view, the enactment of a graduated personal income tax, as proposed to be authorized by constitutional amendment, would have a seriously adverse effect on the economy of the State. The importance of the referendum issue to the people and government of Massachusetts is not disputed. Its merits, however, are the subject of sharp disagreement.

The question in this case, simply put, is whether the corporate identity of the speaker deprives this proposed speech of what otherwise would be its clear entitlement to protection. We turn now to that question.

We find no support in the First or Fourteenth Amendment, or in the decisions of this Court, for the proposition that speech that otherwise would be within the protection of the First Amendment loses that protection simply because its source is a corporation that cannot prove, to the satisfaction of a court, a material effect on its business or property. The "materially affecting" requirement is not an identification of the boundaries of corporate speech etched by the Constitution itself. Rather, it amounts to an impermissible legislative prohibition of speech based on the identity of the interests that spokesmen may represent in public debate over controversial issues and a requirement that the speaker have a sufficiently great interest in the subject to justify communication.

The Act permits a corporation to communicate to the public its views on certain referendum subjects—those materially affecting its business— but not others. It also singles out one kind of ballot question—individual taxation—as a subject about which corporations may never make their ideas public. The legislature has drawn the line between permissible and impermissible speech according to whether there is a sufficient nexus, as defined by the legislature, between the issue presented to the voters and the business interests of the speaker.

In the realm of protected speech, the legislature is constitutionally disqualified from dictating the subjects about which persons may speak and the speakers who may address a public issue. Especially where, as here, the legislature's suppression of speech suggests an attempt to give one side of a debatable public question an advantage in expressing its views to the people, the First Amendment is plainly offended.

Commercial Speech and the Right to Receive Information

Not only persons, but corporations as well, are guaranteed the right of free speech. The public benefits from hearing all sides to a story. The more information presented to the public, the more likely members of the public are to make intelligent decisions. This concept is important to a business that advertises.

The seminal case in the commercial speech area is *Valentine* v. *Chrestensen* (1942). In this case, a submarine owner protested an ordinance that prohibited him from distributing handbills to advertise the exhibition of his submarine. The Court upheld the ordinance because of the commercial nature of his message. In a unanimous opinion the Court stated: "This Court has unequivocally held that the streets are proper places for the exercise of communicating information and disseminating opinion. . . . We are equally clear that the Constitution imposes no such restraint on government as respects purely commercial advertising." The courts interpreted this opinion as meaning that commercial speech was not entitled to the protections afforded by the Constitution to noncommercial speech. The Supreme Court continued to adhere to the decision in *Valentine* for many years.

In the mid-1970s the Court discarded the commercial speech doctrine. In *Virginia State Board of Pharmacy* v. *Virginia Citizens Consumer Council, Inc.* it decided that speech which does no more than propose a commercial transaction is also protected by the First Amendment. The Court based its decision on the need of the public for the free flow of commercial information.

The following case enunciated the current standard for evaluating commercial speech cases. It created a four-step process to be applied in deciding First Amendment cases involving commercial speech.

Central Hudson Gas v. Public Service Commission of New York

United States Supreme Court
447 U.S. 557 (1980)

Central Hudson Gas brought suit to challenge the constitutionality of the Public Service Commission's ban on promotional advertising. The New York Court of Appeals upheld the complete ban on the ground that the state's interest in decreasing energy consumption justified the limitation on commercial speech. The United States Supreme Court reversed.

Justice Powell

In commercial speech cases a four-part analysis has developed. At the outset, we must determine whether the expression is protected by the First Amendment. For commercial speech to come within that provision, it at least must concern lawful activity and not be misleading. Next, we ask whether the asserted governmental interest is substantial. If both inquiries yield positive answers, we must determine whether the regulation directly advances the governmental interest asserted, and whether it is not more extensive than is necessary to serve that interest.

We now apply this four-step analysis for commercial speech to the Commission's arguments in support of its ban on promotional advertising.

Because appellant holds a monopoly over the sale of electricity in its service area, the state court suggested that the Commission's order restricts no commercial speech of any worth. The Court stated that advertising in a "non-competitive market" could not improve the decision making of consumers. The Court saw no constitutional problem with barring commercial speech that it viewed as conveying little useful information.

This reasoning falls short of establishing that appellant's advertising is not commercial speech protected by the First Amendment. Monopoly over the supply of a product provides no protection from competition with substitutes for that product.

Even in monopoly markets, the suppression of advertising reduces the information available for consumer decisions and thereby defeats the purpose of the First Amendment. The New York court's argument appears to assume that the providers of a monopoly service or product are willing to pay for wholly ineffective advertising. Most businesses—even regulated monopolies—are unlikely to underwrite promotional advertising that is of no interest or use to consumers. Indeed, a monopoly enterprise legitimately may wish to inform the public that it has developed new services or terms of doing business.

The Commission offers two state interests as justifications for the ban on promotional advertising. The first concerns energy conservation. Any increase in demand for electricity—during peak or off-peak periods—means greater consumption of energy. The Commission argues, and the New York court agreed, that the State's interest in conserving energy is sufficient to support suppression of advertising designed to increase consumption of electricity. In view of our country's dependence on energy resources beyond our control, no one can doubt the importance of energy conservation. Plainly, therefore, the state interest asserted is substantial.

The Commission also argues that promotional advertising will aggravate inequities caused by the failure to base the utility's rates on marginal cost. The utilities argued to the Commission that if they could promote the use of electricity in periods of low demand, they would improve their utilization of generating capacity. The Commission responded that promotion of off-peak consumption also would increase consumption during peak periods. The choice among rate structures involves difficult and important questions of economic supply and distributional fairness. The State's concern that rates be fair and efficient represents a clear and substantial governmental interest.

Next, we focus on the relationship between the State's interests and the advertising ban. Under this criterion, the Commission's laudable concern over the equity and efficiency of appellant's rates does not provide a constitutionally adequate reason for restricting protected speech. The link between the advertising prohibition and appellant's rate structure is, at most, tenuous. The impact of promotional advertising on the equity of appellant's rates is highly speculative. Advertising to increase off-peak usage would have to increase peak usage, while other factors that directly affect the fairness and efficiency of appellant's rates remained constant. Such conditional and remote eventualities simply cannot justify silencing appellant's promotional advertising.

We come finally to the critical inquiry in this case: whether the Commission's complete suppression of speech ordinarily protected by the First Amendment is no more extensive than necessary to further the State's interest in energy conservation.

The Commission's order prevents appellant from promoting electric services that would reduce energy use by diverting demand from less efficient sources, or that would consume roughly the same amount of energy as do alternative sources. In neither situation would the utility's advertising endanger conservation or mislead the public. To the extent that the Commission's order violates the First and Fourteenth amendments it must be invalidated.

The Commission also has not demonstrated that its interest in conservation cannot be protected adequately by more limited regulation of appellant's commercial expression. To further its policy of conservation, the Commission could attempt to restrict the format and content of Central Hudson's advertising. It might, for example, require that the advertisements include information about the relative efficiency and expense of the offered service, both under current conditions and for the foreseeable future. In the absence of a showing that more limited speech regulation would be ineffective, we cannot approve the complete suppression of Central Hudson's advertising.

Starting with the case *Goldfarb* v. *Virginia State Bar* (1975), the Supreme Court showed a growing interest in the activities of professionals such as lawyers and doctors. In this case, the Supreme Court struck down the power of attorneys to jointly agree upon the minimum prices they would charge for certain professional services. The Court characterized the activities of attorneys in drafting minimum fee schedules as a clear example of illegal price-fixing in violation of the Sherman Antitrust Act. *Goldfarb* represents the first step by the Court to inject some competition in the field of professional services.

Commercial Speech by Professionals

The Court in 1977 considered the question of advertising by two attorneys for the purpose of increasing their business—clearly commercially motivated speech. In *Bates* v. *State Bar of Arizona*, two Arizona attorneys, John Bates and Van O'Steen, had decided to advertise in order to attract the volume of business necessary to sustain their legal clinic. They reasoned that it would be necessary to advertise to attract a large number of clients.

The clinic performed only routine services, such as uncontested bankruptcies, uncontested divorces, uncontested adoptions, and changes of names. To attract more business, they placed an advertisement in the *Arizona Republic*, a daily newspaper of general circulation in the Phoenix metropolitan area. The advertisement stated that the clinic offered "legal services at very reasonable fees," and the fees for certain services were listed. This advertisement violated the Arizona rules governing the practice of law, under which attorneys were forbidden to advertise.

The Court decided that the First Amendment of the United States Constitution invalidated the prohibition on advertising by attorneys. A majority of the members of the Court concluded that a state may not prevent the publication in a newspaper of a truthful advertisement concerning the terms and availability of routine legal services. The state may regulate advertising by attorneys, but it may not prohibit advertising outright. The Court listed some permissible limitations: False, deceptive, or misleading advertising may be restrained, and reasonable restrictions on the time, place, and manner of advertising may be required.

SUMMARY   In addition to providing individuals with basic rights, the Constitution of the United States created the general structure of our government. The governmental structure is one of relationships between sources of power. The Constitution provided that the executive, judicial, and legislative powers be confined to separate units of the federal government.

The Constitution grants extensive power in the commerce clause to the federal government. This power has been used to pass innumerable rules that control the conduct of business in America. The states get their power from the police power. They also extensively regulate the activities of business people. Both the power of the states and the power of the federal government are limited by various provisions in the United States Constitution.

Provisions for individual-rights guarantees from government infringement may be found in a number of places in the Constitution. The Bill of Rights and the Civil Rights Amendments are prime sources of those protected individual freedoms. One of the most important areas of constitutional protection for business is the First Amendment's freedom-of-speech guarantee. Corporations are protected by that provision, and recently the concept of speech has been interpreted by the Supreme Court to include business advertising, or commercial speech.

REVIEW QUESTIONS

1. Define the following terms:
   a. Separation of powers
   b. Due process
   c. Equal protection clause
   d. Commercial speech doctrine
   e. Commerce clause

2. Discuss the structure and organization of government created by the United States Constitution. What was the purpose of this type of organization?

3. Why are most of the protections for individual rights in the Constitution procedural protections?

4. Discuss the "unwritten rules" of the doctrine of judicial review.

5. The Township of Smithville enacted an ordinance that banned "For Sale" and "Sold" signs from front lawns in the township. The stated purpose of the ordinance was to prevent panic selling by white owners and to preserve the racially integrated nature of the township. Linmark, a property owner, sought an injunction against the enforcement of the ban and a declaration that the ban violated the First Amendment guarantee of free speech. The township argued that only one of many available forms of commercial speech was being restricted. The township further argued that the vital goal of the ordinance, namely to promote a stable, racially integrated housing pattern, conferred substantial benefits upon the residents and overrode the constitutional considerations of freedom of commercial speech. Is the ordinance an impermissible restriction on commercial speech?

6. McLain represented a class of purchasers and sellers of real estate in the New Orleans area. The Real Estate Board represented various real estate associations and brokers in the New Orleans areas. McLain filed an antitrust suit against the Real Estate Board under the Sherman Antitrust Act, alleging that its practice of setting uniform brokerage commissions for

real estate was a price-fixing conspiracy in restraint of interstate commerce, and had a substantial effect upon interstate commerce. It was established that brokers sometimes participated in or helped arrange financing for purchasers and that the financing and title insurance involved substantial interstate movement of funds. The Real Estate Board responded that brokers acted in a purely local manner and did not do anything that had a substantial effect on interstate commerce. The lower court dismissed the complaint, holding that the activities of brokers were not an integral part of the interstate aspects of the transactions and that they were not directly "in" interstate commerce. Should the Supreme Court affirm or reverse the lower court?

7. Explain the concept of "state action" in constitutional law.

8. Should business speech be protected by the First Amendment?

9. The United States Jaycees was a civic organization whose regular membership was limited to men between the ages of eighteen to thirty-five. The Minnesota Human Rights Act makes it illegal to deny any person "full and equal enjoyment of goods, services, facilities, privileges, advantages, and accommodations of a place of public accommodation because of . . . sex." The Jaycees argued that, by requiring it to accept women as regular members, the Minnesota Act would violate the male members' constitutional rights of free speech and association. Was the Jaycees correct?

10. An association of coal producers challenged the constitutionality of the Surface Mining Control and Reclamation Act of 1977. The act was passed by Congress to protect the environment from the adverse effects of surface coal mining operations. Congress held extended hearings in both houses concerning the effects of surface mining on the environment. The House committee documented the adverse effects of surface coal mining on interstate commerce as the source of damage to eleven thousand miles of streams, the loss of forests, the destruction of wildlife habitat, and the sedimentation of river systems. Is the application of this act to the coal companies a lawful exercise of Congressional power under the commerce clause? Would it be useful for the coal producers to argue they were engaged in local activities only?

11. The state of Texas required notaries to be United States citizens. A resident alien who had lived in the United States since 1961 asserted that the Texas citizenship requirement violated the equal protection clause of the Fourteenth Amendment. Does this act violate the equal protection clause?

12. The Cleburne Living Center (CLC) desired to operate a group home for thirteen retarded men and women, who would be under the constant supervision of CLC staff members. The CLC applied for a special use permit to operate a group home at a particular location. Under city zoning regulations, a special permit was required for the construction of a facility for the feeble-minded. After holding a public hearing, the city council voted to deny the special use permit. The CLC filed suit. It alleged that the zoning ordinance discriminated against the mentally retarded in violation of their equal protection rights. Is the CLC correct?

13. The federal government passed a statute that prohibited the mailing of unsolicited advertisements for contraceptives. Youngs Drug Product Company wished to mail to the public unsolicited advertisements including informational pamphlets promoting the use of contraceptives. Youngs Drug Product brought an action for declaratory and injunctive relief that alleged, as applied to the proposed mailings, the statute violated the First Amendment. Is Youngs Drug Product correct?

14. After his resignation from the presidency, Richard Nixon entered into an agreement with the administrator of general services concerning his presidential papers. The agreement provided, in part, that the papers and tapes would be destroyed as Nixon directed, at the time of his death or on September 1, 1984, whichever occurred first. Soon thereafter, Congress enacted legislation designed to abrogate this agreement. Does the act encroach on the president's ability to control the oper- ation of the office of the president, thereby offending the doctrine of separation of powers?

15. The Virginia Board of Pharmacy adopted a rule that prohibited pharmacists within the state from advertising the prices of prescription drugs. The plaintiff, in this case, wished to receive drug price information. It challenged the rule, asserting that it violated the First Amendment. Did this rule violate the First Amendment?

CHAPTER 7

The Administrative Agency

Administrative Agencies and Administrative Law
Functions of Administrative Agencies

An administrative agency is a governmental body other than a court or a legislature. Agencies exist at all levels of government and affect individuals and businesses through rule making, adjudicating, and enforcing laws and policies that have been delegated to them. In the past thirty years, administrative agencies have become increasingly involved in various aspects of American life. Their power and lawmaking ability have affected the ways in which the largest corporations conduct day-to-day business. Their ability to dispense government funds has affected even the poorest individuals' daily lives.

Administrative agencies control various substantive areas of the law. Such diverse legal topics as air and water pollution, safety in the workplace, product safety, and equal employment opportunities are covered by different administrative agencies. Volumes might be written on the workings of just one agency and the areas of substantive law that it covers. Therefore, rather than review new substantive legal rules that happened to be produced by the administrative law system, this chapter will focus on several general issues concerning the administrative agency in our legal system.

This chapter is divided into two sections. First, a general discussion of administrative agencies and administrative law will be presented, which will identify some general characteristics of agencies. Second, three main functions of administrative agencies will be explored: the investigative or enforcement function, the adjudicative function, and the rule-making function. Various issues and limits imposed on the agency in the carrying out of those functions will also be discussed.

ADMINISTRATIVE AGENCIES AND ADMINISTRATIVE LAW

Importance of Agencies

Although the great influence of administrative agencies in the legal environment is a relatively recent development, administrative agencies are not new to our form of government. The first agencies were established by Congress in 1789. They were created to affix duties on foreign imports (the forerunner of today's customs office) and to provide pensions for the soldiers who were disabled in the Revolutionary War (the forerunner of today's Veterans' Administration).

The First Congress created those agencies for practical reasons. Processing applications for disability benefits and administering duties on imported products would take an enormous amount of congressional time. Furthermore, use of the judicial branch for these matters would similarly overload it so that the cases and disputes normally associated with the judicial process would be left waiting. The decision-making bodies established by the Constitution were not appropriate for handling such matters, and specialized bodies were necessary to carry out congressional policy. The rationale of practicality that led the First Congress to establish those agencies is still the driving force behind new ones being created today.

Administrative agencies exist at all levels of government. Federal agencies regulate such areas as the environment, workplace safety, and civil rights, as well as distribute welfare and social security payments. States are also filled with various administrative agencies. Such state offices as the division of motor vehicles, workmen's compensation department, and the fish and game control board are examples. Local government also contains a number of administrative agencies—police and fire departments, zoning commissions, and park boards.

Virtually no business decision can be made without complying with a rule or regulation concerning the type of decision, the outcome of the decision, or the decision-making process itself. For example, personnel questions in business often involve rules and regulations of the Equal Employment Opportunities Commission (EEOC). Business decisions involving finance or capital accumulation may bring into play rules and regulations of the Securities and Exchange Commission (SEC). The workplace and its design often involve the Environmental Protection Agency (EPA) or the Occupational Safety and Health Administration (OSHA). Selling and marketing the product that has been produced may involve the Federal Trade Commission (FTC) (see Figure 7.1) or the Federal Reserve Board. State or local regulation may also affect these business decisions. Administrative regulation of business is a pervasive force in the legal system and in the business world. Some writers call agencies the fourth branch of government, even though they are not mentioned in the Constitution.

Agencies: Created by the Legislature

Administrative agencies are creations of the legislature. Their lives are begun through the enactment of a statute, called an **enabling act,** which briefly outlines the desired policy goals. Often, however, the specific implementation provisions for those goals are not included in the statute. Instead, the agency is charged with the responsibility of carrying out the intention of the legislature within its rather broadly defined goals. Note that the legislature need not create a new agency to administer the areas it chooses to regulate. Frequently, an existing agency is given the authority.

Two of the most important features of an administrative agency are its expertise

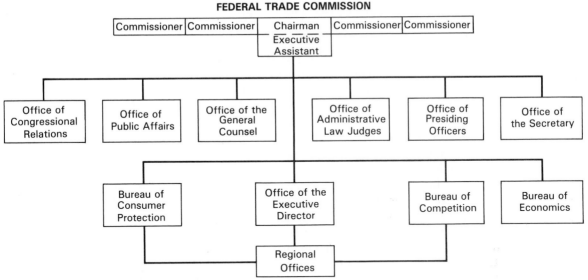

FIGURE 7.1 *Source:* Office of the Federal Register, *The United States Government Manual, 1983/84* (Washington, D.C.: U.S. Government Printing Office, 1983), p. 838.

and its ability to constantly monitor and review regulatory programs. Agencies are staffed with experts in the area over which the agency has jurisdiction. They can provide the technical skill needed to properly carry out the legislative policies that led to the agency's creation.

General Functions of an Agency. The doctrine of separation of powers places the legislative power, the judicial power, and the executive power in separate branches. This doctrine was an important element in the Constitution's plan to minimize the risk of too much power being concentrated in one governmental body. However, administrative agencies are deliberately created with all these powers concentrated in one agency.

The agency is able to legislate; that is, to make rules and draft regulations that serve as statutory guidelines for the type of conduct necessary to follow the regulatory scheme. Agencies may also exert the power of the executive; that is, an agency may investigate whether the rules it enacted have been properly followed by businesses and individuals. Some agencies are empowered to assess fines against those who violate their rules as well as to file complaints in court against them. Finally, an administrative agency is able to perform the same tasks as the judiciary; that is, to decide cases in the area of its expertise and, like the courts, to make law by virtue of its decisions in those cases.

The National Labor Relations Board (**NLRB**), for example, is very active in its role as an agency that adjudicates. Its decisions are published in bound volumes, much the same as court decisions, and the NLRB uses its past decisions as precedent in current cases. Most interestingly, the NLRB rarely makes rules or drafts regulations in its capacity as an agency. Instead, it relies on its case decisions to make the law and create rules of conduct in interpreting congressional policy under the National Labor Relations Act (NLRA) governing labor-management relations in the private sector.

Criticism of Administrative Agencies. The increased influence of administrative agencies and the effect of their regulations on business have caused a dissatisfaction with them. Certain agency decisions restrict formerly allowable business activity. For example, the EPA has set emission standards for certain types of pollutants created by factories. Companies constrained by this standard must modify their production practices. Laws that compel certain activities seem antithetical to our system, and those encumbered by them can be expected to harbor distaste for the body that applies them.

In addition, administrative agencies are insulated from voter control. Although the heads of agencies are often political appointees, the general functionaries often remain in their jobs regardless of a change in political climate. In the federal government, those jobs are protected by the civil service system. Thus, voters have no input into the activities of administrative agencies, another source of dissatisfaction.

Karl Llewellyn, a renowned American legal scholar, once wrote: "A man's rights must be accessible, but to be right rights, they must call also for some share on his part in initiating or working out their procurement, their fulfillment. Else law remains remote, the government becomes an enemy or a dairy cow, and the morale of official, citizen, and group alike bogs in morass, and pressure-groups become a by-word."[1]

Writers frequently describe a typical evolution of an agency. At the outset, the agency, usually with public and political support, will work with enthusiasm and flexibility in carrying out the goals set in its enabling act. After a few years of operation, complaints begin to arise that the agency has lost its sense of purpose and that complacency has set in. Public and political support wanes, perhaps because early agency successes have solved the most pressing problems, perhaps because more urgent problems gain public attention. In its third stage, the agency falls into a routine, and the focus of its attention is making sure others abide by the norms of the bureaucracy rather than initiating innovative approaches to the problems that may still exist. There is no final stage in the life of a typical administrative agency. The legislature rarely phases one out of existence.

Thus, as administrative agencies become more important in the legal environment, concern over their role seems to increase. Politicians, quick to detect these feelings, frequently campaign for office against the bureaucracy. Ronald Reagan has made reducing the burdens of government on business a major theme of his administration.

Checks on Agency Power. Checks do exist in the law on the activities of administrative agencies. The agencies are not simply loose guns going off in whatever direction they see fit. Courts exercise review over the decisions of agencies. The legislature also has tools available to check the agency. Since the legislature created the agency, the legislature can abolish or change the agency in virtually any way it sees fit. Furthermore, since the legislature controls the funding of the various agencies, subtle pressures may be exerted on the agencies by legislators during the time that funding decisions are being made for the next fiscal year.

Congress has enacted general statutes that affect the processes and procedures of administrative agencies. The Administrative Procedure Act sets forth standards and procedures an agency must follow in its rule-making and adjudication functions. These standards are due process protections for those who may be affected by agency activity. Hearing procedures must contain the general processes similarly available to parties in a judicial hearing. The procedural requirements for rule making require public notice of the proposed rule making and the opportunity for interested or affected parties to comment. In short, the Administrative Procedure Act legislatively commands the federal agencies to follow minimum standards of procedural fairness.

Sunset legislation exists that requires that an agency cease to exist after a set period of years, unless the legislature re-creates it. In effect, this control plan envisions legislative study of the work of the agency to determine if a further extension of its existence is warranted.

However, legislative oversight of agency activities primarily occurs indirectly. Use of the budgetary process to forbid the expenditure of funds for certain programs or to designate that funds be used in a certain way can channel agency activity. Furthermore, agency commissioners generally owe their appointments (and reappointments) to Congress. Unless the president makes those decisions a major part of his policies, that leverage remains with Congress. Finally, hearings and investigations of agency activities are used by legislators to influence agency activities and to thwart unwanted agency policy initiatives. Thus, agencies generally consult with Congress informally before undertaking policy initiatives.

FUNCTIONS OF ADMINISTRATIVE AGENCIES

Inspection and Data Gathering. An administrative agency could not function without the ability to gather and analyze information. Information is vital to the agency in its tasks of rule making and adjudication. One of the reasons that agencies are created is to have experts available to study and respond to a problem that the legislature seeks to regulate. Without the ability to acquire information, agencies would be unable to fulfill their assigned tasks.

Function of the Executive

Most of the information received by agencies is voluntarily transmitted to them. Private parties respond to requests by the agency to produce documents and other data. Some agencies also inspect public records and reports in order to gather the information needed for their work.

However, agencies are not dependent upon the voluntary cooperation of individuals and business for their information. Agencies generally have the power to legally require the necessary cooperation. In fact, the first administrative agencies created by Congress in 1789 had the power to require that records and reports be kept. The record-keeping power is necessary so that an agency can monitor a business in order to effectively regulate pursuant to commands from the legislature. Business managers often complain about this function of administrative regulation. Record keeping and reporting are both costly and time consuming, especially when a business is required to do so by several agencies. Some critics question whether the need for this information outweighs the burden placed on businesses.

Administrative agencies can also subpoena witnesses and documents. This power is important in any hearing process that may be undertaken by an agency, either as a means of gathering information as a part of the rule-making process, or as a part of a hearing before an administrative law judge or hearing examiner.

The third information-gathering power of an agency is the power to investigate by inspection of the business's books and records or to visit the premises of parties subject to the agency's regulation. Inspection is a very important tool for enforcement of administrative rules and regulations. For example, local health and safety regulation for housing would be difficult to enforce without the agency's having the ability to inspect premises where such regulations may be violated. Spot inspections by OSHA investigators of various workplaces determine if any workplace safety rules have been violated. Although inspections are an important form of law enforcement, they need to be balanced against the general rights provided to the people by the Constitution.

Marshall v. Barlow's, Inc.
United States Supreme Court
436 U.S. 30 (1978)

Petitioner, Barlow's, Inc., brought this action to obtain an injunction against a warrantless search of his business premises in accordance with the Occupational Safety and Health Act of 1970 (OSHA), which allows agents of the secretary of labor to search the work area of any employment facility under OSHA's jurisdiction for safety hazards and violations of OSHA regulations. The three-judge district court ruled in petitioner's favor, holding that a warrantless search violated the Fourth Amendment. The United States Supreme Court affirmed.

Justice White

The Warrant Clause of the Fourth Amendment protects commercial buildings as well as private homes. To hold otherwise would belie the origin of that Amendment, and the American colonial experience. An important forerunner of the first 10 Amendments to the United States Constitution, the Virginia Bill of Rights, specifically opposed general warrants, whereby an officer or messenger may be commanded to search suspected places without evidence of a fact committed. The general warrant was a recurring point of contention in the Colonies immediately preceding the Revolution. The particular offensiveness it engendered was acutely felt by the merchants and businessmen whose premises and products were inspected for compliance with the several parliamentary revenue measures that most irritated the colonists.

Against this background, it is untenable that the ban on warrantless searches was not intended to shield places of business as well as of residence.

The businessman, like the occupant of a residence, has a constitutional right to go about his business free from unreasonable official entries upon his private right placed in jeopardy if the decision to enter and inspect for violation of regulatory laws can be made and enforced by the inspector in the field without official authority evidenced by a warrant.

Certain industries have such a history of government oversight that no reasonable expectation of privacy could exist for a proprietor over the stock of such an enterprise. Liquor and firearms are industries of this type; when an entrepreneur embarks upon such a business, he has voluntarily chosen to subject himself to a full arsenal of governmental regulation.

The element that distinguishes these enterprises from ordinary businesses is a long tradition of close government supervision, of which any person who chooses to enter such a business must already be aware. The clear import of our cases is that the closely regulated industry is the exception.

We are unconvinced, however, that requiring warrants to inspect will impose serious burdens on the inspection system or the courts will prevent inspections necessary to enforce the statute, or will make them less effective. In the first place, the great majority of businessmen can be expected in normal course to consent to inspection without warrant; the Secretary has not brought to this Court's attention any widespread pattern of refusal.

Whether the Secretary proceeds to secure a warrant or other process, with or without prior notice, his entitlement to inspect will not depend on his demonstrating probable cause to believe that conditions in violation of OSHA exist on the premises. Probable cause in the criminal law sense is not required. For purposes of an administrative search such as this, probable cause justifying the issuance of a warrant may be based not only on specific evidence of an existing violation but also on a showing that reasonable legislative or administrative standards for conducting an inspection are satisfied with respect to a particular establishment.

Nor do we agree that the incremental protections afforded the employer's privacy by a warrant are so marginal that they fail to justify the administrative burdens that may be entailed.

The authority to make warrantless searches devolves almost unbridled discretion upon executive and administrative officers, particularly those in the field, as to when to search and whom to search. A warrant, by contrast, would provide assurances from a neutral officer that the inspection is reasonable under the Constitution, is authorized by statute, and is pursuant to an administrative plan containing specific neutral criteria. Also, a warrant would then and there advise the owner of the scope and objects of the search, beyond which limits the inspector is not expected to proceed. These are important functions for a warrant to perform, functions which underlie the Court's prior decisions that the Warrant Clause applies to inspections for compliance with regulatory statutes. We conclude that the concerns expressed by the Secretary do not suffice to justify warrantless inspections under OSHA or vitiate the general constitutional requirements that for a search to be reasonable a warrant must be obtained.

Giving Advice. One of the most common activities of an administrative agency is giving advice to individuals and businesses who have questions concerning their duties under the law. Inquirers are often seeking information concerning how to comply with the various rules and rulings of the agency. As a practical matter, in the vast majority of the cases, the information received from the agency is reliable. The individual or business can follow that advice with the virtual assurance of compliance with the rules of the agency.

However, the agency is not bound to follow the advice given by one of its employees. Of course, when that happens the result may be devastating to the person who has relied on that advice. Yet there is an important reason in the public interest why an agency may not be considered legally bound by advice given by an employee. If such advice could bind the agency, there would be a danger that the agency could begin to assume powers that the legislature did not wish it to have solely because of its inability to disavow any acts by its employees. In a sense, this doctrine, although sometimes unfair to the inquiring individual who erroneously relies on agency advice, is a protective device to control the powers and activities of an administrative agency. The following case is an example.

Federal Crop Insurance Corp. v. Merrill
United States Supreme Court
332 U.S. 380 (1947)

The Federal Crop Insurance Corporation is a government-owned corporation created for the purpose of insuring wheat producers against crop losses due to unavoidable causes, including drought. The corporation promulgated and published in the *Federal Register* regulations specifying the conditions on which it would insure wheat crops, including a provision making "spring wheat which has been reseeded on winter wheat acreage" ineligible for insurance. The corporation accepted an application for insurance from a wheat grower, who, without knowledge of the provision, informed the local Federal Crop Insurance Corporation agent that most of the wheat to be insured was being reseeded on winter wheat acreage. Later, most of the wheat on the reseeded acreage was destroyed by drought. The corporation, after discovering that the destroyed acreage had been reseeded, refused to pay the loss, and this litigation was begun in one of the lower courts of Idaho. The supreme court of Idaho affirmed the judgment of the lower court, in effect adopting the theory of the trial judge: Since the knowledge of the agent of a private insurance company, under the circumstances of this case, would be attributed to, and thereby bind, a private insurance company, the corporation is equally bound. The United States Supreme Court reversed.

Justice Frankfurter

We assume that recovery could be had against a private insurance company. But the Corporation is not a private insurance company. It is too late in the day to urge that the Government is just another private litigant, for purposes of charging it with liability, whenever it takes over a business theretofore conducted by private enterprise or engages in competition with private ventures. Government is not partly public or partly private, depending upon the governmental pedigree of the type of a particular activity or the manner in which the Government conducts it. The Government may carry on its operations through conventional executive agencies or through corporate forms especially created for defined ends. Whatever the form in which the Government functions, anyone entering into an arrangement with the government takes the risk of having accurately ascertained that he who purports to act for the Government stays within the bounds of his authority. The scope of this authority may be explicitly defined by Congress or be limited by delegated legislation, properly exercised through the rule-making power. And this is so even though, as here, the agent himself may have been unaware of the limitations upon his authority.

Congress has legislated in this instance, as in modern regulatory enactments it so often does, by conferring the rule-making power upon the agency created for carrying out its policy. Just as everyone is charged with knowledge of the United States Statutes at Large, Congress has provided that the appearance of rules and regulations in the Federal Register gives legal notice of their contents.

Accordingly, the Wheat Crop Insurance Regulations were binding on all who sought to come within the Federal Crop Insurance Act, regardless of actual knowledge of what is in the Regulations or of the hardship resulting from innocent ignorance. The oft-quoted observation in that "Men must turn square corners when they deal with the Government," does not reflect a callous outlook. It merely expresses the duty of all courts to observe the conditions defined by Congress for charging the public treasury. The "terms and conditions" defined by the Corporation, under authority of Congress, for creating liability on the part of the Government preclude recovery for the loss of the reseeded wheat no matter with what good reason the respondents thought they had obtained insurance from the Government. Indeed, not only do the Wheat Regulations limit the liability of the Government as if they had been enacted by Congress directly, but they were in fact incorporated by reference in the application, as specifically required by the Regulations.

Function of the Judiciary

An administrative agency not only investigates rule violations, but also hears complaints brought concerning those violations either by the agency or by private parties. **Agency adjudication** of a dispute is very similar to the adjudicative function of a court. Witnesses are heard, evidence is submitted, the law and policy are applied to the facts at hand and a decision is reached. The materials on judicial decision making would be applicable also to decision making by an administrative law judge or hearing examiner.

Basic adjudication practices and procedures followed by federal administrative agencies are contained in the Administrative Procedure Act. The act codifies traditional court practices as a means of providing fair procedures in administrative hearings. For example, the act provides that notice or appraisal of an agency complaint be provided to the affected party or parties. These parties are given the opportunity to respond to the complaint and to have counsel available to assist them at the hearing. The conduct of a hearing is similar to a court proceeding. Witnesses are called and examined. The opposing party has the opportunity to confront and cross examine the witnesses as well as provide evidence. The proceeding is conducted by a hearing examiner who performs much the same function as a judge in a courtroom hearing.

In addition to procedures provided to parties by the Administrative Procedure Act, various administrative agencies have adopted rules of practice for the hearings that they hold. This is similar to the judicial practice in which various jurisdictions create rules governing cases to be heard. Administrative agency rules of practice are published in the *Federal Register*, which is the official public notice organ of the federal administrative agencies.

Comparison: Court and Agency Hearings. A few general observations may be made in comparing the administrative agency adjudication process and a trial before a court. Both are usually open to the public and conducted formally, although agency hearings are often not as formal as those in a court. The hearing process, from its initiation to its rendered decision, is also similar. Initiation of the proceeding by a complaint, response by answer, prehearing discovery, and pretrial conferences are common to both forums. Additionally, evidence is presented in a question-answer format with the opportunity for the parties to call witnesses and cross-examine the opposing party's witnesses.

An agency hearing is presided over by a hearing examiner who performs functions similar to those of a judge. The hearing examiner conducts the hearing and rules on motions raised by the parties. The examiner also renders a decision based on the evidence presented. Usually this decision is written and accompanied by findings of fact.

However, some major differences exist between hearings conducted by the judicial system and by administrative agencies. Agency hearings are never heard by a jury. The decisions are made solely by a hearing examiner. As a result, the evidentiary rules designed to insulate juries from unreliable evidence are not applied with the same degree of strictness in an administrative hearing. Furthermore, since some agencies use the adjudicative process more as a rule-making than a dispute-settling mechanism, they are more willing to accept general evidence about the problem surrounding the hearing than information solely relating to the parties to the action. The National Labor Relations Board (NLRB) is an example of such an agency.

Decisions by administrative agencies under their adjudication function have precedential effect, much like judicial decisions. These decisions are often published and made available as are judicial decisions. These decisions are often cited as authority by the agency (and by courts) to justify a decision in a similar case.

Doctrines of Judicial Review of Agency Adjudications. Courts will exercise review of agency adjudicative decisions on four levels. In general, courts will review them for questions of law and constitutional procedure. A court will determine whether the agency (1) had exceeded its authority as provided in its enabling statute or (2) had properly interpreted and applied the law in the case. Courts will also (3) review the hearing conducted by the agency to determine whether it was fair; that is, whether it was in keeping with constitutional due process requirements. Courts will also (4) review whether the agency has acted reasonably and not arbitrarily in its decision making.

This type of review is generally not a trial de novo. It is more of an appellate review of the agency decision. Courts will usually not substitute their own view of the facts for that of the agency. Instead the facts will be reviewed to determine if the agency decision was rationally based upon the evidence presented at the hearing.

The following cases are examples of judicial review of the adjudicatory function of administrative agencies.

Federal Trade Commission v. Colgate-Palmolive, Co.
United States Supreme Court
380 U.S. 374 (1964)

The Federal Trade Commission charged Colgate-Palmolive with deceptive advertising under Section 5 of the Federal Trade Commission Act. Commercials purported to give viewers visual proof that Colgate-Palmolive's shaving cream could soften sandpaper. Unknown to viewers, the "sandpaper" test was actually done with simulated sandpaper made of plexiglass to which sand had been applied. This became "moisturized" by the shaving cream differently from actual sandpaper. The prop was shaved of sand immediately after the application of Rapid-Shave shaving cream. Actual sandpaper would require an approximately eighty-minute soaking before it could be shaved. The commission ordered respondent to cease and desist. On appeal, the court of appeals reversed, holding that the order could be broadly interpreted to forbid the use of all undisclosed simulations. This appeal to the United States Supreme Court followed.

Chief Justice Warren

In reviewing the substantive issues in the case, it is well to remember the respective roles of the Commission and the courts in the administration of the Federal Trade Commission Act. When the Commission was created by Congress in 1914, it was directed by Section 5 to prevent "[u]nfair methods of competition in commerce." Congress amended the Act in 1938 to extend the Commission's jurisdiction to include "unfair or deceptive acts or practices in commerce"—a significant amendment showing Congress' concern for consumers as well as for competitors. It is important to note the generality of these standards of illegality; the proscriptions in Section 5 are flexible, "to be defined with particularly by the myriad of cases from the field of business."

This statutory scheme necessarily gives the Commission an influential role in interpreting Section 5 and in applying it to the facts of particular cases arising out of unprecedented situations. Moreover, as an administrative agency which deals continually with cases in the area, the Commission is often in a better position than are courts to determine when a practice is "deceptive" within the meaning of the Act. This Court has frequently stated that the Commission's judgment is to be given great weight by reviewing courts. This admonition is especially true with respect to allegedly deceptive advertising since the finding of a Section 5 violation in this field rests so heavily on inference and pragmatic judgment. Nevertheless, while informed judicial determination is dependent upon enlightenment gained from administrative experience, in the last analysis the words

"deceptive practices" set forth a legal standard and they must get their final meaning from judicial construction.

We agree with the Commission, therefore, that the undisclosed use of plexiglass in the present commercials was a material deceptive practice. We find unpersuasive respondents' objections to this conclusion. Respondents claim that it will be impractical to inform the viewing public that it is not seeing an actual test, experiment or demonstration, but we think it inconceivable that the ingenious advertising world will be unable, if it so desires, to conform to the Commission's insistence that the public be not misinformed. If, however, it becomes impossible or impractical to show simulated demonstrations on television in a truthful manner, this indicates that television is not a medium that lends itself to this type of commercial, not that the commercial must survive at all costs.

We turn our attention to the order issued by the Commission. It had been repeatedly held that the Commission has wide discretion in determining the type of order that is necessary to cope with the unfair practices found, and that Congress has placed the primary responsibility for fashioning orders upon the Commission. For these reasons the courts should not "lightly modify" the Commission's orders. However, this Court has also warned that an order's prohibitions "should be clear and precise in order that they may be understood by those against whom they are directed," and that "[t]he severity of possible penalties prescribed for violations of orders which have become final underlines the necessity for fashioning orders which are, at the outset, sufficiently clear and precise to avoid raising serious questions as to their meaning and application."

The Court of Appeals has criticized the reference in the Commission's order to "test, experiment or demonstration" as not capable of practical interpretation.

The crucial term of the present order—test, experiment or demonstration represented as actual proof of a claim—are as specific as the circumstances will permit. If respondents in their subsequent commercials attempt to come as close to the line of misrepresentation as the Commission's order permits, they may without specifically intending to do so cross into the area proscribed by this order. However, it does not seem unfair to require that one who deliberately goes perilously close to an area of proscribed conduct shall take the risk that he may cross the line. In commercials where the emphasis is on the seller's word, and

not on the viewer's own perception, the respondents need not fear that an undisclosed use of props is prohibited by the present order. On the other hand, when the commercial not only makes a claim, but also invites the viewer to rely on his own perception for demonstrative proof of the claim, the respondents will be aware that the use of undisclosed props in strategic places might be a material deception. We believe that respondents will have no difficulty applying the Commission's order to the vast majority of their contemplated future commercials. If, however, a situation arises in which respondents are sincerely unable to determine whether a proposed course of action would violate the present order, they can, by complying with the Commission's rules, oblige the Commission to give them definitive advice as to whether their proposed action, if pursued, would constitute compliance with the order.

Citizens to Preserve Overton Park v. Volpe
United States Supreme Court
401 U.S. 402 (1971)

Overton Park is a 342-acre city park located near the center of Memphis. The park contains a zoo, a nine-hole municipal golf course, an outdoor theater, nature trails, a bridle path, an art academy, picnic areas, and 170 acres of forest. The proposed highway, which is to be a six-lane, high-speed expressway, will sever the zoo from the rest of the park. Although the roadway will be depressed below ground level except where it crosses a small creek, twenty-six acres of the park will be destroyed. The highway is to be a segment of Interstate Highway I-40, part of the National System of Interstate and Defense Highways. I-40 will provide Memphis with a major east-west expressway that will allow easier access to downtown Memphis from the residential areas on the eastern edge of the city.

Justice Marshall

Section 4(f) of the Department of Transportation Act and section 138 of the Federal-Aid Highway Act are clear and specific directives. Both the Department of Transportation Act and the Federal-

Aid to Highway Act provide that the Secretary shall not approve any program or project that requires the use of any public parkland unless (1) there is no feasible and prudent alternative to the use of such land, and (2) such program includes all possible planning to minimize harm to such park. This language is a plain and explicit bar to the use of federal funds for construction of highways through parks—only the most unusual situations are exempted.

In most cases considerations of cost, directness of route, and community disruption will indicate that parkland should be used for highway construction whenever possible. Although it may be necessary to transfer funds from one jurisdiction to another, there will always be a smaller outlay required from the public purse when parkland is used since the public already owns the land and there will be no need to pay for right-of-way. And since people do not live or work in parks, if a highway is built on parkland no one will have to leave his home or give up his business. Such factors are common to substantially all highway construction. Thus, if Congress intended these factors to be on an equal footing with preservation of parkland there would have been no need for the statutes.

Congress clearly did not intend that cost and disruption of the community were to be ignored by the Secretary. But the very existence of the statutes indicates that protection of parkland was to be given paramount importance. The few green havens that are public parks were not to be lost unless there were truly unusual factors present in a particular case or the cost of community disruption resulting from alternative routes reached extraordinary magnitudes. If the statutes are to have any meaning, the Secretary cannot approve the destruction of parkland unless he finds that alternative routes present unique problems.

But the existence of judicial review is only the start: the standard for review must also be determined. For that we must look at section 706 of the Administrative Procedure Act which provides that a reviewing court shall hold unlawful and set aside agency action, findings, and conclusions found not to meet six separate standards. In all cases agency action must be set aside if the action was arbitrary, capricious, an abuse of discretion, or otherwise not in accordance with law or if the action failed to meet statutory, procedural,

or constitutional requirements. In certain narrow, specifically limited situations, the agency action is to be set aside if the action was not supported by substantial evidence. And in other equally narrow circumstances the reviewing court is to engage in a de novo review of the action and set it aside if it was unwarranted by the facts.

The court is first required to decide whether the Secretary acted within the scope of his authority. This determination naturally begins with a delineation of the scope of the Secretary's authority and discretion. As has been shown, Congress has specified only a small range of choices that the Secretary can make. Also involved in this initial inquiry is a determination of whether on the facts the Secretary's decision can reasonably be said to be within that range. The reviewing court must consider whether the Secretary properly construed his authority to approve the use of parkland as limited to situations where there are no feasible alternative routes or where feasible alternative routes involve uniquely difficult problems. And the reviewing court must be able to find that the Secretary could have reasonably believed that in this case there are no feasible alternatives or that alternatives do involve unique problems.

Scrutiny of the facts does not end, however, with the determination that the Secretary has acted within the scope of his statutory authority. Section 706(2)(A) requires a finding that the actual choice made was not arbitrary, capricious, an abuse of discretion, or otherwise not in accordance with law. To make this finding the court must consider whether the decision was based on a consideration of the relevant factors and whether there has been a clear error of judgment. Although this inquiry into the facts is to be searching and careful, the ultimate standard of review is a narrow one. The court is not empowered to substitute its judgment for that of the agency.

The final inquiry is whether the Secretary's action followed the necessary procedural requirements. Here the only procedural error alleged is the failure of the Secretary to make formal findings and state his reason for allowing the highway to be built through the park.

The administrative record is not before us.

The lower courts based their review on the litigation affidavits that were presented. And they clearly do not constitute the "whole record" compiled by the agency: the basis for review required by section 706 of the Administrative Procedure Act.

Thus, it is necessary to remand this case to the District Court for review of the Secretary's decision. That review is to be based on the full administrative record that was before the Secretary at the time he made his decision.

Function of the Legislature

A third function of an administrative agency is promulgating rules and regulations, much as a legislature enacts a statute. These rules are agency statements of policy or interpretation that will be applied in the future. Administrative rules and regulations have the same force and effect as a statute enacted by a legislature. Agencies work together with the legislature in carrying out the representatives' desires for regulating a certain area.

An administrative agency's **rule-making** process resembles that of a legislature. Its rules and regulations set forth guidelines to govern the conduct of those individuals and businesses that are subject to its jurisdiction. Since the commands of the legislature in the agency's enabling act are rather general in nature, the rules and regulations crafted by the administrative agency will often be of greater practical importance to individuals and businesses than the actual legislation. Frequently, the administrative agency will make rulings interpreting the statute, giving guidance to those who must abide by its terms. In some commercial law areas, the agency may draft a business form that, if used, will virtually insure compliance with the regulatory requirements.

The Administrative Procedure Act provides basic practices to be followed by a federal agency involved in formal rule making. These practices, like those pertaining to administrative agency judicial functions, are guidelines to insure fairness in the agency activity. In general, three steps are required. First, the administrative agency must give notice to the public of its proposed rule-making activity. This notice is made through publication in the *Federal Register*. Thereafter, interested persons are given the opportunity to participate in the process. Such participation may be limited to filing written comments, arguments, or facts with the agency. Additionally, the agency may provide for oral testimony by having formal presentations made at a rule-making hearing. However, the agency is not limited in the construction of the rule to information presented during the public participation phase of the procedure. The purpose of the participation procedures is to give interested parties some voice in the rule-making process. Finally, once the rule has been promulgated, it must be made public, through publication in the *Federal Register,* at least thirty days before it becomes effective. This gives those who are affected by the rule the opportunity to learn of it and conform to its provisions.

Administrative rules, like statutes, are uniform in treatment. However, this uniformity exists at the cost of a loss of flexibility on the part of the agency. Case-by-case adjudication of issues over which the agency has jurisdiction does grant the individual more tailored justice. A uniform rule does not necessarily do this. Rather than deciding each case on its merits, the existence of rules and regulations allows disposal of the cases and problems based on pre-existing rules. The efficiency that rules bring also helps the agency plan its work. People who are required to conform to the commands of the agency are better able to do so if there is an existing body of rules to follow. However, in practice some of the rules are so complex that many individuals and businesses have great difficulty in understanding what their conduct requirements are. As a result, new rules and official explanations of the rules are given by the agency, increasing the amount of material that must be digested by those who are subject to the regulations.

The advantages and disadvantages of administrative agency rule making raise questions that have already been considered in studying the American legal environment. These questions revolve around the struggle in the law between certainty and stability on the one hand and fairness and flexibility on the other.

Did the Agency Have the Authority to Make the Rule? Although an agency action need not pass muster with the other branches of government before it is effective, there are standards of review that the courts apply to agency rules and regulations that serve to keep the agency rule-making process in line. First, an agency rule may be reviewed to determine whether it was within the power of the agency to enact. Agencies are creatures of their enabling acts, limited in scope and power by the act's terms. For example, the EPA, which was created to respond to pollution problems, would not have the ability to promulgate rules concerning discrimination in employment. Discrimination may be an important issue deserving legal control, but the powers of the EPA do not include the power to act on employment discrimination matters. This limitation on agency power is called an **ultra vires** limitation, which means that no act outside the power granted to the agency may be performed.

Forging Industry Association v. Secretary of Labor
United States Court of Appeals, Fourth Circuit
748 F.2d 210 (1984)

An occupational noise exposure standard has existed since OSHA's inception in 1971. The current standard was promulgated for the purpose of protecting employees from workplace exposure to damaging levels of noise. The standard establishes a permissible workplace limit of 90 decibels (db) calculated using an eight-hour time-weighted average. If the 90 db exposure limit is exceeded, the employer must reduce noise to or below this level by using feasible engineering or administrative controls. If such controls are infeasible, employers may use hearing protectors, such as ear muffs or plugs, to reduce employee noise exposure to permissible limits. The standard also contained a generally phrased requirement that employers administer a continuing effective hearing conservation program in workplaces where sound levels exceeded the permissible exposure level.

When studies revealed that many employees suffered significant hearing impairment at noise levels below the 90 db threshold, OSHA began the process of collecting and evaluating the information necessary to issue a comprehensive new regulation with a reduced permissible exposure level of 85 db. As an interim measure, OSHA adopted a hearing conservation amendment to replace the general conservation program requirement.

Despite its interim nature, the requirements of the amendment are substantial. The amendment requires employers to determine which employees are exposed to or above an "action level" of 85 db measured as an eight-hour time-weighted average. Such employees must be notified of the amount of sound they are exposed to and provided with an audiometric test to determine their hearing level.

Chapman, Circuit Judge

An initial inquiry that must be made in determining the validity of any regulation adopted by a federal agency is whether the regulation is within the scope of the agency's statutory authority. Examining the language of the Occupational Safety and Health Act and the Supreme Court decisions interpreting it, we find it clear that Congress only authorized the Secretary to adopt those standards which relate to health and safety at the workplace.

A standard is invalid if it requires an employer to take actions in regard to hazards existing outside the workplace. It is clear from the language of the hearing conservation amendment, that employers may be subjected to requirements and penalties may be imposed as a result of non-workplace hazards. The amendment's requirements are triggered whenever an employee suffers a standard threshold shift loss in hearing. It is obvious that such a hearing loss can result from non-occupational noise exposure just as easily as it can from occupational exposure. Airplanes, hunting rifles, loud music and a myriad of other sources produce noise potentially as damaging as any at the workplace.

Yet the Amendment makes no distinction between hearing loss caused by workplace sources and loss caused by non-workplace sources. The rule-making record clearly provides that once a hearing loss is found, the amendment requires the same actions by the employer whether or not the loss is work-related, and that the subject rule contains no requirement that there be a determination of work relatedness.

Thus the hearing conservation amendment clearly imposes responsibilities on employers based on non-work-related hazards. Under the amendment, an employer whose workers are unaffected by workplace noise may be subject to numerous requirements simply because its workers choose to hunt, listen to loud music or ride motorcycles during their non-working hours. Hearing loss caused by such activities is regretable but it is not a problem that Congress delegated to OSHA to remedy. The amendment is therefore vacated and remanded to OSHA for the creation of a valid standard.

Was the Rule-Making Procedure Fair? A second type of judicial review over agency rule making is review of the agency rule-making procedures to determine if the agency followed the proper course outlined in its enabling act, the Administrative Procedure Act, or other relevant statutes. If the agency failed to follow the required procedures, then its regulations may be attacked through judicial review.

Is the Rule Reasonably and Not Arbitrarily Made? Courts will also review the regulation itself. However, they will not simply impose their judgment for that of the agency. Relevant judicial opinions often state that, although the court disagrees with the wisdom of a certain rule, it will not substitute its own judgment concerning the rule for the expertise of the agency. (In understanding this limitation on the scope of judicial review, refer to Chapter 4 on judicial reasoning.) However, in practice, predicting when the court will defer to the agency's expertise and when it will attack a regulation is problematic. Nonetheless, deferring to agency expertise is the most frequent action.

Administrative regulations that are found to be unreasonable or arbitrary will be stricken. The court will review the agency rule-making record to determine whether there is a rational relationship between the rule and the enabling act passed by the legislature, or with the information used by the agency to study the problem before drafting the rule. The following cases illustrate the reasonable-and-not-arbitrarily-made review standard being applied.

Federal Security Administration v. Quaker Oats Co.
United States Supreme Court
318 U.S. 218 (1943)

The federal security administrator promulgated regulations under the Federal Food, Drug, and Cosmetic Act establishing standards of identity for certain milled wheat products. Under the new regulations, the respondent's product could not be marketed as "farina" because it contained vitamin D, which was permitted only in "enriched farina." On the other hand, the product could not be marketed as "enriched farina" because it did not contain the minimum quantities of vitamin B_1, riboflavin, nicotinic acid, and iron required by the regulations. The respondent, Quaker Oats Co., argued that the regulations are not valid as applied to it.

Chief Justice Stone

In recent years millers of wheat have placed on the market flours and farinas which have been enriched by the addition of various vitamins and minerals. The composition of these enriched products varies widely. There was testimony of weight before the Administrator, principally by expert nutritionists, that such products, because of the variety and combination of added ingredients, are widely variable in nutritional value; and that consumers generally lack knowledge of the relative value of such ingredients and combinations of them.

These witnesses also testified, as did representatives of consumer organizations which had made special studies of the problems of food standardization, that the number, variety and varying combinations of the added ingredients tend to confuse the large number of consumers who desire to purchase vitamin-enriched wheat food products but who lack the knowledge essential to discriminating purchase of them; that because of this lack of knowledge and discrimination they are subject to exploitation by the sale of foods described as "enriched" wheat products which would ensure fairly complete satisfaction of dietary needs, and a somewhat lesser number recommended the disallowance, as optional ingredients in the standards for unenriched wheat products, of individual vitamins and minerals whose addition would suggest to consumers an adequacy for dietary needs not in fact supplied.

The court below characterized this evidence

as speculative and conjectural, and held that because there was no evidence that respondent's product had in fact confused or misled anyone, the Administrator's finding as to consumer confusion was without substantial support in the evidence.

None of the testimony which we have detailed can be said to be speculative or conjectural unless it be the conclusion of numerous witnesses, adopted by the Administrator, that the labeling and marketing of vitamin-enriched foods, not conforming to any standards of identity, tend to confuse and mislead consumers. The exercise of the administrative rule-making power necessarily looks to the future. The statute requires the Administrator to adopt standards of identity which in his judgment will promote honesty and fair dealing in the interest of consumers. Acting within his statutory authority he is required to establish standards which will guard against the probable future effects of present trends.

We cannot say that the Administrator made an unreasonable choice of standards when he adopted one which defined the familiar "farina" of commerce without permitting addition of vitamin enrichment, and at the same time prescribed for "enriched farina" the restoration of those vitamins which had been removed from the whole wheat by milling, and allowed the optional addition of vitamin D, commonly found in milk but not present in wheat. Consumers who buy farina will have no reason to believe that it is enriched. Those who buy enriched farina are assured of receiving a wheat product containing those vitamins naturally present in wheat, and, if so stated on the label, an additional vitamin D, not found in wheat.

We conclude that the Administrator did not depart from statutory requirements in choosing these standards of identity for the purpose of promoting fair dealing in the interest of consumers, that the standards which he selected are adapted to that end, and that they are adequately supported by findings and evidence.

Home Box Office, Inc. v. Federal Communications Commission
United States Court of Appeals, District of Columbia Circuit
567 F.2d 9 (1977)

Fifteen consolidated cases challenged four orders of the Federal Communications Commission that regulate and limit the programing that can be offered by cablecasters and subscription broadcast television stations to the public for a fee set on a per-program or per-channel basis. The four 1975 orders prohibited pay exhibitions of (1) feature films between three and ten years old; (2) specific sports events shown on broadcast television within the previous five years; (3) more than the minimum number of regular-season sports events that had not been broadcast in any of the five preceding years, and in some cases only half that number; and (4) all series programs. The FCC also prohibited commercial advertising with pay programing and limited the overall number of hours of pay operation that could be devoted to sports and feature films to ninety percent of total pay operations.

The FCC's stated purpose for these orders was to prevent competitive bidding away (also known as "siphoning") of popular program material from the free television service to a service for which the audience would have to pay a fee to see the same material.

Per Curiam

We have recently had occasion to review at length our obligation to set aside agency action which is arbitrary, capricious, an abuse of discretion, or otherwise not in accordance with law. It is axiomatic that we may not substitute our judgment for that of the agency. Yet our review must be searching and careful, and we must ensure both that the Commission has adequately considered all relevant factors, and that it has demonstrated a rational connection between the facts found and the choice made.

Equally important, an agency must comply with the procedures set out in Section 4 of the Administrative Procedure Act. The APA sets out three procedural requirements: notice of the proposed rulemaking, an opportunity for interested persons to comment, and a concise general statement of the basis and purpose of the rule ultimately adopted. As interpreted by recent decisions of this court, these procedural requirements are intended to assist judicial review as well as to provide fair treatment for persons affected by a rule.

At the outset, we must consider whether the Commission has made out a case for undertaking rulemaking at all since a regulation perfectly reasonable and appropriate in the face of a given problem may be highly capricious if that problem does not exist. Here the Commission has framed the problem it is addressing as: ". . . how cable-casting can best be regulated to provide a beneficial supplement to over-the-air broadcasting without at the same time undermining the continued operation of that 'free' television service." To state the problem this way, however, is to gloss over the fact that the Commission has in no way justified its position that cable television must be a supplement to, rather than an equal of, broadcast television. Such an artificial narrowing of the scope of the regulatory problem is itself arbitrary and capricious and is ground for reversal. Moreover, by narrowing its discussion in this way the Commission has failed to crystallize what is in fact harmful about "siphoning."

Setting aside the question whether siphoning is harmful to the public interest, we must next ask whether the record shows that siphoning will occur. The Commission assures us that siphoning is real, not imagined. We find little comfort in this assurance, however, because the Commission has not directed our attention to any comments in a voluminous record which would support its statement. As to the potential financial power of cable television we are left to draw the inference from two facts—that championship boxing matches often appear only on closed-circuit television in theaters and that Evil Knievel chose to televise his jet-cycled dive into the Snake River in the same fashion—and a series of mathematical demonstrations. While the former may be directly relevant to siphoning of what the Commission has characterized as "specific" sports events, it is not at all clear the light they shed on the question of who is going to pay how much to see feature films and nonspecific sports events on pay cable.

We find the Commission's argument that "siphoning" could lead to loss of programming for those too poor to purchase cable television plausible. Here again, however, we find that the Commission has not documented its case that the poor would be deprived of adequate television service and, worse, that the Commission, by prohibiting advertising in connection with subscription operations, has virtually ensured that the price of pay cable will never be within reach of the poor. There is little disagreement at the theoretical level about the mechanism through which the poor would be deprived of broadcast service in markets served by cable television. Cable operators, to be able to sell a show, would require exclusive exhibition rights in the markets they served, with the result that events purchased by cable operators for subscription presentation would be unavailable to broadcasters, or would be available only after a delay. What follows from this scenario, even assuming that cable operators would have the financial strength to outbid broadcasters, is by no means clear. There is uncontradicted evidence in the record, for example, that the popularity of film material does not decline with an increase in the interval between first theater exhibition and first television broadcast. At least as to movies, therefore, "siphoning" may not harm the poor very much.

Equally important, the pay cable rules taken as a whole scarcely demonstrate a consistent solicitude for the poor. Thus, although "free" home viewing relies upon advertise-supported programming, the Commission has in this proceeding barred cable firms from offering advertising in connection with subscription operations. As a result, the Commission forecloses the possibility that some combination of user fees and advertising might make subscription cable television available to the poor, giving them access to the diverse programming cable may potentially bring. The advertising ban section of the regulations was developed to meet wholly different regulatory problems and it has been retained here, not because of its intrinsic merit, but only because no one objected too much. We are thus left with the conclusion that, if the Commission is serious about helping the poor, its regulations are arbitrary; but if it is serious about its rules, it cannot really be relying on harm to the poor. Whatever may be the ultimate validity of this argument, its principal defect in this review is that there is no record evidence to support it.

Rescission of Agency Rule. A similar standard of review is used by the court when an agency wants to rescind a certain regulation. Not all regulations are disliked by those affected. The automobile industry may dislike regulations requiring airbags on cars and welcome agency action that rescinds the rule. However, insurance companies and consumer groups may argue that the regulation is a good idea, since it was made to encourage safety in auto design. Remember, even though a deregulation climate may exist, all regulations benefit some group. No administrative agency creates rules and regulations that bedevil everyone. One can expect that if an agency moves to rescind a particular rule, groups that have benefited from it or that agree with it will seek judicial review.

This is not to suggest that all regulations that are enacted by administrative agencies become permanent legal fixtures. Regulations can certainly be amended or abolished. However, in doing so the agency may not abuse its discretion or act arbitrarily. The following case is an example of an arbitrary change of an existing agency rule. Note how the court reviewed this rescinding action.

State Farm Mutual Automobile Insurance Company v. Department of Transportation
United States Court of Appeals, District of Columbia Circuit
608 F.2d 206 (1982)

Mivka, Circuit Judge

Petitioners in this action seek review of a final order by the National Highway Traffic Safety Administration (NHTSA) rescinding the automatic crash protection requirements of Federal Motor Vehicle Safety Standard 208 ten months before the standard's effective date. The standard would have required that large and mid-size automobiles manufactured after September 1, 1982, and all automobiles manufactured after September 1, 1983, carry passive restraints such as airbags or "passive" seatbelts. Airbags are cushions stored under the dashboard that, when triggered by a frontal collision, fill with stored or rapidly generated gas to protect the rider from collision with the car's interior. Passive seatbelts, also called "automatic" seatbelts, move into place automatically when a passenger enters a vehicle and closes the door. Petitioners challenge NHTSA's rescission of the standard as arbitrary, capricious, an abuse of discretion, and a violation of law as defined by the Administrative Procedure Act.

We agree. This case is complicated because it has far-reaching implications and involves a politically controversial safety standard, but the determining principle is simple. An administrative agency, possessing power delegated by the legislative branch of government, must comply with the legislative requirement that its decisions be reasoned and in accordance with the purposes for which power has been delegated. NHTSA's rescission of the safety standard presents a paradigm of arbitrary and capricious agency action because NHTSA drew conclusions that are unsupported by evidence in the record and then artificially narrowed the range of alternatives available to it under its legislative mandate. NHTSA thus failed to demonstrate the reasoned decisionmaking that is the essence of lawful administrative action.

In February 1981, approximately one month after taking office, Secretary of Transportation Andrew Lewis reopened rulemaking. He based his decision at least in part on "the fact that economic circumstances have changed since the standard was adopted in 1977: and the "difficulties of the automobile industry," citing high unemployment, sales "at a very depressed level," and losses "by even the largest of the domestic manufacturers." Two months later, the agency ordered a one-year delay in the application of the standard to large cars, extending the deadline to September 1982. This notice also observed that the "economic situation of the industry and consumers and the economy as a whole have drastically changed since the standard was adopted in 1977." On the same day, NHTSA proposed the possible rescission of the entire standard. Both decisions were announced by the White House Press Office on April 6, 1981, as part of economic recovery measures. After receiving written comments and hold-

ing public hearings, NHTSA issued a final rule (Notice 25) that rescinded the passive restraint requirement, and amended Standard 208.

Even when there is no claim that the agency has exceeded its jurisdiction, as there is not in this case, sudden and profound alterations in an agency's policy constitute "danger signals" that the will of Congress is being ignored.

Our review of the legislative history of the 1974 Amendments to the Safety Act and the subsequent congressional reaction to Modified Standard 208 suggests that the standard has come as close as an agency-made regulation can come to being affirmatively endorsed by Congress, without Congress actually having done so. Although Congress has always considered the standard politically controversial, the regulation has received sufficient congressional approval to raise doubts that NHTSA's rescission necessarily demonstrates an effort to fulfill its statutory mandate.

Reading the legislative history as a whole suggests a congressional commitment to the concept of automatic crash protection devices for vehicle occupants that we may not take lightly.

Based on the legislative reaction to the passive restraint standard discussed above, we conclude that rescission of the standard must be subject to "thorough probing, in-depth review" lest the congressional will be ignored.

Although there may be situations in which an agency may repeal a regulation on no basis at all, such is not the case here. NHTSA has the burden of explaining why it has changed course, and of showing that rescission of Modified Standard 208 was reasonable.

This does not mean that NHTSA may not revoke the standard. If the agency clearly articulates a reasonable basis for that action, we must defer to the policy judgments and expertise of the agency.

The rescission of Modified Standard 208 on the grounds stated by NHTSA was arbitrary and illogical for two general reasons. The agency has offered no evidence that seatbelt usage will fail to increase as was expected when the standard was first promulgated, and has therefore made no showing that the standard is unjustified as written.

More important, NHTSA has failed to consider and analyze obvious alternatives to rescission, and has thus artificially foreclosed attempts to further the purpose of the Safety Act. When the agency so narrows its options that it fails to heed the goals that Congress has asked it to meet, the agency violates its basic legislative mandate. Simply put, NHTSA's discussion was wholly inadequate, and rescission was therefore arbitrary and unlawful.

On balance, it is difficult to find anything positive to say about NHTSA's decisionmaking in this case. Based on the record and the statements in Notice 25, we must conclude that NHTSA has acted capriciously, wearing blinders that prevented it from reasoned evaluation of methods to fulfill the purposes of the Safety Act. The rescission of Modified Standard 208 is reversed.

SUMMARY

The administrative agency plays an important role in the American legal environment. It is a governmental body that has a profound effect on the law and day-to-day business conduct.

Problems needing expertise and efficiency that fall outside the institutional limits of other branches of government led to the creation of administrative agencies. Within the limits specified by their enabling acts, they were deliberately granted all the powers that the Constitution had carefully divided among the three branches of government. The agency may make rules and regulations, that is, act like a legislature. The agency may also hold hearings to determine whether its rules have been violated or to resolve disputes concerning them. This function is like that generally associated with the judiciary. Finally, the agency is empowered to enforce the rules and laws in the area of its jurisdiction, in effect, to act like the executive branch of government.

However, administrative agency activities are not without limitation or review. The legislature, which created the agency, has powerful tools available to control agency activity. Courts also play a major role in reviewing the work of administrative agencies. Agency hearing decisions and regulations must comply with its enabling act, statutes concerning administrative procedures, and fundamental notions of due process. Although administrative agencies are powerful governmental bodies, their activities may be restrained by other branches of government.

REVIEW QUESTIONS

1. Define the following words and terms:
   a. Agency rule making
   b. Agency adjudication
   c. Ultra vires
   d. Enabling act

2. What are the reasons that a legislature creates an administrative agency?

3. What are the ways in which agency activity may be reviewed by the courts?

4. The Securities and Exchange Commission (SEC) is a federal administrative agency created and authorized by Congress to regulate securities (e.g., stocks, bonds) and securities markets. In July, the SEC filed suit claiming that XYZ, Inc., had discriminated against its female employees by not paying them at the same rate as male employees holding comparable jobs. The SEC based its suit on a regulation it recently made forbidding discrimination in employment. What argument may be raised by XYZ in response to that suit?

5. Assume the SEC rule in question four was drafted without any public opportunity for comment and was promulgated without providing any notice. Furthermore, the rule was never published before it was applied to the XYZ matter. What additional arguments can XYZ make based upon these facts?

6. An administrative agency properly promulgated the following regulation: "All applications for variances and exceptions to the rules of this agency must be filed by March 15 of the year for which such variance or exception is sought." On March 10, Mary Smith called the local office of the agency and asked an employee when an application for a variance must be filed. Smith was told that all applications must be on file no later than April 4 to qualify for a variance that year. If Mary Smith files her variance on April 3, will she be able to rely on the information given to her by the agency employee if the agency cites the regulation as grounds for denying her variance application?

7. What are the three main functions of an administrative agency? Discuss each function.

8. What are the advantages and disadvantages of the functions in question seven being concentrated in one governmental body?

9. Jones owns a small manufacturing business. The by-products of the manufacturing process include some toxic chemicals. The Environmental Protection Agency (EPA) regulates the disposal of those chemicals. One afternoon an investigator from the EPA appears at the factory to inspect its chemical disposal process. No one from the EPA had received a court warrant to search the business. Must Jones permit the investigator to inspect the factory? Give reasons.

10. A new administration takes office in the federal government. One of the major issues on which it was elected was to eliminate government red tape and regulation. On the day after the inauguration, three federal agencies act to rescind over one hundred regulations. No studies were done by the agencies before taking this action, nor was there any evidence that the regulations were not working. They were rescinded in order to satisfy the election's antiregulation mandate. Discuss how a court might review this rescinding action.

11. The Federal Trade Commission (FTC) promolgated a regulation that prohibited the use of sugar in breakfast cereals. The stated purpose for the regulation was to protect children from health problems that can be caused by too much sugar consumption. However, studies presented to the agency showed that presweetened cereals were eaten primarily by adults. Children usually added their own sugar to unsweetened breakfast products. Furthermore, the FTC had no information that sugar consumption was harmful (except statements by commission members complaining about tooth decay that their children experienced). Discuss how a court might review this regulation.

12. In numerous agency adjudications and other actions, the SEC has interpreted the Securities Exchange Act of 1934 to prohibit trading securities based on information that is not public. Is a court bound to follow that agency interpretation?

13. Compare and contrast hearings before an agency and hearings before a court.

NOTE

[1] Karl N. Llewellyn, *Jurisprudence: Realism in Theory and Practice* (University of Chicago Press, 1962), p. 211.

PART III

The Legal Foundations of American Business: Common Law and Its Development

CHAPTER 8

Contracts

Meaning of the Word _Contract_
Sources of the Rules of Contracts
Historical Look at Contract Law Development
Contract Requirements
Changes in the Marketplace
Refusal to Enforce a Contract
Enforcing a Contract When None Exists

The American law, while at one time largely judge-made law, is increasingly becoming codified—that is, the rules appear in statutes. Even so, many rules still are determined by examining cases. This is especially true of the law of contracts. Though statutes have been passed, particularly in the area of consumer protection, that alter traditional contract rules, most of the law of contracts may still be found in cases.

This chapter first discusses what a contract is and covers some of the forces that created contract law as we now know it. The law of contracts evolved over many years, and the body of contract law is a reflection of the political and social forces of the past. Social forces continue today to affect the law of contracts.

The chapter then briefly presents the requirements that must be fulfilled to create a contract. Following this discussion, the text turns to some areas that represent modern departures from traditional contracts law. Most of those changes have taken place in the context of consumer contracts, so the latter portion of the chapter pertains mostly to transactions between consumers and businesses.

Today, in some cases, the courts will refuse to enforce contracts even though all the requirements for a contract are present. In other cases, even though the contractual requirements have not been met, the courts will impose contractual liabilities on the parties. The last section of the chapter discusses cases of this kind.

MEANING OF THE WORD *CONTRACT*

Each day people throughout the United States enter into contracts. Quite often, the persons involved fail to recognize a contract ever came into existence. The average person probably enters into hundreds of contracts a year without realizing it. Buying clothing, purchasing groceries, and subscribing to a magazine are just a few examples of the many contracts we all enter into every year.

A person not trained in the law often assumes that a contract must be drawn up in a formal written document drafted by an attorney. In fact, contracts may result, without either party's signing a formal written agreement, from the exchange of letters between persons, from conversations, or even from the actions of persons who have neither written nor said anything.

Suppose that today you decide to purchase a candy bar. You go to a vending machine on campus, deposit some change, and out comes your selection. Even though you never signed anything or spoke to anyone, your actions created a contract between the seller and yourself. If the machine fails to give you a candy bar after you deposited your money, the contract created by the deposit of money has been breached.

To understand how these actions created a contract, we first need to know what a contract is.

| What Is a Contract? | **Definition.** One source of law in the contract field is the *Restatement of Contracts Second*. The *Restatement of Contracts* is *not* the law in any state. It is an effort of legal scholars, sponsored by the American Law Institute, to analyze the existing judicial decisions and to distill therefrom some sound principles of contract law. The *Restatement* has often been relied on by the courts as a guide in resolving cases involving contracts. |

The drafters of the *Restatement of Contracts* suggest the following definition of a contract: "A contract is a promise or set of promises for breach of which the law gives a remedy, or the performance of which the law in some way recognizes as a duty." The next question, then, is what is a promise? A **promise** is a voluntary commitment by a person to another person to perform in some manner or refrain from some action in the future.

Consider the following example: A agrees to sell his home to B for fifty thousand dollars. B agrees to pay A fifty thousand dollars for the home. All the other major terms are agreed upon, and this agreement is put in a writing signed by both parties. In this example A and B both made a promise. A promised to sell his home to B at a specific price. B promised to purchase the home from A for a specified price. If B tenders the fifty thousand dollars to A for the home, but A refuses to deliver the home to B, B is entitled to a remedy. One remedy of several that B may request a court to grant him is a decree of specific performance; that is, B may ask the court to order A to deliver the home to him. By the same token, the law recognizes A's obligation to deliver the home to B as a duty in light of A's promise. Thus, by making a promise to B to sell the home for fifty thousand dollars, A incurs a duty or obligation to perform by delivering the home to B if B accepts A's offer. If A fails to comply voluntarily with his duty or obligation under this contract, the court will provide a remedy to B to compensate B for A's failure to perform in accordance with his obligation under the contract.

SOURCES OF THE RULES OF CONTRACTS

As noted earlier in this book, several groups possess the power to make law: the legislatures, Congress, the courts, the president, the governors, and administrative agencies. Contract law, unlike other areas of law, primarily is found in legal cases. For this reason, we refer to it as coming from the common law, that is, the rules of contract commonly are found in earlier cases. To some extent, this generalization is no longer valid, as the state legislatures and Congress have passed statutes creating special rules applicable to certain types of contracts. In some cases, state legislatures have passed statutes to restrict the use of certain clauses in all contracts. In other cases, legislatures have chosen to regulate the contracts of an entire industry. The law of insurance, for example, is heavily regulated in most states. On the federal level, a number of statutes have been passed in the consumer protection area. Nonetheless, the basic principles of contract law are still found by examining cases.

The Common Law

The Uniform Commercial Code in General. The Uniform Commercial Code (UCC) covers many areas of commercial law. Before the twentieth century, the law came primarily from cases, and the laws dealing with commercial transactions varied greatly from state to state. In order to simplify the law, model statutes (codes) were drafted covering several areas of commercial law. These codes were enacted by the legislatures in a number of states. Based on the experience gained in these early attempts at simplifying the law, the National Conference of Commissioners on Uniform State Laws and the American Law Institute set about drafting new codes that would eliminate some of the problems associated with the earlier codes.

The Uniform Commercial Code

This effort culminated in what we now call the Uniform Commercial Code. This model code, consisting of ten articles, deals with the sale of goods, commercial paper, secured transactions, and other commercial activities.

Though the UCC is merely a model code, all the states have enacted it (except Louisiana, which adopted parts of it, but not Article Two, dealing with the sale of goods). States have generally followed the language that appears in the model version. Some states have altered the language of the model code in certain places. We will confine our discussion of the UCC to that part of it dealing with the sale of goods.

Article Two of the UCC. One very important area of contract law—the law covering the sale of goods—is now located in a code. Unlike the law of contracts covering items other than the sale of goods, in which the primary source of law is cases, the law dealing with the sale of goods is embodied in Article Two of the UCC. It is still necessary, of course, for the courts to decide cases to elaborate the meaning of the UCC, but the code itself is the primary source of law. Judges and attorneys turn first to the UCC to resolve legal disputes dealing with contracts for the sale of goods.

Section 2-105(1) of the UCC defines goods as all things that are movable at the time of identification to the contract for sale. A contract for the sale of a house is *not* a contract for the sale of goods because the house is permanently attached to ground. It is not movable. Contracts for the sale of services, such as the services of a house painter or a typist in a business office, are not goods either. Such services are covered by the common law of contracts and not by the UCC. On the other hand, an automobile qualifies as a good, and the sale of an automobile is covered by the UCC.

The law of contracts basically comes, therefore, from prior court cases in the area of real estate contracts, employment contracts, service contracts, and other non-sale-of-goods transactions. When goods are involved in a contract, the principles in the UCC control.

Contract As Defined by the UCC. The Uniform Commercial Code actually gives a broader definition to the term *contract* than a mere group of promises that the law will enforce, or the performance of which is recognized as a duty. The UCC does not use the term *promise* but refers to an *agreement* between the parties. An agreement is defined in Section 1-201(3) of the UCC as "the bargain of the parties in fact as found in their language or by implication from other circumstances including course of dealing or usage of trade or course of performance." This definition recognizes that not only words but also acts, prior understandings between the parties, customs in the industry, and the manner in which the parties perform the contract are all relevant in determining what the bargain between the parties is.

It should be noted that while the UCC creates certain special rules dealing with contracts for the sale of goods, in many places the UCC is silent as to the rule of law that should be applied. In this situation, the common law of contracts governs. In certain situations, special statutes passed by the states also have a bearing on sales contracts.

The law of contracts pertaining to the sale of goods is therefore to a great extent found in two places: case law and Article Two of the Uniform Commercial Code.

Before examining the basic requirements of a contract, the next section of the text discusses the forces that contributed to the evolution of contract law. The principles of the law of contracts as we know them today developed to a great extent in the nineteenth century, and the rules are a product of the economic, social, and political thought of that era.

In examining the basic requirements of a contract, bear in mind the forces that produced these rules. The law of contracts is still evolving. Forces at work in society today are contributing to a change in the attitude of the courts and legislatures as to the nature and enforceability of contracts.

After presenting the basic contract requirements, the text discusses some of the factors that have caused, and will continue to cause, changes in the law of contracts. Although the basic principles still apply in most transactions, in certain situations new rules have developed. The text examines some of these changes.

Many of the changes discussed in the latter part of this chapter have taken place in the law relating to consumer transactions—contracts between businesses and consumers—as opposed to the law relating to contracts between businesses. Contracts between businesses generally are negotiated between knowledgeable, sophisticated parties who understand the basic contract rules. Quite frequently the businesses are represented by attorneys who put great thought into drafting the provisions of the contract. In most cases, the businesses possess equal bargaining power. The courts and legislatures have not treated contracts entered into between consumers and businesses like pure business contracts. This is the area of contract law that has changed the most in the last hundred years. It has changed to a great extent because of the many consumer protection statutes passed by Congress and the state legislatures since 1960. The courts also have adopted different rules for these transactions in some situations.

Because this area of the law has changed, it presents special pitfalls to the uninformed. For this reason the text examines the area of consumer contract developments in greater depth than business contracts.

HISTORICAL LOOK AT CONTRACT LAW DEVELOPMENT

If the courts failed to enforce contractual promises, the system of business would collapse. Buyers and sellers count on the delivery of goods and services from the other party to a contract. Because the courts enforce contractual promises, businesses are assured of the delivery of goods and services.

Enforcement of Promises

Yet this was not always the case in contract law. In the very early development of the law of contracts in England, the courts recognized liability only for a faulty performance of a promise, and declined to penalize a failure or refusal to perform a promise. By the sixteenth century, the courts had begun to enforce promises made by parties to a contract.

Later, such writers as Adam Smith (1723–1790) and John Stuart Mill (1806–1873) pleaded for the courts to enforce contractual promises. They believed once a buyer and seller signed a contract, each person needed to be able to count on the other person's promise to deliver or accept these goods and services in the future.

Today the courts recognize a contract as a promise or set of promises that the parties to the contract must perform. A failure to perform gives the injured party a remedy. The courts, for example, may force persons to pay damages if they voluntarily undertake an obligation but without excuse fail to perform. This helps strengthen the stability and reliability of the business system, which relies heavily on contracts.

Complete Freedom? There really never has been *complete* freedom of contract. No court has ever been willing to enforce a contract that contemplated a crime. Today, we refer to such contracts as *illegal*.

Freedom of Contract

Suppose a criminal entered into a contract to kill someone for five thousand dollars. If he or she committed the act called for by the contract, could the murderer go to court to force the other party to live up to the promise to pay five thousand dollars? No. If a court were to enforce such a contract, it would encourage unacceptable behavior in society. This is true today and has always been true.

Even so, the nineteenth century certainly represents the zenith of the freedom-of-contract doctrine.

Philosophical Thought. John Stuart Mill, a major writer of the nineteenth century, advocated the freedom of the individual to guide his own destiny unimpeded by government. Only through individual freedom, he believed, could the greatest human development occur. Mill believed in the school of *laissez-faire* economics. To Mill and his followers, laissez-faire economics permitted the full development of the individual and permitted production and trade to follow their natural courses unimpeded by government. Followers of this theory believed that the government should interfere with free trade only to the minimum extent necessary to preserve order.

Advocates of laissez-faire economic theory, who believed that a contract represented the free choice of individuals, influenced the nature of contract law. This stress on individualism and free choice was manifested in the widespread belief that freedom to contract was essential to the development of the economic system. They encouraged government, by and large, to let the economy operate free of governmental intrusion.

Contract Law in the United States. In the early years of our country's history, the person who actually made the goods also sold them, dealing directly with the customer. If a buyer wished to purchase new horseshoes, he rode down to the local farrier, who forged the shoes and shod the horse. If the customer found the services to be unsatisfactory, he returned to the farrier and voiced a complaint directly to the owner. Because towns were quite small, word of unsatisfactory service spread quickly. A local merchant certainly could not afford to do unsatisfactory work.

The doctrine *caveat emptor*—let the buyer beware—was generally followed at this time in America. The courts expected buyers who dealt directly with the owner-manufacturer to look out for themselves. The courts rarely helped a person out of a bad bargain.

In considering the doctrine of *caveat emptor*, keep several things in mind: the average person purchased very few items; the items purchased were very simple, easily understood products; quite often the items were purchased directly from the maker; and in a small town, the reputation of the seller was extremely important to his or her ability to sell things in the future.

Following the Civil War, technological change slowed down, but the growth of large industrial enterprises flourished. The age of the "robber barons" began. Men such as John D. Rockefeller (Standard Oil), Andrew Carnegie (Carnegie Steel Company, later United States Steel), and Cornelius Vanderbilt (New York Central Railroad) became fabulously wealthy by building massive companies. Various protest movements took root in response to this concentration of economic power. Doubt began to arise among many persons in the country about the wisdom of freedom of contract.

Legislators pushed through legislation dealing with needed reforms in the workplace, but the judges were reluctant to change with the times. In the late nineteenth century, Congress and the state legislatures tried to adopt restrictions on the concept of freedom of contract, but the courts routinely struck down such statutes on a variety of grounds, one ground being the right to freely contract. The following case illustrates this view.

Lochner v. New York
United States Supreme Court
198 U.S. 45 (1905)

Lochner, owner of a bakery, was convicted of violating a New York labor law because he required his employees to work more than ten hours a day and more than sixty hours in one week. His appeals in state court were all denied, so he appealed to the Supreme Court, which reversed the lower court decision.

Justice Peckham

The New York statute necessarily interferes with the right of contract between the employer and employees, concerning the number of hours in which the latter may labor in the bakery of the employer. The general right to make a contract in relation to his business is part of the liberty of the individual protected by the Fourteenth Amendment of the Federal Constitution. Under that provision no State can deprive any person of life, liberty or property without due process of law. The right to purchase or to sell labor is part of the liberty protected by this amendment, unless there are circumstances which exclude the right. There are, however, certain powers, existing in the sovereignty of each State of the Union, somewhat vaguely termed police powers, the exact description and limitation of which have not been attempted by the courts. Those powers, broadly stated, relate to the safety, health, morals and general welfare of the public. Both property and liberty are held on such reasonable conditions as may be imposed by the governing power of the State in the exercise in those powers, and with such conditions the Fourteenth Amendment was not designed to interfere.

The question whether this act is valid as a labor law, pure and simple, may be dismissed in a few words. There is no reasonable ground for interfering with the liberty of person or the right of free contract, by determining the hours of labor, in the occupation of a baker. There is no contention that bakers as a class are not equal in intelligence and capacity to men in other trades or manual occupations, or that they are not able to assert their rights and care for themselves without the protecting arm of the State, interfering with their independence of judgment and of action. Viewed in the light of a purely labor law, with no reference whatever to the question of health, we think that a law like the one before us involves neither the safety, the morals nor the welfare of the public, and that the interest of the public is not in the slightest degree affected by such an act. The law must be upheld, if at all, as a law pertaining to the health of the individual engaged in the occupation of a baker. The limitation of the hours of labor does not come within the police power on that ground.

We think the limit of the police power has been reached and passed in this case. There is, in our judgment, no reasonable foundation for holding this to be necessary or appropriate as a health law to safeguard the public health or the health of the individuals who are following the trade of a baker.

The act is not, within any fair meaning of the term, a health law, but is an illegal interference with the rights of individuals, both employers and employees, to make contracts regarding labor upon such terms as they may think best, or which they may agree upon with the other parties to such contracts. Statutes of the nature of that under review, limiting the hours in which grown and intelligent men may labor to earn their living, are mere meddlesome interferences with the rights of the individual.

The Twentieth Century. What the courts were overlooking was the *inequality of bargaining power* between the parties. They wrote about freedom of contract between two knowledgeable, intelligent, and equally positioned persons. But large companies, perhaps the only company in town, frequently drafted one-sided contracts that required persons to work long hours in unsafe working conditions for unreasonably low wages. Workers accepted the terms offered by the industrialists. But the resulting contracts were hardly freely and voluntarily negotiated agreements.

Another development influenced the ability of parties to freely contract—the increasing use of the form contract.

The courts gradually began to recognize the gross inequality of bargaining power that is present in many bargaining situations, particularly in contracts between consumers and businesses. The more powerful party, often the seller, presents the other party with a choice: Either sign the printed contract presented or go elsewhere. The agent of the seller negotiating the deal often lacks the power to alter the terms of the printed form. The seller deprives the buyer of the opportunity to read the contract. In some cases, the buyer needs additional background to understand the terms of the contract. And even if he or she does have the time and understanding, the buyer lacks the bargaining power to force the other party to alter the terms of a written contract. As a practical matter, the buyer cannot go elsewhere because other businesses use the same terms. Gradually, as the belief in unrestrained individualism and liberty declined, the legislatures, Congress, and the courts began to erode the doctrine of freedom of contract.

By the beginning of the twentieth century, the courts had become more receptive to social legislation. The courts started to sustain social legislation that restricted the number of hours women and children could work. They upheld minimum wage laws and many other restrictions on the ability of an employer to dictate the terms of employment.

With the election of Franklin D. Roosevelt as president and his implementation of the New Deal, Congress made further inroads on the right to freely contract. Congress passed legislation regulating many facets of the economy. Eventually the United States Supreme Court upheld most of this legislation.

The text next discusses what rules have generally developed in the area of contracts. After a brief examination of the basic elements of a contract, the text turns to an examination of the forces that have altered the traditional body of contract law, particularly in the area of consumer contracts. It then discusses some of these relatively new rules. Bear in mind that the basic rules discussed in the following material are more rigidly followed in contracts between businesses. Even so, businesses frequently deal with consumers. Thus managers as well as consumers must be aware of these changes in the law of contracts.

CONTRACT REQUIREMENTS

In General

In considering the following material, bear in mind that the law of contracts varies from state to state to some degree, particularly in the area of consumer contracts. The following remarks are generalizations about the state of the law across the United States.

As suggested at the beginning of the chapter, a contract essentially is an agreement that the courts will recognize and enforce. The following are the elements necessary to fulfill the legal requirements for a *valid* contract:

1. offer

2. acceptance

3. consideration

4. capacity

5. legality

Each of these requirements is discussed in turn. In addition to these, the parties must have truly assented to the agreement. This is discussed in the material that follows on genuine assent. Finally, certain types of contracts must be in writing to be enforceable.

The following material is a very general, extremely simplified overview of the basic provisions necessary to create a contract. The law of contracts is complex, but this material is presented to give you a broad overview.

Offer

An **offer** is a manifestation by the person making the offer of a desire to enter into a contract. The person making the offer is called the **offeror** and the person to whom the offer is made is referred to as the **offeree.**

Preliminary Negotiations. Some contracts are very simple, such as the purchase of candy from a vending machine. Others are more complex, like the purchase of a home. The more complex the transaction, the more likely there will be some bargaining before the making of an offer.

Suppose a major corporation wishes to dispose of some but not all of its properties located in Los Angeles. An officer of the corporation then decides to write a letter to other corporations the president feels might be interested in the properties. The president's letter merely states: "We are considering selling some of our commercial properties located in Los Angeles. Please write us if you are interested in acquiring property in the Los Angeles market." A recipient of this letter could not write back and state: "I accept your offer." The recipient cannot accept because no offer has yet been made. The parties are in the preliminary negotiations stage. The negotiations between the parties may give rise to a specific offer at a later date.

There was no offer in this example because the letter was too indefinite. The recipient of the letter would not know which properties were being offered, or the terms of the offer, or the price. Until these and perhaps some other matters are specified by the seller, no offer to sell has been made. The seller in this instance has merely invited other businesses to indicate their interest in acquiring these properties.

To constitute a valid offer, the statement in question must (1) indicate an intention to enter into a contract, (2) be certain and definite, and (3) be communicated to the offeree.

Intention to Contract. In the preceding example, no intention to contract could be implied. The corporation merely wanted to learn of the interest of other parties in purchasing Los Angeles property. In order to determine if a statement or writing indicates an intent to contract, one must look at such factors as the language of the statement or writing, the surrounding circumstances, the relationship of the parties, and the method of communication.

Certain and Definite. To constitute an offer, the statement or writing must cover enough terms so that a contract could be enforced. At the minimum, the following terms must be included in the offer for a common law contract to be certain and definite: who the offeree is, the subject matter of the contract, the price, the terms of payment, delivery, or performance.

Offers involving the *sale of goods*, which are covered under Article Two of the Uniform Commercial Code, need not be this precise. This is because many terms, such as price, time of performance, and time of delivery, will be supplied by reference to specific provisions in the UCC. These provisions enable a court to fill in the blanks in a contract. All that is necessary for a valid offer of the sale of goods is a manifestation of an intent to contract by the offeror, expressed to the offeree, which states some quantity of goods is being offered for sale. Thus, the UCC provides that the absence of some terms will not invalidate an offer.

Communicated to Offeree. An offer must also be communicated to the offeree. One cannot accept an offer one does not know about. For example, suppose Mrs. Rich offers a one-hundred-dollar reward for the return of her dog, FuFu. This is an offer made to the general public. Nancy never saw or heard about the reward. While walking down the street, she finds FuFu. Noting the address on the dog tag, she realizes the dog is lost. Nancy returns the dog to Mrs. Rich. Nancy's actions are not an acceptance of the offer because the offer was not communicated to her. Had Nancy known of the offer, her actions would have created an acceptance of the offer and created a contract.

Termination of the Offer. An offer may be terminated in a number of ways—both by the offeror and the offeree, and by operation of law. In this limited discussion, we will cover only a few of the ways in which a termination may occur.

Termination By Offeror. The person who makes an offer, the offeror, may terminate the offer by communicating the withdrawal of the offer to the offeree. In general, an offer may be terminated—*revoked*—at any time before the offer has been accepted. A revocation is therefore not effective until it is received by the offeree.

There are several exceptions to the rule that an offer may be withdrawn any time until it has been accepted. One exception is when the parties have signed an **option contract.** If the offeree gives something of value to the offeror to keep the offer open for a certain period of time, the offer may not be revoked during the time period agreed upon by the parties. The offeror and offeree here have created an option contract.

A second situation, which applies *only* to contracts for the sale of goods, is dealt with in Section 2-205 of the UCC. The UCC states that if a merchant in a signed writing agrees to hold an offer open, the offer may not be revoked during the time stated. If no time is stated, it may not be revoked for a reasonable time. A reasonable time, in this situation, may not exceed three months.

Another exception is when the party trying to enforce the bargain relies on the doctrine of promissory estoppel, which is dealt with extensively at the end of this chapter.

Termination By Offeree. An offer may be terminated by an express rejection by the offeree. Suppose Alice offers to sell her watch to Louise for fifty dollars. Louise replies, "I don't want it." This constitutes an express rejection by the offeree. Louise's actions terminate the offer. Unless Alice renews the offer to Louise, Louise no longer possesses the power to accept. Therefore, if the next day Louise says to Alice, "I will take your watch," no contract is created because Louise no longer has the power to accept the offer.

Suppose, instead of expressly rejecting the watch, Louise stated, "I will take your watch for ten dollars." Such a statement is called a *counter-offer*. A counter-offer is an attempted acceptance that varies the terms of the original offer. It operates in effect as a rejection of the original offer. The person making a counter-offer is treated as having made a new offer. An acceptance generally must be in exactly the same language as the offer. The courts refer to this as a mirror-image rule. A counter-offer terminates the power of acceptance by the offeree. After making such a statement, Louise no longer may accept the original offer unless Alice renews it.

The UCC, which controls contracts for the sale of goods, permits an acceptance that varies the terms of the offer under certain circumstances. This is covered in Section 2-207 of the UCC. Because it is a rather complex provision, we will not discuss it, merely note that the UCC permits acceptances that alter the terms of an offer under certain specified conditions.

In several situations, an offer terminates automatically, although the parties fail to take any action. One such situation is when the offer states it will terminate at a particular time. An offer that states that it must be accepted on January 1, automatically terminates at that time. Sometimes an offer does not state a definite time at which it will terminate. In that case, the offer terminates after a reasonable period of time. What constitutes a *reasonable period of time* depends on the circumstances.

Acceptance

An acceptance is a manifestation of assent to the terms of an offer in the manner required or authorized by the offer. Only the offeree, the person to whom the offer has been made, has the power of acceptance.

The person making an offer may specify the manner of acceptance. He or she may indicate a desire for acceptance in a particular manner (by mail, for example), within a specific time period (by June 1, say), and at a particular place (perhaps at his or her place of business).

If the offer does not place any restrictions on the acceptance, then any kind of acceptance that takes place within a reasonable period of time will create a contract.

However, in any nongoods transaction, acceptances must not change the terms of the offer. If they do, the acceptance is treated as a counter-offer, and will automatically terminate the offer.

An acceptance is generally not valid until it is received by the offeror. There is an important exception to this rule called the **implied agency rule** (or mailbox rule). If the offer does not state that the acceptance will not be effective until it is received, the moment an acceptance is sent by an authorized means a contract is effective. In general, the same means or a faster means of communications than that the offer was made by will be an authorized means of communication. For example, if the offer was made by mail, an acceptance by mail is effective when the letter of acceptance is deposited in the mailbox—assuming the letter is properly addressed and stamped.

If the offeree accepts by an unauthorized means, the general rule applies, and the acceptance does not take effect until the offeror receives the offer.

Consider the following case. Morris offers by mail to sell his home to Anne. The offer is clear and definite in every respect. On June 1, Anne deposits a properly stamped and addressed letter of acceptance in the mailbox. Louise, on June 1, after Anne mails her letter of acceptance, meets with Morris personally. She offers to purchase the home, and Morris accepts because he does not know of Anne's acceptance of his offer. On June 2, Morris receives Anne's letter. In this case, a contract between Morris and Anne came into existence on June 1—the date the letter of acceptance was deposited in the mail. Unfortunately for Morris, he also created a contract on June 1 with Louise. Thus, he has sold his home twice! Clearly, Morris cannot deliver the home to both women. Therefore, the person he fails to deliver the home to may sue him for breach of contract.

This example illustrates the pitfalls associated with the mailbox rule. Morris could have protected himself in this example by stating in the original offer to Anne that the acceptance would not be effective until it was received. In that case, when he sold the home to Louise, he could have called Anne on June 1 and withdrawn the offer—even after she had deposited her acceptance in the mailbox on June 1. This is true because under these circumstances, her acceptance would not be effective until it was received.

Consideration

Bargain and Exchange. The parties to a contract must have bargained with one another and exchanged something for something else. In addition to agreement on an exchange, this bargain must impose a legal detriment to one or both of the parties. A legal detriment is an obligation to do something that a person was under no prior obligation to do or to refrain from doing something the person was not previously obligated to refrain from doing.

Consider the example at the beginning of the chapter in which B agreed to purchase A's home for fifty thousand dollars. The exchange of promises by A and B will fulfill the legal requirement for consideration. A agreed to transfer the home in question to B for fifty thousand dollars. There is clearly a bargain and exchange of promises here. B suffered a legal detriment by agreeing to pay fifty thousand dollars to A, which B previously legally was not obligated to do. Likewise, A incurred a legal detriment by agreeing to part with his interest in the home.

Jennings v. Radio Station KSCS
Court of Appeals of Texas, Fort Worth
708 S.W.2d 60 (1986)

Steve Jennings, a prisoner in Texas, filed suit against Radio Station KSCS. He alleged that his only contact with the outside world was through the radio. Jennings claimed that the radio station had a policy to regularly state that they play "at least three-in-a-row, or we pay you $25,000. No bull, more music on KSCS." He contacted the station on several occasions after the station failed to play at least three consecutive songs, but the station refused to pay him $25,000. The station moved for a summary judgment. It argued there can be no enforceable contract because there was no consideration flowing to the station as offeror. The trial court granted the station's motion for summary judgment denying Jennings right of recovery. The Court of Appeals reversed.

Ashworth, Justice (Retired, Sitting by Assignment)

It is elementary contract law that a valuable and sufficient consideration for a contract may consist of either a benefit to the promisor or a loss or detriment to the promisee. Thus when a promisee acts to his detriment in reliance upon a promise, there is sufficient consideration to bind the promisor to his promise. In the instant case, appellant's petition alleged that he stopped listening to KSCS when appellee refused to pay him $25,000.00. Implicit in this statement is an allegation by appellant that he listened to KSCS *because* appellee promised to pay him $25,000.00 if he could catch the radio station playing fewer than three songs in a row. Appellant thus relied to his detriment. He could have listened to *any* station, but he listened to KSCS because of the promise. Appellee also benefitted by the promise. KSCS gained new listeners, like appellant, who listened in the hope of winning $25,000.00. We hold that appellant's petition sufficiently alleges a cause of action sounding in breach of contract to necessitate a trial on the merits.

We reverse the summary judgment and remand the cause to the trial court.

Adequacy. The items in a bargained-for exchange need not be of equal value. Courts refer to this as the *adequacy of the consideration.* If A in the earlier example agrees to take fifty thousand dollars for a home worth fifty-five thousand dollars, A cannot ask the court at a later date to "set aside" the contract because the consideration was not adequate. In general, the courts will not examine the adequacy of the consideration exchanged.

Example Where There Is No Consideration to Support Agreement. Suppose Stacy sells her home to Gertrude. After signing all the papers, Gertrude asks Stacy to give her the refrigerator and stove in the home. Stacy had planned on taking these with her and the contract specified they could be removed by Stacy. If Stacy agrees, is there any consideration to support this new agreement? No. Even if she made such an agreement, no contract would be created. Stacy did not receive anything in exchange for her promise to give the refrigerator and stove to Gertrude. Likewise, Gertrude did not give anything to Stacy in exchange for the new bargain. In light of this fact, there is no consideration to support Stacy's promise, therefore no contract was created.

In order to make a binding deal, Gertrude should have done something that she was not legally already obligated to do. For example, she could have said, "Will you sell me the stove and refrigerator for five dollars?" If Alice accepted this offer, a contract for the sale of these appliances, supported by consideration, would have been created. That the appliances were worth more than five dollars is irrelevant. The courts do not examine the adequacy of consideration exchanged.

Note that two topics related to consideration, promissory estoppel and illusory promises, are dealt with later in this chapter.

Capacity

The parties to a contract must have the capacity to contract. Some persons are legally regarded as lacking the capacity to contract. One such group of persons is the insane. A second important group is minors. The term *minor* is defined by state law. Most states consider a person a minor until he or she reaches the age of eighteen, although a few states require the person to reach twenty-one before he or she has the capacity to contract.

Insanity. People who have been declared insane in a court of law have no capacity to contract whatsoever. Contracts involving such people are *void;* that is, the agreement never has any legal effect because one of the requirements of a valid contract (capacity) is missing. Contracts involving people who are insane, but have not yet been legally declared so, are treated slightly differently. Such contracts are said to be *voidable;* that is, the agreement is said to be binding against the competent party, but may be avoided by the incompetent party.

Minors. Contracts entered into by minors also are treated as *voidable.* A minor may disaffirm (avoid) his or her contract any time up to the time he or she reaches the age of majority (the age specified by the state when a person has the capacity to contract), or a reasonable time thereafter.

Necessaries. It should be noted that contracts by minors for necessaries are generally enforceable. Necessaries are such things as food, clothing, and medical services, if they are not already being provided for the minor.

One method to protect a person dealing with a minor is for that person to require an adult, as well as the minor, to sign the contract. In the event the minor disaffirms, the adult would still be bound by the provisions of the contract.

Legality

A contract must have a lawful purpose or object to be valid. The general rule is that if the parties enter into an illegal bargain, the courts "leave the parties where they find them." That means the courts will do nothing to assist either party to an illegal agreement. There are some exceptions to this rule, but in most cases a party who enters into an illegal bargain may not petition a court for relief.

Suppose Tony entered into a gambling contract, which in his state was illegal. He paid Susan one hundred dollars to bet on a horse. He now wants to receive his hundred dollars back, claiming the contract is illegal. In general, the courts will not require Susan to return the hundred dollars because the contract is illegal. Contracts are also illegal, of course, if it is necessary to do something illegal, such as a crime, to perform the contract. Some contracts are regarded as illegal because they are contrary to public policy or unconscionable. These concepts are discussed in depth later in this chapter.

In the following case, the court discusses the question of whether a contract between a motion-picture producer and a distributor is illegal.

McConnell v. Commonwealth Pictures Corporation
Court of Appeals of New York
166 N.E.2d 494 (1960)

Plaintiff sues for an accounting. Defendant had agreed in writing that, if plaintiff should succeed in negotiating a contract with a motion-picture producer whereby defendant would get the distribution rights for certain motion pictures, defendant would pay plaintiff ten thousand dollars on execution of the contract between defendant and the producer, and would thereafter pay plaintiff a stated percentage of defendant's gross receipts from distribution of the pictures. Plaintiff negotiated the distribution rights for defendant and defendant paid plaintiff the promised ten thousand dollars but later refused to pay him the commissions or to give him an accounting of profits.

Defendant's answer contains, besides certain denials and counter-claims not now before us, two affirmative defenses. In these defenses, it is asserted that plaintiff, without the knowledge of defendant or of the producer, procured the distribution rights by bribing a representative with the ten thousand dollars that defendant paid plaintiff. The courts below held that the defenses were insufficient to defeat plaintiff's suit. Special Term's opinions said that, since the agreement sued upon—between plaintiff and defendant—was not in itself illegal, plaintiff's right to be paid for performing it could not be defeated by a showing that he had misconducted himself in carrying it out. The court found a substantial difference between this and the performance of an illegal contract. The New York Court of Appeals reversed.

Desmond, Chief Justice

New York's policy has been frequently and emphatically announced in the decisions. It is the settled law of this State (and probably of every other State) that a party to an illegal contract cannot ask a court of law to help him carry out his illegal object, nor can such a person plead or prove in any court a case in which he, as a basis for his claim, must show forth his illegal purpose. The money plaintiff sues for was the fruit of an admitted crime and no court should be required to serve as paymaster of the wages of crime. And it makes no difference that defendant has no title to the money since the court's concern is not with the position of the defendant but with the question of whether a recovery by the plaintiff should be denied for the sake of public interests, a question which is one of public policy in the administration of the law. That public policy is the one described in *Riggs v. Palmer*. No one shall be permitted to profit by his own fraud, or to take advantage of his own wrong, or to found any claim upon his own iniquity, or to acquire property by his own crime. These maxims are dictated by public policy, have their foundation in universal law administered in all civilized countries, and have nowhere been superseded by statutes.

We must either repudiate those statements of public policy or uphold these challenged defenses. Here the money sued for was (assuming the truth of the defenses) the fruit of an admitted crime. To allow this plaintiff to collect his commissions would be to let him profit by his own fraud, or to take advantage of his own wrong, or to found a claim upon his own iniquity, or to acquire property by his own crime.

We are not working here with narrow questions of technical law. We are applying fundamental concepts of morality and fair dealing not to be weakened by exceptions. On the whole case (again assuming that the defenses speak the truth) the disclosed situation would be within the rule of our precedents forbidding court assistance to bribers.

It is argued that a reversal here means that the doing of any small illegality in the performance of an otherwise lawful contract will deprive the doer of all rights, with the result that the other party will get a windfall and there will be great injustice. Our ruling does not go as far as that. It is not every minor wrongdoing in the course of contract performance that will insulate the other party from liability for work done or goods furnished. There must at least be a direct connection between the illegal transaction and the obligation sued upon. Connection is a matter of degree. Some illegalities are merely incidental to the contract sued on. We cannot now, any more than in our past decisions, announce what will be the results of all the kinds of corruption, minor and major, essential and peripheral. All we are doing here is labeling the conduct described in these defenses as gross corruption depriving plaintiff of all right of access to the courts of New York State. Consistent with public morality and settled public policy, we hold that a party will be denied recovery even on a contract valid on its face, if it appears that he has resorted to gravely immoral and illegal conduct in accomplishing its performance.

We point out that our holding is limited to cases in which the illegal performance of a contract originally valid takes the form of commercial bribery or similar conduct and in which the illegality is central to or a dominant part of the plaintiff's while course of conduct in performance of the contract.

Genuine Assent   Sometimes parties will agree to a contract, but the agreement will not be freely and voluntarily arrived at by one of the parties to the contract. An obvious example would be if a person held a gun to a man's head and asked him to sign a contract. The man's agreement would not be freely and voluntarily given, consequently the law would refuse to recognize a contract. Assent has not been freely and voluntarily given if it was the result of mistake, duress, fraud, undue influence, or misrepresentation. When any of these are present the courts may refuse to enforce an agreement.

Mistake. Sometimes a person or persons enter into a contract because of a mistake. If the mistake was material, that is, if it involved a fact that induced the party trying to avoid the contract to enter into the bargain, it may be possible to set aside the contract.

ILLEGAL CONTRACTS

H & R Block, Inc., is a corporation that franchises individuals and other concerns to operate a business solely for the preparation of income tax returns under the name of H & R Block.

Earl Lovelace, of Yates Center, Kansas, entered into such a franchise agreement with H & R Block. As part of that agreement, he agreed to not enter into competition with H & R Block for five years should he cease operating an H & R Block franchise. Several years after entering into the agreement, Lovelace terminated the agreement and opened a tax preparation business under his own name at the same location in Yates Center where he had operated under the Block name.

Block felt that it should be entitled to prevent Lovelace from engaging in the tax preparation business for five years. While agreements of this nature, which are called "restrictive covenants," are frequently enforceable, they must be reasonable in the area and the time restrained. An agreement that prevents a person from competing with H & R Block anywhere for a five-year period is an unreasonable restraint on competition and is not an enforceable agreement.

Had Block limited the restrictive covenant to cover only Yates Center for a period such as two years, the agreement would probably be enforceable. However, a restrictive covenant that prevents a person from engaging in a business for an unreasonable period of time or in an unreasonable area will not be enforceable.

The courts examine whether only one person to the contract was in error, or whether all parties to the contract were operating under a mistaken belief. A mistake is *unilateral* if only one party held a mistaken belief, whereas it is *bilateral* if all the parties were mistaken.

If the mistake is a unilateral mistake of fact, the courts generally will not grant relief to the party seeking to avoid the contract. However, the courts do try to achieve a just result, and many courts will grant relief to the mistaken party if it may be granted without causing a hardship or expense to the other party. Furthermore, if the nonmistaken party knows or should know of the mistake, the contract is voidable.

If all the parties were mistaken as to a material fact, the contract is voidable.

Duress. If a party enters a contract because of a wrongful act or threat that overcomes the person's free will, this constitutes duress. Consent to the contract in such a situation is given because the person fears the consequences associated with refusing to agree to the contract. An obvious example noted earlier is holding a gun to someone's head to force the person to consent to a contract.

Fraud. Fraud is a deliberate misrepresentation or nondisclosure of a material fact made with the intent the other party will rely upon it. A fact is material if the person trying to avoid the contract would not have entered into the contract had he or she known of the misrepresentation. If the other party does in fact rely upon such a statement, and this causes an injury, the person may bring an action to rescind (set aside) the contract. The misrepresentation must be of a present or past fact. False statements as to events in the future are not actionable.

Statements of opinion usually may not be used as the basis of a fraud or misrepresentation case. If the seller says, "These dishes are the best buy in town," such a statement is treated as a statement of opinion—not fact. However, if the person making the misrepresentation has superior knowledge, such as the statement of an expert, a person may rely on this statement of opinion.

In general, silence is not fraudulent. However, if a person chooses to speak, he or she must tell the whole truth. Deceptive partial disclosures probably will be treated as fraudulent.

Undue Influence. Undue influence is present if a person agrees to a contract because of the stronger personality or will of the other party. Undue influence differs from duress in that, in the case of duress, a person yields his or her assent because of fear, but in the case of undue influence, the person assents to the contract because he or she is unable to hold out against the will of the other party. A mentally ill person, for example, might assent to a contract because the other person pressured him.

Misrepresentation. A misrepresentation occurs when a person, by words or acts, creates in the mind of another person an impression not in accordance with the facts. If the seller of an automobile states, "The engine of this car has been rebuilt," when it had not been, and the buyer relies upon this statement in deciding to purchase the automobile, the buyer's assent was not freely and voluntarily given. The buyer may ask a court to free him or her of the contractual obligations under this automobile purchase contract.

Unlike fraud, in this cause of action it is not necessary to establish that the person making the misrepresentation did so intentionally. An unintentionally false statement will be sufficient to establish a case.

The concepts of fraud and undue influence come into play in the following case.

Vokes v. Arthur Murray, Inc.
District Court of Appeal of Florida
212 So. 2d 906 (1968)

Audrey E. Vokes filed an action to rescind (set aside) her contracts entered into with Arthur Murray, Inc., alleging fraud and undue influence on the part of agents of this business. Vokes entered into over thirty-one thousand dollars in contracts with the defendant. The trial court dismissed her complaint for failure to state a cause of action. The court of appeals disagreed, stating that Vokes had stated enough facts to merit a trial, and reversed the trial court.

Pierce, Judge

Defendant Arthur Murray, Inc., a corporation, authorizes the operation throughout the nation of dancing schools under the name of "Arthur Murray School of Dancing" through local franchised operators, one of whom was defendant J. P. Davenport whose dancing establishment was in Clearwater.

Plaintiff Mrs. Audrey E. Vokes, a widow of 51 years and without family, had a yen to be "an accomplished dancer" with the hopes of finding "new interest in life." So, on February 10, 1961, she attended a "dance party" at Davenport's "School of Dancing" where she whiled away the pleasant hours, sometimes in a private room during which her grace and poise were elaborated upon and her rosy future as "an excellent dancer" was painted for her in vivid and glowing colors. She was sold eight one-half-hour dance lessons to be utilized within one calendar month therefrom, for the sum of $14.50 cash in hand paid, obviously a baited "come-on."

Thus, she embarked upon an almost endless pursuit of the terpsichorean art during which, over a period of less than sixteen months, she was sold fourteen "dance courses" totalling in the aggregate 2,302 hours of dancing lessons for a total cash outlay of $31,090.45, all at Davenport's dance emporium. All of these fourteen courses were evidenced by execution of a written "Enrollment Agreement—Arthur Murray's School of Dancing" with the addendum in heavy black print. "No one will be informed that you are taking dancing lessons. Your relations with us are held in strict confidence," setting forth the number of "dancing lessons" and the "lessons in rhythm sessions" currently sold to her from time to time, and always of course accompanied by payment of cash of the realm.

At one point she was sold 545 additional hours of dancing lessons to be entitled to award of the "Bronze Medal" signifying that she had reached "the Bronze Standard," a supposed designation of dance achievement by students of Arthur Murray, Inc.

Later she was sold an additional 926 hours in order to gain the "Silver Medal," indicating she had reached "the Silver Standard," at a cost of $12,501.35.

At one point, while she still had to her credit about 900 unused hours of instructions, she was induced to purchase an additional 24 hours of lessons to participate in a trip to Miami at her own expense, where she would be "given the opportunity to dance with members of the Miami Studio."

She was induced at another point to purchase an additional 126 hours of lessons in order to be not only eligible for the Miami trip but also to become "a life member of the Arthur Murray Studio," carrying with it certain dubious emoluments, at a further cost of $1,752.30.

At another point, while she still had over 1,000 unused hours of instruction she was induced to buy 151 additional hours at a cost of $2,049.00 to be eligible for a "Student Trip to Trinidad," at her own expense as she later learned.

Also, when she still had 1,100 unused hours to her credit she was prevailed upon to purchase an additional 347 hours at a cost of $4,235.74, to qualify her to receive a "Gold Medal" for achievement, indicating she had advanced to "the Gold Standard."

On another occasion, while she still had over 1200 unused hours, she was induced to buy an additional 175 hours of instruction at a cost of $2,472.75 to be eligible "to take a trip to Mexico."

Finally, sandwiched in between other lesser sales promotions, she was influenced to buy an additional 481 hours of instruction at a cost of $6,523.81 in order to "be classified as a Gold Bar Member, the ultimate achievement of the dancing studio."

All the foregoing sales promotions, illustrative of the entire fourteen separate contracts, were procured by defendant Davenport and Arthur Murray, Inc., by false representations to her that she was improving in her dancing ability, that she had excellent potential, that she was responding to instructions in dancing grace, and that they were developing her into a beautiful dancer, whereas in truth and in fact she did not develop in her dancing ability, she had no "dance aptitude," and in fact had difficulty in "hearing the musical beat." The complaint alleged that such representations to her "were in fact false and known by the defendant to be false and contrary to the plaintiff's true ability, the truth of plaintiff's ability being fully known to the defendants, but withheld from the plaintiff for the sole and specific intent to deceive and defraud the plaintiff and to induce her in the purchasing of additional hours of dance lessons." It was averred that the lessons were sold to her "in total disregard to the true physical, rhythm, and mental ability of the plaintiff." In other words, while she first exulted that she was entering the "spring of her life," she finally was awakened to the fact there was "spring" neither in her life nor in her feet.

The complaint prayed that the Court decree the dance contracts to be null and void and to be cancelled, that an accounting be had, and judgment entered against the defendants "for that portion of the $31,090.45 not charged against specific hours of instruction given to the plaintiff." The Court held the complaint not to state a cause of action and dismissed it with prejudice. We disagree and reverse.

Defendants contend that contracts can only be rescinded for fraud or misrepresentation when the alleged misrepresentation is as to a material fact, rather than an opinion, prediction or expectation, and that the statements and representations set forth at length in the complaint were in the category of "trade puffing," within its legal orbit.

It is true that "generally a misrepresentation, to be actionable, must be one of fact rather than opinion." But this rule has significant qualifications, applicable here. It does not apply where there is a fiduciary relationship between the parties, or where there has been some artifice or trick employed by the representor, or where the parties do not in general deal at "arm's length" as we understand the phrase, or where the representee does not have equal opportunity to become ap-

prised of the truth or falsity of the fact represented. As stated by Judge Allen of this Court ". . . A statement of a party having . . . superior knowledge may be regarded as a statement of fact although it would be considered as opinion if the parties were dealing on equal terms."

It could be reasonably supposed here that defendants had "superior knowledge" as to whether plaintiff had "dance potential" and as to whether she was noticeably improving in the art of terpsichore. And it would be a reasonable inference from the undenied averments of the complaint that the flowery eulogiums heaped upon her by defendants as a prelude to her contracting for 1944 additional hours of instruction in order to attain the rank of the Bronze Standard, thence to the bracket of the Silver Standard, thence to the class of the Gold Bar Standard, and finally to the crowning plateau of a Life Member of the Studio, proceeded as much or more from the urge to "ring the cash register" as from any honest or realistic appraisal of her dancing prowess or a factual representation of her progress.

Even in contractual situations where a party to a transaction owes no duty to disclose facts within his knowledge or to answer inquiries respecting such facts, the law is if he undertakes to do so he must disclose the whole truth. From the face of the complaint, it should have been reasonably apparent to defendants that her vast outlay of cash for the many hundreds of additional hours of instruction was not justified by her slow and awkward progress, which she would have been made well aware of if they had spoken the "whole truth."

In *Hirschman v. Hodges* it was said that— ". . . what is plainly injurious to good faith ought to be considered as a fraud sufficient to impeach a contract," and that an improvement agreement may be avoided—". . . because of surprise, or mistake, *want of freedom, undue influence, the suggestion of falsehood, or the suppression of truth.*" (Emphasis supplied.)

We repeat that where parties are dealing on a contractual basis at arm's length with no inequities or inherently unfair practices employed, the Courts will in general "leave the parties where they find themselves." But in the case sub judice, from the allegations of the unanswered complaint, we cannot say that enough of the accompanying ingredients, as mentioned in the foregoing author-ities, were not present which otherwise would have barred the equitable arm of the Court to her. In our view, from the showing made in her complaint, plaintiff is entitled to her day in Court.

Statute of Frauds. The basic requirements of a valid contract are offer, acceptance, consideration, capacity, and legality. It is not necessary for a contract to be in writing to be valid. Many oral contracts are perfectly enforceable. In the example given earlier involving the purchase of candy from a vending machine, the contract is valid even though there is no oral or written statement.

A Writing

Certain types of contracts, however, must be in writing to be enforceable. The requirement of a writing has its origins in the British statute of frauds enacted by Parliament in 1677. The British statute was designed to prevent perjury—false testimony under oath. The British thought that certain types of contracts were likely to give rise to perjured testimony in the absence of a writing. To remedy this problem, the British Parliament required proof of certain types of contracts in writing. If the person claiming a contract could not produce a writing reflecting the agreement between the parties, the agreement would not be enforced.

Every state has passed a statute of frauds. These statutes vary from state to state, but in general they prevent the following types of contracts from being enforced in the absence of a writing:

1. contracts to be liable for another person's debts,

2. contracts involving real property, and

3. contracts that cannot be performed within one year from the date the contract was entered into by the parties.

States may require other types of contracts to be in writing, but these contracts generally must be in writing everywhere to be enforceable. Certain exceptions exist. For example, a contract that has been partially performed will take a contract out of the statute of fraud in some cases.

A contract that has been fully performed by both parties to the contract is not subject to the statute of frauds. Suppose A orally offers to sell his home to B for fifty thousand dollars, and B accepts. B pays the fifty thousand dollars and takes title to and possession of the home. Neither party may ask to get out of this contract on the basis of the statute of frauds, because both parties have fully performed.

Contracts involving the sale of goods are subject to a separate statute of frauds found in Article Two of the Uniform Commercial Code. The UCC states that contracts for the sale of goods for a price of five hundred dollars or more are not enforceable unless they are evidenced by some writing sufficient to indicate a contract of sale has been made. As with the statute of frauds that applies to common law contracts, the code statute of frauds is subject to exceptions. For example, a person who admits in court that a contract for sale was made is bound by his admission.

Parol Evidence Rule. The **parol evidence rule** states that oral testimony that adds to, alters, or varies the terms of a written agreement may not be admitted in court. In order for the parol evidence rule to apply, the writing in question must be final and complete.

Even though a writing is intended as the final and complete statement of the agreement between the parties, it is sometimes possible to introduce oral evidence relating to the contract at trial. For example, statements made *after* the contract was signed may be admitted in evidence. Likewise, evidence may be admitted that is necessary to clear up an ambiguity in a written contract.

A Type of Writing Required. A formal writing drafted by an attorney is not required. Generally all that is required is a writing that covers the basic terms of the agreement and is signed by the party against whom enforcement is sought.

Interpretation of the Contract

Once the parties have entered into a valid contract, problems still can arise over the meaning of the contract language itself. The English language, even when the words are carefully chosen by competent attorneys representing all the parties, is subject to varying interpretations. When parties differ on the meaning of contract language, they may be forced to turn to a court for a proper interpretation of the meaning of the contract language, as is illustrated by the following case.

Burroughs v. Metro-Goldwyn-Mayer, Inc.
United States District Court, Southern District New York
519 F. Supp. 388 (1981)

Edgar Rice Burroughs wrote the book *Tarzan of the Apes* in 1912. He later transferred his interest in this book to Edgar Rice Burroughs, Inc. In 1931, MGM acquired the right to use the Tarzan character and other characters appearing in Burroughs's works in an original story to be created by MGM as a screenplay for a motion picture. MGM also acquired the right to produce remakes of the first film. Any remake had to be based substantially on the first MGM film, without material changes or material departures from the original MGM story line. MGM released the first film in 1932. It issued a remake of the film in 1959. By 1980, MGM had begun work on yet another Tarzan film. The heirs of Burroughs brought suit to enjoin release of the new MGM film. They contended this new film, starring Bo Derek, was a material departure from the original film. After viewing all three films in question, the court concluded MGM had not breached the contract.

Werker, District Judge

The 1931 agreement provides as follows: . . . Metro agrees . . . that all 'remakes' of the first

photoplay produced by it hereunder, as well as all other photoplays produced by it hereunder subsequent to the making of said first photoplay, shall be based substantially upon the same story as that used by Metro in connection with said first photoplay and that in such subsequent remakes and/or additional photoplays there will be no material changes or material departures from the story used in connection with said first photoplay. . . .

After viewing the films in question, I must conclude for the reasons that follow that MGM's 1981 remake of the film "Tarzan, The Ape Man" is based substantially on the 1931 photoplay and that there are no material changes or material departures from the story used in that photoplay. My analysis will focus on the story line as well as the portrayal of the characters and their relationships.

The 1931 photoplay is based on the story of an explorer, James Parker, whose daughter Jane joins him in Africa. The movie opens with Jane's arrival and her father's decision shortly thereafter to set off on a safari in search of the fabled "elephants' graveyard" for ivory. In this film, Parker is portrayed as a strong man and Jane as his admiring daughter. There is a suggestion of sexuality in their relationship. The expedition consists of Parker, Jane, Parker's partner Harry Holt, and several natives. On the journey, the party is faced with nearly insurmountable struggles with nature. For example, Jane almost falls off a cliff in the scene of the party crossing the escarpment and Holt is nearly devoured by crocodiles as the party crosses a river on rafts. It is the scene where the party crosses the escarpment that Tarzan's cry is heard for the first time.

After the party crosses the river, Jane is terrorized by an attacking animal and Tarzan appears from the jungle to rescue her. He carries her off and at this point, Jane discovers that Tarzan is human. She gradually begins to trust him and they appear to fall in love. After a brief stay with Tarzan in which Jane seems quite content, she is found by her father and Holt. They are exceedingly distrustful of the ape-man. She rejoins the safari and the group sets out again for the elephants' graveyard. While enroute, the party falls prey to a tribe of pygmies and they are threatened with death when they are thrown into a pit with a huge gorilla. Tarzan, of course, comes to their rescue.

Holt, Parker, Jane and Tarzan then follow a wounded elephant to the elephants' graveyard where Parker dies. Jane decides to stay with Tarzan and Holt returns to civilization.

In the 1981 film, the story similarly opens with Jane's arrival at her father's camp in Africa. This time, however, Parker is a professional adventurer rather than an explorer. He is a strong man and a bit more eccentric than in the first film. Jane, though admiring, is more hostile toward her father. There again is an element of sexuality in their relationship. As in the 1931 photoplay, shortly after Jane's arrival, Parker, Holt, Jane and some natives set out on an expedition to find the elephants' graveyard. While on the journey, the group hears Tarzan's cry and in contrast to the 1931 film, this time Parker speculates that this is the famed 100 foot ape-man. Jane again is imperilled by wild animals enroute and rescued by Tarzan. Holt and Parker are highly distrustful of Tarzan as they were in the original film, but Jane again perceives that he is human. Although his initial encounter with Jane is brief, Tarzan clearly is fascinated by her. He later captures her while she is swimming in a river. She gets away from him, but is then attacked by a snake. As in the original photoplay, Tarzan comes to her rescue. It is at this point that Jane becomes enamored of Tarzan. After what seems to be a couple of days, Parker finally finds his daughter and she rejoins the safari. The group is soon attacked by an African tribe, however, and Tarzan comes to their rescue. Parker nevertheless dies at the hands of the ivory king and Jane and Tarzan leave Holt to live together in the wild.

While there are some differences between the films in the jeopardies and dramatic sequences employed, as well as in the emphasis accorded different elements of the story, they are insufficient to warrant the conclusion that this Tarzan movie is not based substantially upon the 1931 story. The use of the phrase "based substantially" contemplates some deviation from the original story. In addition, the fact that the contract prohibits only material departures and material changes demonstrates that changes and departures were in fact contemplated by the parties.

Plaintiffs argue that the changes and departures in the 1981 photoplay are material. Their principal contention is that the film is no longer suitable for young children. Considering the shift in social mores over the half century from 1931 to 1981, I simply cannot agree that a change of the nature complained of constitutes a material change from the 1931 photoplay. Indeed, the 1931 film itself contained scenes which for its time were rather suggestive.

Since the overall theme of the 1981 film, development of the plot, order of sequence and locus of the 1981 photoplay as edited conform to the 1931 photoplay, I can only conclude that the storyline in the 1981 film is based substantially on the 1931 film and does not contain material departures or changes from that photoplay.

Since I have concluded that the 1981 film as edited is based substantially on the 1931 film and does not contain material changes or material departures from the 1931 film, an injunction permanently restraining release and distribution of the film will not be issued.

Termination of Contract

By Performance. The vast bulk of contracts are terminated by the parties to the contract performing their obligations under the contract. This discharges the parties from the contract.

Discharge by Impossibility of Performance

One of the ways a contract may be terminated is if one of the parties is unable to perform the contract prior to the date set for performance. If an unforeseeable event occurs that makes it impossible for one of the parties to perform, the parties will be released from their obligations under the contract. Generally, what is required is that the promisor can not legally or physically perform the contract, such as when one of the parties becomes seriously ill and his personal performance is required. For example, if a surgeon who is scheduled to perform an operation has a heart attack, he would be excused from his obligation to operate. Courts discharge parties from a contract if a change in the law makes performance of the contract illegal. For example, if a person enters into a contract to sell alcohol, then the state legislature outlaws such sales, the courts will say performance of the contract is impossible. Finally, if the subject matter of the contract is destroyed, performance is regarded as impossible.

Remedies. In some cases, problems arise with respect to the contract. When one of the parties to a contract fails to perform properly under a contract, this is a breach of the contract. A material breach of the contract gives the nonbreaching party various rights. Most important, he or she may sue for any damages sustained as a result of the breach of contract.

While it is true that a party that is injured by a breach of contract has a right to collect damages, the injured party has a duty to limit the losses that result from the breach. The obligation to keep the losses as low as possible is known as **mitigation of damages.** Suppose that a person rents an apartment for one year. After living in the apartment only a month, the tenant moves out. While it is true the landlord is entitled to damages resulting from the wrongful breach of the contract by the tenant, the landlord nonetheless must try to rent the apartment. If the landlord succeeds in finding another tenant, the damages owed by the first tenant are reduced by whatever rent the landlord receives from the substitute tenant.

This does not mean that the landlord must rent to anyone who comes along simply in order to reduce the first tenant's losses. The landlord certainly could refuse to rent to someone with a poor credit history, for example, even if this person was willing to take over the apartment in question. Similar problems arise in the employment context. If an employee who is working under a contract is wrongfully fired, he or she has an obligation to find employment elsewhere. This does not mean, however, that the worker must take just any job. Courts generally require the employee only to take comparable work. This point is discussed in the following case.

Parker v. Twentieth Century–Fox Film Corp.
California Supreme Court
474 P.2d 689 (1970)

Shirley MacLaine Parker, a film star, entered into a contract with Twentieth Century–Fox to act in a picture entitled *Bloomer Girl*. It was to be filmed starting May 23, 1966, and she was to be paid for fourteen weeks. In April 1966, Fox decided not to make the film. It requested MacLaine to act instead in a film tentatively entitled *Big Country, Big Man*. Although it agreed to pay her the same compensation, the films were different. *Bloomer Girl* was to have been a musical, but *Big Country* was a western. *Bloomer Girl* was to have been filmed in California. *Big Country* was scheduled to be filmed in Australia. MacLaine was given one week to accept. She brought this suit seeking compensation for breach of contract. Fox defended by arguing MacLaine had failed to mitigate damages. The court ruled for MacLaine.

Burke, Justice

The general rule is that the measure of recovery by a wrongfully discharged employee is the amount of salary agreed upon for the period of service, less the amount which the employer affirmatively proves the employee has earned or with reasonable effort might have earned from other employment.

However, before projected earnings from other employment opportunities not sought or accepted by the discharged employee can be applied in mitigation, the employer must show that the other employment was comparable, or substantially similar, to that of which the employee has been deprived; the employee's rejection of or failure to seek other available employment of a different or inferior kind may not be resorted to in order to mitigate damages.

The sole issue is whether plaintiff's refusal of defendant's substitute offer of "Big Country" may be used in mitigation. Nor, if the "Big Country" offer was of employment different or inferior when compared with the original "Bloomer Girl" employment, is there an issue as to whether or not plaintiff acted reasonably in refusing the substitute offer. Despite defendant's arguments to the contrary, no case cited or which our research has discovered holds or suggests that reasonableness is an element of a wrongfully discharged employee's option to reject, or fail to seek, different or inferior employment lest the possible earnings therefrom be charged against him in mitigation of damages.

Applying the foregoing rules to the record in the present case, with all intendments in favor of the party opposing the summary judgment motion—here, defendant—it is clear that the trial court correctly ruled that plaintiff's failure to accept defendant's tendered substitute employment could not be applied in mitigation of damages because the offer of the "Big Country" lead was of employment both different and inferior, and that no factual dispute was presented on that issue.

In view of the determination that defendant failed to present any facts showing the existence of a factual issue with respect to its sole defense—plaintiff's rejection of its substitute employment offer in mitigation of damages—we need not consider plaintiff's further contention that for various reasons, plaintiff was excused for attempting to mitigate damages.

The judgment is affirmed.

This concludes our brief overview of the requirements of the law of contracts. Let us stress again that many other issues could be covered. This presentation offers only the skeleton of the law of contracts to give the reader a general idea of the nature of a contract.

We will now move on to an examination of changes in American society that have had an impact on the law of contracts in the last hundred years. Certain developments have made the courts, legislatures, and Congress alter some of the basic rules we have just discussed. Most of the changes have taken place in the law dealing with consumer contracts, although to a limited extent the rules dealing with business contracts also have changed.

CHANGES IN THE MARKETPLACE

Earlier Times

How have things changed for consumers? While at the beginning of the nineteenth century individual craftsmen produced most products, new manufacturing processes, using interchangeable parts to produce standardized goods, gradually replaced individual craftsmen in the industrial sector. Businessmen discovered, following the example set by Eli Whitney's firearms factory (constructed in 1798), that by using standardized parts and assigning specific, repetitive tasks to each worker, they produced more goods. Mass production of products produced more goods in less time at a greater profit.

More complicated products slowly began to enter the marketplace—products produced by manufacturers in distant cities. As the nineteenth century unfolded, the Industrial Revolution spread. Corporations grew larger and larger. Manufacturers could offer a wider selection of more complicated products because of mass production. Rising affluence allowed more and more people to purchase these new products. At the same time, metropolitan areas, because of an influx of foreigners and a high birth rate, grew larger and larger. The development of the railroads also enabled manufacturers to ship goods greater and greater distances, further contributing to the demise of locally owned businesses.

In the 1920s, another important development occurred—the chain store. This took root quite rapidly, with stores such as Woolworth's cropping up in virtually every community. This trend has continued throughout the twentieth century.

More recently, another trend has been operating in the marketplace—the growth of self-service stores, such as K-Mart.

Today, the typical consumer confronts the following environment. (1) A wide variety of items are available. (2) They are complex and technologically sophisticated. (3) They are often produced by a manufacturer from another city, and increasingly, from another country. (4) The products are sold not by reputation but by marketing, and in particular, by advertising. The consumer no longer goes to the manufacturer to purchase goods as in the early nineteenth century. He or she no longer purchases goods from a local retailer whose name and reputation the purchaser knows. Purchase decisions are no longer made on the basis of the personal recommendation of the retailer, but—because of chain, self-service merchandising—on the basis of information contained in advertising.

The Market Today

Today, the courts increasingly recognize that little real bargaining takes place in consumer contract negotiations. Quite often, in a consumer transaction, the seller presents the buyer with a standard form contract prepared by the seller. The seller insists the buyer take the contract in the form it is presented to him or her.

Current View on Consumer Contracts

In the typical consumer transaction, the seller has a form drafted by an attorney. It is so designed that all the seller needs to do is fill in the appropriate blanks on the contract. Such contracts are very useful in businesses that engage in the sale of the same product or service over and over, as in the sale of real estate, insurance, and automobiles. It would be very expensive and time consuming to draft custom contracts every time a sale was made. Furthermore, the agent acting on behalf of the seller would need additional training as to the drafting of a contract.

With a form contract, an agent needs to know just enough about the contract to correctly fill in the blanks. This simplifies employee training and helps assure correctly prepared contracts. Real estate agents might know a great deal about real estate contracts. However, with a preprinted form, an agent may be able to fill out the form correctly with a minimum of knowledge. The agent merely needs to be told to put certain information in the blanks.

Many people, when faced with a form contract, simply sign it without reading. The impact of such an action is discussed later in this chapter.

From a consumer's standpoint, such forms speed up the process of completing a sale. As most people generally are satisfied with the provisions in a fairly drawn standard contract, there really is not any need for individually drafted contracts.

However, there is a danger associated with form contracts. The person creating the form may draft an overly one-sided contract that favors only the drafter. If such a form is presented on a take-it-or-leave-it basis, and the buyer has few alternative sources to purchase from, such a contract might be quite unfair. When a person or company heavily weights a contract in his or her favor and possesses significantly more bargaining power than the other party to the contract, the courts refer to the agreement as a **contract of adhesion.** Judges in some cases have been reluctant to enforce contracts they regard as contracts of adhesion.

Businesses also sign form contracts. The courts tend to treat businesses differently from consumers, even if a form contract is involved. Businesspersons usually are more familiar with contracts and often more aware of the need to consult an attorney. Even so, there are cases where even a pure business contract has been set aside because it is too unfair.

Business Contracts

The material that follows tends to apply mostly to consumer transactions, although it applies to a lesser extent to pure business transactions. It deals with some important changes that have taken place in the last hundred years with respect to the traditional requirements of contracts.

As we discussed earlier, the elements of offer, acceptance, consideration, capacity, and legality must be established to create a valid contract. Today, however, the courts will sometimes enforce a contract when no contract exists. In other situations, the courts will refuse to enforce a contract even though a valid contract exists. The text first discusses the latter situation.

REFUSAL TO ENFORCE A CONTRACT

In the material on traditional contract requirements, the text already has covered some situations in which the courts refuse to enforce a contract. If fraud, misrepresentation, mistake, duress, or undue influence is present, the courts sometimes will treat a contract as voidable or void, thus permitting a party to escape his or her obligations under the contract. Likewise, certain contracts that are valid, but are not in writing, also will not be enforced.

But the law has developed to the extent that other situations also enable a party to avoid his or her obligations under a contract even though the person signed after reading the contract.

The following material discusses the issues of public policy, unconscionability, and duty to read.

Public Policy

A court may refuse to enforce a contract that has been found to be contrary to public policy. Alternatively, a clause within a contract may be ruled contrary to public policy, and the court may elect to enforce all of the contract except the offensive clause.

What Courts Mean by Public Policy. In general, conduct that conflicts with generally accepted standards of conduct in the community violates public policy. By examining the applicable statutes and judicial precedents, a judge determines what these community standards are. There is no precise rule or formula for a judge to determine what is and what is not contrary to public policy. As social, economic, moral, and ethical values change, the concept of public policy also changes.

Public policy has recently evolved into another concept. Today, the courts will refuse to enforce contracts not only if they are illegal or contrary to public policy, but also if they are unconscionable. The concept of unconscionability is an evolution of judicial thinking, building on the ideas of illegality, contracts of adhesion, and contracts that are contrary to public policy.

Unconscionability

The doctrine of unconscionability is as murky a concept as the concept of public policy. The courts recognize it as a ground for invalidating contracts under both the common law and the Uniform Commercial Code.

The Uniform Commercial Code. The drafters of the Uniform Commercial Code adopted the concept of unconscionability in Section 2-302.

The UCC gives a court that finds a contract or a clause in a contract to be unconscionable *at the time it was made* several options. It may: (1) refuse to enforce the contract, (2) enforce the remainder of the contract without the unconscionable clause, or (3) limit the application of any unconscionable clause so as to avoid any unconscionable result.

The UCC fails to clearly define the term **unconscionability.** The drafters of the UCC offer this test: "The basic test is whether, in the light of the general commercial background and the commercial needs of the particular trade or case, the clauses involved are so one-sided as to be unconscionable under the circumstances existing at the time of the making of the contract. . . . The principle is one of the prevention of oppression and unfair surprise . . . and not of disturbance of allocation of risks because of superior bargaining power." The UCC seems to be directed at contracts with provisions that heavily favor one party over the other. Such a contract must be unconscionable *at the time the contract was entered into* by the parties—as opposed to a contract that, at a later date, becomes unfair because of some event the parties had not anticipated.

The failure to adequately define the term unconscionability or at least to set some standards for guiding the courts has met with criticism, as has the broad authority given to the courts to remake a contract. This provision clearly gives judges vast power and discretion to tamper with the provisions of a contract negotiated between private parties.

Typical Case. Generally, it would seem that the party in the best position to assert the doctrine of unconscionability as a defense would be a person who was not engaged in business (for example, a consumer), who did not regularly enter into contracts, and who had a limited education, especially in business affairs. This person probably dealt with a businessperson who presented the consumer with a form contract drafted by an attorney in such a manner that it unfairly favored the businessperson over the consumer. The contract probably was presented on a take-it-or-leave-it basis, and the consumer had few other places to go to obtain these goods or services. Generally, the purchaser had little time to examine the terms of the contracts. Very possibly he or she had been pressured into signing "at once" without being given the opportunity to reflect on the terms.

In many cases, the courts have struck down a contract because the sale price was unconscionable, as the following case illustrates.

Frostifresh Corp. v. Reynoso
District Court, Nassau County, New York, Second District
274 N.Y.S.2d 757 (1966)

A contract for a refrigerator-freezer was negotiated orally in Spanish between the Reynosos and a Spanish-speaking salesman representing Frostifresh. In that conversation, Mr. Reynoso told the salesman that he had but one week left on his job and he could not afford to buy the appliance. The salesman distracted and deluded the Reynosos by advising them that the appliance would cost them nothing because they would be paid bonuses or commissions of $25 each on the numerous sales that would be made to their neighbors and friends. Thereafter the Reynosos signed a retail installment contract entirely in English. The retail contract was neither translated for nor explained to the defendants. In that contract, there was a cash sales price set forth of $900. To this was added a credit charge of $245.88, making a total of $1,145.88 to be paid for the appliance. The cost to Frostifresh for the freezer was $348.00.

Frostifresh brings this action for $1,364.10, alleging that this amount is owed by the Reynosos on account of the purchase of the refrigerator-freezer, for which they agreed to pay $1,145.88. The balance of the amount consists of a claim for attorney fees of $227.35 and a late charge of $22.87. The only payment made by the Reynosos is the sum of $32.

Donavan, Judge

The court finds that the sale of the appliance at the price and terms indicated in this contract is shocking to the conscience. The service charge, which almost equals the price of the appliance is in and of itself indicative of the oppression which was practiced on these defendants. Defendants were handicapped by a lack of knowledge, both as to the commercial situation and the nature and terms of the contract which was submitted in a language foreign to them.

The question presented in this case is simply this: Does the court have the power under section 2-302 of the Uniform Commercial Code to refuse to enforce the price and credit provisions of the contract in order to prevent an unconscionable result.

It is normally stated that the parties are free to make whatever contracts they please so long as there is no fraud or illegality.

However, it is the apparent intent of the Uniform Commercial Code to modify this general rule by giving the courts power "to police explicitly

against the contracts or clauses which they find to be unconscionable. . . . The principle is one of the prevention of oppression and unfair surprise."

In the instant case the court finds that here it was "too hard a bargain" and the conscience of the court will not permit the enforcement of the contract as written. Therefore the plaintiff will not be permitted to recover on the basis of the price set forth in the retail installment contract, namely $900.00 plus $245.85 as a service charge.

However, since the defendants have not returned the refrigerator-freezer, they will be required to reimburse the plaintiff for the cost to the plaintiff, namely $348.00. No allowance is made on account of any commissions the plaintiff may have paid to salesmen or for legal fees, service charges or any other matters of overhead.

Accordingly the plaintiff may have judgment against both defendants in the amount of $348.00 with interest, less the $32.00 paid on account, leaving a net balance of $316.00 with interest from December 26, 1964.

Unconsciona-bility—Busi-nesspersons

While unconscionability enables consumers on occasion to avoid their contractual obligations, businesspersons fare poorly under this doctrine. By and large, the courts tend to reject unconscionability as a ground for escaping contracts when persons in business assert it.

The reasons for the declining to apply this doctrine to business contracts essentially are: (1) the parties generally are knowledgeable, sophisticated corporations; (2)

the negotiations leading up to the consummation of the contract are deliberate and detailed; (3) they are not presented on a take-it-or-leave-it basis but are generally negotiated transactions; and (4) usually the parties have the assistance of legal counsel or are aware they could use legal counsel. Such contracts rarely involve a person who is unaware of his or her legal rights and has very little bargaining power. The parties rarely have been oppressed or surprised by the terms.

Typically, the businessperson asserting unconscionability as a defense simply made a bad deal and is looking for the courts to relieve him or her of the consequences of his or her bad judgment. The courts, in light of the unusual negotiations and awareness of the terms of the contract, are quite unlikely to be receptive to the argument of unconscionability in the business context. The following case is typical of the treatment of businesspersons who assert unconscionability as grounds for not enforcing the contract.

Potomac Electric Power Co. v. Westinghouse Electric Corp.
United States District Court, District of Columbia
385 F. Supp. 572 (1974)

After several years of contract negotiations, in the summer of 1970, a turbine-generator was placed in commercial operation in Maryland. A few months later, a malfunction developed, causing substantial damage to the turbine. As a consequence, the unit was out of service for six months.

Potomac Electric Power Company (PEPCO) seeks compensatory and punitive damages from Westinghouse arising from an alleged contract breach for the manufacture and sale of the steam turbine-generator. The complaint alleges negligence, gross negligence, misrepresentation, breach of contract to repair or replace, breach of warranties, breach of express guarantees, and unconscionability. In response to the complaint, Westinghouse relies upon various defenses and contends that PEPCO is estopped from asserting any claim and has waived any right to consequential damages by virtue of the express provisions of the contract.

Parker, Judge

The rights and obligations of the parties are contained in a fully detailed and integrated written contract. Under the first subsection the defendant expressly warranted that the equipment would be of the kind and quality described in the contract and would be free of defects in workmanship or material for one year. In the event of a breach of this warranty, upon notification of the defect and substantiation of proper maintenance and operation, the defendant was only required to repair or replace the nonconforming part at its expense. The parties further agreed that there were no other warranties, express or implied, or merchantability, fitness for purpose, or other warranties. This last provision of the warranty was conspicuously underlined. The liability limitation subsection of the contract also specifically provided that the defendant would in no event be liable ". . . for special, or consequential damages, such as, but not limited to, damage or loss of other property or equipment, loss of profits or revenue, loss of use of power system, cost of capital, cost of purchased or replacement power, or claims of customers of Purchaser for service interruption. . . ."

Within the framework of this commercial transaction the Court perceives no valid legal reason why PEPCO should not be held to the clear and express provisions of the written agreement between the parties. Warranty and limitation of liability clauses such as found in the present contract, which restrict PEPCO's remedies to the repair and replacement of nonconforming parts and limit Westinghouse's liability, regardless of its negligence in causing such nonconformities, are valid and enforceable and have been consistently upheld by the courts. They are also consistent with Section 2-316(4) and 2-719(1)(a) and (3), Uniform Commercial Code. Provisions such as those precluding PEPCO from recovering consequential damages have likewise been upheld as valid and enforceable.

Finally, plaintiff raises the issue of the unconscionability of the exculpatory clauses. The negotiated agreement between these parties was not a contract between two small unknowledgeable shop keepers but between two sophisticated corporations each with comparable bargaining power and fully aware of what they were doing. The negotiations leading to the consummation of the contract were deliberate, detailed and consumed more than two years. PEPCO's representatives were experienced and the final agreement was reviewed by their corporate legal staff. While the evidence shows that other than Westinghouse, there was only one other domestic manufacturer with the capability of marketing the turbine-generator, there is nothing to indicate that PEPCO was precluded from contracting with that manufacturer or even foreign manufacturers. Nor is there any evidence in the record showing that PEPCO was a reluctant and unwilling purchaser, overreached and forced to yield to onerous terms imposed by Westinghouse.

In short, the facts have been sufficiently developed and the Court finds that there is no genuine issue as to any material fact and concludes that the law clearly supports the defendant.

Duty to Read

General Rule. The general rule regarding the duty to read before signing a contract is that a person is bound by what he or she signs. The *Restatement of Contracts*, Section 70 (1932), states: "One who makes a written offer which is accepted, or who manifests acceptance of the terms of a writing which he should reasonably understand to be an offer or proposed contract, is bound by the contract through ignorant of the terms of a writing or of its proper interpretation."

This rule suggests that before signing a written contract, a person read the contract provisions. If a person signs without reading, he or she runs the risk of being bound by the contract even though failing to read or comprehend its terms.

This general rule, as this chapter has already indicated, is subject to some exceptions. Certainly people are not bound by an illegal contract. Other exceptions also exist.

Rationale for Rule. By enforcing a contract against someone who failed to read a document or failed to comprehend it, the courts lend certainty to the law of contracts. No one could rely on a signed document if the other party could avoid the transaction by saying he or she had not read or did not understand the writing. If the courts let a person out of a contract under these circumstances, all predictability and certainty of business contractual relationships would be destroyed. Parties to a contract would never be certain whether the contract would be enforced or not. The way to avoid the harsh results that might flow from the doctrine of the duty to read is to read contracts before signing them.

Modern Trend. The more modern cases search for a true assent to the terms of a contractual agreement. Simply having presented a complex contract to the other party for an immediate signature quite frequently will not be sufficient to convince a court that the person signing really agreed to all the terms in the contract. To adopt a contrary rule would reward the unethical seller who cleverly drafts a contract with many inconspicuous, harsh provisions and then pressures the other person into signing the contract without reading it.

Thus, in determining whether a person actually assented to the terms of a contract, a court should determine whether that person had the opportunity to read the contract, understood the provisions in question, and had a real opportunity to accept or reject the provisions.

This view is not necessarily followed by all courts: The law in this area is changing and uniformity of results does not exist. Nonetheless, many of the more modern cases do seem receptive to the idea that when a form contract that contains very harsh provisions is used, the court should be able to find true assent by the person who signed the contract before recognizing a contract.

The doctrine of freedom of contract seems to be giving way to the idea of enforcing fairness in the particular circumstances of the case. Some modern cases on duty to read either refuse to find an actual assent to the terms, or if they find such an assent, refuse to enforce the clause in question because it is unconscionable or contrary to public policy.

Business Contracts. Even in cases involving businesses, some court decisions, as well as legislation, have recognized the inequality in bargaining power that exists between large manufacturers and retailers. Because of this inequality in bargaining power, steps have been taken to protect the weaker party. *Hoffman* v. *Red Owl Stores*, at the end of this chapter, is one such case, in which the doctrine of promissory estoppel (discussed later) was used to help out a small businessman.

As an example of a situation in which the courts have acted to protect business-persons, consider **illusory promises.** An illusory promise is one in which the obligation to perform is entirely optional on the part of one of the parties. Illusory contracts have been treated by the courts in many cases as agreements *not* supported by consideration, as one of the parties had in effect received nothing in exchange for his or her promise to do something. Therefore, the courts have in many cases refused to enforce an alleged contract. For example, XYZ business might enter a contract with Al's Tires stating, "XYZ agrees to sell our tires as, when, and if deemed desirable." Such an agreement would be treated as illusory, because XYZ would not be obliged to do anything under the contract.

One situation in which the courts have begun to protect businesses that arguably have made an illusory promise involves a contract that may be canceled at any time without notice. The older cases held such a promise to be illusory. The more recent cases have upheld such contracts. In *Sylvan Crest Sand & Gravel Co.* v. *U.S.*, the contract provided a right to cancel without notice. The court interpreted this as meaning that notice of cancellation must be given within a reasonable time from the time of acceptance and therefore held that the contract was not an illusory promise unsupported by consideration.

The trend in the area of illusory promises has been to sustain such agreements when possible.

Legislation has been passed to protect small businesses. For example, retail auto dealers sought legislation to prevent unfair termination of automobile franchise contracts. The Automobile Dealers Day in Court Act permits the termination of an auto franchise only in good faith. This act was passed in response to the arbitrary terminations of franchises by manufacturers who had drafted extremely one-sided contracts.

One can no longer be absolutely certain, especially when using a form contract, that the courts will enforce a contract. Some courts may choose to examine whether a person actually assented to the terms of the contract. Other courts may examine whether the actual terms used are fair. If a court finds the term was not assented to or was unfair, it may refuse to enforce the contract.

ENFORCING A CONTRACT WHEN NONE EXISTS

The preceding material illustrates situations in which a valid contract will not be enforced by the courts. In this section the text examines two situations in which no contract exists, but the courts impose contractual obligations on the parties anyway. The doctrines of quasi contract and promissory estoppel are discussed in turn.

Quasi Contract

Before signing the typical contract, the parties often discuss the subject matter and major terms of a contract. After they come to an agreement on the major terms, one of the parties makes an offer and the other person accepts the offer. In such a case, whether the contract is oral or written, there is a clear express intention to contract. But in some situations the parties never indicate, nor do they in fact have, an intent to contract.

Suppose that today a student decides to drive his car to the record store. On the way to the store, another vehicle collides with his automobile. Because of the serious injuries he sustains, he is in a comatose state. An ambulance driver rushes him to a hospital. While the student is unconscious, the hospital attendants rush him to the operating room for emergency surgery to save his life. The physician in charge operates on him to stop his bleeding. The next day he awakens in a hospital bed. After several days in the hospital attempting to recover, he finally decides to go home. When he leaves the hospital, the cashier presents him with a bill for the use of the emergency room, the hospital room, and various services and supplies. When he arrives home, he discovers the physician's bill in his mailbox.

Although the student *never had an intent to contract*, the law requires him to pay the reasonable value of the services rendered. Suit may be brought against him based on a quasi-contractual theory of recovery.

Quasi contracts (also called *contracts implied in law*) are not technically contracts, because one of the parties never intended to contract. Even so, the law recognizes an implied contract in order to do justice. If the student received hospital and medical services but was not required to pay for them, he would be unjustly enriched. Thus, the duty to pay is imposed to prevent the unjust enrichment of one person at the expense of another.

Another situation in which recovery may be had based on a quasi contract is one in which a minor purchases necessaries, assuming the minor does not have a parent or guardian who is able and willing to supply him or her with such necessities as food, clothing, and medical services. In such a situation, the minor must pay for the items purchased, even though one of the elements for a valid contract is missing— capacity. No contract technically ever comes into existence. Nonetheless, to let the minor purchase these things without an obligation to pay for them would unjustly enrich the minor at the expense of the adult or business. Consequently, the courts will permit such a person or business to contract under a quasi-contractual theory of recovery.

Clearly, the doctrine of quasi contract may be used in many situations where it appears one party has been unjustly enriched at the expense of another. The courts have used it in instances in which a contract was too indefinite to be enforced, where a person who partially performed personal services had died, and in innumerable other situations to insure that one party was not unjustly enriched at the expense of another.

The case that follows presents an implied in law contract.

County of Champaign v. Hanks
Court of Appeals of Illinois
353 N.E.2d 405 (1976)

Gary Hanks was accused of a crime. Hanks claimed at the time of his arrest that he had no money to hire an attorney to defend himself. This statement was in fact false because he owned real estate worth over fifty thousand dollars. Relying on these false statements, the state provided a free attorney to Hanks. When it discovered that the statements were false, the state sued to recover the cost of providing an attorney to Hanks. Hanks argued that there was no contract on his part to pay for the legal services. The court ruled Hanks had to pay for the services rendered by the state.

Stengel, Justice

A quasi contract, or contract implied in law, is one which reason and justice dictate and is founded on the equitable doctrine of unjust enrichment. A contract implied in law does not depend on the intention of the parties, but exists where there is a plain duty and a consideration. The essential element is the receipt of a benefit by one party under circumstances where it would be inequitable to retain that benefit without compensation.

The county does not officiously confer the benefits of free legal representation, but furnishes legal services to those criminal defendants who qualify by virtue of their indigency. The undisputed facts reveal that defendant received free legal representation when he clearly was not entitled to such representation and that defendant failed to disclose his assets. Under these circumstances the law will imply a promise by defendant to compensate the county and, accordingly, we find that summary judgment was properly granted.

The measure of damages for an implied in law contract is the amount by which defendant has been unjustly enriched or the value of the actual benefit received by defendant, and recovery is usually measured by the reasonable value of the services performed by plaintiff.

Defendant, by his misrepresentations, received legal services which were found by the trial court to have a reasonable value of $2000. The services rendered by three different attorneys from the Public Defender's Office were not only competent but lengthy and most thorough. The record reveals that between March 28, 1972, and July 17, 1972, they appeared in court at least nine days on various matters from preliminary hearing and arraignment to motions to suppress the in-court identification. The jury trial consumed four days from July 17 to July 20, 1972. Motions for mistrial, post-trial motions, probation hearing and finally sentencing hearing were not completed until October 6, 1972. Thus the damage award does not exceed the extent of defendant's unjust enrichment as it is no more than defendant would have paid for such services had he not misrepresented his assets. This damage award more nearly reflects the value of the benefit received by defendant, and a lesser measure of damages would be tantamount to allowing defendant to profit from his wrongful conduct.

Promissory Estoppel

Section 90 of the *Restatement of Contracts Second* states the doctrine of promissory estoppel:

> A promise which the promisor should reasonably expect to induce action or forbearance on the part of the promisee or a third person and which does induce such action or forbearance is binding if injustice can be avoided only by enforcement of the promise. The remedy for breach may be limited as justice requires.

A person may, by making a promise to another person, cause the person to whom the statement is made to take some sort of action or to abstain from taking action of some sort. In this situation the person making the statement should not be able to avoid his or her promise by asserting that the promise in question was not supported by consideration. A court in this situation may treat the promise as enforceable even though it is not supported by consideration.

As promissory estoppel is currently being applied, however, it serves as much more than a simple substitute for the doctrine of consideration. *Hoffman* v. *Red Owl Stores*, the case that follows, is a good illustration of the broad application some courts make of the promissory estoppel doctrine. Even when many of the terms have never been agreed upon, as in *Hoffman*, courts have been willing to recognize a contract where no contract ever existed.

The *Restatement of Contracts Second* requires a court to find:

1. that the promise was one that the promisor should have reasonably expected would induce action or forbearance of a definite and substantial character on the part of the person to whom the promise was made; and

2. the promise induced such action or forbearance; and

3. injustice can be avoided only by enforcement of the promise.

The trend of the cases is to apply the doctrine of promissory estoppel to any promise that meets these requirements. Many cases have applied this doctrine.

For example, promissory estoppel has come up frequently in construction cases. Suppose a general contractor is building a ten-story building. The contractor asks for bids from various subcontractors. An electrical subcontractor, XYZ, makes the low bid for the electrical work on the building, which the general contractor uses in making his bid for the job. On August 1, the general contractor is awarded the contract. He then goes to XYZ, which informs him its bid has been withdrawn. Some courts have taken the position that once a subcontractor makes a bid, because of the doctrine of promissory estoppel, the subcontractor may not withdraw the bid. The rationale is that the subcontractor, at the time it made its bid, knew the general contractor might rely upon the bid to its detriment, because it would use the subcontractor's bid in making a bid for the entire building. In effect, these courts have altered the general rule that an offeror may withdraw his offer any time before it is accepted in the construction contract situation.

The following case is a well-known illustration of the rule of promissory estoppel.

Hoffman v. Red Owl Stores

Supreme Court of Wisconsin
133 N.W. 2d 267 (1965)

In this case, the Hoffmans claimed that Red Owl's representatives made a number of representations to them upon which they relied to their detriment. They urged the court to apply the doctrine of promissory estoppel to create an enforceable bargain. The Wisconsin Supreme Court rules that it was properly applied in this case.

Currie, Chief Justice

Many courts of other jurisdictions have seen fit over the years to adopt the principle of promissory estoppel, and the tendency in that direction continues. As Mr. Justice McFaddin, speaking in behalf of the Arkansas court, well stated, that the development of the law of promissory estoppel "is an attempt by the courts to keep remedies abreast of increased moral consciousness of honesty and fair representations in all business dealings."

Because we deem the doctrine of promissory estoppel, as stated in sec. 90 of Restatement, 1

Contracts, is one which supplies a needed tool which courts may employ in a proper case to prevent injustice, we endorse and adopt it.

The record here discloses a number of promises and assurances given to Hoffman by Lukovitz on behalf of Red Owl upon which plaintiffs relied and acted upon to their detriment.

Foremost were the promises that for the sum of $18,000 Red Owl would establish Hoffman in a store. After Hoffman had sold his grocery store and paid the $1,000 on the Chilton lot, the

$18,000 figure was changed to $24,000. Then in November, 1961, Hoffman was assured that if the $24,000 figure were increased by $2,000 the deal would go through. Hoffman was induced to sell his grocery store fixtures and inventory in June, 1961, on the promise that he would be in his new store by fall. In November, plaintiffs sold their bakery building on the urging of defendants and on the assurance that this was the last step necessary to have the deal with Red Owl go through.

There remains for consideration the question of law raised by defendants that an agreement was never reached on essential factors necessary to establish a contract between Hoffman and Red Owl. Among these were the size, cost, design, and layout of the store building; and the terms of the lease with respect to rent, maintenance, renewal, and purchase options. This poses the question of whether the promise necessary to sustain a cause of action for promissory estoppel must embrace all essential details of a proposed transaction between promisor and promisee so as to be the equivalent of an offer that would result in a binding contract between the parties if the promisee were to accept the same.

Originally the doctrine of promissory estoppel was invoked as a substitute for consideration rendering a gratuitous promise enforceable as a contract. In other words, the acts of reliance by the promisee to his detriment provided a substitute for consideration. If promissory estoppel were to be limited to only these situations where the promise giving rise to the cause of action must be so definite with respect to all details that a contract would result were the promise supported by consideration, then the defendants' instant promises to Hoffman would not meet this test. However, sec. 90 of Restatement, 1 Contracts, does not impose the requirement that the promise giving rise to the cause of action must be so comprehensive in scope as to meet the requirements of an offer that would ripen into a contract if accepted by the promisee. Rather the conditions imposed are:

1. Was the promise one which the promisor should reasonably expect to induce action or forbearance of a definite and substantial character on the part of the promisee?

2. Did the promise induce such action or forbearance?

3. Can injustice be avoided only by enforcement of the promise?

We conclude the injustice would result here if plaintiffs were not granted some relief because of the failure of defendants to keep their promises which induced plaintiffs to act to their detriment.

SUMMARY   The law of contracts has evolved over hundreds of years into the court-enforced laws of today. Over a period of centuries, the courts gradually accepted the notion that they should enforce a contract freely entered into by the parties to a contract. Nineteenth-century philosophers, many of whom espoused the doctrine of freedom of contract, argued that the free enterprise system depended upon the willingness of the courts to enforce every contract. The courts, persuaded by this thinking, developed the doctrine *caveat emptor*—let the buyer beware. For many years few persons succeeded in escaping their contractual obligations.

More recently, the courts have moved away from this doctrine because of the harsh consequences associated with enforcing certain contracts. The courts have come to recognize that many contracts are not the product of the free will of individuals, as John Stuart Mill believed, but rather are the product of an inequality of bargaining power between the parties. This inequality of bargaining power often gives the stronger party the opportunity to insert unfair clauses into a contract. Today, the courts are inclined to set aside unfair contracts.

Before any contract comes into existence, certain requirements must have been fulfilled. The person making the offer must manifest a desire to enter into a contract, referred to as an offer. The person to whom this offer is made must manifest an assent to the terms of the offer in a manner required or authorized by the offer, referred to as an acceptance. The entire transaction must be supported by consideration; that is, the contract must have been the product of a bargain and exchange between the parties to the contract. No contract will be enforced if the parties to the contract lack the capacity to contract or if the bargain in question is illegal. Even if all of these requirements have been met, a contract still will not be enforceable, in certain cases, if it is not evidenced by a writing.

Simply signing a contract does not ensure the enforceability of an agreement. In some cases, the courts refuse to enforce agreements because the agreements are basically unfair. The courts use the doctrines of public policy and unconscionability to set aside these unfair contracts. This approach reflects an evolution in thinking as to the degree of protection that should be afforded to people who enter into contracts. Courts and legislatures are more willing to protect people, and even some businesses, who enter into unfair contracts. In other instances, the courts, in the interest of justice, will impose contractual obligations where no such obligations exist.

A sense of history helps in understanding the evolution of contract law. What has happened in society has influenced the law. What happens today and in the future will continue to influence the rules in every area of the law.

REVIEW QUESTIONS

1. Define the following terms:
   a. *Restatement of Contracts*
   b. Contract
   c. Promise
   d. Uniform Commercial Code
   e. Contract of adhesion
   f. Caveat emptor

2. Why did the concept of freedom of contract develop as part of our contract law?

3. Is the meaning of *unconscionability* understood by everyone?

4. Capitol sued Mary for the $406 balance due under a contract for household goods. The merchandise was valued at $595 plus $18 sales tax. The credit charge for purchase over a two-year period equaled $219. The cost of the goods to Capitol was $234. Mary claimed that the goods were grossly over-priced, that she had already paid their fair market value, and that the contract terms were unconscionable. Are the contract terms unconscionable?

5. The parties entered into a contract to repair MacIver's home. The contract was for $1,759, payments to be made over sixty months. Five days later, the MacIvers notified American Home to cease work on their home. American Home had done a negligible amount of work up to that point, but they had paid an $800 sales commission in reliance upon the contract. American Home sued the MacIvers for damages for their breach of contract. The MacIvers moved to dismiss the suit on the ground that the contract terms were unconscionable. How should the court rule?

6. After three years of talks, Westinghouse and a public service utilities company entered into a contract for the purchase of a turbine generator manufactured by Westinghouse. Both parties are very large industrial organizations. Westinghouse is one of only two companies

that can manufacture the required generator. The contract involved over ten million dollars, and limited Westinghouse's liability to corrections of defects in workmanship and material appearing within one year of installation. Is this liability limitation unconscionable?

7. Vargas is an artist, and a native of Peru. He has lived in the United States for over thirty years. He entered an employment contract with the publishers of *Esquire* magazine, after having looked at and signed it. The contract was written in plain English. Vargas now wishes to cancel the contract on the ground that he failed to know and understand its contents when it was signed. Is this a good defense to a breach of contract claim?

8. In 1898, Congress passed a law prohibiting employers from requiring employees, as a condition of employment, to agree not to join labor unions. Adair required his employee, Coppage, to sign such an agreement and fired him when he joined a union. In the absence of a valid contract between the parties, can Congress make it a crime for Adair to fire Coppage without just cause?

9. Colburn contracted for the construction of a home on his property and executed a mortgage to secure his purchase. He signed a mortgage in the presence of a notary public, but had some questions about the instrument. Colburn paid the installments as they became due for four years. Then he sought to void the mortgage on the ground that he failed to read and understand it when he signed it. Will the court accept this argument?

10. Smith signed a contract with Standard Oil to sell a piece of property. In a suit to enforce the contract against Smith, Smith argued that she was unable to read the contract when it was presented for signature because of her faulty eyesight. She did not have eyeglasses with her, so she signed the contract only upon the assurances given to her by Standard Oil. As soon

as she arrived home, she put on her glasses and discovered that the contract did not contain a provision that she was led to believe was in it. Can she have the contract set aside?

11. Parker, a thirty-seven-year-old bachelor, entered into a series of contracts with Arthur Murray for dancing lessons. During the lessons, he was told he had "exceptional potential to be a fine and accomplished dancer." The contracts he signed stated in bold type at the bottom, "Noncancellable Contract," and also stated, "I understand that no refunds will be made under the terms of this contract." He was thereafter severely injured in an automobile accident and was incapable of continuing his dancing lessons. At that time, he had contracted for a total of 2,734 hours of lessons. He contends he should be released from these contracts based on impossibility. Should he win?

12. Marie Bredemann worked for the Vaughan Manufacturing Company for a number of years. The president of Vaughan orally promised to pay her $375 per month for life when she retired. In reliance on his statement, she retired. Several years later, the company, which had been paying her $375 per month, stopped making payments. It argued there was no consideration to support the alleged contract between Vaughan and Bredemann. What could Bredemann argue?

13. Massie, who had been licensed as a real estate agent, let his license lapse. A farmer asked Massie to find a buyer for his farm, for which the farmer would pay Massie five percent of the sale price. State law required persons to have a license in order to sell real estate. Massie found a buyer for the farmer's land, but the farmer refused to pay Massie for his work. Must the farmer pay?

14. Christopher Kitsos claimed that he was offered an oral contract for lifetime employment by the Mobile Gas Service Corporation. The com-

pany fired him. When sued by Kitsos, it argued that this contract had to be in writing in order to be enforceable. Is the company correct?

15. Troutman, an attorney, was hired by the Southern Railway to attempt to influence the president of the United States to oppose the position of the Interstate Commerce Commission in a case filed by Southern against the ICC. Troutman was successful. The Department of Justice intervened in the case in support of Southern's position. Troutman asked for two-hundred thousand dollars for his services. When Southern refused to pay, he filed suit. Southern argued this was an illegal contract. Is it correct?

CHAPTER 9

Torts

Definition and General Discussion
Intentional Torts
The Tort of Negligence
Tort Law and History
Developments in Tort Law

DEFINITION AND GENERAL DISCUSSION

Many writers have attempted to draft a good working definition of the term **tort.** They have failed, mainly because of the nature of the legal concept of the term. Tort law is a certain body of civil (noncriminal) law covering civil wrongs other than breaches of contract. In cases involving torts, a court will usually provide money damages to parties injured by the acts of others. Torts encompass a wide range of conduct. Causing an automobile collision, punching someone in the nose, printing untrue statements about your roommate in the student newspaper, and opening a bottle of pop that explodes are all examples of torts.

General Factors That Make Up the Law of Torts

Tort law is based upon a multitude of factors or aims. One aim of tort law is to provide compensation for injuries. The goal of the compensation award or damages in tort is to restore, through the award of money, the injured parties to their condition before the injury. This means that the elements of a damage award are made up of a number of possible factors, depending on the nature of the case. The more tangible elements in the computation of a damage award are out-of-pocket costs and expenses incurred by the injured party (doctor bills and medical expenses, for example) and income lost because of the injury. However, the injured party may have suffered in less clearly measurable ways. Pain and suffering or embarrassment may certainly be consequences of an injury. These intangible factors, too, may be included in the total compensation awarded to the plaintiff in order to make the injured party whole (that is, by awarding money damages, put the injured party in the same position as before the accident occurred). However, tort law is not a general social insurance system by which members of society who somehow receive an injury automatically are compensated for it.

Tort law is also an allocation of risks and losses between those who cause the harm and those who must incur it. One of the major features of tort law, therefore, is the striking of a balance based upon this allocation. As will be seen in the discussion of tort law and history in this chapter, the balance often shifts. Courts that decide cases and develop doctrine in tort law are aware that their decisions do not operate in a vacuum. Holding that certain conduct may be an actionable tort may have the effect of inhibiting that conduct, because compensation will be awarded to those injured. If the effect is to make manufacturers take greater care in their production procedures, society benefits. However, if the effect is to inhibit the development of new and useful tools, one might question the overall benefit to society. Yet limiting the types of conduct that lead to tort liability might result in the inevitable misfortunes of a complex and highly industrialized society being borne by the unlucky few who are injured. Tort law, therefore, is additionally a means to regulate the conduct of members of society. It encourages socially reasonable conduct in that it requires people to pay for certain injuries they cause. It is expected that unreasonable conduct will be inhibited because of the risk of the actor having to pay damages or pay larger insurance premiums. In a sense, for economic reasons an individual will choose a more reasonable mode of behavior.

Tort Law, Business Behavior, and Insurance

When activities of a business cause injury, tort law is available to impose damages on that business. As a result, an additional "cost" must be computed for all business activities—the cost of potential tort liability arising from that activity. However, an exact figure for these costs may be difficult to compute for any individual company. For example, the Acme Grocery Store would be able to compute labor costs by reviewing the contract with its employees' union and making reasonable assumptions about industry labor costs over the long term. However, the store would have no way to predict how many people will slip on cottage cheese spilled in an aisle or the severity of any of their injuries. Nonetheless, Acme Grocery Store may become liable for a damage award and thus needs to determine how to factor those awards, overtime, into its pricing.

The usual way to approach the problem would be for Acme to purchase liability insurance. In fact, most businesses (and individuals) hedge against the risk of major damage awards depleting their assets by purchasing insurance. The insurance company will, consistent with the terms and coverage purchased, defend Acme and, if necessary, ultimately pay any customers injured in the store. The cost of the insurance policy, like labor costs, will be used to make grocery pricing decisions.

Thus, tort law and insurance together operate to further the major goals of tort doctrine. Through insurance, a compensation pool is readily available to satisfy tort damage awards. Otherwise a **defendant** without either insurance or sufficient assets will be unable to pay the award, thereby causing the injured party to forego compensation for injuries even though a court provided an award. Furthermore, an ongoing business, like Acme Groceries, can plan its liability costs and need not realistically fear a loss of its assets. Finally, the insurance company, in order to minimize tort claims, may cause Acme Grocery Store to modify some of its business procedures. For example, employees may be assigned to police aisles for spilled food. Lower rates or perhaps the availability of insurance itself may be conditioned on such actions. A safer shopping environment and ultimately fewer accidents will result.

Thus, day-to-day activities of business are tied to tort law and insurance. However, the relationship between tort law and insurance today is a tenuous one. Recently, business insurance premiums have skyrocketed or the coverage itself has become very difficult to obtain. Why this problem has arisen is subject to great dispute.

Some people suggest that jury damage awards and the tort law system have run amuck. As will be seen by the developments section of this chapter, the compensation of victims policy of tort doctrine has become dominant. Legal doctrines once available as defenses to tort claims have been eliminated or weakened. The *Flagiello* v. *Pennsylvania Hospital* case in Chapter 4 illustrates the abandonment of the charitable immunity doctrine, a tort rule that prevented charitable institutions from being held liable for torts. Furthermore, the scope of tort liability has been expanded to provide remedies for once uncompensated injuries. However, tort law changes are merely reflecting a social belief that injured individuals should not have to absorb certain losses on their own.

Other people suggest that the liability insurance crisis is a ruse under which insurance companies have been able to shift the loss of their investment miscalculations. Tort law doctrine has been slowly evolving for the past thirty years, while the insurance crisis is of very recent vintage. No sudden change occurred to precipitate the problem. The only sudden change that did occur was economic: Inflation and interest rates fell very rapidly. Insurance companies were writing insurance at bargain rates, counting on continued inflation and a large return from their investments. When interest rates fell, the companies were responsible for far greater tort liability losses than premium income and their investments could cover. (Some people, however, contend that skillful accounting had as much to do with the claimed "loss" as did the change in the economy.) As a result, insurance companies began to demand huge premium increases for business insurance.

Some businesses have been unable to cope with the large insurance rate increases. Their price structures could not support passing the increase along to their consumers. Thus, in some instances, insurance protection has diminished, risking a loss of assets if a major damage award is assessed. Some businesses have decided to forego all insurance. A few have quit doing business in the areas in which rate increases have been the highest.

Predictably, legislative solutions have been proposed. Tort law "reforms" that limit damage awards or modify tort law doctrine have been enacted. Tighter regulation of insurance companies has also been suggested.

However, basic to the current concerns are general tort law principles that are embodied in the close relationship between tort law doctrine and insurance. Two questions should be central to any response to the current crisis: First, how (or should) society provide for compensation to be paid to those persons injured as a result of someone else's activity; and second, how can business best hedge against potential tort liability? These are issues seeking a solution.

INTENTIONAL TORTS

An **intentional tort** focuses on whether the aim of a certain act was to result in an injury. The conduct involved may be malicious or may actually be designed to cause harm (punching someone in the nose). A defendant who commits an intentional tort may be liable to the injured party for damages caused by the tort and may be assessed punitive damages, an award not linked to the injury, but instead designed to penalize the defendant. Furthermore, some intentional torts may also cause criminal charges to be filed against the wrongdoer. For example, assume that Mary was fired from her job with an investment firm. In a rage, she hit her supervisor with an umbrella, causing massive injuries. Mary committed an intentional tort. The purpose of her action was to harm her supervisor. Furthermore, criminal charges of assault and battery may be filed against Mary.

However, the scope of what is considered an intentional tort is considerably broader than might first appear. Determining the precise intent of a person who has committed a tort is an impossible undertaking. The best that can be done is to establish a standard based on all the facts surrounding the act in order to determine whether that act would be considered intentional. The legal standard is, Would a reasonable person in the position of one who committed the act in question believe that the injury that did occur was certain to follow from that act? For example, assume that a practical joker pulls a chair from under another person about to sit. The person then falls to the ground and is injured. It is unlikely that the practical joker acted maliciously or actually intended to harm the other person. At most the joker hoped to get a few laughs from the pratfall. Yet such an act has been held to be an intentional tort. A reasonable person pulling a chair out from another would expect that person to fall on the floor and could reasonably expect injury to occur. It may be considered that the wrongdoer knew or was certain that the other person would fall on the floor even though injury was not meant to occur.

Even though the legal standard for "intentional" may not be precisely fulfilled, similar tort liability can still arise, as the following case illustrates.

Hackbart v. Cincinnati Bengals, Inc.
United States Tenth Circuit Court of Appeals
601 F.2d 516 (1979)

The question in this case is whether in a regular season professional football game an injury inflicted by one professional football player on an opposing player can give rise to liability in tort where the injury was inflicted by the intentional striking of a blow during the game.

The injury occurred in 1973, in Denver, during a game between the Denver Broncos and the Cincinnati Bengals. A Broncos defensive back, Dale Hackbart, was the recipient of the injury, and a Bengals' offensive back, Charles "Booby" Clark, inflicted the blow that produced it.

Just before the injury, Clark had run a pass pattern to the right side of the Denver Broncos' end zone. The pass was intercepted by Billy Thompson, a Denver free safety, who returned it to midfield. The subject injury occurred as an aftermath of the pass play.

As a consequence of the interception, the roles of Hackbart and Clark suddenly changed. Hackbart, who had been defending, instantaneously became an offensive player. Clark, on the other hand, became a defensive player. Acting as an offensive player, Hackbart attempted to block Clark by throwing his body in front of him. He thereafter remained on the ground. He turned, and with one knee on the ground, watched the play following the interception.

The trial court's finding was that Charles Clark, "acting out of anger and frustration, but without a specific intent to injure stepped forward and struck a blow with his right forearm to the back of the kneeling plaintiff's head and neck with sufficient force to cause both players to fall forward to the ground." Both players, without complaining to the officials or to one another, returned to their respective sidelines, since the ball had changed hands and the offensive and defensive teams of each had been substituted. Clark testified at trial that his frustration was brought about by the fact that his team was losing the game.

The officials did not notice the incident, and no foul was called. However, the game film showed very clearly what had occurred. The plaintiff did not report the happening to his coaches or to anyone else during the game. However, because of the pain he experienced, he was unable to play golf the next day. He did not seek medical attention, but the continued pain caused him to report this fact and the incident to the Bronco trainer, who gave him treatment. Apparently he played on the specialty teams for two successive Sundays, but after that the Broncos released him on waivers. (He was in his thirteenth year as a player.) He sought medical help, and it was then that it was discovered by the physician that he had a serious neck fracture injury.

Doyle, Circuit Judge

The evidence at the trial uniformly supported the proposition that the intentional striking of a player in the head from the rear is not an accepted part of either the playing rules or the general customs of the game of professional football. The trial court, however, believed that the unusual nature of the case called for the consideration of underlying policy which it defined as common law principles which have evolved as a result of the case to case process and which necessarily affect behavior in various contexts. From these considerations the belief was expressed that even intentional injuries incurred in football games should be outside the framework of the law.

We are forced to conclude that the result reached is not supported by evidence.

Contrary to the position of the trial court then, there are no principles of law which allow a court to rule out certain tortious conduct by reason of general roughness of the game or difficulty of administering it.

The general customs of football do not approve the intentional punching or striking of others. That this is prohibited was supported by the testimony of all of the witnesses. They testified that the intentional striking of a player in the face

or from the rear is prohibited by the playing rules as well as the general customs of the game. Punching or hitting with the arms is prohibited. Undoubtedly these restraints are intended to establish reasonable boundaries so that one football player cannot intentionally inflict a serious injury on another. Therefore, the notion is not correct that all reason has been abandoned, whereby the only possible remedy for the person who has been the victim of an unlawful blow is retaliation.

The Restatement of Torts Second, section 500, distinguishes between reckless misconduct and intentional wrongdoing. To be reckless the act must have been intended by the actor. At the same time, the actor does not intend to cause the harm which results from it. It is enough that he realized, or from the facts should have realized, that there was a strong probability that harm would result even though he may hope or expect that his conduct will prove harmless. Nevertheless, existence of probability is different from substantial certainty which is an ingredient of intent to cause the harm which results from the act.

Therefore, recklessness exists where a person knows that the act is harmful but fails to realize that it will produce the extreme harm which it did produce. It is in this respect that recklessness and intentional conduct differ in degree.

In the case at bar the defendant Clark admittedly acted impulsively and in the heat of anger, and even though it could be said from the admitted facts that he intended the act, it could also be said that he did not intend to inflict serious injury which resulted from the blow which he struck.

In ruling that recklessness is the appropriate standard and that assault and battery is not the exclusive one, we are saying that these two liability concepts are not necessarily opposed one to the other. Rather, recklessness under section 500 of the Restatement might be regarded, for the purpose of analysis at least, a lesser included act.

THE TORT OF NEGLIGENCE

The most common form of tort is the tort of **negligence.** Torts of negligence involve an injury caused by the actions or conduct of a wrongdoer. However, being the wrongdoer in a tort of negligence does not require an evil mental state or purposeful act. The focus of the doctrine is not the intent of the action that caused the injury, but the conduct itself. Negligence involves a lapse in an acceptable pattern of conduct that creates an unreasonable risk of injury. When injury occurs, a tort of negligence exists.

Most often, torts of negligence involve carelessness on the part of the wrongdoer. Perhaps the wrongdoer should have taken a precaution or two to prevent the possibility of an injury occurring. A common example of a tort of negligence is an automobile accident. Safely driving an automobile involves paying attention to the road. Drivers create a risk to others when their minds or eyes wander from the task at hand. Suppose Mary is driving her new car along a city street. As she reaches to change a tape in her cassette player, she looks from the road. Tom, who is crossing the street, is hit by Mary's car and suffers a broken leg.

Mary committed a tort of negligence. She did not intend to hit Tom as he crossed the street, nor was she driving in a reckless manner (for example, at a high speed or while intoxicated). Mary's attention was simply diverted from her driving. As a result of her careless behavior, Tom was injured.

A tort of negligence has four elements. First, a legal duty must exist that establishes a standard of care that a person must follow. This standard of care is based upon reasonableness. For example, the driver of an automobile is required to act as a reasonable and prudent person would act in the operation of that automobile. That is the driver's legal duty of care. Second, there must be a breach of the duty of care. For example, the driver of the automobile looks from the road in order to change a tape. This conduct breaches the duty of care. Reasonable and prudent drivers do not take their eyes from the road. Third, this breach of legal duty must cause an injury to another. Mary's car crashes into Tom, who was crossing the street. Fourth, actual loss or damage must occur. In our example, Tom's leg was broken. These elements must be proven by an injured party (the **plaintiff**) in order to prevail in a tort action for negligence.

The law of negligence imposes liability on all persons who deviate from a certain standard of care. This standard of care is not derived from a list of approved rules of behavior for all types of human activity. There is no book to consult. Instead the

Standard of Care

law creates a general standard, which it imposes on all types of behavior. This standard is called the **reasonable person** standard of care.

The reasonable person is a fictitious individual in the law whose behavior sets the standard that all other persons must meet. The issue in a tort of negligence is whether the wrongdoer acted as a reasonable person would have acted under similar circumstances. In the previous example, a reasonable person would not have looked from the road in order to change a tape in a cassette player. Therefore, by not meeting the reasonable person standard, Mary was negligent. An old English case defined the tort of negligence as follows: "Negligence is the omission to do something which a reasonable man, guided upon those considerations which ordinarily regulate the conduct of human affairs, would do, or doing something which a prudent and reasonable man would not do."[1]

Causation

Not every negligent act will create a tort of negligence. The negligent act must cause the injury. If Mary, in our example, had simply changed the tape and had not hit Tom, no tort would have occurred. Her conduct still fell below the reasonable person standard, but no injury arose from it.

However, a more difficult problem of causation occurs when injuries are less closely related to the negligent conduct. In the example, Mary's negligence was clearly the cause of Tom's injury. Her inattentiveness directly led to her car's striking Tom. However, what if Tom had been carrying a package, which fell from his arms when he was struck? A passer-by tripped over the package, falling into a ladder. A painter on the ladder slipped and fell onto a second passer-by. The second passer-by was injured. Did Mary's negligence cause the injury to the second passer-by?

This issue of causation is called **proximate cause.** Proximate cause is a term of art in the law. It essentially means that the injury in question must be within the scope of foreseeability of the defendant's conduct. Or to put it another way, the injury must be a "natural and probable" consequence of the conduct of the defendant. Proximate cause responds to a need in tort law to limit the liability exposure of a negligent person to injuries reasonably related to the negligent conduct. In the example, it is unlikely that Mary's negligence would be found to be the proximate cause of the injury to the second passer-by. That injury was not foreseeable, nor was it a natural consequence of her inattentiveness.

The following case involves a tort of negligence. See if you can identify the duty, the breach of duty, the breach being the cause of an injury, and an actual damage or loss to the plaintiff. What element was found to be missing by the court?

Palsgraf v. Long Island R. Co.
Court of Appeals of New York
162 N.E. 99 (1928)

Palsgraf was standing on a platform of defendant's railroad after buying a ticket to go to Rockaway Beach. A train stopped at the station, bound for another place. Two men ran forward to catch it. One of the men reached the platform of the car without mishap, though the train was already moving. The other man, carrying a package, jumped aboard the car but seemed unsteady, as if about to fall. A guard on the car, who had held the door open, reached forward to help him in, and another guard on the platform pushed him from behind. In this act, the package was dislodged, and fell upon the rails. It was a small package, about fifteen inches long, and was covered by a newspaper. In fact it contained fireworks, but there was nothing in its appearance to give notice of its contents. The fireworks exploded when they fell. The shock of the explosion threw down some scales used for weighing at the other end of the platform many feet away. The scales struck the plaintiff, Palsgraf, causing injuries for which she sued.

Cardozo, Chief Justice

The conduct of the defendant's guard, if a wrong in its relation to the holder of the package, was not a wrong in its relation to the plaintiff, standing far away. Nothing in the situation gave notice that the falling package had in it the potency of peril to persons thus removed. Negligence is not actionable unless it involves the invasion of a legally protected interest, the violation of a right. "Proof of negligence in the air, so to speak, will not do." If no hazard was apparent to the eye of ordinary vigilance, an act innocent and harmless, at least to outward seeming, with reference to her, did not take to itself the quality of a tort because it happened to be a wrong, though apparently not one involving the risk of bodily insecurity, with reference to some one else. "In every instance, before negligence can be predicated of a given act, back of the act must be sought and found a duty to the individual complaining, the observance of which would have averted or avoided the injury." "The ideas of negligence and duty are strictly correlative."

One who jostles one's neighbor in a crowd does not invade the rights of others standing at the outer fringe when the unintended contact casts a bomb upon the ground. The wrongdoer as to them is the man who carries the bomb, not the one who explodes it without suspicion of the danger. Life will have to be made over, and human nature transformed, before prevision so extravagant can be accepted as the norm of conduct, the customary standard to which behavior must conform.

The risk reasonably to be perceived defines the duty to be obeyed, and risk imports relation; it is risk to another or to others within the range of apprehension. Here, by concession, there was nothing in the situation to suggest to the most cautious mind that the parcel wrapped in newspaper would spread wreckage through the station. If the guard had thrown it down knowingly and willfully, he would not have threatened the plaintiff's safety, so far as appearances could warn him. His conduct would not have involved, even then, an unreasonable probability of invasion of her bodily security. Liability can be no greater where the act is inadvertent.

Negligence is not a tort unless it results in the commission of a wrong, and the commission of a wrong imports the violation of a right.

Andrews, Justice (dissenting)

Negligence may be defined roughly as an act or omission which unreasonably does or may affect the rights of others, or which unreasonably fails to protect one's self from the dangers resulting from such acts.

There must be both the act or the omission, and the right. It is the act itself, not the intent of the actor, that is important.

Where there is the unreasonable act, and some right that may be affected there is negligence whether damage does or does not result. That is immaterial. Should we drive down Broadway at a reckless speed, we are negligent whether we strike an approaching car or miss it by an inch. The act itself is wrongful. It is a wrong not only to those who happen to be within the radius of danger, but to all who might have been there—a wrong to the public at large.

Due care is a duty imposed on each one of us to protect society from unnecessary danger, not to protect A, B, or C alone.

Negligence does involve a relationship between man and his fellows, but not merely a relationship between man and those whom he might reasonably expect his act would injure; rather, a relationship between him and those whom he does in fact injure. If his act has a tendency to harm some one, it harms him a mile away as surely as it does those on the scene.

The proposition is this: Every one owes to the world at large the duty of refraining from those acts that may unreasonably threaten the safety of others. Such an act occurs. Not only is he wronged to whom harm might reasonably be expected to result, but he also who is in fact injured, even if he be outside what would generally be thought the danger zone.

As we have said, we cannot trace the effect of an act to the end, if end there is. Again, however, we may trace it part of the way. An overturned lantern may burn all Chicago. We may follow the fire from the shed to the last building. We rightly say the fire started by the lantern caused its destruction.

A cause, but not the proximate cause. What we do mean by the word "proximate" is that, because of convenience, of public policy, of a rough sense of justice, the law arbitrarily declines to trace a series of events beyond a certain point. This is not logic. It is practical politics.

We look back to the catastrophe, the fire kindled by the spark, or the explosion. We trace the consequences, not indefinitely, but to a certain point. And to aid us in fixing that point we ask what might ordinarily be expected to follow the fire or the explosion.

This last suggestion is the factor which must determine the case before us. The act upon which defendant's liability rests is knocking an apparently harmless package onto the platform. The act was negligent. For its proximate consequences the defendant is liable. If its contents were broken, to the owner; if it fell upon and crushed a passenger's foot, then to him; if it exploded and injured one in the immediate vicinity, to him also as to A in the illustration. Mrs. Palsgraf was standing some distance away. How far cannot be told from the record—apparently 25 to 30 feet, perhaps less. Except for the explosion, she would not have been injured. We are told by the appellant in his brief, "It cannot be denied that the explosion was the direct cause of the plaintiff's injuries." So it was a substantial factor in producing the result—there was here a natural and continuous sequence—direct connection. The only intervening cause was that, instead of blowing her to the ground, the concussion smashed the weighing machine which in turn fell upon her. There was no remoteness in time, little in space. And surely, given such an explosion as here, it needed no great foresight to predict that the natural result would be to injure one on the platform at no greater distance from its scene than was the plaintiff. Just how no one might be able to predict. Whether by flying fragments, by broken glass, by wreckage of machines or structures no one could say. But injury in some form was most probable.

Under these circumstances I cannot say as a matter of law that the plaintiff's injuries were not the proximate result of the negligence.

Res Ipsa Loquitur

Res ipsa loquitur is a doctrine that shifts the burden of proof from the injured party (the plaintiff) to the wrongdoer (the defendant) in a claim of negligence. The term translates to "the act speaks for itself." It is a combination of two concepts. First, that there is circumstantial evidence that someone was negligent. (A barrel falls from a warehouse window onto a passing pedestrian. The falling of the barrel is sufficient circumstantial evidence to show that someone at the warehouse must have somehow been negligent.) The second concept is the switching of the burden of proof of the negligence from the plaintiff to the defendant. (Under res ipsa loquitur, the plaintiff need only establish that the barrel fell. The presumption would then be that its falling was caused by the warehouse's negligence. The warehouse defendant would then need to establish that there was no negligence on its part.)

Generally three factors (in some states, four) must exist before res ipsa loquitur will apply. First, the event must have been one that would usually not occur without negligence. Second, the event must have been caused by something within the exclusive control of the defendant. Third, the event must not have been caused by any voluntary act of the plaintiff's. Fourth, evidence concerning the event must have been more accessible to the defendant than to the plaintiff.

Rose v. Melody Lane of Wilshire
Supreme Court of California
247 P.2d 335 (1952)

At about 11:00 P.M., plaintiff and a friend entered defendant's cocktail room for a drink on their way home from a lodge meeting. There is no question of intoxication; the injuries were sustained before any liquor was consumed. Almost immediately upon their sitting down at the bar, and while his companion was giving their order to the attendant, plaintiff's chair separated from its supporting base and he fell backward to the floor, sustaining injury.

Traynor, Justice

Defendant contends that the accident resulted from a latent defect in the pin, that defendant did not know of the defect, and that reasonable inspection to ascertain the condition of the stools had been made. Since defendant is not an insurer of the safety of its premises but is liable only for negligence in constructing, maintaining, or inspecting them, it argues that the evidence is insufficient to sustain the verdict.

The very fact that it is virtually impossible to detect this type of defect made it all the more important that defendant install stools so designed that the possibility of a break is reduced to a minimum. In denying defendant's motion for a directed verdict, the trial judge said, "I believe there is sufficient evidence for the jury to decide whether or not there was a latent defect, or whether the rod was perhaps too small to support the weight." It may even have been the conclusion of the jury that an additional pin or other safety device was reasonably necessary to guard against injury.

Plaintiff was entitled to rely upon the doctrine of res ipsa loquitur. That doctrine applies if the accident in question would not ordinarily have happened in the absence of negligence and if defendant had exclusive control over the instrumentality causing the injury.

Seats designed for use by patrons of commercial establishments do not ordinarily collapse without negligence in their construction, maintenance, or use.

Here it was the condition of the stool, not the use made of it, that was responsible for the fall. Plaintiff had done no more than sit upon it when it gave way, and there is no suggestion that his conduct was in any way improper. So far as construction, inspection, or maintenance of the stool were concerned, defendant had exclusive control. Plaintiff's actions had no more legal significance as a cause of the accident than those of the innocent bystander in the typical res ipsa loquitur case.

When res ipsa loquitur is applicable, as it is here, an inference of defendant's negligence may be drawn. On appeal that inference is sufficient to sustain a verdict against defendant unless it is overcome by plaintiff's own evidence, or unless it is conclusively rebutted by evidence that is "clear, positive, uncontradicted, and of such a nature that it can not rationally be disbelieved."

The inference in this case was not dispelled by plaintiff's own evidence. Nor did defendant's countershowing conclusively establish absence of negligence on its part. The jury may have rejected defendant's evidence that the accident resulted from a latent defect in the pin. The credibility of defendant's expert witness and the probative value of his testimony were questions for the triers of fact.

TORT LAW AND HISTORY

Developments in the tort of negligence in the United States reflect changes in lifestyle and technology. Much of the increased capacity of negligent acts to cause injuries is an outgrowth of the availability of machines and new technology. For example, if a person walking along a pathway bumps into another walker it is unlikely that an injury would occur. However, if that same person was daydreaming while driving an automobile, thereby causing a collision, the probability of injury would be very great.

Tort law, especially the law of negligence, was a child of the Industrial Revolution, before which the law of negligence was not well developed. Most actions for tort concerned intentional torts, usually arising out of the use of physical force. In fact, the first major work on negligence law was not written until 1850. The leading commentators on the law before that time mentioned it only briefly. But as the machine age began, and especially as the railroads began to spread throughout the country, a great number of machine-related injuries began to occur. Not only did the Industrial Revolution change the way people lived, where people lived, and how people worked, but it also had a profound effect on the law of torts. As Lawrence Friedman wrote: "The modern law of torts must be laid at the door of the industrial revolution, whose machines had a marvelous capacity for smashing the human body."[2]

However, tort law requires a balancing of interests. The same machines that smashed human bodies also created wealth, provided jobs, and were the key to growth and development of the country. Railroads served to open the West by linking wilderness and farm areas to cities and markets. An inherent problem, one that continues to surface in tort law, became apparent. Courts, in creating tort law doctrines, must continually be aware that too narrow a reading of the tort doctrines may impose harsh consequences on injured victims, while a very broad concept of tort could cripple a new industry by draining its resources.

Nineteenth-Century Limitations on Tort Law Recovery

In the latter part of the nineteenth century, courts were rather sympathetic to the interests of developing industry and created a number of doctrines that limited the ability of the injured individual to collect damages. Three major doctrines arose that were defenses to be used by a defendant in an action for negligence. The effects of these defenses were particularly severe to the worker who happened to be injured on the job. These legal rules favored the developing industrial base of the country by limiting its exposure to liability claims.

Contributory Negligence. One of these doctrines was called the doctrine of contributory negligence. It provided that if the plaintiff (the injured party) and the defendant were both negligent, resulting in the plaintiff's injury, then the plaintiff would be unable to recover damages in tort from the defendant. The injured party would in a sense have to establish that the defendant alone was at fault. Some writers have suggested that even the slightest degree of negligence by the injured party was enough to deny recovery from the defendant.

Assumption of the Risk and the Fellow Servant Rule. Two other doctrines were even more effective in limiting the ability of workers who were injured on the job to successfully bring a tort claim against an employer. One doctrine, assumption of the risk, basically provides that if a person is voluntarily in a position where risk of injury exists, and that injury occurs, then no tort will be found to have occurred. For example, if you knowingly and voluntarily enter the cage of a hungry and ferocious lion, which then uses your leg for lunch, you have no tort claim against its owner, since you will have assumed the risk of being attacked by the beast upon entering the cage. Although this seems to be a fair doctrine, in the nineteenth century, workers were frequently held to have assumed the risks involved in their jobs merely upon accepting the job.

A second rule that further limited the ability of workers to collect damages was called the fellow servant rule. This rule provided that workers could not sue employers for job-related injuries caused by another employee. Since very few employers were actually on the shop floor or in the mine or in the railroad yard, this doctrine too limited the ability of the worker to recover for injuries. The only tort claim would be against the negligent fellow employee. A damage claim is worthless unless the party who is liable has the funds to pay it. Few ordinary laborers would have such money.

The following two cases are examples of these doctrines at work in the nineteenth-century courts. Note the harshness of the result to the injured party. By reading these cases with twentieth-century eyes, you may be able to foresee a major change in tort law, which involves a shift in the policies balance toward a system of providing compensation for those who are injured.

Haring v. New York and Erie Railroad

Supreme Court of New York
13 Barb. 2 (N.Y. 1851)

The complaint alleged that Haring was thrown out of his sleigh with great force and violence and was so severely and seriously injured as to cause his death in a few hours, and that the injury was caused by the gross carelessness, negligence, or willful mismanagement of the defendants. The defendants denied that the death of Haring was caused by their carelessness, or negligence, or willful misconduct, but alleged that it was caused by the gross carelessness and negligence of Haring and of the person who was with him in the sleigh at the time.

Barculo, Justice

The undisputed evidence introduced by the plaintiff, established the fact that her deceased husband, whose death is the subject of the action, was riding in a sleigh with another person, who was driving at the rapid rate of a mile in four or five minutes, across the track of the railroad when the collision occurred. It also appeared that near the point of intersection, high embankments between the railroad, and highway, render it impossible for a person on the highway to see the cars coming until he gets on the track. Upon this state of facts, the simple question was presented to the circuit judge, whether such fast driving at such a place, constituted a degree of negligence that defeated the plaintiff's right of recovery.

That the deceased was guilty of negligence, cannot for a moment be doubted. A man who rushes headlong against a locomotive engine, without using the ordinary means of discovering his danger, cannot be said to exercise ordinary care. And the rule is well settled that where the carelessness and imprudence of the person injured contributed to the injury, an action for damages cannot be sustained.

It is contended by the counsel for the plaintiff, that the question of negligence should have been submitted to the jury. But when, upon the plaintiff's own showing, he has defeated his claim by his own misconduct, there can be no propriety in requiring the jury to pass upon the evidence. We can not shut our eyes to the fact that in certain controversies between the weak and the strong—between a humble individual and a gigantic corporation, the sympathies of the human mind naturally, honestly and generously, run to the assistance and support of the feeble, and apparently oppressed; and that compassion will sometimes exercise over the deliberations of a jury, an influence which, however honorable to them as philanthropists, is wholly inconsistent with the principles of law and the ends of justice. There is, therefore, a manifest propriety in withdrawing from the consideration of the jury, those cases in which the plaintiff fails to show a right of recovery.

The facts here are plain, simple and undisputed; and upon them the law is clear that the plaintiff cannot recover.

Farwell v. Boston and Worcester Railroad

Supreme Court of Massachusetts
45 Mass. 49 (1842)

The plaintiff was employed by the defendant as an engineer. His duties included the management and care of the engines and cars running on the railroad between Boston and Worcester. He alleged that on October 30, 1837, another employee, Whitecomb, negligently operated the switching apparatus, causing the engine and cars upon which the plaintiff was working to be thrown from the tracks. In the process, the plaintiff was thrown to the ground, and his hand was crushed and destroyed when one of the wheels of one of the cars passed over it.

Shaw, Chief Justice

The question is, whether, for damages sustained by Farwell by means of the carelessness and negligence of Whitecomb, the party injured has a remedy against their common employer.

The general rule, resulting from considerations of justice as well as of policy, is, that he who engages in the employment of another for the performance of specified duties and services, for compensation, takes upon himself the natural and ordinary risks and perils incident to the performance of such services, and in legal presumption, the compensation is adjusted accordingly. And we are not aware of any principle which should except the perils arising from the carelessness and negligence of those who are in the same employment. These are perils which the servant is as likely to know, and against which he can as effectually guard, as the master. They are perils incident to the service, and which can be as distinctly foreseen and provided for in the rate of compensation as any others.

We are of opinion that where several persons are employed in the conduct of one common enterprise or undertaking, and the safety of each depends much on the care and skill with which each other shall perform his appropriate duty, each is an observer of the conduct of the others, can give notice of any misconduct, incapacity or neglect of duty, and leave the service, if the common employer will not take such precautions, and employ such agents as the safety of the whole party may require. By these means, the safety of each will be much more effectually secured, than could be done by a resort to the common employer for indemnity in case of loss by the negligence of each other. Regarding it in this light, it is the ordinary case of one sustaining an injury in the course of his own employment, in which he must bear the loss himself, or seek his remedy, if he have any, against the actual wrong-doer.

In applying these principles to the present case, it appears that the plaintiff was employed by the defendants as an engineer, at the rate of wages usually paid in that employment, being a higher rate than the plaintiff had before received as a machinist. It was a voluntary undertaking on his part, with a full knowledge of the risks incident to the employment; and the loss was sustained by means of an ordinary casualty, caused by the negligence of another servant of the company. Under these circumstances, the loss must be deemed to be the result of a pure accident, like those to which all men, in all employments, and at all times, are more or less exposed; and like similar losses from accidental causes, it must rest where it first fell, unless the plaintiff has a remedy against the person actually in default; of which we give no opinion.

Of course not all courts and cases exactly paralleled these situations. Juries were often very sympathetic to the injured party. But the legal doctrines of contributory negligence and assumption of the risk, and the fellow servant rule often provided the means to remove the case from the sympathy of the jury. These and other doctrines were criticized even at the time for their harsh treatment of the injured. Attorneys began attacking those doctrines, and a number of exceptions were developed by the courts. As the nineteenth century moved toward its end, political pressure arose from labor unions and other groups for reforms in this area of law.

DEVELOPMENTS IN TORT LAW

Tort law is an ever-changing, ever-expanding field. The United States in the 1980s is vastly different from the United States in the latter half of the nineteenth century, when many of the basic doctrines of tort law arose. The railroad, which some writers suggest was central in the development of many of the doctrines, today has been replaced by the automobile and consumer products as a generator of tort law claims. No longer a new, undeveloped nation, the United States is now heavily industrialized.

Insurance has arisen to cushion the effects of tort liability for individuals and industry. Many of the rules designed to protect the capital of new industry have been questioned and seriously challenged. In fact, the tort law system itself is being scrutinized to discover whether it is a viable system for providing compensation to the victims in modern society. The following discussion will examine the movement and growth of some tort law doctrines today.

Developments in Tort Law: Compensation of Injured Workers

In response to the effect of the nineteenth century application of contributory negligence, assumption of the risk, and the fellow servant rule to the workplace, states in 1910 began to enact **workmen's compensation** statutes. By the early 1920s, virtually every state legislature, and the Congress in the case of government employees, had enacted a plan. The statutes removed accidents and injuries to a worker on the job from the tort law system. Workmen's compensation was a system of no-fault social insurance. The injured worker would collect a sum of damages, prescribed by statute, from the workmen's compensation fund. The employer would be assessed premiums to pay into the fund, and the employee would be barred from bringing a negligence suit against the employer. The system provided a number of advantages. The employer was no longer subject to lawsuit by an employee negligently injured on the job. The employer knew what payments would be made and would be able to plan for them, as for any other regular cost of doing business. The employee would be assured of reasonably prompt payment for work-related injuries. The doctrines that made it extremely difficult to collect for injuries from an employer no longer would have an effect. Furthermore, the new system eliminated much litigation, which had formerly caused a great deal of delay in the injured worker's receiving any money. The costs and attorney fees associated with the lawsuit had often substantially decreased the money actually paid to the worker.

Today, however, complaints are being raised against the workmen's compensation system by injured workers—not because of its structure, but because in many states the statutory amount awarded for a work-related injury is very low. Frequently the amount of money received by the injured worker would be less than if a tort law remedy had been available. Furthermore, with government assistance plans available, as well as private insurance and disability coverage, an injured worker is often no longer without a source of funds and could better afford to await the outcome of litigation than a nineteenth-century counterpart. Additionally, although the workplace today is certainly not injury-free, it in no way resembles the conditions in factories and industries prior to the enactment of the compensation acts. The government now regulates safety in the workplace and inspects factories, mines, and other areas to determine if the employer is complying with safety regulations. Lack of compliance could well mean government action being taken against the employer. The relationship between the employer and employee is much different today from what it was in the nineteenth century, and the attitude of the courts is certainly less protective of industry than it was in the nineteenth century.

Some states have raised and improved the benefits available to workers under the workmen's compensation statutes. However, this action required increased payments by employers into the compensation fund. Consequently, some have argued that, other things being equal, a new employer may decide not to locate in that state in order to save money on a cost of doing business. This, they argue, may cost the state jobs in the long run.

Given the many changes in American society just mentioned, one might expect new law to be made in workmen's compensation, which would begin to permit certain types of worker lawsuits against employers for on-the-job injuries. Attorneys are attempting to skirt the prohibition against employee suits by convincing the courts that tort law suits other than those based on negligence are not barred by the statute. One such attempt is to show the injury was caused by an intentional tort. As previously discussed, an intentional tort is different from one based on negligence and is not limited to situations in which the action was hostile or was meant to cause harm, like a punch in the nose. A practical joke that results in an injury may be considered an intentional tort. The key is the concept of intent, which has been interpreted by courts to mean whether a reasonable person would expect that the result was almost certain to follow from an act. Plaintiffs' attorneys have filed cases arguing that clients' injuries on the job, caused by exposure to dangerous chemicals, were suffered as a result of an intentional tort of the employer. The employer would not actually have intended that an employee be injured by exposure to the chemicals, but by failing to correct the unsafe working conditions, the employer created a situation in which a reasonable person would expect injuries to occur. Thus, it is argued, the conduct would be considered an intentional tort.

Blankenship v. Cincinnati Milacron Chemicals
Supreme Court of Ohio
433 N.E.2d 572 (1982)

On February 22, 1979, eight current or former employees of Cincinnati Milacron instituted an action seeking compensatory and punitive damages against their employer (Milacron). They alleged in their complaints that while they were stationed at Milacron's chemical manufacturing facility in Reading, Ohio, they were exposed to the fumes and otherwise noxious characteristics of certain chemicals within the scope of their employment. They further alleged that notwithstanding the knowledge of Milacron that such conditions existed, Milacron failed to correct the conditions, failed to warn the employees of the dangers and conditions that existed, and failed to report conditions to the various state and federal agencies to which they were required to report by law. They alleged that the failure was intentional, malicious, and in willful and wanton disregard of the health of employees, and that as a direct and proximate result of this failure they have been injured.

The trial court issued an order on October 5, 1980, that dismissed the action on the ground that the action was barred by relevant sections of the Ohio Workers' Compensation Act, which afforded an employer and his employees total immunity from civil suit.

This holding was appealed and subsequently affirmed by the court of appeals on January 14, 1980.

Brown, Justice

The sole issue raised in this appeal is whether the trial court properly granted appellees' motion to dismiss appellants' complaint.

The primary focus of the dispute between the parties centers upon the question of whether the Workers' Compensation Act is intended to cover an intentional tort committed by employers against their employees.

The pertinent statutory language does not expressly extend the grant of immunity to actions alleging intentional tortious conduct by employers against their employees. The statutory language clearly limits the categories of injuries for which the employer is exempt from civil liability. By designating as compensable only those injuries received or contracted in the course of or arising out of employment the General Assembly has expressly limited the scope of compensability. By its use of this phrase, the General Assembly has seemingly allowed the judiciary the freedom to determine what risks are incidental to employment in light of the humanitarian purposes which underlie the Act.

Where an employee asserts in his complaint a claim for damages based on an intentional tort, the substance of the claim is not an "injury . . . received or contracted by any employee in the course of or arising out of his employment." No reasonable individual would equate intentional and unintentional conduct in terms of the degree of risk which faces an employee nor would such individual contemplate the risk of an intentional tort as a natural risk of employment. Since an employer's intentional conduct does not arise out of employment, the Act does not bestow upon employers immunity from civil liability for their intentional torts and an employee may resort to a civil suit for damages.

The worker's compensation system is based on the premise that an employer is protected from a suit for negligence in exchange for compliance with the Workers' Compensation Act. The Act operates as a balance of mutual compromise between the interests of the employer and the employee whereby employees relinquish their common law remedy and accept lower benefit levels coupled with the great assurance of recovery and employers give up their common law defenses and are protected from unlimited liability. But the protection afforded by the Act has always been for negligent acts and not for intentional tortious conduct. Indeed, workers' compensation Acts were designed to improve the plight of the injured worker, and to hold that intentional torts are covered under the Act would be tantamount to encouraging such conduct, and this clearly cannot be reconciled with the motivating spirit and purpose of the Act.

In addition, one of the avowed purposes of the Act is to promote a safe and injury-free work environment. Affording an employer immunity for his intentional behavior certainly would not promote such an environment, for an employer could commit intentional acts with impunity with the knowledge that, at the very most his worker's compensation premiums may rise slightly. The judgment of the Court of Appeals is reversed.

Krupansky, Justice (dissenting)

The majority opinion, while appearing on the surface to be a humanitarian gesture, in effect undermines the beneficient purposes for which the Ohio Workers' Compensation Act was created.

Nowhere in the language of the statute is there support for the conclusion that the workers compensation system was designed to compensate employees solely for employer negligence. The majority claims, if intentional torts are covered under the Act then intentional torts are encouraged. If this is true, then are not negligence and industrial accidents similarly encouraged, since they are covered under the Act?

Such reasoning leads ultimately to releasing the floodgates to a whole vista of lawsuits, each claiming exceptions to the all-inclusive language of the Act. The majority opinion represents a foot in the door policy to encourage workers to sue their employers for damages in addition to compensation provided under the Act.

The intent of the General Assembly, was to eliminate all damage suits outside the Act for injury or disease arising out of employment, including suits based on intentional tort. If the General Assembly desired to create an exception for intentional misconduct it surely could have done so.

The majority's myopic approach disrupts the delicate balance struck by the Act between the interests of labor, management and the public and signals the erosion of a valuable system which has served its purpose of providing a common fund for the benefit of all workers.

While that Act provides for a liberal construction, it must not be used as a panacea to justify reasoning which suffers from logical malnutrition. One of the long-range effects of permitting recovery in these types of cases is the additional costs that will ultimately have to be borne by the consumer through increased product prices. Goods manufactured in this state will thereby suffer a competitive disadvantage, and a less hospitable climate is created to attract and maintain industry in this state. Since industry provides jobs, the labor force has an interest in encouraging industry. Thus, while some workers may benefit from recovery against the employer for intentional torts in addition to collecting workers' compensation benefits, we would be ill-advised to engage in such irresponsibility for the benefit of a few at the detriment of so many.

Earlier in the discussion of the development of the tort of negligence in the nineteenth century, the doctrine of contributory negligence was briefly discussed. This doctrine served to deny recovery to an injured party whose own negligence contributed to the injuries, even if the defendant was also negligent. This doctrine has fallen into disfavor. Today a majority of the states have abandoned the doctrine and have substituted **comparative negligence.** Comparative negligence provides a proportional recovery to the injured party, based upon a comparison of the plaintiff's negligence with that of the defendant in causing the accident. This doctrine reflects a trend in tort law toward compensation of injured parties, weighing that factor more heavily than the factor of assigning fault to the wrongdoer.

Developments in Tort Law: The Demise of Contributory Negligence

---

Alvis v. Ribar
Supreme Court of Illinois
421 N.E.2d 886 (1981)

Plaintiffs ask the court to abolish the doctrine of contributory negligence and to adopt in its place the doctrine of comparative negligence as the law in Illinois.

A motor vehicle operated by defendant Ribar skidded out of control and collided with a metal barrel that anchored an official intersection stop sign. The sign had been temporarily placed at the intersection while construction work on the intersecting road was being done by the defendant Cook County. Plaintiff Alvis, who was a passenger in defendant Ribar's vehicle, sustained injuries as a result of the collision. He filed a multicount personal injury complaint seeking damages from Ribar, Cook County, and the construction company.

Moran, Justice

Generally, under the doctrine of contributory negligence, a plaintiff is barred from recovering compensation for his injuries if his negligence contributed to the accident.

Criticism of the harshness of the doctrine came as swiftly as did its acceptance into the law, and courts found exceptions to soften that harshness.

In 1910, Mississippi became the first State to adopt a comparative negligence statute applicable to negligence cases generally. The statute adopted the "pure" form of comparative negligence under which each responsible party would pay for the injuries sustained according to the relative percentage of his fault. Another form of comparative negligence was enacted by Wisconsin in 1931. This "modified" form allowed a negligent plaintiff to recover for his injuries only if his negligence was "not as great as that of the defendant."

The contributory negligence defense has been subject to attack because of its failure to apportion damages according to the fault of the parties. Under a comparative negligence standard, the parties are allowed to recover the proportion of damages not attributable to their own fault. The basic logic and fairness of such apportionment is difficult to dispute. We believe that the concept of comparative negligence which produces a more just and socially desirable distribution of loss is demanded by today's society.

Defendants contend that the apportionment of relative fault by a jury cannot be scientifically done, as such precise measurement is impossible. The simple and obvious answer to this contention is that in 36 jurisdictions of the United States such apportionment is being accomplished by juries. Although it is admitted that percentage allocations of fault are only approximations, the results are far superior to the "all or nothing" results of the contributory negligence rules.

There remains the question of the form of comparative negligence to be adopted. Under a "pure" form, the plaintiff's damages are simply reduced by the percentage of fault attributable to him. Under a "modified" form, a negligent plaintiff may recover so long as the percentage of his fault does not exceed 50 percent of the total.

The "pure" form of comparative negligence is the only system which truly apportions damages according to the relative fault of the parties and, thus, achieves total justice. The '50 percent' system simply shifts the lottery aspect to the contributory negligence rule to a different ground. There is no better justification for allowing a defendant who is 49 percent at fault to completely escape liability than there is to allow a defendant who is 99 percent at fault under the old rule to escape liability.

Mindful of the facts stated and that the vast majority of legal scholars who have studied the area recommend the "pure" approach, we are persuaded that the "pure" form of comparative negligence is preferable, and we therefore adopt it as the law of Illinois.

| Developments in Tort Law: New Torts—Wrongful Life | Given the relationship between tort law and social change, one can expect to find new and very difficult questions of injury and liability coming before the courts. The following case raises a very difficult issue—that of the concept of wrongful life. With abortion available in the United States, parents may decide to abort a fetus that is shown by new and sophisticated medical technology to be deformed. If the tests were negligently performed, showing no deformity, and the child was carried to full term and born deformed, would the child have a claim against the doctor for wrongful life? That is, if the doctor had properly performed the tests, the plaintiff would have been aborted and would not be alive. But since the doctor erred, the plaintiff was born, although deformed. Are damages called for? If so, how are damages to be figured? Damages in tort attempt to put plaintiffs in the position they would have |

been had the tort not occurred. Is no life at all preferable to life in an impaired state? Are plaintiffs worse off because they are alive? Thus, technological advances today (like the rise of the railroad in the nineteenth century) can create new issues in tort that can have a profound influence on the use of new technology and on social values.

Turpin v. Sortini

Supreme Court of California

643 P.2d 954 (1982)

This case presents the question of whether a child born with a hereditary affliction may maintain a tort action against a medical care provider who—before the child's conception—negligently failed to advise the child's parents of the possibility of the hereditary condition, depriving them of the opportunity to choose not to conceive the child.

On September 24, 1976, James and Donna Turpin, acting on the advice of their pediatrician, brought their first—and at that time their only—daughter, Hope, to the Leon S. Peters Rehabilitation Center at the Fresno Community Hospital for evaluation of a possible hearing defect. The complaint alleges that Dr. Sortini and other persons at the hospital negligently examined, tested, and evaluated Hope and incorrectly advised her pediatrician that her hearing was within normal limits when, in reality, she was "stone deaf" as a result of a hereditary ailment. Hope's parents did not learn of her condition until October 15, 1977, when it was diagnosed by other specialists. According to the complaint, the nature of the condition is such that there is a reasonable degree of medical probability that the hearing defect would be inherited by any offspring of James and Donna. The complaint further alleges that in December 1976, before learning of Hope's true condition and relying on defendant's diagnosis, James and Donna conceived a second child, Joy. The complaint avers that had the Turpins known of Hope's hereditary deafness they would not have conceived Joy. Joy was born August 23, 1977, and suffers from the same total deafness as Hope.

Kaus, Justice

A plaintiff's remedy in tort is compensatory in nature and damages are generally intended not to punish a negligent defendant but to restore an injured person as nearly as possible to the position he or she would have been in had the wrong not been done. Because nothing defendants could have done would have given plaintiff an unimpaired life, it appears inconsistent with basic tort principles to view the injury for which defendants are legally responsible solely by reference to plaintiff's present condition without taking into consideration the fact that if defendants had not been negligent she would not have been born at all.

Although it is easy to understand and to endorse the desire to affirm the worth and sanctity of less-than-perfect life, we question whether these considerations alone provide a sound basis for rejecting the child's tort action. To begin with, it is hard to see how an award of damages to a severely handicapped or suffering child would "disavow" the value of life or in any way suggest that the child is not entitled to the full measure of legal and nonlegal rights and privileges accorded to all members of society.

In this case, in which the plaintiff's only affliction is deafness, it seems quite unlikely that a jury would ever conclude that life with such a condition is worse than not being born at all. Other wrongful life cases, however, have involved children with much more serious, debilitating and painful conditions, and the academic literature refers to still other, extremely severe hereditary diseases. Considering the short life span of many of these children and their frequently very limited ability to perceive or enjoy the benefits of life, we cannot assert with confidence that in every situation there would be a societal consensus that life is preferable to never having been born at all.

While it thus seems doubtful that a child's claim for general damages should properly be denied on the rationale that the value of impaired life, as a matter of law, always exceeds the value of nonlife, we believe that the out-of-state decisions are on sounder grounds in holding that—with respect to the child's claim for pain and suffering or other general damages—recovery should be denied because (1) it is simply impossible to determine in any rational or reasoned fashion whether the plaintiff has in fact suffered an injury in being born impaired rather than not being born, and (2) even if it were possible to overcome the first hurdle, it would be impossible to assess general damages in any fair, nonspeculative manner.

Justice Weintraub captured the heart of the problem simply and eloquently. "Ultimately, the infant's complaint is that he would be better off not to have been born. Man, who knows nothing of death or nothingness, cannot possibly know whether that is so. We must remember that the choice is not being born with health or being born without it. Rather the choice is between a worldly existence and none at all. To recognize a right not to be born is to enter an area in which no one can find his way."

Although we have determined that the trial court properly rejected plaintiff's claim for general damages, we conclude that her claim for the extraordinary expenses for specialized teaching, training and hearing equipment that she will incur during her lifetime because of her deafness stands on a different footing.

Realistically, a defendant's negligence in failing to diagnose a hereditary ailment places a significant medical and financial burden on the whole family unit. Unlike the child's claim for general damages, the damage here is both certain and readily measurable. Furthermore, in many instances these expenses will be vital not only to the child's well-being but to his or her very survival. Thus, while the child may not recover general damages for being born impaired as opposed to not being born at all, the child may recover special damages for the extraordinary expenses necessary to treat the hereditary ailment.

Developments in Tort Law: New Torts—Wrongful Discharge

The employer-employee relationship is sometimes a precarious affair. Most people are employees and earn their living working for someone else. Yet frequently these employees do not have job security. Their employment may be terminated at any time, for any reason. This notion is called the at-will employment doctrine.

The at-will employment doctrine holds that in the absence of an express contract to the contrary, an employee may be fired for no cause or for any cause whatsoever without a legal wrong being committed by the employer. However, the doctrine gives like rights to the employee, who may quit for any reason, in absence of express contract terms to the contrary, without committing a compensable legal wrong against the employer. Practically the doctrine works most often against the interests of the employee. The doctrine recognizes the great degree of control the employer has over an employee.

The doctrine arose in the late nineteenth century and became the general rule throughout the country. The Wagner Act in the 1930s limited the scope of the discharge right by making it unlawful for employers to fire employees who engaged in union activities. However, employees without contractual protection remained at the mercy of their employers. Examples of past judicially approved at-will discharges involve an employee fired because of refusal to falsify reports being submitted to the government.

Recently, a trend in the law has been to limit the absolute right of an employer to fire an employee in absence of contractual protection. Employees who have been unjustly fired from their jobs have instituted lawsuits alleging damages for tortious discharge by an employer. The following case is an example.

Wagenseller v. Scottsdale Memorial Hospital

Supreme Court of Arizona
710 P.2d 1025 (1985)

Catherine Wagenseller began her employment at Scottsdale Memorial Hospital as a staff nurse in March 1975, having been personally recruited by the manager of the emergency department, Kay Smith. Wagenseller was an "at-will" employee—one hired without a specific contractual term.

Most of the events surroundiing Wagenseller's work at the Hospital and her subsequent termination are not disputed. For more than four years, Smith and Wagenseller maintained a friendly professional, working relationship. In May 1979, they joined a group consisting largely of personnel from other hospitals for an eight-day camping and rafting trip down the Colorado River. According the Wagenseller, "an uncomfortable feeling" developed between her and Smith as the trip progressed—a feeling that Wagenseller ascribed to "the behavior that Kay Smith was displaying." Wagenseller states that this included public urination, defecation and bathing, heavy drinking, and "grouping up" with other rafters. Wagenseller did not participate in any of these activities. She also refused to join in the group's staging of a parody of the song "Moon River," which allegedly concluded with members of the group "mooning" the audience. Smith and others allegedly performed the "Moon River" skit twice at the hospital following the group's return from the river, but Wagenseller declined to participate there as well.

Wagenseller contends that her refusal to engage in these activities caused her relationship with Smith to deteriorate and was the proximate cause of her termination. She claims that following the river trip Smith began harassing her, using abusive language and embarrassing her in the company of other staff. Other emergency department staff reported a similar marked change in Smith's behavior toward Wagenseller after the trip, although Smith denied it. On November 1, 1979, Wagenseller was terminated.

Up to the time of the river trip, Wagenseller had received consistently favorable job performance evaluations. Two months before the trip, Smith completed an annual evaluation report in which she rated Wagenseller's performance as "exceed[ing] results expected," the second highest of five possible ratings.

Feldman, Justice

As early as 1562, the English common law presumed that an employment contract containing an annual salary provision or computation was for a one-year term. In the early nineteenth century, American courts borrowed the English rule. The legal rationale embodied in the rule was consistent with the nature of the predominant master-servant employment relationship at the time because it reflected the master's duty to make provision for the general well-being of his servants. The late nineteenth century, however, brought the Industrial Revolution; with it came the decline of the master-servant relationship and the rise of the more impersonal employer-employee relationship. In apparent response to the economic changes sweeping the country, American courts abandoned the English rule and adopted the employment-at-will doctrine. This new doctrine gave the employer freedom to terminate an at-will employee for any reason, good or bad. Thus, an employer was free to fire an employee hired for an indefinite term "for good cause, for no cause, or even for cause morally wrong, without being thereby guilty of legal wrong."

In recent years there has been apparent dissatisfaction with the absolutist formulation of the common law at-will rule. With the rise of large corporations conducting specialized operations and employing relatively immobile workers who often have no other place to market their skills, recognition that the employer and employee do not stand on equal footing is realistic. In addition, unchecked employer power, like unchecked employee power, has been seen to present a distinct threat to the public policy carefully considered and adopted by society as a whole. As a result, it is now recognized that a proper balance must be maintained among the employer's interest in operating a business efficiently and profitably, the employee's interest in earning a livelihood, and society's interest in seeing its public policies carried out. Today, courts in three-fifths of the states have recognized some form of a cause of action for wrongful discharge.

The most widely accepted approach is the

"public policy" exception, which permits recovery upon a finding that the employer's conduct undermined some important public policy. There is no precise definition of the term, "public policy." In general, it can be said that public policy concerns what is right and just and what affects the citizens of the state collectively. It is to be found in the State's constitution and statutes and, when they are silent, in its judicial decisions. Although there is no precise line of demarcation dividing matters that are the subject of public policies from matters purely personal, a survey of cases in other states involving retaliatory discharges shows that a matter must strike at the heart of a citizen's social rights, duties, and responsibilities before the tort will be allowed.

It may be argued, of course, that our economic system functions best if employers are given wide latitude in dealing with employees. We assume that it is in the public interest that employers continue to have that freedom. We also believe, however, that the interests of the economic system will be fully served if employers may fire for good cause or without cause. However, the interests of society as a whole will be promoted if employers are forbidden to fire for cause which is "morally wrong." We hold that an employer may fire for good cause or for no cause. He may not fire for bad cause—that which violates public policy.

In the case before us, Wagenseller refused to participate in activities which arguably would have violated our indecent exposure statute. While this statute may not embody a policy which "strikes at the heart of a citizen's social rights, duties and responsibilities" we believe that it was enacted to preserve and protect the commonly recognized sense of public privacy and decency. The statute does, therefore, recognize bodily privacy as a "citizen's social right." The nature of the act, and not its magnitude, is the issue. The legislature has already concluded that acts fitting the statutory description contravene the public policy of this state. The relevant inquiry here is not whether the alleged "mooning" incidents were either felonies or misdemeanors or constituted purely technical violations of the statute, but whether they contravened the important public policy interests embodied in the law. The law enacted by the legislature establishes a clear policy that public exposure of one's anus is contrary to public standards of morality. We are compelled to conclude that termination of employment for refusal to participate in public exposure of one's buttocks is a termination contrary to the policy of this state, even if, for instance, the employer might have grounds to believe that all of the onlookers were voyeurs and would not be offended. In this situation, there might be no crime, but there would be a violation of public policy to compel the employee to do an act ordinarily proscribed by the law.

We have little expertise in the techniques of mooning. We cannot say as a matter of law, therefore, whether mooning would always violate the statute. We deem such an inquiry unseemly and unnecessary in a civil case. Compelled exposure of the bare buttocks, on pain of termination of employment, is a sufficient violation of the policy embodied in the statute to support the action, even if there would have been no technical violation of the statute.

SUMMARY

Various doctrines of tort law (such as negligence, contributory negligence, comparative negligence, wrongful life, wrongful discharge) are judicial creations. These creations are based on a number of policies in the law concerning the notion of compensating injuries. These policies include compensating injured parties, deterring socially unreasonable conduct, adjusting the competing claims of litigating parties, weighing the interests of society that are affected by the legal rule, and assigning fault for the mishap among the conflicting parties.

Since these policies often conflict, there is continued tension within a given tort law doctrine. As shown by the historical material, judicial weight placed on any one of these policies may change over time, resulting in a change in the law. You should understand that the law is not static. It, like society as a whole, is constantly changing to meet the needs of today.

REVIEW QUESTIONS

1. Define the following terms:
   a. Tort
   b. Negligence
   c. Intentional tort
   d. Workmen's compensation
   e. Comparative negligence

2. What are the major differences between a tort of negligence and an intentional tort? Give an example of each.

3. What are the functions of tort law?

4. Discuss the defenses to tort claims that arose during the nineteenth century and that limited an injured person's right to recover damages.

5. Sandra brought suit against a grocery store, alleging that the manager of the store included a dead rat with the groceries that were delivered to her home. She alleged that, as a practical joke, the manager caused the package to be prepared for delivery with the dead rat inside. When the package was delivered, the person who delivered it stated, "The store manager said you had better open the package while I am here." When Sandra opened the package, she saw the dead rat, whereupon she fainted, fell to the floor, and was injured.

   What type of tort should Sandra allege took place? Would your answer change if a rat from the grocery store's storage area had simply crawled into the package without the knowledge of anyone in the store? Could a tort still be said to exist?

6. The plaintiff is the infant son of the defendant. He seeks damages from his father because he is an illegitimate child.

    The defendant is the plaintiff's father; the defendant induced the plaintiff's mother to have sexual relations by promising to marry her. This promise was not kept and could not be kept because, unknown to the mother, the defendant was already married. The complaint charges that the promise was fraudulent, that the acts of the defendant were willful, and that the defendant injured the plaintiff in his person, property, and reputation by causing him to be born an adulterine bastard. The plaintiff seeks damages for the deprivation of his right to be a legitimate child, to have a normal home, to have a legal father, to inherit from his father, and to inherit from his paternal ancestors, and for being stigmatized as a bastard. The essence of the complaint is the concept of wrongful life.

    Analyze this case in light of the material on tort law and on the *Turpin* case.

7. Discuss at-will employment. How is that doctrine affected by the tort of wrongful discharge?

8. Tom owned a fast-food restaurant business. The restaurant sold sandwiches. It stocked a table with ketchup, mustard, and relish for customers to use. One afternoon while filling the mustard container, Tom accidentally spilled some mustard on the floor. Before he had a chance to clean it, a customer entered the restaurant. Tom promptly waited on the customer and soon forgot about the mustard on the floor. A few hours later, another customer entered the restaurant, slipped on the mustard, fell, and broke a leg. Does the injured customer have a tort claim against Tom? Explain.

9. Discuss the relationship between tort law and

insurance as they affect the behavior of a business.

10. Jack was walking in the city. While strolling past a high-rise construction site, a board fell and struck him, causing injury. Jack was walking in a safety area, and no one could tell exactly how that board happened to fall. Discuss how Jack might proceed with his claim against the construction company.

11. The ABC Corporation owned a delivery business. One evening one of its trucks was parked negligently, in neutral with its parking brake only partly engaged. Furthermore, the truck was parked on a steep incline. That evening the truck rolled downhill and struck a car causing that car to hit a telephone pole. The pole fell to the ground and demolished a fire hydrant. Water began to spray. Before the hydrant could be turned off, Smith's basement was flooded. Does Smith have a tort claim against the ABC Corporation?

12. Mary Jones was jogging. She was wearing a Walkman with the volume nearly on maximum. She was concentrating on the music instead of watching where she was running. As a result, she entered a busy intersection against the light and a clearly noted "Do Not Walk" sign. She was struck by a car that was exceeding the speed limit by fifteen miles per hour. If Mary brings a tort action against the driver of the car, what defenses could be raised? First, assume the case arose in a state that retained its nineteenth-century tort law doctrines and note the argument. Thereafter, assume the state has adopted doctrines in line with a majority of other states today and note the arguments anew.

13. Jenkins worked for the ABC Chemical Corporation. The factory where he worked produced a certain chemical that emitted dangerous fumes during the production process. Exposure to those fumes over a period of time could cause permanent injury. ABC Corpora-

tion knew about the dangers in the production process and also knew that its safety procedures were below standard. The only time the corporation met required safety procedures was when a government inspector toured the factory. At other times, the procedures were such that fumes were likely to be emitted. One day Jenkins was exposed to a dangerous level of fumes and was injured. What contentions and claims could Jenkins and ABC Chemical Corporation make?

14. Smith was an executive with the XYZ Corporation, which sells gasoline products. The corporation is governed by the antitrust laws and is prohibited from agreeing with its competitors to fix prices charged for the products. Smith worked for the company without any written contract. One day he was asked by the vice-president of marketing to meet with executives from competing companies in order to set prices on the firms' kerosine, which sold in various regions throughout the country. Smith refused and was therefore fired. Does Smith have a claim against the XYZ Corporation?

NOTES

[1] *Blyth* v. *Birmingham Waterworks Co.*, 156 Eng. Rep. 1047 (1856).

[2] Lawrence Friedman, *A History of American Law* (New York: Simon & Schuster, 1974), p. 409.

CHAPTER 10

Property Rights and Land Use Regulation

The Nature of Property
Where Does a Rule of Property Come From?
Property Rights and Individual Rights
Eminent Domain, Zoning Law, and Land Use Controls

Although this chapter focuses on property rights, the importance of local government in the legal environment should also be considered. The regulations of local government can affect business decision making as much as state and federal level regulation. Zoning and eminent domain are tools used by local government to regulate the use of land. Local government, through land use planning, may have a profound effect on business.

THE NATURE OF PROPERTY

Property As a Relationship

Property is a relationship between the holder of rights and all others. These rights, recognized and enforced by the government, have been created by the law either through statute, through judicial decision, or through long-time common law recognition. **Rights,** in our system of laws, refers to the adjustment and balance of relationships between individuals, government, and business, or any combination of them. Lawyers consider property to be a bundle of rights.

Often people speak of property as it relates to a thing. This is my car, my book, or my land. Although it is a convenient way of describing property, what is really meant is that the person has rights in that car, book, or land, and those rights describe certain legally recognized and protected relationships. In the novel *Robinson Crusoe* by Daniel Defoe, Crusoe was shipwrecked on a deserted island and lived alone for many years. During that time he captured and raised a herd of goats. Could it be said that Robinson Crusoe had property rights in those goats? Think about this question and compare Robinson Crusoe's "rights" with those of Mary in the following paragraph.

Mary purchased this textbook from the bookstore for a class. One might say she owns the book, or more accurately, that she has rights in the book called **property rights.** Those rights include the right to sell the book, perhaps to the bookstore or to a friend taking the course next semester. If she needs to borrow ten dollars from her roommate, Mary can use the book as collateral for the loan; that is, in the event Mary does not repay the loan, her roommate may sell the book to get back her ten dollars. Mary has the right to use the book or to let someone else use it. If a thief takes the book, Mary may call upon the police to arrest the thief and return the book to her. These are just a few of the property rights Mary acquired when she purchased the book from the bookstore.

Now compare Mary with Robinson Crusoe. Can Robinson Crusoe sell the goats or use any of them as collateral for a loan? Is there any difference between what Crusoe and Mary can do with their "property"? Anything that Crusoe can do with the goats he is able to do simply because he is in control of them and is alone. One cannot say that Crusoe has property rights in the goats. Against whom would such rights exist? Mary's rights regulate her relationship with others concerning the textbook. Property rights have meaning only as they regulate certain relationships.

Property and Government

Later in Defoe's novel, another person appears on the island—Friday. Since there is now more than one person, there can be relationships that property rights concepts can regulate. For example, Crusoe may sell a goat to Friday or permit Friday to borrow a number of them to begin his own herd. But there is still something very important missing to establish that Robinson Crusoe has property rights in the goats, as Mary has property rights in her book. Who says that Crusoe, who captured the goats, should own them rather than Friday? If Robinson Crusoe is stronger or better-armed than Friday, that would settle the matter. But Mary need not be a weight lifter in order to have her rights enforced against the thief who stole her textbook. The government is there to recognize and enforce her property rights. On Robinson Crusoe's island, there is no government or system of laws to confer and enforce property claims he might want to make with respect to the goats. Therefore, it is not accurate to say that Robinson Crusoe has any property rights with respect to the goats. In summary, for property rights to exist, two things must first exist. First, there must be others against whom property rights claims may be asserted because property rights describe a certain relationship among people. Second, there must be a system of government or laws that can confer, adjust, and enforce claims of property rights.

This is a very basic yet very sophisticated concept of property. It raises the question whether property rights are absolute. Are relationships absolute? Do others not have rights too, which may affect a property owner's rights? The following case illustrates the basic concept of property. It involves a college professor and claims of property rights in the professor's lectures. The professor had a property right in his lectures, called a **common law copyright.** Under this right the professor has exclusive control of the use and publication of his lectures. The relationship between the professor and others with respect to those notes is regulated by the government.

Williams v. Weisser

California Court of Appeals

78 Cal. Rptr. 542 (1962)

Plaintiff is assistant professor at UCLA in the Anthropology Department. Defendant's business, Class Notes, in Westwood, California, sells outlines for various courses given at UCLA. In 1965, defendant paid Karen Allen, a UCLA student, to attend plaintiff's class in Anthropology 1, to take notes from the lectures, and to type up the notes. Allen delivered the typed notes to defendant, and defendant placed a copyright notice thereon in defendant's name, reproduced the typed notes, and offered them for sale. Plaintiff objected. Defendant did not cease these activities until served with summons, complaint, and temporary restraining order. Plaintiff seeks a permanent injunction, general damages, and punitive damages.

One of the grounds on which the judgment was based was that the defendant infringed on the plaintiff's common law copyright (property right) in his lectures.

Kaus, Presiding Judge

The oral delivery of the lectures did not divest plaintiff of his common law copyright to his lectures. Nothing tangible was delivered to the students. The principle which pervades the whole of that reasoning is, that where the persons present at a lecture are not the general public, but a limited class of the public, selected and admitted for the sole and special purpose of receiving individual instruction, they may make any use they can of the lecture, to the extent of taking it down in shorthand, for their own information and improvement, but cannot publish it. It is defendant's position that, copyright aside, he was privileged to publish the notes and to use plaintiff's name in connection with such publication because "[p]laintiff intentionally placed himself in the public eye when he undertook his employment as an instructor."

An author who owns the common law copyright to his work can determine whether he wants to publish it and, if so, under what circumstances. Plaintiff had prepared his notes for a specific purpose—as an outline to lectures to be delivered to a class of students. Though he apparently considered them adequate for that purpose, he did not desire a commercial distribution with which his name was associated. Right or wrong, he felt that his professional standing could be jeopardized. There is evidence that other teachers at UCLA did not object to representatives of Class Notes being in the classroom, indeed some cooperated with defendants in revising the product of the note takers. Plaintiff considered the Anthropology 1 notes sold by defendant as defective in several respects, chiefly because of certain omissions. Any person aware of the cooperation given by other faculty members could reasonably believe that plaintiff had assisted in the final product. We think that these considerations easily bring the case within the ambit of *Fairfield* v. *American Photocopy*. There the defendant used the plaintiff's name in advertising a certain product. He was said to be one of the many satisfied users of the product. He had been a user, but had returned the product to the defendant. The court held that defendant's conduct was "an unauthorized and unwarranted appropriation of plaintiff's personality as a lawyer for pecuniary gain and profit." We think that the *Fairfield* case is indistinguishable from the one at bar.

WHERE DOES A RULE OF PROPERTY COME FROM?

Property rights and rules that establish property rights do not exist in a vacuum. They are the results of a careful consideration of a variety of factors that society values. Some of those factors may conflict. But the end result is a rule of property or the establishment of a property right that reflects a number of important things. The best way to understand this notion is to take a long-established rule for the creation of property rights and seek to determine why that rule is as it is.

In an article published over thirty years ago, Felix Cohen, a prominent legal scholar, discusses the values and balances inherent in a timeless rule of property.[1] He begins with a discussion of who owns a newborn mule, and through the discussion the reader is led to understand the reasons for the legal rule, in existence for thousands of years in numerous places, that the newborn mule belongs to the owner of its mother. One reason is that the rule seems to be in accordance with the laws of nature. Cohen asks whether it would be just as consistent with the laws of nature if the owner of the father owned the newborn mule. An additional factor then becomes apparent, based upon the difficulty in determining a newborn mule's paternity: the basic need for certainty in the establishment of property law rules. Cohen then asks whether an alternative simple and definite rule for newborn mule ownership should be that the first person to rope or capture it would be its owner. Two final factors are raised from this inquiry: a concept of fairness and the contribution the rule makes to economic productivity. The owner of the mother had cared for it during pregnancy, and thereafter the newborn depends on its mother for its survival. Furthermore, without ownership vesting in the mother's owner, one could expect problems in the livestock business because of the disincentive to breed one's herd.

The interesting thing about Cohen's dialogue is that the values and considerations that make up the rule seem to flow so effortlessly to the result. Yet it is not

COMPUTER SOFTWARE "CLONES" AND PROPERTY RIGHTS

Lotus Development Corp. recently filed a lawsuit against the makers of computer software that compete with Lotus's successful business spreadsheet package, "1-2-3." The suit alleges that the competitors' products are clones or look-alike programs and therefore infringe on Lotus's property rights in 1-2-3. The clone programs are alleged to contain only minor variations from 1-2-3 and copy its command names as well as the sequence and range of choices available to users. Lotus is seeking compensatory damages, ten million dollars in punitive damages, and an injunction to keep the defendants from selling their products.

The suit has been described as a potentially important application of copyright law to look-alike software, but may also be considered an admission by Lotus that they are worried about losing market share to clone programs. For example, the defendants' programs list for $100, but are often discounted by forty to fifty percent. By contrast, Lotus's 1-2-3 lists for $495, and when discounted, it sells for $325. Analysts note that the timing of the suit is noteworthy because inexpensive foreign-made software clones will soon become available.

difficult to imagine major disputes arising thousands of years ago over this issue. Property rights disputes today reflect a similar weighing of considerations. Four considerations should be noted: productivity, or contribution to the economy; certainty and ease of application; enforceability; and fairness.

Consider the following problem. Biotechnology is a major area of scientific research and high-technology corporate activity. Discoveries from research in this field may provide vastly improved treatment for many diseases. Corporations that develop products from these discoveries can expect large profits. Smith contracted a rare form of virus-caused cancer. After his spleen was removed, Smith's body increased its immunity defenses to ward off the disease. This was the only hope given for his survival, and fortunately it worked. Smith's spleen was analyzed by medical researchers. They discovered that through gene manipulation and cloning, certain of Smith's cells could be used to produce anticancer substances. The university hospital where Smith was treated obtained a patent on the discovery and intends to market it. Smith contends that since the spleen was his, so should be the discovery. Who should own the new anticancer biotechnological substance?

Rule of Property Example: Fixtures

The following discussion of a common rule of property law—fixtures—illustrates the various considerations that make up a rule of property law. Note the factors courts consider in order to determine whether an item of property is a part of the real property or is instead a separable item of personal property.

Classification of Property. The law divides property into a number of classifications. Once property is found to fit within one of the classifications, various legal rules and procedures, which differ from one classification to another, apply to determine the extent of the rights held by the owner of that property. For example, more formalities are required by the law in buying or selling a home than in buying or selling a textbook or a pencil. Yet legally the same thing is accomplished in each situation; that is, the owner of the property rights is transferring those property rights to another person, who will then be considered the owner upon completion of the transfer.

The law provides three major categories of property. Property may be either real property (land and anything firmly attached to it) or personal property (everything else). Personal property may be either tangible (it can be seen, felt, touched—it has a physical existence) or intangible (ideas, accounts receivable, other items with economic value but without a physical existence). When a person buys a new home, that purchase is considered a purchase of real property. The land and the house, firmly attached to the land, are transferred to the buyer. This textbook is personal property, as are shoes, as are the songs heard on the radio, as is a new short story. Such types of personal property may be tangible (the shoes or the textbook) or intangible (the song or the short story). If someone steals a textbook, the owner has a claim against that person. Similarly, if another band records a songwriter's work without permission or a company publishes a story without the author's consent, the songwriter or author would have claims for property rights infringement even though the song and the short story by themselves do not have a physical existence. They have a physical existence only when placed upon a record or printed on paper.

Fixture Rules. Sometimes property that would ordinarily be considered personal property is instead categorized as real property. At other times, items of property usually classified as real property may instead be categorized as personal property. This area of property law is called **fixtures.**

A fixture may be defined as personal property that is so attached to or used with real property that it is considered to be part of that real property. One example may be a doorknob. A doorknob at the hardware store is personal property. It is simply stacked on a shelf and is in no way connected with the land or the building. But as soon as a home owner purchases the doorknob and affixes it to the front door, that item of personal property has been transformed into a part of the house, part of the real property.

The legal standard courts generally apply to fixtures questions is a reasonable person standard. That is, would a reasonable person familiar with the community and with the facts and circumstances of the case be justified in assuming that the person attaching or using the personal property with the real property intended the item of personal property to become a fixture and therefore part of the real property? The law labels property real or personal not according to its general appearance but according to its use in any given situation—as the doorknob may be personal property in a hardware store, but real property when it becomes part of a home.

Although the definition of fixture and the standard for determining whether a given item of property is a fixture may seem clear in the case of the doorknob, it is not always that easy to apply. Courts will frequently look for at least four indications that assist them in settling the dispute. A dispute may arise in a situation where Jack purchases a home from Jill. The contract conveys the real property of Jill to Jack, but exactly what is included in the conveyance of the real property—the curtain rods? the fireplace grill? the doorknob?

One item the courts will look for is a written agreement labeling an item as a fixture. The written agreement shows intent and is a strong, but not conclusive factor in determining whether something is a fixture. Courts will also analyze the facts concerning the relationship of the item of personal property to the real property in order to determine whether it should be considered a fixture. These facts revolve around three general concepts. The first is the degree of attachment or annexation of the item of personal property to the real property. The greater the attachment, the more a part of the real property the item appears to be. Certainly a brick that becomes part of the wall of a building is more solidly affixed to the real property than a throw rug lying on one of the room's floors. Second, courts analyze the ease or difficulty of removing the item of personal property, and whether such removal would damage the real property or the item of personal property. Ease of removal suggests that the item is not a part of the real property. Removing the brick from a wall in the building would without question result in damage to the wall and probably also result in damage to the brick. Since the throw rug could easily be rolled up and carried out of the room there would be no damage occasioned by its removal. Third, the appropriateness of the use of the personal property item with the real property; that is, by its use alone, should the item of personal property be considered part of the real property? For example, the throw rug in the above examples may fit into this category if it was custom designed to fit wall-to-wall in an unusually shaped room—perhaps a room shaped as a star—as well as being a necessary part of the particular decor of that room. In such a case, the easy-to-remove, unaffixed throw rug begins to appear to have been intended to be a part of the real property.

Sigrol Realty Corp. v. Valcich

Supreme Court, Appellate Division, New York
212 N.Y.S. 2d 224 (1961)

In 1891, six members of the Wilmore family acquired the tract of waterfront land in Richmond County known as Robinson's Beach. During the Wilmore ownership, seven frame bungalows were placed on the land by various tenants who rented the land space from the landowners for that purpose. The tenants paid rent for the use of the land; they paid for the maintenance and insurance of the bungalows; and from time to time they repaired, altered, and sold the bungalows without hindrance from the landowners. The tenants occupied the bungalows during the summer months only.

The bungalows rested on cinder blocks that were not sunk into the ground. The bungalows were not bolted to the ground, and they had no basements. It is not disputed that the bungalows were so constructed that, upon severance of the water and electrical connections, they could be removed without injury either to them or to the land.

On April 9, 1959, the Wilmores, for the sum of $12,250, contracted to sell to the plaintiff the land with the buildings and improvements thereon, subject to the rights of tenants, if any. The contract contained the printed provision that fixtures and articles of personal property attached or appurtenant to the premises "which are owned by the seller, are free from all liens and encumbrances."

When defendants, the sellers of the land, attempted to remove the bungalows, plaintiff, on October 6, 1959, instituted this action to declare that it had title to the bungalows and to restrain defendants from removing them.

Beldock, Justice

For the purpose of determining whether chattels annexed to realty remain personalty or become realty, chattels are divided into three classes: (1) some chattels, such as gas ranges, because of their character as movables, remain personalty even after their annexation, regardless of any agreement between the chattel owner and the landowner; (2) other chattels, such as brick, stone and plaster placed in the walls of a building, become realty after annexation, regardless of any agreement to the contrary between the chattel owner and the

landowner; such personal property does not retain its character as such if it be annexed to the realty in such manner as to become an integral part of the realty and be immovable without practically destroying the personal property, or if all or a part of it be essential to the support of the structure to which it is attached; and (3) still other chattels, after attachment, continue to be personalty or become realty, in accordance with the agreement between the chattel owner and the landowner.

In my opinion, these bungalows were movables which continued to be personalty. The bungalows were erected by defendants or by their predecessors in title without any intention of making them permanent accessions to the realty. The manner of their annexation was such as to make them easily removable without injury either to them or to the land. Defendants repaired, maintained, insured, altered, and sold the bungalows without the consent or interference by the Wilmores.

Only the fixtures and articles of personalty owned by the Wilmores were sold. Under the contract the Wilmores sold and the plaintiff purchased the land subject to the rights of the defendants in the bungalows.

PROPERTY RIGHTS AND INDIVIDUAL RIGHTS

Some people have described property ownership, especially the ownership of land, as a system of protection of the rights of the minority against the wishes of the majority. The minority in this case is the person labeled the property owner, the majority is the rest of society or the government. The legal system confers rights on the property owner, within limits, which enable the individual to exercise power in relationships with others concerning those property rights. Property owners may prohibit certain people from using their property. That private decision will be enforced by the government.

For example, if Jack owned a tract of land, he would be considered to have property rights in that land. Jack could cultivate corn on the land, thus making productive and reasonable use of it. Or Jack could let the land lie fallow and use it for picnics—even if the corn he could have grown would be needed by the community for food. Jack could prohibit anyone else from picnicking on his land or charge a fee for the privilege. The government would, through its laws, enforce such personal choices made by Jack. Under classic property rights theory, Jack, the owner, is generally not answerable to the community, his neighbors, or the government for his use of his land. The majority yields to the dictates of the minority when the minority has property rights.

Individual rights (or liberty) work much the same way. The major distinction is the focus of those rights. Property rights focus on the creation and protection of items of economic value, whether that value was great (a gold mine) or negligible (a mangy, old dog or a swamp). Individual rights are the other rights the law recognizes. Examples of individual rights are the right to travel, the right to vote, the right not to be discriminated against on the basis of sex, the right to a jury in a criminal case, and the right to stay out of jail except upon the state's following a rigorous procedure to prove guilt. These rights, too, involve relationships. In fact, historically, liberty and property concepts were treated much the same. Each allowed the individual who possessed any of those rights to make personal (and perhaps illogical, unreasonable, or stupid) choices. The rights insulated the individual from the necessity to conform to the norms of the community through the force of the government.

Today those concepts of rights have been divided, with many writers and courts favoring individual rights (liberty) over property rights. One of the major reasons for this was the abuse of property rights by a few owners in the nineteenth and early twentieth centuries. As the historical material in Chapters 13, 14, and 15 on antitrust law demonstrates, ownership of property and decisions about use of the property became separated. In major corporations and trusts, the owners of the property were not necessarily the individuals making the decisions about the use of that property. Great concentrations of wealth and power came into relatively few hands. Many people became subject to the control of the property owner, whether that owner was a landlord or an employer. People became subject to the private choices of the property owner on whom they relied for their livings. In *Hard Times* and other works, Charles Dickens, writing about England, graphically pointed out the abuses inherent in a legal system that recognized such large amounts of private power in the hands of the property owner. The nonowner or the owner who did not possess a great deal of property had little if any control over the use of others' property. The labor union movement, the populist movement, the grange movement, and the enactment of antitrust laws around the turn of the century were attempts to regulate the private decision-making power of property owners by those individuals who felt exploited by that power. The tool for such regulation was the law.

Limitations on Property Rights

Today property rights are subject to a great deal of regulation. Although the general concept of property rights still holds, the government has taken over the task of monitoring the use of property for the "general health, safety, welfare and morals" of the community. Courts are frequently called upon to decide the permissible extent to which the government may regulate decisions made by the holders of private property rights. Most frequently, the government will prevail. The zoning materials focus on this issue.

The turn-of-the-century property-rights reform movement did not result in a shift of power from the few to all. The classic theory of property rights would work well in theory if property ownership were widespread. However, no property redistribution or corporate breakup occurred to return control to the individual. Instead, the reform movement resulted in the power and control being transferred to the government, another large and powerful body. As a result, individuals remained subject to decisions made by those who control large amounts of property, but at the same time any individual's property has become subject to the control of the government.

In the following two cases, property rights and individual rights seem to be in conflict. Each case seems to favor individual rights, thereby relegating property rights to a lower status. Can the cases be characterized another way?

State of New Jersey v. Shack and Tejeras

Supreme Court of New Jersey
277 A.2d 369 (1971)

Tedesco, a farmer, employed migrant workers for his seasonal needs. As part of their compensation, these workers were housed at a camp on his property.

Defendant Tejeras was a field worker for the Farm Workers Division of the Southwest Citizens Organization for Poverty Elimination, known by the acronym

SCOPE, a nonprofit corporation funded by the Office of Economic Opportunity pursuant to an act of Congress. The role of SCOPE included providing for the health services of the migrant farm worker.

Defendant Shack was a staff attorney with the Farm Workers Division of Camden Regional Legal Services, Inc., known as CRLS, also a nonprofit corporation funded by the Office of Economic Opportunity pursuant to an act of Congress. The mission of CRLS included legal advice and representation for these workers.

Differences had developed between Tedesco and these defendants before the events that led to the trespass charges in this case. Hence, when defendant Tejeras wanted to go upon Tedesco's farm to find a migrant worker who needed medical aid for the removal of twenty-eight sutures, he called upon defendant Shack for his help with respect to the legalities involved. Shack, too, had a mission to perform on Tedesco's farm; he wanted to discuss a legal problem with another migrant worker. Defendants arranged to go to the farm together.

Defendants entered upon Tedesco's property, and as they neared the campsite where the farmworkers were housed, they were confronted by Tedesco, who inquired as to their purpose. Tejeras and Shack stated their missions. In response, Tedesco offered to find the injured worker. Tedesco also offered to locate the worker who needed legal advice but insisted that the consultation take place in Tedesco's office and in his presence. Defendants declined, saying they had the right to see the workers in the privacy of their living quarters and without Tedesco's supervision. Tedesco thereupon summoned a state trooper, who, however, refused to remove defendants except upon Tedesco's written complaint. Tedesco then executed the formal complaints charging violations of the trespass statute.

Weintraub, Chief Justice

Property rights serve human values. They are recognized to that end, and are limited by it. Title to real property cannot include dominion over the destiny of persons the owner permits to come upon the premises. Their well-being must remain the paramount concern of a system of law. Indeed the needs of the occupants may be so imperative and their strength so weak, that the law will deny the occupants the power to contract away what is deemed essential to their health, welfare, or dignity.

Here we are concerned with a highly disadvantaged segment of our society. The migrant farmworkers come to New Jersey in substantial numbers. The migrant farmworkers are a community within but apart from the local scene. They are rootless and isolated. Although the need for their labors is evident, they are unorganized and without economic or political power. It is their plight alone that summoned government to their aid. In response, Congress provided under the Economic Opportunity Act of 1964 for "assistance for migrant and other seasonally employed farmworkers and their families."

These ends would not be gained if the intended beneficiaries could be insulated from efforts to reach them. It is in this framework that we must decide whether the camp operator's rights in his lands may stand between the migrant workers and those who would aid them. The key to that aid is communication. Since the migrant workers are outside the mainstream of the communities in which they are housed and are unaware of their rights and opportunities and of the services available to them, they can be reached only by positive efforts tailored to that end.

A man's right in his real property is not absolute. It was a maxim of the common law that one should so use his property as not to injure the rights of others. Although hardly a precise solvent of actual controversies, the maxim does express the inevitable proposition that rights are relative and there must be an accommodation when they meet. Hence, it has long been true that necessity, private or public, may justify entry upon the lands of another.

This process involves not only the accommodation between the right of the owner and the interests of the general public in his use of this property, but involves also an accommodation between the right of the owner and the right of individuals who are parties with him in consensual transactions relating to the use of the property.

We see no profit in trying to decide this case upon a conventional category and then forcing the present subject into it. That approach would be artificial and distorting. The quest is for a fair adjustment of the competing needs of the parties, in the light of the realities of the relationship between the migrant worker and the operator of the housing facility.

Thus, approaching the case, we find it unthinkable that the farmer-employer can assert a right to isolate the migrant worker in any respect significant for the worker's well-being. The farmer, of course, is entitled to pursue his farming activities without interference, and this defendants readily concede. But we see no legitimate need for a right in the farmer to deny the worker the opportunity for aid available from federal, State, or local services, or from recognized charitable groups seeking to assist him. Hence, representatives of these agencies and organizations may enter upon the premises to seek out the worker at his living quarters. So, too, the migrant worker must be allowed to receive visitors there of his own choice, so long as there is no behavior hurtful to others, and members of the press may not be denied reasonable access to workers who do not object to seeing them.

It is not our purpose to open the employer's premises to the general public if in fact the employer himself has not done so. We do not say, for example, that solicitors or peddlers of all kinds may enter on their own; we may assume for the present that the employer may regulate their entry or bar them, at least if the employer's purpose is not to gain a commercial advantage for himself or if the regulation does not deprive the migrant worker of practical access to things he needs.

And we are mindful of the employer's interest in his own and in his employees' security. Hence, he may reasonably require a visitor to identify himself, and also to state his general purpose if the migrant worker has not already informed him that the visitor is expected. But the employer may not deny the worker his privacy or interfere with his opportunity to live with dignity and to enjoy associations customary among our citizens. These rights are too fundamental to be denied on the basis of an interest in real property and too fragile to be left to the unequal bargaining strength of the parties.

It follows that defendants here invaded no possessory right of the farmer-employer. Their conduct was therefore beyond the reach of the trespass statute.

Katko v. Briney
Supreme Court of Iowa
183 N.W. 2d 657 (1971)

In 1957, defendant Bertha L. Briney inherited her parents' farmland. Included was an eighty-acre tract where her grandparents and parents had lived. No one occupied the farmhouse. Her husband, Edward, attempted to care for the land. He kept no farm machinery thereon. The outbuildings became dilapidated.

From 1957 to 1967, there was a series of trespassings and housebreakings with loss of some household items, the breaking of windows, and "messing up of the property in general." The latest occurred June 8, 1967.

Defendants through the years boarded up the windows and doors in an attempt to stop the intrusions. They had posted "no trespass" signs on the land several years before 1967. The nearest one was thirty-five feet from the house. On June 11, 1967, defendants set "a shotgun trap" in the north bedroom. After Mr. Briney cleaned and oiled his twenty-gauge shotgun, the power of which he knew well, defendants took it to the old house where they secured it to an iron bed with the barrel pointed at the bedroom door. It was rigged with wire from the doorknob to the gun's trigger so it would fire when the door was opened. Mr. Briney admitted he set the trap "because I was mad and tired of being tormented," but he did not intend to injure anyone. He gave no explanation of why he used a loaded shell and set it to hit a person already in the house. Tin was nailed over the bedroom window. The spring gun could not be seen from the outside. No warning of its presence was posted.

Plaintiff lived with his wife and worked regularly as a gasoline station attendant in Eddyville, seven miles from the old house. He had observed it for several years while hunting in the area and considered it as being abandoned. He knew it had long been uninhabited. In 1967, the area around the house was covered with high weeds. Before July 16, 1967, plaintiff and McDonough had been to the premises and found several old bottles and fruit jars, which they took and added to their collection of antiques. An old organ fascinated plaintiff. Arriving at the house a second time, they found that the window by which they had entered before was now a "solid mass of boards" and walked around the house until they found the porch window, which offered less resistance. They crawled through this window. While searching the house, the plaintiff came to the bedroom door and pulled it open, thus triggering the gun, which delivered a charge that struck him in the leg.

Much of his leg, including part of the tibia, was blown away. Only by McDonough's assistance was plaintiff able to get out of the house. After crawling some distance, he was put in his vehicle and rushed to a doctor and then to a hospital. He remained in the hospital for forty days.

Plaintiff's doctor testified he seriously considered amputation, but eventually the healing process was successful. Some weeks after his release from the hospital, plaintiff returned to work on crutches. He was required to keep the injured leg in a cast for approximately a year and wear a special brace for another year. He continued to suffer pain during this period.

There was undenied medical testimony plaintiff had a permanent deformity, a loss of tissue, and a shortening of the leg.

Plaintiff knew he had no right to break into and enter the house with intent to steal bottles and fruit jars therefrom. He entered a plea of guilty, was fined fifty dollars and costs, and paroled during good behavior from a sixty-day jail sentence. Other than minor traffic charges, this was plaintiff's first brush with the law.

Plaintiff sued the defendant for damages for his injuries, which is the subject of this case.

[You write the opinion. How should these rights be balanced?]

Property Rights May Change

Property rights, like other rights, in general are subject to change. As society changes, relationships with respect to property also change. As a result, the law will adjust and modify what is meant by property rights in order to reflect the needs of society. Most towns in the United States have grown a great deal during the last forty years. Parents or grandparents will frequently point to a subdivision or a shopping center and remark that they used to picnic in that area, once an open field. Perhaps your home is in a subdivision that years ago was part of a farm outside of the city. A farmer probably kept cows and chickens on that farm. Can your family keep cows and chickens in the backyard of their home, now virtually in the middle of town? Of course not. Yet your home is in the exact location where a previous owner of the land could legally keep livestock. The law today prohibits your family from doing the same. The change of conditions has resulted in a change in the property rights that the owner has in that piece of land. Livestock is inappropriate in a city neighborhood—farm animals infringe upon the rights of neighbors with their smells and their noises. Yet that same livestock was appropriate years ago when the entire area was farmland. Changes in the relationships and proximity of people have resulted in a change in the property rights of the landowner.

This is not an isolated example, nor does it mean that the bundle of rights we call property will always change in the future. The following cases and materials illustrate these points. In the nineteenth century, land was considered by many in this country to be a commodity to be bought, sold, and used, like a plow or a horse. Land was valued for its economic return. Farmers would grow crops on their farm and then move to another farm in the West when the land began to be used up. Speculators quickly moved to newly opened territory in the West to stake their claims to land and to begin the creation of towns on the prairie. The land they purchased was to be sold quickly for a profit. The new owners too would hope to profit from the land as the town grew and the land in it therefore became more valuable. Progress, growth, and boosterism for various towns reflected the notion of growth and change in the use of land. Land that was once open prairie became divided into city lots, then further divided as the need for more commercial space arose and taller buildings were constructed to meet the needs of growing towns. All of this reflected the values of the society and consequently the property rights recognized by the law also reflected these values. Claims for property rights that conflicted with these values were often not recognized by the courts. This is clearly shown by the following *Parker* v. *Foote* case in which a claim for sunlight access rights was denied by the court.

In property law, legal rights may be obtained involuntarily from another person merely through long-term use (usually twenty years) of that other person's property. This doctrine is called **prescription** or adverse possession, depending upon the type of property right being claimed. It requires that the user enjoy the property of another under a claim of right for a number of years. This enjoyment must be known to the property owner, who acquiesces in it without asserting legal right to either stop or give permission for such a use.

An example of this doctrine is a pathway which crosses Farm A, connecting Farm B with a highway. For a long period of time, Bill, the owner of Farm B, has crossed the same spot over Farm A to reach the highway. During the winter, Bill plows the pathway, and during the summer, he grades it to make it smooth. Sam, the owner of Farm A, knows of this use and does nothing to stop it, nor does he assert his rights by giving permission to Bill to use the pathway. After a time, Bill will be said to have acquired a legal right to use that pathway through prescription. Thereafter, Sam will be unable to halt Bill's use of it. In the case that follows, it is sunlight that is being used by one landowner. Note how the court distinguishes the types of use. Also note the values inherent in the court's decision.

Parker v. Foote

Supreme Court of New York
19 Wend. 309 (1838)

This was an action arising from the obstruction of sunlight flowing into a house.

In 1808, the defendant, who owned two adjoining lots, sold one of them to Joseph Stebbins. Stebbins erected a house with windows in it overlooking the other lot. The defendant, in the same year, built an addition to a house that stood on the lot that he retained, leaving a space of about sixteen feet between the house erected by Stebbins and the addition put up by himself. This space was subsequently occupied by the defendant as an alley leading to buildings situated on the rear of his lot, and was so used by him until the year 1832, when (twenty-four years after the erection of the house by Stebbins) he erected a store on the alley, filling up the whole space between the two houses, and consequently obstructing the sunlight flowing into the house erected by Stebbins. At the time of the erection of the store, the plaintiffs were the owners of the lot originally conveyed to Stebbins. Stebbins (the original purchaser from the defendant) was a witness for the plaintiffs, and on his cross examination, testified that he never had any written agreement, deed, or writing granting permission to have his windows overlook the defendant's lot, and that nothing was ever said upon the subject.

Bronson, Justice

Most of the cases on the subject of obtaining legal rights through the long term use of another's property relate to ways, commons, markets, watercourses, and the like, where the use if not rightful, has been an immediate and continuing injury to the person against whom the use is made. His property has either been invaded, or his beneficial interest in it has been rendered less valuable by the use. The injury has been of such a character that he might have immediate redress by action. But in the case of windows overlooking the land of another, the injury, if any, is merely ideal or imaginary. The light and air which they admit are not the subjects of property beyond the moment of actual occupancy. The party has no remedy but to build on the adjoining land opposite the offensive window. Upon what principle the courts in England have applied the same rule to these two classes of cases so essentially different in character, I have been unable to discover. If one commit a daily trespass on the land of another, under a claim of right to pass over, or feed his cattle upon it, or divert the water from his mill, or throw it back upon his land or machinery; in these and the like cases, long continued use affords strong evidence of right. But in the case of sunlight, there is no use whatever of another's property; and no foundation is laid for indulging any presumption against the rightful owner.

The learned English judges who have laid down this doctrine have not told us upon what principle or analogy in the law it can be maintained. They tell us that a man may build at the extremity of his own land, and that he may lawfully have windows looking out upon the lands of his neighbor. The reason why he may lawfully have such windows, must be, because he does his neighbor no wrong; and indeed, so it is adjudged as we have already seen; and yet, somehow or other, by the exercise of a lawful right in his own land for 20 years, he acquires a beneficial interest in the land of his neighbor. The original proprietor still owns the land, with the privilege of paying taxes and assessments: but the right to build on the land, without which city and village lots are of little or no value, has been destroyed by a lawful window. How much land can thus be rendered useless to the owner, remains yet to be settled.

Now what is the acquiescence which concludes the owner? No one has trespassed upon his land, or done him a legal injury of any kind. He had submitted to nothing but the exercise of a lawful right on the part of his neighbor. How then has he forfeited the beneficial interest in his property? He has neglected to incur the expense of building a wall 20 or 50 feet high, as the case may be—not for his own benefit, but for the sole purpose of annoying his neighbor. That was his only remedy. A wanton act of this kind, although done on one's own land, is calculated to render a man odious.

The principle of a right to sunlight being acquired by its use may do well enough in England. But it cannot be applied in the growing cities and villages of this country, without working the most mischievous consequences.

In this case the evidence of Stebbins, who built the house, in connection with the other facts which appeared on the trial, proved most satisfactorily that the windows were never enjoyed under a claim of right, but only as a matter of favor.

Sunlight and the free circulation of air through windows was certainly important in an era before electric lights and air-conditioning. Yet legally conferring the right to sunlight and air upon a property owner—as one of the bundle of rights associated with the concept of owning that piece of land—had important consequences for adjoining landowners, who would be unable to build on their land if that building would interfere with the sunlight and air flow to their neighbor. This would have a profound effect on the growth of cities.

The following case raises issues very similar to those discussed in *Parker* v. *Foote* over one hundred twenty years before. One landowner wants unobstructed sunlight to flow onto its property. The other landowner wants to construct a building that, when completed, will obstruct that sunlight. This time the sunlight is for sunbathing rather than for illumination, but the values inherent in each decision remained the same.

Fontainebleau Hotel Corp. v. Forty-Five Twenty-Five, Inc.

Florida District Court of Appeal
114 So.2d 357 (1959)

Appellee, plaintiff below, owns the Eden Roc Hotel, which was constructed in 1955, about a year after the Fontainebleau Hotel, owned by the defendant, and adjoins the Fontainebleau on the north. Both are luxury hotels facing the Atlantic

Ocean. The Fontainebleau is constructing an addition. During the winter months, from around two o'clock in the afternoon for the remainder of the day, the shadow of the addition will extend over the cabana, swimming pool, and sunbathing areas of the Eden Roc, which are located in the southern portion of its property.

In this action, plaintiff-appellee sought to enjoin the defendants-appellants from proceeding with the construction of the addition to the Fontainebleau (it appears to have been roughly eight stories high at the time suit was filed), alleging that the construction would interfere with the light and air on the beach in front of the Eden Roc and cast a shadow of such size as to render the beach wholly unfit for the use and enjoyment of its guests, to the irreparable injury of the plaintiff. It was alleged that the construction would interfere with the sunlight and air enjoyed by plaintiff and the previous owners of that property for more than twenty years.

Per Curiam

It is well settled that a property owner may put his own property to any reasonable and lawful use, so long as he does not thereby deprive the adjoining landowner of any right of enjoyment of his property which is recognized and protected by law, and so long as his use is not such a one as the law will pronounce a nuisance.

No American decision has been cited, and independent research has revealed none, in which it has been held that—in the absence of some contractual or statutory obligation—a landowner has a legal right to the free flow of light and air across the adjoining land of his neighbor. Even in English common law, the landowner had no legal right, in the absence of an easement or uninterrupted use and enjoyment for a period of 20 years, to unobstructed light and air from the adjoining land. And that doctrine has been unanimously rejected in this country.

There being, then, no legal right to the free flow of light and air from the adjoining land, it is universally held that where a structure serves a useful and beneficial purpose, it does not give rise to a cause of action, either for damages or for an injunction.

If, as contended, public policy demands that a landowner in the Miami Beach area refrain from constructing buildings on his premises that will cast a shadow on the adjoining premises, an amendment of the city's comprehensive planning and zoning ordinance, applicable to the public as a whole, is the means by which such purpose should be achieved.

The *Fontainebleau* case contains a very interesting comment. The court in *Fontainebleau* refers to **zoning** and suggests that a zoning ordinance could have protected the Eden Roc in the dispute over sunlight.

Land use regulation (or zoning) involves local rules concerning the extent to which landowners may use their land. Zoning sets up a general framework for land use through local ordinance by attempting to balance the conflicting interests of members of the community. For example, a corporation deciding to erect a factory on land it purchased will often make a valuable contribution to the community. Jobs will be created, and more tax revenue will be available to run the city. However, if the factory is noisy and the corporation's land is in a residential area, the rights of the homeowners near that factory who must put up with the noise, fumes, and increased traffic will be jeopardized. As Samuel Johnson once said, "A cow is a very good animal in the field; but we turn her out of a garden."[2] Land use regulation acts in much the same way. It recognizes that various uses of land may be valuable, but that clashes in landowner rights may result if the various uses are mixed. The following case illustrates the clash of land use rights of neighbors in absence of a zoning rule.

Rodrigue v. Copeland

Supreme Court of Louisiana
475 So.2d 1071 (1985)

Plaintiffs, three residents of the Pontchartrain Shores Subdivision in Jefferson Parish, instituted this action to enjoin defendant, Alvin C. Copeland, from erecting and operating his annual Christmas display. The plaintiffs sought injunctive relief due to problems associated with an enormous influx of visitors to their limited access, residential neighborhood.

Since 1977, defendant has annually maintained a Christmas display on his premises at 5001 Folse Drive. The display consists of an extravagant array of lights and lighted figures accompanied by traditional Christmas music.

Since 1982, defendant's exhibition has drawn numerous spectators to the neighborhood during the hours while the display is in operation. The spectators view the display either from their automobiles or on foot after parking their vehicles in the surrounding neighborhood. The increased congestion in the neighborhood has created numerous problems for some of the defendant's neighbors, such as restricted access to their homes, noise, public urination, property damage, and a lack of on-street parking.

After trial, the court granted limited injunctive relief, directing Copeland to limit his display to thirty days, commencing the first Saturday in December, and ordering him to turn off the display at 11:00 P.M. nightly. The court also permanently enjoined defendant from using the public property adjacent to his premises for any purpose. Injunctive relief was otherwise denied. The court of appeal affirmed the district court's denial of injunctive relief.

Dixon, Chief Justice

As a general rule, the landowner is free to exercise his rights to ownership in any manner he sees fit. He may even use his property in ways which occasion some inconvenience to his neighbor. However, his extensive rights do not allow him to do "real damage" to his neighbor. At issue in this case is whether Copeland's light and sound display has caused a mere inconvenience or real damage to his neighbors and their right to enjoy their own premises. In determining whether an

activity or work occasions real damage or mere inconvenience, a court is required to determine the reasonableness of the conduct in light of the circumstances. This analysis requires consideration of factors such as the character of the neighborhood, the degree of the intrusion and the effect of the activity on the health and safety of the neighbors.

Defendant's exhibition constitutes an unreasonable intrusion into the lives of his neighbors when considered in light of the character of the neighborhood, the degree of the intrusion and its effect on the use and enjoyment of their properties by his neighbors. The damage suffered by plaintiffs during the operation of defendant's display is extensive, both in terms of its duration and its size. Defendant's display becomes operative in early December and remains in operation until January 5. During this period, plaintiffs are forced to contend with a flow of bumper to bumper traffic through their limited access neighborhood. In addition, they must endure the noise and property abuse associated with the crowd of visitors who congregate near the display.

The display begins operation at dusk each evening and continues until 11:00 P.M. on weekdays and 12:00 midnight on weekends. The display is occasionally operational beyond midnight. While in operation, it features an extravagant display of lights which are located across the front of defendant's residence, on the roof and in the enclosed yard to the west of the residence. Some of the lights comprising the display are shaped into figures such as a star, a reindeer, a snowman, three angels and a depiction of Santa and his reindeer. Lights are also located in the trees and shrubs. In addition to the lights, the display features a tapestry proclaiming "Glory to God in the Highest" and a creche.

Noise emanates from the display and from visitors. The display is accompanied by traditional Christmas music which is amplified through loudspeakers located on the second floor of defendant's residence. The plaintiffs also complain of noise emanating from car engines, car horns, the slamming of car doors and police whistles.

The record clearly indicates that traffic in the neighborhood is congested due to the slow progress of vehicles carrying spectators by the display. The traffic has seriously impaired the ability of plaintiffs to gain access to and from their premises. Furthermore, on-street parking for plaintiffs or their guests becomes virtually nonexistent. As a result of the traffic congestion and lack of parking, plaintiffs and children of defendant's neighbors cannot have their own Christmas celebrations and gatherings.

Plaintiff's injury stems from the nature and size of the display which render it incompatible with a restricted access, residential neighborhood. Thus, defendant is enjoined from erecting and operating a Christmas exhibition which is calculated to and does attract an unusually large number of visitors to the neighborhood. In complying with our order, defendant is specifically enjoined from placing oversized lighted figures, such as the reindeer and snowman, in his yards or upon the roof of his residence. The proper place for these "commercial size" decorations is not within a quiet, residential neighborhood. Defendant is also specifically ordered to reduce the volume of any sound accompanying the display so that it is not audible from within the closest homes of his neighbors. In limiting his display, the burden is placed on defendant to reduce substantially the size and extravagance of his display to a level at which it will not attract the large crowds that have been drawn to the neighborhood in the past.

EMINENT DOMAIN, ZONING LAW, AND LAND USE CONTROLS

Land use planning is basically a local decision. Yet it raises questions of state and federal law and touches on emotional values of the local citizens. Within the context of land use planning disputes arises one of the key conflicts of modern American law—the tensions between the ideal of individual liberty and the needs and desires of the community. Although land use disputes may be primarily local in nature, they raise profound questions concerning individual values and constitutional rights.

Eminent Domain

The ownership of property is the ownership of rights. Property is a bundle of legal rights. One right that is held by the government in relation to all property is the right of **eminent domain.** Eminent domain is the right of the government to take private property from an individual or business. Government may take the property upon the payment of just compensation to the owner. For example, City A may need to widen a street because of changes in housing and traffic patterns over the years. In order to do this, the city will have to acquire part of the front lawn of Sally's residence. Normally, one person has no right to force others to sell or convey any part of their property. However, the city, through the eminent domain power, has that right. If Sally will not voluntarily convey the needed strip of lawn to the city for the widening of the street, the city can condemn the needed property and simply take it away from her upon payment of just compensation.

The right of eminent domain is contained in the Fifth Amendment to the United States Constitution as well as being contained in the constitutions of the states. Although eminent domain may seem harsh to an individual landowner, it is in fact a device to protect the individual from the powers of the government. The government must pay just compensation (generally fair market value) to the landowner for the property. Furthermore, the property the government condemns must be intended for **public use.** The provision limits the power of the government and provides compensatory remedies to the landowner. Without such a protection, the government would have the power to take whatever property it chose for whatever reason it desired. A glance at the newspaper would show that this exercise of governmental power is not uncommon in other parts of the world. Our Constitution simply limits the burden such activities of the government place on individual landowners.

Furthermore, the provision recognizes the claim a community may have upon certain parcels of property. Without the right to condemn property, the government could be stymied by one landowner who refused to convey needed property or demanded a very high price. The result would be a severe hindrance on government in building public works projects.

The requirement for "public use" of the property is a much broader concept than one may first think. It covers not only property taken by the government to be used by the general public (such as roads, schools, or hospitals), but also property that is used to produce a public advantage, convenience, or benefit, even if the general public makes no use of the property. For example, local governments have condemned slum areas, taking the property from its owners upon paying them just compensation. The local government will then clear the land and sell it to a developer, who will construct new housing, commercial, or industrial buildings. The general public will certainly not have the use of that property. The use will be limited to the new developer and those who purchase or rent from the developer. However, such use has been considered by the courts as a permissible public use of the property.

In *Berman* v. *Parker,* for example, the United States Supreme Court held that condemnation of land on which a department store was located as a part of an area-wide redevelopment plan was consistent with the public use requirement of the Constitution. Even though the store itself was not blighted and the land was to be transferred to a private developer, the Court upheld the decision to remove a slum in total instead of on a piecemeal basis. The elimination of a slum was considered well within the public use limitation, since it was found to further the public welfare. As Justice Douglas, writing for the Court, noted: "Miserable and disreputable housing conditions may do more than spread disease and crime and immorality. They may also suffocate the spirit by reducing the people who live there to the status of cattle. They may indeed make living an almost insufferable burden. They may also be an ugly sore, a blight on the community which robs it of charm, which makes it a place from which men turn. The misery of housing may despoil a community as an open sewer may ruin a river."[3]

As a practical matter, it is not often that a use to which the local government wants to put condemned property will be successfully challenged as a nonpublic use. The definition of the term is very broad. Most of the fights in the eminent domain area of law are over the amount of compensation paid to the property owner.

Although the power and right of the government to condemn property for public use is generally used to acquire land, it is not so limited. Personal property may also be acquired by the government for public purposes. The following case is an example. Note the virtual lack of practical restrictions on local government's taking an individual's property.

City of Oakland v. Oakland Raiders

Supreme Court of California

183 Cal. Rptr. 673 (1982)

In 1966, the Oakland Raiders football team signed a five-year licensing agreement for use of the Oakland Coliseum. The Raiders subsequently exercised three of its three-year renewal options but failed to do so for the 1980 football season. The City of Oakland brought this action in eminent domain to prevent the football team from moving to Los Angeles, when plans were announced to do so. The city argues that it is seeking to condemn "property," which is the subject of eminent domain law. The Raiders contend that the law of eminent domain does not apply to "intangible property not connected with realty," like a football franchise. Thus, the case presents two issues, one dealing with the intangible nature of the property the city proposes to take, and the second focusing on the scope of the condemning power as limited by the doctrine of public use.

Richardson, Justice

We conclude that the trial court erred in granting the summary judgment and we reverse and remand the case for trial of the issues on the merits.

Because the power to condemn is an inherent attribute of general government, we have observed that "constitutional provisions merely place limitations upon its exercise." The two constitutional restraints are that the taking be for a "public use" and that "just compensation" be paid therefor. No constitutional restriction, federal or state, purports to limit the nature of the property that may be

taken by eminent domain. In contrast to the broad powers of general government, "a municipal corporation has no inherent power of eminent domain and can exercise it only when expressly authorized by law." We examine briefly the source of that statutory power.

The statutory power appears to impose no greater restrictions on the exercise of the condemnation power than those which are inherent in the federal and state Constitutions. Further, the power which is statutorily extended to cities is not limited to certain types of property, nor was it intended to be. In discussing the broad scope of property rights which are subject to a public taking under the new law, the Law Revision Commission comment significantly notes that "Section 1235.170 is intended to provide the broadest possible definition of property and to include any type of right, title or interest in property that may be required for public use." To that end the commission eliminated the "duplicative listings of property types and interests subject to condemnation" which had appeared in the earlier eminent domain statutes.

We are aware of nothing peculiar to a franchise which can class it higher, or render it more sacred, than other property. A franchise is property, and nothing more; it is incorporeal property.

For eminent domain purposes, neither the federal nor the state Constitution distinguishes between property which is real or personal, tangible or intangible. Nor did the 1975 statutory revision. Bearing in mind that the Law Revision Commission, after an extensive national study, made its legislative recommendations, including a definition of condemnable property which is characterized as "the broadest possible," we conclude that our eminent domain law authorizes the taking of intangible property. To the extent that the trial court based its summary judgment on a contrary conclusion it erred.

In fairness it must be said that the trial court fully acknowledged "the intent of the Legislature to allow the taking of any type of property, real or personal, if it was in fact necessary for a public use." But the court concluded as a matter of law that (1) no statutory or charter provision specifically authorized the taking of a professional football franchise, and (2) the operation of such a franchise is not a recognized public use which would permit its taking under general condemnation law. Assuming, for purposes of discussion, the propriety of the first premise, this fact alone is insufficient to support summary judgment, and we cannot agree with the second premise which we now explore.

Is City's attempt to take and operate the Raider's football franchise a valid public use? We have defined "public use" as "a use which concerns the whole community or promotes the general interest in its relation to any legitimate object of government." Further, "Public uses are not limited, in the modern view, to matters of mere business necessity and ordinary convenience, but may extend to matters of public health, recreation and enjoyment."

The examples of Candlestick Park in San Francisco and Anaheim Stadium in Anaheim, both owned and operated by municipalities, suggest the acceptance of the general principle that providing access to recreation to its residents in the form of spectator sports is an appropriate function of city government. In connection with the latter stadium, the appellate court upheld the power of the City of Anaheim to condemn land for parking facilities at the stadium on the ground that "the acquisition, construction, and operation of a stadium by a county or city represents a legitimate public purpose."

The obvious difference between managing and owning the facility in which the game is played, and managing and owning the team which plays in the facility, seems legally insubstantial. If acquiring, erecting, owning and/or operating a sports stadium is a permissible municipal function, we discern no valid legal reason why owning and operating a sports franchise which fields a team to play in the stadium is not equally permissible.

We caution that we are not concerned with the economic or governmental wisdom of City's acquisition or management of the Raider's franchise, but only with the legal propriety of the condemnation action. In this period of fiscal constraints, if the city fathers of Oakland in their collective wisdom elect to seek the ownership of a professional football franchise are we to say to them nay? And, if so, on what legal ground? Constitutional? Both federal and state Constitutions permit condemnation requiring only compensation and public use. Statutory? The applicable statutes authorize a city to take any property, real or personal. Decisional? Courts have consistently expanded the eminent domain remedy permitting property to be taken for recreational purposes with the public either as playing participants or observing spectators.

Bird, Chief Justice (concurring and dissenting)

The power of eminent domain claimed by the City in this case is not only novel but virtually without limit. This is troubling because the potential for abuse of such a great power is boundless. Although I am forced by the current state of the law to agree with the result reached by the majority, I have not signed their opinion because it endorses this unprecedented application of eminent domain law without even pausing to consider the ultimate consequences of their expansive decision. It should be noted that research both by the parties and by this court has failed to disclose a single case in which the legal propositions relied on here have been combined to reach a result such as that adopted by the majority.

There are two particularly disturbing questions in this case. First, does a city have the power to condemn a viable, ongoing business and sell it to another private party merely because the original owner has announced his intention to move his business to another city? For example, if a rock concert impresario, after some years of producing concerts in a municipal stadium, decides to move his productions to another city, may the city condemn his business, including his contracts with the rock stars, in order to keep the concerts at the stadium? If a small business that rents a storefront on land originally taken by the city for a redevelopment project decides to move to another city in order to expand, may the city take the business and force it to stay at its original location? May a city condemn any business that decides to seek greener pastures elsewhere under the unlimited interpretation of eminent domain law that the majority appear to approve?

Second, even if a city were legally able to do so, is it proper for a municipality to drastically invade personal property rights to further the policy interests asserted here?

At what point in the varied and complex business relationships involved herein would this power to condemn end? In my view, this court should proceed most cautiously before placing a constitutional imprimatur upon this aspect of creeping statism. These difficult questions are deserving of more thorough attention than they have yet received in this litigation.

It strikes me as dangerous and heavy-handed for the government to take over a business, including all of its intangible assets, for the sole purpose of preventing its relocation. The decisional law appears to be silent as to this particular question. It appears that the courts have not yet been confronted with a situation such as that presented by this case. However, a review of the pertinent case law demonstrates that decisions as to the proper scope of the power of eminent domain generally have been considered legislative, rather than judicial, in nature. Therefore, in the absence of a legislative bar to the use of eminent domain in this manner, there appears to be no ground for judicial intervention.

Not all property use decisions made by local governments involve condemning and paying for private property. Government could not afford it. The most common decision made concerning property involves regulation concerning its use. These regulations are commonly referred to as zoning ordinances or land use planning rules.

Regulation of land use does not involve any compensation being paid to the landowner whose property is affected by the regulation. The government is empowered to enact such regulations under its police power. That is, the government has the right to enact land use regulations if they protect the health, safety, morals, or welfare of the general public. For example, a city may prohibit the keeping of livestock on property within the community. This regulation clearly hinders property

Land Use Regulation

owners' rights to use their property. However, livestock with its smells and sounds would infringe on the rights of neighboring property owners to enjoy their land. Therefore the city, in balancing the rights of individual landowners with the needs of the community, prohibits the keeping of livestock within the city limits.

Zoning regulation is a means for a local government to plan the growth and development of the community. It is a way to balance the needs and rights of the community against the rights of the individual landowner. It recognizes that as we advance as a society, what some people do with their property may well affect how others enjoy their property. Zoning provides orderly regulation of the varied uses of property. Typically, certain areas of a community will be zoned for industrial use, while others will be zoned for residential or commercial use. In that way, an individual who purchases a home need not fear that a tannery or pig farm will be put on the land next door or that an all-night bistro will open across the street.

Of course, there is a limit to the extent to which local government may regulate land use. Regulation (which does not require compensation to the landowner whose property is subject to the regulation) may so affect the use and value of a property as to make it seem that the government has almost taken the property away from the landowner. This problem—how much regulation before compensation must be paid—is one of the thorniest problems in land use law.

If the regulation goes too far, then it will be considered a "taking," similar to condemnation of the land under eminent domain, and the government will be required to pay just compensation to the affected landowner and the regulation will be declared unconstitutional. In *First Lutheran Church* v. *County of Los Angeles* (1987), the United States Supreme Court held that when an ordinance is found to be a "taking" of private property, the Fifth Amendment requires that just compensation be paid to the landowner. However, no set standard or predictable test exists to determine when a certain amount of regulation of land use by a local government will lead a court to hold that the landowner must be compensated. Oliver Wendell Holmes, Jr., writing in the *Pennsylvania Coal Co.* v. *Mahon* case, stated: "Government hardly could go on if to some extent values incident to property could not be diminished without paying for every such change in the general law. As long recognized, some values are enjoyed under an implied limitation and must yield to the police power."[4]

Zoning controls basically involve a redistribution of property rights from a landowner to other community residents. These residents, through local government, are able to determine the uses of property within the community. In essence, the means of control over property use is removed from those who own the property and transferred to those who have political control in the community. The goal, no matter who exercises control, is for the land to be efficiently and wisely used. However, it is not clear that government control, as opposed to control by the owner, will necessarily lead to wise choices.

One of the problems with land use control is that it sometimes places an inequitable burden on the affected landowner. It is one thing to prohibit the keeping of a piggery in the city limits, but it is another thing to prohibit the construction of homes or businesses in an area that already has similar homes or businesses. Benefits may flow to the community, but is it fair for the burdens of no or little additional similar development to be borne by an individual landowner?

RAISING A LANDMARK BUILDING

St. Bartholomew's Episcopal Church is located on Park Avenue and Fiftieth Street, across from the Waldorf-Astoria Hotel in New York City. It has been designated as a landmark pursuant to New York City's landmark preservation ordinance. Church officials want to demolish the community house, located on Fiftieth Street, and build a high-rise office tower in its place. They contend that the income from the proposed forty–seven-story building is needed in order to continue the church's mission of helping the poor and to maintain the church building itself. In late September 1986, church members voted, 403 to 240, to approve the development. The Episcopal bishop of New York was quoted in *The New York Times* as saying "There's no other possible financial way by which that church can survive, the church should be allowed to make the decision to build an office building nearby or to open a parking lot or whatever."

This plan, however, has been rejected by New York's Landmarks Preservation Commission and is strongly op-posed by a local committee. Opponents of St. Bartholomew's plan contend that development in New York City must be regulated so that important buildings will not be raized merely to make room for more profitable commercial development. Otherwise, older structures that greatly contribute to the quality of life in the city and lend it a distinctive character will be irretrievably lost. For example, the loss of the Pennsylvania Railroad Station to more lucrative development has been called "one of the blasphemies of New York." Over seven hundred buildings in New York City have been designated as landmarks pursuant to the ordinance.

The matter is in litigation. St. Bartholomew's has spent over $2 million promoting the plan. Opponents have spent over $300 thousand fighting it. Another landmark Episcopal church, the Church of the Holy Communion, did not survive as a church and was converted into the Limelight discotheque, a fate that concerns supporters of St. Bartholomew's.

The following case is an example of land use regulations that had a profound effect on the individual landowner's future use of the land. In the case, the landowner argued that the effect of the regulation on his property was so great as to involve a "taking" of that land by the government, thereby requiring the government to pay compensation. Note that the landowner intended to construct residential housing in a residential area, although the proposal was for a high-rise development.

William C. Haas & Co. v. San Francisco
United States Court of Appeals, Ninth Circuit
605 F.2d 1117 (1979)

After it procured a site permit from the City Planning Commission to build a high-rise project, the plaintiff William C. Haas & Co. purchased the land in question, paying $1,650,000 to the vendor of the property and brokers' commissions, real estate taxes, and other fees of more than $165,000. The site permit was subsequently invalidated because of violations of the California Environmental Quality Act of 1970 and the 1972 amendments thereto. Reapplication was unsuccessful because in the interim the property was rezoned and more stringent land use restrictions were imposed.

The plaintiff brought this action against the City and County of San Francisco claiming that the city's rezoning of its property and the imposition of other land use restrictions so diminished the value of its property as to constitute a taking for which it is entitled to just compensation.

Hufstedler, Circuit Judge

As the City recognizes, governmental action in the form of regulation can "be so onerous as to constitute a taking which constitutionally requires compensation." Moreover, the Supreme Court has acknowledged that it "has been unable to develop any 'set formula' for determining when 'justice and fairness' require that economic injuries caused by public action be compensated by the Government, rather than remain disproportionately concentrated on a few persons."

Land use restrictions, reasonably related to the promotion of the health, safety, morals, or general welfare, have been repeatedly upheld even though the challenged regulations destroyed or adversely affected recognized real property interests or flatly prohibited the most beneficial use of the property. Haas necessarily agrees that the zoning and land use restrictions applied to its property did promote the general welfare by decreasing population density in the Russian Hill area, preserved light and air available to the neighbors, and served the aesthetic values enjoyed by the City as a whole. But, accepting as true the valuation evidence most favorable to Haas, the value of Haas' property was reduced from about $2,000,000 to about $100,000.

Decisions sustaining other land use regulations reasonably related to the promotion of the general welfare, uniformly reject the proposition that diminution in property value, standing alone, can establish a taking, and that the taking issue in these contexts is resolved by focusing on the uses the regulations permit. The regulations do not prevent Haas from developing the property, even though the planned development cannot be undertaken. Of course, Haas would not have paid as much for the property as it did if it had known that it would not be able to build high-rises on it. But its disappointed expectations in that regard cannot be turned into a taking, nor can Haas transform a regulation into a taking by recharacterizing the diminution of the value of its property as an inability to obtain a favorable return on its investment.

Haas has suffered a serious economic loss, and a frustration that it is not equally borne by the owners of adjacent parcels. That the loss is heavy and that Haas must bear more than its proportionate share of the burden for the sake of the general welfare, however, did not convert the regulation into a taking.

**Quality of Life
Land Use
Controls**

Traditionally, land use control issues regulated land-related issues. For example, the government created zones in a city where factories or apartments could be located. Regulations that concerned the height and size of buildings and regulations that required a certain number of parking spaces for a new retail establishment are other examples. Such controls may be considered traditional, because they apply to general uses of property. However, today, communities are also concerned about various other issues involving quality of life standards.

Since land use controls are generally looked upon with favor by the courts, some communities have been enacting regulations that go far beyond the traditional land use controls. These new controls sometimes attempt to insulate the community residents from outside elements they consider undesirable or to preserve their current way of life.

Agins v. City of Tiburon
Supreme Court of California
598 P.2d 25 (1979)

The plaintiffs are landowners in the City of Tiburon, Marin County, California. Tiburon is a very desirable and wealthy suburban residential area. The plaintiffs' property (five acres) is ridgeland and possesses views of San Francisco Bay. It was acquired by the plaintiffs for residential development. By Ordinance No. 124 N.S., effective June 28, 1973, Tiburon adopted a zoning modification plan that will permit a maximum of five dwellings and a minimum of one—depending on the architectural design contemplated—on the plaintiffs' land. The plaintiffs filed their complaint alleging a claim in inverse condemnation for two million dollars damages and asserting that Ordinance No. 124 N.S. is unconstitutional in that it "constitutes a taking of [plaintiffs'] property without payment of just compensation." The trial held for the defendants and the plaintiffs appealed.

Richardson, Justice

Community planners must be permitted the flexibility which their work requires. As we ourselves have recently observed, "If a governmental entity and its responsible officials were held subject to a claim for inverse condemnation merely because a parcel of land was designated for potential public use, the process of community planning would either grind to a halt, or deteriorate to publication of vacuous generalizations regarding the future use of land."

Accepting as we must the general proposition that whether a regulation is excessive in any particular situation involves questions of degree, turning on the individual facts of each case, we hold that a zoning ordinance may be unconstitutional and subject to invalidation only when its effect is to deprive the landowner of substantially all reasonable use of his property. The ordinance before us had no such effect. According to the wording of the ordinance, of which we may take note, the RPD-1 zoning allows plaintiffs to build between one and five residences on their property. This belies plaintiffs' claim that development of their land is forever prevented. Taking cognizance of the use which plaintiffs were entitled to make of their land the trial court was justified in finding that the ordinance did not unconstitutionally interfere with plaintiffs' entire use of the land or impermissibly decrease its value. The trial court acted properly in determining that plaintiffs were not, as a matter of law, entitled to a favorable judgment in declaratory relief.

Clark, Justice (dissenting)

Particular concern must be seen arising from to-day's decision. Tiburon—and many other governmental agencies enacting similar land use plans—will price properties within their control out of reach of most people. Only the most wealthy will be able to afford purchase of and construction on land in such areas. The environment which Ti-buron seeks to preserve will disproportionately benefit that wealthy landowner, whose home will be surrounded by open space, unobstructed view and unpolluted atmosphere.

Today's decision must further encourage city councils and their zoners to politically preserve entrenched property use.

Quality of life for people in a community may not be limited to the number of new homes that can be built in the community or the amount of open space in the community. It may also involve the kind of people who live in the community. Homeowners may not want to have student renters living in their community. Wealthy people may want to associate only with other wealthy people. Are the political and legal systems properly used by a local government when its land use regulations act to restrict people who may live in the community by "class"? Consider the conflicting approaches to this problem in the following two cases.

Village of Belle Terre v. Boraas

United States Supreme Court

416 U.S. 1 (1974)

The village of Belle Terre near the State University of New York at Stonybrook, located on the north shore of Long Island, has an area of less than one square mile. In 1973, it had two hundred homes with a total population of about seven hundred people. The village passed a zoning ordinance requiring that only single-family homes be built and that households of more than two unrelated persons be prohibited. The owners of a house who rented to six college students were ordered to remedy their violation. The district court held the ordinance constitutional. The court of appeals reversed. The United States Supreme Court reversed, holding that such an ordinance was constitutional.

Justice Douglas

The present ordinance is challenged on several grounds: that it interferes with a person's right to travel; that it interferes with the right to migrate to and settle within a State; that it bars people who are uncongenial to the present residents; that it expresses the social preferences of the residents for groups that will be congenial to them; that social homogeneity is not a legitimate interest of government; that the restriction of those whom the neighbors do not like trenches on the newcomers' rights of privacy; that it is of no rightful concern to villagers whether the residents are married or unmarried; that the ordinance is antithetical to the Nation's experience, ideology, and self-perception as an open, egalitarian, and integrated society.

We find none of these reasons in the record

before us. It is not aimed at transients. It involves no procedural disparity inflicted on some but not on others. It involves no "fundamental" right guaranteed by the Constitution, or any rights of privacy. We deal with economic and social legislation where legislatures have historically drawn lines which we respect against the charge of violation of the Equal Protection Clause if the law be "reasonable, not arbitrary" and bears a rational relationship to a permissible state objective.

It is said, however, that if two unmarried people can constitute a "family," there is no reason why three or four may not. But every line drawn by a legislature leaves some out that might well have been included. That exercise of discretion, however, is a legislative, not a judicial, function.

The ordinance places no ban on other forms of association, for a "family" may, so far as the ordinance is concerned, entertain whomever it likes.

The regimes of boarding houses, fraternity houses, and the like present urban problems. More people occupy a given space; more cars rather continuously pass by; more cars are parked; noise travels with crowds.

A quiet place where yards are wide, people few, and motor vehicles restricted are legitimate guidelines in a land-use project addressed to family needs. This goal is a permissible one. The police power is not confined to elimination of filth, stench, and unhealthy places. It is ample to lay out zones where family values, youth values, and the blessings of quiet seclusion and clean air make the area a sanctuary for people.

Hope, Inc. v. County of DuPage
United States Court of Appeals, Seventh Circuit
717 F.2d 1061 (1983)

In March, 1971, ten individual plaintiffs, some of whom resided in DuPage County, Illinois, and others who lived in the Chicago metropolitan area, and HOPE, Inc., a DuPage County based not-for-profit fair housing organization, filed suit against DuPage County, the members of its county board, and certain landowners and land developers in DuPage County claiming deprivation of rights protected by the Thirteenth and Fourteenth Amendments of the Constitution.

They alleged that DuPage County and large land developers had engaged in a practice of exclusionary housing whereby all new housing units in the county were built for and sold or rented to the relatively wealthy. The net result of the county's alleged use of its state-delegated housing regulatory policy and the contractor's housing regulatory policy was that poor and black persons were denied the opportunity of housing in DuPage County. This denial of housing resulted in the perpetuation and increase of racial and economic segregation in the Chicago metropolitan area.

DuPage County, measured by per capita income, is the fourth richest county in the United States. It has the lowest percentage of inexpensive housing, both owner-occupied and rental, of any county in the eight-county Chicago metropolitan area. DuPage County is also predominately white. In 1970, there were 1,276 black persons residing in DuPage County households, representing 0.26 percent of the total population. DuPage County's population in the two decades from 1950 to 1970 grew from 150,052 to 485,181, an increase of 223 percent, the largest of any of the eight counties in the Chicago Metropolitan area. While the population increase in the other counties of the Chicago metropolitan area has resulted primarily from natural growth, DuPage County is uniquely the recipient of white persons migrating from Chicago.

On February 3, 1982, the district court entered its judgment and decree. The decree enjoined the enforcement of provisions of the DuPage County Zoning Ordinance.

Grant, Senior District Judge

It was the district court's conclusion that DuPage County zoning practices effectively excluded non-white residents. The court found the County's pattern of preventing moderate and low income families from being residents coincided with its objective of excluding non-whites. The court finally concluded that the legislative and administrative history reflected that DuPage County desired to exclude certain types of people. The court found that the DuPage County zoning ordinances do not serve a legitimate state interest which justifies any incidental discriminatory impact. In fact, their impact far outweighed any legitimate state interest which they might have served. The summary conclusion found that DuPage County and its Board knowingly and intentionally, through housing policies and practices, excluded racial and low–moderate income minorities from living in the County.

We recognize that zoning is a local governmental function. The district court's Decree does not usurp that local power. The Decree does not, as argued by the County Board, require federal intervention in disputes over zoning for low and moderate income housing. The Decree enjoins the enforcement of the minimum lot sizes, acreage, etc. in respect to low and moderate income hous-

ing. It similarly suspends the requirement of a special use permit for construction of low and moderate income multi-family dwellings. It was through the requirements and enforcement of these two areas that adequate low and moderate income housing was prevented. The district court did not mandate the construction of a specified number of housing units, rather it directed the County to develop its own ten-year plan to significantly increase the number of units.

The Decree of the district court was targeted to what it viewed as the violation—the use of the zoning powers and ordinances to create a homogeneous, racially and economically compatible community. Such an equitable remedy was not overly broad as to usurp the local zoning powers and hence, did not constitute an abuse of discretion. This Decree was simply an attempt to implement the purported housing goals of DuPage County. The purpose of the Decree was to simply make the application of zoning equitable to all citizens and to assure "a meaningful amount of housing for families with low and moderate incomes" actually available in DuPage County. The decision of the district court is affirmed.

Social Issues and Land Use Controls

The First Amendment of the United States Constitution provides that government may not pass any law infringing upon the freedom of speech. It has long been held that not all utterances or publications are protected by this provision. A jokester who yells "fire" in a crowded theater may not claim its protection. Obscenity is not protected. However, the problem with obscenity is not that it is not constitutionally protected speech, it is deciding what is obscene, or to put it another way, deciding who in society may act as censor on behalf of the government.

Courts have been very strict in prohibiting the censorship of what some people may believe is pornography. However, some communities, under political pressure from local groups, have used land use control laws to control the location of businesses that sell objectionable material, as the following case illustrates.

City of Renton v. Playtime Theatres, Inc.

United States Supreme Court
106 S. Ct 925 (1986)

This case involves a constitutional challenge to a zoning ordinance, enacted by the city of Renton, Washington, that prohibits adult motion picture theaters from locating within one thousand feet of any residential zone, single- or multiple-family dwelling, church, park, or school. In early 1982, the respondents, Playtime Theatres, acquired two existing theaters in downtown Renton, with the intention of using them to exhibit feature-length adult films. The theaters were located within the area proscribed by the ordinance. At about the same time, the respondents filed a lawsuit challenging the ordinance on First and Fourteenth Amendment grounds.

Justice Rehnquist

This Court has long held that regulations enacted for the purpose of restraining speech on the basis of its content presumptively violate the First Amendment. On the other hand, so-called "content-neutral" time, place, and manner regulations are acceptable so long as they are designed to serve a substantial governmental interest and do not unreasonably limit alternative avenues of communication.

To be sure, the Renton ordinance treats theaters that specialize in adult films differently from other kinds of theaters. Nevertheless the ordinance is aimed not at the content of the films shown at "adult motion picture theaters," but rather at the secondary effects of such theaters on the surrounding community.

The ordinance by its terms is designed to pre-

vent crime, protect the city's retail trade, maintain property values, and generally protect and preserve the quality of the city's neighborhoods, commercial districts, and the quality of urban life, not to suppress the expression of unpopular views.

The Renton ordinance is completely consistent with our definition of "content-neutral" speech regulations as those that are justified without reference to the content of the regulated speech. Cities may regulate adult theaters by dispersing them or by effectively concentrating them, as in Renton. It is not our function to appraise the wisdom of the city's decision to require adult theaters to be separated rather than concentrated in the same areas. The city must be allowed a reasonable opportunity to experiment with solutions to admittedly serious problems.

Justice Marshall (dissenting)

The fact that adult movie theaters may cause harmful "secondary" land use effects may arguably give Renton a compelling reason to regulate such establishments; it does not mean, however, that such regulations are content-neutral. Because the ordi-

nance imposes special restrictions on certain kinds of speech on the basis of content, I cannot simply accept, as the Court does, Renton's claim that the ordinance was not designed to suppress the content of adult movies. Other motion picture theaters, and other forms of "adult entertainment," such as bars, massage parlors, and adult bookstores, are not subject to the same restrictions as adult theaters. This selective treatment strongly suggests that Renton was interested not in controlling the "secondary effects" associated with adult businesses, but in discriminating against adult theaters based on the content of the films they exhibit.

Additionally, shortly after this lawsuit commenced, the Renton City Council amended the ordinance, adding a provision explaining that its intention in adopting the ordinance had been to promote the City of Renton's great interest in protecting and preserving the quality of its neighborhoods, commercial districts, and the quality of urban life through effective land use planning. Prior to the amendment, there was no indication that the ordinance was designed to address any "secondary effects" a single adult theater might create. The ordinance greatly restricts access to lawful speech, and is plainly unconstitutional.

Abortion is one of the most controversial issues of the day. Ever since the Supreme Court upheld the right of women to have abortions if they so chose, various pressure groups have attempted to limit that right. The following case involves an attempt to limit the availability of medical facilities that performed abortions through the use of land use planning techniques.

Framingham Clinic, Inc. v. Board of Selectmen

Supreme Court of Massachusetts
367 N.E.2d 367 (1977)

The town of Southborough, Massachusetts, passed a zoning bylaw that prohibited the operation of abortion clinics within the town. Framingham Clinic, Inc., a corporation that had been attempting to establish a gynecological clinic in the town, wished to provide first-trimester abortions in that clinic. The corporation sued the town.

Kaplan, Justice

We hold for the corporation. The by-law amendment is invalid. The conclusion becomes clear when attention is paid to the constitutionally protected rights of a woman in respect to termination of her pregnancy (and the correlative rights of an attending physician or a health facility), as expounded by the Supreme Court of the United States in the line of cases beginning with *Roe v. Wade.*

The by-law amendment would have the effect of banishing from the town any clinic in which first-trimester abortions, themselves admittedly lawful, were performed. But clinics offering other lawful medical procedures could locate themselves and carry on in this or any other industrial park district that might appear on the town map. This indicates strongly that discrimination was at work against the constitutional right.

The desires of members of the community to disfavor an "abortion clinic"—desires which, reflexively, may cause these persons to see an economic detriment to themselves in the existence of the clinic—cannot extenuate such a violation. The report of the Southborough planning board about public sentiment was thus an irrelevancy, and a dangerous one, for that way would lie the extinction of many liberties which are, indeed, constitutionally guaranteed against invasion by a majority.

Neither could Southborough justify its own exclusionary rule by saying that a woman might overcome it by going elsewhere in the Commonwealth. May a "fundamental" right be denied in Worcester County because it remains available in Suffolk or Barnstable? Such a proposition cannot be seriously maintained. The picture of one community attempting thus to throw off on others would not be a happy one.

SUMMARY   The study of property in the American legal environment involves more than focusing on a variety of legally protected ownership rights. Property is a relationship among people that is recognized and enforced by the government. Property as a bundle of rights, therefore, is subject to change as the relationships of people in society change. Property rights are much like liberty or individual rights. Each provides certain freedoms to people. However, the permissible government controls are greater in property rights than in individual rights situations.

A major example of property rights and relationships can be found by examining land use planning. Local governments have the power under eminent domain to condemn and pay for private property to be used for a public purpose. Additionally, an owner's property-use choices may be limited without compensation through zoning or land use planning regulations. Issues of eminent domain and zoning raise constitutional questions, since they may have a profound effect on the rights of landowners. Often in the study of the American legal environment, local government is overlooked. However, local governments can have a great influence on the ability of business and individuals to function.

REVIEW QUESTIONS

1. Define the following terms:
   a. Property
   b. Eminent domain
   c. Fixtures
   d. Public use
   e. Zoning

2. List and discuss the factors and values that make up a rule of property or a property right.

3. List the factors a court may consider in determining whether something is a fixture.

4. Determine from the following facts whether rain should be considered a property right associated with ownership of land. What factors or values make up the arguments of each side in the dispute?

   Weather Research, Inc., began a program of cloud seeding for the purpose of suppressing hail. A number of farmers had hired Weather Research because their lands were frequently ravaged by damaging hailstorms. However, a group of ranchers brought suit against Weather Research, contending that the cloud seeding destroyed potential rain clouds over their property. Seeding was done on clouds directly over the ranchers' property. Ten to twenty minutes thereafter a potential rain cloud or thunderhead would be destroyed, leaving only a fuzzy or wispy mist. The ranchers' claim that they have a property right in the precipitation that nature deigns to bestow and that Weather Research, Inc., is interfering with that right.

5. Jones is an archaeologist. He has traveled the world seeking archaeological treasures. Some of his finds have been placed in his home. For example, in the family room there is a huge

stone slab that he pried from the tomb of an Egyptian pharaoh. Jones brought the slab to his house while it was being constructed. He had the family room specially designed so that the slab would stretch from wall to wall. It is used as a table or shelf. The room also has a triple-size door through which the slab was transported into the room. The slab weighs two thousand pounds. The balance of the room is designed and painted to look like the inside of an Egyptian tomb. The slab adds authenticity to the decor.

In July 1986, Jones sold his "house and real property" to Smith. When Smith moved into the house, he noticed that the slab in the family room was missing. He demanded that Jones return it. Jones refused. Discuss in full.

6. Prah constructed a home with a solar heating system. The properties to the north and south of Prah's home were vacant. Therefore, sunlight could, without obstruction, strike the solar collectors that were installed on Prah's roof. Subsequently, Maretti began to construct a home on vacant land adjacent to Prah's residence. Completion of the home would result in a shading of Prah's solar collectors during the cold Wisconsin winters. The shading would reduce the system's efficiency. In addition, there was a possibility of damage through freezing to the solar energy system and to Prah's home itself. The parties attempted, unsuccessfully, to negotiate a settlement concerning the location of Maretti's home.

Should Prah have a property right to the sunlight needed for his solar energy collector? Discuss in light of *Parker* and *Fontainebleau*.

7. Is land use planning a proper tool to use to further social or quality of life goals?

8. Smith owns a one-hundred-acre tract of land, or more accurately, holds the legal rights to that one-hundred-acre tract. He intends to transfer all his legal rights to Jones in the year 2000. Will Jones be able to use the property then as Smith could use it now? Discuss ways

in which the property rights that Smith now holds could change between today and the year 2000.

9. Compare individual rights (liberty) and property rights.

10. Jones is a rock concert impresario. He brings the most popular groups to the city for concerts. All concerts are held in Municipal Auditorium, which was built with tax revenues. The city built the auditorium primarily as a place where concerts could be held to encourage people to visit the community and to enhance its urban renewal goals. In addition, when Jones began to use the auditorium fifteen years ago, the city agreed to abate his taxes by fifty percent. Jones's business, which is made up of contracts with various rock musicians, has grown, and he intends to move his concerts from Municipal Auditorium to a privately owned facility in a community thirty miles away. What action might the city take, based on the Oakland Raiders' case (see *City of Oakland* v. *Oakland Raiders*, pp. 271–273)?

11. What are the advantages and disadvantages of zoning and land use controls?

12. You are an executive with the XYZ Corporation, a real estate development firm. The corporation purchased some land, zoned for industrial development, for ten million dollars. One of XYZ's clients intends to construct a large factory there, and XYZ will thereby make a large profit on the transaction. Assume, however, that the county commission rezones the land to make it usable only for agricultural use. As a result, the land is worth two million dollars, and XYZ's client will seek another site for its factory. Does XYZ Corporation have a claim against the commission for its loss on the project? Explain.

13. Hut is a very exclusive suburb with many wealthy residents. Twenty years ago, Hut was a small rural community. Today it has a very

large, urban population. Most of its growth is attributable to white upper-middle-class residents who have left the city, which Hut adjoins. Although areas surrounding Hut are economically and racially integrated, Hut's population is almost all white. It ranks as one of the wealthiest, per capita, communities in the nation. One reason for Hut's particular development is a series of land use regulations. These regulations are such as to virtually foreclose any low or moderately priced housing from being built. Furthermore, the acknowledged purpose of those regulations is to keep low-income people from moving to Hut and to keep the town homogeneous. Construct an argument that questions the validity of those regulations.

NOTES

[1] F. Cohen, Dialogue on Private Property, 9 *Rutgers L. Rev.* 357 (1954).
[2] James Boswell, *The Life of Samuel Johnson,* 421 (1791).
[3] *Berman* v. *Parker,* 348 U.S. 26 (1954).
[4] 260 U.S. 393 (1922).

PART IV

Legal Aspects of the Firm and the Regulation of Its Power

CHAPTER 11

Corporations, Agency, and Other Forms of Business Organization

Nature of the Corporation
Fiduciary Duties
Sole Proprietorship and Agency Law
The Partnership
The Limited Partnership

Marital, parent-child, and buyer-seller relationships are examples of interactions of individuals that are governed by law. A business organization is a type of human relationship, one among workers, managers, owners, investors, and creditors. These individuals and their interactions with one another make up the business organization.

The corporation is the dominant form of business organization in the American legal environment. However, it is not the only form a business may take. Numerically, there are far fewer corporations than other forms of business. Consequently, this chapter will focus on the corporation, but will thereafter briefly explore the other major forms for business organizations: the sole proprietorship and agency, the partnership, and the limited partnership. The basic legal structure of each type of business organization will be outlined, and the factors that distinguish one form from another will be examined. In addition, the legal implications of conducting business under a certain organizational form will be discussed.

CREATING A BUSINESS ORGANIZATION

In late January 1987, Steve Jobs, formerly of Apple Computers, Inc., and H. Ross Perot, the outspoken founder of Electronic Data Systems, Inc., which is now a part of General Motors, joined forces in Jobs's latest venture. Next, Inc. Next, Inc., will be developing computers and software aimed at universities. Its first product has been called a "scholar's work station."

Prior to Perot's investment, the company had fifty employees involved in product development, but no manufacturing facility. Most of Jobs's initial seven million dollar investment had been spent, and the corporation needed to move from the product developmental stage to the marketing stage. After careful review, Perot invested twenty million dollars for a sixteen percent share of the company. He also received a seat on Next's three-member board of directors. Additionally, Carnegie-Mellon University and Stanford University were invited to participate and received a one percent share for their combined $1.3 million investment.

Although initially Jobs rejected outside investment in Next, the infusion of new capital, he indicated, will enable the company to begin supplying its products within a year.

NATURE OF THE CORPORATION

The corporation is the response of a legal system to business and commercial needs of society. The concept of an organization of individuals having a single personality has deep historical roots. Some writers date this idea to primitive societies; others contend that the seeds of the modern business corporation can be found in ancient Greece. Still others submit that it was first developed in Rome. Under Roman law, a corporation was empowered to do many things that an actual person could do: hold and convey property, inherit land and goods, and acquire assets or incur liabilities. Early Christianity continued to use a corporate concept of organization. These early forms of incorporation greatly influenced the development of English law, which became the basis for American corporate law.

The first corporation to be chartered in the American colonies was chartered in 1768, in what would become the state of Pennsylvania. The company was called "The Philadelphia Contributionship for Insuring Houses from Loss by Fire." As the name implied, it was an insurance company, and it was the only corporation organized in this country before the Revolution. Thereafter, a number of American businesses received corporate charters. Most of these companies were involved in banking, insurance, turnpikes, canals, and toll bridges.

Early American corporations were granted their charters by state legislatures. Later, states passed enabling acts, which relieved the legislature of this task. These acts are the same means by which a corporation may be organized today. In brief, corporate organization statutes provide a set procedure that must be followed for a business to be granted a corporate charter. These requirements usually include the filing of the articles of incorporation with the secretary of state. If the filed documents meet the requirements of the enabling statute, the secretary will issue a certificate of incorporation signifying the formal beginning of a corporation's legal existence.

The materials on corporations may be divided into two sections. The first section discusses the nature of the corporate entity—that is, the ways in which the corporation is considered a person in the eyes of the law. This section emphasizes the formalistic nature of the corporate organization and the important attributes the law grants to a corporation. The reader should make careful note that although most business corporations are legally alike, individual corporations differ in size, power, organization, and personality. The second section discusses one of the most important legally regulated relationships—the fiduciary relationship. Corporate directors owe duties of care and loyalty to the shareholders beyond what is normally required in business relationships. Note that the fiduciary duty, although discussed in the context of a corporate organization, applies to numerous business relationships in which one party has the power to exercise control over another's property for that person's benefit.

The corporation is a unique form of business organization. Legally, it is a separate entity—a person in the eyes of the law, distinguishable and apart from any of its members. The separate entity concept of the corporation was described by Chief Justice John Marshall of the United States Supreme Court in the famous case of *Dartmouth College* v. *Woodward* in 1819.

Characteristics of the Corporate Form

> A corporation is an artificial being, invisible, intangible, and existing only in contemplation of law. Being the mere creature of law, it possesses only those properties which the charter of its creation confers upon it, either expressly or as incidental to its very existence. These are such as are supposed best calculated to effect the object for which it was created. Among the most important are immortality, and if the expression may be allowed, individuality.

Individuality. A corporate individual cannot be seen or touched. It is an intangible organizational idea that is given life, personality, and an existence by the law. It is solely a creature of the law, being formed pursuant to statute. Corporations have many of the legal characteristics of any natural person. For example, the corporation can sue and be sued. It can own property and invest it. A corporation can make money, lose money, and go bankrupt. Corporations can enter into contracts.

Since a corporation has no physical form, its individuality is somewhat limited. A corporation can only act through agents. Agents are people (workers, managers, vice-presidents, and so on) who are empowered to do certain tasks on behalf of the corporation. For example, when General Motors produces a new type of sports car, legally the corporation used its capital and resources to design a new car for the market. However, practically speaking, people, acting on behalf of General Motors, actually produced the car. Corporate agents made decisions concerning all aspects of design and production. Other agents built the car, tested it, and developed its unique features. In addition, since the corporation can only act through agents, it may be liable for torts committed by them. For example, if the car was negligently developed by the people in the company's design department, the corporation, General Motors, may be sued for the tort. Furthermore, the corporation may be found guilty of certain criminal activity of its members. Thus, the organization itself incurs liability, even though all its activities must be performed by its members.

Limited Liability. Another important characteristic of the corporation is **limited liability:** The members of the corporation, the people who make up the organization, will not be liable for claims made against the corporation. Corporate debts belong to the corporation, and creditors may not seek contribution from individuals within the organization to pay them, even if the corporation is insolvent. Directors, officers, shareholders, or employees of the corporation may not be charged with corporate liabilities.

Corporate shareholders can only lose the amount of their investment in the business. For instance, if a shareholder buys one hundred dollars' worth of stock in Corporation X, the most the shareholder could lose is the one-hundred-dollar investment. Limited liability is a protective device that encourages people to contribute capital to business enterprises. The investor need not fear calamitous personal financial exposure should the business fail.

Piercing the Corporate Veil. Although a corporation has legal existence and confers limited liability protection upon its members, there are times when the law will not recognize the corporate form. As a result, the limited liability shield is ignored and a court may hold various members liable for obligations of the business. This occurrence is known as **piercing the corporate veil.**

Piercing the corporate veil is an equitable doctrine through which a court has the power to reach a just result in a case by ignoring the corporate form. The doctrine may be involved when there is an abuse of the law. This abuse may occur, for example, when the corporation becomes the "alter ego" of its members or when recognition of the corporation as a separate entity would perpetrate a fraud. Piercing the corporate veil is infrequently invoked. Limited liability is usually upheld even if the result in a particular case may seem unfair.

A corporate entity becomes the alter ego of its members when they fail to treat the corporation as a separate legal being. This may involve ignoring organizational formalities. Perhaps, after a business receives a corporate charter from the state, corporate documents, such as bylaws and minutes of meetings, are never prepared. Perhaps neither directors nor officers are elected. Perhaps shares of stock are never issued. Making the corporation an alter ego may also involve intermingling of personal and corporate property to such an extent that the financial individuality of the corporation is lost. Members of the corporation may be guilty of using their own funds for the benefit of the business or using the firm's funds for personal benefit without loans or other documentation. In short, making the corporation an alter ego abuses the corporate form by using it as an empty shell containing the personal property of its members. Since the members of the corporation have not treated it as a separate entity, the court may also refuse to do so, holding its members liable for claims against the corporation.

Courts will also intervene when to recognize the corporation as an entity apart from its members would perpetrate a fraud. For reasons of equity and justice, the court will not recognize the corporate entity separate from its members. It will look behind the corporate shield to find the individuals.

A classic example of corporate fraud committed by a corporation's members is an arson case from the early part of this century. X was the principal behind a small corporation whose sole asset was a warehouse of tailor clippings worth approximately thirty thousand dollars. X was corporate president, was a director, and owned nearly all the shares of stock in the corporation. He was also a creditor of the corporation for over twenty-nine thousand dollars. X arranged to have the warehouse burned by an arsonist. Later, X was tried and convicted of the crime. However, the corporation filed a claim with its insurance company to collect approximately thirty thousand dollars on its policy for the loss. The insurance company refused to pay, and the court upheld it. The court pierced the corporate veil and refused to allow X to gain through the corporate personality what he would not have gained individually. A person may not collect insurance on property that the person willfully destroyed. In this case, recognizing the legal entity would have allowed just that result to occur, although circuitously.

The following case is another example of the piercing the corporate veil doctrine. Note that although the company was granted a charter of incorporation, none of the corporate formalities were complied with.

Minton v. Cavaney
Supreme Court of California
364 P.2d 473 (1961)

The Seminole Hot Springs Corporation was duly incorporated in California on March 8, 1954. It operated a public swimming pool that it leased from its owner. On June 24, 1954, plaintiffs' daughter drowned in the pool, and plaintiffs recovered a judgment of ten thousand dollars against Seminole for her wrongful death. The judgment remained unsatisfied.

On January 30, 1957, plaintiffs brought the present action to hold defendant Cavaney personally liable for the judgment against Seminole.

Plaintiffs introduced evidence that Cavaney was a director and secretary and treasurer of Seminole and that on November 15, 1954, about five months after the drowning, Cavaney, as secretary of Seminole, and Edwin A. Kraft, as president of Seminole, applied for permission to issue three shares of Seminole stock, one share to be issued to Kraft, another to F. J. Wettrick, and the third to Cavaney. The commissioner of corporations refused permission to issue these shares unless additional information was furnished. The application was then abandoned and no shares were ever issued. There was also evidence that for a time Seminole used Cavaney's office to keep records and to receive mail. Cananey was asked if Seminole "ever had any assets." Cavaney stated, "[I]nsofar as I know, this corporation had no assets of any kind or character. The corporation was duly organized but never functioned as a corporation."

Traynor, Justice

The figurative terminology "alter ego" and "disregard of the corporate entity" is generally used to refer to the various situations that are an abuse of the corporate privilege. The equitable owners of a corporation, for example, are personally liable when they treat the assets of the corporation as their own and add or withdraw capital from the corporation at will or when they hold themselves out as being personally liable for the debts of the corporation or when they provide inadequate capitalization and actively participate in the conduct of corporate affairs.

In the instant case the evidence is undisputed that there was no attempt to provide adequate capitalization. Seminole never had any substantial assets. It leased the pool that it operated, and the lease was forfeited for failure to pay the rent. The evidence is also undisputed that Cavaney was not only the secretary and treasurer of the corporation but was also a director. The evidence that Cavaney was to receive one-third of the shares to be issued supports an inference that he was an equitable owner and the evidence that for a time the records of the corporation were kept in Cavaney's office supports an inference that he actively participated in the conduct of the business. The trial court was not required to believe his statement that he was only a "temporary" director and officer "for accommodation." In any event it merely raised a conflict in the evidence that was resolved adversely to defendant. Moreover, section 800 of the Corporations Code provides the business and affairs of every corporation shall be controlled by a board of not less than three directors. Defendant does not claim that Cavaney was a director with specialized duties. It is immaterial whether or not he accepted the office of director as an "accommodation" with the understanding that he would not exercise any of the duties of a director. A person may not in this manner divorce the responsibilities of a director from the statutory duties and powers of that office.

Cavaney was the "alter ego" of Seminole Hot Springs Corporation.

Members of the Corporate Organization

A corporation may be defined as an organization of people—officers, directors, employees, and shareholders—all having certain functions within the corporate organization. Two of the most important groups of members from a legal perspective are the shareholders and the directors.

Shareholders. The shareholders in a corporation are considered to be its owners. They invest money in the enterprise through the purchase of stock. However, shareholders do not participate in the management or operation of the corporation unless they occupy some position other than shareholder, for example, shareholder-director or shareholder-division manager. The only corporate control that shareholders exercise is through the election of the board of directors.

Generally, each share of common stock is entitled to one vote. Thus, the shareholders who control sufficient shares can indirectly control the corporation through the election of a board of directors who will carry out those shareholders' aims. The other shareholders, although able to vote, will have no effective voice in corporate affairs. In large publicly held corporations, shareholders who are dissatisfied with management may simply sell their shares on the market. But in small, privately held corporations in which there is no market for the shares, this is not an alternative.

Directors. The board of directors of a corporation is vested with the duty to manage the corporation. This does not mean that they are involved in the day-to-day decision making of the business. These decisions are made by the officers of the corporation, who are elected by the directors. However, the board of directors is legally responsible for the management of the corporation. In fulfilling this responsibility, the directors must operate as a board. One or two directors may not act independently. Also, the board only has authority to act as a group.

In a sense, the directors act as the representatives of the shareholders in corporate management. They have control over the shareholders' investments and the assets of the corporation. Their decisions affect the future of the business. Consequently, the law imposes specific duties of care and loyalty upon them. These are called the directors' fiduciary duties.

FIDUCIARY DUTIES

A **fiduciary duty** arises in certain legal relationships, such as that between corporate directors and shareholders. It also occurs in agent-principal, trustee-beneficiary, attorney-client, and accountant-client relationships. Each of these relationships involves one party (the fiduciary) being vested with power and authority over the property or person of another. The other party consequently places trust and confidence in the work of the fiduciary. In a corporate setting, the directors have the power to control the corporation. They are vested with this power by the shareholders whose money is invested in corporate stock. Activities of the board of directors, therefore, can have a profound effect on shareholder property.

The directors' fiduciary duty obligates them to use the utmost good faith and loyalty and to exercise care and prudence in all matters concerning the management of the corporation. Normally acceptable standards of business practice are not sufficient to satisfy the fiduciary duty. Extraordinary conduct and diligence are demanded of the fiduciary.

In general, the fiduciary duty may be divided into two categories: The fiduciary duty of care concerns diligent decision making by the board; the fiduciary duty of loyalty concerns the relationship between an individual director and the corporation. It requires that the interests of the corporation be placed ahead of any personal interests of the director.

Fiduciary Duty of Care

Directors have a fiduciary duty to exercise care in their decision making. The standard is the amount of care an ordinarily prudent person in a like position would use under similar circumstances. This is not an easy standard to apply. In effect, it is a standard of hindsight. Shareholders will argue breach of this duty or will review the directors' decision making when a particular decision turns out to be wrong or costs the shareholders potential profits. The standard, therefore, requires the directors to exercise careful and prudent decision-making procedures. However, the standard is no guarantee that all decisions will be correct.

The following case is an example of the fiduciary duty of care. It involves a bank fraud and claims that the fiduciaries violated their duty of care by not detecting the fraud before it became a disaster. Note that the duty of care was applied differently to the board of directors than it was to the president (who also owed a fiduciary duty). Although each owed the shareholders a fiduciary duty of care, their positions in the day-to-day operation of the bank were different. Thus, the diligence each needed to exercise on behalf of the corporation was found to be factually different.

Bates v. Dresser
United States Supreme Court
251 U.S. 524 (1920)

The bank was a little bank at Cambridge with a capital of $100,000 and average deposits of somewhere about $300,000. Coleman, who made the trouble, entered the service of the bank as messenger in September 1903. In January 1904, he was promoted to bookkeeper.

In November 1906, he began the thefts that come into question here. Having a small account at the bank, he would draw checks for the amount he wanted, exchange checks with a Boston broker, get cash for the broker's check, and, when the checks came to the bank through the clearinghouse, abstract his own from the envelope, enter the others on his book, and conceal the difference by a charge to some other account or a false addition in the column of drafts or deposits in the depositors' ledger. He handed to the cashier only the slip from the clearinghouse that showed the totals. The cashier paid whatever appeared to be due, and thus Coleman's checks were honored. So far as Coleman thought it necessary, in view of the absolute trust in him on the part of all concerned, he took care that his balances should agree with those in the cashier's book.

By May 2, 1907, Coleman had abstracted $17,000, concealing the fact by false addition in the column of total checks and false balances in the deposit ledger. Then for the moment a safer concealment was effected by charging the whole to Dresser's inactive account. Coleman adopted this method when a bank examiner was expected. Of course, when the fraud was disguised by overcharging a depositor, it could not be discovered except by calling in the passbooks, or taking all the deposit slips and comparing them with the depositors' ledger in detail. By February 21, 1910, when the bank closed, the amount taken by Coleman was $310,143.02.

The directors considered the matter in September 1909, but concluded that the falling off in deposits was due in part to the springing up of rivals, whose deposits were increasing, but was parallel to a similar decrease in New York. An examination by a bank examiner in December 1909 disclosed nothing wrong.

In this connection it should be mentioned that in the previous semi-annual examinations by national bank examiners, nothing was discovered pointing to malfeasance. The cashier was honest, and everybody believed that they could rely upon him, although in fact he relied too much upon Coleman, who also was unsuspected by all. If the cashier had opened the envelopes from the clearinghouse and had seen the checks, or had examined the deposit ledger with any care, he would have found out what was going on. The scrutiny of anyone accustomed to such details would have discovered the false addition and other indicia of fraud that were on the face of the book. But it may be doubted whether anything less than a continuous pursuit of the figures through pages would have done so except by a lucky chance.

Justice Holmes

The question of the liability of the directors in this case is the question whether they neglected their duty by accepting the cashier's statement of liabilities and failing to inspect the depositors' ledger. The statements of assets always were correct. Of course liabilities as well as assets must be known to know the condition and, as this case shows, speculations may be concealed as well by a false understatement of liabilities as by a false show of assets. But the former is not the direction in which fraud would have been looked for, especially on the part of one who at the time of his principal abstractions was not in contact with the funds. A debtor hardly expects to have his liability understated. Some animals must have given at least one exhibition of dangerous propensities before the owner can be held. This fraud was a novelty in the way of swindling a bank so far as the knowledge of any experience had reached Cambridge before 1910.

We are not prepared to reverse the finding of the master and the Circuit Court of Appeals that the directors should not be held answerable for taking the cashier's statement of liabilities to be as correct as the statement of assets always was. If he had not been negligent without their knowledge it would have been. Their confidence seemed warranted by the semi-annual examinations by the government examiner and they were encouraged in their belief that all was well by the president, whose responsibility, as executive officer; interest, as large stockholder and depositor; and knowledge, from long daily presence in the bank, were greater than theirs. They were not bound by virtue of the office gratuitously assumed by them to call in the pass-books and compare them with the ledger, and until the event showed the possibility they hardly could have seen that their failure to look at the ledger opened a way to fraud. We are not laying down general principles, however, but confine our decision to the circumstances of the particular case.

The position of Dresser, the president, is different. Practically he was the master of the situation. He was daily at the bank for hours, he had the deposit ledger in his hands at times and might have had it at any time. He had had hints and warnings in addition to those that we have mentioned, warnings that should not be magnified unduly, but still would have induced scrutiny but for an invincible repose upon the status quo. In 1908 one Fillmore learned that a package containing $150 left with the bank for safe keeping was not to be found, told Dresser of the loss, wrote to him that he could but conclude that the package had been destroyed or removed by someone connected with the bank, and in later conversation said that it was evident that there was a thief in the bank. He added that he would advise the president to look after Coleman, that he believed he was living at a pretty fast pace, and that he had pretty good authority for thinking that he was supporting a woman. In the same year or the year before, Coleman, whose pay was never more than twelve dollars a week, set up an automobile, as was known to Dresser and commented on unfavorably, to him. There was also some evidence of notice to Dresser that Coleman was dealing in copper stocks. In 1909 came the great and inadequately explained seeming shrinkage in the deposits. No doubt plausible explanations of his conduct came from Coleman and the notice as to speculations may have been slight, but taking the whole story of the relations of the parties, we are not ready to say that the two courts below erred in finding that Dresser had been put upon his guard.

In accepting the presidency Dresser must be taken to have contemplated responsibility for losses to the bank, whatever they were, if chargeable to his fault. Those that happened were chargeable to his fault, after he had warnings that should have led to steps that would have made fraud impossible, even though the precise form that the fraud would take hardly could have been foreseen.

Business Judgment Rule. The defense of the directors to any shareholder claim of breach of fiduciary duty of care is called the business judgment rule. The business judgment rule provides that when an act or omission involves a question of policy or business judgment, the directors will not be liable for an erroneous decision, in absence of a showing of fraud or bad faith. This defense recognizes that mistakes may be made and that people may disagree about the proper business policies in a given situation. If the directors make their business decisions honestly and use sound business judgment, then they have not breached their fiduciary duty of care.

However, the directors may not choose to ignore what is happening around them in the business in order to protect themselves from a breach of duty claim. Furthermore, the standard of honest judgment reflects the notion that the directors have used proper decision-making procedures. Generally, this requires the directors to make reasonable efforts to gather information concerning the decisions to be made.

The following case illustrates the business judgment rule defense. Note that the court was not concerned with whether the business decision was correct or whether it was the decision the court would have made in a similar situation. Instead, the court held that the decision was proper because it found that the directors had exercised sound business judgment in reaching it.

Shlensky v. Wrigley et al.

Appellate Court of Illinois
237 N.E.2d 776 (1968)

Plaintiff is a minority stockholder of defendant corporation, Chicago National League Ball Club (Inc.), a Delaware corporation with its principal place of business in Chicago, Illinois. Defendant corporation owns and operates the major league professional baseball team known as the Chicago Cubs. The individual defendants are directors of the Cubs and have served for varying periods of years. Defendant Philip K. Wrigley is also president of the corporation and owner of approximately eighty percent of the stock therein.

Plaintiff alleges that since night baseball was first played in 1935, nineteen of the twenty major league teams have scheduled night games. In 1966, out of a total of 1,620 games in the major leagues, 932 were played at night. Plaintiff alleges that every member of the major leagues, other than the Cubs, scheduled substantially all its home games in 1966 at night, exclusive of opening days, Saturdays, Sundays, holidays, and days prohibited by league rules. This has been done for the specific purpose of maximizing attendance and thereby maximizing revenue and income.

The Cubs, in the years from 1961 to 1965, sustained operating losses from its direct baseball operations. Plaintiff attributes those losses to inadequate attendance at Cubs' home games. He concludes that if the directors continue to refuse to install lights at Wrigley Field and schedule night baseball games, the Cubs will continue to sustain comparable losses, and its financial condition will continue to deteriorate.

Plaintiff alleges that defendant Wrigley has refused to install lights, not because of interest in the welfare of the corporation but because of his personal opinions "that baseball is a 'daytime sport' and that the installation of lights and night baseball games will have a deteriorating effect upon the surrounding neighborhood." It is alleged that he has admitted that he is not interested in whether the Cubs would benefit financially from such action because of his concern for the neighborhood, and that he would be willing for the team to play night games if a new stadium were built in Chicago.

Sullivan, Justice

Plaintiff in the instant case argues that the directors are acting for reasons unrelated to the financial interest and welfare of the Cubs. However, we are not satisfied that the motives assigned to Philip K. Wrigley, and through him to the other directors, are contrary to the best interests of the corporation and the stockholders. For example, it appears to us that the effect on the surrounding neighborhood might well be considered by a director who was considering the patrons who would or would not attend the games if the park were in a poor neighborhood. Furthermore, the long run interest of the corporation in its property value at Wrigley Field might demand all efforts to keep the neighborhood from deteriorating. By these thoughts we do not mean to say that we have decided that the decision of the directors was a correct one. That is beyond our jurisdiction and ability. We are merely saying that the decision is one properly before directors and the motives alleged in the amended complaint showed no fraud, illegality or conflict of interest in their making of that decision.

There is no allegation that the night games played by the other nineteen teams enhanced their financial position or that the profits, if any, of those teams were directly related to the number of night games scheduled. There is an allegation that the installation of lights and scheduling of night games in Wrigley Field would have resulted in large amounts of additional revenues and incomes from increased attendance and related sources of in-

come. Further, the cost of installation of lights, funds for which are allegedly readily available by financing, would be more than offset and recaptured by increased revenues. However, no allegation is made that there will be a net benefit to the corporation from such action, considering all increased costs. No mention was made of operation and maintenance of the lights or other possible increases in operating costs of night games and we cannot speculate as to what other factors might influence the increase or decrease of profits if the Cubs were to play night home games.

Finally, we do not agree with plaintiff's contention that failure to follow the example of the other major league clubs in scheduling night games constituted negligence. Plaintiff made no allegation that these teams' night schedules were profitable or that the purpose for which night baseball had been undertaken was fulfilled. Furthermore, it cannot be said that directors, even those of corporations that are losing money, must follow the lead of the other corporations in the field. Directors are elected for their business capabilities and judgment and the courts cannot require them to forego their judgment because of the decisions of directors of other companies. Courts may not decide these questions in the absence of a clear showing of dereliction of duty on the part of the specific directors and mere failure to "follow the crowd" is not such a dereliction.

**Fiduciary Duty
of Loyalty**

The directors' fiduciary duty of loyalty does not regulate their decision-making process. Instead, it regulates the relationship between an individual director and the corporation. Shareholders are concerned not only that careful business decisions are made, but also with the conduct of the individuals who occupy positions on the board. These individuals are privy to secret corporate plans and information. By virtue of their powerful position they have the ability to influence corporate decisions for their own benefit. They have the ability to make investments and personal business decisions that could garner large profits at the expense of the corporation.

The danger the fiduciary duty of loyalty seeks to avoid is that of individual directors' taking advantage of their positions on the board for personal gain. Such directors, therefore, are held to a duty of loyalty in all personal dealings with the corporation to promote the interests of the corporation without regard for individual profit.

Dealings with the Corporation. The law does not prohibit a director from engaging in business deals with the corporation. However, there exists the danger of a conflict of interest in such transactions. The director owes a duty to the corporation, yet stands to gain financially from the terms of the contract. Furthermore, by virtue of a position on the board, a director may have an undue advantage in securing or negotiating the contract.

The directors' fiduciary duty requires a standard different from that which exists in the marketplace. For example, the director must make a full disclosure concerning all aspects of the contract affecting the value of the property or services involved, as well as the amount of profit to be made. This full disclosure must be made to an independent board of directors. Essentially, this means that the other directors of the corporation must not be influenced by the contracting director. Alternatively, the contract must, in all respects, be fair and reasonable to the corporation. If one or the other of these standards is not met, then the contract is considered legally voidable.

Under either of these standards, fairness in the contractual dealing with the corporation is the key. It can be expected that a board that is not under undue influence of a particular director will exercise its fiduciary duty of care in reviewing the contract proposal. In any event, the duty of loyalty standard responds to a concern that directors may take advantage of their position in dealing with the corporation.

The following case is an example of a breach of the fiduciary duty of loyalty. Note that the director who negotiated the startlingly one-sided contract was on the boards of both corporations. Yet he owned stock only in one of them—the corporation for whose benefit the contract was drafted.

Globe Woolen Co. v. Utica Gas & Electric Co.
Court of Appeals of New York
121 N.E. 378 (1918)

The plaintiff is the owner of two mills in the city of Utica. One is for the manufacture of worsteds and the other for the manufacture of woolens. The defendant generates and sells electricity for light and power. For many years, John F. Maynard has been the plaintiff's chief stockholder, its president, and a member of its board of directors. He has also been a director of the defendant and chairman of its executive committee. He received a single share of the defendant's stock to qualify him for office. He returned the share at once, and he has never held another. His property interest in the plaintiff is large. In the defendant he has none.

At the beginning, the mills were run by steam, and the plant was antiquated and inadequate. Greenidge, the general manager of the defendant's electrical department, suggested to Mr. Maynard the substitution of electric power. Mr. Maynard was fearful that the cost of equipment would be too great unless the defendant would guarantee a saving in the cost of operation. Nonetheless, a change was felt to be important. The plaintiff's books were thrown open to Greenidge, who calculated for himself the cost of operation with steam and the probable cost with electricity.

When the investigation was over, a contract was closed. The defendant proposed to supply the plaintiff's mills with electricity at a maximum rate of $.0104 per kilowatt hour, and to guarantee that the cost for heat and light and power would show a saving each month of $300 each as compared with the cost for the corresponding month in the year previous to the change. In addition, the contract would apply to "current used for any purposes in any extensions or additions to the mills." There was to be a trial period ending July 1, 1907. Then, at the plaintiff's option, the contract was to run for five years, with a privilege of renewal for a like term. Six weeks later, on December 1, 1906, Mr. Maynard laid the contract before the defendant's executive committee. He went to the meeting with Mr. Greenidge. The contract was read. Mr. Lewis, the vice-president, asked Mr. Greenidge what the rate would be, and was told about $.0104 per kilowatt hour. Mr. Beardsley, another director, asked whether the contract was a profitable one for the company, and was told by Mr. Greenidge that it was. Mr. Maynard kept silent. A resolution was moved and carried that the contract be ratified. Mr. Maynard presided at the meeting, and put the resolution, but was excused from voting.

It quickly appeared that the defendant had made a losing contract, but only gradually did the extent of the loss, its permanence, and its causes unfold themselves. Greenidge had miscalculated. The plaintiff dyed more yarn and less slubbing than before. But the dyeing of yarn takes twice as much heat as that of slubbing, and thus doubles the cost of fuel. These and like changes in the output of the mills had not been foreseen by Greenidge, and Maynard had not warned of them. In 1909, the defendant became alarmed at the mounting loss. Finally, in February 1911, the defendant gave notice of rescission. At that time, it had supplied the plaintiff with electricity worth $69,500.75 if paid for at the maximum rate fixed by the contract, and $60,000 if paid for at the lowest rate charged to any customer in Utica. Yet not only had it received nothing, but it owed the plaintiff under its guaranty $11,721.41. The finding is that a like loss prolonged to the end of the term would amount to $300,000.

Cardozo, Justice

We think the evidence supports the conclusion that the contracts are voidable at the election of the defendant. The plaintiff does not deny that this would be true if the dual director had voted for their adoption. But the argument is that by refusing to vote he shifted the responsibility to his associates, and may reap a profit from their errors. One does not divest oneself so readily of one's duties as director. A dominating influence may be exerted in other ways than by a vote. A beneficiary, about to plunge into a ruinous course of dealing, may be betrayed by silence as well as by the spoken word.

The director is free to stand aloof, while others act, if all is equitable and fair. He cannot rid himself of the duty to warn and to denounce, if there is improvidence or oppression, either apparent on the surface, or lurking beneath the surface, but visible to his practiced eye.

There was an influence here, dominating, perhaps, and surely potent and persuasive, which was exerted by Mr. Maynard from the beginning to the end. In all the stages of preliminary treaty he dealt with a subordinate, who looked up to him as to a superior, and was alert to serve his pleasure. There was no clean-cut cleavage in those stages between his conflicting offices and agencies. No label identified the request of Mr. Maynard, the plaintiff's president, as something separate from the advice of Mr. Maynard, the defendant's chairman. The members of the committee, hearing the contract for the first time, knew that it had been framed by the chairman of the meeting. They were assured in his presence that it was just and equitable. Faith in his loyalty disarmed suspicion.

There was, then, a relation of trust reposed, of influence exerted, of superior knowledge on the one side and legitimate dependence on the other.

At least, a finding that there was this relation was evidence to sustain it. A director may not cling to contracts thus won, unless their terms are fair and just.

The contracts before us do not survive these tests. The unfairness is startling, and the consequences have been disastrous. The mischief consists in this: No matter how large the business, no matter how great the increase in the price of labor or of fuel, no matter what the changes in the nature or the proportion of the products, no matter even though there be extensions of the plant, the defendant has pledged its word that for ten years there will be a saving of $600 a month, $300 for each mill, $7,200 a year. As a result of that pledge it has supplied the plaintiff with electric current for nothing, and owes, if the contract stands, about $11,000 for the privilege. These elements of unfairness Mr. Maynard must have known, if indeed his knowledge be material. He may not have known how great the loss would be. But he cannot have failed to know that he held a one-sided contract which left the defendant at his mercy. He was not blind to the likelihood that in a term of ten years there would be changes in the business.

We hold that the constant duty rests on a director to seek no harsh advantage to the detriment of his corporation, but rather to protest and renounce if through the blindness of those who treat with him he gains what is unfair. And, because there is evidence that in the making of these contracts that duty was ignored, the power of equity was fittingly exercised to bring them to an end.

Corporate Opportunity Doctrine. The corporate opportunity doctrine imposes two more loyalty standards. First, a director may not enter into any business competition with the corporation, for a director has access to corporate strategy and plans that would make a competitive enterprise particularly harmful to the corporation. In effect, the director would be using the position for personal gain rather than for the benefit of the corporation.

A second standard of the corporate opportunity doctrine prohibits a director from taking advantage of a business opportunity that may have been of interest to or could have been used by the corporation. The director owes the corporation a right of first refusal, that being the right to acquire a particular opportunity at the same terms and conditions as were first offered to the individual director. If the opportunity is presented and the corporation refuses it, the director is generally able to legally take advantage of it. For example, a director may know that the corporation has plans for expansion at some undetermined future date, and a real estate agent may offer the director land adjacent to the corporation, making a prime location for future expansion. The director may not purchase this land, even though it may be an outstanding investment, without first giving the corporation the opportunity to do so.

A further example illustrates the operation of the corporate opportunity doctrine. Assume that Jane Jones is a member of the board of directors of XYZ, Inc., which owns a large chain of fast food restaurants. The restaurants specialize in a wide variety of soft drinks, its most popular being an orange-flavored beverage. The corporation has attempted to negotiate bulk rates with the small firm that supplies the popular orange drink, but to no avail. On February 15, Jones learns that the small firm that supplies the orange drink is in financial trouble. She purchases a controlling interest in the company and thereafter decides to expand operations to include quick stop restaurants that sell the orange drink and sandwiches.

Jane Jones has violated her fiduciary duty of loyalty to XYZ, specifically, the corporate opportunity doctrine. First, Jones, through her controlling interest in the small firm, is in direct competition with XYZ. The Jones-controlled firm will be selling products similar to XYZ's, including the most popular item at XYZ's restaurants. Furthermore, since both businesses will be selling fast food, their clientele will be similar. Thus, the danger to XYZ shareholders is that Jones's personal success conflicts with the success of the corporation, and her access to corporate plans and strategies can be used to harm it. A director's duty of loyalty requires that corporate interests supersede individual ones.

Furthermore, Jones took for herself an opportunity that rightfully belonged to XYZ when she purchased a controlling interest in the small beverage-supply firm. Since XYZ sold the very popular orange drink, the opportunity to acquire the firm that produces it would be a business opportunity that would most likely interest the corporation. A director's duty of loyalty requires that such business opportunities be made available to the corporation before the individual director can consider them. Since Jones did not provide the corporation with the chance to purchase the beverage-supply firm that was offered to her, she breached her duty of loyalty.

SOLE PROPRIETORSHIP AND AGENCY LAW

Although the corporation is the major form of business organization, other forms exist, primarily for small business or investment purposes. During the discussion that follows, three of these forms will be discussed: the sole proprietorship, the partnership, and the limited partnership. However, note that some of the issues discussed in this chapter may apply to any of the organization. The fiduciary duty arises in all the organizations, as does the agency principles. Keep in mind the nature of the relationship that is being regulated by law.

The sole proprietorship, the least complex form of business, consists of one owner, the proprietor. No legal formalities precede its creation. A sole proprietorship may be any size, although most are small businesses. In fact, the sole proprietorship need not have employees. The sole proprietor could be the only one involved in the

The Sole Proprietorship

business. As an illustration, assume that Mary Smith opened a store that sold computer software. She had complete control of the business, was its sole owner, and made all the management decisions. She secured a loan from a local bank, using her home as collateral. She purchased the inventory and worked in the store throughout the day. Although her conduct is regulated by certain bodies of law (contracts or consumer law in her dealings with customers, licensing requirements of the state and local governments, and so forth), she is not required to follow any legal procedure to become a sole proprietor. If the computer software store is successful, Mary will reap the benefits. If it is a failure, then she will be responsible for its losses. Therefore, there is no legal distinction between Mary and the business.

No separate body of "sole proprietorship law" exists. Since there is only one owner, no special legal rules are needed to regulate co-owner relations. Since the sole proprietor is also the manager of the business, no legal rules are necessary to govern the separation of owner and manager. The sole proprietor and the business have a single identity. Therefore, the "law of the sole proprietorship" is the law of contracts, torts, property, agency, government regulation, and others applicable to any business.

The Law of Agency	A sole proprietorship need not be a one-person business. If the sole proprietorship has employees, the law will regulate the relationship between sole proprietor and employees through agency law.

The law of agency may be traced to ancient Rome, where "agents" were actually slaves, who had no legal status under Roman law. Their legal identities were absorbed into the Roman families they served. Since the master (male head of the household) represented the family in the eyes of the law, he also became liable for the actions of his slaves. Today, the law of agency carries forward the legal consequences of the Roman relationship, even though the relationship no longer exists in its original form.

An agency relationship is created by consent of two persons, **agent** and **principal**. The agent has the power to act on behalf of the principal. Consequently, the agent also owes legal duties to the principal. On the other hand, the principal has the legal right to control the activities of the agent. In the example of Mary Smith's computer software store, if she hires an employee, George Jones, an agency relationship is created. Mary is the principal. She has control over the actions of George and is the one on whose behalf George will be acting. George, the agent, has the power to act in place of Mary and owes her a fiduciary duty throughout this employment.

However, not every consensual relationship between two persons creates an agency relationship. Buyer-seller relations are consensual, but the parties are not each other's agents and principals. A debtor-creditor relationship is another example. Although the creditor may have control over certain aspects of the debtor's business, the debtor is not given the power to act on behalf of the creditor. Therefore, no agency relationship arises.

In order for an agency relationship to be formed, two factors must exist. First, the principal must have the right to control the activities of the agent. In a typical employer-employee agency relationship, the employer (principal) has the right to control work activities of the employee (agent). Second, the agent must have the power to act on behalf of the principal.

The following case concerns the issue of identifying a principal-agent relationship. Before the legal doctrines that bind the principal to the consequences of certain actions by the agent can arise, the relationship must be established.

Hurla v. Capper Publications, Inc.
Supreme Court of Kansas
87 P.2d 552 (1939)

The defendant Arthur Capper and Capper Publications, Incorporated, operated several routes of the Topeka *Daily Capital* in the neighborhood of Delia, Kansas. The defendant John Lane collected subscriptions and delivered the Sunday edition of that paper. On September 26, 1937, the Hurla family was driving east on a county highway in a Chevrolet coach. At a point two miles east of Delia, the county highway is intersected by a township road running north and south. At the intersection, the Hurla car collided with a Ford V-8 car traveling north on the township road. The Ford car was owned by the defendant John Lane.

As a result of the collision, the plaintiff Michael Hurla suffered severe injuries for which he asks damages.

The defendant Arthur Capper denied that he at any time, either in his personal capacity or as owner of the Topeka *Daily Capital,* operated any newspaper route or routes in the neighborhood of Delia. He also denied that John Lane was his agent, servant, or employee. Capper further alleged that the defendant John Lane was the owner of and was operating a newspaper route on his own responsibility for the purpose of delivering the Sunday edition of the Topeka *Daily Capital.*

Allen, Justice

A principal employing another to achieve a result but not controlling nor having the right to control the details of his physical movement is not responsible for incidental negligence while such person is conducting the authorized transaction. Thus, the principal is not liable for the negligent physical conduct of an attorney, a broker, a factor, or a rental agent, as such. In their movements and their control of physical forces, they are in the relation of independent contractors to the principal. It is only when to the relationship of principal and agent there is added that right to control physical details as to the manner of performance which is characteristic of the relationship of master and servant, that the person in whose service the act is done becomes subject to liability for the physical conduct of the actor.

The general rule is that when a person lets out work to another, the contractee reserving no control over the work or workmen, the relation of contractor and contractee exists, and not that of master and servant, and the contractee is not liable for the negligence or improper execution of the work by the contractor.

Under the established rule in this state it is necessary to show by competent testimony that the relation of master and servant existed between John Lane and Arthur Capper. It is not sufficient to show that John Lane had a paper route, and that he solicited and collected subscriptions and delivered papers to the subscribers. These acts are consistent with the conduct of an independent contractor. On the subscription card delivered by Lane to the subscriber appeared the title "Topeka Daily

Capital," "Topeka Sunday Capital" and was endorsed "Carrier, J. A. Lane." It is argued that this establishes the relation of master and servant between the parties. We think however this is consistent with the view that Lane was an independent contractor. Giving the plaintiff the benefit of every reasonable inference arising from the evidence adduced it fails to show that Arthur Capper controlled or had the right to control the physical conduct of John Lane in the performance of his duties as a paper carrier over the route.

Doctrines of agency law occur in every business organization where one person (the agent) works on behalf of another (the principal). For example, in a corporation, the corporate entity is the principal, and all who perform its tasks are agents. The principal-agent relationship is sometimes referred to as an employer-employee or master-servant relationship.

Relationship between Agent and Principal

Agents and principals owe legal duties to each other. The principal's duty is to abide by the terms of the agreement reached with the agent. Essentially, this means paying the agent for the work performed on the principal's behalf.

The agent owes the principal a fiduciary duty that requires the agent to use great care and to exercise utmost loyalty when acting on behalf of the principal. Since the agent has the power to expose the principal to liability, the law imposes a high standard of conduct on the agent as a means of protecting the principal. Note that the concept of a fiduciary duty was discussed in the relationship between corporate directors and shareholders. The doctrines are the same for agent and principal.

Relationship between Agents, Principals, and Third Parties

Torts and Vicarious Liability. A tort committed by an agent within the course and scope of the agency relationship (or the principal's business) binds the principal. This is known as the doctrine of respondeat superior or vicarious liability. (The agent who committed the tort, of course, would also be liable.) Vicarious liability is a doctrine under which the principal is liable for certain torts of the agent. The principal did not commit a tort but is liable simply because of the relationship with the agent. Vicarious liability may, at first, seem at odds with notions of fairness or justice; liability is imposed on someone who has committed no wrong. However, the doctrine serves some major purposes. It provides that those who have others act in their stead may not thereby escape liability. If the principal had committed the tort, liability would exist; thus, by hiring an agent as a substitute, liability should also follow. Today, probably the strongest rationale for vicarious liability is the "deep pocket." The injured party will be more likely to receive damages from the principal (a business with assets or insurance) than from the individual who committed a tort.

Determining whether a tort is within the course and scope of the business is often not an easy task. The basic question is whether the tort was committed by the agent while performing business of the principal. Some agent torts may involve both business and nonbusiness (personal) elements. For instance, while on route, a delivery driver stops at home to check the mail and has an accident. Or, a delivery driver has an order to deliver a special package to an important customer by 3:00 P.M., but cannot because the road is blocked by a person protesting high taxes. The driver, unable to convince the protester to move and concerned because the deadline is near, throws the protester to the side of the road causing injury. Neither example involves solely business or personal activities by the agent.

Generally, the courts analyze these and other situations case by case. Courts use a number of factors in deciding whether or not an agent has acted in the course and scope of the business. Some pertinent questions are:

1. Were the agent's actions common among other employees? Consider again the case of the delivery driver making a convenient stop at home. If delivery drivers commonly stopped at home on personal errands while delivering goods for the employer, then the tort may be considered in the course of the business.

2. Was the agent's action unexpected by the employer? For example, if personal errands by delivery drivers were tolerated and therefore not unexpected by the employer, then the tort may be considered normal business conduct.

3. When and how did the act occur? (Did it occur during normal business hours, on the premises of the business, or with property owned by the business?)

4. If physical violence by the agent was involved, was it fully unexpected by the employer? Recalling the example of the delivery driver with a deadline, it might be expected that an employee take whatever actions necessary in order to make an important delivery. At least, the reaction in the example would seem less unexpected than if the employee had punched an innocent passerby.

In studying these considerations, note that there is no single answer to the ultimate question posed by the court: Was an activity within the course and scope of the business? Since the trend in tort law is toward victim compensation, the scope of principal liability under vicarious liability is broadly interpreted.

Harris v. Trojan Fireworks Company
California Court of Appeals
174 Cal. Rptr. 452 (1981)

Anthony Barajas was an employee of defendant Trojan Fireworks Company. On Friday, December 21, 1979, at the Trojan manufacturing plant in Rialto, commencing at noon and continuing until 4 P.M., Trojan held a Christmas party for its employees at which, it is alleged, the employees were caused to attend and caused to imbibe large quantities of alcoholic beverages. Barajas attended the party and became intoxicated to the extent that his ability to drive an automobile was substantially impaired. Nevertheless, he attempted to drive home. In this attempt he was involved in the accident which resulted in the death of James Harris and injury to Dawn and Steven Griffin.

Garst, Associate Justice

Plaintiffs contend that Barajas' intoxication occurred in the course and scope of his employment so that under the doctrine of respondeat superior his employer, defendant Trojan, is liable for the resulting injuries and wrongful death. Trojan contends that the respondeat superior doctrine is not here applicable because the accident did not occur until after Barajas had left the defendant's plant and was on his way home.

As a general rule, a principal is responsible for the acts of his agent; however, an employer is often exempted from liability for injury caused to or by the employee while the employee is traveling to or from work. In third party liability cases, the negligent employee's employer is often excused from liability under the "going and coming" rule on the rationale that the employer should not be liable for acts of the employee which occur when the employee is not rendering service to his employer.

As we depart from liability for one's own act or conduct and enter into the arena of vicarious liability, the quest of liability is frequently determined by who is best able to spread the risk of loss through the prices charged for its product or liability insurance. The underlying philosophy which holds an employer liable for an employee's negligent acts is the deeply rooted sentiment that a business enterprise should not be able to disclaim responsibility for accidents which may fairly be said to be the result of its activity.

Thus, we think it can be fairly said that liability attaches where a nexus exists between the employment or the activity which results in an injury that is foreseeable. Foreseeable is here used in the sense that the employee's conduct is not so unusual or startling that it would seem unfair to include the loss resulting from it among the other costs of the employer's business.

Applying these standards of business purpose or business activity and foreseeability to the facts of the instant case it appears that there is sufficient connection between the employment or the employer's Christmas party and the employee's negligent act to justify holding the employer financially responsible for the injuries occasioned by the employee's accident. It may be inferred that the party was for the benefit of the employer. It may be argued that the purpose of the party was to improve employer/employee relations or to increase the continuity of employment by providing employees with the fringe benefit of a party, or to improve relations between the employees by providing them with this opportunity for social contact. That Trojan intended for Barajas to attend the party is indicated by the fact that the party was held at work during work hours and Barajas was paid to attend. That Trojan intended for Barajas to consume alcohol is implied from the fact that the employer furnished the alcoholic beverages and it is further alleged that Trojan, its agents and employees caused him to imbibe large quantities of alcoholic beverages. It is further alleged that he became intoxicated at the party, to such an extent that his ability to operate a motor vehicle was substantially impaired.

We hold that plaintiffs have pleaded sufficient facts, which, if proved, would support a jury's determination that Barajas' intoxication occurred at the Christmas party and that his attendance at the party as well as his state of intoxication occurred within the scope of his employment. That he would attempt to drive home while still intoxicated and might have an accident was foreseeable.

Averill v. Luttrell

Court of Appeals of Tennessee
311 S.W.2d 812 (1957)

In this action, the plaintiff, Lyle Luttrell, a professional baseball player with the Chattanooga Baseball Club, sued the defendants, Nashville Baseball Club, a corporation, and Earl Averill, Jr., one of its players, for damages for an assault and battery committed by Averill upon plaintiff during the playing of one of the regularly scheduled games between these two teams at Engel Stadium in Chattanooga, Tennessee, on the night of August 20, 1955. The clubs, known as the Chattanooga Lookouts and Nashville Vols, are both members of the Southern Baseball Association.

The assault occurred during the sixth inning of the game while the plaintiff, who played the position of shortstop for the Chattanooga Lookouts, was batting for his team. Pitching for the Nashville Vols was Gerry Lane, a resident of Chattanooga, and catching was the defendant Averill. The contest between the teams was keen, and the players as well as the fans were tense with excitement, some of which was probably due to Lane's pitching against his hometown team. Lane had made three pitches known as curves or sliders, called by the umpire as "balls," and on each Luttrell had stepped forward to meet the ball before the break or curve started. These balls barely missed Luttrell, who had to dodge, and his teammates and the crowd got the impression that he was being, in baseball parlance, "dusted off" by Lane, who on his fourth pitch hit Luttrell on the seat of his pants.

Immediately thereafter Luttrell threw his bat in the direction of the pitcher's mound. Averill, without any warning whatsoever, stepped up behind Luttrell and struck him a hard blow on the side or back of the head with his fist. The force of the blow rendered Luttrell unconscious, and on falling face first to the ground, he sustained a fractured jaw. Thereafter the players and the fans who rushed out upon the field, generally, engaged in what was described as a "free for all" until the police arrived in sufficient force to restore order, after which the game was continued. Meantime Luttrell was removed by ambulance to the hospital, and Averill, who was put out of the game by the umpire, was arrested.

It was undisputed that there was no previous "animosity or malice" between Averill and Luttrell, who testified that when they spoke "it was on friendly terms." Nor was there any proof showing that Averill had ever committed a similar act or that his employer should have anticipated his unwarranted assault.

Howard, Judge

The assault made by Averill was no part of the ordinary risks expected to be encountered in sportsmanlike play. Nor was there any proof showing that the assault was other than a wilful independent act on Averill's part, entirely outside the scope of his duties. The assault was neither incident to nor in the furtherance of his employer's business, and under the circumstances we think that the Nashville Baseball Club would not be liable under the doctrine of respondent superior.

It seems to be the rule generally that a master is not liable for the wilful acts of his servant who steps aside from his master's business and commits an act wholly independent and foreign to the scope of his employment.

In support of the above rule, there are numerous cases cited, including *Atlanta Baseball Co. v. Lawrence* in which the Court said: "The conduct of McLaughlin, the pitcher, in leaving his place upon the grounds and coming into the grandstand, and assaulting the plaintiff, was not within the scope of his employment, nor in the prosecution of his master's business, but was his own personal affair in resenting a real or fancied insult. If a servant steps aside from his master's business, for however short a time, to do an act entirely disconnected from it, and injury results to another from such independent voluntary act, the servant may be liable; but the master is not liable."

Accordingly, for reasons indicated, the judgment against the Nashville Baseball Club will be reversed.

Contracts and Agent Authority. An agent has the power to bind the principal to contracts. However, not every agent contract binds the principal. The agent must have the authority to make the contract. Note, usually the agent will not become a party to the contract.

Three doctrines regulate an agent's power to bind a principal to a contract: actual authority, apparent authority, and ratification. The doctrine of **actual authority** requires that the principal has given expressly or by implication some specific contracting powers to the agent. Determining whether an agent has actual authority requires a review of the directions given by the principal to that agent. If the power given to the agent is definite and precise, the agent is considered to have express authority. For example, if the principal directs the agent to purchase a certain type of computer software for the business, the agent, when purchasing the software, is using the express authority given by the principal.

However, not all instructions given to the agent will be so unequivocal. Sometimes the agent will be assigned a job with a general description—computer supplies manager—or the agent will be given somewhat vague directions—"Buy some computer software for the business." Although the principal has empowered the agent to do some act, the exact contours of the act have not been stated. Nonetheless the agent has actual authority from the principal. To determine the scope of that authority will require some assumptions to be made about the nature of the business and the intent of the principal. In short, the inquiry is to determine whether certain agent contracts can be implied from the general grant of authority. This doctrine is called implied authority.

Implied authority is a very practical doctrine. No principal could be expected to precisely convey every action for the agent to take. Furthermore, some contracting activities may require choices to be made that can readily be delegated to the agent. Thus, the doctrine of implied authority works together with express authority to describe the contracting rights given by the principal to the agent.

Consider the following example as an illustration. Warren was recently hired by ABC, Inc., as a warehouse manager and is therefore its agent. His job description grants him the power to "hire employees and generally manage the warehouse." If Warren hires a fork-lift operator, he will be acting with express authority. That is, Warren has expressly been given the right to hire warehouse workers on behalf of

ABC. Therefore, his principal (the corporation) is bound by the employment contract. However, assume Warren hired a local pest control firm to rid the warehouse of vermin. Nothing in his job description expressly states that he was empowered to hire pest control firms. However, his position as warehouse manager and the general language of his grant of authority, to "generally manage the warehouse," clearly suggests that the authority to hire the pest control firm was intended to be granted to him by ABC.

A second doctrine concerning agents and contracts with third parties is known as **apparent authority.** Apparent authority exists in the absence of actual authority. The agent does not have the right to enter into the contract on behalf of the principal. However, due to certain circumstances, the agent has the power to do so. In this event the principal would be bound to the contract even though no such authority was granted to the agent.

Apparent authority has two elements. First, the principal must have created the impression that the agent had the authority to enter into the contract. Second, the third party must have reasonably relied upon an agent's having the authority. For example, assume that Jill has the actual authority to negotiate spare automobile parts contracts worth no more than ten thousand dollars, that is, she has been given an express limit on her actual authority. Jill, however, enters into a contract on behalf of her principal to purchase eleven thousand dollars in spare automobile parts. Note that she does not have the actual authority to enter into such a contract. Her authority is limited to ten thousand dollars. However, under the doctrine of apparent authority, she would have the power to bind her principal to such a contract.

By granting Jill the actual authority to enter into automobile parts contracts, her principal created the impression that she was empowered to enter into the contract at issue. The principal would have had to give notice of Jill's authority limitation for the contract to be voidable. The principal, by failing to do so, established the appearance that Jill's actual authority did not have an express dollar ceiling. Furthermore, the party with whom Jill contracted had no way of knowing about the ten-thousand-dollar limitation. Apparent authority may be seen as a fairness device designed to protect the interests of third parties contracting with agents. Principals cannot escape liability for the misimpressions of agent authority they allow to reasonably exist with a third party.

A final doctrine concerning agents and contracts is **ratification.** Ratification binds the principal to an agent's contract in the absence of either actual or apparent authority. If the principal accepts the benefits of an unauthorized contract or in some other way affirms that contract, then the principal is bound. For example, assume in the previous example that Jill signed a promissory note borrowing five thousand dollars from a third party. She had no actual authority, since she was limited to purchasing spare automobile parts. Furthermore, she had no apparent authority because the principal created no impression that she was empowered to borrow money for the firm. However, if the principal were to take the five thousand dollars and use it for business, then the contract would be ratified and the principal would be bound by it. The doctrine of ratification is based on common sense. If the principal accepts the benefits of the contract, then the obligations of that contract should also apply.

The most important aspect of an agent's contracting authority is that the law provides a mechanism for one person to legally act on behalf of another. No business could function if concepts of agency were not in existence.

Lind v. Schenley Industries Inc.
United States Court of Appeals, Third Circuit
278 F.2d 79 (1960)

Lind, the plaintiff-appellant, sued Park & Tilford Distiller's Corporation for compensation that he asserts is due him by virtue of a contract expressed by a written memorandum supplemented by oral conversations. Lind also sued for certain expenses he incurred when moving from New Jersey to New York when his position as New Jersey State Manager of Park & Tilford terminated. Lind has been employed for some years by Park & Tilford. In July 1950, Lind was informed by Herrfeldt, then Park & Tilford's vice-president and general sales manager, that he would be appointed assistant to Kaufman, Park & Tilford's sales manager for metropolitan New York. Subsequently, Lind received a communication, dated April 19, 1951, signed by Kaufman, informing Lind that he would assume the title of "District Manager." The letter went on to state: "I wish to inform you of the fact that you have as much responsibility as a State Manager and that you should consider yourself to be of the same status." The letter concluded with the statement: "An incentive plan is being worked out so that you will not only be responsible for increased sales in your district, but will benefit substantially in a monetary way." Lind assumed his duties as district sales manager for metropolitan New York. During the weeks following Lind's new appointment, Lind inquired of Kaufman frequently what his remuneration would be under the incentive plan and was informed that details were being worked out. In July 1951, Kaufman informed Lind that he was to receive one-percent commission on the gross sales of the men under him. This was an oral communication and was completely corroborated by Kaufman's former secretary. On subsequent occasions, Lind was assured by Kaufman that he would get his money. Lind was also informed by Herrfeldt in the autumn of 1952, that he would get a one-percent commission on the sales of the men under him. Early in 1955, Lind negotiated with Brown, then president of Park & Tilford, for the sale of Park & Tilford's New Jersey Wholesale House, and Brown agreed to apply the money owed to Lind by reason of the one-percent commission against the value of the goodwill of the Wholesale House.

Biggs, Chief Judge

The problems of "authority" are probably the most difficult in that segment of law loosely termed, "Agency." Two main classifications of authority are generally recognized, "actual authority," and "apparent authority."

"Actual authority" means, as the words connote, authority that the principal, expressly or implicitly, gave the agent. "Apparent authority" arises when a principal acts in such a manner as to convey the impression to a third party that an agent has certain powers which he may or may not actually possess. "Implied authority" has been variously defined. It has been held to be actual authority given implicitly by a principal to his agent. Another definition of "implied authority" is that it is a kind of authority arising solely from the designation by the principal of a kind of agent who ordinarily possesses certain powers. It is this concept that is called "inherent authority." Usually it is not necessary for a third party attempting to hold a principal to specify which type of authority he relies upon.

From the evidence it is clear that Park & Tilford can be held accountable for Kaufman's action on the principle of "inherent authority." Kaufman was Lind's direct superior, and was the man to transfer communications from the upper executives to the lower. Moreover, there was testimony tending to prove that Herrfeldt, the vice-president in charge of sales, had told Lind to see Kaufman for information about his salary and that Herrfeldt himself had confirmed the 1 percent commission arrangement. Thus Kaufman, so far as Lind was concerned, was the spokesman for the company.

There is no doubt that New York accepts the "apparent authority" doctrine if change of position is shown. "[T]he principal is often bound by the act of his agent in excess or abuse of his actual authority, but this is only true between the principal and third person, who believing and having a right to believe that the agent was acting within and not exceeding his authority, would sustain loss if the act was not considered that of the principal."

Testimony was adduced by Schenley tending to prove that Kaufman had no authority to set salaries, that power being exercisable solely by the president of the corporation, and that the president had not authorized Kaufman to offer Lind a commission of the kind under consideration here. However, this testimony, even if fully accepted, would only prove lack of actual or implied authority in Kaufman but is irrelevant to the issue of apparent authority.

The opinion below seems to agree with the conception of the New York agency law as set out above but the court reversed the jury's verdict and the judgment based on it on the conclusion, as a matter of law, that Lind could not reasonably have believed that Kaufman was authorized to offer him a commission that would, in the trial judge's words "have almost quadrupled Lind's then salary." But Lind testified that before he had become Kaufman's assistant in September 1950, he had earned $9,000 for the period from January 1, 1950 to August 31, 1950, that figure allegedly representing half of his expected earnings for the year. Lind testified that a liquor salesman can expect to make 50 percent of his salary in the last four months of the year owing to holiday sales. Thus Lind's salary two years before his appointment as district manager could have been estimated by the jury at $18,000 per year, and his alleged earnings, as district manager, a position of greater responsibility, do not appear disproportionate. On the basis of the foregoing it appears that there was sufficient evidence to authorize a jury finding that Park & Tilford had given Kaufman apparent authority to offer Lind 1 percent commission of gross sales of the salesmen under him and that Lind reasonably had relied upon Kaufman's offer.

It must be remembered that when dealing with internal corporate management matters an employee must be able to rely on the word of his superiors, or their apparent spokesmen, lest operation of such organizations become impossible. A salesman cannot check every promise made to him by a superior with the president and the board of directors of the corporation.

THE PARTNERSHIP

The partnership is a unique form of business organization. Its existence, structure, actions, and relationships among its members are governed by a separate body of law called the law of partnership. In addition to having its own body of law, the partnership is affected by the laws of contracts, agency, property, and other legal areas that regulate general business conduct.

Creation of a Partnership

The partnership as a profit-seeking business organization has existed at least since Babylonian times. It is a special relationship among co-owners of a business in which they share profits, losses, and management responsibility. The Uniform Partnership Act defines a partnership as "an association of two or more persons to carry on as co-owners of a business for profit." Partnerships may vary in size from a small two-owner business to a large law or accounting firm having hundreds of partners.

No formal legal procedures are needed for the creation of a partnership. All that is required is that the co-owners intend to act in accordance with the definition of partnership. Although no written document is needed to create a partnership, frequently a detailed partnership agreement is prepared. The Uniform Partnership Act provides that many aspects of the partnership relationship may be regulated by partner agreement rather than by the act. Therefore, many partners use the agreement to clearly state certain rights and responsibilities of the partners.

However, no conscious agreement is required to conduct a business as a partnership. The key to the matter is whether the persons in the business are acting as co-owners. Some features of doing business as a partnership are profit and loss sharing, investment of capital, and decision making for the business. Courts will look to the actual operation of the business (and the just-mentioned features) rather than to any expressed intent (or lack thereof) by the members of the firm in determining if a partnership exists.

The following case is an example of the process of determining whether a partnership exists. Though there was no indication that the parties consciously decided to act as partners, the nature of their business relationship fulfilled the requirements of a partnership.

Zajac v. Harris
Supreme Court of Arkansas
410 S.W.2d 593 (1967)

The appellee, George Harris, brought this suit to compel the appellant, Carl A. Zajac, to account for the profits and assets of a partnership that assertedly existed between the parties for two years. Zajac denied that a partnership existed, insisting that Harris was merely an employee in a business owned by Zajac.

Smith, Justice

At first blush the testimony appears to be in such hopeless conflict that the controlling issue at the trial must have been one of credibility. Upon reflection, however, we arrive at a somewhat different view of the case. The business association that is known in the law as a partnership is not one that can be defined with precision. To the contrary, a partnership is a contractual relationship that may vary, in form and substance, in an almost infinite variety of ways.

These two laymen went into business together without consulting a lawyer or attempting to put their agreement into writing. It is apparent from the testimony that neither man had any conscious or deliberate intention of entering into a particular legal relationship. When the testimony is viewed in this light the conflicts are not so sharp as they might otherwise appear to be. Our problem is that of determining from the record as a whole whether the association they agreed upon was a partnership or an employer-employee relationship.

Before the two men became business associates Zajac had conducted a combination garage-and-salvage company, filling station, and grocery store. In the salvage operation now in controversy the parties bought wrecked automobiles from insurance companies and either rebuilt them for resale or cannibalized them by reusing or reselling the parts. Harris, the plaintiff, testified that he and Zajac agreed to go into business together, splitting the profits equally—except that Harris was to receive one fourth of the proceeds from any parts sold by him. Harris borrowed $9,000 from a bank, upon the security of property that he owned, and placed the money in a bank account that he used in buying cars for the firm. The profits were divided from time to time as the cars were resold, so that Harris's capital was used and reused. He identified checks totaling more than $73,000 that he signed in making purchases for the business.

Zajac, by contrast, took the position that Harris was merely an employee working for a commission of one half the profits realized from cars that Harris himself had bought. Zajac denied that he had ever agreed that Harris would spend his own money in buying cars. "I told him, when you go out there, when you bid on a car, make a note that I will pay for it." We have no doubt, however, that Harris did use his own money in the venture and that Zajac knew that such expenditures were being made.

Zajac and his wife and their accountant had charge of the books and records. No partnership income tax return was ever filed. Harris was ostensibly treated as an employee, in that federal withholding and Social Security taxes were paid upon his share of the profits. The firm also carried workmen's compensation insurance for Harris's protection. In our opinion, however, any inferences that might ordinarily be drawn from these bookkeeping entries are effectively rebutted by the undisputed fact that Harris, apart from being able to sign his name, was unable to read or write. There is no reason to believe that he appreciated the significance of the accounting practices now relied upon by Zajac. They were unilateral.

Zajac paid Harris one half of the profits derived from cars that Zajac bought with his own money and sold by his own efforts. Zajac has insisted from the outset that Harris was working upon a commission basis, but that view cannot be reconciled with Harris's admitted right to receive his share of the profits derived from business conducted by Zajac alone.

Harris invested, as we have seen, substantial sums of his own money in the acquisition of cars for the firm. Zajac concedes that Harris was entitled to a share of the profits from transactions that Harris certainly did not handle on a commission basis. When the testimony is reconciled, as we have attempted to do, it does not appear that the chancellor was wrong in deciding that a partnership existed.

Each member of a partnership is dependent on the others; each benefits (or loses) from the others' efforts. Partners are one another's agents and principals. Each has the power to bind fellow partners to contracts and to create liability for torts committed in the course and scope of the business. Consequently, the partners owe fiduciary duties to one another. The law does not consider the partnership to be a legal entity apart from its partners. The legal identity of a partnership, therefore, is the individual partners. Note how this is different from the legal definition of a corporation. The corporation is a separate legal entity. Thus, its shareholders, directors, managers, and so forth have no individual liability for claims against the corporation. Partners, however, may be personally liable for claims against the business.

Determining who should be one's partners is a very important business decision. Existing partners want new partners to be able to add to the profitability of the firm, to fit in, to be a part of the close relationship that derives from each partner's being legally dependent on the others. However, the right of partners to freely choose their fellow partners is not absolute. Although the reasons for selecting someone as a partner may be varied, they are not without limit.

The following case is an example of that limitation. Large partnerships often hire new employees, called associates, with the expectation that they will be considered for membership in the partnership within a few years. Not all associates are invited to become partners. Although the firm is given wide discretion in making that decision, invitations to partnership may not be based upon reasons proscribed by Title VII of the Civil Rights Act. (See Chapter 22 for a more complete discussion of employment discrimination.)

Hishon v. King & Spalding
United States Supreme Court
81 L. Ed.2d 59 (1984)

In 1972, petitioner Elizabeth Anderson Hishon accepted a position as an associate with respondent, a large Atlanta law firm established as a general partnership. When this suit was filed in 1980, the firm had more than fifty partners and employed appproximately fifty attorneys as associates. Up to that time, no woman had ever served as a partner at the firm.

Petitioner alleges that the prospect of partnership was an important factor in her initial decision to accept employment with respondent. She alleges that respondent used the possibility of ultimate partnership as a recruiting device to induce petitioner and other young lawyers to become associates at the firm. According to the complaint, respondent represented that advancement to partnership after five or six years was "a matter of course" for associates "who receive[d] satisfactory evaluations" and that associates were promoted to partnership "on a fair and equal basis."

In May 1978, the partnership considered and rejected Hishon for admission to the partnership. One year later, the partners again declined to invite her to become a partner. Once an associate is passed over for partnership at respondent's firm, the associate is notified to begin seeking employment elsewhere. Petitioner's employment as an associate terminated on December 31, 1979.

Hishon filed a charge with the Equal Employment Opportunity Commission on November 19, 1979, claiming that respondent had discriminated against her on the basis of her sex in violation of Title VII of the Civil Rights Act.

The District Court dismissed the complaint on the ground that Title VII was inapplicable to the selection of partners by a partnership. A divided panel of the United States Court of Appeals for the Eleventh Circuit affirmed.

Chief Justice Burger

The issue before us is whether petitioner's allegations state a claim under Title VII.

Petitioner alleges that respondent is an "employer" to whom Title VII is addressed. She then asserts that consideration for partnership was one of the "terms, conditions, or privileges of employment" as an associate with respondent. If this is correct, respondent could not base an adverse partnership decision on "race, color, religion, sex, or national origin."

Once a contractual relationship of employment is established, the provisions of Title VII attach and govern certain aspects of that relationship.

Here, petitioner in essence alleges that respondent made a contract to consider her for partnership. Indeed, this promise was allegedly a key contractual provision which induced her to accept employment. If the evidence at trial establishes that the parties contracted to have petitioner considered for partnership, that promise clearly was a term, condition, or privilege of her employment. Title VII would then bind respondents to consider petitioner for partnership as the statute provides, i.e., without regard to petitioner's sex.

Several allegations in petitioner's complaint would support the conclusion that the opportunity to become a partner was part and parcel of an associate's status as an employee at respondent's firm. These allegations, if proved at trial, would suffice to show that partnership consideration was a term, condition, or privilege of an associate's employment at respondent's firm, and accordingly that partnership consideration must be without regard to sex.

Respondent asserts that elevation to partnership entails a change in status from an "employee" to an "employer." However, even if respondent is correct that a partnership invitation is not itself an offer of employment, Title VII would nonetheless apply and preclude discrimination on the basis of sex. The benefit a plaintiff is denied need not be employment to fall within Title VII's protection; it need only be a term, condition, or privilege of that employment relationship. Pension benefits, for example, qualify as terms, conditions, or privileges of employment even though they are received only after employment terminates. Accordingly, nothing in the change in status that advancement to partnership might entail means that partnership consideration falls outside the terms of the statute.

We conclude that petitioner's complaint states a claim cognizable under Title VII. Petitioner therefore is entitled to her day in court to prove her allegations. The judgment of the Court of Appeals is reversed, and the case is remanded for further proceedings consistent with this opinion.

THE LIMITED PARTNERSHIP

The **limited partnership** may be described as a mixture of partnership and corporation concepts. In fact, the push for adoption of the limited partnership as a business form in the United States arose in the early nineteenth century as a response to concerns stemming from the partner's liability to third persons, as well as the difficulty of obtaining a corporate charter. In 1822, New York became the first state to enact a limited partnership statute. It was based on the French Commercial Code. Chancellor Kent, in *Commentaries on American Law,* described it as the first instance in which non-British law was adopted in the United States.

As a form of business organization, the limited partnership contains elements of other major organizational forms. Like a corporation, a limited partnership must be formed pursuant to a statute. Formalities prescribed by the statute and required filings must take place before the limited partnership is created. Once the limited partnership exists, the investors (limited partners) have limited liability. Furthermore, the limited partners do not take part in the management of the business. A limited partnership is also similar in some ways to a partnership. The persons who manage the business are called general partners and are governed by the terms of partnership law. Also, limited partners share in the profits of the business.

Limited partnerships are primarily used for investments in rather risky businesses. Broadway shows, professional sports franchises, and oil exploration are examples. Limited partnerships and tax shelters are virtually synonymous. Investors in limited partnerships generally can be assured that their loss will be no more than what they invested since they have limited liability. Furthermore, since the limited partnership is not a legal entity like a corporation, income and losses for tax purposes are apportioned among the investors. Thus, the limited partnership is an attractive business organization for investment purposes. Note, however, if limited partners are found to be taking part in managing the business, they lose their limited liability protection. The following case is an example.

Holzman v. De Escamilla

California District Court of Appeal
195 P.2d 833 (1948)

Early in 1943, Hacienda Farms, Limited, was organized as a limited partnership with Ricardo de Escamilla as the general partner and James L. Russell and H. W. Andrews as limited partners.

The partnership went into bankruptcy in December 1943, and Lawrence Holzman was appointed and qualified as trustee of the estate of the bankrupt. On November 13, 1944, he brought this action for the purpose of determining that Russell and Andrews, by taking part in the control of the partnership business, had become liable as general partners to the creditors of the partnership. The trial court found in favor of the plaintiff on this issue and rendered judgment to the effect that the three defendants were liable as general partners.

Marks, Justice

The record shows the following testimony of de Escamilla:

"Q. Did you have a conversation or conversations with Mr. Andrews or Mr. Russell before planting the tomatoes? A. We always conferred and agreed as to what crops we would put in.

"Q. Who determined that it was advisable to plant watermelons? A. Mr. Andrews.

"Q. Who determined that string beans should be planted. A. All of us. There was never any crop that was planted or contemplated in planting that

wasn't thoroughly discussed and agreed upon by the three of us; particularly Andrews and myself."

De Escamilla further testified that Russell and Andrews came to the farms about twice a week and consulted about the crops to be planted. He did not want to plant peppers or egg plant because, as he said, "I don't like that country for peppers or egg plant; no, sir," but he was overruled and those crops were planted. The same is true of the watermelons.

Hacienda Farms, Limited, maintained two

bank accounts. It was provided that checks could be drawn on the signatures of any two of the three partners. The general partner had no power to withdraw money without the signature of one of the limited partners.

The Civil Code provides as follows:

"A limited partner shall not become liable as a general partner, unless, in addition to the exercise of his rights and powers as a limited partner, he takes part in the control of the business."

The foregoing illustrations sufficiently show that Russell and Andrews both took "part in the control of the business." The two men had absolute power to withdraw all the partnership funds in the banks without the knowledge or consent of the general partner. Either Russell or Andrews could take control of the business from de Escamilla by refusing to sign checks for bills contracted by him and thus limit his activities in the management of the business. They were active in dictating the crops to be planted, some of them against the wish of Escamilla. This clearly shows they took part in the control of the business of the partnership and thus became liable as general partners.

SUMMARY

Although the corporation is the dominant form of business organization in the American legal environment, there are three other forms of business organization that are noteworthy. These are the sole proprietorship, the partnership, and the limited partnership.

A corporation is a legal entity. It is separate and apart from its members and provides a limited liability shield. However, in some circumstances—if the corporate form is being abused, for example—the court may ignore the corporate form and hold the principals behind it liable. One of the most important corporate relationships is the fiduciary relationship between a corporation's directors and its shareholders. Fiduciary duties also exist in other relationships, such as agent-principal and between partners in a partnership.

The sole proprietorship has only one owner. No separate body of law regulates its form. The "law of sole proprietorship," therefore, is simply the general legal doctrines that affect all business. One such legal doctrine, the law of agency, applies when the proprietor begins to hire employees. Agency law creates duties and powers in situations where one person is acting on behalf of another.

The partnership is a business association with more than one owner. The co-owners share in profits, losses, and the management of the firm. They are agents and principals of one another and may be personally liable for claims arising from the business. A related form of business organization is the limited partnership. A limited partnership contains features of both the corporation and the partnership. It is designed for investors who do not want to take part in the business or be exposed to liability beyond what was originally invested, but who want to share in the profits.

Business managers should be aware of the many forms that business organizations may take. They should especially note how the law regulates the relationships of members of the various organizations, imposing duties upon and granting powers to them.

REVIEW QUESTIONS

1. Define the following terms:
   a. Limited liability
   b. Fiduciary duty
   c. Apparent authority
   d. Limited partnership
   e. Agent

2. Discuss the major characteristics of a corporation. How does the doctrine of piercing the corporate veil operate to remove the corporate shield?

3. Smith, Inc., received an offer to purchase its assets in September for $500 million. The offer was made after months of negotiations and evaluation of the assets of the corporation. However, the deal was never consummated. On December 18, another offer of $500 million was received. The offer must be accepted or rejected by December 21. A special meeting of the board of directors was called to consider the offer. The directors met for one hour and heard a report roughly outlining the offer. They neither asked questions nor requested that corporate experts be called to advise them concerning its soundness. Furthermore, general inflation had increased by ten percent in the last quarter of the year. The directors accepted the offer. Have the directors fulfilled their duty to the shareholders?

4. Mary is a member of the board of directors of XYZ, Inc., which operates a popular restaurant in the city. In February, the directors met to discuss the possibility of expanding the restaurant onto the vacant lot next to it. However, because interest rates were high, the board deferred action on the proposal. In April, Mary was approached by the owner of the lot, who offered Mary an excellent deal, including low-interest financing, to purchase the lot. Mary immediately agreed. Discuss this problem with relation to Mary's duty to the shareholders of XYZ.

5. Explain the differences between a sole proprietorship, a partnership, and a limited partnership.

6. Tom was the sole proprietor of a grocery store. He hired Jane to stock the shelves in his store. One afternoon, Jane was putting bars of soap in a large basket located in an aisle of the store. She was bored with the task so to make it more enjoyable, she invented a game in which, for each bar of soap placed in the basket, the next one would have to be tossed in from one step further away. A bar of soap missed the basket and skidded down the aisle. A customer stepped on the soap, fell, and was injured. Would Tom be liable for that tort?

7. Jim began working at Harry's Book Shop. His job was to sell books to customers. One Thursday afternoon a bedraggled old professor was browsing and noted an early edition of Walt Whitman poetry. The price marked on the book was $150. Jim approached the professor and they began to speak and haggle about the price. They agreed, finally, that the professor could purchase the book for $128. When the professor attempted to pay for the book, Harry refused to accept the agreed-upon $128 and insisted on the full $150. Must Harry sell the book for the price negotiated by Jim? (Note that negotiating over the price of books is standard practice in many used-book stores.)

8. Lilly and Yolanda wanted to begin a fitness center where people could go to work out and get in condition. They decided that the best organizational form for them would be the partnership. They thereafter began to call one another "partner" and considered themselves to be co-owners. Do Lilly and Yolanda have a partnership? If so, why? If not, why not?

9. Assume that your answer to question 8 was that there was no partnership formed. What facts might you add to show that Lilly and Yolanda did create a partnership?

10. Bill decided to invest ten thousand dollars in a Broadway show. The show was being operated as a limited partnership. The investors were the limited partners, and the producers of the show were general partners. Unfortunately, the show was a flop, and after all the assets were liquidated, two hundred thousand dollars was still owed to various creditors. Is Bill liable for all or any portion of that debt?

Note that there are twenty limited partners in this organization.

11. Maude invested five thousand dollars in a limited partnership. There were three other limited partners and one general partner. The limited partnership was engaged in growing and marketing avocados. After two years, with no return on her investment, Maude became rather concerned. She visited Jack, the general partner, and demanded his resignation. Instead, he agreed, at her urging, to allow her to co-sign all checks the firm issued. Thereafter, she had input into all expenditures of the limited partnership. Within six months the firm was bankrupt, and forty thousand dollars remained in unpaid debts. Do the creditors have claims against the limited partners?

12. Jane Jones is the sole owner of a small business that manufactures pencils. She is also a member of the board of directors of XYZ Corporation. May Jones legally enter into a contract to sell pencils manufactured by her business to XYZ Corporation? If so, is she legally able to negotiate with XYZ to the same extent she is able to do so with all other pencil manufacturers?

13. Smith took care of the formalities necessary for his computer programming business to be incorporated. Upon issuance of the certificate of incorporation, the business was known as ABC, Inc. Although Smith was to own all the shares of stock in the business, no shares were ever issued. Furthermore, the corporation kept no formal records as required by law. Money that the business produced was frequently used by Smith for his personal expenses. He also used his home and car in the business. Neither of these events were accounted for. If a disgruntled customer sues ABC, will Smith be successful in interposing the corporation's limited liability to protect his personal assets? Explain.

14. What are the roles of a shareholder and a director in a corporation?

CHAPTER 12

 Federal
Securities
Regulation

Historical Background of the Federal Securities Laws
Objectives of the 1933 and 1934 Acts
Federal Securities Law

Capital formation is a business activity with great national importance. In a private, free-market economy the availability of capital from nongovernmental sources is vital. If business could not rely on a ready source of investment funds, then either the economy would wither or it would become state-directed. Neither development would preserve the current American business system.

One major source of private capital is the securities markets. Corporations seeking new funds will sell securities, the most common being shares of stock, to investors who risk their private funds for a share of the business. Most major corporations are publicly traded; their stock is available for purchase or sale through a national exchange. Many individuals are investors, at least indirectly, through pension or retirement plans that purchase corporate shares. Thus, the workings of the private securities markets has a major influence on capital formation as well as a great effect on the wealth of corporations and the financial security of individuals.

As a result, the issuance, purchase, and sale of securities is subject to strict government regulation. Most of the regulatory activity is by the federal government through the federal securities laws. However, individual states also regulate securities through what have become known as "blue-sky laws."

The law of securities regulation is very broad and complex. Therefore, this chapter will provide only a brief introduction and overview of some of the major provisions. The focus will be on federal securities regulation, since most major issues occur under its provisions. Throughout the chapter, consider whether the regulatory approach taken by the securities laws is the best way to implement their goals.

HISTORICAL BACKGROUND OF THE FEDERAL SECURITIES LAWS

A common misconception about the major federal securities statutes, the Securities Act of 1933 and the Securities Exchange Act of 1934, is that they grew directly from the stock market crash of 1929. Although the crash and various practices that led to the crash provided the political impetus, the issue of securities regulation had long preceded it.

In Great Britain, concern about controlling the private capital markets can be seen as early as 1285. Edward I authorized the Court of Aldermen to license London brokers as a means of controlling the developing capital markets. The early part of the eighteenth century saw vast speculative investments fueled by the success of a few trading companies in the New World. Many of the investments were dubious schemes. During one morning, a thousand investors paid two guineas each as a first installment for the purchase of a share in a company whose business was advanced to be of major importance, but no one knew what it was. Available speculative investments at one point exceeded the value of all the land in Britain. As a result, in 1720, Parliament passed the "Bubble Act," which was designed to eliminate abuses. Thereafter, many of the schemes collapsed, causing major investor losses. During the nineteenth century, various securities regulation statutes were enacted in Britain, reflecting its maturing industrial economy.

Interest in securities regulation arose later in the United States. In 1903, roughly one-third of the transactions on the New York Stock Exchange were estimated to be a result of attempted manipulation of the market. Federal legislation was proposed in the late nineteenth century, but the first regulations began to appear in the states. Kansas, in 1911, enacted the first major securities regulation statute, which reflected the strong Populist current of the times: the moneyed Eastern interests were exploiting the honest tillers of the soil. By 1913, twenty-two states had followed suit.

However, these state **blue sky laws** were not particularly effective. The laws were limited to the states of their enactment, while the scope of the capital markets was national in character. Furthermore, not all states had such laws, and often no proper enforcement mechanism was available where regulations existed. Nonetheless, at the time, federal intervention was not considered a proper course.

Political philosophies changed by the early 1930s. The Great Depression had begun, heralded by the stock market crash in 1929. In the autumn of that year, the value of the securities traded on the New York Stock Exchange was eighty-nine billion dollars. By 1932, the value had fallen to fifteen billion dollars. The Roosevelt administration had taken office, and federal intervention into economic activity was the byword. Furthermore, revelations about market abuses during the 1920s combined with the other factors to create the political climate for the enactment of federal securities laws. For example, a report of the House of Representatives noted that approximately one-half of the securities issued during the 1920s were worthless.

The Securities Act of 1933 and the Securities Exchange Act of 1934 were enacted to regulate the securities markets. However, Congress did not intend to create a system of insurance to protect bad investments or to cushion the shock of market fluctuations. Instead, the acts were designed to limit market abuses. The acts protect investors from potentially unfair and manipulative practices in the securities markets.

They also provide that investors not have less information than corporate insiders when analyzing potential securities transactions.

OBJECTIVES OF THE 1933 AND 1934 ACTS

Full Disclosure

The Federal Securities Acts of 1933 and 1934 have two major objectives. First, the acts are designed to provide the investing public with adequate information about securities so that the investor may make an informed decision. No attempt is made to approve or recommend various types of investments. Instead, the law permits the individual investor to make ill-founded, unwise, or foolish investments as long as the information for a more rational approach was available. Thus, the first objective of the securities laws is aimed at market efficiency. One of the major problems with the securities markets in the 1920s was a general unavailability of reliable information on which investors could base their decisions. Furthermore, people with information would withhold it until they had purchased or sold securities. Congress was concerned that such practices inhibited the proper functioning of the securities markets, which requires an informed buying and selling public.

The informational objective of the securities laws not only provides the facts to individual investors, but, more importantly, permits professional financial advisers, brokers, and money managers to devise sophisticated tools of investment analysis. Their efforts and advice, which require access to reliable information, can filter down to the ordinary individual investor. The individual investor may take advantage of the advice by subscribing to a newsletter, using a stockbroker to recommend securities, or by purchasing shares in a mutual fund. The informational objective of the federal securities laws may be described as encouraging the markets to work properly.

Fair Securities Markets

A second major objective of the federal securities laws is to provide a fair market for the investor. If the investing public loses confidence in the securities market, its funds will be spent elsewhere. Abuses that occurred in the 1920s created a market that was subject to manipulation and therefore not one in which the ordinary investor would want to participate. For example, corporate insiders would issue false or misleading information about company stock and take advantage of the market's reaction to it. In addition, if the insiders had important, accurate information, they would sometimes withhold it until they had acted upon it for their own accounts. Then, when the market responded to the information, those insiders profited.

Thus, the second major objective of the federal securities laws may be described as working to deter market abuses by elevating the ethical standards of conduct in the buying and selling of securities. Compare the regulation of typical securities transactions, discussed later, with those of other types of property. Note that commonly acceptable buying and selling practices, if used in securities transactions, would violate the law. Since the capital markets are of national interest, keeping them free of manipulative practices is an important goal. If the ordinary investor believes that the markets are rigged, then less money will be invested in securities.

The balance of this chapter will discuss the major, basic issues of federal securities regulation: the definition of "security," the disclosure duty imposed when securities are first issued, and the prohibition placed upon trading in securities on the basis of undisclosed corporation information.

FEDERAL SECURITIES LAW

The initial inquiry in a securities regulation issue is whether the items involved in the disputed transaction are considered securities by the acts. The legal definition of **securities** is actually very broad. The 1933 and 1934 acts define securities in list fashion, including stocks and bonds. The listing of items that constitute securities also specifies investment contracts. The term **investment contracts** has been used by courts as a means to include a large number of unusual schemes within the scope of securities covered by the acts. For example, schemes to sell self-improvement lessons, beauty products, and orange groves have all been held to be securities by the courts.

Definition of
Securities

The United States Supreme Court has devised a three-part test to determine if a particular scheme is an investment contract covered by the securities laws: First, there must be money paid from one person to another; second, the money must be an investment in a common enterprise in which the investor is led to expect profits; and third, the profits must arise primarily from the efforts of persons other than the investor.

The following case is one of the more unusual examples of a scheme that was found to be an investment contract by the courts and therefore covered by the securities acts. Note the application of the three-part test to the facts of the case.

Miller v. Central Chinchilla Group, Inc.
United States Court of Appeals, Eighth Circuit
494 F.2d 414 (1974)

The sole issue on this appeal is whether the district court erred in holding that certain contracts for sale of chinchillas were not investment contracts subject to the Securities Act of 1933 and the Securities Exchange Act of 1934.

The plaintiffs initiated a class action in the Southern District of Iowa against the chinchilla corporations and individual defendants in March of 1971. The plaintiffs complained that because of material misrepresentations and omissions, they were persuaded to enter into contracts with the chinchilla corporations under which those firms sold chinchillas to the plaintiffs at prices many times in excess of their true market value. The plaintiffs agreed to raise and breed these chinchillas in accordance with the corporations' directions. The chinchilla corporations agreed to repurchase the offspring for one hundred dollars per pair. The plaintiffs maintain, in part, that they were misinformed by the defendants that it was a simple task to raise chinchillas and that the venture would be highly profitable. They assert that in reality, chinchillas are difficult to raise and have a high mortality rate. More important, they contend that the market for chinchillas is such that the venture could return the promised profits only if the defendants repurchased the offspring at the hundred-dollar price and, in turn, resold them to other prospective chinchilla raisers at an inflated price. Thus, they assert, in essence, that the defendants were operating a pyramiding scheme under which profits could be made by the plaintiffs only if the defendants were successful in encouraging new victims to buy into the scheme.

Heaney, Circuit Judge

We consider the fundamental question before us— whether the contracts were investment contracts and hence securities subject to the federal securities laws. The starting point in this determination is the Supreme Court's definition.

The record shows that the plaintiffs invested money in a common enterprise with the expectation that they would profit if the defendants secured additional investors. It also shows that the plaintiffs would not profit from the venture unless they exerted efforts in raising the chinchillas. But this fact does not preclude the conclusion that they had entered into investment contracts because the plaintiffs have alleged: (1) that the defendants persuaded them to invest by representing that the efforts required of them would be very minimal; and (2) that if they did diligently exert themselves, they still would not gain the promised profits because those profits could be achieved under the scheme only if the defendants secured additional investors at the inflated prices. The defendants by their own actions have admitted that the plaintiffs' contributions to the scheme were nominal, and

what the plaintiffs really purchased was the defendants' skill at persuading others to become chinchilla raisers.

In determining whether the plaintiffs' contributions were nominal or significant, the issue is not what efforts, in fact, were required of them. Rather, it is what efforts the plaintiffs were reasonably led to believe were required of them at the time they entered into the contracts.

Viewed in this context, it becomes apparent that the plaintiffs' efforts in raising the chinchillas are really of no significance to the venture's ultimate success. The investors had to contribute two things: his money and his efforts in raising the chinchillas. The latter contribution is alleged to have been represented as being minimal. In both cases, the investor's profit was dependent upon the defendants' efforts to persuade additional persons to invest in the enterprise.

We are convinced on the record before us that the effort to persuade others to invest was the significant effort here. The decision of the District Court is reversed.

Initial Issuance of Securities: The 1933 Act

The 1933 Act is primarily concerned with the initial issuance of securities. For example, if a major corporation decides to offer to the public a new series of shares or if the corporation seeks to raise capital through the sale of debentures, then the 1933 Act must be complied with. However, not all new issuances of securities must comply with the general provisions of the act. Some securities are exempt (government securities). Other securities that would ordinarily be covered by the act are exempt because of the particular transaction that is the subject of the offering (an offering of securities that is private rather than public). For the most part, however, initial offerings of securities must comply with the terms of the act.

The 1933 Act is sometimes called the *truth-in-securities act*. This reflects its purpose, which is to ensure full disclosure of all material information about the new security to the investing public. The information is contained in filings that must be made by the issuer of the securities to the **Securities and Exchange Commission** (SEC), the administrative agency created to implement and monitor the federal securities laws (see Figure 12.1). These filings are called a **registration statement.**

SECURITIES AND EXCHANGE COMMISSION

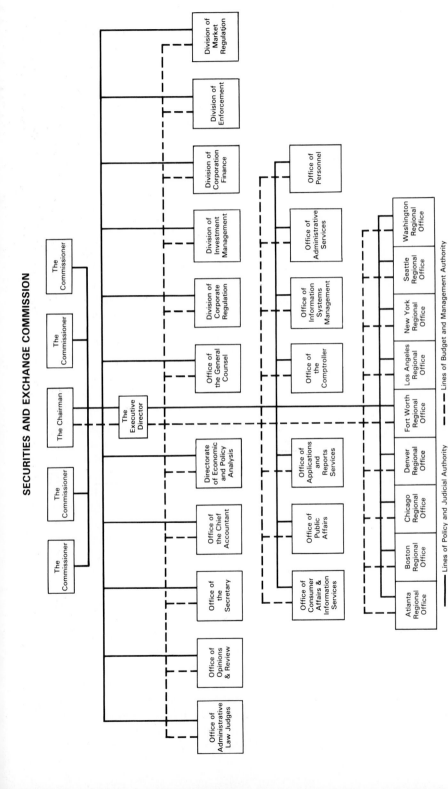

FIGURE 12.1 *Source*: Office of the Federal Register, *The United States Government Manual, 1983/84* (Washington, D.C.: U.S. Government Printing Office, 1983).

A summary of its contents is called a **prospectus** and must be provided to the investors. The SEC reviews the filed registration statement for full disclosure purposes. It does not judge the wisdom or the soundness of the investment being proposed. Rather, the scheme of the 1933 Act imposes that responsibility upon the individual investor. Securities markets operate more efficiently and investors are able to make rational investment decisions if they have the necessary information.

However, some people suggest that the registration statement process of the 1933 Act is not effective in reaching its goals. The cost of preparation and filing the documents to comply with the regulations is argued to exceed the informational benefit that they were designed to provide.

A number of arguments have been advanced supporting this proposition. First, the registration statements and prospectus are written in legal and accounting jargon and are very difficult for the ordinary investor to understand. Thus, the unsophisticated investor relies on professional advisors rather than the information filed by the corporation issuing the securities. These professional advisors have access to similar information without the filing as they seek to serve their clients. Therefore, requiring 1933 Act filing is redundant. Second, the issuer does not actively market the new securities. This task is performed by sophisticated middlemen, underwriters, who would risk professional credibility by misleading investors. Finally, most investors are large institutions, such as brokerage houses, pension and mutual funds, and trust companies. These investors can adequately protect their own interests.

In short, some people argue that the capital markets are sufficiently competitive so that accurate, full information concerning new securities would be readily available even without the full disclosure required by the 1933 Act. Nonetheless, the full disclosure requirement remains. Failure to comply with its provisions may be considered a fraud.

Section 11 of the 1933 Act attempts to eliminate fraud by requiring the filing of the registration statement. **Fraud,** under this section, is a much broader concept than the general legal concept of fraud. This general legal concept requires an intentional distortion of the truth to secure reliance of a person who subsequently parts with money or other legal right. The 1933 Act does not question the intentions of the persons involved. Under the act, fraud has occurred if the full disclosure mandate for the initial issuance of the securities has not been complied with. The act provides that where the registration statement contains a misstatement or omission of material fact, the holder of that security may bring a legal action for violation of the act. Material facts are those which would be of interest to the ordinary, prudent investor.

Several people are responsible for full disclosure of material information. They include the issuer of the securities (the corporation that issues the new series of shares), anyone who signs the registration statement, directors at the time the registration statement is filed, and accountants or other experts who have prepared or certified any report or valuation used in connection with the registration statement.

Although the 1933 Act seems to place a very large burden on people associated with the issuance of new securities, the act does provide a defense, called the **due diligence defense,** which is available to all who may be liable under the act except the issuer of the securities. The issuer has no defense and will be held liable if a fraud in the registration statement is established.

The due diligence defense is maintained when the person against whom a claim has been made has reasonable ground to believe that all statements in the registration statement are true and that no omissions of material fact have been made. A standard of reasonableness imposed by the defense amounts to the reasonable care that would be required of a prudent person in the management of his own property.

The following case is the leading 1933 Act judicial opinion. The business events that led to the 1933 Act claim are explained in some detail. Note the application of the antifraud provisions of the act by the court. Note also the due diligence defenses argued by the various defendants.

Escott v. BarChris Construction Corp.

United States District Court, Southern District of New York

283 F. Supp. 643 (1968)

On the main issue of 1933 Act liability, the questions to be decided are (1) did the registration statement contain false statements of fact, or did it omit to state facts that should have been stated in order to prevent it from being misleading; (2) if so, were the facts that were falsely stated or omitted "material" within the meaning of the act; (3) if so, have defendants established their affirmative defenses?

BarChris was engaged primarily in the construction of bowling alleys, referred to here as "bowling centers." These were rather elaborate affairs. They contained not only a number of alleys or "lanes," but also, in most cases, bar and restaurant facilities. The introduction of automatic pin-setting machines in 1952 gave a marked stimulus to bowling. It rapidly became a popular sport, with the result that bowling centers began to appear throughout the country in rapidly increasing numbers. BarChris benefited from this increased interest in bowling. Its construction operations expanded rapidly. It is estimated that in 1960 BarChris installed approximately three percent of all lanes built in the United States.

In general, BarChris's method of operation was to enter into a contract with a customer, receive at that time a comparatively small down payment on the purchase price, and proceed to construct and equip the bowling alley. When the work was finished and the building delivered, the customer paid the balance of the contract price in notes, payable in installments over a period of years. BarChris discounted these notes with a factor and received part of their face amount in cash. The factor held back part as a reserve.

In 1960, BarChris began a practice that has been referred to throughout this case as the "alternative method of financing." In substance, this was a sale and leaseback arrangement. It involved a distinction between the "interior" of a building and the building itself, that is, the outer shell. In instances in which this method applied, BarChris would build and install what it referred to as the "interior package." Actually, this amounted to constructing and installing the equipment in a building. When it was completed, it would sell the interior to a factor, James Talcott Inc. (Talcott), who would pay BarChris the full contract price therefor. The factor then proceeded to lease the interior either directly to BarChris's customer or back to the subsidiary of BarChris. In the latter case, the subsidiary in turn would lease it to the customer.

Under either financing method, BarChris was compelled to expend considerable sums in defraying the cost of construction before it received reimbursement. As a consequence, BarChris was in constant need of cash to finance its operations, a need that grew more pressing as operations expanded. By early 1961, BarChris needed additional working capital. The proceeds of the sale of the debentures involved in this action were to be devoted, in part at least, to filling that need.

Although BarChris continued to build alleys in 1961 and 1962, it became increasingly apparent that the industry was overbuilt. Operators of alleys, often inadequately financed, began to fail. Precisely when the tide turned is a matter of dispute, but at any rate, its ebbing was painfully apparent in 1962. In October 1962, BarChris came to the end of the road. On October 29, 1962, it filed in this court a petition for an arrangement under Chapter XI of the Bankruptcy Act. BarChris defaulted in the payment of the interest due on November 1, 1962, on the debentures.

The registration statement, filed before the sale of debentures, contained a prospectus as well as other information. The prospectus contained, among other things, a description of BarChris's business, a description of its real property, some material pertaining to certain of its subsidiaries, and remarks about various other aspects of its affairs. It also contained financial information. It included a consolidated balance sheet as of December 31, 1960, with elaborate explanatory notes. These figures had been audited by Peat, Marwick.

Plaintiffs challenge the accuracy of a number of these figures. They also charge that the text of the prospectus, apart from the figures, was false in a number of respects, and that material information was omitted. Each of these contentions, after eliminating duplications, will be separately considered.

The various falsities and omissions are as follows:

1. 1960 Earnings
   (a) Sales

As per prospectus	$9,165,320
Correct figure	8,511,420
Overstatement	$ 653,900

   (b) Net Operating Income

As per prospectus	$1,742,801
Correct figure	1,496,196
Overstatement	$ 246,605

   (c) Earnings per Share

As per prospectus	$	.75
Correct figure		.65
Overstatement	$	.10

2. 1960 Balance Sheet
   Current Assets

As per prospectus	$4,524,021
Correct figure	3,914,332
Overstatement	$ 609,689

3. Contingent liabilities as of December 31, 1960 on alternative method of financing

As per prospectus	$ 750,000
Correct figure	1,125,795
Understatement	$ 375,795
Capitol Lanes should have been shown as a direct liability	$ 325,000

4. Contingent liabilities as of April 30, 1961

As per prospectus	$ 825,000
Correct figure	1,443,853
Understatement	$ 618,853
Capitol Lanes should have been shown as a direct liability	$ 314,166

5. Earnings figures for quarter ending March 31, 1961

(a) Sales

As per prospectus	$2,138,455
Correct figure	1,618,645
Overstatement	$ 519,810

(b) Gross Profit

As per prospectus	$ 483,121
Correct figure	252,366
Overstatement	$ 230,755

6. Backlog as of March 31, 1961

As per prospectus	$6,905,000
Correct figure	2,415,000
Overstatement	$4,490,000

7. Failure to disclose officers' loans outstanding and unpaid on May 16, 1961 ... $ 386,615

8. Failure to disclose use of proceeds in manner not revealed in prospectus

Approximately ... $1,160,000

9. Failure to disclose customers' delinquencies in May 1961 and BarChris's potential liability with respect thereto ... Over $1,350,000

10. Failure to disclose the fact that BarChris was already engaged, and was about to be more heavily engaged, in the operation of bowling alleys

McLean, District Judge

It is a prerequisite to liability under Section 11 of the Act that the fact which is falsely stated in a registration statement, or the fact that is omitted when it should have been stated to avoid misleading, be "material."

The average prudent investor is not concerned with minor inaccuracies or with errors as to matters which are of no interest to him. The facts which tend to deter him from purchasing a security are facts which have an important bearing upon the nature or condition of the issuing corporation or its business.

Judged by this test, there is no doubt that many of the misstatements and omissions in this prospectus were material. This is true of all of them which relate to the state of affairs in 1961.

The misstatements and omissions pertaining to BarChris's status as of December 31, 1960, however, present a much closer question. These debentures were rated "B" by the investment rating services. They were thus characterized as speculative, as any prudent investor must have realized. It would seem that anyone interested in buying these convertible debentures would have been attracted primarily by the conversion feature, by the growth potential of the stock. The growth which the company enjoyed in 1960 over prior years was striking, even on the correct figures. It is hard to see how a prospective purchaser of this type of investment would have been deterred from buying if he had been advised of these comparatively minor errors in reporting 1960 sales and earnings.

Since no one knows what moves or does not move the mythical "average prudent investor," it comes down to a question of judgment. It is my best judgment that the average prudent investor would not have cared about these errors in the 1960 sales and earnings figures, regrettable though they may be. I therefore find that they were not material within the meaning of Section 11. The same is true of the understatement of contingent liabilities by approximately $375,000.

This leaves for consideration the errors in the 1960 balance sheet figures. Would it have made any difference if a prospective purchaser of these debentures had been advised of these facts? There must be some point at which errors in disclosing a company's balance sheet position become material, even to a growth-oriented investor. On all the evidence I find that these balance sheet errors were material within the meaning of Section 11.

Since there was an abundance of material misstatements pertaining to 1961 affairs, whether or not the errors in the 1960 figures were material does not affect the outcome of this case except to the extent that it bears upon the liability of Peat, Marwick. That subject will be discussed hereinafter.

THE "DUE DILIGENCE" DEFENSES

Every defendant, except BarChris itself, to whom, as the issuer, these defenses are not available, has pleaded this affirmative defense. Each claims that (1) as to the part of the registration statement purporting to be made on the authority of an expert (which, for convenience, I shall refer to as the "expertised portion"), he had no reasonable ground to believe and did not believe that there were any untrue statements or material omissions, and (2) as to the other part of the registration statement, he made a reasonable investigation, as a result of which he had reasonable ground to believe and did believe that the registration statement was true and that no material fact was omitted. As to each defendant, the question is whether he has sustained the burden of proving these defenses.

The only expert, in the statutory sense, was Peat, Marwick, and the only parts of the registration statement which purported to be made upon the authority of an expert were the portions which purported to be made on Peat, Marwick's authority.

The registration statement contains a report of Peat, Marwick as independent public accountants dated February 23, 1961. This relates only to the consolidated balance sheet of BarChris and consolidated subsidiaries as of December 31, 1960, and the related statement of earnings and retained earnings for the five years then ended. This is all that Peat, Marwick purported to certify. It is perfectly clear that it did not purport to certify the 1961 figures, some of which are expressly stated in the prospectus to have been unaudited.

I turn now to the question of whether defendants have proved their due diligence defenses. The position of each defendant will be separately considered.

TRILLING

Trilling was BarChris's controller. He signed the registration statement in that capacity, although he was not a director. Trilling entered BarChris's employ in October 1960. He was Kircher's subordinate. When Kircher asked him for information, he furnished it. On at least one occasion he got it wrong. Trilling was not a member of the executive committee. He was a comparatively minor figure in BarChris.

Trilling may well have been unaware of several of the inaccuracies in the prospectus. But he must have known of some of them. As a financial officer, he was familiar with BarChris's finances and with its books of account.

He did not prove that as to the parts of the prospectus expertised by Peat, Marwick he had no reasonable ground to believe that it was untrue. He also failed to prove, as to the parts of the prospectus not expertised by Peat, Marwick, that he made a reasonable investigation which afforded him a reasonable ground to believe that it was true. As far as it appears, he made no investigation. He did what was asked of him and assumed that others would properly take care of supplying accurate data as to the other aspects of the company's business. This would have been well enough but for the fact that he signed the registration statement. As a signer, he could not avoid responsibility by leaving it up to others to make it accurate. Trilling did not sustain the burden of proving his due diligence defenses.

AUSLANDER

Auslander was an "outside" director, i.e., one who was not an officer of BarChris. He was chairman of the board of Valley Stream National Bank in Valley Stream, Long Island. In February 1961 Vitolo, the president and a founder of BarChris asked him to become a director. Vitolo gave him an enthusiastic account of BarChris's progress and prospects. As an inducement, Vitolo said that when BarChris received the proceeds of a forthcoming issue of securities, it would deposit $1,000,000 in Auslander's bank.

In February and early March 1961, before accepting Vitolo's invitation, Auslander made some investigations of BarChris. He obtained Dun & Bradstreet reports which contained sales and earnings figures for periods earlier than December 31, 1960. He caused inquiry to be made of certain of BarChris's banks and was advised that they regarded BarChris favorably.

On March 3, 1961, Auslander indicated his willingness to accept a place on the board. Shortly thereafter, on March 14, Kircher sent him a copy of BarChris's annual report for 1960. Auslander observed that BarChris's auditors were Peat, Marwick. They were also the auditors for the Valley Stream National Bank. He thought well of them.

Auslander was elected a director on April 17, 1961. The registration statement in its original form had already been filed, of course without his signature. On May 10, 1961, he signed a signature page for the first amendment to the registration statement which was filed on May 11, 1961. This was a separate sheet without any document attached. Auslander did not know that it was a signature page for a registration statement. He vaguely understood that it was something "for the SEC."

Auslander attended a meeting of BarChris's directors on May 15, 1961. At that meeting he, along with the other directors, signed the signature sheet for the second amendment which constituted the registration statement in its final form. Again, this was only a separate sheet without any document attached. Auslander never saw a copy of the registration statement in its final form.

At the May 15 directors' meeting, however, Auslander did realize that what he was signing was a signature sheet to a registration statement. This was the first time that he had appreciated that fact. A copy of the registration statement in its earlier form as amended on May 11, 1961 was passed around at the meeting. Auslander glanced at it briefly. He did not read it thoroughly.

At the May 15 meeting, the officers stated that everything was in order and that the prospectus was correct. Auslander believed this statement.

In considering Auslander's due diligence defenses, a distinction is to be drawn between the expertised and non-expertised portions of the prospectus. As to the former, Auslander knew that Peat, Marwick had audited the 1960 figures. He believed them to be correct because he had confidence in Peat, Marwick. He had no reasonable ground to believe otherwise.

As to the non-expertised portions, however, Auslander is in a different position. He seems to have been under the impression that Peat, Marwick was responsible for all the figures. This impression was not correct, as he would have realized if he had read the prospectus carefully. Auslander made no investigation of the accuracy of the prospectus. He relied on the assurance of the officers, and upon the information he had received in answer to his inquiries back in February and early March. These inquiries were general ones, in the nature of a credit check. The information which he received in answer to them was also general, without specific reference to the statements in the prospectus, which was not prepared until some time thereafter.

It is true that Auslander became a director on the eve of the financing. He had little opportunity to familiarize himself with the company's affairs. The question is whether, under such circumstances, Auslander did enough to establish his due diligence defense with respect to the non-expertised portions of the prospectus.

Section 11 imposes liability in the first instance upon a director, no matter how new he is. He is presumed to know his responsibility when he becomes a director. He can escape liability only by using the reasonable care to investigate the facts which a prudent man would employ in the management of his own property. In my opinion, a prudent man would not act in an important matter without any knowledge of the relevant facts, in sole reliance upon representations of persons who are comparative strangers and upon general information which does not purport to cover the particular case. To say that such minimal conduct measures up to the statutory standard would, to all intents and purposes, absolve new directors from responsibility merely because they are new. This is not a sensible construction of Section 11, when one bears in mind its fundamental purpose of requiring full and truthful disclosure for the protection of investors.

I find and conclude that Auslander has not established this due diligence defense with respect to the misstatements and omissions in those portions of the prospectus other than the audited 1960 figures.

PEAT, MARWICK

The part of the registration statement purporting to be made upon the authority of Peat, Marwick as

an expert was, as we have seen, the 1960 figures. But because the statute requires the court to determine Peat, Marwick's belief, and the grounds thereof, "at the time such part of the registration statement became effective," for the purposes of this affirmative defense, the matter must be viewed as of May 16, 1961, and the question is whether at that time Peat, Marwick, after reasonable investigation, had reasonable ground to believe and did believe that the 1960 figures were true and that no material fact had been omitted from the registration statement which should have been included in order to make the 1960 figures not misleading. In deciding this issue, the court must consider not only what Peat, Marwick did in its 1960 audit, but also what it did in its subsequent "S-1 review." The proper scope of that review must also be determined.

Most of the actual work was performed by a senior accountant, Berardi, who was then about thirty years old. He was not yet a C.P.A. He had had no previous experience with the bowling industry. This was his first job as a senior accountant. He could hardly have been given a more difficult assignment.

The purpose of reviewing events subsequent to the date of a certified balance sheet (referred to as an S-1 review when made with reference to a registration statement) is to ascertain whether any material change has occurred in the company's financial position which should be disclosed in order to prevent the balance sheet figures from being misleading. The scope of such a review, under generally accepted auditing standards, is limited. It does not amount to a complete audit.

Peat, Marwick prepared a written program for such a review. I find that this program conformed to generally accepted auditing standards. Among other things, it required the following:

Review minutes of stockholders, directors and committee meetings.

Review latest interim financial statements and compare with corresponding statements of preceding year. Inquire regarding significant variations and changes.

Review the more important financial records and inquire regarding material transactions not in the ordinary course of business and any other significant items.

Inquire as to changes in material contracts.

Inquire as to any significant bad debts or accounts in dispute for which provision has not been made.

Inquire as to newly discovered liabilities, direct or contingent.

Berardi made the S-1 review in May 1961. He devoted a little over two days to it, a total of 20½ hours. He did not discover any of the errors or omissions pertaining to the state of affairs in 1961 which I have previously discussed at length, all of which were material. The question is whether, despite his failure to find out anything, his investigation was reasonable within the meaning of the statute.

What Berardi did was to look at a consolidating trial balance as of March 31, 1961 which had been prepared by BarChris, compare it with the audited December 31, 1960 figures, discuss with Trilling certain unfavorable developments which the comparison disclosed, and read certain minutes. He did not examine any "important financial records" other than the trial balance. As to minutes, he read only what minutes he was given, which consisted only of the board of directors' minutes of BarChris.

In substance, what Berardi did was he asked questions, he got answers which he considered satisfactory, and he did nothing to verify them.

Berardi had no conception of how tight the cash position was. Since he never read the prospectus, he was not even aware that there had ever been any problem about loans from officers.

During the 1960 audit Berardi had obtained some information from factors, not sufficiently detailed even then, as to delinquent notes. He made no inquiry of factors about this in his S-1 review. He was content with Trilling's assurance that no liability theretofore contingent had become direct.

There had been a material change for the worse in BarChris's financial position. That change was sufficiently serious so that the failure to disclose it made the 1960 figures misleading. Berardi did not discover it. As far as results were concerned, his S-1 review was useless.

Accountants should not be held to a standard higher than that recognized in their profession. I do not do so here. Berardi's review did not come up to that standard. He did not take some of the steps which Peat, Marwick's written program prescribed. He did not spend an adequate amount of time on a task of this magnitude. Most important of all, he was too easily satisfied with glib answers to his inquiries.

This is not to say that he should have made a complete audit. But there were enough danger signals in the materials which he did examine to require some further investigation on his part. Generally accepted accounting standards required such further investigation under these circumstances. It is not always sufficient merely to ask questions.

Here again, the burden of proof is on Peat, Marwick. I find that that burden had not been satisfied. I conclude that Peat, Marwick has not established its due diligence defense.

The primary focus of the 1934 Act is the secondary purchase or sale of securities, covering securities transactions other than those involved in an initial offering. The act provides a legal mechanism to combat deceptive or manipulative practices in the securities marketplace. These prohibited practices impose a higher standard of conduct in the securities industry than in others. Retaining confidence in the fair operation of the securities markets is deemed essential to their continued viability. If investors begin to believe that the market is fixed, they will put their investment money elsewhere.

A typical violation of the 1934 Act occurs when a corporate insider trades on the basis of information that was not available to the market in general. For example,

Trading in Securities: The 1934 Act

the purchase, by the president of a major corporation, of large quantities of shares of that corporation on the basis of secret favorable corporate information would be such a violation. Given the nature of the information, the corporate president could well expect that the price of the purchased securities would rise once the market received the information. Thus, the president is considered to have taken unfair advantage of the sellers of those securities, who acted without the benefit of the secret corporate information.

The major provision to combat such problems in the 1934 Act is Section 10(b). That section makes it unlawful to use or employ any manipulative or deceptive device in connection with the purchase or sale of any security. Section 10(b) was implemented by an administrative regulation drafted by the Securities and Exchange Commission. The SEC is the agency charged with the oversight of federal securities laws. This regulation, known as Rule 10b-5, makes it unlawful for any person to:

1. Employ any device, scheme, or artifice to defraud, or

2. Make any untrue statement of a material fact or omit a material fact which would be necessary in order that the statements made not be misleading, or

3. Engage in any act, practice or course of business that operates as a fraud or deceit upon any person in connection with the purchase or sale of any security.

Compare the language of Section 10(b) and Rule 10b-5 with the concept of fraud in the registration statement materials in the 1933 Act. Note that the 1934 Act suggests that a purposeful intent or scienter (guilty knowledge in a matter) will be required in order to violate its provisions. In the 1934 Act, such words as *deceptive, manipulative,* and *scheme* connote a purposeful mental state that is not evident or required in the 1933 Act's antifraud provisions.

The following United States Supreme Court opinion discussed the issue of the intent or scienter requirement of Section 10(b) and Rule 10b-5 of the 1934 Act. The Court used the plain meaning approach (see Chapter 5) to interpret the statute and determined that scienter is required in order for a violation to exist.

Ernst & Ernst v. Hochfelder
United States Supreme Court
425 U.S. 185 (1976)

Petitioner, Ernst & Ernst, is an accounting firm. From 1946 through 1967, it was retained by First Securities Company of Chicago (First Securities), a small brokerage firm, to perform periodic audits of the firm's books and records. In connection with these audits, Ernst & Ernst prepared for filing with the Securities and Exchange Commission (Commission) the annual reports required of First Securities.

Respondents were customers of First Securities who invested in a fraudulent securities scheme perpetrated by Leston B. Nay, president of the firm and owner of ninety-two percent of its stock. Nay induced the respondents to invest funds in "escrow" accounts that he represented would yield a high rate of return. Respondents did so from 1942 through 1966, with the majority of the transactions occurring in the 1950s. In fact, there were no escrow accounts, as Nay converted respondents' funds to his own use immediately upon receipt. These transactions were not in the customary form of dealings between First Securities and its customers. The respondents drew their personal checks payable to Nay or a designated bank for his account. No such escrow accounts were reflected on the books and records of First Securities, and none was shown on its periodic accounting to respondents in connection with their other investments. Nor were they included in First Securities' filings with the Commission or the Exchange.

This fraud came to light in 1968 when Nay committed suicide, leaving a note that described First Securities as bankrupt and the escrow accounts as "spurious." Respondents subsequently filed this action for damages against Ernst & Ernst. The complaint charged that Nay's escrow scheme violated Section 10(b) and Commission Rule 10b-5, and that Ernst & Ernst had "aided and abetted" Nay's violations by its "failure" to conduct proper audits of First Securities. Respondents' cause of action rested on a theory of negligent nonfeasance. The premise was that Ernst & Ernst had failed to utilize "appropriate auditing procedures" in its audits of First Securities, thereby failing to discover internal practices of the firm said to prevent an effective audit. The practice principally relied on was Nay's rule that only he could open mail addressed to him at First Securities or addressed to First Securities to his attention, even if it arrived in his absence. Respondents contended that if Ernst & Ernst had conducted a proper audit, it would have discovered this "mail rule." The existence of the rule then would have been disclosed in reports to the Exchange and to the Commission by Ernst & Ernst as an irregular procedure that prevented an effective audit. This would have led to an investigation of Nay that would have revealed the fraudulent scheme. Respondents specifically disclaimed the existence of fraud or intentional misconduct on the part of Ernst & Ernst.

Justice Powell

Courts and commentators long have differed with regard to whether scienter is a necessary element of such a cause of action under Section 10(b), or whether negligent conduct alone is sufficient. Section 10(b) makes unlawful the use or employment of "any manipulative or deceptive device or contrivance" in contravention of Commission rules. The words "manipulative or deceptive" used in conjunction with "device or contrivance" strongly suggest that Section 10(b) was intended to proscribe knowing or intentional misconduct.

In its amicus curiae brief, however, the Commission contends that nothing in the language "manipulative or deceptive device or contrivance" limits its operation to knowing or intentional practices. The Commission then reasons that since the "effect" upon investors of given conduct is the same regardless of whether the conduct is negligent or intentional, Congress must have intended to bar all such practices and not just those done knowingly or intentionally. The logic of this effect-oriented approach would impose liability for wholly faultless conduct where such conduct results in harm to investors, a result the Commission would be unlikely to support. The argument simply ignores the use of the words "manipulative," "device," and "contrivance"—terms that make unmistakable a congressional intent to proscribe a type of conduct quite different from negligence. Use of the word "manipulative" is especially significant. It is and was virtually a term of art when used in connection with securities markets. It connotes intentional or willful conduct designed to deceive or defraud investors by controlling or artificially affecting the price of securities.

Ascertainment of congressional intent with respect to the standard of liability created by a particular section of the Acts must therefore rest primarily on the language of that section. Where, as here, we deal with a judicially implied liability, the statutory language certainly is no less important.

It is difficult to believe that any lawyer, legislative draftsman, or legislator would use words such as "manipulative" if the intent was to create liability for merely negligent acts or omissions. Neither the legislative history nor the briefs supporting respondents identify any usage or authority for construing "manipulative [or cunning] devices" to include negligence.

When a statute speaks so specifically in terms of manipulation and deception, and of implementing devices and contrivances—the commonly understood terminology of intentional wrongdoing—and when its history reflects no more expansive intent, we are quite unwilling to extend the scope of the statute to negligent conduct.

Insider Trading

The action of the corporate president who illegally purchased shares of stock in the corporation on the basis of secret corporate information is known as **insider trading.** Insider trading violates Section 10 and Rule 10b-5 of the 1934 Act. It involves someone (not necessarily an officer or employee of the corporation) trading in securities on the basis of material inside information, knowing that information is not available to the investing public. Material information is information that would be of interest to an investor in making an investment decision. Inside information is that which is not disseminated to the general investing public. Persons possessing material inside information must either refrain from trading in the securities or wait until the information is disseminated to responsibly perform their duty to the corporation and to the public investor. (See the box, "Ivan Boesky and Insider Trading," on pages 344–345.)

Illegal inside information trading will exist as long as the potential for enormous profits exist. This may be shown by an example using call options. A call option is the right to purchase shares of a certain corporation's stock at a fixed price at some future date. Consider, for example, call options for Santa Fe International stock that was selling for less than one dollar before a takeover bid by Kuwait Petroleum. As soon as the bid was announced (usually such bids involve the offering of a large premium over market price for the shares of the company being taken over), the call option price for Santa Fe rose to over fourteen dollars. Someone with inside information concerning the takeover bid could have made a great deal of money if call options were purchased before the news of the takeover was made public.

A leading case concerning insider trading is *SEC* v. *Texas Gulf Sulphur.* In November 1963, during some geological surveys and exploratory drilling, a potentially vast and very rich area of ore was discovered. No further drilling or exploration was performed at the site until the end of March 1964. The corporation kept the information secret as it sought to acquire the balance of the section of land surrounding the rich exploratory core. During this five-month period of drilling inactivity, a number of corporate personnel who knew of the discovery, as well as some others who had been told, invested in Texas Gulf Sulphur stock. Before these come-lately investments, the persons owned 1,135 shares and no calls. After the investments, they owned 8,235 shares and 12,300 calls.

By early April, rumors abounded that a rich strike had been made. On April 12, the corporation issued a press release aimed at quelling them. On April 16, the corporation released the information about the ore strike through an article in a Canadian mining journal and via a news conference held that morning. Some corporate officials purchased Texas Gulf Sulphur stock between April 12 and April 16. One official left the press conference early to place an order with his broker.

These purchases were later attacked as being illegal insider trades in violation of the 1934 Act. The information was found to be material, since news of a major ore strike would affect the decisions of the investing public whether to buy or sell the stock. The information was secret. The individuals who purchased stock or calls had therefore traded on the basis of material inside information. The officials who purchased between April 12 and April 16 clearly knew of the materiality of the information. They should not have traded until the information was disseminated to the general investing public, yet they chose to do so.

It is interesting to note that at the time of the initial find, in November 1963, Texas Gulf Sulphur stock was selling at 17⅜. On April 16, after the information was disseminated, the stock closed at 36⅜. By May 15, shares in Texas Gulf Sulphur were selling for 58¼.

Texas Gulf Sulphur also illustrates the point that the standard of business conduct imposed by the securities regulations is different from that which is acceptable in other types of business transactions. Purchasing land surrounding the ore strike without releasing the information was an acceptable (and probably prudent) business practice. If landowners had known that valuable ore was beneath their property, Texas Gulf Sulphur would have had to pay much higher prices. However, purchasing Texas Gulf Sulphur securities on the basis of the same secret information was considered illegal insider trading under the 1934 Act.

The following case is yet another example of insider trading under the 1934 Act. The person who was found to have violated the act was not an officer or employee of the corporation.

In the Matter of Cady, Roberts & Co.
Securities and Exchange Commission
40 S.E.C. 907 (1961)

Early in November 1959, Roy T. Hurley, then president and chairman of the board of Curtiss-Wright Corporation, invited two thousand representatives of the press, the military, and the financial and business communities to a public unveiling, on November 23, of a new type of internal combustion engine being developed by the company. On November 24, 1959, press announcements concerning the new engine appeared in certain newspapers. On that day Curtiss-Wright stock was one of the most active issues on the New York Stock Exchange, closing at 35¼, up 3¼ on a volume of 88,700 shares. From November 6 through November 23, Gintel had purchased approximately 11,000 shares of Curtiss-Wright stock for some thirty discretionary accounts of customers of registrant. With the rise in the price on November 24, he began selling Curtiss-Wright shares for these accounts and sold on that day a total of 2,200 shares on the Exchange.

The activity in Curtiss-Wright stock on the Exchange continued the next morning, November 25, and the price rose to 40¾, a new high for the year. Gintel continued sales for the discretionary accounts and, between the opening of the market and about 11:00 A.M., he sold 4,300 shares.

On the morning of November 25, the Curtiss-Wright directors, including J. Cheever Cowdin (Cowdin), then a registered representative of registrant, met to consider, among other things, the declaration of a quarterly dividend. The company had paid a dividend of $.625 per share for each of the first three quarters of 1959. The Curtiss-Wright board, over the objections of Hurley, who favored declaration of a dividend at the same rate as in the previous quarters, approved a dividend for the fourth quarter at the reduced rate of $.375 per share. At approximately 11:00 A.M., the board authorized transmission of information of this action by telegram to the New York Stock Exchange. The secretary of Curtiss-Wright immediately left the meeting room to arrange for this communication. There was a short delay in the transmission of the telegram because of a typing problem, and the telegram, although transmitted to Western Union at 11:12 A.M., was not delivered to the Exchange until 12:29 P.M. It had been customary for the company also to advise the Dow Jones News Ticker Service of any dividend action. However, apparently through some mistake or inadvertence, the *Wall Street Journal* was not given the news until approximately 11:45 A.M., and the announcement did not appear on the Dow Jones ticker tape until 11:48 A.M.

Sometime after the dividend decision, there was a recess of the Curtiss-Wright directors' meeting, during which Cowdin telephoned registrant's office and left a message for Gintel that the dividend had been cut. Upon receiving this information. Gintel entered two sell orders for execution on the Exchange, one to sell 2,000 shares of Curtiss-Wright stock for ten accounts, and the other to sell short 5,000 shares for eleven accounts. Of the 5,000 shares, 400 were sold for three of Cowdin's customers. According to Cowdin, pursuant to directions from his clients, he had given instructions to Gintel to take profits on these 400 shares if the stock took a "run-up." These orders were executed at 11:15 and 11:18 A.M. at 40¼ and 40⅜, respectively.

When the dividend announcement appeared on the Dow Jones tape at 11:48 A.M., the Exchange was compelled to suspend trading in Curtiss-Wright because of the large number of sell orders. Trading in Curtiss-Wright stock was resumed at 1:59 P.M. at 36½, and ranged during the balance of the day between 34⅛ and 37, and closed at 34⅞.

Cary, Chairman

The ingredients are here and we accordingly find that Gintel willfully violated Section 10(b) and Rule 10b-5. We also find a similar violation by the registrant, since the actions of Gintel, a member of registrant, in the course of his employment are to be regarded as actions of registrant itself. It was obvious that a reduction in the quarterly dividend by the Board of Directors was a material fact which could be expected to have an adverse impact on the market price of the company's stock. The rapidity with which Gintel acted upon receipt of the information confirms his own recognition of that conclusion.

The anti-fraud provisions are phrased in terms of "any person" and that a special obligation has been traditionally required of corporate insiders, e.g., officers, directors and controlling stockholders. These three groups, however, do not exhaust the classes of persons upon whom there is such an obligation. Analytically, the obligation rests on two principal elements; first, the existence of a relationship giving access, directly or indirectly, to information intended to be available only for a corporate purpose and not for the personal benefit of anyone, and second, the inherent unfairness involved where a party takes advantage of such information knowing it is unavailable to those with whom he is dealing. In considering these elements under the broad language of the anti-fraud provisions we are not to be circumscribed by fine distinctions and rigid classifications. Thus, our task here is to identify those persons who are in a special relationship with a company and privy to its internal affairs, and thereby suffer correlative duties in trading in its securities. Intimacy demands restraint lest the uninformed be exploited.

The facts here impose on Gintel the responsibilities of those commonly referred to as "insiders." He received the information prior to its public release from a director of Curtiss-Wright, Cowdin, who was associated with the registrant. Cowdin's relationship to the company clearly prohibited him from selling the securities affected by the information without disclosure. By logical sequence, it should prohibit Gintel, a partner of registrant. This prohibition extends not only over his own account, but to selling for discretionary accounts and soliciting and executing other orders.

We do not accept respondents' contention that Gintel was merely carrying out a program of liquidating the holdings in his discretionary accounts—determined and embarked upon prior to this receipt of the dividend information. In this connection, it is further alleged that he had a fiduciary duty to these accounts to continue the sales, which overrode any obligations to unsolicited purchasers on the Exchange.

The record does not support the contention that Gintel's sales were merely a continuance of his prior schedule of liquidation. Upon receipt of the news of the dividend reduction, which Gintel knew was not public, he hastened to sell before the expected public announcement all of the Curtiss-Wright shares remaining in his discretionary accounts, contrary to his previous moderate rate of sales. In so doing, he also made short sales of securities which he then allocated to his wife's account and to the account of a customer whom he had never seen and with whom he had had no prior dealings. Moreover, while Gintel undoubtedly occupied a fiduciary relationship to his customers, this relationship could not justify any actions by him contrary to law. Even if we assume the existence of conflicting fiduciary obligations, there can be no doubt which is primary here. On these facts, clients may not expect of a broker the benefits of his inside information at the expense of the public generally.

Under all the circumstances we conclude that the public interest and the protection of investors will be adequately and appropriately served if Gintel is suspended from the New York Stock Exchange for 20 days and if no sanction is imposed against the registrant.

Gintel, the stockbroker in the preceding case, was not a member of the Curtiss-Wright Corporation. Yet he was held to have violated the insider trading provisions of the 1934 Act. His "wrong" was the use of secret corporate information in the sale of securities. However, the extent of noncorporate members' liability when they act on nonpublic material information has been the subject of much dispute. The

Securities and Exchange Commission argued that possessors of such information must refrain from trading until the information has been disseminated to the general public. The purpose of the act would otherwise be thwarted. The following case is the Supreme Court's response to this position. Note that the Court rejected it and thereby limited the class of "outsider" traders who would be subject to a 1934 Act violation.

Dirks v. Securities and Exchange Commission
United States Supreme Court
103 S. Ct. 3255 (1983)

Dirks was an officer of a New York broker-dealer firm who specialized in providing investment analysis of insurance company securities to institutional investors. On March 6, Dirks received information from Ronald Secrist, a former officer of Equity Funding of America. Secrist alleged that the assets of Equity Funding were vastly overstated as the result of fraudulent corporate practices. He urged Dirks to verify the fraud and disclose it publicly.

Dirks decided to investigate the allegations. He visited Equity Funding's head-quarters in Los Angeles and interviewed several officers and employees of the corporation. The senior management denied any wrongdoing, but certain corporation employees corroborated the charges of fraud. Neither Dirks nor his firm owned or traded any Equity Funding stock, but throughout his investigation, he openly discussed the information he had obtained with a number of clients and investors. Some of these persons, including five investment advisors who liquidated holdings of more than sixteen million dollars, sold their holdings of Equity Funding securities.

During the two-week period in which Dirks pursued his investigation and spread word of Secrist's charges, the price of Equity Funding stock fell from twenty-six dollars per share to less than fifteen dollars per share. This led the New York Stock Exchange to halt trading on March 27. Shortly thereafter, California insurance authorities impounded Equity Funding's records and uncovered evidence of the fraud.

The SEC began an investigation into Dirk's role in the exposure of the fraud. After a hearing, the SEC found that Dirks had aided and abetted violations of the Securities Exchange Act of 1934 by repeating the allegations of fraud to members of the investment community who later sold their Equity Funding stock. The SEC concluded: "Where 'tippees'—regardless of their motivation or occupation—come into possession of material 'information that they know is confidential and know or should know came from a corporate insider,' they must either publicly disclose that information or refrain from trading." Recognizing, however, that Dirks "played an important role in bringing Equity Funding's massive fraud to light," the SEC only censured him.

Dirks sought review in the Court of Appeals for the District of Columbia Circuit. The court entered judgment against Dirks "for the reasons stated by the Commission in its opinion."

Justice Powell

The SEC's theory of liability appears rooted in the idea that the antifraud provisions require equal information among all traders. We reaffirm today that a duty to disclose arises from the relationship between parties and not merely from one's ability to acquire information because of his position in the market.

Imposing a duty to disclose or abstain solely because a person knowingly receives material nonpublic information from an insider and trades on it could have an inhibiting influence on the role of market analysts, which the SEC itself recognizes is necessary to the preservation of a healthy market. It is commonplace for analysts to ferret out and analyze information and this often is done by meeting with and questioning corporate officers and others who are insiders. And information that the analysts obtain normally may be the basis for judgments as to the market worth of a corporation's securities. The analyst's judgment in this respect is made available in market letters or otherwise to clients of the firm. It is the nature of this type of information, and indeed of the markets themselves, that such information cannot be made simultaneously available to all of the corporation's stockholders or the public generally.

The conclusion that recipients of inside information do not invariably acquire a duty to disclose or abstain does not mean that such tippees always are free to trade on the information. Not only are insiders forbidden by their fiduciary relationship from personally using undisclosed corporate information to their advantage, but they may not give such information to an outsider for the same improper purpose of exploiting the information for their personal use.

Thus, some outsiders must assume an insider's duty to the shareholders not because they receive inside information, but rather because it has been made available to them improperly.

In determining whether an outsider is under an obligation to disclose or abstain, it thus is necessary to determine whether the insider's "tip" constituted a breach of the insider's fiduciary duty. All disclosures of confidential corporate information are not inconsistent with the duty insiders owe to shareholders. In contrast to the extraordinary facts of this case, the more typical situation in which there will be a question whether disclosure violates the insider's Cady, Roberts duty is when insiders disclose information to analysts. In some situations, the insider will act consistently with his fiduciary duty to shareholders, and yet release of the information may affect the market. For example, it may not be clear—either to the corporate insider or to the recipient analyst—whether the information will be viewed as material nonpublic information. Corporate officials may mistakenly think the information already has been disclosed or that it is not material enough to affect the market. Whether disclosure is a breach of duty therefore depends in large part on the purpose of the disclosure. This standard was identified by the SEC itself in Cady, Roberts: a purpose of the securities laws was to eliminate "use of inside information for personal advantage." The test is whether the insider personally will benefit, directly or indirectly, from his disclosure. Absent some personal gain, there has been no breach of duty to stockholders. And absent a breach by the insider, there is no derivative breach.

For example, there may be a relationship between the insider and the recipient that suggests a quid pro quo from the latter, or an intention to benefit the particular recipient. The elements of fiduciary duty and exploitation of nonpublic information also exist when an insider makes a gift of confidential information to a trading relative or friend. The tip and trade resemble trading by the insider himself followed by a gift of the profits to the recipient. Determining whether an insider personally benefits from a particular disclosure is a question of fact.

Under the inside-trading and tipping rules set forth above, we find that there was no actionable violation by Dirks. It is undisputed that Dirks himself was a stranger to Equity Funding, with no preexisting fiduciary duty to its shareholders. He took no action, directly or indirectly, that induced the shareholders or officers of Equity Funding to repose trust or confidence in him. There was no expectation by Dirks' sources that he would keep their information in confidence. Nor did Dirks misappropriate or illegally obtain the information about Equity Funding. Unless the insiders breached their Cady, Roberts duty to shareholders in disclosing the nonpublic information to Dirks, he breached no duty when he passed it on to investors.

It is clear that neither Secrist nor the other Equity Funding employees violated their Cady, Roberts duty to the corporation's shareholders by providing information to Dirks. The tippers received no monetary or personal benefit for revealing Equity Funding's secrets, nor was their purpose to make a gift of valuable information to Dirks. As the facts of this case clearly indicate, the tippers were motivated by a desire to expose the fraud. In the absence of a breach of duty to shareholders by the insiders, there was no derivative breach by Dirks. Dirks therefore could not have been a participant after the fact in an insider's breach of a fiduciary duty.

We conclude that Dirks, in the circumstances of this case, had no duty to abstain from use of the insider information that he obtained. The judgment of the Court of Appeals therefore is reversed.

Influencing the Price of Securities

Another problem in the securities marketplace involves individuals' attempting to influence the price of securities. Persons who occupy certain positions may attempt to cause swings in the market price of stock in order to benefit their own investments. For example, a large trader in securities may attempt to create an interest in the stock of a small company by "wash sales." A "wash sale" involves successive buy and sell orders for the securities. The trader, in effect, creates a false picture of activity in the market. Other investors, noticing the activity in the market, may be drawn to purchase shares, thereby driving the price upward. The original trader, who created the interest in the securities, could then sell at a profit. This profit would not arise from any natural or lucky swing in investor interest. Instead it would be caused by the manipulative activities of the trader who created a false interest in the stock.

The following case, *Zweig* v. *Hearst Corp.*, on pages 345–347, is another example of Section 10(b) and Rule 10b-5 violations. It involved a financial columnist who dealt in the stocks that he wrote about in his column. Note the duty that the court maintains is imposed upon the individual by the securities laws.

IVAN BOESKY AND INSIDER TRADING

Ivan Boesky was one of the top arbitrage traders on Wall Street. He started his own investment firm in 1975, using $700 thousand of family money. By 1980 the firm's capital had reached $90 million. In 1986, his personal fortune had been estimated in the $200 million range.

Beginning in early 1985 and lasting for about one year, Boesky entered into a business relationship with Dennis Levine. Levine, managing director of Drexel Burnham Lambert, Inc., arranged to give Boesky secret information concerning pending corporate mergers, acquisitions, and restructurings. These corporate activities, when announced, would likely lead to higher stock prices for the firms involved. Boesky agreed to pay Levine five percent on profits made on information that caused Boesky to invest in a certain corporation's stock and one percent on profits earned on stock that Boesky already held.

This illegal arrangement produced a $4 million dollar profit for Boesky in the R. J. Reynolds takeover of Nabisco Brands whose stock was purchased after a Levine tip. He made an additional $4.1 million when he purchased Houston Natural Gas Corporation stock prior to its acquisition by InterNorth Inc. By spring of 1986, Boesky had agreed to pay Levine $2.4 million pursuant to their ar-rangement. However, Levine was never paid because soon thereafter he was charged by the SEC with a variety of illegal insider trades that resulted in $12.6 million in profit.

Levine, cooperating with the SEC, implicated Boesky, and in November 1986, Boesky signed a consent decree settling insider trading claims against him. He agreed to put $50 million in an escrow account to benefit investors harmed by his insider trades. He also agreed to pay a $50 million fine and will be barred from the securities business for life. Finally, Boesky pleaded guilty to one criminal charge and was sentenced to three years in jail.

Zweig v. Hearst Corp.

United States Court of Appeals, Ninth Circuit

594 F.2d 1261 (1979)

Richard Zweig and Muriel Bruno sued Alex Campbell, a financial columnist for the *Los Angeles Herald-Examiner,* for violations of Section 10(b) of the Securities Exchange Act of 1934, and of Rule 10b-5. Campbell wrote and the *Herald-Examiner* published a column that contained a highly favorable description of ASI. The plaintiffs alleged that the directors of ASI had made material misrepresentations and omissions in an interview with Campbell and hoped that he would publish false information "puffing" ASI shares. This is essentially what he did, but only after first buying five thousand shares from the company at a substantial discount below their market price.

Zweig and Bruno claimed that Campbell's column about ASI caused the price of ASI stock to rise, and that they were damaged when they merged their company with ASI in exchange for a quantity of temporarily inflated stock. The plaintiffs were under a contractual duty to exchange stock at the market price as of a certain time. They alleged that Campbell had violated Rule 10b-5 by publishing his column about ASI without disclosing to his readers that he had bought ASI stock at a discount and intended to sell some of it upon the rise in market price that he knew his column would cause. In addition, plaintiffs contended, Campbell should have revealed to his readers that the column was likely to be republished as an advertisement for ASI in an investment periodical in which Campbell held a substantial ownership interest.

Goodwin, Circuit Judge

The appropriate test for the materiality of an omitted fact is whether there is a substantial likelihood that a reasonable investor would consider the fact important in making his or her investment decision. The facts revealing Campbell's lack of objectivity were material under this test. Reasonable investors who read the column would have considered the motivations of a financial columnist such as Campbell important in deciding whether to invest in the companies touted.

Had Campbell's story objectively reported an undisputed fact or news event, such as the discovery of a valuable mineral deposit or the declaration of a dividend, his ownership of ASI stock might not have been significant in reasonable investors' minds. But given the column's style and tone, with its glowing praise of ASI and conclusion that the firm was a worthy investment despite its risks, the effect of Campbell's stock ownership on his objectivity would be important to his readers. We conclude, therefore, that the omitted facts alleged as violations were material. Unless some doctrine limits Campbell's duty to disclose the facts, he must be held liable for intentionally withholding them. Rule 10b-5 makes no distinction between material misrepresentations and nondisclosure of material facts necessary to keep other statements from being misleading.

Campbell was an informal financial adviser in a medium that the plaintiffs offer to prove influenced the market for ASI stock. He controlled the information that he owned the stock and intended to sell, and he kept those facts secret. As a salaried columnist for a large newspaper, he benefited from his relationship with his readers, on whom his employment ultimately depended. Zweig and Bruno have offered to prove that his column initiated many of the stock transactions that caused the quick rise in the stock's price. Campbell's duty to his readers is well established.

In order for Campbell to be liable to nonreaders Zweig and Bruno, however, a further duty must be shown. To recover damages, these plaintiffs must prove that Campbell owed them a duty. They must show that they were in a relationship with Campbell similar to his readers' relationship with him. We believe that RGC, and its shareholders Zweig and Bruno, were in a position similar to that of Campbell's readers. RGC and the readers had strikingly similar stakes in the processes of the market.

At the time the Campbell column was published, RGC had already contractually committed itself to sell its assets to ASI. ASI agreed to pay at a future date stock worth $1,800,000 for the RGC assets. The number of ASI shares was to be fixed by the market value of ASI stock on given dates. In making this deal, RGC relied on the existence of an honest market. A market presumes the ability of investors to assess all the relevant data on a stock, including the credibility of those who recommend it, in creating a demand for that stock.

In effect, RGC in good faith placed its fate in the hands of market investors, including Campbell's readers. RGC relied on the forces of a fully informed market. Instead, it was forced to sell in a manipulated market. If Campbell was unaware of RGC's reliance on the market, he could have discovered it with minimal effort by asking ASI or RGC about the terms of the merger, or by checking the reorganization agreement that had been signed several months before. RGC was a foreseeable plaintiff.

Furthermore, the more readers the Campbell column influenced, the greater the distortion of the market. As the price of ASI stock rose, the added losses caused by the deception did not fall upon the readers, but shifted to RGC. Each reader who bought into ASI at the inflated price reduced the number of shares that ASI would have to issue to RGC in the merger. The more shares the readers bought in reliance on Campbell, the less real value the ASI shareholders as a whole had to give up in the merger, and the more RGC had to absorb the adverse effects of the deception. In this unusual situation, the duty Campbell owed his readers must also extend to RGC.

While Rule 10b-5 should not be extended to require every financial columnist or reporter to disclose his or her portfolio to all of his or her readers, it does cover the activities of one who uses a column as part of a scheme to manipulate the market and deceive the investing public.

The federal securities laws, in guarding the public from abuses, strictly circumscribe the opportunities of persons holding certain positions to profit from their positions. We hold that these laws also require a financial columnist, in recommending a security that he or she owns, to provide the public with all material information he or she has on that security, including his or her ownership, and any intent he or she may have (a) to score a quick profit on the recommendation, or (b) to allow or encourage the recommendation to be published as an advertisement in his or her own periodical.

SUMMARY

The securities markets are regulated by state blue sky laws and by the federal securities laws. Most of the major issues that arise, however, involve two federal statutes: the Securities Act of 1933 and the Securities Exchange Act of 1934. Two major objectives of that regulatory scheme may be discerned. The first objective is that the investor should have full disclosure of important information surrounding the securities transaction at issue. No law requires that an investor actually use the information. However, the requirement is meant to create an informed securities marketplace, thereby increasing its efficiency. A second objective of federal securities regulation is to raise the ethical standards of participants in securities transactions. Acceptable business behavior may well run afoul of those regulations. Investor confidence in the fairness of the market is an important factor in their continued participation. A vigorous private capital market is necessary for the economy, and investor participation is to be encouraged.

Although federal securities regulation is complex and wide-ranging, a few issues recur and also clearly illustrate the objectives of the law. When securities are being newly offered, the first-time buyers need to have full information in order to be able to make an informed purchase decision. The 1933 Act requires public filing of this information. Once the securities are in the marketplace, concerns arise about certain investors taking advantage of others. One such problem is the trading of securities based on information that has not been made public. Those who possess such information are able to make a more complete investment decision. The 1934 Act prohibits certain insider trading, thereby placing a higher ethical standard on securities traders than exists in other businesses.

REVIEW QUESTIONS

1. Define the following terms:
   a. Investment contract
   b. Insider trading
   c. Blue sky laws
   d. Securities and Exchange Commission

2. Discuss the historical background that led to the enactment of the Securities Act of 1933 and the Securities Exchange Act of 1934.

3. What are the purposes of the federal securities laws?

4. The ABC Corporation plans to issue a new series of bonds to be offered to the general public throughout the United States. The bonds are valued at fifty million dollars. What must the corporation do to avoid problems with the SEC? Limit your discussion to materials contained in the chapter.

5. Your spouse is the administrative assistant to the president of Oil Co., Inc., a major petroleum concern. On August 1 your spouse comes home and tells you that the board of directors was told at that day's meeting of a major corporate petroleum discovery. This discovery, it is believed, will be the largest ever recorded. It was decided at the board meeting to withhold announcement of the find until the corporation can purchase the land rights to cover all the drilling sites. The next day you and your spouse use all joint savings to purchase Oil Co. stock. In October, the find is announced and the stock price jumps. Are there any potential problems for you and your spouse under the 1934 Act? Discuss.

6. You are a member of the board of directors of the XYZ Corporation. At the annual meeting of the board held in January, you are given a lengthy document that you are told is to be filed with the SEC in the morning. Since the document was distributed about fifteen minutes before the meeting was to adjourn, you do not have an opportunity to read it. What concerns should you have about signing this document?

7. Horace operates a large number of swimming pools throughout the country. He plans to sell memberships in the pools. Current members will get a share of the fee paid by each prospect they recommend who joins the pools. However, no member actually sells memberships. Instead members bring prospects to a meeting, which Horace leads. The meeting is carefully orchestrated by Horace, and no pool member has any part in the meeting other than bringing the new prospects. Horace then attempts to convince the prospects to become one of three types of pool members. The types of memberships vary in price. But the more one pays to become a member the higher percentage of new member fees is received from prospects who later join the pool. Is this plan a sale of securities?

8. You are having dinner in a nice restaurant in the financial district of a city you are visiting. At the next table is a group that is discussing their decision to decrease the dividend being paid on ABC Corporation stock. The corporation has never before cut its dividends. You suddenly realize that the group is the board of directors of that company. Furthermore, you enjoy investing in stock and have studied the fortunes of ABC. You are very surprised to hear about the dividend decision. If you sell your ABC stock before the corporation announces its dividend cut, can you expect problems to arise with the SEC? Explain.

9. The XYZ Corporation filed a registration statement with the SEC concerning a new issuance of securities. The statement fails to note that most of the proceeds from the sale of those securities will be paid to executives as a year-end bonus. The language of the document states that: "The funds will be used to enhance corporate productivity." In addition, the document significantly understates corporate liabilities and overvalues corporate assets. Finally, the document fails to indicate that most of the accounts receivable are actually bad debts. Would a purchaser of those new securities have a claim under federal securities law. Explain.

10. Referring to question 9, discuss defenses that XYZ Corporation may raise to that claim.

11. Jones organizes two corporations. He is the sole shareholder and director for each. Jones intends to use the corporations in a securities investment plan that he believes will earn large profits. The plan involves Jones and the two corporations he controls becoming active in the purchase and sale of large amounts of stock in the ABC Corporation. The total holdings of Jones and the two corporations in ABC will not change because for each purchase by one entity, another will sell a like amount. Assume that some investors will become interested in

ABC because of the volume of trading activity generated by Jones. Is Jones's plan advisable?

12. Jenkins is a close friend of Smith, the president of XYZ Mining Corporation. One afternoon while playing golf, Smith tells Jenkins that XYZ has discovered a very large deposit of diamonds in Montana and that the corporation is quietly purchasing land surrounding the initial find in order to fully exploit the discovery. Smith also tells Jenkins that the information is highly confidential. If Jenkins thereafter begins to purchase land in Montana near the discovery site, will he have problems with the SEC? Explain. If not, change the facts to raise a potential securities law problem.

13. Accounting Firm audits the books and records of Joe's House of Investments, a small brokerage firm. Through negligence, Accounting Firm did not discover that the brokerage firm was engaged in numerous fraudulent investment practices in which client funds were not invested as promised. Instead the funds were stolen. After the discovery of the fraud and the bankruptcy of Joe's House of Investments, the investors bring an action under the 1934 Act against Accounting Firm. They claim that the negligence of Accounting Firm aided and abetted the 1934 Act violations committed by Joe's House of Investments. Should Accounting Firm be liable as claimed?

CHAPTER 13

Introduction to Antitrust

What Is the Meaning of Antitrust?
Forces That Produced the Antitrust Laws
Objectives of the Antitrust Laws
Overview of the Major Federal Antitrust Laws
Enforcement of the Antitrust Laws
Remedies
Jurisdiction Under Federal Statutes
Exemptions from the Antitrust Laws
Pre-emption
Political Action

Antitrust laws have had and continue to have a profound effect on the manner in which business is conducted in the United States. Business executives for many years have been greatly concerned with this area of the law owing to the rather large judgments in antitrust cases. It is not uncommon for judgments against major corporations to run into the hundreds of millions of dollars.

The goal of the antitrust laws is to promote competition and the efficient allocation of resources. The federal government, and to a lesser extent the state governments, as well as private parties have the power to enforce the antitrust laws—subject to some of the exemptions noted in this chapter.

After a basic introduction to the federal antitrust laws, the next chapter discusses some of the specific activities that have been outlawed by these acts.

WHAT IS THE MEANING OF ANTITRUST?

Trusts

Many people are familiar with trusts. As commonly used, the term **trust** refers to a property right, held by one person (the trustee) for the benefit of the other (the beneficiary). The trustee controls and manages property for the benefit of the ben-

350

eficiary of the trust. Many people today utilize trusts to lower their estate taxes, designate that their funds be used in a particular manner, or protect their spouses and children. The trustee invests the money and distributes the interest to the beneficiaries. Trusts of this nature are perfectly legal and quite common.

The antitrust laws are not directed at this type of trust, but are directed at unlawful restraints of trade and monopolies. The term *antitrust* in this sense applies to the trusts created by men like John D. Rockefeller, who founded the Standard Oil Trust, the trustees of which managed the business affairs of a number of independent oil companies. Many industries developed large trusts that in effect constituted single businesses run by a board of trustees.

Antitrust

In 1890, Congress tried to put a stop to the consolidation of businesses by enacting the Sherman Antitrust Act. The act outlaws unreasonable attempts to monopolize or restrain trade. Additional legislation in the antitrust field was passed in 1914, when Congress enacted the Clayton Antitrust Act and the Federal Trade Commission Act. Congress strengthened the Clayton Act in the 1930s, through the passage of the Robinson-Patman Act, and again in the 1950s, with the passage of the Cellar-Kefauver amendment to the Clayton Act.

FORCES THAT PRODUCED THE ANTITRUST LAWS

At the heart of the movement for the passage of the antitrust laws lies the American Dream of equal opportunity for those people willing and able to work—the right of people to advance through their own efforts. Vast amounts of unowned land beckoned the early settlers of this country. Many immigrants from Europe arrived hoping to own a piece of that land. Successive waves of settlers moved farther and farther west seeking free land to homestead, until eventually, no more free land was available. Frederick Jackson Turner called this the closing of the American frontier.

Equal Opportunity

What of those immigrants who planned to start small businesses? Many millions arrived over the years and started businesses: drug stores, restaurants, grocery stores, shipping lines, newspapers, feed stores, banks, insurance companies, dressmaking, millinery, oil companies, meat packing, and lumber yards—every type of business imaginable. And why not? The opportunity to engage in a wide variety of businesses was available to anyone who wanted to take a chance. Often there were no competing businesses in a town, and a man or woman could simply move to the town and set up shop.

Many persons believed in laissez-faire economics; that is, they opposed governmental interference in economic affairs beyond the minimum necessary for the maintenance of peace and property rights. The public opposed governmental interference with individual freedom of choice and action. People felt they should have the opportunity to better themselves.

Why, then, would Congress pass the antitrust laws?

One of the many forces behind the antitrust movement arose from the concentration of enormous sums of money in the hands of very few persons. As business enterprises like steel, oil, and railroads became larger, their owners became extremely wealthy. At the same time, the average factory worker often lived in poverty. The concentra-

Concentration of Wealth

tion of wealth in the hands of a few monopolists (persons or groups of persons who exclusively control a particular field of business) offended the public. Some argued that the industrialists profited at the expense of the average man. While many workers lived in slums and worked twelve hours a day, six days a week, fifty-two weeks a year, the industrialists lived in luxury. Many people immigrated to the United States to escape the aristocratic structure of Europe. Is it surprising these same people would object to an aristocracy of wealth being created in the United States?

Individualism

The American frontier contributed to the growth of a belief in individualism—the right to live life in the manner a person feels is best. The men and women who settled the West wished to live free of government restraints. These self-reliant individuals believed man could advance through individual enterprise. Once the farmland was all settled, it seemed to many that only small business remained as a means to self-betterment. But in the late nineteenth century, many persons also saw wealth gradually falling into the hands of the elite; indeed, with businesses growing larger and larger, some persons foresaw the day when a few persons would control all businesses.

Mass Production

Mass production contributed heavily to the growth of large national and international enterprises. For example, where formerly a rifle had been created by a craftsman, step by step, industrialists learned to assemble rifles by assigning particular steps to various workers on a line. With each person performing a single repetitive task, a manufacturer could produce many more rifles. Industrialists applied this same process to the manufacture of shoes, the slaughter and dressing of beef, the weaving of materials, and the sewing of clothes. Every manufacturing enterprise produced more products faster by using the techniques of mass production. Over time, the neighborhood tailor or cobbler gave way to large, national manufacturers.

Businesses learned how to produce goods cheaply and in quantity. However, they needed a market for the large quantity of goods being produced. A cobbler who sold shoes only to his townsmen did not have any problems disposing of his goods. But a company that manufactured enough goods for hundreds of towns needed new methods to get the goods into the consumer's hands.

This increasingly became a possibility in the 1870s and 1880s, with the rapid expansion of the American railway system, which became one of the finest and most extensive systems in the world. The railway system created a means for the mass producer to get its goods to a larger market. Large companies began to compete in many sections of the country virtually overnight. These big businesses became formidable competitors for local manufacturers. The sudden competition created a sort of "shock of the new," and a consequent distaste, among many persons, for big business.

The growth of mass production and the expansion of the railway system, the indigenous American quest for individualism, the growing inequality in the distribution of wealth, and the desire to maximize opportunity for all willing workers all contributed to the legal environment in the late nineteenth century.

The Populists and Farmers

One interest group that worried over the changing structure of America—the move away from small farms and small businesses—was the Populists. The Populists objected to the growth of large oil, packing, and steel companies. They favored small, local, individually owned businesses, which they claimed were more accountable and less corrupt than the large, national enterprises springing up across America.

Another group particularly upset by higher prices was the farmers. While the large meat-packing companies and grain elevators kept prices for farm products low, the farmers paid high prices for farm equipment. The farmers argued that big business kept farm prices artificially low, and at the same time sold them products at artificially inflated prices.

Populists, farmers, and small business owners saw competition as the method by which markets could be kept open. They viewed competition as the means to assure that individual enterprise would be rewarded. The obstructions to competition created by the industrialists appeared to be unfairly eroding the rewards for hard work by the siphoning off of large profits to big business. These groups favored competition as the means for keeping prices to consumers as low as possible.

The widespread belief in the virtues of free, unfettered competition led ultimately to the election of Congressmen committed to passing antitrust legislation. These elected representatives passed the Sherman Act of 1890.

OBJECTIVES OF THE ANTITRUST LAWS

The Sherman Act reflected the wishes of many diverse groups—farmers, Populists, small business owners, frontiersmen, and others—that wished to stop unfair business practices. Congress complied with their desires in passing the Sherman Act.

Not all people agree the Sherman Act really satisfied the needs of these groups. Congress chose very vague language, rather than specifically spelling out the acts or practices it wished to prohibit. Neither the legislative history of the Sherman Act nor the language of the act itself gave the courts clearcut directions as to what the Congress wished to accomplish and how Congress intended the act to be enforced. It was therefore up to the courts to develop a body of law in the antitrust field on a case-by-case basis.

Some commentators view the original act as a lukewarm attempt to appease various groups without clearly adopting their aims. Indeed, in the first antitrust case to reach the Supreme Court, *United States* v. *E. C. Knight Co.* (1895), the Court interpreted the power of the government to act pursuant to the Sherman Act very narrowly. The *Knight* case held that manufacturing was not commerce, and therefore a monopoly of the sugar manufacturing industry was not covered by the Sherman Act. Subsequent decisions avoided this doctrine, but the case illustrates the point that the Supreme Court initially construed the act quite narrowly, thus hampering antitrust enforcement, and certainly the Court did not offer the broad interpretation the people who worked for its passage probably hoped for.

Whether or not Congress intentionally watered down the language of the act so as to make vigorous enforcement impossible, the vague language of the act did give the Court great latitude in deciding which business actions Congress intended to prohibit. But it was clear that Congress chose market competition—not government regulation—as the method best suited for achieving its goals.

Over the years, the courts have identified the furtherance of competition as one of the foremost goals of the antitrust laws. Almost without exception, the courts have

Competition

favored the promotion of competition over any other social goal that might be accomplished through the enforcement of the antitrust laws. Many people argue that vigorous competition lowers the price of goods and promotes the efficient allocation of resources. Competition also limits business power; in a competitive market, individuals cannot take advantage of the people with whom they deal. If a seller charges too high a price for wares, buyers are able to purchase them from someone else. Many people regard this alternative as producing fairer results than would decisions by private people or the government as to what and how much to produce. Arguably competition also helps to keep businesses small and opportunity open for everyone, and to distribute money throughout society rather than to a few powerful people.

Economic Efficiency

Another aim of the antitrust laws is to improve the economic performance of individual firms and the economy as a whole. Through vigorous enforcement of the antitrust laws, the government hopes to insure that those companies which need resources the most, and are willing to pay the most for them, will receive a proper allocation of society's funds. By this means, it is hoped, output will be increased, new techniques of production will be utilized, and new and better products will be developed. One might label this "progressiveness."

Picture what might happen if we had no competition; if, for example, the government regulated all production. Suppose the government had ordered the production of buggy whips. This would have consumed some of our resources. When someone came along who wished to make automobiles, extra resources might not be available to develop this new mode of transportation. The automobile might never have been developed if the government had misallocated the available resources to the buggy whip manufacturer.

In general, the courts apply the antitrust law to encourage efficiency. In this way, the courts help those enterprises which can most efficiently utilize our valuable resources and which are best able to devise cheaper methods of production and improved products. These firms will be permitted to prosper. The less efficient, more poorly run business will fall by the wayside. In the final analysis, society will prosper because it will be getting the biggest return on its investment of resources.

The courts also favor competition so long as competition does not interfere with efficiency. *United States v. Grinnell Corp.* supports this proposition in noting that a monopoly resting on economies of scale or obtained by skill, foresight, and industry does not violate the antitrust laws. To the extent that competition promotes efficiency, the courts favor the maintenance of a competitive economic environment.

Limitation on Size

Another possible goal of the antitrust laws is the limitation on the growth of big business—or the protection of small, independent businesses. Essentially, people who espouse this view wish to limit the size of big business, not so much because of the economic advantages of small businesses as because of the political problems associated with big business. These persons fear the power held by large businesses because of its implications for democracy. Concentration of wealth and power in the hands of a very few people, in their eyes, opens the door to abuse of our political system.

The other goals of fairness and the Populist goals of distribution of wealth, limitation on the size of business, and promotion of business opportunities really have not been given great emphasis by the courts in the enforcement of the antitrust laws. Some commentators assert that these Populist goals should not be given *any* weight in formulating rules in the antitrust field, that the courts should focus on a procompetitive policy that promotes economic efficiencies. They contend that to promote these other Populist goals over economic efficiency would make the antitrust laws costly, futile, and impossible to administer. Not every scholar in the antitrust field shares this view. Some argue that noneconomic goals—such as the distribution of economic power, the increase in opportunity for more people to enter business, and the preference for small businesses—are laudable goals that should be promoted through antitrust enforcement. Nonetheless, the cases over the years and the more recent cases, in particular, do seem to be favoring the goals of economic efficiency and competition. The Populists' goals seem to have been ignored over the decades as the courts have chosen not to emphasize them at the expense of economic efficiency.

Other Possible Goals

OVERVIEW OF THE MAJOR FEDERAL ANTITRUST LAWS

This book covers only the broadest principles in antitrust. It does not attempt to discuss every issue or rule covered by the antitrust laws. The goal here is to provide a general introduction to the area of antitrust. The first piece of antitrust legislation, as indicated earlier, was the Sherman Act, which was enacted in 1890. Two important acts followed in 1914—the Clayton Act and the Federal Trade Commission Act. In 1936, Congress passed the Robinson-Patman Act, which amended the Clayton Act, and in 1950, amended it again through the Cellar-Kefauver Act. In order to strengthen antitrust enforcement in the United States, the Congress passed the 1976 Antitrust Improvements Act and the 1980 Antitrust Procedural Improvements Act.

Exactly what does the Sherman Act cover? Section 1 of the act states: "Every contract, combination in the form of trust or otherwise, or conspiracy, in restraint of trade or commerce among the several States, or with foreign nations, is declared to be illegal." This means that no person or company may enter into any arrangement with another person or company to restrain trade (restraints restrict production, affect prices, or otherwise control the market to the detriment of purchasers or consumers of goods and services). Congress provided no definition of restraint of trade, but left it up to the courts to clarify this term on a case-by-case basis.

Sherman Act

Section 2 of the act states: "Every person who shall monopolize, or attempt to monopolize, or combine or conspire with any other person or persons, to monopolize any part of the trade or commerce among the several States, or with foreign nations, shall be deemed guilty of a felony." The act declares that any actions by any person that attempt to create or succeed in creating a monopoly violate Section 2 of the Sherman Act. The act also failed to define these terms.

The first antitrust act thus gave the courts broad discretion in creating a body of antitrust law. As noted earlier, the Supreme Court's initial cases dealing with the antitrust laws construed the act very narrowly. As time passed, the Court chose to interpret the words of the act more broadly to cover more situations. In the 1930s, Congress decided small businesses deserved further protection. The feeling spread that a manufacturer should be able to set the price at which its product sold at the retail level. In 1937, Congress passed the Miller-Tydings Act, which exempted from Section 1 of the Sherman Act agreements of this nature. In 1952 Congress passed the McGuire Act, which also related to this issue. In the 1970s, both acts were repealed.

Clayton Act

The next antitrust act was passed in 1914 in response to a public outcry for more effective restraints on big business. The public lacked confidence in the adequacy of the Sherman Act and the interest of the Department of Justice in enforcing the Sherman Act. The Supreme Court also contributed to a climate favorable to the passage of new legislation by announcing its Rule of Reason principle in *Standard Oil Co. v. United States*, 221 U.S. 1 (1911), which is discussed in the next chapter. People who opposed big business pushed for new legislation, as did business executives who wished for further clarification of permissible business conduct.

All this activity culminated in the adoption of the Clayton Act in 1914. The act prohibited price discrimination, sales on the condition that the buyer cease dealing with the seller's competitors, certain types of mergers, and interlocking corporate directorates. This act was amended in 1936 by the Robinson-Patman Act, which rewrote the price discrimination provisions of the original Clayton Act. In 1950, Congress again amended the act to strengthen its merger provisions when it passed the Cellar-Kefauver Act. The Clayton Act is discussed in greater depth in the next chapter.

Federal Trade Commission Act

Also in 1914, the Congress created the Federal Trade Commission (FTC) when it passed the Federal Trade Commission Act. This act, like the Clayton Act, was passed in response to the misuse of economic power by the trusts. All of the candidates for president in the election of 1912 vowed to further strengthen the laws to combat the trusts. President Wilson vowed in his State of the Union Message to Congress to seek new legislation in the antitrust field. The act stated: "Unfair methods of competition in commerce are hereby declared unlawful." Once again, the Congress chose not to define this terminology, but left it up to the FTC to determine on a case-by-case basis the meaning of this phrase. Congress could have chosen to specify certain acts as "unfair methods of competition," but it elected not to do so. In 1938, the Congress decided the Federal Trade Commission act needed further strengthening. It passed the Wheeler-Lea Amendment to the act, which declared illegal, in addition to unfair methods of competition, "unfair or deceptive acts or practices in commerce." This amendment was an express statement by Congress that consumers needed direct protection.

These acts constitute the substantive law in the antitrust field. Clearly, they attempt to prohibit monopolies, attempts to monopolize, restraints of trade, unfair methods of competition, and unfair or deceptive acts or practices by business. Just what all these acts meant was left up to the courts and the Federal Trade Commission to decide. For this reason, the cases in the antitrust field, as opposed to the statutes, assume great importance. A careful examination of all cases is necessary to understand the meaning given by the courts and the FTC to these acts.

ENFORCEMENT OF THE ANTITRUST LAWS

Department of Justice

The Department of Justice represents the federal government in the courts. The head of the department is the attorney general—a cabinet member. The Department of Justice has many functions, among them, working on civil rights issues, federal crimes, and tax questions, and advising the president and other executive agencies on legal matters. One of the most important functions of the Department of Justice is enforcement of the antitrust laws (see Table 13.1). A special division of the department, the antitrust division, has the power to bring either criminal suits or civil suits pursuant to the Sherman Act, and civil suits under the Clayton Act.

Federal Trade Commission

The Department of Justice has the exclusive power to enforce the Sherman Act. It shares the enforcement responsibilities involving the Clayton Act with the Federal Trade Commission, which has the power to enforce Sections 2, 3, 7, and 8 of the Clayton Act. The Department of Justice and the Federal Trade Commission coordinate their enforcement activities to avoid conflicts. The Federal Trade Commission has sole authority to enforce Section 5 of the Federal Trade Commission Act. The Federal Trade Commission Act gives the FTC power to challenge any conduct that would violate the Sherman Act or any conduct that violates the spirit of either the Clayton Act or the Sherman Act though not technically a violation of either act. The power of the FTC to reach improper actions of business is greatest under Section 5 of the Federal Trade Commission Act.

Private Parties

The Department of Justice has the exclusive right to bring criminal actions pursuant to the Sherman Act, but private parties who think themselves injured by a violation of the Sherman Act may bring civil actions for either treble damages or the equitable remedies called **injunctions.** Likewise, the Department of Justice shares its power to enforce the Clayton Act with the FTC and private parties who may request treble damages or equitable relief for a violation of the Clayton Act. Section 4 of the Clayton Act states that "any person who shall be injured in his business or property by reason

TABLE 13.1   Parties with Power to Enforce Federal Antitrust Laws

	DEPARTMENT OF JUSTICE	FEDERAL TRADE COMMISSION	PRIVATE PARTIES AND STATE ATTORNEYS GENERAL
SHERMAN ACT	Enforces criminal and civil litigation	No power to enforce	Enforces civil litigation
CLAYTON ACT	Enforces civil litigation	Enforces civil litigation	Enforces civil litigation
FEDERAL TRADE COMMISSION ACT	No power to enforce	Enforces Federal Trade Commission Act	No power to enforce

of anything forbidden in the antitrust laws may sue therefore . . . and shall recover threefold the damages by him sustained, and the cost of the suit, including a reasonable attorney's fee." Section 16 of the Clayton Act permits private parties to sue for injunctive relief.

In many instances, a private action follows upon successful government prosecution of a case. However, many private actions are brought separate and apart from action by the government. The reason most private litigants wait for the government to establish its case is that a final judgment rendered against the defendant in any civil or criminal proceeding brought by the United States is prima facie evidence against the defendant in any suit brought by a private plaintiff in a civil treble damages suit. This means the private litigant need only establish the extent of its injuries and that the injuries resulted from a violation of the antitrust laws. The private plaintiff need not establish a violation of the antitrust laws because the government established the violation in the earlier case. The burden of proving an antitrust violation is formidable and the cases often take many years. Many private parties prefer to let the government establish this part of the case for them.

While a person, firm, corporation, or association may sue for treble damages or injunctive relief for a violation of either the Sherman or the Clayton acts, several other devices may be utilized to enforce the antitrust laws. One is the **class action**— a lawsuit brought by members of a large group of persons on behalf of all members of the group. Another possibility is a **parens patriae** action—a suit brought by the attorney general of a state on behalf of persons living in that state.

Class Actions. The Supreme Court, in deciding *Eisen* v. *Carlisle & Jacquelin* (1974), essentially eliminated mass class action suits brought on behalf of a huge class of persons, when each person in that class has sustained only a small loss. *Eisen* increased the cost of litigation in class action suits. A plaintiff faced with the problems of proving manageability, notifying class members, and paying for the notification is quite likely to be deterred from bringing suit in the first place. Following the *Eisen* case, consumer class action suits for small claims simply have not been feasible.

Parens Patriae. As class actions had fallen by the wayside, Congress moved to create an alternative method of enforcement of the antitrust laws. The Department of Justice and the Federal Trade Commission lack the funds to pursue every antitrust violation. Because of the difficulties of proof, the high costs, and the extended litigation, private parties often choose not to bring suit even when an antitrust violation appears. This means many antitrust violations are not prosecuted. Many violators reap the benefits of violating the law without fear of suit, as both the detection and prosecution of such activities present formidable hurdles to every potential litigant.

Congress amended Section 4 of the Clayton Act in 1976 with the passage of the Hart-Scott-Rodino Antitrust Improvements Act, which provides for additional means of enforcement beyond those previously provided for in the act. The amendment did not create any new substantive law but provided for a new enforcement mechanism. The most significant feature of the act is that it permits *state* attorneys general to bring treble damage actions as parens patriae, on behalf of consumers in their states, for injury to their property caused by any violation of the Sherman Act. An attorney general, suing on behalf of consumers in his or her state, may recover from the defendant whatever damages the persons he or she is suing on behalf of sustained. The court will then triple this amount and award this sum to the attorney general. That is, if the attorney general proves consumers in his or her state lost one million dollars due to illegal activities by the defendant, the court will award the attorney general three million dollars. The court also will award the attorney general the cost of the suit, including reasonable attorney's fees. Any monetary relief recovered is distributed as the trial court authorizes or may be deposited in the state treasury as general revenues.

One major problem exists with respect to the enforceability of the Hart-Scott-Rodino Antitrust Improvements Act. In many cases, the persons on whose behalf the attorney general is suing did not purchase the product directly from the defendant. In many cases, the manufacturer may have fixed prices with other manufacturers. The manufacturer then sells its product to a wholesaler who in turn sells the product to a retailer. Suppose a shoe manufacturer set the price of shoes five cents higher than would have been the price in the absence of a price-fixing scheme. These shoes often are sold to distributors and resold to retailers. How do we know the consumer paid five cents more per shoe when he or she purchased the shoes from a retailer? Quite possibly, either the distributor or the retailer absorbed this overcharge in order to make a sale. This problem is referred to as the "pass-on" defense. Did the distributor pass on the five-cent overcharge to the retailer and did the retailer pass on the five-cent overcharge to the public? This issue involves very complex issues of proof.

Pass-on presents significant problems in those cases in which the consumer did not deal directly with the defendant, but dealt instead with another party in the chain of distribution.

In *Illinois Brick Co.* v. *Illinois*, the United States Supreme Court ruled that an indirect purchaser may not bring suit for overcharges allegedly passed on to it by someone further up in the distributive chain. Only the direct purchaser may sue for any alleged overcharge. When the direct purchaser sues, the defendant may not use as a defense the fact that the direct purchaser may have passed on the overcharge to its customers.

REMEDIES

As we have noted, several organizations, as well as persons or corporations, may attempt to enforce the antitrust laws. The primary goals to be achieved through the enforcement of these acts is the furtherance of competition and economic efficiency in the American economy.

In spite of the rather clear preference for competition and economic efficiencies, businesses still run afoul of the antitrust laws. This section discusses how the courts deal with persons who violate the antitrust laws.

The government, if it establishes an antitrust violation, may pursue two remedies: equitable relief and criminal sanctions. Private parties may seek equitable relief and damages.

Equitable Actions

A suit in equity seeks as its objective the control of future behavior rather than punishment for past acts. Section 4 of the Sherman Act and Section 15 of the Clayton Act give the government the power to seek equitable relief from the federal courts. The federal courts have a great deal of discretion in deciding what type of remedy is appropriate in a given situation. The courts may enjoin companies from restraining trade. They may force a company to divest itself of a company it acquired. They may force a company to share its patents with other companies. There are many, many different types of actions a federal court may order a company to take in order to create a remedy for a violation of the antitrust laws.

Section 16 of the Clayton Act also permits private persons to obtain injunctive relief against any threatened loss or damage by a violation of the antitrust laws.

Criminal Sanctions

In certain cases, the activity in question may be of such an unjustifiable nature that the party or parties in question should be punished. In this case, the government will attempt to have fines imposed on the parties or seek prison terms. Only the government may institute a criminal suit. The Department of Justice handles all criminal prosecutions pursuant to the antitrust laws.

The Sherman Act provides that any violation of the act shall be punished by a fine not exceeding one million dollars for a corporation or one hundred thousand dollars for a person.

A violation of Section 1 or 2 of the Sherman Act also is punishable as a crime. Such a violation is a felony. In general, violations of the Clayton Act are not crimes.

In 1974, the Antitrust Procedures and Penalties Act revised the Sherman Act to increase the criminal penalty from a misdemeanor to a felony. Officers and employees of the corporation who are substantially responsible for a criminal offense may be indicted along with the corporation. Changing the penalty from a misdemeanor to a felony has very significant implications for management.

Pleas. Prior to this change, it used to be in the best interest of the company and the executives to dispose of an alleged antitrust violation by entering a plea of **nolo contendere;** that is, the defendants pleaded no contest to the charges brought by the Department of Justice. The advantage of a nolo contendere plea, as opposed to a guilty or not guilty plea, is that a nolo contendere plea may not be used as prima facie evidence of liability in a subsequent suit brought by a private litigant for its damages. On the other hand, a guilty plea or a finding of guilty by a court after a trial is prima facie evidence of liability in any subsequent damages suit. Private persons injured by an antitrust violation still may bring damage suits following a plea of nolo contendere, but they must prove an antitrust violation as well as damages. Many companies forgo suing in light of the substantial problems of proof. A plea of nolo contendere also is advantageous because it avoids a costly trial and possibly more widespread adverse publicity.

Today, more individual defendants are indicted along with the corporation, and there is an increasing tendency to send persons who are convicted to jail. While a plea of nolo contendere might strike the corporation as advantageous, many individuals probably will resist such pleas as the consequences, as far as punishment is concerned, are the same whether the plea is nolo contendere or guilty. A judge can and will sentence executives to prison whether the defendant pleads guilty or nolo contendere. Since the penalty for such a plea has been increased from a misdemeanor to a felony, many indicted executives probably will desire to take the case to trial rather than pleading guilty.

In the event the government institutes either a civil or criminal antitrust suit, this will toll the running of the statute of limitations on any private right of action under the antitrust laws. In other words, the time within which a private suit must be brought to enforce the antitrust laws is temporarily halted pending the outcome of the government's case. This rule applies, however, only if the government wins a case at trial or obtains a plea of guilty from the defendant. In such a situation, Section 5(b) of the Clayton Act gives a private party one year to file a civil suit following the termination of the government's case.

Tolling of Statute of Limitations

However, if the government files a case against a defendant but fails to win at trial or fails to obtain a plea of guilty from the defendant, the statute of limitations will be treated as having *not* been tolled. In such a situation, a person wishing to bring a private suit for damages must have filed his or her action within four years of the antitrust violation.

Suppose that the government files an antitrust case against XYZ Corporation for fixing prices. As a result of this price-fixing scheme, a customer of XYZ, Acme Corporation, believes it has been damaged. Acme has two options: It may file suit immediately, or it may wait until the government's case comes to a conclusion. If it files suit immediately after the antitrust violation, it unquestionably has brought suit within the four-year period. However, it may be forced to incur some heavy expenses in litigating the case. Instead, Acme may wait to see what the outcome of the government's suit is. If the government wins, or the defendant pleads guilty, Acme has one year in which to file a suit for damages. At that trial, Acme need only prove its damages—the government has already established a violation of the antitrust laws. But what if, instead of litigating the case, four years and two months after the government files suit, XYZ pleads nolo contendere or enters into a consent decree (discussed later) with the government? In this case, the statute is treated as having run from the date of the initial violation. All persons who wished to bring suits for civil damages must have filed their cases within the four-year period. Because Acme did not file within the four-year period, it will be precluded from filing now by the statute's four-year statute of limitations. In this situation, Section 5(b) does *not* apply, and the private parties are *not* entitled to file suit within one year following the termination of the government's case.

As indicated earlier, private persons may enforce the Sherman and Clayton acts. Section 4 of the Clayton Act provides that the plaintiff may recover treble damages if it is able to establish an antitrust violation, and damages resulting from that violation. That is, if the plaintiff establishes losses of one hundred thousand dollars because of an antitrust violation by the defendant, he or she will actually recover three times this amount, or three hundred thousand dollars plus the cost of the action, including reasonable attorney's fees. As noted earlier, Section 16 of the Clayton Act also permits suits by private parties for injunctive relief.

Treble Damages

The reason the law permits treble damages is not only to compensate a private party for its injuries, but also to *punish* the defendant for violating the law. As the award for an antitrust violation might be very large, treble damage suits encourage private persons to enforce the antitrust law by bringing these suits. This helps encourage compliance with the antitrust laws and supplements public enforcement.

Even with private treble damage actions and the enforcement powers of the FTC, the Department of Justice, and state attorneys general, the rewards for violating the antitrust laws are very great, and the chances of detection often are slim. One might argue that the remedies are inadequate to deter violations.

Consent Decree

While a plea of guilty or nolo contendere may be utilized to dispose of a criminal case, a consent decree is the device utilized by a corporation should it wish not to go to trial on a civil antitrust case brought by the government. Most cases brought by the Department of Justice terminate with a settlement known as a *consent decree*. A consent decree is a voluntary agreement entered into by a corporation and a governmental agency in which the business agrees to cease engaging in certain activities. It is not an admission of a violation of the law. A company may enter into a consent decree with the government at any time—even after the case has gone to trial and the government has lost. It might be simpler to enter into a consent decree at this point than to involve the corporation in a costly, time-consuming appeal.

Consent decrees are advantageous to both parties. The government can handle more suits if the parties settle suits in this fashion instead of going to trial. The defendant saves money and time and avoids adverse publicity. Most important, a consent decree may *not* be used by a private party seeking damages to prove the defendant violated the antitrust laws. Thus, a consent decree minimizes the possibility of subsequent damage suits. If the corporation takes the civil suit to trial and loses, the judgment may be used by persons or companies injured by an antitrust violation in a subsequent suit for damages. A consent decree usually states it is not an adjudication on the merits nor an admission of liability on the part of the defendants. Consent decrees must be approved by a court.

Both consent decrees and pleas of nolo contendere are valuable tools for the government. The government is understaffed and inadequately funded. It lacks the manpower to pursue every antitrust violation. If it were forced to try every case it handled, the government would be unable to pursue many antitrust violators.

JURISDICTION UNDER FEDERAL STATUTES

While these remedies may be sought in antitrust cases, the antitrust laws do not extend to every imaginable type of activity. This section discusses the type of activities that the antitrust laws apply to.

When lawyers refer to jurisdiction, they are speaking of the power of a court to hear and determine a case. If a court lacks the jurisdiction to hear a case, it should dismiss the case. As noted in Chapter 6, Congress possesses substantial power with respect to the regulation of commerce. Its power in this field is practically without limits, as it possesses the power to regulate interstate commerce and commerce substantially affecting interstate commerce. This means that even if an activity is purely intrastate, Congress has the power to regulate the activity if it has a substantial impact on interstate commerce.

The Supreme Court has so interpreted the Clayton Act that its scope is somewhat less than that of the Sherman Act. The Sherman Act reaches to the utmost extent of Congress's constitutional power. The reason the antitrust laws must reach so far is the damage done by anticompetitive acts to our entire economy. Any act that damages interstate commerce must be within the reach of the Sherman Act. There must be a restraint that "substantially and adversely affects interstate commerce."

Unlike the Sherman Act, which in Section 1 used the words "among the several states," the Clayton Act used the words "in commerce." While the Supreme Court has given a broad interpretation to the grant of power under the Sherman Act, it has more narrowly construed the Clayton Act. The courts have interpreted this language as exempting local commerce from the act but reaching every transaction that crosses a state line.

EXEMPTIONS FROM THE ANTITRUST LAWS

Labor

Certain groups are exempt from the antitrust laws. Labor unions are one such group. Section 6 of the Clayton Act provides: "The labor of a human being is not a commodity or article of commerce. Nothing contained in the antitrust laws shall be construed to forbid the existence and operation of labor . . . organizations, instituted for the purpose of mutual help . . . or to forbid or restrain individual members of such organizations from lawfully carrying out the legitimate objects thereof." Section 20 of the Clayton Act prohibits federal courts from issuing injunctions in cases between employers and employees involving or growing out of a dispute concerning the terms or conditions of employment.

While this language indicates an intent by Congress to exempt labor unions from the antitrust laws, the Supreme Court soon made it clear that not all types of union activity were protected from the antitrust laws. Congress responded in 1932 by passing the Norris-LaGuardia Act, which further clarified its wish to prohibit the use of injunctions against labor unions by federal courts. The activities protected by the Clayton Act and the Norris-LaGuardia Act are activities between employees and unions. The activities between a union and an employer are not expressly exempted. Labor unions generally need not concern themselves with the antitrust laws so long as they do not combine with a nonlabor group in order to restrain trade.

Agricultural Cooperatives

Another group excluded from the antitrust laws is agricultural cooperatives. Congress wanted to reach restraints on competition and monopolization by big trusts when it passed the Sherman Act. It did not intend to reach cooperatives. After all, the farmers pushed hard for the Sherman Act. They felt at a disadvantage in dealing with the large packing companies. They probably did not visualize the antitrust laws being applied against them, yet it was in cases early in the 1900s. Congress, as it had done for labor unions in 1914, attempted to clarify the exemption for agricultural cooperatives when it passed the Clayton Act. In 1922, Congress enacted the Capper-Volstead Act to make it crystal clear it wished to exempt agricultural cooperatives from the antitrust laws. The object of the act was to protect farmers, planters, ranchmen, and the like from the antitrust laws to permit them to collectively process, prepare for market, handle, and market their products.

Congress thought farmers needed additional legislation because of the farmer's economic plight. Most farms were relatively small, but the processors with whom farmers dealt were few and very powerful. Furthermore, problems with the weather compounded the farmer's difficulties with the processors. In spite of the rather clear exemption, the act has been construed narrowly so that in some instances the antitrust laws have been applied to the cooperatives.

The following case discusses a recent application of the antitrust laws to cooperatives.

National Broiler Marketing Association v. United States

United States Supreme Court
436 U.S. 816 (1978)

The question presented at the trial court level was whether all members of the National Broiler Marketing Association (NBMA), the defendant, qualified as farmers. If so, the NBMA was entitled to a limited exemption from the antitrust laws. The trial court ruled in favor of the NBMA. The Fifth Circuit Court of Appeals reversed. The Supreme Court affirmed the decision of the court of appeals.

Justice Blackmun

NBMA is a nonprofit cooperative association organized in 1970 under Georgia law.

It performs various cooperative marketing and purchasing functions on behalf of its members.

These members are all involved in the production and marketing of broiler chickens. Production involves a number of distinct stages: the placement, raising, and breeding of breeder flocks to produce eggs to be hatched as broiler chicks; the hatching of the eggs and placement of those chicks; the raising of the broiler chicks for a period, not to exceed, apparently, 10 weeks; the catching, cooping, and hauling of the "grown-out" broiler chickens to processing facilities; and the operations of facilities to process and prepare the broilers for market.

All the members of NBMA are "integrated," that is, they are involved in more than one of these stages of production. Many, if not all, directly or indirectly own and operate a processing plant where the broilers are slaughtered and dressed for market. All contract with independent growers for the raising or grow-out of at least part, and usually a substantial part, of their flocks.

It is established, however, that six NBMA members do not own or control any breeder flock whose offspring are raised as broilers, and do not own or control any hatchery where the broiler chicks are hatched. And it appears from the record that these members do not own a breeder flock or hatchery, and also do not maintain any grow-out facility. These members, who buy chicks already hatched and then place them with growers, enter the production line only at its later processing stages.

The Capper-Volstead Act removed from the proscription of the antitrust laws cooperatives formed by certain agricultural producers that otherwise would be directly competing with each other in efforts to bring their goods to market. But if the cooperative includes among its members those not so privileged under the statute to act collectively, it is not entitled to the protection of the Act. Thus, in order for NBMA to enjoy the limited exemption of the Capper-Volstead Act, and, as a consequence, to avoid liability under the antitrust laws for its collective activity, all its members must be qualified to act collectively. It is not enough that a typical member qualify, or even that most of NBMA's members qualify. We therefore must determine not that the typical integrated broiler producer is qualified under the Act, but whether all the integrated producers who are members of NBMA are entitled to the Act's protection.

The Act protects those who are "engaged in the production of agricultural products as farmers, planters, ranchmen, dairymen, nut or fruit growers." A commonsense reading of this language clearly leads one to conclude that not all persons engaged in the production of agricultural products are entitled to join together and to obtain and enjoy the Act's benefits: the quoted phrase restricts and limits the broader preceding phrase "[p]ersons engaged in the production of agricultural products. . . ."

The purposes of the Act, as revealed by the legislative history, confirm the conclusion that not all those involved in bringing agricultural products to market may join cooperatives exempt under the statute, and have the cooperatives retain that exemption.

The congressional debates demonstrate that the Act was meant to aid not the full spectrum of the agricultural sector, but, instead, to aid only those whose economic position rendered them comparatively helpless. It was very definitely, special interest legislation. Indeed, several attempts were made to amend the Act to include certain processors who, according to preplanting contracts, paid growers amounts based on the market price of processed goods; these attempts were roundly rejected. Clearly, Congress did not intend to extend the benefits of the Act to the processors and packers to whom the farmers sold their goods, even when the relationship was such that processor and packer bore a part of the risk.

We, therefore, conclude that any member of NBMA that owns neither a breeder flock nor a hatchery, and that maintains no grow-out facility at which the flocks to which it holds title are raised, is not among those Congress intended to protect by the Capper-Volstead Act. The economic role of such a member in the production of broiler chickens is indistinguishable from that of the processor that enters into a preplanting contract with its supplier, or from that of a packer that assists its supplier in the financing of his crops. Their participation involves only the kinds of investment that Congress clearly did not intend to protect. We hold that such members are not "farmers," as that term is used in the Act, and that a cooperative organization that includes them—or even one of them—as members is not entitled to the limited protection of the Capper-Volstead Act.

State Action Exemption

Another important exception to the application of the antitrust laws is the *state action exemption* created by the *Parker* v. *Brown* case. In that case, a producer and packer of raisins in California brought suit to enjoin the state director of agriculture from enforcing a program for marketing the raisins produced in the state. The state of California wished to restrict competition among growers to maintain the price of raisins. In an earlier case, the Supreme Court had held states were "persons" within the meaning of the Sherman Act, and therefore entitled to maintain an action for treble damages. Essentially, *Parker* boiled down to the question of whether the California statute was rendered invalid by the Sherman Act. The Supreme Court held the Sherman Act did not invalidate the California statute (although the statute quite obviously restricted competition in the raisin-growing market). Instead, the Supreme Court enunciated an exception to the Sherman Act:

> [W]e find nothing in the language of the Sherman Act or in its history which suggests that its purpose was to restrain a state or its officers or agents from activities directed

by its legislature. . . . [I]n view of the (Act's) words and history, it must be taken to be a prohibition of individual and not state action. . . . The state . . . imposed the restraints as an act of government which the Sherman Act did not undertake to prohibit.

What the Supreme Court wished to do in deciding *Parker* v. *Brown* was to recognize the fact that states are free to establish their own set of laws absent a conflict with the United States Constitution or preemption of the area by Congress.

Parker reflects the idea of dual federalism. In our system of government, both the federal government and the states are sovereign. The states gave up part of their power in forming the United States government. They retained the power not delegated to the United States or reserved to the people. As states are sovereign, states may pass laws in the same areas as the federal government. Only if the state law violates the Constitution, or if Congress preempts the field, must the courts strike down a state law. In the case of the Sherman Act, Congress failed to indicate that it intended to restrain state action in this field. As nothing about the Sherman Act indicated any intent upon the part of Congress to prohibit states from legislating in a manner contrary to the Sherman Act, the Supreme Court upheld the California statute.

Following this decision, the Supreme Court decided a number of cases that further refined the state action exemption. In one case, in Virginia, purchasers of a home wished to obtain the lowest price possible for a title examination on their home. After contacting a number of attorneys, they discovered the attorneys all charged a given price. No attorney offered to charge less than a certain price because the Fairfax County Bar Association required all attorneys to charge a minimum fee for title examinations. Any attorney charging below this price violated the ethical code of the Bar Association. The plaintiffs challenged the agreement to adhere to a minimum fee as a violation of the antitrust laws. The Supreme Court found a violation of the antitrust laws. It rejected the state action exemption defense because the State of Virginia permitted attorneys to set minimum fees but did not require the attorneys in the state to adhere to a minimum fee.

In a later case, *Bates* v. *State Bar of Arizona* (1977), the Court reviewed the actions of an attorney licensed to practice law in Arizona. In order to keep his prices low, he felt it necessary to advertise in order to attract more customers to his clinic. The clinic performed only such routine legal services as uncontested bankruptcies, uncontested divorces, uncontested adoptions, and changes of name. He placed an advertisement in the *Arizona Republic*, a daily newspaper of general circulation in the Phoenix metropolitan area, which stated the clinic offered "legal services at very reasonable fees" and listed fees for certain services. This advertisement directly violated the state law. As to the question of whether the Sherman Act applied to this case, the Court ruled Bates's claim based on the Sherman Act was barred by the *Parker* v. *Brown* state action exemption. As the State of Arizona *compelled* attorneys not to advertise (unlike the minimum fee case, in which the prices set were a voluntary act of the attorneys), the Court ruled the Sherman Act did not apply even if this was a restraint of trade by forbidding advertising. The Supreme Court ruled that as the State of Arizona compelled the attorneys not to advertise, this activity fell within the state action exemption and the Sherman Act did not apply to the actions of the state in prohibiting advertisements by attorneys.

It should be noted that the Supreme Court ruled that attorneys could advertise, not on the basis of the Sherman Act, but because the First Amendment guarantees free speech to everyone, including professionals.

Southern Motor Carriers Rate Conference, Inc. v. United States
United States Supreme Court
105 S.Ct. 1721 (1985)

The Southern Motor Carriers Rate Conference is a rate bureau composed of common carriers which submits, on behalf of its members, joint rate proposals to the Public Service Commission in North Carolina, Georgia, Tennessee, and Mississippi. The collective rate making is authorized, but not compelled, by these states. The United States brought suit against Southern Motor Carriers. It contended that the collective rate making violated federal antitrust laws. Southern Motor Carriers claimed its actions were immune from the federal antitrust laws by virtue of the state action doctrine of *Parker* v. *Brown*. The Supreme Court ruled for Southern Motor Carriers.

Justice Powell

In *Midcal,* we affirmed a state-court injunction prohibiting officials from enforcing a statute requiring wine producers to establish resale price schedules. We set forth a two-pronged test for determining whether state regulation of private parties is shielded from the federal antitrust laws. First, the challenged restraint must be "one clearly articulated and affirmatively expressed as state policy." Second, the State must supervise actively any private anticompetitive conduct. This supervision requirement prevents the state from frustrating the national policy in favor of competition by casting a "gauzy cloak of state involvement" over what is essentially private anticompetitive conduct.

We hold *Midcal's* two-pronged test applicable to private parties' claims of state action immunity. Moreover, a state policy that expressly *permits,* but does not compel, anticompetitive conduct may be "clearly articulated" within the meaning of *Midcal.* Our holding today does not suggest, however, that compulsion is irrelevant. To the contrary, compulsion often is the best evidence that the State has a clearly articulated and affirmatively expressed policy to displace competition. Nevertheless, when other evidence conclu-

sively shows that a State intends to adopt a permissive policy, the absence of compulsion should not prove fatal to a claim of *Parker* immunity. A private party may claim state action immunity only if both prongs of the *Midcal* test are satisfied. Here the Court of Appeals found, and the Government concedes, that the State Public Service Commissions actively supervise the collective ratemaking activities of the rate bureaus. Therefore, the only issue left to resolve is whether the petitioners' challenged conduct was taken pursuant to a clearly articulated state policy. *Parker* immunity is available only when the challenged activity is undertaken pursuant to a clearly articulated policy of the State itself, such as a policy approved by a state legislature, or a state supreme court.

A private party acting pursuant to an anticompetitive regulatory program need not "point to a specific, detailed legislative authorization" for its challenged conduct. As long as the State as sovereign clearly intends to displace competition in a particular field with a regulatory structure, the first prong of the *Midcal* test is satisfied.

If more detail than a clear intent to displace competition were required of the legislature, States would find it difficult to implement through regulatory agencies their anticompetitive policies. Agencies are created because they are able to deal with problems unforeseeable to, or outside the competence of, the legislature. Requiring express authorization for every action that an agency might find necessary to effectuate state policy would diminish, if not destroy, its usefulness. Therefore, we hold that if the State's intent to establish an anticompetitive regulatory program is clear, as it is in Mississippi, the State's failure to describe the implementation of its policy in detail will not subject the program to the restraints of the federal antitrust laws.

We hold that the petitioners' collective rate-making activity is immune from Sherman Act liability. This anticompetitive conduct is taken pursuant to a "clearly articulated state policy." The legislatures of North Carolina, Georgia, and Tennessee expressly permit motor common carriers to submit collective rate proposals to public service commissions, which have the authority to accept, reject, or modify any recommendation. Mississippi, the fourth State in which the petitioners operate, has not expressly approved of collective ratemaking, but it has articulated clearly its intent to displace price competition among common carriers with a regulatory structure. Anticompetitive conduct taken pursuant to such a regulatory program satisfies the first prong of the *Midcal* test. The second prong of the *Midcal* test likewise is met, for the government has conceded that the relevant States, through their agencies, actively supervise the conduct of private parties.

We conclude that the petitioners' collective ratemaking activities, although not compelled by the States, are immune from antitrust liability under the doctrine of *Parker v. Brown.* Accordingly, the judgment of the Court of Appeals is reversed.

Regulated Industries

Many businesses operate in industries subject to extensive government regulation. In some cases, government regulation specifies in great detail the manner in which companies must conduct their business. A federal agency or state agency might order a business to conduct itself in a manner contrary to the broad requirements of the antitrust laws. Does this mean that a business that obeys the regulation at the same time violates the antitrust laws? The law in the regulated-industries area cannot be explained in a few general statements. A given action may be subject to the antitrust laws, depending on a number of factors, even when a business operates within a regulated industry.

Such industries as insurance and banking are subject to extensive government regulation. Many professionals in areas like law, medicine, and dentistry must follow rules set down by state regulatory agencies. While precise general rules as to when an industry must comply with the antitrust laws are difficult to state in many instances, if Congress expressly indicated an intent to displace the antitrust laws with agency regulation, the Sherman Act does not apply to matters regulated by the agency. If Congress failed to grant an express immunity, the Courts try to avoid finding an implied immunity unless such a rule is necessary to make the regulation work.

It should be noted that there is a trend to extend the antitrust laws to as many industries as possible, even though they are regulated to some extent by the government.

PREEMPTION

Consider the following case, which examines the extent to which a city can force landlords to charge a maximum level of rents. It examines the extent to which the provisions of the antitrust law prohibit local and state governments from enacting legislation.

Alexandra Fisher v. City of Berkeley, California
United States Supreme Court
106 S.Ct. 1045 (1986)

The city of Berkeley, California, enacted an ordinance that imposed rent ceilings on residential real property in the city. The rent ceilings may be adjusted on an annual basis by a Rent Stabilization Board. The landlords argued that the ordinance was unconstitutional because it was preempted by the federal antitrust laws. The California Supreme Court held that there was no conflict between the ordinance and the Sherman Act. The United States Supreme Court affirmed.

Justice Marshall

What distinguishes the operation of Berkeley's Ordinance from the activities of a benevolent landlords' cartel is not that the Ordinance will necessarily have a different economic effect, but that the rent ceilings imposed by the Ordinance and maintained by the Stabilization Board have been unilaterally imposed by government upon landlords to the exclusion of private control.

The distinction between unilateral and concerted action is critical here. Adhering to the language of § 1, this Court has always limited the reach of that provision to "unreasonable restraints of trade effected by a 'contract, combination . . . or conspiracy' between *separate* entities."

Recognizing this concerted action requirement, appellants argue that the Ordinance "forms a combination between [the City of Berkeley and its officials], on the one hand, and the property owners on the other. It also creates a horizontal combination among the landlords." In so arguing, appellants misconstrue the concerted action requirement of § 1. A restraint imposed unilaterally by government does not become concerted action within the meaning of the statute simply because it has a coercive effect upon parties who must obey the law. The ordinary relationship between the government and those who must obey its regulatory commands whether they wish to or not is not enough to establish a conspiracy. Similarly, the mere fact that all competing property owners must comply with the same provisions of the Ordinance is not enough to establish a conspiracy among landlords. Under Berkeley's Ordinance, control over the maximum rent levels of every affected residential unit has been unilaterally removed from the owners of those properties and given to the Rent Stabilization Board.

POLITICAL ACTION

The antitrust laws to a great extent are designed to further competition. What if a businessman decided that he disliked competition? Could he seek a special rule for his business or industry that exempts it from competition? The answer is yes.

In the discussion of constitutional law, we noted the United States Constitution in the First Amendment provides that "Congress shall make no law . . . abridging the freedom of speech . . . or the right of the people . . . to petition the Government for a redress of grievances."

Because the Constitution permits all persons to freely speak their minds and to petition (that is, request some action from) the government, there is nothing improper about asking government officials for special treatment. To create another rule would be a denial of free speech and the right to petition as guaranteed by the First Amendment. Whether a particular business or industry will succeed in convincing Congress of the need for special protection is another question.

Quite clearly, if a business or industry seeks special legislation from Congress and obtains it, the passage of the legislation constitutes a sort of stamp of approval on its efforts. Congress apparently judged the public interest as being furthered by such a law. This is a legislative judgment. Congress is free to determine how much competition our system needs. Of course, a business might succeed in its lobbying effort even though the public interest was not served by a given piece of legislation. Nonetheless, absent a conflict with the Constitution, the courts must defer to the judgment of Congress.

A business also might elect to lobby a state legislature for favorable treatment. Absent a conflict with federal legislation or with the state constitution or United States Constitution, such efforts may result in special favorable treatment for a business. Once again, the degree of competition in our society is a legislative judgment.

What if a business engaged in a ruthless lobbying effort to obtain favorable anticompetitive legislation? Suppose this legislation was aimed to harm its rivals. Suppose further that the business engaged in unethical and perhaps illegal conduct to induce the Congress or a state legislature to pass this anticompetitive bill. Does all this mean its actions violated the antitrust laws? The following case discusses these issues.

Eastern Railroad Presidents Conference
v. Noerr Motor Freight, Inc.
United States Supreme Court
365 U.S. 127 (1961)

The plaintiffs, Noerr Motor Freight and other truck operators, allege that the defendants, Eastern Railroad Presidents Conference, twenty-four Eastern railroads, and a public relations firm, conspired to restrain trade in and monopolize the long-distance freight business. The railroads allegedly hired a public relations firm to foster the adoption and retention of laws and law enforcement practices destructive to the trucking business, to create an atmosphere of distaste for the truckers among the general public, and to impair the relationships existing between the truckers and their customers. The truckers asked for treble damages and an injunction against future acts of this nature. The railroads brought similar charges against the truckers. The trial court ruled that the railroads' publicity campaign violated the Sherman Act. Insofar as the publicity campaign was directed at lawmakers, the court found that it was fraudulent and salacious and that its only purpose was to destroy the truckers as competitors. The court of appeals affirmed the judgment of the trial court. The Supreme Court reversed.

Justice Black

We accept, as the starting point for our consideration of the case, the same basic construction of the Sherman Act adopted by the courts below—that no violation of the Act can be predicated upon mere attempts to influence the passage or enforcement of laws.

We think it equally clear that the Sherman Act does not prohibit two or more persons from associating together in an attempt to persuade the legislature or the executive to take particular action with respect to a law that would produce a restraint or a monopoly. In the first place, such a holding would substantially impair the power of government to take actions through its legislature and executive that operate to restrain trade. In a representative democracy such as this, these branches of government act on behalf of the people and, to a very large extent, the whole concept of representation depends upon the ability of the people to make their wishes known to their representatives. To hold that the government retains the power to act in this representative capacity and yet hold, at the same time, that the people cannot freely inform the government of their wishes would impute to the Sherman Act a purpose to regulate, not business activity, but political activity, a purpose which would have no basis whatever in the legislative history of that Act. Secondly, and of at least equal significance, such a construction of the Sherman Act would raise important constitutional questions. The right of petition is one of the freedoms protected by the Bill of Rights, and we cannot, of course, lightly impute to Congress an intent to invade these freedoms. We are thus called upon to consider whether the courts below were correct in holding that, notwithstanding this principle, the Act was violated here because of the presence in the railroads' publicity campaign of additional factors sufficient to take the case out of the area in which the principle is controlling.

The first such factor relied upon was the fact, established by the finding of the District Court, that the railroads' sole purpose in seeking to influence the passage and enforcement of laws was to destroy the truckers as competitors for the long-distance freight business. But we do not see how this fact, even if adequately supported in the record, could transform conduct otherwise lawful into a violation of the Sherman Act. All of the considerations that have led us to the conclusion that the Act does not apply to mere group solicitation of government action are equally applicable in spite of the addition of this factor. The right of the people to inform their representatives in government of their desires with respect to the passage or enforcement of laws cannot properly be made to depend upon their intent in doing so. It is neither unusual nor illegal for people to seek action on laws in the hope that they may bring about an advantage to themselves and a disadvantage to their competitors.

In addition the courts below rested their holding that the Sherman Act had been violated upon a finding that the purpose of the railroads was "more than merely an attempt to obtain legislations. It was the purpose and intent to hurt the truckers in every way possible even though they secured no legislation."

There may be situations in which a publicity campaign, ostensibly directed toward influencing governmental action, is a mere sham to cover what is actually nothing more than an attempt to interfere directly with the business relationships of a competitor and the application of the Sherman Act would be justified. But this certainly is not the case here. No one denies that the railroads were making a genuine effort to influence legislation and law enforcement practices. Indeed, if the version of the facts set forth in the truckers' complaint is fully credited, as it was by the courts below, that effort was not only genuine but also highly successful. Under the circumstances, we conclude that no attempt to interfere with business relationships in a manner proscribed by the Sherman Act is involved in this case.

In rejecting each of the grounds relied upon by the courts below to justify application of the Sherman Act to the campaign of the railroads, we have rejected the very grounds upon which those courts relied to distinguish the campaign conducted by the truckers. In doing so, we have restored what appears to be the true nature of the case—a "no-holds-barred fight" between two industries both of which are seeking control of a profitable source of income. Inherent in such fights, which are commonplace in the halls of legislative bodies, is the possibility, and in many instances even the probability, that one group or the other will get hurt by the arguments that are made. In this particular instance, each group appears to have utilized all the political powers it could muster in an attempt to bring about the passage of laws that would help it or injure the other. But the contest itself appears to have been conducted along lines normally accepted in our political system, except to the extent that each group has deliberately deceived the public and public officials. And that deception, reprehensible as it is, can be of no consequence so far as the Sherman Act is concerned. That Act was not violated by either the railroads or the truckers in their respective campaigns to influence legislation and law enforcement.

Noerr suggests that any attempt to influence any branch of government—legislative, executive, judicial, or administrative—may be exempt from the antitrust laws. As one moves away from the legislative area, however, the courts may be more willing to find the action of a company a mere sham or undertaken in bad faith. Clearly, instituting a suit in bad faith may lead to a countersuit. The standards for when and how a litigant uses the courts are fairly clear. A company might also attempt to seek favorable treatment by the president of the United States or by the governor of a state. These persons possess the power to make law through such devices as the executive order. Furthermore, the executive branch enforces legislation. A company might petition the executive branch to not enforce a piece of legislation against it. Once again, such actions are consistent with the Constitution and do not violate the antitrust law absent a bad faith attempt to injure competition.

Neither bad acts, unethical conduct, nor anticompetitive intent make a company's actions in attempting to influence government illegal under the antitrust laws. Only misuse of the process results in an application of the antitrust laws. While some efforts to influence the administrative branch also fit within this political action exception, the Supreme Court will not permit competitors to abuse the administrative process by instituting proceedings against competitors without probable cause and regardless of the merits.

In *California Motor Transport Co.* v. *Trucking Unlimited* (1972), the Supreme Court discussed the sham exception to the *Noerr* doctrine. In this case, the plaintiffs alleged the defendants engaged in concerted action to institute state and federal administrative proceedings to defeat plaintiff's applications to conduct trucking business over certain routes. The plaintiffs alleged that the defendant's real purpose in instituting proceedings was to destroy them as competitors. Administrative cases had been instituted sometimes without cause, and regardless of the merits of the case. The Court ruled that a pattern of baseless, repetitive claims constitutes an abuse of process. Such actions barred the plaintiffs from access to the agencies and courts.

While all trucking companies legally could use the agencies and the courts, using them with intent to eliminate a competitor by denying it free and meaningful access to the agencies and courts comes within the sham exception to the *Noerr* case.

The defendants' wrongdoing in using the agencies to prevent their competitors from obtaining licenses consisted of contesting every request for a license by the plaintiffs—even when the defendants lacked any grounds for such action. Repeatedly contesting every request for a license constituted an abuse of the administrative process. Consequently, the Court applied the Sherman Act to the defendants in this case.

Business executives should not be deterred by the *California Motor Transport* case from exercising their legitimate rights under the Constitution. Many valid arguments may lawfully be presented to Congress, state legislatures, the president, a governor, or the courts. The Constitution guarantees businesses the right of free speech and the right to petition the government. Business executives need not fear the antitrust laws even if they seek anticompetitive legislation of value only to their business and harmful to their competitors. *Noerr* illustrates the point that even bad acts in seeking favorable legislation will not alone trigger the application of the Sherman Act. However, when a person's actions constitute a mere sham to cover up an attempt to interfere directly with the business relationships of a competitor, such actions result in the application of antitrust laws. If a business crosses this line, and seeks legislative, executive, judicial, or administrative relief solely for this purpose, and without any legitimate political aims, the courts will impose the antitrust sanctions on its activities.

SUMMARY

Many forces contributed to the passage of the Sherman Act: the growth of mass production, the expansion of the railway system, American individualism, a desire to redistribute wealth, and a desire to maximize opportunity for workers. Populists, farmers, and small businessmen in 1890 succeeded in convincing Congress that the best way to achieve these goals was through an act which promoted competition and economic efficiency.

Since the passage of the Sherman Act, Congress has passed a number of other acts in order to keep our economic system competitive. It vested the Department of Justice and the Federal Trade Commission with the primary responsibility for enforcing these acts. Private businesses and individuals, as well as state attorneys general, also may to some extent enforce the federal antitrust laws. Businesses that violate the antitrust laws may be enjoined from certain types of conduct, may be fined, or their employees may be sentenced to prison. Furthermore, civil suits may be filed for damages wrought by antitrust violations and treble damages may be assessed against an erring company.

Certain groups and businesses are not subject to the federal antitrust laws. In general, labor unions and agricultural cooperatives are not subject to these laws. States also may elect to exempt certain types of business activity from antitrust scrutiny.

The United States Constitution also strongly affects the law in this area. Businesses are free to seek legislation even if it has an anticompetitive effect. The constitution permits businesses and people to petition the government for redress of grievances. The Supreme Court has interpreted this clause in the Constitution as creating a right to seek political action from the government.

REVIEW QUESTIONS

1. Define the following terms:
   a. Class actions
   b. Parens patriae
   c. Nolo contendere

2. What forces produced the antitrust laws?

3. What objectives do the courts regard as furthered by the antitrust laws?

4. Class actions and parens patriae actions have been used to enforce the antitrust laws. Discuss these enforcement methods.

5. What groups, if any, are exempt from the antitrust laws?

6. Why is the state action exemption, as announced in *Parker* v. *Brown*, important?

7. Is it a violation of the Sherman Act to seek legislation that destroys some other person or company as a competitor?

8. The state of Michigan regulated the rates charged by public utilities operating within the state boundaries. The Michigan Public Service Commission, which set these rates, authorized the Detroit Edison Company also to distribute free electric light bulbs to its customers. A retail druggist who sells light bulbs alleged that the company violated the Sherman Act by using its monopoly power in the distribution of electricity to restrain competition in the sale of light bulbs. Is the druggist correct?

9. Sunkist Growers, Inc., permitted some people who were not growers or producers to join its organization. Sunkist at the time was organized into local associations, which in turn elected members of the Sunkist board. Is Sunkist an association of persons engaged in the production of agricultural products within the meaning of the Capper-Volstead Act?

10. The State of Illinois brought suit under Section 4 of the Clayton Act on behalf of itself and various other local governmental entities. It charged that the defendants, all of whom manufacture or sell concrete block, violated the Sherman Act by combining and conspiring to fix the price of concrete blocks. The governmental entities purchased buildings in which concrete block was merely one component part, rather than purchasing the concrete block outright. This meant that the concrete block passed through at least two separate, unrestrained levels in the chain of distribution—the masonry contractors who purchased the concrete block from the defendants, and the general contractors who purchased the concrete block along with other goods and services from the masonry contractors. Can the State of Illinois recover for any pass-on of the alleged overcharge in the price of concrete block?

11. The Arizona Supreme Court delegated the power to administer the bar examination to the state bar examiners, although it retained the final power to determine who would be admitted to the bar in Arizona. Ronwin failed to pass the Arizona bar. He brought suit against the bar examiners who administered and graded the bar exam. Ronwin alleged that the bar examiners had conspired to restrain trade in violation of the Sherman Act by attempting to reduce the number of attorneys in the state of Arizona by setting the grading scale on the examination with reference to the number of attorneys it thought desirable. The defendants contended they were immune from liability under the state action doctrine. Are the defendants correct?

CHAPTER 14

Antitrust Law

Monopolies
Attempts to Monopolize
Restraint of Trade
Resale Price Maintenance
Vertical Nonprice Restraints
Group Boycotts
Tying Contracts
Section 5 of the Federal Trade Commission Act

In the preceding chapter, we discussed the scope and enforcement procedures of the antitrust laws. This chapter discusses briefly some major antitrust rules. Antitrust law is very complex. Unlike many other areas of law, the statutes creating the antitrust laws leave it up to the courts to precisely define the limits of corporate activity in the antitrust field. The Sherman and Clayton Acts were written in broad, general terms. This gives the courts considerable discretion in creating a body of antitrust law. Careful attention to the pronouncements by the courts is essential. We will present in-depth discussions of some cases in this chapter to make it easier to understand the current view of the courts on selected antitrust issues.

The cases should enable you to gain a broad overview of the goals of the antitrust laws as interpreted by the courts. Some important issues have been left out because of the complexity and lack of clear-cut rules. Nonetheless, this chapter presents most of the major issues confronting the courts today in this area. The primary emphasis of this chapter is on monopolies and restraints of trade. We have tried to deal with both of these areas in sufficient depth to cover most of the major issues. A number of other important areas have been presented briefly to alert readers to potential problem areas in the antitrust field.

MONOPOLIES

As noted in Chapter 13, the Sherman Act outlawed monopolies and attempts to monopolize. Section 2 of the act reads as follows:

Every person who shall monopolize, or attempt to monopolize, or combine or conspire with any other person or persons, to monopolize any part of the trade or commerce among the several states, or with foreign nations, shall be deemed guilty of a felony, and, on conviction thereof, shall be punished by fine not exceeding one million dollars if a corporation, or, if any other person, one hundred thousand dollars, or by imprisonment not exceeding three years or by both said punishments, in the discretion of the court.

Most challenges to monopolistic behavior are brought under Section 2 of the Sherman Act.

What Is a Monopoly?

When the courts speak of a **monopoly,** they are referring to a firm that deliberately engages in conduct to obtain or maintain the power to control prices or exclude competition in some part of trade or commerce. The courts do not require a firm to be the sole business operating in a particular market—other firms may be operating in the market but they must lack the power to influence prices or output in the market. Contrast a monopolistic industry with an industry composed of several large firms each possessing a major part of the trade in a given market. The courts refer to these firms as **oligopolists.** In a *competitive system,* there are many firms each producing the same product, with none of the firms possessing the power to control prices or output.

Picture a business that operates the parking lot at the airport in your city. Does not this business, in a sense, have a monopoly? Either you park your automobile at the airport in the airport lot, or you take the bus or a cab or arrange to be driven to the airport. If you want to park your car at the airport, you must park at this lot. Such a parking facility faces competition only from other parking lots, but an airport miles from town really need not concern itself with such lots. The airport parking lot in this situation has a monopoly in the parking business. Contrast this with a person operating a downtown parking lot in a big city. The big city parking lot competes with every other lot downtown, as well as with parking on the street. People also may see the bus or a cab as a substitute for driving and parking if parking downtown becomes too expensive. Which business is in the best position to obtain a premium price for renting its space, the lot downtown or the lot at the airport? Clearly, the airport parking lot ought to earn more money.

In labeling the airport parking lot a monopoly, we must make certain assumptions, assumptions that courts make when they designate a business as a monopoly.

Geographic Market. First of all, we must consider the *geographic market.* Implicit in this analysis is the assumption that we will exclude all other parking lots outside the geographical boundaries of the airport. If we include all parking lots in the city as well as those at the airport, the airport business probably rents only a tiny portion of the parking spaces in the city. However, if the geographic market is the airport, the lot probably rents one hundred percent of the spaces. The latter case looks a lot more like a monopoly. A business that controls one hundred percent of the market probably has the power to control prices. Courts must examine the geographic market in which a business operates.

Product Market. Likewise, courts inspect the nature of the *product sold by a business.* While the airport parking lot sells one hundred percent of the parking spaces at the airport, the parking lot sells only a tiny portion of all goods and services sold at the airport. By first defining the product market as the rental of parking spaces and the geographic market as the airport, we arrive at the conclusion that the parking lot business is a monopolist because it sells one hundred percent of the parking lot spaces (the product market) at the airport (the geographic market). If the court defined the geographic market as the whole city, and the product market as all goods and services sold in the city, would the airport parking lot be a monopolist? Clearly not. Courts go through a very similar analysis in monopoly cases. A court first determines the *geographic market* in which a business operates, then the court decides the *product market,* and then it determines the *anticompetitive effects* of a particular company's activities.

Not all people share the view that monopolies are bad. Some economists think the most efficient use of resources occurs when market power is concentrated in the hands of one efficient firm—or a few efficient firms—in each industry. They see economic waste and inefficiency resulting from the competitive rivalry of industrial corporations. Many executives at large companies share the view that big business operates more efficiently than a number of small competitors.

> **Is Monopolizing Trade Bad?**

Diametrically opposed to those who favor monopoly are those who believe the consumer needs protection through the furtherance of competition. Classic economic theory supports this view. It tells us that competition weeds out inefficiency, results in the most productive use of resources, encourages technological advances, and assures the consumer of an adequate supply of goods at the lowest possible price. Whichever theory is correct, some monopolies violate the Sherman Act.

Not every monopoly violates the antitrust laws. Some businesses, such as utilities, are natural monopolies. The states give these businesses the exclusive right to operate in a certain territory. Other businesses fall within an exemption to the antitrust laws. Article I, Section 8, of the United States Constitution gives monopolies to authors in the form of copyrights and gives patents to inventors. The framers of the Constitution reasoned that such protection for authors and inventors encourages work in these areas. One object of marketing certainly is to give a product a unique identification in the minds of consumers. If consumers perceive a company's product as different from any other product on the market, they may pay a higher price for its product. There is nothing illegal about a company trying to project a unique, favorable image of its products in the minds of the public. To the extent such a campaign succeeds, the company has obtained a kind of monopoly.

> **Are All Monopolies Illegal?**

Absent one of these situations, a company that becomes a monopoly in a given geographic and product market may violate the Sherman Act.

In determining whether a monopoly violates the antitrust laws, the Supreme Court has altered its position over the years. In an early landmark case in the antitrust area, *Standard Oil Co.* v. *United States* (1911), Justice White stated, "The dread of enhancement of prices . . . which . . . would flow from the undue limitation on competitive conditions caused by contracts or other acts . . . led . . . to the prohi-

> **Changing the Law**

bition . . . of all contracts or other acts which were unreasonably restrictive of competitive conditions." Justice White did not interpret Section 2 as condemning all monopolies. On this point he noted that the act "by the omission of every direct prohibition against monopoly . . . indicates a consciousness that the freedom of the individual to contract when not unduly or improperly exercised was the most efficient means for the prevention of monopoly."

Justice White viewed the statutory purpose of the act as directed at the "dread of enhancement of prices." What he probably meant by his opinion in *Standard Oil* is that if a company is headed towards a monopoly fairly, the extra profits it earns will attract others into the market. For this reason, there will never be a monopoly unless the company is guilty of bad acts. Essentially his views reflect the early analysis of Section 2 of the Sherman Act—that a court must find a firm has monopolized its market and engaged in *bad acts* in order to find the company in violation of the Sherman Act.

The view currently applied in the courts no longer follows White's opinion. Today, the focus has shifted from an emphasis on reprehensible behavior to the issue of *monopoly power*. Courts examine the relevant *geographic market* a firm operates in and the *product line* it sells. Once a court defines these markets, it determines the *degree of power* a firm possesses in this market. If a firm reaches the position where it sells forty to sixty percent of the goods in a given geographical and product market, it must act with caution. A firm selling sixty percent or more of such a market probably will be in violation of Section 2.

Rule of Reason

Standard Oil Co. v. *United States* was decided under Section 2 of the Sherman Act. Although Justice White dissolved the Standard Oil Trust, he also announced the famous **Rule of Reason** in this case. In what looks very much like a reversal of earlier cases, he stated that only *unreasonable* restraints of trade and *unreasonable* attempts to monopolize violate the Sherman Act. The courts still follow the Rule of Reason in interpreting the Sherman Act.

Starting with *United States* v. *Aluminum Co. of America*, the courts embarked on a new approach to the handling of monopoly cases. The opinion, written by the distinguished judge, Learned Hand, has served as a model for subsequent judges handling monopoly cases. In this famous decision, Judge Hand analyzed the activities of Alcoa by examining the structure of the aluminum market.

United States v. Aluminum Co. of America
Circuit Court of Appeals, Second Circuit
148 F.2d 416 (1945)

Aluminum Co. of America (Alcoa) was a corporation engaged in the production and sale of aluminum. The issue in this case was whether its production of "virgin" ingot was an illegal monopoly after 1912. During this time period, it was the sole producer of virgin ingot in the United States. Alcoa argued that this fact did not make it a monopolist because of imported virgin ingot and secondary (recycled) ingot. It also claimed its growth was not a product of bad acts.

The judges had to decide how to categorize the aluminum market. One characterization could have been that its market consisted only of aluminum produced by Alcoa and secondary aluminum, but did not include aluminum produced by Alcoa that was fabricated by Alcoa directly into products. In that case, Alcoa would have thirty-three percent of the market. On the other hand, if all of Alcoa's production, as well as imported and secondary ingot, were included in the market, Alcoa's share of the aluminum market would have been sixty-four percent. Alternatively, if the market consisted of all of Alcoa's production and the imported ingot, but none of the secondary ingot, Alcoa's market share rose to ninety percent. The judges chose ninety percent as Alcoa's market share.

Following is the portion of the opinion in which the judges discuss whether Alcoa monopolized the market. Parts of the opinion dealing with unlawful practices by Alcoa and its cartel arrangements are omitted. The court found that Alcoa had unlawfully monopolized the ingot market. The court chose not to dissolve Alcoa, but it did enjoin some activities by Alcoa in the future.

Hand, Circuit Judge

The judge found that, over the whole half century of its existence, Alcoa's profits upon capital invested, after payment of income taxes, had been only about ten percent, and although the plaintiff puts this figure a little higher, the difference is negligible. This assumed, it would be hard to say that Alcoa had made exorbitant profits on ingot.

But the whole issue is irrelevant anyway, for it is no excuse for "monopolizing" a market that the monopoly has not been used to extract from the consumer more than a "fair" profit. The Act has wider purposes. Indeed, even though we disregarded all but economic considerations, it would by no means follow that such concentration of producing power is to be desired, when it has not been used extortionately. Many people believe that possession of unchallenged economic power deadens initiative, discourages thrift and depresses energy; that immunity from competition is a narcotic, and rivalry is a stimulant, to industrial progress; that the spur of constant stress is necessary to counteract an inevitable disposition to let well enough alone. Such people believe that competitors, versed in the craft as no consumer can be, will be quick to detect opportunities for saving and new shifts in production, and be eager to profit by them. In any event the mere fact that a producer, having command of the domestic market, has not been able to make more than a "fair" profit, is no evidence that a "fair" profit could not have been made at lower prices. Congress did not condone "good trusts" and condemn "bad" ones; it forbad all. Moreover, in so doing it was not necessarily actuated by economic motives alone. It is possible, because of its indirect social or moral effect, to prefer a system of small producers, each dependent for his success upon his own skill and character, to one in which the great mass of those engaged must accept the direction of a few.

We have been speaking only of the economic reasons which forbid monopoly; but, as we have already implied, there are others, based upon the belief that great industrial consolidations are inherently undesirable, regardless of their economic results. In the debates in Congress Senator Sherman himself showed that among the purposes of Congress in 1890 was a desire to put an end to great aggregations of capital because of the helplessness of the individual before them. Throughout history it has been constantly assumed that one of their purposes was to perpetuate and preserve, for its own sake and in spite of possible cost, an organization of industry in small units which can effectively compete with each other. We hold that Alcoa's monopoly of ingot was of the kind covered by Section 2.

It does not follow because Alcoa had such a monopoly, that it "monopolized" the ingot market: it may not have achieved monopoly; monopoly may have been thrust upon it. Persons may unwittingly find themselves in possession of a monopoly, automatically so to say: that is, without having intended either to put an end to existing competition, or to prevent competition from arising when none had existed; they may become monopolists by force of accident. Since the Act makes "monopolizing" a crime, as well as a civil wrong, it would be not only unfair, but presumably contrary to the intent of Congress, to include such instances. A market may, for example, be so limited that it is impossible to produce at all and meet the cost of production except by a plant large enough to supply the whole demand. Or there may be changes in taste or in cost which drive out all but one purveyor. A single producer may be the survivor out of a group of active competitors, merely by virtue of his superior skill, foresight and industry. In such cases a strong argument can be made that, although the result may expose the public to the evils of monopoly, the Act does not mean to condemn the resultant of those very forces which is its prime object to foster; finis opus coronat. The successful competitor, having been urged to compete, must not be turned upon when he wins.

It would completely misconstrue Alcoa's position in 1940 to hold that it was the passive beneficiary of a monopoly, following upon an involuntary elimination of competitors by automatically operative economic forces. The only question is whether it falls within the exception established in favor of those who do not seek, but cannot avoid, the control of a market. It seems to us that that question scarcely survives its statement. It was not inevitable that it should always anticipate increases in the demand for ingot and be prepared to supply them. Nothing compelled it to keep doubling and redoubling its capacity before others entered the field. It insists that it never excluded competitors; but we can think of no more effective exclusion than progressively to embrace each new opportunity as it opened, and to face every newcomer with new capacity already geared into a great organization, having the advantage of experience, trade connections and the elite of personnel. Only in case we interpret "exclusion" as limited to manoeuvres not honestly industrial, but actuated solely by a desire to prevent competition, can such a course, indefatigably pursued, be deemed not "exclusionary." So to limit it would in our judgment emasculate the Act; would permit just such consolidations as it was designed to prevent.

In order to fall within Section 2, the monopolist must have both the power to monopolize, and the intent to monopolize. To read the passage as demanding any "specific" intent, makes nonsense of it, for no monopolist monopolizes unconscious of what he is doing. So here, Alcoa meant to keep, and did keep, that complete and exclusive hold upon the ingot market with which it started. That was to "monopolize" that market, however innocently it otherwise proceeded.

The *Alcoa* case suggests the following rule: Unless a company can prove a thrust-upon defense, if the government proves a company possesses monopoly power in a given market, it has violated Section 2 of the Sherman Act.

Since the *Alcoa* case, the courts have focused more attention on *monopoly power* and *market structure*. The courts determine the relevant market—geographic and product—and then examine whether a firm possesses power within that market. Remember, a monopolist is one who possesses the power to exclude competition or control prices in a given market.

Relevant Market. Determining the relevant product market often is critical to the outcome in a case. In *United States* v. *E. I. du Pont de Nemours & Co.* (1956), the

Supreme Court expanded the test for relevant product market. The Court ruled that the relevant product market is composed of products that are reasonably interchangeable for the purposes for which they are produced. It examined the price, use, and quality of all products that might compose a given market. The government, in that case, charged du Pont with monopolizing interstate commerce in cellophane in violation of Section 2. Du Pont produced seventy percent of all cellophane during the relevant period, but cellophane constituted less than twenty percent of all flexible packaging material sales. The government argued the proper product market definition was cellophane. The company argued the market definition should include all flexible packaging materials.

A company has a monopoly in violation of Section 2 only if it has the power to control prices or unreasonably restrict competition. Taking this definition of monopoly into consideration, the Court stated that if it defined the product market as cellophane, du Pont had monopoly power over that market. The company possessed the power to control the price of cellophane. The Court rejected cellophane as the proper product market definition, however, and adopted flexible packaging materials as the proper market definition. The Court reasoned that control in a market depends upon the availability to buyers of alternative commodities. To determine if buyers will substitute one product for another, a court must examine the price, characteristics, and adaptability of competing commodities. The Court found purchasers were willing to substitute other wrapping papers for cellophane (wax paper, brown wrapping paper, and so on). It therefore ruled for du Pont.

While a company controlling a product possesses monopoly power if no substitutes are available for that product, it does not follow that merely because a product differs from others an illegal monopoly exists. Although cellophane differs from other wrapping papers, the Court found these other papers to be reasonably interchangeable with cellophane for the purpose of wrapping articles. In making this determination, the Court examined the price, use, and qualities of the substitute products. It found the proper product market definition, in light of these factors, to be flexible wrapping materials.

The *du Pont* case suggests that courts will pay more attention to product market definitions and will take into consideration partial substitutes. Du Pont clearly possessed substantial market power over cellophane. It lowered the price and increased its sales over time. But it escaped any sanctions by convincing the Court to adopt flexible wrapping materials as opposed to cellophane as the proper definition of relevant product market. This meant du Pont controlled only twenty percent of the relevant product market—not enough to constitute a monopoly.

Geographic Market. Not only must a court examine the relevant product market before determining if a firm possesses monopoly power, it must also determine the relevant geographic market. Quite often the geographic market for purposes of the Sherman Act is the nation.

In *United States v. Grinnell Corp.*, 384 U.S. 563 (1966), the Supreme Court essentially announced a two-part test for monopolization. The defendant must (1) possess monopoly power in the relevant market, and (2) have willfully acquired or maintained that power as distinguished from growth or development as a consequence of a superior product, business acumen, or historical accident.

**Aggressive
Competition Not
Based on
Efficiency**

In the following case, Aspen Skiing Co. was acting aggressively. Aspen Skiing Co. used its monopoly power to exclude a rival on some basis *other than* efficiency. It did not maintain its monopoly power due to its superior business ability and efficiency.

Aspen Skiing Co. v. Aspen Highlands Skiing Corp.

United States Supreme Court
105 S.Ct 2847 (1985)

Aspen is a ski resort. Private investors in Aspen operated three facilities (Ajax, Highlands, and Buttermilk) for downhill skiing between 1945 and 1960. A fourth mountain (Snowmass) opened in 1967. It is no longer possible to open additional facilities in the area. Starting in 1962, the three independent firms that operated the facilities introduced a six-day, all Aspen ticket that permitted skiers to ski on any of the three mountains then in service. This six-day ticket was offered at a discount from the price of six daily tickets.

Aspen Skiing Co. (called Ski Co.), the owner of Ajax, purchased Buttermilk in 1964 and opened Snowmass in 1967. It continued to offer all-Aspen tickets in conjunction with Aspen Highlands, but over the years evinced a hostility to the all-Aspen ticket. In 1978, due to a difference of opinion as to the sharing of revenues, the parties were unable to come to an agreement, and Ski Co. discontinued selling the all-Aspen ticket. Ski Co. then began to promote its own three-area six-day ticket in a national advertising campaign that strongly implied there were only three mountains in Aspen. Highlands continued to try to market an all-Aspen ticket, but Ski Co. took additional actions to make it difficult for Highlands to market the all-Aspen ticket—such as refusing to sell Highlands any lift tickets for use in its all-Aspen ticket. Without the convenient all-Aspen ticket, Highlands's share of the market for downhill skiing services steadily declined from 20.5 percent in 1976 to 11 percent in 1980 to 1981. Its other revenues declined sharply as well.

Highlands brought suit against Ski Co. in 1979. It alleged that Ski Co. had monopolized the market for downhill skiing services at Aspen in violation of Section 2 of the Sherman Act and asked for treble damages. The jury ruled for Highlands and found Ski Co. had violated Section 2 of the Sherman Act. It calculated Highlands actual damages at $2.5 million. The district court entered a judgment awarding Highlands treble damages of $7.5 million, plus costs and attorney's fees. The Supreme Court affirmed this judgment.

Justice Stevens

In her instructions to the jury, the District Judge explained that the offense of monopolization under § 2 of the Sherman Act has two elements: (1) the possession of monopoly power in a relevant market, and (2) the willful acquisition, maintenance, or use of that power by anticompetitive or exclusionary means or for anticompetitive or exclusionary purposes. Although the first element was vigorously disputed at the trial and in the Court of Appeals, in this Court Ski Co. does not challenge the jury's special verdict finding that it possessed monopoly power.

The central message of the Sherman Act is that a business entity must find new customers and higher profits through internal expansion—that is, by competing successfully rather than by arranging treaties with its competitors. Ski Co., therefore, is surely correct in submitting that even a firm with monopoly power has no general duty to engage in a joint marketing program with a competitor. Ski Co. is quite wrong, however, in suggesting that the judgment in this case rests on any such proposition of law. For the trial court unambiguously instructed the jury that a firm possessing monopoly power has no duty to cooperate with its business rivals.

The absence of an unqualified duty to cooperate does not mean that every time a firm declines to participate in a particular cooperative venture, that decision may not have evidentiary significance, or that it may not give rise to liability in certain circumstances. The absence of a duty to transact business with another firm is, in some respects, merely the counterpart of the independent businessman's cherished right to select his customers and his associates. The high value that we have placed on the right to refuse to deal with other firms does not mean that the right is unqualified.

In the actual case that we must decide, the monopolist did not merely reject a novel offer to participate in a cooperative venture that had been proposed by a competitor. Rather, the monopolist elected to make an important change in a pattern of distribution that had originated in a competitive market and had persisted for several years.

Ski Co.'s decision to terminate the all-Aspen ticket was a decision by a monopolist to make an important change in the character of the market. Such a decision is not necessarily anticompetitive, and Ski Co. contends that neither its decision, nor the conduct in which it engaged to implement that decision, can fairly be characterized as exclusionary in this case.

We must assume that the jury followed the court's instructions. The jury must, therefore, have drawn a distinction between practices which tend to exclude or restrict competition on the one hand, and the success of a business which reflects only a superior product, a well-run business, or luck, on the other. Since the jury was unambiguously instructed that Ski Co.'s refusal to deal with Highlands "does not violate § 2 if valid business reasons exist for that refusal," we must assume that the jury concluded that there were no valid business reasons for the refusal. The question then is whether that conclusion finds support in the record.

The question whether Ski Co.'s conduct may properly be characterized as exclusionary cannot be answered by simply considering its effect on Highlands. In addition, it is relevant to consider its impact on consumers and whether it has impaired competition in an unnecessarily restrictive way. If a firm has been attempting to exclude rivals on some basis other than efficiency, it is fair to characterize its behavior as predatory. It is, accordingly, appropriate to examine the effect of the challenged pattern of conduct on consumers, on Ski Co.'s smaller rival, and on Ski Co. itself.

The evidence supports a conclusion that consumers were adversely affected by the elimination of the 4-area ticket. The actual record of competition between a 3-area ticket and the all-Aspen ticket in the years after 1967 indicated that skiers demonstrably preferred four mountains to three.

The adverse impact of Ski Co.'s pattern of conduct on Highlands is not disputed in this Court.

Perhaps most significant, however, is the evidence relating to Ski Co. itself, for Ski Co. did not persuade the jury that its conduct was justified by any normal business purpose. Ski Co. was apparently willing to forgo daily ticket sales both to skiers who sought to exchange the coupons contained in Highlands' Adventure Pack, and to those who would have purchased Ski Co. daily lift tickets from Highlands if Highlands had been permitted to purchase them in bulk. The jury may well have concluded that Ski Co. elected to forgo these short run benefits because it was more interested in reducing competition in the Aspen market over the long run by harming its smaller competitor.

The record in this case comfortably supports an inference that the monopolist made a deliberate effort to discourage its customers from doing business with its smaller rival.

Thus the evidence supports an inference that Ski Co. was not motivated by efficiency concerns and that it was willing to sacrifice short run benefits and consumer good will in exchange for a perceived long-run impact on its smaller rival.

ATTEMPTS TO MONOPOLIZE

A firm may violate Section 2 of the Sherman Act not only by achieving a monopoly, but also by *attempting* to monopolize a market. As stated earlier, a monopolist possesses the power to control prices or exclude competition in some part of the trade or commerce. Thus, a firm attempting to monopolize a market is trying to achieve a position in a market whereby the firm may control prices or exclude competition.

Presumably, such a company desires to achieve a monopoly position in the market in order to charge prices higher than those which would prevail in a competitive market. The antitrust laws, by preventing monopolies, help keep prices low.

The approach taken by courts in the attempt-to-monopolize cases is to require a demonstration that the defendant has a specific intent to monopolize a market, is engaging in conduct likely to lead to a monopoly, and possesses significant market power in the relevant geographical and product market.

With respect to intent, Judge Hand observed in the *Alcoa* case: "Conduct falling short of monopoly is not illegal unless it is part of a plan to monopolize, or to gain such other control of a market as is equally forbidden. To make it so, the plaintiff must prove what in the criminal law is known as a 'specific intent'; an intent which goes beyond the mere intent to do the act." In other words, by engaging in certain behavior, the firm intends to achieve a monopoly. Most courts merely require proof of improper conduct to establish a specific intent. The defendant is presumed to intend the likely consequences of its acts.

In an attempt-to-monopolize case, courts require evidence the defendant possesses a significant market share. A firm that intends to monopolize a market and engages in conduct designed to achieve this goal is not guilty of a violation of Section 2 until it achieves a significant market share. The firm must have enough of the market in question to pose a dangerous probability of succeeding in achieving a monopoly.

In monopoly cases, the defendant is accused of trying to control all or a significant portion of a market. In restraint of trade cases, a discussion of which follows, the defendant is accused of interfering with free trade.

RESTRAINT OF TRADE

Section 1 of the Sherman Act outlaws **restraint of trade.** The act reads as follows:

Every contract, combination in the form of trust or otherwise, or conspiracy, in restraint of trade or commerce among the several States, or with foreign nations, is declared to be illegal. Every person who shall make any contract or engage in any combination or conspiracy . . . shall be deemed guilty of a felony, and, on conviction thereof, shall be punished by fine not exceeding one million dollars if a corporation, or, if any other person, one hundred thousand dollars, or by imprisonment not exceeding three years, or by both said punishments, in the discretion of the court.

What does the Sherman Act require before a corporation or person may be deemed in violation of Section 1? There must be (1) a contract, combination, or conspiracy, and (2) a restraint of trade. Generally, we need not concern ourselves with a careful definition of geographical and product markets or market power when analyzing restraints of trade. Though a careful definition of markets and market power can be useful in some restraint-of-trade cases, such as exclusive dealing agreements (agreements by a buyer to deal only from a particular seller), we will not discuss this type of case.

Elements of Case

Although the act used the phrase "in restraint of trade or commerce," Congress left it to the courts to define this phrase. One possible construction of those words is that any action that restrains trade violates the act. If you read the words literally, they imply the act outlaws all restraints of trade. If a person enters into an employment contract, does this violate the Sherman Act? Obviously, to some extent trade is restrained by this person's agreeing to work for only a certain employer. A more reasonable interpretation of "in restraint of trade or commerce" is that it is intended to outlaw only a subset of all contracts that restrain trade or commerce, namely, those that are bad for various reasons.

In the early cases dealing with the Sherman Act, the Supreme Court read Section 1 literally. When faced with the question whether the act outlawed all restraints of trade and commerce, or merely unreasonable restraints of trade and commerce, the Supreme Court chose the former option. In *United States* v. *Trans-Missouri Freight Association* (1897), the Court stated: "The plain and ordinary meaning of such language is not limited to that kind of contract alone which is in unreasonable restraint of trade, but all contracts are included in such language." As noted, outlawing all contracts that restrain trade makes very little sense. Many contracts that restrain trade are highly beneficial to society.

Early Interpretation of the Act

The Supreme Court eventually changed its position in the landmark case *Standard Oil Co.* v. *United States* (1911). In this case, brought against the Standard Oil Trust, the Supreme Court again reconsidered the question of whether the Sherman Act outlaws all restraints of trade. The defendants in this case had entered into agreements to fix prices, limit production, and control the transportation of oil and its products. They turned over the management of all aspects of their businesses to nine trustees. In return for surrendering the control of their businesses to the Standard Oil trustees, they received trust certificates. The Supreme Court decided this trust agreement violated the Sherman Act. The Court enjoined Standard Oil of New Jersey from voting the stocks or otherwise controlling the thirty-seven subsidiaries, and the individuals and corporations from entering into any similar combination to evade the decree. The Court enjoined the defendants from engaging in the petroleum business as long as the illegal combination existed.

Justice White, in his opinion in the *Standard Oil* case, described the Sherman

The Rule of Reason

Act as an act designed to promote the free marketplace and competition. Congress was concerned with enhancement of prices caused by undue limitations on the competitive process. However, Congress chose to outlaw only *unreasonable* restraints of trade or *unreasonable* attempts to monopolize. The facts of the *Standard Oil* case presented a situation so clearly in violation of the Sherman Act that the trust device used by Standard was found to be illegal without extensive analysis.

Many people viewed the *Standard Oil* case as an outrage. They argued the Supreme Court adopted this interpretation of the Sherman Act in order to favor big business. As noted in the monopoly section, the Court subsequently held the United States Steel Corporation not to be an illegal monopoly in violation of the Sherman Act. This also probably contributed to a feeling of uneasiness among the general population as to the Court's orientation.

Look back at the language of Section 1 of the Sherman Act, quoted on pages 384–385. Does the act refer to "unreasonable" restraints of trade? No. The Court *read the term unreasonable into the statute* though the word does not actually appear in the statute. The Court felt it necessary to interpret the language of the act in this fashion in order to make it workable.

The Supreme Court found support in the common law dealing with restraints of trade. The common law also followed the reasonableness standard, which arguably was incorporated into the Sherman Act by Congress's deliberate use of the common law term **restraint of trade.** Thus there was legislative intent and precedential support for the rule of reason announced in the *Standard Oil* case.

It should be borne in mind that courts have the final say as to the actual meaning of a statute. In the case of the Supreme Court, its interpretation of a statute is final and can only be overruled by the decision of Congress or a constitutional amendment. As Congress has never reversed the Court's interpretation on restraints of trade, we continue to apply what is referred to as the Rule of Reason in analyzing some restraints of trade under Section 1 of the Sherman Act.

Per Se Rule

In following the Rule of Reason, a court must examine whether a contract, combination, or conspiracy hinders or promotes the purposes of the Sherman Act. This analysis enmeshes the court in a complex web of facts. Antitrust cases tend to be long and very involved. Yet some types of restraints of trade clearly contravene the spirit of the Sherman Act. Why not adopt a rule that outlaws certain types of practices without an extended analysis of the impact of certain conduct on the economic system? This is exactly what the courts have done with respect to certain business practices. Rather than examining whether a particular act has a bad effect, the courts sometimes rule that if a given set of facts exist, the defendant's conduct violates the antitrust law. This is referred to as the **Per Se Rule,** as opposed to the Rule of Reason. When a situation presents a clear-cut violation of the Sherman Act, the courts use the Per Se Rule and find a violation without extended consideration of the effects of a defendant's conduct. Conversely, if the situation is one in which a violation is not evident, the court follows the Rule of Reason and examines the impact of particular behavior to determine if it constitutes an *unreasonable* restraint of trade.

The following case discusses the question of whether the National Collegiate Athletic Association violated the antitrust laws.

NCAA v. Bd. of Regents of Univ. of Oklahoma
United States Supreme Court
104 S.Ct. 2948 (1984)

The University of Oklahoma and the University of Georgia brought suit against the National Collegiate Athletic Association (NCAA). They contended the NCAA had violated Section 1 of the Sherman Act by adopting a plan for the televising of college football games for its member institutions for the 1982 through 1985 seasons. The plan limited the total number of televised intercollegiate football games. It also limited the number of games that any one college could televise. No member of the NCAA was permitted to make any sale of television rights except in accordance with the basic plan. The Court ruled against the NCAA, rejecting all NCAA justification in support of its conduct.

Justice Stevens

There can be no doubt that the challenged practices of the NCAA constitute a "restraint of trade" in the sense that they limit members' freedom to negotiate and enter into their own television contracts. In that sense, however, every contract is a restraint of trade, and as we have repeatedly recognized, the Sherman Act was intended to prohibit only unreasonable restraints of trade.

By participating in an association which prevents member institutions from competing against each other on the basis of price or kind of television rights that can be offered to broadcasters, the NCAA member institutions have created a horizontal restraint—an agreement among competitors on the way in which they will compete with one another. A restraint of this type has often been held to be unreasonable as a matter of law.

Horizontal price-fixing and output limitation are ordinarily condemned as a matter of law under an "illegal *per se*" approach because the probability that these practices are anticompetitive is so high; a *per se* rule is applied when the practice facially appears to be one that would always or almost always tend to restrict competition and decrease output. In such circumstances a restraint is presumed unreasonable without inquiry into the particular market context in which it is found. Nevertheless, we have decided that it would be inappropriate to apply a *per se* rule to this case.

What is critical is that this case involves an industry in which horizontal restraints on competition are essential if the product is to be available at all.

As Judge Bork has noted: "[S]ome activities can only be carried out jointly. Perhaps the leading example is league sports." What the NCAA and its member institutions market in this case is competition itself—contests between competing institutions. Of course, this would be completely ineffective if there were no rules on which the competitors agreed to create and define the competition to be marketed.

The NCAA plays a vital role in enabling college football to preserve its character, and as a result enables a product to be marketed which might otherwise be unavailable. In performing this role, its actions widen consumer choice—not only the choices available to sports fans but also those available to athletes—and hence can be viewed as procompetitive. Thus, despite the fact that this case involves restraints on the ability of member institutions to compete in terms of price and output, a fair evaluation of their competitive character requires consideration of the NCAA's justifications for the restraints.

Our analysis of this case under the Rule of Reason, of course, does not change the ultimate focus of our inquiry. Both *per se* rules and the Rule of Reason are employed to form a judgment about the competitive significance of the restraint. But whether the ultimate finding is the product of a presumption or actual market analysis, the essential inquiry remains the same—whether or not the challenged restraint enhances competition. Under the Sherman Act the criterion to be used in judging the validity of a restraint on trade is its impact on competition.

The anticompetitive consequences of this arrangement are apparent. Individual competitors lose their freedom to compete. Price is higher and output lower than they would otherwise be, and both are unresponsive to consumer preference. This latter point is perhaps the most significant, since Congress designed the Sherman Act as a 'consumer welfare prescription.' A restraint that has the effect of reducing the importance of consumer preference in setting price and output is not consistent with this fundamental goal of antitrust law. Restrictions on price and output are the paradigmatic examples of restraints of trade that the Sherman Act was intended to prohibit.

Petitioner argues, however, that its television plan can have no significant anticompetitive effect since the record indicates that it has no market power—no ability to alter the interaction of supply and demand in the market. We must reject this argument for two reasons, one legal, one factual.

As a matter of law, the absence of proof of market power does not justify a naked restriction on price or output. To the contrary, when there is an agreement not to compete in terms of price or output, no elaborate industry analysis is required to demonstrate the anticompetitive character of such an agreement.

Petitioner does not quarrel with the District Court's finding that price and output are not responsive to demand. Thus the plan is inconsistent with the Sherman Act's command that price and supply be responsive to consumer preference. We have never required proof of market power in such a case. This naked restraint on price and output requires some competitive justification even in the absence of a detailed market analysis. As a factual matter, it is evident that petitioner does possess market power.

Thus, the NCAA television plan on its face constitutes a restraint upon the operation of a free market, and the findings of the District Court establish that it has operated to raise price and reduce output. Under the Rule of Reason, these hallmarks of anticompetitive behavior place upon petitioner a heavy burden of establishing an affirmative defense which competitively justifies this apparent deviation from the operations of a free market.

The NCAA plays a critical role in the maintenance of a revered tradition of amateurism in college sports. There can be no question but that it needs ample latitude to play that role, or that the preservation of the student-athlete in higher education adds richness and diversity to intercollegiate athletics and is entirely consistent with the goals of the Sherman Act. But consistent with the Sherman Act, the role of the NCAA must be to *preserve* a tradition that might otherwise die; rules that restrict output are hardly consistent with this role. Today we hold only that the record supports the District Court's conclusion that by curtailing output and blunting the ability of member institutions to respond to consumer preference, the NCAA has restricted rather than enhanced the place of intercollegiate athletics in the Nation's life. Accordingly, the judgment of the Court of Appeals is affirmed.

Subsidiaries

In *Copperweld Corporation* v. *Independence Tube Corporation*, 104 S.Ct. 2731 (1984), the United States Supreme Court ruled that a corporation and its *wholly owned* subsidiary are incapable of conspiring with each other for the purposes of violating Section 1 of the Sherman Act because they have a complete unity of interest. It is irrelevant whether the subsidiary is an unincorporated division or a wholly owned subsidiary. Congress *exempted* unilateral conduct from Section 1 of the antitrust law.

This brings us to the issue of price fixing. Price fixing is one of those areas of conduct treated by the courts as a per se violation of Section 1 of the Sherman Act. No extended analysis of the effect of the defendant's activities is necessary. The proof that a defendant entered into a contract, combination, or conspiracy to fix prices is sufficient to find him or her in violation of the Sherman Act.

Price Fixing

In *United States* v. *Trenton Potteries* (1927), the Supreme Court explained why it regarded price-fixing agreements as so offensive to the purposes of the Sherman Act. Trenton Potteries manufactured vitreous pottery. It fixed prices and limited the sale of its pottery to specific companies. Justice Stone, speaking for the majority, wrote the following concerning price-fixing agreements:

> The aim and result of every price fixing agreement, if effective, is the elimination of one form of competition. . . . The reasonable price fixed today may through economic or business changes become the unreasonable price of tomorrow. Once established, it may be maintained unchanged because of the absence of competition secured by the agreement. . . . Agreements which create such potential power may well be held to be in themselves unreasonable unlawful restraints, without necessity of minute inquiry whether a particular price is reasonable or unreasonable.

Trenton Potteries argued that it fixed only *reasonable* prices. The Court rejected the reasonable price defense in this case. This means that even a company that sets a price for its product at the same level that competition would have produced violates Section 1, if it enters into a contract, combination, or conspiracy with any other firm or person to fix prices at this level. The contracts in this case were between Trenton Potteries and the people to whom Trenton sold its products.

The question remained, however, whether price fixing was illegal per se if the persons or companies that set the prices *lacked* the *market power* actually to fix prices. The Supreme Court answered this question definitively in the following case.

United States v. Socony-Vacuum Oil Co.
United States Supreme Court
310 U.S. 150 (1940)

At the time of this suit, the major oil refiners were able to respond to changes in demand by increasing or decreasing their inventories, or production, or price. The major refiners thought they were being hurt by the independent refiners who lacked storage capacity for their gasoline. Because of this, the independents were forced to offer their gasoline on the spot market for immediate delivery to dealers. This caused the price of gasoline to vary greatly.

To eliminate the price fluctuations, the major producers entered into a program of bidding for and buying gas on the spot market that they were capable of storing. The major producers entered into this arrangement in order to stabilize the price of gasoline. There was no actual formal contractual commitment to purchase the gasoline, either between the majors or between the majors and the independent refiners. It was more of a gentlemen's agreement, or understanding. The prices did rise and stabilize in the markets in which the parties were operating during 1935 and 1936. The government charged the major oil companies had violated Section 1 of the Sherman Act. The Supreme Court agreed.

Justice Douglas

There was abundant evidence that the combination had the purpose to raise prices. And likewise, there was ample evidence that the buying programs at least contributed to the price rise and the stability of the spot markets, and to increases in the price of gasoline sold in the Mid-Western area during the indictment period. That other factors also may have contributed to that rise and stability of the markets is immaterial. Proof that there was a conspiracy, that its purpose was to raise prices, and that it caused or contributed to a price rise is proof of the actual consummation or execution of a conspiracy under Section 1 of the Sherman Act.

The fact that sales on the spot markets were still governed by some competition is of no consequence. For it is indisputable that that competition was restricted through the removal by respondents of a part of the supply which but for the buying programs would have been a factor in determining the going prices on those markets.

Any combination which tampers with price structures is engaged in an unlawful activity. Even though the members of the price-fixing group were in no position to control the market, to the extent that they raised, lowered, or stabilized prices they would be directly interfering with the free play of market forces. The Act places all such schemes beyond the pale and protects that vital part of our economy against any degree of interference. Congress has not left with us the determination of whether or not particular price-fixing schemes are wise or unwise, healthy or destructive. It has not permitted the age-old cry of ruinous competition and competitive evils to be a defense to price-fixing conspiracies. It has no more allowed genuine or fancied competitive abuses as a legal justification for such schemes than it has the good intentions of the members of the combination.

Under the Sherman Act a combination formed for the purpose and with the effect of raising, depressing, fixing, pegging, or stabilizing the price of a commodity in interstate or foreign commerce is illegal per se. Where the machinery for price-fixing is an agreement on the prices to be charged or paid for the commodity in the interstate or foreign channels of trade, the power to fix prices exists if the combination has control of a substantial part of the commerce in that commodity. Where the means for price-fixing are purchases or sales of the commodity in a market operation or, as here, purchases of a part of the supply of the commodity for the purpose of keeping it from having a depressive effect on the markets, such power may be found to exist though the combination does not control a substantial part of the commodity. In such a case that power may be established if as a result of market conditions, the resources available to the combinations, the timing and the strategic placement of orders and the like, effective means are at hand to accomplish the desired objective. But there may be effective influence over the market though the group in question does not control it. Price-fixing agreements may have utility to members of the group though the power possessed or exerted falls far short of domination and control. Monopoly power is not the only power which the Act strikes down, as we have said. Proof that a combination was formed for the purpose of fixing prices and that it caused them to be fixed or contributed to that result is proof of the completion of a price-fixing conspiracy under Section 1 of the Act. The indictment in this case charged that this combination had that purpose and effect. And there was abundant evidence to support it. Hence the existence of power on the part of members of the combination to fix prices was but a conclusion from the finding that the buying programs caused or contributed to the rise and stability of prices.

Accordingly we conclude that the Circuit Court of Appeals erred in reversing the judgments on this ground. A fortiori the position taken by respondents in their cross petition that they were entitled to direct verdicts of acquittal is untenable.

Socony-Vacuum Oil **Case.** The *Socony* case illustrates several points. Whether the price established through a contract, combination, or conspiracy is reasonable is irrelevant. The Court also rejected the argument that the manufacturers needed to set prices in order to avoid the ruinous competition created by sellers on the spot market. Ruinous competition is *not* a defense to a price-setting scheme. The Court stated: "Under the Sherman Act a combination formed for the purpose and with the effect of raising, depressing, fixing, pegging or stabilizing the price of a commodity in interstate commerce is illegal per se." The Court also implied that even if the defendants lacked the power to influence prices, that is, even if they lacked market power to influence the price of oil, they violated the Sherman Act simply by entering into such an agreement to fix prices.

Why was the Court so hard on price fixers? After all, if the price that is fixed is the price that would have prevailed in a fully competitive market, how is the public interest prejudiced? The Court answered this in *Trenton Potteries.* The reasonable price fixed today could become an unreasonable price tomorrow. It would place an unreasonable burden on the courts to recognize the reasonable price defense. The government would be forced to monitor prices and relitigate a case if it appeared the price fixers changed their price from a reasonable price to an unreasonable price. A Per Se Rule minimizes the time the courts must spend on a price-fixing scheme. Furthermore, it provides a clear-cut rule for people in business to follow. Anyone who fixes the price of his or her product does so at the risk of being prosecuted for a violation of the antitrust laws. As we noted in Chapter 13, such a violation may lead to substantial civil penalties and even criminal sanctions.

Maximum Prices. What if, rather than agreeing upon a given price, several manufacturers enter into an agreement in which they agree to charge buyers no more than a certain price—a maximum price. Setting a maximum price, as well as any other tampering with the price system of the free market, violates the antitrust laws.

Rather than agreeing to require their purchasers to resell a commodity at a maximum price, manufacturers may agree simply to charge their customers a minimum price. Agreements among manufacturers to charge all customers no less than a stated price also violates the Sherman Act.

We now know that setting a minimum or a maximum price, stabilizing prices, or fixing prices in any way all violate the Sherman Act.

When faced with a Section 1 case, the Court first asks if the parties entered into an agreement. If so, should the agreement be covered by a Per Se Rule? Activities that clearly violate Section 1, such as price fixing, fall under a per se form of analysis.

Analysis of Section 1 Cases

The government, in a price-fixing case, need only prove an agreement to fix prices between two or more parties. It need not prove any harmful effects.

If the Court analyzes a case under the Rule of Reason, it looks for harmful effects. It then examines the legitimate beneficial effects of the agreement—that is, those which are procompetitive. In determining the effects, courts often look at the *purposes* of the defendants as a guide to interpreting effects. This is often a very critical move by the courts in their application of the Rule of Reason approach. (The Court does not examine broader social policy arguments other than the furtherance of competition and efficiency.) Finally, the Court examines whether *less restrictive alternatives* exist for achieving the goals the defendants wish to achieve. If they are able to achieve the same results in another way, which does not injure competition, the Court likely will rule against the defendants.

Ruinous Competition. What if a company entered into a price-fixing agreement with its competitors in order to stay in business? Suppose competition within the industry reached such a fever pitch that every company was near bankruptcy. Should the competitors be allowed to fix prices in order to stay in business, in light of the otherwise ruthless competition within the industry?

In *Appalachian Coal, Inc.* v. *United States* (1933), the Court examined the social costs of business failure. The coal industry was in disarray. In order to prevent a collapse of the companies in the coal industry, the coal companies formed a cooperative, Appalachian Coal, Inc., to market their coal. The cooperative charged a single price for its coal. While these companies produced only a small percentage of United States coal, the cooperative did tend to stabilize the price of coal in this geographical area. Not all mines in the area belonged to the cooperative. Was this a violation of the Sherman Act? The Supreme Court ruled it was not! The Court noted that the cooperative was formed to combat evils inherent in the coal industry. The cooperative stabilized prices, but to the Court this was insufficient to make out an antitrust violation.

Does the *Appalachian Coal* case make any sense in light of the subsequent decision in 1940 in *Socony?* The Court in *Socony* found any contract, combination, or conspiracy to fix prices violated the Sherman Act, whether the conspirators had market power to influence prices or not. This suggests the *Appalachian Coal* decision no longer is valid. However, the case illustrates an important point. The Supreme Court in most cases has been unresponsive to fear of ruinous competition. Normally, courts reject social arguments—such as the argument that if competition is not stopped in a given industry, it will destroy all companies within that industry. The Supreme Court probably accepted this argument in 1933 because the United States was in the Great Depression. This caused the Court to be more responsive to arguments that excessive competition was an evil from which companies had a right to protect themselves.

In examining antitrust or any part of the law, keep in mind the *historical forces at work* at the time a court renders a decision or Congress passes an act. All institutions are influenced to some degree by events in society. So it is in the case of *Appalachian Coal*. The Court reflected the basic distrust of competition evident in the New Deal legislation. After the country passed through the Great Depression, the Court reaffirmed its original position that any tampering with prices violates the Sherman Act.

But for a few years, the Court listened to and accepted social arguments that put forth goals other than competition as legitimate goals of the antitrust laws. Today, the Court no longer accepts such social arguments as a legitimate justification for price fixing.

RESALE PRICE MAINTENANCE

Suppose a single manufacturer and a retail seller or a distributor agree to set the price at which a commodity may be resold. An arrangement like this between suppliers and customers is commonly referred to as a **resale price maintenance** scheme. Resale price maintenance schemes often run afoul of Section 1 of the Sherman Act. They are a form of *vertical* price fixing (between a manufacturer and a distributor or a retailer). The problem with such an arrangement is that it prevents competition between retailers. If a television manufacturer required all television sets be sold at no more than a certain price, every retailer would be forced to sell the televisions at a price somewhere between the wholesale price and the maximum price. This would lead, possibly, to very little competition at the retail level. Furthermore, a maximum price might result in a price below that level which would occur in the presence of a competitive retail market. In this situation, the retailer's earnings would be lower than he or she would achieve in the absence of such an agreement. Alternatively, the price set by the manufacturer might be too high.

In an early resale price maintenance case, *Dr. Miles Medical Co.* v. *John D. Park & Sons Co.* (1911), the Supreme Court ruled that when a manufacturer parts with title to his property, he may not require the person or company with whom he dealt to resell the product at a particular price. In that case, a manufacturer of patent medicines entered into an agreement with its dealers on the minimum price at which the patent medicine could be resold. The Court acknowledged that such a price-fixing scheme helped increase the profits of dealers handling this patent medicine and seemed to imply there may also be some advantage to Dr. Miles as well. Without determining what that advantage might be, the Court held that a manufacturer may not enter into an agreement with its dealers that restrains trade in this fashion. A resale price maintenance scheme of this nature is illegal per se.

In two subsequent cases, the Court refused to invalidate restrictions on the price at which dealers could resell goods. In *United States* v. *General Electric Company* (1926), the Court ruled in favor of General Electric. General Electric held a patent on electric lamps and used agents to resell its products to consumers. Unlike the *Dr. Miles* case, in this case General Electric held a patent on its products and used agents to distribute the products. The Court held that sales through this type of agency relationship were *not* violations of the antitrust laws. In 1964, the Supreme Court decided a case very similar to *General Electric—Simpson* v. *Union Oil Co.* The plaintiff, Simpson, leased a retail gasoline station owned by Union Oil. Simpson signed a consignment agreement under which *Union* set the price at which he could resell the gasoline. He sold below this price and Union terminated his lease. Simpson asserted this agreement violated the Sherman Act. Without overruling *General Electric*, the Court ruled against Union Oil. The Court held that a resale price maintenance agreement utilizing a coercive consignment agreement violates the antitrust laws.

These cases seem to create a set of rules whereby certain agreements are per se illegal, as those in the *Dr. Miles* case. Agreements that set resale prices and use agents and patented products arguably are legal under the *General Electric* decision. In the middle, probably analyzed under the Rule of Reason, are such agreements as the one discussed in the *Simpson* case. One might argue, however, that the decision in *Simpson* overrules *General Electric*. As to whether a firm may sell to another company (to a jobber or wholesaler, for example) and control the resale price of its product, it may still be possible to enter into such an arrangement if the other firm is an agent of the manufacturer. The *Simpson* case stressed the comprehensiveness of the arrangement and the fact that the consignment agents appeared to be independent businesspersons. In the absence of these factors, the *Simpson* rule might not apply.

The *Simpson* case has been criticized. Justice Stewart wrote a dissent in that case in which he argues that *Simpson* is virtually indistinguishable from *General Electric*.

In *Monsanto Co.* v. *Spray-Rite Service Co.* 104 S.Ct. 1464 (1984), the United States Supreme Court upheld the *Dr. Miles* case. It ruled that it is illegal per se to engage in *concerted* activities to set prices. Thus, in distributor cases, it is illegal per se to engage in a resale price maintenance scheme with distributors.

Whether a case involves an agreement between two manufacturers and their customers, or an agreement between a supplier and a customer, resale price maintenance agreements that fix the price at which the buyer may resell its products are a per se violation of Section 1 of the Sherman Act.

In any event, a firm is still free to integrate forward and undertake its own distribution of its products. In such a case, as the firm would not be forcing independent businessmen to resell its products at a particular price, the rule in *Simpson* would not apply.

The following case is a recent decision of the Supreme Court on retail price maintenance.

California Retail Liquor Dealers Association v. Midcal Aluminum, Inc.

United States Supreme Court
100 S. Ct. 937 (1980)

In this case, Midcal Aluminum, the plaintiff-respondent, a wine distributor, challenged California's wine-pricing scheme. The state required all wine producers and wholesalers to file with the state fair trade contracts or price schedules. If a wholesaler sold below these prices, he could be fined or his license could be suspended or revoked. Midcal sold below these prices and the state challenged its prices. Midcal claimed this was an illegal resale price maintenance scheme in violation of Section 1 of the Sherman Act. The California Court of Appeals agreed, and the Supreme Court affirmed the ruling for Midcal.

Portions of its opinion dealing with the Twenty-first Amendment to the Constitution have been deleted. The Court noted that the amendment gives the states substantial discretion to establish liquor regulations. However, the federal government also has the power to regulate in this area, and therefore the Sherman Act applies in spite of the Twenty-first Amendment.

Justice Powell

Under Section 24866(b) of the California Business and Professions Code, all wine producers, wholesalers, and rectifiers must file with the State fair trade contracts or price schedules. If a wine producer has not set prices through a fair trade contract, wholesalers must post a resale price schedule for that producer's brands. No state-licensed wine merchant may sell wine to a retailer at other than the price set "either in an effective price schedule or in an effective fair trade contract. . . ."

The State is divided into three trading areas for administration of the wine pricing program. A single fair trade contract or schedule for each brand sets the terms for all wholesale transactions in that brand within a given trading area. Similarly, state regulations provide that the wine prices posted by a single wholesaler within a trading area bind all wholesalers in that area. A licensee selling below the established prices faces fines, license suspension, or outright license revocation. The State has no direct control over wine prices, and it does not review the reasonableness of the prices set by wine dealers.

The threshold question is whether California's plan for wine pricing violates the Sherman Act. This Court has ruled consistently that resale price maintenance illegally restrains trade. In *Dr. Miles Medical Co. v. Park & Sons Co.* (1911), the Court observed that such arrangements are "designed to maintain prices . . . and to prevent competition among those who trade in [competing goods]." For many years, however, the Miller-Tydings Act of 1937 permitted the States to authorize resale price maintenance. The goal of that statute was to allow the States to protect small retail establishments that Congress thought might otherwise be driven from the marketplace by large-volume discounters. But in 1975 that congressional permis-

sion was rescinded. The Consumer Goods pricing Act of 1975 repealed the Miller-Tydings Act and related legislations. Consequently, the Sherman Act's ban on resale price maintenance now applies to fair trade contracts unless an industry or program enjoys a special antitrust immunity.

California's system for wine pricing plainly constitutes resale price maintenance in violation of the Sherman Act. The wine producer holds the power to prevent price competition by dictating the prices charged by wholesalers. As Mr. Justice Hughes pointed out in *Dr. Miles,* such vertical control destroys horizontal competition as effectively as if wholesalers "formed a combination and endeavored to establish the same restrictions . . . by agreement with each other."

We must consider whether the State's involvement in the price-setting program is sufficient to establish antitrust immunity under *Parker v. Brown* (1943).

Our decisions establish two standards for antitrust immunity under *Parker v. Brown*. First, the challenged restraint must be "one clearly articulated and affirmatively expressed as state policy"; second, the policy must be "actively supervised" by the State itself. *City of Lafayette v. Louisiana Power & Light Co.* (1978). The California system for wine pricing satisfies the first standard. The legislative policy is forthrightly stated and clear in its purpose to permit resale price maintenance. The program, however, does not meet the second requirement for *Parker* immunity. The State simply authorizes price-setting and enforces the prices established by private parties. The State neither establishes prices nor reviews the reasonableness of the price schedules; nor does it regulate the terms of fair trade contracts. The State does not monitor market conditions or engage in any "pointed reexamination" of the program. The national policy in favor of competition cannot be thwarted by casting such a gauzy clock of state involvement over what is essentially a private price fixing arrangement. As *Parker* teaches, "a state does not give immunity to those who violate the Sherman Act by authorizing them to violate it, or by declaring that their action is lawful. . . ."

Why would a company wish to engage in a program to fix the price at which its product is resold? Normally, one would assume that a manufacturer would want more competition at the retail level. With more competition at the retail level, the manufacturer would sell more of its product. If the manufacturer requires its dealers to sell at a minimum price, this may depress its retail sales. There are, however, several reasons a manufacturer might attempt to set retail prices: (1) the manufacturer may wish to protect its dealers from price cutters; (2) the manufacturer may wish to cultivate a prestige image for its product by selling the product at a high price; (3) retailers may wish to have the manufacturer set a high resale price in order to increase their profits (a dealer cartel); (4) price setting may encourage retailers to increase their promotional expenses (dealer services); or (5) resale price maintenance programs may help a manufacturer who has entered into a price-fixing agreement with other manufacturers.

If a price cutter handles a company's products, many consumers will purchase the product from the discounter. Local retailers may then drop the company's product from their shelves, as they need a sufficient volume of sales in order to profitably stock a particular line of products.

Given the right product—that is, one which consumers will pay a premium price for over other similar products—retailers will earn larger profits if the manufacturer sets a minimum price for its product. If all manufacturers set a minimum price for their products, retailers will earn large profits.

Another rationale for minimum prices at the retail level is to enhance a company's image. If its perfume sells for fifty dollars an ounce at a prestige store, few manufacturers wish to see that product sold at a discounter for five dollars an ounce.

A manufacturer might engage in setting the resale price of its products if all the manufacturers in the industry have entered into an illegal price-fixing agreement. If four manufacturers sold all the electric irons in the United States, they could enter into an agreement to sell all their irons at a certain price to distributors or retailers. But what if one of the parties to a price-fixing scheme decided not to abide by the scheme? Suppose this firm sells to buyers at a price lower than that at which the other manufacturers agreed to sell to their customers. If there were a number of different prices charged by retailers, then it would be more difficult to determine that one of the manufacturers was failing to comply with the unlawful agreement to fix prices. If retailers cut their prices, it would be unclear whether a manufacturer had cut its price to the retailers, or the retailers had cut prices on their own. A retail price maintenance agreement makes it clear that if Company X's retailers cut their prices, Company X must have cut its prices to its retailers. The members of the group that agreed to fix prices would then know they must take some action to force Company X to stop cutting its price to the retailers.

The dealer cartel is also often cited as a reason for the manufacturer's setting a resale price. The dealers might ask the manufacturer to act as their agent in administering the cartel by fixing a uniform resale price. Of course, dealers could enter into such an agreement on their own, but the agreement can be more easily enforced if the manufacturer agrees to it.

One argument that has been vigorously asserted as a justification for a price-fixing scheme is the dealer service theory. If a price is set at a given level, this may encourage retailers to compete by providing more services to purchasers. Many products require substantial retailer service. For example, an automobile manufacturer may wish for its dealerships to give customers a great deal of presale attention. If the price were fixed, the dealers might compete by giving customers more services (often called point-of-sale services).

As none of these reasons for price maintenance schemes strikes the courts as fair, the courts normally invalidate retail price-fixing agreements.

While today these agreements often violate the Sherman Act, at one point Congress permitted such retail price setting by manufacturers. The McGuire Act and the Miller-Tydings amendment to the Sherman Act allowed states to adopt fair trade acts. These acts granted an exemption to the Sherman Act if a state passed a fair trade law. In a state with such a law, manufacturers could require retailers to resell a product at a certain minimum price. The Consumer Goods Pricing Act of 1975 repealed the states' ability to pass fair trade laws.

Colgate Doctrine

One last device should be mentioned before leaving the resale price maintenance area. It is possible for a company to attempt to maintain retail prices by announcing it will not deal with customers who resell the product at a price different from that set by the manufacturer. The Supreme Court announced this rule in *United States v. Colgate Co.* (1919). The *Colgate* doctrine permits a unilateral announcement by a manufacturer that it will not deal with customers who fail to abide by the price set by the manufacturer. The manufacturer may terminate dealers who sell above the stated price.

The Court in *Colgate* basically recognized the right of a company to exercise its own independent judgment as to whom it would deal with—assuming the company has no purpose to create or maintain a monopoly. *Colgate* has been criticized because the Court really did not offer a sound economic argument for adopting such a rule. The *Colgate* doctrine creates an exception to the resale price rule adopted by the Court for no apparent economic reason.

The *Colgate* doctrine has been greatly limited by other decisions, but it remains a valid doctrine today. In *United States v. Parke, Davis & Co.* (1960), the Court held that a manufacturer may not threaten to cut off wholesalers who sell to retailers selling below the price specified by the manufacturer. The effect of the *Parke, Davis* case is that a manufacturer may avail itself of the *Colgate* doctrine only when it is selling directly to retailers. Even then, of course, the manufacturer may only announce it will not sell to retailers who sell below a certain price, and terminate retailers who sell below the stated price.

In *Monsanto Co. v. Spray-Rite Service Co.*, the Supreme Court reaffirmed the validity of the *Colgate* doctrine. So long as a manufacturer acts independently when it announces its resale prices and its refusal to deal with those who fail to comply, it acts lawfully.

Generally, a company can safely warn retailers in advance of a sale that it will not deal with anyone who undercuts its recommended prices. But any action taken by a company to enforce that warning—threatening retailers, for example—can run afoul of the law. This doctrine is not precisely clear. A company must act with *extreme* caution when making such statements.

VERTICAL NONPRICE RESTRAINTS

While it is quite clear that the United States Supreme Court has adopted a per se condemnation of vertical price fixing, that is not the case with respect to vertical nonprice restraints. In *Continental T.V., Inc.* v. *GTE Sylvania, Inc.* the United States Supreme Court ruled that vertical nonprice restraints are to be judged under the rule of reason standard.

There are many agreements that businesses can enter into that do not involve an agreement to fix the price of goods. For example, a company might wish that retailers it sells its goods to only sell those goods in a certain geographic area. There are a variety of reasons that a manufacturer might want a retailer to enter into such an agreement. For example, a manufacturer might be concerned that purchasers need service after a sale. In order to encourage a retailer to give good service to its customers, the manufacturer might want to give the retailer the exclusive right to sell its products in a particular city.

The important thing to keep in mind with respect to such restraints is that they are judged under the Rule of Reason rather than the Per Se Rule.

GROUP BOYCOTTS

A business that does not intend to create or maintain a monopoly may choose the parties with whom it deals. While a simple unilateral refusal to deal with another business does not violate the antitrust laws, a business must take care not to act in concert with other businesses when it decides not to deal with a given company.

A good example of unlawful concerted activity would be if a group of wholesalers asked retailers not to buy from wholesaler X, and threatened the retailers that if they bought from wholesaler X, the other wholesalers would stop selling to them. Such an action would constitute a classic boycott and is unlawful per se. Another example would be if a group of retailers asked some manufacturers not to sell to a retailer—with the sole desire of limiting competition at the retail level. Such a conspiracy would be illegal per se.

In order to be covered by this Per Se Rule, the activity in question must fit within the definition of a boycott. Concerted activity in which the parties agree not to deal with a company or companies or demand that others not deal with a company or companies will be treated as a classic boycott when the purpose of the conspirators is to deprive a competitor of a needed resource and make it harder for the competitor to compete. Such concerted activity constitutes a per se violation of the Sherman Act. The courts regard such activity as inherently harmful to competition.

Even the United States Supreme Court has acknowledged that there is considerable confusion about the operation of the Per Se Rule against group boycotts. The Court has applied a Per Se Rule when a firm (or firms) either directly denies or persuades or coerces suppliers or customers to deny relationships the competitors need to survive. The boycott often cuts off access to a supply facility or market necessary to enable the boycotted firm to compete, and frequently the boycotting firm possesses a dominant position in the relevant market. Furthermore, the activities of the boycotting firm or firms do not enhance overall efficiency and make markets more competitive.

Fashion Originators' Guild of America v. *Federal Trade Commission* is a classic boycott case. Members of the guild agreed, in order to drive certain manufacturers out of business, to refuse to deal with retailers who stocked the boycotted manufacturers' products. The guild agreed to this course of action because the boycotted manufacturers were copying original dress designs and selling them at a lower price. These designs could not be copyrighted or patented. The guild members controlled thirty-eight percent of all women's garment wholesaling and sixty percent of the wholesaling of all high-priced garments. *Fashion Originators' Guild* thus involved a classic boycott where competitors were being driven out of the market. The Supreme Court ruled that this combination violated the Sherman and Clayton Acts.

A variety of other situations may fall within the boycott definition, but these arrangements always involve an agreement not to deal with someone when the purpose of the conspirators is to deprive a competitor of a needed resource and make it harder for the competitor to compete.

Absent a showing that the boycotting firm or firms possessed market power or unique access to a business element necessary for effective competition, the courts should apply a Rule of Reason analysis and not the Per Se Rule. Of course, to be safe, a business would be wise not to engage in any boycott, thus avoiding the possibility of being prosecuted for violating the antitrust laws.

TYING CONTRACTS

A seller must be careful when it refuses to deal with another business, and it must also exercise caution if it asks the buyer to purchase certain goods in addition to those the buyer wants.

It may violate the antitrust laws if the seller of a product the buyer wants (the tying product) requires the buyer, as a condition of purchasing the tying product, to also purchase another product (the tied product). Suppose the lessor of a computer (the tying product) required persons leasing the seller's computer to use only punch cards (the tied product) made and sold by the seller. The Supreme Court ruled against International Business Machines Corporation in just such a case. The Court stated that such an agreement violated the antitrust laws.

Tying agreements are outlawed by Section 3 of the Clayton Act, which states:

> It shall be unlawful for any person engaged in commerce, in the course of such commerce, to lease or make a sale of contract for sale of goods, wares, merchandise, machinery, supplies, or other commodities, whether patented or unpatented, for use, consumption, or resale within the U.S. . . . on the condition, agreement, or understanding that the lessee or purchaser thereof shall not use or deal in the goods . . . of a competitor or competitors of the . . . seller, where the effect of such lease, sale, or contract for sale or such condition, agreement, or understanding may be to substantially lessen competition or tend to create a monopoly in any line of commerce.

It should be noted that tying agreements may also violate Section 1 of the Sherman Act. Section 3 of the Clayton Act applies only to the sale or lease of a commodity on the condition that the lessee or purchaser not use or deal in commodities of seller's or lessor's competitors. If a tying arrangement deals with the sale of services, suit must be brought on the basis of Section 1 of the Sherman Act.

In many cases, the Court has indicated that a given tying agreement is per se unlawful under one or both of these acts. However, perhaps tying agreements should be viewed as governed by a complex Per Se Rule.

Certainly not every sale is illegal in which the seller conditions the sale of a product on the purchase of some other product. If a tailor requires the purchaser of a suit to also buy a vest with a suit, the tailor has not violated the antitrust laws.

The following elements would seem necessary for a plaintiff to establish an unlawful tying agreement: (1) that the defendant possess economic power over the tying product; and (2) that a not unsubstantial amount of commerce in the tied product is involved. Even if both these conditions have been met, the defendant probably has a good defense if it can show that the purpose of the tie-in is to protect the goodwill of the tying product.

In some cases, such as when the seller has a patent or copyright, the tying product has been regarded as sufficiently unique to give rise to a presumption of economic power.

Purpose of Tying

Some economists have suggested that one of the purposes of a tie-in is often to facilitate price discrimination.

What a seller might do is to tie the sale of a product that the buyer wants (the tying product) to a product the buyer does not necessarily want (the tied product). Why would a seller do this? Probably the seller intends to charge a higher-than-market price for the tied product. If the seller intends to sell a great deal of the tied product to the buyer, this may be a very profitable arrangement for the seller. Furthermore, it may enable the seller to discriminate in price between different buyers.

An excellent example of this is the *International Salt* case. International Salt leased certain machines on which it held a patent (the tying product) to customers, but required the lessees to purchase only International Salt (the tied product) as a condition of receiving the machines. The Supreme Court held that this arrangement violated Section 3 of the Clayton Act because International Salt controlled a major portion of the market for salt and was attempting to monopolize the market.

Consider the effect of such an arrangement. If International Salt charged the same price to three customers for a machine, it could in effect discriminate in price between them because the buyers would not use the same amount of salt. Suppose A intended to use one thousand pounds of salt, B intended to use two thousand pounds of salt, and C intended to use three thousand pounds of salt. If International Salt charged a higher-than-market price for the salt it sold to A, B, and C, they would in effect be paying different prices for the machine. Suppose the price for salt is ten cents per pound regularly, but International Salt charges its customers fifteen cents per pound. At the end of the year, A will have paid $150 for salt it could have purchased for $100, B will have paid $300 for salt it could have purchased for $200, and C will have paid $450 for salt it could have purchased for $300. In effect, A has paid $50 more for the salt than it could have been purchased for on the open market, B has paid $100 more, and C has paid $150 more.

The next section of the book deals with another important antitrust problem—the power of the FTC to regulate businesses.

SECTION 5 OF THE FEDERAL TRADE COMMISSION ACT

Many actions violate the spirit of the antitrust laws but for some technical reason are beyond the reach of the government under the Sherman or Clayton Acts. Business practices beyond the reach of the Sherman Act may sometimes be struck down by the FTC acting pursuant to Section 5 of the Federal Trade Commission Act. The FTC possesses power to declare invalid trade practices that conflict with the basic policies of the Sherman and Clayton Acts even though such practices may not actually violate these laws.

The Federal Trade Commission Act and the Clayton Act were passed by Congress in 1914 largely in response to a public outcry for more effective control over big business. One important group that supported the creation of the FTC was those people who feared the effect of big business on competition. They favored more competition. President Wilson put his support behind the strengthening of the law in order to promote competition.

To some extent, the Court's lax enforcement of the Sherman Act served as an impetus for this new legislation. In particular, the Supreme Court's decision in 1911 in the *Standard Oil* case, in which it announced the Rule of Reason, created a great demand for new legislation.

Congress, in Section 5 of the Federal Trade Commission Act, outlawed "unfair methods of competition." Many members of Congress believed that a monopoly could be achieved only through unfair competition and that the nation needed an agency designed to check such unfair practices by business.

Congress thought it would be impossible to define every unfair practice. So, rather than defining "unfair methods of competition," Congress left it up to the FTC to determine what constituted unfairness on a case-by-case basis.

In 1938, Congress passed the Wheeler-Lea amendment to the Federal Trade Commission Act. This added the language "unfair or deceptive acts or practices in commerce." Section 5 of the Federal Trade Commission Act, as amended, reads "unfair methods of competition in or affecting commerce, and unfair or deceptive acts or practices in or affecting commerce, are declared unlawful." The goal of Congress in adding this language was to make it clear that it wished to protect not only competition, but also competitors.

As indicated earlier, the FTC may reach conduct that violates the spirit of the Sherman or Clayton Acts, and even conduct that is simply unfair. Thus, the reach of Section 5 is much greater than that of the Sherman or Clayton Acts, and Section 5 may be used by the FTC to reach unfair trade practices in general.

Only the Federal Trade Commission has the power to enforce Section 5. When it believes a company has done something improper, the FTC tries to settle its investigations by entering into a consent order with the company. In such a case, the company agrees not to engage in the designated behavior in the future. The company need not admit to a violation of the law.

If the company refuses to agree not to engage in certain behavior, the FTC conducts a hearing before an administrative law judge. The decision of the administrative law judge may be reviewed by the Federal Trade Commission, and a final order of the FTC may be reviewed by the federal courts.

The FTC may issue "cease and desist" orders. These operate like an injunction issued by a court and prevent further action of the type designated in the order. If a company violates an FTC order, unless it seeks judicial review, a substantial fine may be imposed on the company for each day it violates the order.

The FTC also possesses the power to issue rules, called Trade Regulation Rules, which apply to all companies in an industry. A company that violates such a rule may be fined.

In the late 1970s, substantial efforts to curtail the activities of the FTC were exerted in Congress. Many persons believed the FTC had gone too far in its attempt to regulate business. Some industries were successful in obtaining limitations in the appropriations act that prohibited FTC expenditures to investigate given businesses. This probably reflects a changing sentiment in the nation as to consumer protection. But, in general, the Federal Trade Commission Act has not been altered, although some spending limitations have been imposed.

As noted earlier, the Federal Trade Commission possesses the power under Section 5 of the Federal Trade Commission Act to find a given activity an unfair trade practice even though the activity in question does not violate the Sherman or Clayton Acts. The following case illustrates the power of the FTC when it is acting pursuant to Section 5.

Federal Trade Commission v. Brown Shoe Company

United States Supreme Court
384 U.S. 316 (1966)

The Federal Trade Commission charged that Brown Shoe had violated Section 5 of the Federal Trade Commission Act, which empowers and directs the FTC "to prevent persons, partnerships and corporations . . . from using unfair methods of competition in commerce and unfair or deceptive acts or practices in commerce."

Brown, a shoe manufacturer, entered into a contract with some of its retail stores. In exchange for signing a contract that restricted their purchase of shoes for resale to the Brown lines, and that prohibited them from purchasing, stocking, or reselling shoes manufactured by competitors of Brown, Brown would agree to give certain special treatment. A number of retail customers entered into this agreement.

The FTC concluded the contract program was an unfair method of competition within the meaning of Section 5 and ordered Brown to cease and desist from its use. The court of appeals set aside the FTC's order. The Supreme Court reversed.

Justice Black

The question we have for decision is whether the Federal Trade Commission can declare it to be an unfair practice for Brown, the second largest manufacturer of shoes in the Nation, to pay a valuable consideration to hundreds of retail shoe purchasers in order to secure a contractual promise from them that they will deal primarily with Brown and will not purchase conflicting lines of shoes from Brown's competitors. We hold that the Commission has power to find, on the record here, such an anticompetitive practice unfair, subject of course to judicial review.

In holding that the Federal Trade Commission lacked the power to declare Brown's program to be unfair the Court of Appeals was much influenced by and quoted at length from this Court's opinion in *Federal Trade Comm'n v. Gratz*. That case, decided shortly after the Federal Trade Commission Act was passed, construed the Act over a strong dissent by Mr. Justice Brandeis as giving the Commission very little power to declare any trade practice unfair. Later cases of this Court, however, have rejected the *Gratz* view and it is now recognized in line with the dissent of Mr. Justice Brandeis in *Gratz* that the Commission has broad powers to declare trade practices unfair. This broad power of the Commission is particularly well established with regard to trade practices which conflict with the basic policies of the Sherman and Clayton Acts even though such practices may not actually violate these laws. The record in this case shows beyond doubt that Brown, the country's second largest manufacturer of shoes, has a program, which requires shoe retailers, unless faithless to their contractual obligations with Brown, substantially to limit their trade with Brown's competitors. This program obviously conflicts with the central policy of both section 1 of the Sherman Act and section 3 of the Clayton Act against contracts which take away freedom of purchasers to buy in an open market. Brown nevertheless contends that the Commission had no power to declare the franchise program unfair without proof that its effect "may be to substantially lessen competition or tend to create a monopoly" which of course would have to be proved if the Government were proceeding against Brown under section 3 of the Clayton Act rather than section 5 of the Federal Trade Commission Act. We reject the argument that proof of this section 3 element must be made for our cases hold that the Commission has power under section 5 to arrest trade restraints in their incipiency without proof that they amount to an outright violation of section 3 of the Clayton Act or other provisions of the antitrust laws. This power of the Commission was emphatically stated in *F.T.C. v. Motion Picture Adv. Co.*

"It is . . . clear that the Federal Trade Commission Act was designed to supplement and bolster the Sherman Act and the Clayton Act . . . to stop in their incipiency acts and practices which, when full blown, would violate those Acts . . . as well as to condemn as 'unfair methods of competition' existing violations of them." We hold that the Commission acted well within its authority in declaring the Brown franchise program unfair whether it was completely full blown or not.

SUMMARY

Section 2 of the Sherman Act outlaws monopolies, as well as attempts to monopolize. When a court is confronted with the charge that a firm allegedly has violated Section 2, it must make two important determinations: It must decide what the relevant geographic and product markets are for the purposes of the suit. How the court characterizes these markets will have a great effect on whether a firm is found guilty of violating the law.

Not every monopoly is unlawful—just unreasonable ones. A firm that has monopoly power in the relevant market which was not thrust upon it probably has violated the Sherman Act. It is possible that a firm which arrives at a monopoly position as a result of aggressive competition has not violated the act; however, there is no definitive Supreme Court decision on this point yet.

It is also unlawful to unreasonably restrain trade. The Court has created two rules in this area. Certain types of activities are illegal per se, other conduct is analyzed under the Rule of Reason. Price fixing is a good example of an activity that is always in violation of the Sherman Act. Any attempt to fix prices with another firm violates the law. Attempts by firms to control the price at which the products it sells are resold are governed by a more complex rule but are generally held to be unlawful. A manufacturer, however, may unilaterally announce the price at which it wants the products resold and may terminate customers who fail to abide by the price specified by the manufacturer.

Sellers are also restricted from entering into most tying agreements. If a seller requires buyers to purchase one product only if they buy some other product sold by the seller, such agreements typically are treated as unlawful per se. Group boycotts also are generally treated as per se violations of the antitrust laws.

The Federal Trade Commission Act also places restraints upon the manner of conducting business. Certain practices which do not technically violate the Sherman or Clayton Acts can be held to be violations of the FTC Act.

REVIEW QUESTIONS

1. Define the following terms:
   a. Monopoly
   b. Oligopoly
   c. Rule of Reason
   d. Resale price maintenance
   e. Restraint of trade
   f. *Colgate* doctrine

2. In determining whether a company has unlawfully monopolized an industry, do courts today emphasize bad acts?

3. Initially, the Supreme Court ruled the Sherman Act covered all restraints of trade. What is the practical effect of the *Standard Oil* case on Section 1?

4. What arguments would you advance in favor of accepting ruinous competition as a defense in a price-fixing case? What counter-arguments might be asserted? Why did the Supreme Court accept this defense in the *Appalachian Coal* case?

5. The Grinnell Corp. manufactures plumbing supplies and fire sprinkler systems. It owned 76 percent of the stock in ADT, a burglary and fire protection service, 89 percent of the stock in AFA, a fire protection service, and 100 percent of the stock in Holmes, a burglary protection service. Each company offers central station services under which hazard-detecting devices are installed and a signal is transmitted to a central station. ADT, Holmes, and AFA have 87 percent of the business for central station services. The government asserts this is an illegal monopoly. How should the relevant market be determined?

6. The *Globe-Democrat*, a St. Louis paper, required its deliverymen not to charge above a certain suggested price. Albrecht raised his prices above this price. The *Globe-Democrat* told him if he failed to lower his price to the suggested price, his territory would be taken from him. The paper hired Milne to solicit customers away from Albrecht to get him to lower his prices. He refused to lower his prices, so the paper terminated him and replaced him with another carrier who agreed to charge the suggested price. Has the *Globe-Democrat* violated the antitrust laws?

7. International Business Machines leased its computer to lessees on the condition that lessees use only IBM punch cards. IBM controlled eighty-one percent of the industry at the time. IBM claimed it needed this agree-

ment to prevent patent infringement on the machine. Has it violated the antitrust laws?

8. Klor's alleged that a competing retailer, Broadway-Hale, had placed pressure on certain manufacturers to get the manufacturers not to deal with Klor's. Some of the manufacturers refused to sell to Klor's. Broadway-Hale did not deny the charge. Does this action violate the antitrust laws?

9. USX Corporation's Home Division, a manufacturer of homes, owned a wholly owned subsidiary, Credit Corporation, which provided financing to customers of Home Division. In return for purchasing prefabricated homes, Credit Corporation agreed to finance the Fortner Corporation's cost of acquiring and developing land and purchasing the homes. Credit Corporation lent money only to customers of the Home Division. In return for getting very reasonable financing, Fortner was required to purchase homes at a noncompetitive price. Fortner alleged that the providing of credit (the tying product) was unlawfully tied to the purchase of homes (the tied product) and therefore violated the Clayton Act. How should the court rule?

10. Between 1933 and 1948, the *Lorain Journal*, a newspaper, was the only local business disseminating news and advertising in a small Ohio town. In 1948, a small radio station was started in a nearby town. In order to destroy the radio station as a competitor and to regain its pre-1948 monopoly over the mass dissemination of all news and advertising, the *Journal* refused to sell advertising to advertisers who bought air time from the radio station. The station argued this was an unlawful attempt to monopolize in violation of Section 2 of the Sherman Act. The publisher argued it had a right to select its customers and to refuse to deal with other firms. Who is correct?

11. Seventy percent of the physicians in Maricopa County are members of the Maricopa County Medical Society. They agreed upon the *maxi-*

mum fees that members may claim in full payment for health services provided to policyholders of insurance plans. Is this agreement legal?

12. Regal was a wholly owned subsidiary of Copperweld. Is it possible for Regal to be found guilty of having conspired with Copperweld to violate Section 1 of the Sherman Act?

13. Monsanto on several occasions contacted distributors that were selling Monsanto herbicides below the price suggested by Monsanto. Monsanto advised the price cutters that if they did not maintain the suggested price, they would not receive adequate supplies of Monsanto's herbicides. When one distributor refused to agree, Monsanto complained to the distributor's parent company. The parent instructed its subsidiary to comply, and the distributor informed Monsanto it would charge the suggested price. Has Monsanto violated Section 1 of the Sherman Act?

14. Northwest Wholesale Stationers is a purchasing cooperative made up of approximately one hundred office supply retailers in the Pacific Northwest. The cooperative acts as the primary wholesaler for the retailers. It also provides certain warehousing facilities to members. Pacific Stationery was expelled from membership in this cooperative without any explanation, notice, or hearing. Pacific asserted that its expulsion without procedural protections was a group boycott that should be considered a per se violation of the Sherman Act. Is Pacific correct?

15. If one of a dozen food stores in a community refuses to sell flour unless purchasers also buy sugar, is this an illegal tying arrangement if other sellers offer to sell flour by itself?

16. Dr. Edwin Hyde, an anesthesiologist, was denied admission to the medical staff of East Jefferson Hospital. The hospital denied the application because the hospital had a contract with Roux and Associates that provided Roux

would provide all anesthesiological services required by the hospital's patients. Seventy percent of the patients residing around the East Jefferson Hospital used the services of another hospital. Hyde brought suit against the hospital. He alleged the exclusive contract violated Section 1 of the Sherman Act. Is Hyde correct?

CHAPTER 15

The Clayton Act: Mergers and Price Discrimination

Mergers
Price Discrimination

In the two preceding chapters on antitrust, we examined the scope and enforcement of the antitrust laws as well as various problems associated with this field of law, and in particular, monopolies and restraints of trade.

The goal of the lawmakers in drafting the Sherman Act was primarily to preserve a competitive system in America. As the twentieth century progressed, other goals soon won the favor of the general public and Congress. Many persons perceived large manufacturers and large chain stores as exploiting the advantage they enjoyed. The chain stores succeeded in many situations in obtaining favorable prices not available to smaller purchasers. In order to protect not only a system of competition but also small competitors, Congress passed and later modified the Clayton Act with respect to the issues of mergers and price discrimination.

This chapter deals with the Clayton Act and those modifications made to it by Congress in order to help preserve a system of small businesses.

MERGERS

When speaking of a merger, we are referring to the joining together of two companies that previously operated as separate entities, whereby one company absorbs the other and continues to exist, while the absorbed company ceases to exist as a separate entity. The courts have identified several types of mergers: (1) **horizontal** mergers

Types of Mergers

407

involve a merger between two companies that previously competed with each other; (2) **vertical** mergers join together a customer and a supplier; and (3) all other mergers are classified as **conglomerate** mergers. If General Motors merged with Ford, the action would be referred to as a horizontal merger. These companies compete in the sale of automobiles. On the other hand, if General Motors merged with USX, the courts would call this type of merger a vertical merger. General Motors purchases steel and USX makes steel. Suppose, instead, that American Tobacco merged with Continental Can. Since neither company competes with the other—one produces tobacco, the other produces cans—and neither buys or sells to the other, the courts call such a merger a conglomerate merger.

In the 1960s, the merger law became more restrictive. The Supreme Court invalidated a number of mergers. More recently, the Supreme Court has upheld a number of mergers.

As noted in Chapters 13 and 14, the public sentiment against the growth of big business led to the adoption of the Sherman Act in 1890. The Sherman Act outlawed monopolies, attempts to monopolize, and restraints of trade.

Congress soon decided the antitrust laws needed further strengthening, so in 1914 it passed the Clayton Act, which outlawed certain types of mergers. Congress amended the Clayton Act in 1950 to make it more difficult for firms to lawfully merge.

Opposition to Mergers

Antitrust law generally strives to limit the growth of monopolies and to prohibit restraints of trade, because monopolies and restraints of trade give businesses the power to raise prices above the level that would prevail in a truly competitive market. Thus the courts strive to prevent the raising of prices by vigorously enforcing the antitrust laws.

Many critics of the expansion of big business oppose large businesses because of the vast amount of power concentrated in the hands of managers of these companies. These critics are concerned not with economic arguments dealing with mergers, but with political arguments, and the type of mergers opposed by such critics are often different from the types opposed by persons concerned solely with the issue of high prices.

Opponents of big business view the increasing concentration of wealth and economic power in the hands of a few as a direct threat to democracy. Furthermore, such persons wish to preserve small businesses and the power of local communities over businesses operating in their towns.

Many people also oppose the growth of large businesses because they wish to preserve a lifestyle. Small businesses, like small farms, enable some persons to live in a certain manner. Not everyone desires to work for the government or a large corporation. Many prefer to avoid the politics associated with working in a large enterprise.

Innumerable other arguments in favor of small businesses, as opposed to large businesses, might be asserted. However, the arguments tend not to be economic, but rather deal with political, social, and community control of businesses. Arguments in favor of permitting various types of mergers tend to be economic in nature and seldom consider the social and political ramifications of large businesses.

The *primary* source of law in the area of mergers today is Section 7 of the Clayton Act. The act currently reads as follows:

Clayton Act

> [N]o corporation engaged in commerce shall acquire, directly or indirectly, the whole or any part of the stock or other share capital and no corporation . . . shall acquire the whole or any part of the assets of another corporation engaged also in commerce, where in any line of commerce in any section of the country, the effect of such acquisition may be substantially to lessen competition, or to tend to create a monopoly.

The language, as it presently stands, comes in part from the original Clayton Act passed in 1914 and in part from the Celler-Kefauver amendment to Section 7 in 1950. In 1950, Congress deemed it necessary to clarify the law in this area. At one point, the courts applied Section 7 only to horizontal mergers. The Celler-Kefauver amendment clarified Congress's wish to extend the act to vertical mergers as well. The amendment also extends the act to cover not only acquisitions of the stock of a company, but also acquisitions of the assets of a business.

As the language indicates, Congress wished to reach certain mergers *before* they had an actual anticompetitive impact on trade. Section 7 is designed to reach any merger that *may* substantially lessen competition or that *tends* to create a monopoly. Exactly when a merger may have an anticompetitive effect is not always clear. Therefore, while the Sherman Act requires proof of an actual and substantial adverse effect on competition, the Clayton Act requires only that the action create a probable substantial lessening of competition or a tendency to create a monopoly. The Supreme Court in the 1960s applied Section 7 to a number of cases. Some commentators argue the Court acted overzealously. The Court arguably applied Section 7 to any merger with even a *possibility* of an anticompetitive effect, as opposed to a merger with a *probable* anticompetitive effect.

When analyzing a case under Section 7 of the Clayton Act, two important determinations must be made. The court must determine the *relevant product market* (line of commerce) and the *relevant geographic market*. If a court very narrowly defines these markets, such a definition may have the effect of making the merger look detrimental to competition. Suppose a court defines the relevant product market in a case as rolled steel, as opposed to all types of steel. If two companies that manufacture rolled steel tried to merge, the categorization of the product market as rolled steel makes the merger look more anticompetitive than it would if the court selected all types of steel as the relevant product market. These firms' percentage of the total steel business would be much smaller than their percentage control over the rolled steel business. Likewise, if a defendant operates in St. Louis and the court defines the geographical market as the St. Louis metropolitan area, the defendant's percentage of the business in the relevant geographic market is much larger than the percentage it would have if the market were defined as the nation.

Product and Geographic Markets

The Supreme Court dealt with the issue of determining the relevant market in the following case. This case interprets the original Section 7 of the Clayton Act, not the Clayton Act as amended.

United States v. E. I. du Pont de Nemours & Co.

United States Supreme Court

353 U.S. 586 (1957)

The government in 1949 alleged that du Pont's acquisition of twenty-three percent of the stock in General Motors during the years 1917 to 1919 violated Section 7 of the Clayton Act. The trial court dismissed the case. The Supreme Court on direct appeal reversed the decision of the trial court.

Justice Brennan

The primary issue is whether du Pont's commanding position as General Motors' supplier of automotive finishes and fabrics was achieved on competitive merit alone, or because its acquisition of the General Motors' stock, and the consequent close intercompany relationship, led to the insulation of most of the General Motors' market from free competition, with the resultant likelihood, at the time of suit, of the creation of a monopoly of a line of commerce.

Determination of the relevant market is a necessary predicate to a finding of a violation of the Clayton Act because the threatened monopoly must be one which will substantially lessen competition "within the area of effective competition." Substantiality can be determined only in terms of the market affected. The record shows that automotive finishes and fabrics have sufficient peculiar characteristics and uses to constitute them products sufficiently distinct from all other finishes and fabrics to make them a "line of commerce" within the meaning of the Clayton Act. Thus, the bounds of the relevant market for the purposes of this case are not the total market for finishes and fabrics, but the relevant market for automotive finishes and fabrics.

The market affected must be substantial. Moreover, in order to establish a violation of Section 7 the Government must prove a likelihood that competition may be "foreclosed in a substantial share of . . . [that market]." Both requirements are satisfied in this case. The substantiality of a relevant market comprising the automobile industry is undisputed. The substantiality of General

Motors' share of that market is fully established in the evidence.

General Motors is the colossus of the giant automobile industry. It accounts annually for upwards of two-fifths of the total sales of automotive vehicles in the Nation. Purchases by General Motors of du Pont fabrics in 1948 amounted to $3,700,000—making it the largest account of du Pont's Fabrics Division. Expressed in percentages, du Pont supplied 67% of General Motors' requirements for finishes in 1946 and 68% in 1947. In fabrics du Pont supplied 52.3% of requirements in 1946, and 38.5% in 1947. Because General Motors accounts for almost one-half of the automobile industry's annual sales, its requirements for automotive finishes and fabrics must represent approximately one-half of the relevant market for these materials. Because the record clearly shows that quantitatively and percentagewise du Pont supplies the largest part of General Motors' requirements, we must conclude that du Pont has a substantial share of the relevant market.

The Clayton Act was intended to supplement the Sherman Act. Its aim was primarily to arrest apprehended consequences of intercorporate relationships before those relationships could work their evil, which may be at or any time after the acquisition.

To accomplish the congressional aim, the Government may proceed at any time that an acquisition may be said with reasonable probability to contain a threat that it may lead to a restraint of commerce or tend to create a monopoly of a line of commerce. Even when the purchase is solely for investment, the plain language of Section 7 contemplates an action at any time the stock is used to bring about, or in attempting to bring about, the substantial lessening of competition.

The fact that sticks out in this voluminous record is that the bulk of du Pont's production has always supplied the largest part of the requirements of the one customer in the automobile industry connected to du Pont by a stock interest. The inference is overwhelming that du Pont's commanding position was promoted by its stock interest and was not gained solely on competitive merit.

The statutory policy of fostering free competition is obviously furthered when no supplier has an advantage over his competitors from an acquisition of his customer's stock likely to have the effects condemned by the statute. We repeat, that the test of a violation of Section 7 is whether, at the time of suit, there is a reasonable probability that the acquisition is likely to result in the condemned restraints. The conclusion upon this record is inescapable that such likelihood was proved as to this acquisition.

The judgment must therefore be reversed and the cause remanded to the District Court for a determination, after further hearing, of the equitable relief necessary and appropriate in the public interest to eliminate the effects of the acquisition offensive to the statute.

Brown Shoe

The first case decided under the amended Section 7 of the Clayton Act was *Brown Shoe Co. v. United States.* Congress wanted to stop any incipient trend by a few businesses to produce all the goods in a certain industry. Congress arguably passed this legislation to keep excessive power out of the hands of a few companies.

The *Brown Shoe* case arose after Brown, in 1956, acquired G. R. Kinney Company. Brown was the nation's third-largest shoe manufacturer. Kinney was the nation's eighth-largest retailer. Brown already had some retail outlets, and Kinney had some manufacturing capacity.

The Court observed that a small number of companies produced most of the nation's shoes. (The top four produced twenty-three percent of the shoes.) There had been a trend by shoe manufacturers to acquire retail outlets. Brown already had 845 before the Kinney merger. Once a manufacturer purchased a retail outlet, it tended to stock the store with its own brands, which foreclosed other manufacturers from effectively competing for these retail accounts. The Court also noted that there had been a decline in the number of shoe manufacturers.

The merger really had both vertical and horizontal aspects. It was a vertical merger in that it joined a supplier (Brown) with a customer (Kinney). This deprives rivals of the opportunity to supply shoes to its Kinney outlets. In determining whether such a merger violated Section 7 of the Clayton Act, the Court looked at the product market, the geographical market, and the probable effect of the merger. It defined the product market as men's, women's, and children's shoes for purposes of analysis of the vertical aspects of this merger. The geographical market was defined as the nation. Brown argued that the shoe industry was dynamically competitive. The Court ignored this argument, however, because it felt the Clayton Act required an examination of the probable effect of the merger on the future of the industry. Although the merger foreclosed only one percent of the market, the Court noted the industry already had undergone a cumulative series of vertical mergers, which, if left unchecked, would likely "substantially lessen competition." In light of this fact, the Court held the merger to be in violation of Section 7.

The Court also analyzed the horizontal nature of the merger. Both companies were producers and retailers, though Brown was principally a manufacturer and Kinney principally a retailer. The Court defined the product market here as men's, women's, and children's shoes. However, it regarded the geographical market, for purposes of this analysis, as any city with a population exceeding ten thousand and its immediate surrounding territory. Noting that Congress wished to curb incipient tendencies toward concentration in any industry, and that it wished to promote competition through small businesses, the Court found the merger in its horizontal aspect also violated Section 7 of the Clayton Act. It held that the probable effect of the merger would be to further concentrate control of substantial phases of trade in cities, which would have important adverse effects on competition.

One might criticize the majority opinion in *Brown Shoe* because there really was no trend toward concentration in the manufacturing business or the retail sales business. Brown Shoe sold only a small percentage of the shoes produced in America. Nor did any other shoe company dominate the shoe market. The Court, in striking down this merger, perhaps was more concerned with the potential political dangers associated with a concentration of power in the hands of a few companies than with any adverse economic consequences caused by such mergers.

Beyond Market Share Analysis

An examination of market share alone probably should not establish an anticompetitive effect. In *Brown Shoe*, the Court examined the percentage of the market held by Brown Shoe after the merger. From this examination of market share, it concluded the merger should be invalidated because it might have an anticompetitive impact.

The Court could have examined many factors other than the share of the market held by Brown after the merger. For example, it could have examined the *ease of entry* of other firms into the shoe manufacturing or shoe retailing business. If it is easy to enter a market, in the event one firm begins to earn large profits, other firms will enter that line of business. Another important factor is the *relative vigor* of other firms in the industry. While a business might have a small market share, it might be an aggressive competitor. If a large firm acquired this small aggressive firm, its market share would not be greatly increased. However, the absence of the aggressive competitor might greatly decrease competition in this market. The Court might have examined the *peculiar characteristics* of each firm—does the merging firm have peculiar assets, abilities, patents, and so on? Is this industry already an oligopoly—a few firms producing a large percentage of the products in this line of commerce? If so, another merger certainly should concern the Court. Another factor that could have been examined is the question of the *demand for the industry's products*. Is the demand growing or contracting? If the demand is growing, the Court need not worry as much about the adverse effects of the merger. *Brown Shoe* really focused on market share and ignored these other factors.

The Court in the 1960s placed its primary emphasis on *market share*. In the 1970s, the Court began to show a broader concern with the other factors just mentioned. *United States* v. *General Dynamics* illustrates the current approach of the Court, which focuses on more than just the market share of the company following the merger.

United States v. General Dynamics Corporation

United States Supreme Court
415 U.S. 486 (1974)

The government challenged the acquisition of the stock of United Electric Coal Companies by Material Service Corporation and its successor, General Dynamics Corporation. The trial court did not find a violation of the Clayton Act. The government appealed directly to the Supreme Court, which affirmed the decision of the trial court.

Justice Stewart

The thrust of the Government's complaint was that the acquisition of United Electric by Material Service in 1959 violated Section 7 of the Clayton Act because the take-over substantially lessened competition in the production and sale of coal in either or both of two geographic markets. It contended that a relevant "section of the country" within the meaning of Section 7 was, alternatively, the State of Illinois or the Eastern Interior Coal Province Sales Area, the latter being one of four major coal distribution areas recognized by the coal industry and comprising Illinois and Indiana, and parts of Kentucky, Tennessee, Iowa, Minnesota, Wisconsin, and Missouri.

The Government sought to prove a violation of Section 7 of the Clayton Act principally through statistics showing that within certain geographic markets the coal industry was concentrated among a small number of large producers; that this concentration was increasing; and that the acquisition of United Electric would materially enlarge the market share of the acquiring company and thereby contribute to the trend toward concentration.

These statistics, the Government argued, showed not only that the coal industry was concentrated among a small number of leading producers, but that the trend had been toward increasing concentration.

The question before us is whether the District Court was justified in finding that other pertinent factors affecting the coal industry and the business of the appellees mandated a conclusion that no substantial lessening of competition occurred or was threatened by the acquisition of United Electric.

Much of the District Court's opinion was devoted to a description of the changes that have affected the coal industry since World War II. First, it found that coal had become increasingly less able to compete with other sources of energy in many segments of the energy market.

Second, the court found that to a growing extent since 1954, the electric utility industry has become the mainstay of coal consumption.

Third, and most significantly, the court found that to an increasing degree, nearly all coal sold to utilities is transferred under long-term requirements contracts, under which coal producers promise to meet utilities' coal consumption requirements for a fixed period of time, and at predetermined prices.

Because of these fundamental changes in the structure of the market for coal, the District Court was justified in viewing the statistics relied on by the Government as insufficient to sustain its case. Evidence of past production does not, as a matter of logic, necessarily give a proper picture of a company's future ability to compete. In most situations, of course, the unstated assumption is that a company that has maintained a certain share of a market in the recent past will be in a position to do so in the immediate future. Thus, companies that have controlled sufficiently large shares of a concentrated market are barred from merger by Section 7, not because of their past acts, but because their past performances imply an ability to continue to dominate with at least equal vigor.

In the coal market, as analyzed by the District Court, however, statistical evidence of coal *production* was of considerably less significance. The bulk of the coal produced is delivered under long-term requirements contracts, and such sales thus do not represent the exercise of competitive power but rather the obligation to fulfill previously negotiated contracts at a previously fixed price. The focus of competition in a given time frame is not on the disposition of coal already produced but on the procurements of new long-term supply contracts. In this situation, a company's past ability to produce is of limited significance, since it is in a position to offer for sale neither its past production nor the bulk of the coal it is presently capable of producing, which is typically already committed under a long-term supply contract. A more significant indicator of a company's power effectively to compete with other companies lies in the state of a company's uncommitted reserves of recoverable coal. A company with relatively large supplies of coal which are not already under contract to a consumer will have a more important influence upon competition than a firm with small reserves, even though the latter may presently produce a greater tonnage of coal. In a market where the availability and price of coal are set by long-term contracts rather than immediate or short-term purchases and sales, reserves rather than past production are the best measure of a company's ability to compete.

The testimony and exhibits in the District Court revealed that United Electric's coal reserve prospects were "unpromising." United's relative position of strength in reserves was considerably weaker than its past and current ability to produce. United was found to be facing the future with relatively depleted resources at its disposal, and with the vast majority of those resources already committed under contracts allowing no further adjustment in price. In addition, the District Court found that "United Electric has neither the possibility of acquiring more [reserves] nor the ability to develop deep coal reserves," and thus was not in a position to increase its reserves to replace those already depleted or committed.

Viewed in terms of present and future reserve prospects—and thus in terms of probable future ability to compete—rather than in terms of past production, the District Court held that United Electric was a far less significant factor in the coal market than the Government contended or the production statistics seemed to indicate. Irrespective of the company's size when viewed as a producer, its weakness as a competitor was properly analyzed by the District Court and fully substantiated that court's conclusion that its acquisition by Material Service would not "substantially . . . lessen competition. . . ."

The *General Dynamics* case marks the beginning of the Supreme Court's willingness to consider factors other than market share in analyzing the legality of a merger. Such factors as the ease of entry, the vigor of the industry, the demand for the products, and the characteristics of each firm are now considered in evaluating a merger under Section 7 of the Clayton Act.

Potential Entrants

In a less-than-competitive market, the presence of a few potential entrants on the edge of the market may cause the firms in the market to behave more competitively. The firms know that if they extract too much income from the market, the potential entrant may enter the market.

A problem arises if one of the potential entrants merges with an existing firm in the market. This may reduce competition in the industry because one of the potential entrants is gone. Such a merger can be a violation of the Clayton Act.

Two other points on mergers bear examination. The Court in *Brown Shoe* implied that a company may assert several defenses to a charge brought under Section 7. One is the *failing company defense*. Basically, under this doctrine, if there is a grave possibility of business failure (that is, dim prospects for survival even if the company is reorganized), and if there are no other prospective purchasers, then the merger should be permitted. This defense is justified because there is no anticompetitive consequence when a company acquires a failing company. The failing company would simply go out of business otherwise. Furthermore, this doctrine helps the stockholders, bondholders, employees, and creditors of the soon-to-be-defunct company.

Failing Company Defense

The other defense is the *inadequate resources defense*. The majority discussed this in *General Dynamics* in its examination of the inadequacy of the coal reserves of the acquired company. If a company lacks adequate resources to become a viable competitor, another company may purchase it.

Inadequate Resources Defense

The Department of Justice has issued guidelines that it follows in screening the mergers it examines each year. The purpose of the guidelines is to provide guidance to the public. The guidelines were first issued in 1968. In 1982, the department revised them.

The Department of Justice's Merger Guidelines

The Federal Trade Commission issued its own statement on horizontal mergers the same day the Justice Department released its statement. The FTC indicated it would give considerable weight to the guidelines. However, the FTC merely listed factors it will consider in such cases, without indicating the weight to be given to them.

The new guidelines recognize only two categories of mergers—horizontal and nonhorizontal. The guidelines are designed to prevent either type of merger if such a merger makes it easier for a firm or firms to raise prices above a competitive level.

These guidelines may be consulted to determine if the Department of Justice is likely to challenge a planned merger. Anyone contemplating a merger should examine the Federal Trade Commission's guidelines as well, as they set forth the FTC's policy. The guidelines suggest that a person may obtain advice from the department as to the legality of an intended merger.

The guidelines have evoked a variety of general comments. Some persons have noted the complete reliance on economics in crafting these rules. No consideration was given to the sociopolitical goals alleged to be furthered by the Clayton Act in the *Brown Shoe* case. Furthermore, the guidelines set up standards not previously utilized by the courts in resolving merger cases. Whether the courts, which have the final power of interpretation of statutes, choose to follow the guidelines remains to be seen. Of course, the Department of Justice will file suit only when the guidelines dictate such action—but the Federal Trade Commission and private parties are not bound by these guidelines, nor are the courts.

Until the courts rule in the future, we must assume that the prior cases—which often appear to be more inclined to set mergers aside—are good law. In time, the

Supreme Court may give some further indication whether it agrees with the analysis of the Department of Justice.

PRICE DISCRIMINATION

While the antitrust laws are intended to preserve competition and further efficiency, some antitrust legislation may impede competition. Section 2(a) of the Clayton Act, as amended by the Robinson-Patman Act, makes it unlawful to discriminate in price between different purchasers of commodities of like grade and quality where the effect of such discrimination may be substantially to lessen competition or tends to create a monopoly in any line of commerce, or to injure, destroy, or prevent competition with any person who either grants or knowingly receives the benefit of such discrimination, or with customers of either of them.

In order to establish a violation of the Robinson-Patman Act, the plaintiff must establish the following:

1. A sale of goods. Gifts, leases and other nonsale transactions are not covered by the act. The sale must be of goods—tangible, movable property. If a business provided services, for example, at discriminatory prices, the act would not apply.

2. A sale in interstate commerce; that is, there must be a physical movement of the relevant product across a state line.

3. Evidence that the seller discriminated in price between a buyer and its competitor at roughly the same time.

MERGERS

In 1986, Delta Air Lines agreed to purchase Western Airlines. At that time, Delta was the nation's sixth largest carrier and Western was the nation's ninth largest carrier. The acquisition of Western made Delta the nation's fifth largest carrier. Delta was a carrier that largely served eastern cities. Western was a carrier that primarily served western cities.

During the time period in question there were a great number of mergers in the airline industry. At this same time, Texas Air agreed to acquire both People Express, Inc. (which had very recently purchased Frontier Airlines) and Eastern Airlines. With these acquisitions, Texas Air is the world's largest airline, other than Aeroflot, which is operated by the Soviet Union. It gave Texas Air 24.3 percent of the U.S. domestic market, as opposed to 17.5 for United and 15.1 for American. During this same period, TWA acquired Ozark Airlines.

In the case of the Delta/Western merger it is interesting to note that Western probably would not have been able to survive as an independent company. Perhaps for this reason, in spite of a rather large number of mergers going on in the airline industry, the Transportation Department approved this merger.

4. That the goods in question are of like grade and quality.

5. An injury to competition.

The Robinson-Patman Act is intended to prevent sellers from trying to gain an unfair advantage over their competitors by discriminating as to price among buyers of like commodities. The drafters also hoped to prevent such buyers as chain grocery stores from using their economic power to gain an advantage over competitors.

When a seller provides lower prices to a buyer, or a buyer obtains lower prices from a seller, and the effect of providing this lower price to the favored buyer is (1) to substantially lessen competition, (2) to tend to create a monopoly in any line of commerce; or (3) to injure, destroy, or prevent competition with any person who either grants or knowingly receives the benefit of such discrimination, or with customers of either of them, the act has been violated. Thus, contrary to cases brought pursuant to the Sherman Act, it is *not* necessary to show an actual competitive injury. At least under tests one and two, the plaintiff need only introduce proof of a probable adverse competitive impact in the relevant market. Because of problems of proof, plaintiffs tend to try to establish a case based on the third effect on competition. Under test three, the plaintiff must demonstrate a probability of injury to competition at certain levels of distribution. Competitive injury at these levels is discussed in the following material.

The original Section 2 of the Clayton Act, passed in 1914, was designed to prevent predatory price discrimination by sellers. This is referred to as **primary line competitive injury.** Here a seller is injured by a price discrimination given by a competitive seller. A national firm selling pies might lower the price of its pies in St. Louis, while keeping its prices high throughout the rest of the United States. The aim of the national firm in this situation is to drive the St. Louis pie maker out of business.

In Figure 15.1, Seller 1 might charge Buyer 1 one dollar per unit of a given product, but charge Buyer 2 ninety cents in order to make it more difficult for Seller 2 to compete. Seller 1 keeps its prices high in all areas where the two sellers do not compete. There is a probability of injury to competition at the level of the sellers.

In the 1920s, the nation underwent a change in the manner of doing business at the retail level. Chain stores, especially grocery stores, gradually entered the retailing field in competition with small, locally owned businesses. Manufacturers wished to obtain the business of these chain stores, as they purchased much larger quantities of a product than an independent retailer. The chains demanded larger discounts from the manufacturers because they purchased huge quantities. The chains then were able to sell the goods at a lower retail price than other competing

FIGURE 15.1 Primary Line Price Discrimination

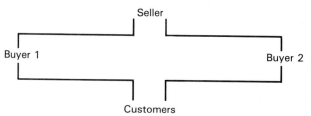

FIGURE 15.2 Secondary Line Price Discrimination

retailers. Here, the courts refer to the injury as a **secondary line competitive injury.** Damage here occurs not to sellers, but to *buyers.* If the large chain stores obtain substantial discounts, these discounts put the chains in a more favorable position than the independent retailer who failed to obtain a discount.

In Figure 15.2, Buyers 1 and 2 are trying to sell to the same customers. The Seller sells at a lower price to Buyer 1, usually because Buyer 1 purchases large quantities, but sells the goods at a higher price to Buyer 2. This enables Buyer 1 to sell to its customers at a lower price than Buyer 2. Thus, there is probability of injury to competition at the level of the buyers. If Buyer 1 and Buyer 2 sold to customers in different markets, the Seller could discriminate in price between them without causing secondary line injury.

A recent example of secondary line competitive injury appears in the following case. It should be noted that the Robinson-Patman Act exempts certain transactions from its coverage. For example, sales to charitable not-for-profit institutions are not covered by the act, as long as the sales are for the organizations' own use. It does not apply to purchases that are resold by the institution. In *Jefferson County Pharmaceutical*, the Supreme Court found that the transaction in question was not exempt.

Jefferson County Pharmaceutical Association, Inc.
v. Abbott Laboratories
United States Supreme Court
103 S.Ct. 1011 (1983)

Jefferson County Pharmaceutical Association, Inc., a trade association of retail pharmacists and pharmacies, brought suit against a number of organizations, including fifteen manufacturers and the University of Alabama Pharmacies. The plaintiff contended that the manufacturers sold products to the university pharmacies, and to a county pharmacy, at a price lower than those charged to its members for like products. It asserted that the hospital pharmacies knowingly induced such lower prices in violation of Section 2(f) and sold these drugs to the general public in direct competition with privately owned pharmacies. It alleged violations of Sections 2(a) and 2(f) of the Clayton Act as amended by the Robinson-Patman Act.

The trial court and court of appeals ruled for the defendants. The Supreme Court reversed and remanded the case for trial.

Justice Powell

The issue presented is whether the sale of pharmaceutical products to state and local government hospitals for resale in competition with private retail pharmacies is exempt from the proscriptions of the Robinson-Patman Act.

The issue here is narrow. We are not concerned with sales to the federal government, nor with state purchases for use in traditional governmental functions. Rather, the issue before us is limited to state purchases for the purpose of competing against private enterprise—with the advantage of discriminatory prices—in the retail market.

The courts below held, and respondents contend, that the Act exempts all state purchases. Assuming, without deciding, that Congress did not intend the Act to apply to state purchases for consumption in traditional government functions, and that such purchases are therefore exempt, we conclude that the exemption does not apply where a State has chosen to compete in the private retail market.

The Robinson-Patman Act by its terms does not exempt state purchases. The only express exemption is that for nonprofit institutions contained in 15 U.S.C. Section 13(c). (Section 13(c) provides: Nothing in [the Robinson-Patman Act] shall apply to purchases of their supplies for their own use by schools, colleges, universities, public libraries, churches, hospitals, and charitable institutions not operated for profit.)

Moreover, as the courts below conceded, "[t]he statutory language—'persons' and 'purchasers' [as covered in Robinson-Patman Section 2(a) and 2(f)]—is sufficiently broad to cover governmental bodies." This concession was compelled by several of this Court's decisions.

The plain language of the Act strongly suggests that there is no exemption for state purchases to compete with private enterprise.

The plain language of the Act is controlling unless a different legislative intent is apparent from the purpose and history of the Act. An examination of the legislative purpose and history here reveals no such contrary intention.

The legislative history falls far short of supporting respondents' contention that there is an exemption for state purchases of "commodities" for "resale." There is nothing whatever in the Senate or House Committee reports, or in the floor debates, focusing on the issue. Some members of Congress were aware of the possibility that the Act would apply to governmental purchases. Most members, however, were concerned not with state purchases, but with possible limitations on the Federal Government. The most relevant legislative history is the testimony of the Act's principal draftsman, H. B. Teegarden, before the House Judiciary Committee. Although the testimony is ambiguous on the application of the Act to state purchases for consumption, one conclusion is certain: Teegarden expressly stated that the Act would apply to the purchase of municipal hospitals in at least some circumstances. Thus, his comments directly contradict the exemption found by the courts below for all such purchasing.

Despite the plain language of the Act and its legislative history, respondents nevertheless argue that subsequent legislative events and decisions of district courts confirm that state purchases are outside the scope of the Act.

Post-enactment developments—whether legislative, judicial, or in commentary—rarely have considered the specific issue before us. There is simply no unambiguous evidence of congressional intent to exempt purchases by a State for the purpose of competing in the private retail market with a price advantage.

The Robinson-Patman Act has been widely criticized, both for its effects and for the policies that it seeks to promote. Although Congress is well aware of these criticisms, the Act has remained in effect for almost half a century. And it certainly is not for [this Court] to indulge in the business of policy-making in the field of antitrust legislation. . . . Our function ends with the endeavor to ascertain from the words used, construed in the light of the relevant material, what was in fact the intent of Congress.

A general application of the Robinson-Patman Act to all combinations of business and capital organized to suppress commercial competition is in harmony with the spirit and impulses of the times which gave it birth. The legislative history is replete with references to the economic evil of large organizations purchasing from other large organizations for resale in competition with the small, local retailers. There is no reason, in the absence of an explicit exemption, to think that congressmen who feared these evils intended to deny small businesses, such as the pharmacies of Jefferson County, Alabama, protection from the competition of the strongest competitor of them all. To create an exemption here clearly would be contrary to the intent of Congress.

We hold that the sale of pharmaceutical products to state and local government hospitals for resale in competition with private pharmacies is not exempt from the proscriptions of the Robinson-Patman Act. The judgment of the Court of Appeals accordingly is reversed and the case is remanded for further proceedings consistent with this opinion.

In Figure 15.3 on page 423, there is a probability of injury to competition at the third line; that is, to Retailer 2, in its retailer operation, as opposed to injury to the sellers, as illustrated by Figure 15.1, or injury to the buyers, as illustrated by Figure 15.2.

The Seller here sells goods to Buyer 1 at a lower price than that at which it sells the goods to Retailer 2. Buyer 1 then is able to sell the goods to a retailer, Retailer 1, who is in competition with Retailer 2. Retailer 1, who purchased the goods from Buyer 1, can then sell the goods at a lower price than Retailer 2. Harm here is done to Retailer 2.

The courts have also considered cases involving discrimination at the fourth level of distribution, as is illustrated by the following case.

Standard Oil Co. v. Perkins

United States Supreme Court
395 U.S. 642 (1969)

Perkins operated gasoline stations in Washington and Oregon. From 1955 to 1957, Standard charged Perkins a higher price for its gasoline and oil than it charged its own dealers, who competed with Perkins, and Signal Oil & Gas Co., a wholesaler. Signal sold its gasoline to Western Hyway (owned sixty percent by Signal), and Western sold the gasoline to Regal Stations (fifty-five percent owned by Western), a competitor of Perkins.

Perkins brought suit against Standard seeking treble damages under Section 2 of the Clayton Act, as amended by the Robinson-Patman Act, for injuries alleged to have resulted from Standard's price discriminations in the sale of gasoline and oil during a period of over two years from 1955 to 1957. Perkins won a judgment for $1,298,213.71 in the trial court.

Both the lower courts and the Supreme Court agreed it was improper to charge the Standard dealers a lower price than Perkins. However, the court of appeals ruled that Regal was too far removed from Standard in the chain of distribution for

Standard to be liable under the Robinson-Patman Act. The Supreme Court reversed, ruling for Perkins and reinstating the verdict in his favor.

Justice Black

With regard to Perkins' damage resulting from Standard's discrimination in favor of Signal Oil, however, the Court of Appeals took a different view (than as to Standard's liability for charging its own dealers less) because of the following circumstances under which the discriminatory sales were made. Standard admittedly sold gasoline to Signal at a lower price than it sold to Perkins. Signal sold this Standard gasoline to Western Hyway, which in turn sold the Standard gasoline to Regal Stations Co., Perkins' competitor. Perkins alleged that the lower price charged Signal by Standard was passed on to Signal's subsidiary Western Hyway, and then to Western's subsidiary, Regal. Regal's stations were thus able to undersell Perkins' stations and, according to Perkins, the resulting competitive harm, along with that he suffered at the hands of Standard's favored Branded Dealers, destroyed his ability to compete and eventually forced him to sell what was left of his business. The Court of Appeals held, however, that any harm suffered by Perkins from impaired competition with Regal stations was beyond the scope of the Robinson-Patman Act because Regal was too far removed from Standard in the chain of distribution. A substantial part of the damages the jury assessed against Standard, as the Court of Appeals viewed it, might have been based upon a finding that Perkins suffered competitive harm from the price advantage held by Regal stations. That court, concluding that "the whole verdict is tainted, since the amount reflected in it by Regal's conduct cannot be ascertained. . . ." reversed the judgment and ordered a new trial.

We disagree with the Court of Appeals' conclusion that Section 2 of the Clayton Act, as amended by the Robinson-Patman Act, does not apply to the damages suffered by Perkins as a result of the price advantage granted by Standard

to Signal, then by Signal to Western, then by Western to Regal. The Act, in pertinent part, provides:

"(a) It shall be unlawful for any person engaged in commerce . . . either directly or indirectly, to discriminate in price between different purchasers or commodities of like grade and quality . . . where the effect of such discrimination may be substantially to lessen competition or tend to create a monopoly in any line of commerce, or to injure, destroy, or prevent competition with any person who either grants or knowingly receives the benefit of such discrimination, or with customers of either of them. . . ."

The Court of Appeals read this language as limiting "the distributing levels on which a supplier's price discrimination will be recognized as potentially injurious to competition." According to that court, the coverage of the Act is restricted to injuries caused by an impairment of competition with (1) the seller ("any person who . . . grants . . . such discrimination"), (2) the favored purchaser ("any person who . . . knowingly receives the benefit of such discrimination"), and (3) customers of the discriminating seller or favored purchaser ("customers of either of them"). Here, Perkins' injuries resulted in part from impaired competition with a customer (Regal) of a customer (Western Hyway) of the favored purchaser (Signal). The Court of Appeals termed these injuries "fourth level" and held that they were not protected by the Robinson-Patman Act. We conclude that this limitation is wholly an artificial one and is completely unwarranted by the language or purpose of the Act.

In *FTC v. Fred Meyer, Inc.*, the Court stated that to read "customer" [as it appears in Section 2(d)] narrowly would be wholly untenable when viewed in light of the purposes of the Robinson-Patman Act. Similarly, to read "customer" more narrowly in this section than we did in the section involved in *Meyer* would allow price discriminators to avoid the sanctions of the act by the simple expedient of adding an additional link to the distribution chain. Here, for example, Standard supplied gasoline and oil to Signal. Signal, allegedly because it furnished Standard with part of its vital supply of crude petroleum, was able to insist upon a discriminatorily lower price. Had Signal then sold its gas directly to the Regal stations, giving Regal stations a competitive advantage, there would be no question, even under the decision of the Court of Appeals in this case, that a clear violation of the Robinson-Patman Act had been committed. Instead of selling directly to the retailer Regal, however, Signal transferred the gasoline first to its subsidiary, Western Hyway, which in turn supplied the Regal stations. Signal owned 60 percent of the stock of Western Hyway; Western in turn owned 55 percent of the stock of the Regal stations. We find no basis in the language or purpose of the Act for immunizing Standard's price discriminations simply because the product in question passed through an additional formal exchange before reaching the level of Perkins' actual competitor. From Perkins' point of view, the competitive harm done him by Standard is certainly no less because of the presence of an additional link in this particular distribution chain from the producer to the retailer. Here Standard discriminated in price between Perkins and Signal, and there was evidence from which the jury could conclude that Perkins was harmed competitively when Signal's price advantage was passed on to Perkins' retail competitor Regal. These facts are sufficient to give rise to recoverable damages under the Robinson-Patman Act.

Before an injured party can recover damages under the Act, he must, of course, be able to show a causal connection between the price discrimination in violation of the Act and the injury suffered. This is true regardless of the "level" in the chain of distribution on which the injury occurs. The court below held that, as a matter of law, "Section 2(a) of the Act does not recognize a causal connection, essential to liability, between a supplier's price discrimination and the trade practices of a customer as far removed on the distributive ladder as Regal was from Standard." As we have noted above, we do not accept such an artificial limitation. If there is sufficient evidence in the record to support an inference of causation, the ultimate conclusion as to what that evidence proves is for the jury. Here the trial judge properly charged the jury that Perkins had the burden of showing that any damage to his business was proximately caused by Standard's price discriminations and there was substantial evidence from which the jury could infer causation. There was evidence that Signal received a lower price from Standard than did Perkins, that this price advantage was passed on, at least in part, to Regal, and that Regal was thereby able to undercut Perkins' price on gasoline. Furthermore, there was evidence that Perkins repeatedly complained to Standard officials that the discriminatory price advantage given Signal was being passed down to Regal and evidence that Standard officials were aware that Perkins' business was in danger of being destroyed by Standard's discriminatory practices. This evidence is sufficient to sustain the jury's award of damages under the Robinson-Patman Act.

Congress passed the Robinson-Patman amendment to Section 2 of the Clayton Act in 1936. No doubt different legislators sought different goals—some wished to protect competition, others wished to protect small businesses. To the extent the act favors small businesses, it may injure competition. If a large retailer operates more efficiently, it may be able to sell goods cheaper to consumers. To the extent that some members of Congress wished to favor small business even at the expense of competition, the Robinson-Patman amendment creates problems in the enforcement

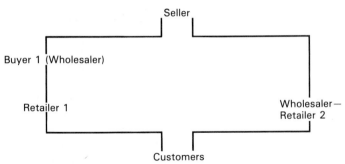

FIGURE 15.3 Tertiary Line Price Discrimination

of the antitrust laws. It reflects the belief of some congressmen and senators that other goals (such as the preservation of small business, the dispersal of economic power, and the preservation of opportunity) rank equally with the goals of competition and efficiency as set forth in the original Sherman Act. In the 1930s, 1940s, and 1950s, Congress saw the demise of small business. It perceived that certain problems arise when too much power falls into the hands of too few persons. To some extent, Congress wished to stop this trend toward concentration of business in the hands of very few companies. This goal conflicts with the goal of reducing prices through the furtherance of competition and efficiency.

As Congress never repealed the earlier acts, the antitrust laws conflict with one another to some extent. Those persons favoring competition and efficiency find the alternative goal of preservation of small, independently owned businesses offensive. Perhaps efficiency and competition ought not to be the sole goal of the law—even if it results in higher prices for consumers. At least some members of Congress thought so in the 1930s.

The Robinson-Patman Act has been criticized by the Federal Trade Commission as legislation designed to protect small, independent businesspeople against the growth of chain stores. The FTC stated that this protectionist legislation has cost consumers money.

Although the last Department of Justice suit was in 1963 and the Federal Trade Commission has filed very few suits to enforce the Robinson-Patman Act, suits still can be filed by private parties seeking treble damages and injunctions pursuant to Sections 4 and 16 of the Clayton Act.

The Robinson-Patman Act may be enforced by either the Department of Justice or the Federal Trade Commission. Normally, the FTC handles the cases. However, in those instances in which a criminal penalty applies, the Department of Justice handles the cases. Where applicable, the penalty for a criminal violation is up to five thousand dollars and imprisonment for a maximum of one year.

Enforcement of the Act

Section 4 of the Clayton Act, which the Robinson-Patman Act also amended, also permits injured parties to bring treble damage actions for injuries arising out of a violation of the antitrust laws, including court costs and reasonable attorneys' fees. Section 16 gives such persons the right to injunctive relief. The Department of Justice also may seek to have violations of the act enjoined.

Other Illegal Practices

Section 2(c) of the Clayton Act makes it unlawful for a seller to pay or a buyer to receive anything of value as a commission, brokerage, or other compensation, or any allowance or discount in lieu thereof, except for services rendered in connection with the sale or purchase of goods, wares, or merchandise. This provision is designed to prevent disguised price concessions to the buyer.

Section 2(d) of the Clayton Act prohibits the seller from giving promotional allowances or payments on goods bought for resale unless the allowances are available to all other competing customers on proportionally equal terms.

Section 2(e) prohibits the seller from giving promotional services and facilities on goods bought for resale unless they are made available to all other competing customers on proportionally equal terms.

Unlike cases brought under 2(a) for an alleged discrimination in price, persons suing pursuant to sections 2(c), (d), and (e) need not establish a substantial lessening of competition or a tendency to create a monopoly in any line of commerce.

Promotional Allowances and Services

Promotional allowances and services may not be granted unless they are available to all competing customers on proportionally equal terms.

In *Fred Meyer, Inc.* v. *FTC* (1968), the courts decided that if a seller offers a promotional allowance or service to a direct purchasing retailer, a proportional offer must also be made to competitors of that retailer who obtain the seller's goods from distributors. This can be handled by the seller's simply offering a promotional allowance directly to customers of distributors.

It is permissible to limit advertising and promotional offers to specific geographic areas or functional levels. For example, an offer could be made only to wholesalers.

While there is a private cause of action against a buyer who knowingly induces a price discrimination, there is no private cause of action if a business knowingly induces a discrimination in advertising or promotional allowances. It is subject to challenge only by the FTC under Section 5 of the Federal Trade Commission Act. Since the government has not been overly active in this area, it is possible such an action would never be challenged.

Statutory Prerequisites Necessary to Establish a Case

As noted earlier, a plaintiff must prove five elements in order to establish a case. If the plaintiff fails to prove any of these elements, he or she cannot prevail at trial. Companies have relied upon various techniques related to these five elements in order to avoid being found to have violated the act.

For example, a seller does not violate the act by giving price concessions on the condition that the customer purchase a certain minimum quantity of goods. As long as the price is made known to all competing customers, and all the conditions that must be met to obtain the favorable price are attainable by most customers, no violation of the act has taken place simply because certain customers do not take advantage of the lower price.

Some companies create special lines of merchandise they sell only to certain buyers. Since this merchandise is never offered at a lower price to anyone else, there never can be any charge of price discrimination brought against the company. In this manner, the seller can favor volume buyers. Of course, the merchandise in question must be of a different grade and quality than is being offered to small customers.

These are just a few examples of the numerous ways sellers have discovered to circumvent the provisions of the Robinson-Patman Act.

Section 2(a) of the Clayton Act permits a seller to select his or her own customers. Certain other exceptions to the rule prohibiting price discrimination are provided for in Section 2(a) of the act.

Defenses

The *cost justification defense* provides that sellers may charge different prices to different buyers of the same type of goods in order to "make due allowance for differences in the cost of manufacture, sale or delivery resulting from the differing methods or quantities in which such commodities are to such purchasers sold or delivered." Establishing a successful defense based on differences in the cost of producing a large volume of goods, as opposed to a smaller sale, is very difficult and seldom successful. The burden of establishing this defense is on the seller.

Cost Justification

Another defense permits "price changes from time to time where in response to changing conditions affecting the market for or the marketability of the goods concerned." This defense protects a seller who sells strawberries at one price today, then lowers this price the next day because of the perishable nature of the strawberries. Likewise, a Christmas tree seller might lower his or her price to various buyers as the number of days to Christmas decreases.

Changing Market Conditions

Another important defense is the *meeting competition defense* created by Section 2(b) of the Clayton Act. This defense permits a seller to show "that his lower price or the furnishing of services or facilities to any purchaser or purchasers was made in good faith to meet an equally low price of a competitor, or the services or facilities furnished by a competitor." Once again, the burden of establishing this defense is on the seller.

Meeting Competition

As an illustration of the meeting competition defense, suppose Amoco sold gasoline to two gasoline stations in Los Angeles—A and B. Another manufacturer offered to sell gasoline at a lower price to station A. In this situation, Amoco could, in good faith, lower its price to the price offered by the other manufacturer in order to retain A's business. However, it could continue to charge a higher price to B. Thus, even though A and B would be paying a different price for gasoline from Amoco, this would be lawful because Amoco lowered its price to A in good faith to meet the equally low price of a competitor.

Good faith essentially means acting as a reasonable, prudent business executive would in response to a competitive situation. The FTC in *Continental Baking Company* stated that "at the heart of Section 2(b) is the concept of 'good faith.' This is a flexible and pragmatic, not a technical or doctrinaire, concept. The standard of good faith is simply the standard of the prudent businessman responding fairly to what he reasonably believes is a situation of competitive necessity."

The act permits a seller merely to meet competition—it does not permit a seller to *beat* competition.

In the following case, the Court deals with the question of whether a business may lower its price to meet a competitor's lower price to gain new customers, and whether a seller may lower a price in an entire territory rather than to specific customers.

Falls City Industries, Inc. v. Vanco Beverage, Inc.
United States Supreme Court
103 S.Ct. 1281 (1983)

Falls City, a brewer, sold its beer to Vanco, a wholesale distributor in Vanderburgh County, Indiana, at a higher price than that it charged its only wholesale distributor in Henderson County, Kentucky, Dawson Springs, Inc. These two counties formed a single metropolitan area across the state line. Indiana wholesalers were allowed by state law to sell only to Indiana retailers. While the wholesalers did not sell to the same retailers, the retailers competed for the sale of beer to consumers in the same market area. Because the prices for retail beer were lower in Kentucky as a result of Falls City's pricing policy, many Indiana customers purchased beer in Kentucky. Vanco claimed that Falls City's pricing policy prevented it from competing effectively with the Kentucky wholesaler and caused it to sell less beer in Indiana. Vanco accused Falls City of violating Section 2(a) of the Clayton Act, as amended by the Robinson-Patman Act, by charging Vanco a higher price than it charged Dawson Springs.

The district court ruled for Vanco, as did the United States Court of Appeals for the Seventh Circuit. The court held that Vanco had established a prima facie case of illegal price discrimination. It rejected Falls City's meeting competition defense. The United States Supreme Court ruled in favor of Falls City Industries.

Justice Blackmun

When proved, the meeting-competition defense of Section 2(b) exonerates a seller from Robinson-Patman Act liability.

On its face, Section 2(b) requires more than a showing of facts that would have led a reasonable person to believe that a lower price was available to the favored purchaser from a competitor. The showing required is that the "lower price . . . *was made* in good faith to *meet* the competitor's low price." 15 U.S.C. Section 13(b) (emphasis added). Thus, the defense requires that the seller offer the lower price in good faith *for* the *purpose* of meeting the competitor's price, that is, the lower price must actually have been a good faith response to that competing low price. In most situations, a showing of facts giving rise to a reasonable belief that equally low prices were available to the favored purchaser from a competitor will be sufficient to establish that the seller's lower price was offered in good faith to meet that price.

Almost 20 years ago, the FTC set forth the standard that governs the requirement of a "good faith response":

> "At the heart of Section 2(b) is the concept of 'good faith'. This is a flexible and pragmatic, not a technical or doctrinaire, concept. The standard of good faith is simply the standard of the prudent businessman responding fairly to what he reasonably believes is a situation of competitive necessity."

Whether this standard is met depends on " 'the facts and circumstances of the particular case, not abstract theories or remote conjectures.' "

Vanco contends that Falls City did not satisfy Section 2(b) because its price discrimination "was not a *defensive* response to competition." According to Vanco, the Robinson-Patman Act permits price discrimination only if its purpose is to retain a customer. We agree that a seller's response must be defensive, in the sense that the lower price must be calculated and offered in good faith to "meet not beat" the competitor's low price. Section 2(b), however, does not distinguish between one who meets a competitor's lower price to retain an old customer and one who meets a competitor's lower price in an attempt to gain new customers.

The Court of Appeals ruled that the meeting-competition defense places emphasis on individual competitive situations, rather than upon a general system of competition, and does not justify the maintenance of discriminatory pricing among classes of customers that results merely from the adoption of a competitor's discriminatory pricing structure. The Court of Appeals was apparently invoking the District Court's findings that Falls City set prices statewide rather than on a "customer to customer basis," and the District Court's conclusion that this practice disqualified Falls City from asserting the meeting-competition defense.

There is no evidence that Congress intended to limit the availability of Section 2(b) to customer-specific responses. We conclude that Congress did not intend to bar territorial price differences that are in fact responses to competitive conditions.

Section 2(b) specifically allows a "lower price . . . to any purchaser or purchasers" made in good faith to meet a competitor's equally low price. A single low price surely may be extended to numerous purchasers if the seller has a reasonable basis for believing that the competitor's lower price is available to them. Beyond the requirement that the lower price be reasonably calculated to "meet not beat" the competition, Congress intended to leave it a "question of fact . . . whether the way in which the competition was met lies within the latitude allowed." 80 Cong.Rec. 9418 (1936) (Rep. Utterback). Once again, this inquiry is guided by the standard of the prudent businessman responding fairly to what he reasonably believes are the competitive necessities.

A seller may have good reason to believe that a competitor or competitors are charging lower prices throughout a particular region.

Of course, a seller must limit its lower price to that group of customers reasonably believed to have the lower price available to it from competitors. A response that is not reasonably tailored to the competitive situation as known to the buyer, or one that is based on inadequate verification, would not meet the standard of good faith. Similarly, the response may continue only as long as the competitive circumstances justifying it, as reasonably known by the seller, persist. One choosing to price on a territorial basis, rather than on a customer-by-customer basis, must show that this decision was a genuine, reasonable response to prevailing competitive circumstances. Unless the circumstances call into question the seller's good faith, this burden will be discharged by showing that a reasonable and prudent businessman would believe that the lower price he charged was generally available from his competitors throughout the territory and throughout the period in which he made the lower price available.

The judgment of the Court of Appeals is vacated, and the case is remanded for further proceedings consistent with this opinion.

Not only is it illegal for a seller to discriminate in prices charged to customers, but it is also illegal under Section 2(f) of the Robinson-Patman Act for a person to knowingly induce or receive a discrimination in price that is prohibited by Section 2 of the act. This provision and the meeting competition defense are discussed in the following case.

Great Atlantic & Pacific Tea Co. v. Federal Trade Commission
United States Supreme Court
440 U.S. 69 (1979)

A&P decided to sell private label milk (milk sold under its label) to its two hundred A&P stores in Chicago. It asked the Borden Company to submit an offer to supply milk under a private label. After receiving the Borden bid, it solicited offers from other dairies. Bowman Dairy then submitted an offer lower than Borden's. A&P's Chicago buyer then contacted Borden's chain store sales manager and indicated Bowman's had underbid Borden. A&P did not indicate the amount of the Bowman bid. Because the account was important to Borden, it rebid. The bid was made in good faith to retain A&P as a customer. A&P accepted the Borden bid.

The FTC charged A&P with, among other things, violating Section 2(f) of the Robinson-Patman Act. The administrative law judge ruled against A&P, as did the Federal Trade Commission. A&P filed a petition for review with the Court of Appeals for the Second Circuit. The Second Circuit affirmed. A&P, the petitioner in this case, appealed to the Supreme Court. The Supreme Court reversed.

Justice Stewart

The question presented in this case is whether the petitioner, the Great Atlantic and Pacific Tea Company (A&P), violated Section 2(f) of the Robinson-Patman Act, as amended, by knowingly inducing or receiving illegal price discriminations from the Borden Company (Borden).

As finally enacted, Section 2(f) provides:

That it shall be unlawful for any person engaged in commerce, in the course of such commerce, knowingly to induce or receive a discrimination in price *which is prohibited by this section.*: (Emphasis added.)

Liability under Section 2(f), thus, is limited to situations where the price discrimination is one "which is prohibited by this section." While the phrase "this section" refers to the entire Section 2 of the Act, only subsections (a) and (b) dealing with seller liability involve discriminations in price. Under the plain meaning of Section 2(f), therefore, a buyer cannot be liable if a prima facie case could not be established against a seller or if the seller has an affirmative defense. In either situation, there is no price discrimination "prohibited by this section." The legislative history of Sec-

tion 2(f) fully confirms the conclusion that buyer liability under Section 2(f) is dependent on seller liability under Section 2(a).

The petitioner, A&P, relying on this plain meaning of Section 2(f), argues that it cannot be liable under Section 2(f) if Borden had a valid meeting competition defense. The respondent, on the other hand, argues that the petitioner may be liable even assuming that Borden had such a defense. The meeting competition defense, the respondent contends, must, in these circumstances, be judged from the point of view of the buyer. Since A&P knew, for a fact, that the final Borden bid beat the Bowman bid, it was not entitled to assert the meeting competition defense even though Borden may have honestly believed that it was simply meeting competition. Recognition of a meeting competition defense for the buyer, in this situation, the respondent FTC argues, would be contrary to the basic purpose of the Robinson-Patman Act to curtail abuses by large buyers.

The short answer to these contentions of the respondent is that Congress did not provide in Section 2(f) that a buyer can be liable even if the seller has a valid defense. The clear language of

Section 2(f) states that a buyer can be liable only if he receives a price discrimination "prohibited by this section." If a seller has a valid meeting competition defense, there is simply no prohibited price discrimination.

Under the view advanced by the respondent, however, a buyer, to avoid liability, must either refuse a seller's bid or at least inform him that his bid has beaten competition. Such a duty of affirmative disclosure would almost inevitably frustrate competitive bidding and, by reducing uncertainty, lead to price matching and anticompetitive cooperation among sellers.

We decline to adopt a construction of Section 2(f) that is contrary to its plain meaning and would lead to anticompetitive results. Accordingly, we hold that a buyer who has done no more than accept the lower of two prices competitively offered does not violate Section 2(f) provided the seller has a meeting competition defense.

The test for determining when a seller has a valid meeting competition defense is whether a seller can show the existence of facts which would lead a reasonable and prudent person to believe that the granting of a lower price would in fact meet the equally low price of a competitor. A good faith belief, rather than absolute certainty, that a price concession is being offered to meet an equally low price offered by a competitor is sufficient to satisfy the Robinson-Patman's section 2(b) defense. Since good faith, rather than absolute certainty, is the touchstone of the meeting competition defense, a seller can assert the defense even if it has unknowingly made a bid that, in fact, not only met but beat his competition.

Under the circumstances of this case, Borden did act reasonably and in good faith when it made its second bid.

Borden was informed by the petitioner that it was in danger of losing its A&P business in the Chicago area unless it came up with a better offer. It was told that its first offer was "not even in the ball park" and that a $50,000 improvement "would not be a drop in the bucket." In light of Borden's established business relationship with the petitioner, Borden could justifiably conclude that A&P's statements were reliable and that it was necessary to make another bid offering substantial concessions to avoid losing its account with the petitioner.

Borden was unable to ascertain the details of the Bowman bid. It requested more information about the bid from the petitioner, but this request was refused. It could not, then, attempt to verify the existence and terms of the competing offer from Bowman without risking Sherman Act liability. Faced with a substantial loss of business and unable to find out the precise details of the competing bid, Borden made another offer stating that it was doing so in order to meet competition. Under these circumstances, the conclusion is virtually inescapable that in making that offer Borden acted in a reasonable and good-faith effort to meet its competition and, therefore, was entitled to a meeting competition defense.

Since Borden had a meeting competition defense and it could not be liable under Section 2(b), the petitioner, who did no more than accept that offer, cannot be liable under Section 2(f).

Accordingly the judgment is reversed.

SUMMARY

When two companies that previously operated as separate entities join together, the transaction is called a *merger*. The courts typically use one of three terms in referring to mergers: *horizontal*, *vertical*, or *conglomerate*.

Because many persons regarded mergers as threatening to the economy, as well as a possible threat to democratic principles, Congress passed the Clayton Act. Section 7 of the Clayton Act is the primary source of law in this area. The Clayton Act was amended in 1950 to strengthen its prohibitions on mergers.

In identifying whether a merger violates the Clayton Act, a court must first identify the relevant product and geographic markets for purposes of the merger.

Once these markets have been determined, a court decides whether a given merger may substantially lessen competition or tends to create a monopoly. If so, the court will find the merger violates Section 7. At one point, the court placed almost exclusive reliance on the market shares of the merging firms. Today the courts look at a number of other factors, such as ease of entry in a market or the vigor of an industry, in deciding whether a merger will have an anticompetitive effect.

In the 1930s, Congress amended the Clayton Act by passing the Robinson-Patman Act. The original Clayton Act outlawed certain forms of price discrimination. Congress broadened the scope of the act to outlaw more forms of price discrimination by passing the Robinson-Patman Act. Congress hoped to make price discrimination by businesses more difficult to engage in, thereby helping to preserve small businesses. There are several important defenses to a charge of price discrimination: cost justification, changing market conditions, and the meeting-competition defense.

The goals of the Robinson-Patman Act seem to conflict with the overall goal of the Sherman Act to preserve competition. Consequently, some of the antitrust laws appear to favor competition, while other laws—in particular, the Robinson-Patman Act—seem to promote a system of small competitors.

REVIEW QUESTIONS

1. Define the following terms:
   a. Primary line competitive injury
   b. Secondary line competitive injury
   c. Vertical merger
   d. Horizontal merger
   e. Conglomerate merger

2. What does a court look at in determining whether a merger violates Section 7 of the Clayton Act? What must the government demonstrate?

3. What must be established by the plaintiff in order to prove a violation of the Robinson-Patman Act?

4. In 1960, Von's Grocery Co. acquired Shopping Bag Food Store's capital stock and assets. Von's was the third-largest grocery chain in the Los Angeles market. Shopping Bag was the sixth-largest grocery chain in the Los Angeles market. Together, these firms had joint sales of 7.5 percent of the Los Angeles market. In the period from 1948 to 1958, the number of single stores in Los Angeles had declined.

Does such a merger violate Section 7 of the Clayton Act?

5. The Federal Trade Commission alleged that Standard Oil had violated the Robinson-Patman Act. Standard sold gasoline to four large wholesalers in Detroit at a lower price per gallon than it sold like gasoline to many comparatively small service station customers in Detroit. Standard introduced evidence that it lowered the price to the jobbers in good faith to retain them as customers. The FTC concluded that this defense was not available in light of evidence introduced that the effect of the discrimination was to injure competition between the retail stations. Is the FTC correct?

6. What part do social and political goals play in the current Department of Justice merger guidelines?

7. Morton Salt is a manufacturer of table salt. It sells its "Blue Label" brand on what it terms a standard quantity discount system available to all customers. The prices are as follows:

Less than carload purchases, $1.60 per case; carload purchases, $1.50 per case; 5,000-case purchases in any consecutive twelve months, $1.40 per case; 50,000-case purchases in any consecutive twelve months, $1.35 per case. Only five companies ever bought sufficient quantities of Morton salt to attain the $1.35 price. These companies were able to buy in such quantities because of the volume in the large chains of retail stores they operated. The result is that these companies could sell Blue Label at the retail level at a price lower than wholesalers buying from Morton Salt could sell to independently operated retail stores, many of whom competed with the local outlets of the chain stores. Answering to a charge of price discrimination under the Robinson-Patman Act, Morton Salt argues that the discounts are available to everyone. All that is required is that a purchaser buy a certain quantity, which is the standard to everyone with no favoritism. Is this a good defense for Morton to a charge of violation of the Robinson-Patman Act?

8. Bird & Sons, Inc., was in the business of selling hard-surfaced felt-base floor covering. Bird is charged with price discrimination under Section 2(a) of the Clayton Act, as amended by the Robinson-Patman Act, for selling to Montgomery Ward at prices lower than the price charged Ward's retail competitors. Ward's is charged with the violation of Section 2(f) of the act for receiving the benefits of such discrimination. As a result of a change in sales policy a year and a half before the passage of the Robinson-Patman Act, at the time of the act's passage, only about one percent of all Bird sales were made to ordinary retailers. The remainder was being sold to mail order houses, such as Ward's, and to jobbers for resale to retailers. With respect to the price discrimination existing during the four months following the passage of the act, Bird showed the cost of selling to mail order houses was 18.6 percent, while the cost of selling to ordinary

retailers was 47.1 percent. This is one reason for Bird's shift in customers. Thus, costs differed by 28 percent while the difference in prices was less than 20 percent. Who, if anyone, is liable and what section of the amended act is relevant?

9. Alcoa is the country's leading producer of aluminum conductor, maintaining a 27.8 percent market share. Alcoa acquires Rome, which primarily manufactures insulated copper products, but has a 1.3 percent share of the aluminum conductor market. Rome ranks ninth among all companies and fourth among the independents in the aluminum conductor market. In the insulated aluminum field, a submarket of the aluminum conductor market, Rome ranked eighth among all companies and fourth among independents. Also, in the aluminum conductor market, no more than a dozen companies could account for as much as one percent of the industry production in any of the five years prior to the acquisition. Do you think the acquisition was allowed or disallowed and what are your reasons for thinking so?

10. Proctor & Gamble acquired the assets of Clorox Chemical Co. Clorox at that time was the leading manufacturer in the heavily concentrated household liquid bleach industry. Because of the high shipping cost and low sales price, it was not feasible to ship liquid bleach more than three hundred miles from the point of manufacture. Clorox had thirteen plants distributed throughout the nation. At the time of the acquisition, Clorox was the leading manufacturer of household liquid bleach with 48.8 percent of the national sales. Its market share had been steadily increasing for five years before the merger. In 1957, Clorox and Purex, its nearest rival, accounted for almost 65 percent of the nation's household liquid bleach sales, and together with four other firms, for almost 80 percent. Proctor & Gamble was a formidable competitor in the general area of

soaps, detergents, and cleaners. Proctor had been considering diversifying into other product lines related to its basic detergent-soap-cleanser business. Liquid bleach was a distinct possibility. Did this merger of Proctor and Clorox violate Section 7 of the Clayton Act?

11. GAF Corporation operated a cooperative advertising program. It paid the yellow pages advertising for its distributors. Marty's Floor Covering objected because GAF did not make this same offer to it. Marty's purchased tile from a distributor, not from GAF. Does it violate the Robinson-Patman Act to fail to offer to pay Marty's advertising expenses?

12. ITT Continental Baking Company sold its bread in the Northern California market at a lower price than it sold it elsewhere in the country. It did so because it believed that competitors were charging an equally low price in this area. Did Continental violate the Robinson-Patman Act?

13. Ranchero Motors, Inc., and Valley Plymouth were competing franchised dealers of defendant Studebaker-Packard Corporation. Due to excess production of its 1960 models, Studebaker had too many cars on hand after the introduction of the 1961 models, which were offered for sale in the early fall of 1960. Studebaker sold a large number of cars to Ranchero on December 31, 1960, at a price substantially lower than Valley had paid for the same cars earlier in the year. Valley argued that Studebaker violated the Robinson-Patman Act by selling these cars to Ranchero without according to it the same reduced prices of that sale. Is Valley correct?

14. Black Gold needed to purchase blown wool to use in the insulation of older homes. It needed this wool for participation in a program operated by the Public Service Company of Colorado. The only brand approved for use in this program was manufactured by Rockwool. Black Gold claimed that Rockwool violated the Robinson-Patman Act by refusing to supply it with as much blown wool as it required for the Public Service program. Is Black Gold correct?

CHAPTER 16

White-Collar and Business Crime: Regulation of Business through the Criminal Process

Classes of Crimes
Prosecution of Cases
Constitutional Protection
White-Collar Crime

Many people read about, and in some cases are the victims of, crimes. Businesses suffer billions of dollars in losses each year due to crime (see Table 16.1). In spite of the enormous impact of crime on society, many people have no idea how the criminal system operates. This chapter is designed to briefly explain what activities are classified as criminal and how criminal cases are handled within the American judicial system. The chapter also covers some of the limitations in the United States Constitution on the operation of the criminal system. The Constitution protects the rights of all people accused of a crime to make certain that every person receives a fair trial. The final section discusses the topic of white-collar crime, which is increasingly recognized as a major problem in society. Every year, more effort is devoted by the government to prosecuting such crimes.

TABLE 16.1   Estimated Cost of "Ordinary" Crime by Sector of Business—1971, 1973 and 1974, 1975 (billions of dollars)

BUSINESS SECTORS	1971	1973	1974	1975
Retailing	$ 4.8	5.2	$ 5.8	$ 6.5
Manufacturing	1.8	2.6	2.8	3.2
Wholesaling	1.4	1.8	2.1	2.4
Services	2.7	3.2	3.5	4.3
Transportation	1.5	1.7	1.9	2.3
Arson	0.2	0.3	0.3	0.4
Preventive	3.3	3.5	3.9	4.5
	$15.7	$18.3	$20.3	$23.6

Source: Bureau of Domestic Commerce, U.S. Department of Commerce.

CLASSES OF CRIMES

Crimes

A *crime* is an act or omission for which a sentence or a fine may be imposed by the presiding judge. Crimes are thought of as wrongs not only against the injured parties but also against society. The federal government, state governments, and city and county governments make certain types of behavior criminal.

Felonies

The most serious crime is called a **felony.** A felony generally is punishable by imprisonment in a penitentiary for more than a year. A fine may also be imposed in some cases. Theft of property worth more than a specified sum of money (for example, over one hundred dollars) usually constitutes a felony. Other examples of felonies are murder, rape, and possession of such drugs as heroin. Persons in business who violate the antitrust laws in certain cases may be guilty of a felony, as discussed in Chapters 13, 14, and 15.

Misdemeanors

All crimes that are not felonies normally are classified as **misdemeanors.** Misdemeanors are punishable by up to one year in jail. A fine also may be imposed. Theft of property of small value and assaulting another person are examples of misdemeanors. Violations of county and city laws sometimes may be punished by a jail sentence. Driving while intoxicated is a good example of an offense in violation of a local law. People refer to crimes that violate city and county laws as *petty crimes*. It should be noted that violations of local ordinances are frequently civil violations rather than criminal violations. In the case of felonies, misdemeanors, or petty crimes, the judge may impose a jail sentence.

PROSECUTION OF CASES

Criminal As Opposed to Civil

The American legal system handles cases in two separate ways: *civil litigation* and *criminal litigation*. The same action may result in both a civil case and a criminal case, but usually a set of facts gives rise to either one or the other.

Civil Cases. In a **civil case,** the plaintiff institutes suit against the defendant for some civil wrong allegedly committed by the defendant. Civil suits may be instituted by private citizens, businesses, or the government. The law creates the right and duties of persons. The term *civil law* refers to suits dealing with the rights and duties of persons other than those created in the criminal law. The plaintiff quite often seeks monetary damages in these cases. The goal of the civil system, in general, is to restore the injured party to the position he or she occupied prior to the defendant's wrongful actions. For example, if a person drives a vehicle at an excessive speed, and as a result, an accident occurs, that individual probably has committed a civil wrong—a tort. If the injured party broke a leg, the courts would require the defendant to compensate the plaintiff for the damages caused to the plaintiff. By the payment of a certain sum of money, the plaintiff in theory is restored to his or her position before the accident.

Criminal Cases. In a **criminal case,** a prosecutor representing either the state or the federal government brings suit against the defendant for an alleged violation of the state or federal criminal laws. The prosecutor in effect represents the public at large. The law penalizes a violation of the criminal law with a fine or imprisonment. The victim is not, as a general rule, compensated for the damages done.

The following are the typical stages of a felony case after the arrest of a person. Practices vary from state to state. The federal procedure is somewhat different from the states' procedure. This material is presented to give readers a general idea of the steps of a criminal case.

Steps in a Criminal Prosecution

The Arraignment or Appearance. The first appearance before a judge of a person accused of a crime is generally called the *arraignment* or appearance. At this stage, the charges are read to the accused, and the judge inquires how that person pleads—guilty or not guilty. The judge also determines whether the person is assisted by an attorney. If not, the judge inquires whether the person has the funds to hire an attorney. A person who lacks the money to hire an attorney will be provided one. The question of a person's release on bond or on his own recognizance (without posting a bond) is also discussed. A person may also at this point waive presentment of the case to a grand jury or waive presentment of the preliminary hearing.

The prosecutor is required to take a person before a judge without an unreasonable delay following his arrest.

The Preliminary Hearing. In place of a grand jury (when one is not required), most states use a preliminary hearing. At this stage the prosecution must prove that some evidence exists to establish that a crime was committed and that evidence exists that indicates the accused committed the crime. A formal hearing is conducted in front of the judge. If the judge agrees the case merits further prosecution, the judge "binds the defendant over" for trial—that is, the judge holds the person for trial.

Grand Jury. It is the function of a grand jury to determine if evidence that merits a trial exists. (Grand juries were discussed in Chapter 3.) A state may use a grand jury or a preliminary hearing, or both, and practice varies from state to state.

The Arraignment. At this point the defendant appears before the trial judge and the charges are read to the accused. The judge inquires how the defendant pleads. If the defendant pleads not guilty, the judge sets the case for trial. Some persons plead guilty at this stage. Others plead not guilty, but enter a guilty plea at a later date before the date set for trial.

A common practice in the United States is for the prosecution to agree to drop or reduce the charges against the defendant if the defendant will agree to plead guilty to certain charges. This is called a *plea bargain.*

The Trial. If the case is not settled before this time, the case will be tried. Most criminal cases are settled by a plea of guilty by the accused to reduced charges. The prosecution must prove at trial, beyond a reasonable doubt, (1) that a crime was committed, and (2) that the accused committed the crime in question. If the prosecution fails to establish its case, the person will go free.

Sentencing. Following either a plea or a conviction, court personnel generally study a person's past history and talk with the convicted person to decide whether the person should go to prison or not. The findings or recommendations are made to the judge. The judge takes this information into consideration in deciding whether to send a person to prison. If a judge decides to send a person to prison, the statute governing the crime typically specifies the length of time a person must be confined.

Appeal. If a person is convicted, he or she may appeal the conviction to a higher court. In general, the state may not appeal when the defendant is found to be not guilty as charged. The appeals court, if it disagrees with the decision of the trial court, may dismiss the case against the defendant. In most cases, if a prejudicial error took place at trial, the appeals court orders a new trial. This new trial does not violate the double jeopardy clause of the Constitution.

A person in prison who feels his or her conviction ought to be set aside may also file a writ of habeas corpus. The sole function of such a suit is to obtain the release of a person from unlawful imprisonment.

CONSTITUTIONAL PROTECTION

Bill of Rights

Many of the issues litigated in a criminal case involve constitutional principles. The Constitution guarantees each person in the United States a fair trial. The persons who wrote the Constitution feared abuse of the rights of innocent persons. For this reason, they adopted ten amendments to the United States Constitution that collectively are referred to as the **Bill of Rights.** These first ten amendments ensure that every person is treated in a fair and just manner. Several of them protect persons appearing in a court in a criminal case.

Fourteenth Amendment

For many years, the provisions in the first ten amendments were applied only to actions of the federal government. In the 1950s, the mood on the Supreme Court shifted, and the Court began to extend some of the provisions of the Bill of Rights to state actions as well as federal. The device used to extend some of the provisions in the Bill of Rights to state action was the due process clause of the Fourteenth

Amendment. The Court essentially was saying that the failure of the states to abide by certain provisions in the Bill of Rights was a denial of due process. Today, most of the provisions in the Bill of Rights apply to both federal and state proceedings.

We next turn to the three constitutional amendments most frequently dealt with in criminal cases—the Fourth, Fifth, and Sixth Amendments to the Constitution.

The Fourth Amendment protects the public from *unreasonable* searches and seizures. It does not prohibit all searches and seizures. It also requires that no warrants be issued "but upon probable cause, supported by oath or affirmation, and particularly describing the place to be searched, and the persons or things to be seized." A cursory examination of this language reveals a certain degree of vagueness in the language adopted. What is an *unreasonable* search and seizure? What is *probable cause?* The Constitution leaves a number of points unresolved, and the courts must examine and interpret the material in the Constitution. Because the members of the courts change over time, *the meaning attributed to various phrases in the Constitution also changes over time.* Different factual situations give rise to different applications of these rules. For this reason, people charged with a crime quite often challenge the introduction of evidence against them. They assert that somehow the Constitution was violated when certain evidence was obtained. A matter frequently contested is the failure of the police to obtain a search warrant prior to conducting a search.

The Fourth Amendment

Search Warrants. A **search warrant** is a written order by a court that gives the police the right to search certain premises or property for certain items, which if found may be seized and used as evidence in a criminal trial. A warrant also may be issued by a court to the police directing them to arrest someone.

Once an officer is in possession of sufficient information to warrant a search, the Constitution requires a review of this information by a judge to determine if probable cause for a search exists. After discussing the matter, if the judge thinks probable cause for a search exists, he or she will issue a warrant. Probable cause is more than a mere suspicion that certain facts are true—there should be sufficient evidence that a reasonable person would believe the facts alleged to be true. The warrant must be precisely worded—it must particularly describe the place to be searched and the item or items to be seized.

Justice Jackson, a former justice of the Supreme Court, made the following statement in *Johnson* v. *U.S.*, 333 U.S. 10, 13 (1948) concerning the purpose of the warrant requirement:

> The point of the Fourth Amendment, which often is not grasped by zealous officers, is not that it denies law enforcement the support of the usual inference which reasonable men draw from evidence. Its protection consists in requiring that those inferences be drawn by a neutral and detached magistrate instead of being judged by the officer engaged in the often competitive enterprise of ferreting out crime. Any assumption that evidence sufficient to support a magistrate's disinterested determination to issue a search warrant will justify the officers in making a search without a warrant would reduce the amendment to a nullity and leave the people's homes secure only in the discretion of police officers.

The drafters of the Constitution struck a balance between the need to apprehend criminals and the right to privacy. If the police have a reason to search a place, they must first convince a third party (a judge) of the merits of the search. If the judge agrees, a warrant is issued.

While the Fourth Amendment refers to "The right of people to be secure in their persons, houses, papers, and effects, against unreasonable searches and seizures," this right has been interpreted by the Supreme Court to extend to businesses as well as people. The government must comply with the Fourth Amendment when dealing with businesses as well as people, as is illustrated by the following case.

G. M. Leasing Corp. v. United States
United States Supreme Court
429 U.S. 338 (1977)

The Internal Revenue Service (IRS) determined that a taxpayer owed it money. The IRS, after determining that the corporation was the alter ego of the taxpayer, made a warrantless seizure of several automobiles in its possession and made a warrantless forced entry into a building owned by the corporation. Two days later, they again returned without a warrant and seized certain books, records, and other property. The corporation, claiming it was not the taxpayer's alter ego, brought a suit for damages based on the warrantless search conducted by the IRS. The district court ruled for the plaintiff. The court of appeals reversed. The Supreme Court ruled for the plaintiff. It held the IRS had violated the Fourth Amendment rights of the corporation by conducting a warrantless search. The portion of the Court's opinion dealing with the search of the business premise follows.

Justice Blackmun

The seizure of the books and records involved intrusion into the privacy of petitioner's offices. Significantly, the Court has said:

"[O]ne governing principle, justified by history and by current experience, has consistently been followed: except in certain carefully defined classes of cases, a search of private property without proper consent is 'unreasonable' unless it has been authorized by a valid search warrant."

The respondents do not contend that business premises are not protected by the Fourth Amendment. Such a proposition could not be defended in light of this Court's clear holdings to the contrary nor can it be claimed that corporations are without some Fourth Amendment rights.

The Court, of course, has recognized that a business, by its special nature and voluntary ex-

istence, may open itself to intrusions that would not be permissible in a purely private context.

In the present case, however, the intrusion into petitioner's privacy was not based on the nature of its business, its license, or any regulation of its activities. Rather, the intrusion is claimed to be justified on the ground that petitioner's assets were seizable to satisfy tax assessments. This involves nothing more than the normal enforcement of the tax laws, and we find no justification for treating petitioner differently in these circumstances simply because it is a corporation.

One of the primary evils intended to be eliminated by the Fourth Amendment was the massive intrusion on privacy undertaken in the collection of taxes pursuant to general warrants and writs of assistance.

The intrusion into petitioner's office is governed by the normal Fourth Amendment rule that "except in certain carefully defined classes of cases, a search of private property without proper consent is 'unreasonable' unless it has been authorized by a valid search warrant."

We therefore conclude that the warrantless entry into petitioner's office was in violation of the commands of the Fourth Amendment.

The Fifth Amendment creates a number of safeguards to protect persons accused of crimes from being prosecuted unfairly. In certain federal cases, it requires a grand jury to first issue an indictment before a person is tried for a crime. After an indictment by a grand jury, if one is used, the defendant is arraigned in trial court. The Fifth Amendment prevents people from being tried twice for the same offense.

The Fifth Amendment

Self-incrimination. The Fifth Amendment prohibits the government from compelling a person to be a witness against himself or herself. The drafters of the Bill of Rights feared the police might abuse a suspect in order to extract a confession. At one point in history, prosecutors placed people accused of crimes on the rack. They tortured suspects until they admitted a violation of the law. Naturally, the rack proved to be an effective device in obtaining confessions. People either admitted their guilt or died.

The courts have held that a confession may be used against a defendant—but only when the confession was *knowingly, freely,* and *voluntarily* given. The United States Supreme Court has decided that before confessions may be used against defendants, they must first be informed of certain rights guaranteed to all persons under the Constitution.

Business Records. The Fifth Amendment is also relevant to the question of attempts by the government to obtain business records from companies. The argument has been made that requiring a person to turn over certain records violates the Fifth Amendment privilege that prevents a person from being compelled in a criminal case to be a witness against himself or herself.

Over the years, the Court has interpreted the Fifth Amendment in such a manner that it applies only when the accused is compelled to make some testimonial communication that is incriminating. The Court has refused to extend the Fifth Amendment privilege to the giving of blood samples, voice samples, and other nontestimonial evidence.

The following case discusses an attempt by the Internal Revenue Service to obtain documents from an attorney that were produced by an accountant.

Fisher v. United States
United States Supreme Court
425 U.S. 391 (1976)

In two cases, the government brought an action to compel the production of accountants' documents in possession of taxpayers' attorneys. These documents involved the accountants' workpapers relating to the clients' books and records, copies of income tax returns, and certain other correspondence between the accountants and the clients. The taxpayers argued that to force the attorneys to turn over these papers would violate their Fifth Amendment privilege rights. The lower courts, as well as the Supreme Court, ruled that the Fifth Amendment was not violated by requiring these papers to be turned over to the Internal Revenue Service. The Court also ruled that the attorney-client privilege did not bar the production of these records.

Justice White

In these two cases we are called upon to decide whether a summons directing an attorney to produce documents delivered to him by his client in connection with the attorney-client relationship is enforceable over claims that the documents were constitutionally immune from summons in the hands of the client and retained that immunity in the hands of the attorney.

All of the parties in these cases and the Court of Appeals for the Fifth Circuit have concurred in the proposition that if the Fifth Amendment would have excused a taxpayer from turning over the accountant's papers had he possessed them, the attorney to whom they are delivered for the purpose of obtaining legal advice should also be immune from subpoena. Although we agree with this proposition we are convinced that it is not the taxpayer's Fifth Amendment privilege that would excuse the attorney from production.

The relevant part of that Amendment provides:

"No person . . . shall be compelled in any criminal case to be a *witness against himself*." (Emphasis added.)

The taxpayer's privilege under this Amendment is not violated by enforcement of the summonses involved in these cases because enforcement against a taxpayer's lawyer would not "compel" the taxpayer to do anything—and certainly would not compel him to be a "witness" against himself. The Court has held repeatedly that the Fifth Amendment is limited to prohibiting the use of "physical or moral compulsion" exerted on the person asserting the privilege. The taxpayer's Fifth

Amendment privilege is not violated by enforcement of the summonses directed toward their attorneys. This is true whether or not the Amendment would have barred a subpoena directing the taxpayer to produce the documents while they were in his hands.

The fact that the attorneys are agents of the taxpayers does not change this result. In *Hale v. Henkel* the Court said that the privilege "was never intended to permit [a person] to plead the fact that some third person might be incriminated by his testimony, even though he were the agent of such person. . . . [T]he Amendment is limited to a person who shall be compelled in any criminal case to be a witness against himself." It is extortion of information from the accused himself that offends our sense of justice. Agent or no, the lawyer is not the taxpayer. The taxpayer is the "accused," and nothing is being extorted from him.

We feel obliged to inquire whether the attorney-client privilege applies to documents in the hands of an attorney which would have been privileged in the hand of the client by reason of the Fifth Amendment. "It follows that when the client himself would be privileged from production of the document, either as a party at common law . . . or as exempt from self-incrimination, the attorney having possession of the document is not bound to produce." 8 Wigmore, Section 2307.

Since each taxpayer transferred possession of the documents in question from himself to his attorney in order to obtain legal assistance in the tax investigations in question, the papers, if unobtainable by summons from the client, are unobtainable by summons directed to the attorney by reason of the attorney-client privilege. We accordingly proceed to the question whether the documents could have been obtained by summons addressed to the taxpayer while the documents were in his possession. The only bar to enforcement of such summons asserted by the parties or the courts below is the Fifth Amendment's privilege against self-incrimination.

A subpoena served on a taxpayer requiring him to produce an accountant's workpapers in his possession without doubt involves substantial compulsion. But it does not compel oral testimony; nor would it ordinarily compel the taxpayer to restate, repeat, or affirm the truth of the contents of the documents sought. Therefore, the Fifth Amendment would not be violated by the fact alone that the papers on their face might incriminate the taxpayer, for the privilege protects a person only against being incriminated by his own compelled testimonial communications. The accountant's workpapers are not the taxpayer's.

They were not prepared by the taxpayer, and they contain no testimonial declarations by him. Furthermore, as far as this record demonstrates, the preparation of all of the papers sought in these cases was wholly voluntary, and they cannot be said to contain compelled testimonial evidence, either of the taxpayers or of anyone else. The taxpayer cannot avoid compliance with the subpoena merely by asserting that the item of evidence which he is required to produce contains incriminating writing, whether his own or that of someone else.

Whether the Fifth Amendment would shield the taxpayer from producing his own tax records in his possession is a question not involved here; for the papers demanded here are not his "private papers." We do hold that compliance with a summons directing the taxpayer to produce the accountant's documents involved in these cases would involve no incriminating testimony within the protection of the Fifth Amendment.

In a later case involving a sole proprietorship, the Supreme Court ruled that, where the businessman was being investigated concerning corruption in the awarding of county and municipal contracts, the act of producing certain business records of his company was privileged. The act of producing subpoenaed documents cannot be compelled without a statutory grant of immunity (*United States* v. *Doe*, 104 S.Ct. 1237 [1984]).

The Sixth Amendment guarantees anyone tried in either federal or state court the following rights: (1) a speedy and public trial, (2) trial by an impartial jury of the state and district where the crime was committed, (3) the right to be informed of the charges against him or her, (4) the right to confront witnesses against him or her, (5) the right to an attorney, and (6) the right to subpoena witnesses in his or her favor. The right to a trial would mean very little if the government conducted it unfairly. These safeguards merely help ensure that a person receives a trial likely to achieve a just result.

The Sixth Amendment

The Right to Counsel. The Sixth Amendment specifically states: "In all criminal prosecutions, the accused shall . . . have the assistance of counsel for his defense." The Constitution guarantees everyone the right to an attorney.

The Constitution is silent on the question of providing attorneys for poor persons accused of crimes. Many people were tried by the government without the assistance of an attorney because they lacked the funds to hire one. The state or federal government, of course, was represented by an attorney.

The Court, in *Gideon* v. *Wainwright*, decided the Constitution requires the government to provide an attorney for a person who is accused of a felony but who lacks the funds to hire an attorney. Since the *Gideon* decision, the Court has expanded this doctrine to cover any situation in which a conviction on the charges brought by the government would result in a jail sentence. This means that even for less serious offenses, the state or federal government must provide an attorney to indigent persons if there is a chance a jail sentence could be imposed.

Having examined the major constitutional provisions related to criminal trials, we will now focus on a problem of great concern to business—white-collar crime.

WHITE-COLLAR CRIME

The most widely talked about form of crime often involves violence (as in murder or rape) or a loss of property (as in theft or arson). These crimes may be distinguished from some less frequently discussed crimes, which are often referred to under the general heading of "white-collar crime." The term *white-collar crime* was first popularized by Edwin H. Sutherland in 1939. He defined it as "crime committed by a person of respectability and high social status in the course of his occupation." Since that time, the term has taken on a much broader significance. A possible definition, although there is widespread disagreement on the meaning of this term, is *an illegal act or series of illegal acts committed by nonphysical means and by concealment or guile, to obtain money or property, or to obtain business or personal advantage.* While definitions of white-collar crime vary, most people in using this phrase are referring to criminal activity by persons who use neither force nor violence. The people who commit white-collar crimes tend to bilk the public through fraud, not strong-arm tactics.

White-collar crimes often are committed against businesses or by businesses.

Types of White-Collar Crime

Innumerable actions by persons may result in criminal liability. Some of these activities might be regarded as white-collar crimes. The Federal Bureau of Investigation, in its work dealing with white-collar crimes, looks at such activities as bank fraud and embezzlement, federal program fraud, corruption of public officials, and theft of copyrighted material.

Other types of fraud include theft by employees, bribery, insurance fraud, and consumer fraud. Much of the merchandise stolen from retail businesses leaves the stores not in the hands of shoplifters, but in those of store employees. Many employees feel entitled to take a dress or shirt or pair of shoes every now and then. In order to get the business of a firm, a company may pay the purchasing agent a bribe. To induce unions to refer good workers, companies may bribe union officials. To obtain lucrative government contracts, companies might grease the palms of the appropriate officials. Fraudulent insurance claims cost insurance companies millions of dollars—for example, when an accident victim falsely claims a whiplash, or a businessman sets fire to his building to collect the insurance. Likewise, some insurance companies have signed policyholders up, and after collecting a few premiums, the companies have folded. In other cases, collecting under the terms of the policy is virtually impossible.

Consumer Fraud. Every day, many types of consumer fraud result in losses to gullible consumers. Advertisements for products that fraudulently promise weight loss dot newspapers and magazines. Promises to restore hair appear daily in the papers. Promises that they will get rich quick lure unsuspecting consumers to part with their cash.

Antitrust Violations. Antitrust law is discussed in depth in Chapters 13, 14, and 15. For our purposes here, it is sufficient to realize that federal law prohibits activities by businesses that restrain trade, or monopolize it, or even attempt to monopolize it. Several federal acts—the Sherman Act, the Clayton Act, and the Federal Trade Commission Act—govern the resolution of antitrust cases.

Although the Federal Trade Commission (FTC) can enforce much of the antitrust law, criminal actions are instituted only by the Department of Justice. The department brings antitrust criminal cases pursuant to the Sherman Act, which permits fines of up to two million dollars against corporations and penalties of up to one-hundred thousand dollars for individuals as well as up to three years in prison. The penalties under the Clayton Act are largely civil. The FTC Act also provides for civil penalties.

Computer Crime. Since the introduction of the computer to the business world, its impact has grown by leaps and bounds. The use of the computer to generate and store data has gone from limited use by large businesses to the point where today hundreds of thousands of businesses use computers. Even small businesses rely on computers in day-to-day transactions. Everyone deals with companies using computers.

As the use of computers spreads, so does the possibility of misuse of these machines. People run, maintain, and receive data from them. This opens the door to such crimes as fraud, embezzlement, espionage, and sabotage. Businesses must be vigilant to prevent computer crimes, as the average computer crime easily can cost a business thousands of dollars.

People working with computers may be tempted to misuse the machines. Maintenance personnel, analysts, intruders making unauthorized use of the computer system, or other users may commit a computer crime. People who wish to destroy business records might attempt to physically destroy a computer or its programs. False data can be provided to the machine. People can attempt to unlawfully obtain information stored in the computer. Information can also be improperly fed into the machine. These are just a few of the dangers associated with the storage of information. Realizing the dangers associated with such machines, businesses have tried to install security controls to minimize such crime, but people continue to commit them.

The main types of computer crimes are: (1) entering fraudulent data into a computer system, (2) unauthorized use of computer-related facilities, (3) alteration or destruction of information or files, and (4) theft by use of the computer.

Although many of these crimes have been committed, businesses have not consistently reported them. There are several reasons for this. Such crimes are often difficult to detect. Furthermore, management is often reluctant to report them because it feels persons will lose respect for the management.

Mail and Wire Fraud

Businesspeople frequently use the mail, the telephone, and other devices to communicate with the public. By transmitting messages to other people, a person may be opening himself up for prosecution under the federal statutes relating to mail and wire fraud.

With respect to mail fraud, merely using the mail as an incident to an essential part of a fraudulent scheme is sufficient to make the person subject to possible prosecution under the mail fraud act. For example, a real estate promoter might try to induce people to purchase worthless land from him by mailing letters to prospective buyers concerning the land he is offering for sale. Sending the letter may make the sender subject to prosecution under the mail fraud act. Alternatively, using a telephone, telegraph, telecopier, television, radio, or other device to transmit the same message may result in the sender being subject to prosecution under the federal wire fraud act.

The mail and wire fraud statutes outlaw the same type of behavior; that is, using the mails (or wire) for the purpose of executing a scheme or artifice to defraud the public in order to obtain money or property. The acts do not define the term *defraud*. However, the courts have given this term a very broad interpretation. A "scheme or artifice" to defraud refers to the use of some plan or devising some trick to perpetrate a fraud upon another.

In order to prosecute a person, the government must establish that the scheme or artifice was reasonably calculated to deceive persons of ordinary prudence and intelligence in order to bring about some harm or to obtain some undeserved advantage. In other words, the defendant must have intended to defraud an average person.

Suppose someone plans to try to encourage people to invest in a business he is organizing. The promoter intends to abscond with the funds once he tricks investors out of their money. Use of the mail or wire by the promoter to further his fraudulent scheme will make it possible to prosecute him under these acts.

These statutes can be used in a wide variety of situations. Each violation is subject to a fine of not more than one thousand dollars and/or imprisonment of not more than five years. Needless to say, because of the broad scope of these acts, a business person should be exceedingly careful when using the mail or transmission devices. It should also be noted that these acts are quite often used with other federal statutes. For example, a person might be charged by federal prosecutors with both securities fraud and mail fraud.

These acts are especially important because violations of these acts can give rise to liability under the Racketeer Influenced Corrupt Organization Act, which is discussed in the next section.

Racketeer Influenced Corrupt Organizations Act (RICO)

When persons violate the law by engaging in illegal activities, their actions sometimes generate great sums of money. Suppose a group of college students decide to deal in cocaine. Even if they sell the drugs to a limited number of people, the drug dealers very likely will take in more money than the cocaine cost them. Just as in legitimate businesses, the object in many criminal enterprises is to make a profit. The people from whom the college students purchase the cocaine hope to make a profit, as do other individuals in the chain of distribution.

Criminal behavior can generate immense sums of money for everybody concerned. The college students may cease dealing in drugs after graduating from school, but many dealers belong to a more complex organization that operates for years.

Such enterprises often resemble the organizational structure of a corporation. When a member dies or retires, another person moves up in the enterprise to take his or her place.

The traditional approach to dealing with crime has emphasized the detection of crime and imprisonment of those responsible for the crimes in question. The police often find it difficult to establish any evidence against mobsters high up in such organizations. Even when prosecutors succeed in obtaining convictions, crime never halts for a moment. That is because a criminal enterprise, much like a corporation, fills the vacant slot with another person. Just like a legitimate corporation, a criminal enterprise has a life of its own.

In the course of engaging in criminal conduct, such enterprises generate considerable sums—quite often, in cash. The money obtained through an activity such as drug peddling then needs to be "cleaned" so that the source of such money will be hidden. One device frequently used to cleanse money is to acquire control of a seemingly legitimate business—such as a bank, restaurant, motel, or auto dealership. Alternatively, a legitimate business may be operated in a perfectly legal manner and not used to cleanse money, but may have been acquired with funds generated by criminal activities. Thus, sooner or later, some or all of the illicit profits produced by an unlawful venture winds up in "legitimate" businesses. Competitors of these businesses, who acquired their companies by investing money they accumulated through lawful means, find themselves in competition with criminals.

To effectively deter crime, Congress deemed it necessary to seize the funds generated by enterprises that break the law. Without such a law, criminal enterprises would continue to flourish even after placing one or more of their members behind bars. Congress wished to halt the infiltration of legitimate businesses by organized crime.

To accomplish this, Congress passed the Racketeer Influenced Corrupt Organizations Act (**RICO**) which was enacted as part of the Organized Crime Control Act of 1970. This Act is designed to economically cripple organized crime by attacking its economic base. Congress hoped that if the underworld lost the money it generated through its illicit activities, eventually its members would find it unprofitable to continue to break the law.

RICO makes it unlawful to conduct or acquire an interest in an "enterprise" through a "pattern of racketeering activity" or through the collection of an "unlawful debt."

Collecting an illegal gambling debt is an example of a violation of the latter provision. It is largely addressed to loan sharking. Most RICO defendants, however, are alleged to be engaged in a "pattern of racketeering."

Suppose that the college students mentioned earlier eventually acquire a substantial sum of money as a result of selling cocaine. They then invest their profits by purchasing a college pizza parlor. The students violated RICO because the income in this instance was produced by a pattern of racketeering activity.

RICO prohibits using money generated by a pattern of racketeering activity (1) to gain or maintain control over an enterprise, (2) to invest in an enterprise, or (3) to participate in the conduct or the affairs of an enterprise. The term *enterprise* includes all legal entities and any union or group of individuals associated in fact even though they are not a legal entity.

In *United States* v. *Turkette*, 452 U.S. 576 (1981), the United States Supreme

Court ruled that RICO applies to the activities of illegitimate enterprises. In that case, the enterprise in question dealt with the trafficking of narcotics. The Supreme Court decided that a group of persons dealing in drugs was an "enterprise" because of the use of the language in the statute that defines an enterprise as "a group of persons associated together for a common purpose of engaging in a course of conduct." The government established an enterprise at trial by introducing evidence that the defendants participated in an on-going organization, formal or informal, and by introducing evidence that the various associates functioned as a continuing unit. Thus, a wholly criminal organization can be a RICO enterprise. In addition to establishing that the defendants are engaged in an enterprise, the government must also prove they conducted or acquired this enterprise through a "pattern of racketeering activity."

A "pattern of racketeering activity" is defined in the act as "at least two acts of racketeering activity . . . committed within ten years of each other. . . ." There are four basic types of racketeering activities. First, certain activities that are felonies under state law, for example, arson, are categorized as racketeering under RICO. Second, acts indictable under Title 18 of the United States Code, such as mail fraud, are racketeering activities. Third, violations of Title 29 of the United States Code, which prohibits such activities as loans to labor organizations, also constitute racketeering. Finally, bankruptcy fraud and fraud in the sale of securities and drug-related offenses also are regarded as racketeering activities.

Because the act defines drug-related offenses as racketeering activities, if the college students mentioned earlier engaged in two sales of cocaine within a ten-year period, a court could find they had been engaged in a "pattern of racketeering activity" for purposes of establishing a violation of the RICO Act. RICO is very important to individuals engaged in legitimate businesses as well as to persons involved in a criminal organization.

What makes RICO such a significant statute in the field of white-collar crime is the type of offenses that the statute defines as racketeering activities (predicate acts). Within a ten-year period, if a person engages in two acts such as mail (or wire) fraud, securities fraud, arson, bribery, bankruptcy fraud, embezzlement from pension funds or a host of other criminal activities, he or she has engaged in a "pattern of racketeering activity" insofar as RICO is concerned.

Obviously, since many transactions in business utilize the mail or wire, if these transactions are subsequently established to be fraudulent, they may give rise to a RICO suit. This creates an enormous likelihood that any white-collar crime perpetrated by a business person may subsequently be attacked as a violation of the RICO Act.

Congress included significant penalties in RICO. RICO authorizes the government to bring actions to enjoin RICO violations. Each violation may be punished by a maximum fine of twenty-five thousand dollars and/or a maximum sentence of twenty years. Furthermore, RICO permits a judge to order a forfeiture of any interest in property that was acquired or maintained in violation of the act, or a forfeiture of any interest in property that gives the defendant influence over an enterprise that the defendant has "established, operated, controlled, conducted or participated in the conduct of" in violation of the Act.

The purpose of the forfeiture penalty is to take the property in question from the racketeer, thus depriving him or her of the ability to continue to control the property.

A recent case decided by the Supreme Court dealt with the forfeiture provision. Russello had been convicted of violating the RICO Act because of his involvement in an arson ring. He received compensation from an insurance company for a fire he caused to a building he owned. A person convicted under the RICO Act shall forfeit to the United States "any interest he has acquired or maintained in violation" of the act. Russello argued that this language permitted the United States to seize only interests in an enterprise. The Supreme Court rejected his interpretation of this provision. It ruled that the insurance proceeds he received as a result of a violation of the RICO Act were subject to forfeiture to the United States government.

RICO creates a very significant right for *private parties*—the right to sue for any damages a person sustains as a result of a violation of RICO. These damages, if established, will be *trebled* by the court. Attorney fees also may be recovered.

Civil RICO

Civil RICO claims have been asserted in a wide variety of cases, such as securities, commodities and contract disputes.

A person who engages in mail fraud can be sued under RICO. Because the federal mail fraud statute is so broad, it is relatively easy for private litigants to establish a case under the RICO Act. Each mailing is generally treated as a separate violation of the mail fraud act. Thus, two such mailings can be treated as a "pattern of racketeering activity." Every transaction involving the wrongful use of the mails, telephone, or interstate wire facilities creates the potential for a civil lawsuit under RICO.

Although Congress was concerned with the takeover of legitimate businesses by organized crime when it passed RICO, the primary focus of the act is now civil lawsuits. As the categories of racketeering activities are so broad, it is relatively easy for a plaintiff to state a case. Therefore, it is highly likely that RICO suits will become even more common as time passes. Businesspeople should be aware of the possibility that any unlawful actions they engage in could result in a civil suit under RICO. In the following case, the Supreme Court considered civil RICO suits.

Sedima, S.P.R.I. v. Imrex Co., Inc.
United States Supreme Court
105 S.Ct. 3275 (1985)

Sedima, a Belgian corporation, entered into a joint venture with Imrex Company to provide electronic components to a Belgian firm. A dispute arose between the parties. Sedima filed suit in federal court and alleged a number of claims against Imrex, including claims against two of its officers. The complaint alleged that Imrex had engaged in the predicate acts of mail and wire fraud. The district court and Court of Appeals for the Second Circuit ruled for Imrex. The Second Circuit in its ruling expressed concern about the use of the RICO Act in civil suits against people other than mobsters. It ruled that, to bring a civil suit, the defendant must have first been convicted of a crime. Second, it ruled that an injury separate and apart from any injury caused by the defendant's commission of the predicate acts must be established. The United States Supreme Court reversed the Second Circuit on both points.

Justice White

The language of RICO gives no obvious indication that a suit can proceed only after a criminal conviction. The word "conviction" does not appear in any relevant portion of the statute. As defined in the statute, racketeering activity consists not of acts for which the defendant has been convicted, but of acts for which he could be. Indeed, if either § 1961 or § 1962 did contain such a requirement, a prior conviction would also be a prerequisite, nonsensically, for a criminal prosecution, or for a civil action by the government to enjoin violations that had not yet occurred.

The legislative history also undercuts the reading of the court below. Had Congress intended to impose this novel requirement, there would have been at least some mention of it in the legislative history, even if not in the statute.

Finally, we note that a prior conviction requirement would be inconsistent with Congress' underlying policy concerns. Such a rule would severely handicap potential plaintiffs. A guilty party may escape conviction for any number of reasons—not least among them the possibility that the Government itself may choose to pursue only civil remedies. Accordingly, the fact that Imrex and the individual defendants have not been convicted under RICO or the federal mail and wire fraud statutes does not bar Sedima's action.

In considering the Court of Appeals' second prerequisite for a private civil RICO action—"injury . . . caused by an activity which RICO was designed to deter"—we are somewhat hampered by the vagueness of that concept. We need not pinpoint the Second Circuit's precise holding, for

we perceive no distinct "racketeering injury" requirement. Given that "racketeering activity" consists of no more and no less than commission of a predicate act, we are initially doubtful about a requirement of a "racketeering injury" separate from the harm from the predicate acts. A reading of the statute belies any such requirement. If the defendant engages in a pattern of racketeering activity in a manner forbidden by these provisions, and the racketeering activities injure the plaintiff in his business or property, the plaintiff has a claim under § 1964(c). There is no room in the statutory language for an additional, amorphous "racketeering injury" requirement.

A violation of § 1962(c), the section on which Sedima relies, requires (1) conduct (2) of an enterprise (3) through a pattern (4) of racketeering activity. The plaintiff must, of course, allege each of these elements to state a claim. Conducting an enterprise that affects interstate commerce is obviously not in itself a violation of § 1962, nor is mere commission of the predicate offenses. In addition, the plaintiff only has standing if, and can only recover to the extent that, he has been injured in his business or property by the conduct constituting the violation.

But the statute requires no more than this. Any recoverable damages occurring by reason of a violation of § 1962(c) will flow from the commission of the predicate acts.

The decision below is reversed, and the case is remanded for further proceedings consistent with this opinion.

Justice Powell (dissenting)

In both *Turkette* and *Russello,* we found that the "declared purpose" of Congress in enacting the RICO statute was "to seek the eradication of organized crime in the United States." That orga-

nized crime was Congress's target is apparent from the Act's title, is made plain throughout the legislative history of the statute. The legislative history cited by the Court today amply supports this conclusion and the Court concedes that in its private civil version, RICO is evolving into something quite different from the original conception of its enactors. Yet, the Court concludes that it is compelled by the statutory language to construe § 1964(c) to reach garden variety fraud and breach of contract cases such as those before us today. Nonetheless, the legislative history makes clear that the statute was intended to be *applied* to organized crime, and an influential sponsor of the bill emphasized that any effect it had beyond such crime was meant to be only incidental. RICO has been interpreted so broadly that it has been used more often against respected businesses with no ties to organized crime, than against the mobsters who were the clearly intended target of the statute. While I acknowledge that the language of the statute *may* be read as broadly as the Court interprets it today, I do not believe that is *must* be so read. The statute may and should be read narrowly to confine its reach to the type of conduct Congress had in mind. It is the duty of this Court to implement the unequivocal intention of Congress.

White-collar crimes cost society billions of dollars. Many persons allege that this type of crime today costs society over two hundred billion dollars—far more than the costs associated with crimes of violence.

Cost of Crime

What efforts are being made by the government to counteract this tide of criminal activity? Many prosecutors have expressed a desire to devote an increasing amount of time to white-collar crimes. Their efforts are hampered, however, by the difficulty of detecting such crimes and the complexity of proof. Most departments lack the training and manpower to go after many of the complex white-collar crimes, such as computer crime. For this reason, prosecutors may prefer to devote the bulk of their effort to crimes of violence. However, a move in the direction of increasing prosecution of white-collar crimes is clearly taking place. The great public outcry due to the widespread publicity some of these schemes attract eventually will lead to more and more prosecutions.

Enforcement Efforts

Few Go to Jail. Of the cases that actually go to trial and result in a conviction, many historically have been disposed of through the use of a *fine* or a suspended sentence. Very few white-collar criminals go to jail for any extended period. Many people have charged that our system of justice follows a double standard—a harsh, unbending attitude towards crimes other than white-collar crimes, and lenient treatment of white-collar offenses. On the average, a white-collar criminal stands a far smaller chance of spending even a day in jail than a person who commits an act of violence.

While it is true that businesses often are the victim of crimes, sometimes, acting through their employees, businesses commit crimes. Many major companies have been convicted of major violations of the law. Companies have been found guilty of violating the antitrust laws, giving kickbacks, and evading their tax liabilities, to name just a few of the crimes.

Criminal Liability of Officers of Corporations

Some scholars attribute business crimes to excessive competitive pressure in certain industries. As managers are evaluated only in the short run and quite often only on the basis of financial returns, the temptation to violate the law sometimes proves irresistible. Another possible explanation for criminal activities is industry custom and structure. The problems associated with certain industries encourage criminal activities. For example, in the construction industry, the need to meet deadlines may contribute to bribery. The fact that crime frequently pays also contributes to criminal activity. If it is profitable to violate the law, many people will do so—hoping, of course, they will be able to escape detection.

In the following case, the United States Supreme Court found the chief executive of a corporation criminally liable even though there was no direct proof of wrongful action by the president. The issue in the *Park* case essentially deals with the issue of accountability. Park held a responsible position within the corporation, and by virtue of this position, he had authority and responsibility to deal with the problems for which he was subsequently held accountable. This case perhaps reflects a trend among courts and lawmakers toward forcing chief executive officers to assume more direct responsibility for their actions. It should be noted, however, that this case was brought pursuant to the Food, Drug, and Cosmetic Act, which creates special standards of behavior for covered businesses.

United States v. Park
United States Supreme Court
421 U.S. 658 (1974)

Acme Markets, Inc., a large national food chain, and its president were charged with violating Section 301(k) of the Federal Food, Drug, and Cosmetic Act, which prohibits the adulteration of food held for sale after shipment in interstate commerce. The government alleged that Acme had caused food shipments to be exposed to rodent contamination. Acme pleaded guilty but its president did not. Evidence was admitted that tended to show that the president was "responsible for . . . the entire operation of the company" and that he knew of the unsanitary conditions at Acme's warehouse. The president was advised by the Food and Drug Administration (FDA) of unsanitary conditions at Acme's Philadelphia warehouse in April 1970, and of similar conditions in 1971, at the Baltimore warehouse. In January 1972, after receiving an FDA letter, the president conferred with the vice-president of legal affairs, who informed him the Baltimore division vice-president was taking corrective action. The president contended he assigned the issue of sanitation to dependable subordinates. The president was convicted at the trial level. He was required to pay a fine of fifty dollars on each violation for which he was found guilty. The court of appeals reversed, arguing that the president could not be found guilty without evidence of "wrongful action" on his part. The government appealed to the Supreme Court. The Supreme Court ruled against Park.

Chief Justice Burger

The question presented by the Government's petition for certiorari in *United States v. Dotterweich,* and the focus of this Court's opinion, was whether the manager of a corporation, as well as the corporation itself, may be prosecuted under the Federal Food, Drug, and Cosmetic Act of 1938 for the introduction of misbranded and adulterated articles into interstate commerce.

In reversing the judgment of the Court of Appeals and reinstating Dotterweich's conviction, this Court looked to the purposes of the Act and noted that they "touch phases of the lives and health of people which, in the circumstances of modern industrialism, are largely beyond self-protection." It observed that the Act is of "a now familiar type" which "dispenses with the conventional requirement for criminal conduct—awareness of some wrongdoing. In the interest of the larger good it puts the burden of acting at hazard upon a person otherwise innocent but standing in responsible relation to a public danger."

Central to the Court's conclusion that individuals other than proprietors are subject to the criminal provisions of the Act was the reality that "the only way in which a corporation can act is through the individuals who act on its behalf."

The Court concluded, settled doctrines of criminal law dictated that the offense was committed "by all who . . . have . . . a responsible share in the furtherance of the transaction which the statute outlaws."

The rule that corporate employees who have "a responsible share in the furtherance of the transaction which the statute outlaws" are subject to the criminal provisions of the Act was not formulated in a vacuum. Cases under the Federal Food and Drugs Act of 1906 reflected the view both that knowledge or intent were not required to be proved in prosecutions under its criminal provisions, and that responsible corporate agents could be subjected to the liability thereby imposed. Moreover, the principle had been recognized that a corporate agent, through whose act, default, or omission the corporation committed a crime, was himself guilty individually of that crime. The principle had been applied whether or not the crime required "consciousness of wrongdoing," and it had been applied not only to those corporate agents who themselves committed the criminal act, but also to those who by virtue of their managerial positions or other similar relation

to the actor could be deemed responsible for its commission.

In the latter class of cases, the liability of managerial officers did not depend on their knowledge of, or personal participation in, the act made criminal by the statute. Rather, where the statute under which they were prosecuted dispensed with "consciousness of wrongdoing," an omission or failure to act was deemed a sufficient basis for a responsible corporate agent's liability. It was enough in such cases that, by virtue of the relationship he bore to the corporation, the agent had the power to prevent the act complained of.

Thus *Dotterweich* and the cases which have followed reveal that in providing sanctions which reach and touch the individuals who execute the corporate mission—and this is by no means necessarily confined to a single corporate agent or employee—the Act imposes not only a positive duty to seek out and remedy violations when they occur but also, and primarily, a duty to implement measures that will insure that violations will not occur. The requirements of foresight and vigilance imposed on responsible corporate agents are beyond question demanding, and perhaps onerous, but they are no more stringent than the public has a right to expect of those who voluntarily assume positions of authority in business enterprises whose services and products affect the health and well-being of the public that supports them.

The Act does not, as we observed in *Dotterweich*, make criminal liability turn on "awareness of some wrongdoing" or "conscious fraud." The duty imposed by Congress on responsible corporate agents is, we emphasize, one that requires the highest standard of foresight and vigilance, but the Act, in its criminal aspect, does not require that which is objectively impossible. The theory upon which responsible corporate agents are held criminally accountable for "causing" violations of the Act permits a claim that a defendant was "powerless" to prevent or correct the violation to "be raised defensively at a trial on the merits." If such a claim is made, the defendant has the burden of coming forward with evidence, but this does not alter the Government's ultimate burden of proving beyond a reasonable doubt the defendant's guilt, including his power, in light of the duty imposed by the Act, to prevent or correct the prohibited condition. Congress has seen fit to enforce the accountability of responsible corporate agents dealing with products which may affect the health of consumers by penal sanctions cast in rigorous terms, and the obligation of the courts is to give them effect so long as they do not violate the Constitution.

The *Park* case establishes the rule that an executive who possesses the authority and responsibility to prevent a violation of the Food, Drug, and Cosmetic Act may be held criminally liable for a failure to comply with the law. Park had the power and authority to take action to bring the corporation in compliance with the law. His failure to take measures to ensure that a violation of the law did not occur resulted in his criminal liability. The absence of personal knowledge of the wrongdoing by Park and the delegation of the task to a dependable subordinate did not prevent him from being found guilty.

Merely having the power and authority to correct a violation of the law does not, however, always result in criminal liability on the part of the officers of a company. In fact, the *Park* case is somewhat unusual. Many criminal statutes require proof that a manager, to be guilty of a crime, have a culpable state of mind—which Park argued he did not have.

Many prosecutors in recent years have attempted to prosecute officers of corporations for violating the criminal law. The following case deals with a charge made against officers of the Warner-Lambert Company that they were somehow criminally responsible for the deaths of six employees. This case is illustrative of a growing trend to attempt to force businesses to behave in a socially responsible manner by attempting to impose criminal sentences on the officers of the company. Ask yourself if the decision in this case furthers or hinders socially responsible actions by business.

People v. Warner-Lambert Co.
Court of Appeals of New York
414 N.E.2d 660 (1980)

The state of New York brought an action against certain officers and employees of the Warner-Lambert Co. for the deaths of six employees. While some employees were cleaning up some dust on a machine, an explosion occurred, followed by a second explosion that injured fifty workers—of whom six did not survive. The cause of the explosion, although it apparently was not caused by a worker, was not definitely established. The officers were charged with manslaughter in the second degree and criminally negligent homicide. These persons were indicted by a grand jury. They challenged the grand jury indictment. The court of appeals decided there was not sufficient evidence before the grand jury to establish the forseeability of the actual immediate triggering cause of the explosion. Therefore, the court found that the defendants were not criminally culpable and dismissed the indictment.

Jones, Judge

Defendant Warner-Lambert Co. is a manufacturing corporation which produces, among other items, Freshen-Up chewing gum. The individual defendants were officers or employees of the corporation. The indictment charges each defendant with six counts of manslaughter in the second degree and six counts of criminally negligent homicide in consequence of the deaths of six employees which resulted from a massive explosion and fire at the Long Island City Warner-Lambert plant about 2:30 A.M. on November 21, 1976.

On the day on which the explosion occurred, Freshen-Up gum was being produced at the Warner-Lambert plant by a process in which filled ropes of the gum were passed through a bed of magnesium stearate (MS), a dry, dustlike lubricant which was applied by hand, then into a die-cut punch (a Uniplast machine) which was sprayed with a cooling agent (liquid nitrogen), where the gum was formed into the square tablets. The process produced a dispersal of MS dust in the air and an accumulation of it at the base of the Uniplast machine and on overhead pipes; some also remained ambient in the atmosphere in the surrounding area.

Both MS and liquid nitrogen are considered safe and are widely used in the industry. In bulk, MS will only burn or smoulder if ignited; however, like many substances, if suspended in the air in sufficient concentration the dust poses a substantial risk of explosion if ignited. The minimum concentration at which an explosion can occur is denominated the "lower explosion level" (LEL). Liquid nitrogen, with a boiling temperature of minus 422 degrees Fahrenheit, is an effective cryogenic which might play a part in the process of "liquefaction"—here, the production of liquid oxygen in the course of the condensation of air on its exposure to a source of intense cold. Liquid oxygen is highly volatile, is easily ignited and, if ignited, will explode. Among possible causes of such ignition of either liquid oxygen or ambient MS are electrical or mechanical sparks.

Although there was no direct proof as to what had triggered the early morning disaster, the Peo-

ple introduced expert testimony hypothesizing that there might have been a mechanical sparking induced by a breakup of metal parts of the Uniplast machine. Also presented was testimony by one of the People's experts who theorized that liquid oxygen produced through liquefaction occurring in the Uniplast machine was ignited by the impact of a moving metal part and that this touched off the dispersed MS dust present.

With respect to the quantity of ambient MS dust in the area of the Uniplast machines (the presence of which was the basis for the People's submission to the Grand Jury of evidence against the defendants ultimately indicted), there was proof that an inspection of the plant by Warner-Lambert's insurance carrier in February, 1976 had resulted in the advice to the insured that the dust condition in the Freshen-Up gum production area presented an explosion hazard and that the MS concentration was above the LEL, together with recommendations for installation of a dust exhaust system and modification of electrical equipment to meet standards for dust areas. Although a variety of proposals for altering the dust condition were considered by the individual defendants in consultations and communications with each other and some alterations in the MS application were made, both ambient and settled MS dust were still present on November 21, 1976, as the result of an executive decision to work toward the eventual elimination of MS entirely by modification of the Freshen-Up equipment. This modification had been accomplished with respect to only one Uniplast machine at the date of the explosion, when approximately 500 pounds of MS a day were still being used in Freshen-Up production. Employees were wearing face masks and goggles to protect their eyes and breathing passages, and just prior to the tragedy, when sweeping and airhosing of accumulated MS were in progress, there was rising dust and a "heavy fog" or "mist" all around.

The charges of manslaughter in the second degree and criminally negligent homicide laid against the corporate and individual defendants are each dependent on two interrelated provisions of the Penal Law. As to manslaughter in the second degree, the following provisions are pertinent:

"125.15 Manslaughter in the second degree

"A person is guilty of manslaughter in the second degree when:

"1. He recklessly causes the death of another person."

"15.05 Culpability; definitions of culpable mental states

"The following definitions are applicable to this chapter. . . .

"3. 'Recklessly.' A person acts recklessly with respect to a result or to a circumstance described by a statute defining an offense when he is aware of and consciously disregards a substantial and unjustifiable risk that such result will occur or that such circumstance exists. The risk must be of such nature and degree that disregard thereof constitutes a gross deviation from the standard of conduct that a reasonable person would observe in the situation. A person who creates such a risk but is unaware thereof solely by reason of voluntary intoxication also acts recklessly with respect thereto."

As to criminally negligent homicide the following provisions are pertinent:

"Section 125.10 Criminally negligent homicide

"A person is guilty of criminally negligent homicide when, with criminal negligence, he causes the death of another person."

"Section 15.05 Culpability; definitions of culpable mental states

"The following definitions are applicable to this chapter:

"4. 'Criminal negligence.' A person acts with criminal negligence with respect to a result or to a circumstance described by a statute defining an offense when he fails to perceive a substantial and unjustifiable risk that such result will occur or that such circumstance exists. The risk must be of such nature and degree that the failure to perceive it constitutes a gross deviation from the standard of care that a reasonable person would observe in the situation."

For each of these crimes there must be "a substantial and unjustifiable risk," and "[t]he risk must be of such nature and degree that disregard thereof [or, the failure to perceive it] constitutes a gross deviation from the standard of conduct [or, care] that a reasonable person would observe in the situation." The essence of manslaughter in the second degree is awareness accompanied by disregard of the risk; for criminally negligent homicide the essence is failure to perceive the risk. With respect to each crime the culpable conduct of the defendant must have been the cause of the death of other person or persons.

The issue before us, is whether defendants could be held criminally liable for what actually occurred, on theories either of reckless or negligent conduct, based on the evidence submitted to this Grand Jury, viewed in the light most favorable to the People. The focus of our attention must be on the issue of culpability, taking into account the conduct of defendants and the factors both of foreseeability and of causation, all of which in combination constitute the ultimate amalgam on which criminal liability may or may not be predicated.

Viewed most favorably to the People, the proof with respect to the actual cause of the explosion is speculative only, and as to at least one of the major hypotheses—that involving oxygen liquefaction—there was no evidence that that process was foreseeable or known to any of the defendants. In sum, there is no proof sufficient to support a finding that defendants foresaw or should have foreseen the physical cause of the explosion. This being so there was not legally sufficient evidence to establish the offenses charged or any lesser included offense.

It has been the position of the People that but-for causation is all that is required for the imposition of criminal liability. Thus, it is their submission, reduced to its simplest form, that there was evidence of a foreseeable and indeed foreseen risk of explosion of MS dust and that in consequence of defendants' failure to remove the dust a fatal explosion occurred. The chain of physical events by which the explosion was set off, i.e., its particular cause, is to them a matter of total indifference.

We have rejected the application of any such sweeping theory of culpability under our criminal law, however.

In view of our disposition of this appeal on the ground that, inasmuch as the evidence before the Grand Jury was not legally sufficient to establish the foreseeability of the actual immediate, triggering cause of the explosion, defendants cannot be held criminally culpable, we have no occasion to reach or consider whether the steps that they took with respect to the general risk of explosion were a gross deviation from the standard of care or conduct that a reasonable person would have observed in the situation.

For the reasons stated, we conclude that there was not legally sufficient evidence in this case on the premise of which any jury could permissibly have imposed criminal liability on any of these defendants.

Accordingly, the order of the Appellate Division should be reversed and the indictment dismissed.

The New York Court of Appeals in the *Warner-Lambert* case decided that in order to establish causation, each link in the chain of events leading to the two explosions must have been foreseeable. The crime of negligent homicide required proof of some culpable conduct by the defendants. Apparently, the prosecutor thought causation could be established by showing the officers' direct participation in the offense, or at least their knowledge of and willingness to permit the existence of the conditions leading up to the explosions. The court, however, also required that the officers be able to foresee exactly how such an event might occur.

A corporation may be held liable for the acts of its agents. Even low-level employees can, under certain circumstances, commit acts which will result in a corporation's being held criminally responsible.

Corporate Liability for Crimes of Its Agents

Under federal criminal law, if an employee was acting in the course of his employment and within the scope of his authority, a corporation may subsequently be prosecuted for the employee's acts.

A corporation may be prosecuted for a crime that requires a specific intent, so long as the corporate agent was acting with the intent to benefit the corporation. This point is discussed in the following case.

Standard Oil Company of Texas v. United States
Fifth Circuit Court of Appeals
307 F.2d 120 (1962)

Employees of several corporations engaged in activities that violated the Connally Hot Oil Act. The issue in this case was whether the corporations could be held liable for the crimes committed by the employees. In this case, the court held for the corporations.

Brown, Circuit Judge

This appeal by two corporate defendants, from fines imposed on judgments of conviction under the Connally Hot Oil Act, raises this basic question. May a corporate employer be held liable for a crime committed by employees who, although ostensibly acting in the performance of their duties, were really cooperating with a third person in the accomplishment of a criminal purpose for the benefit of that third person, and whose acts not only did not benefit the employer, but in some instances, at least, result in a theft of its property? Here the statute expressly requires that the forbidden act be knowingly done. It punishes only persons "knowingly violating" the statute or regulations. . . . The corporations can be found guilty, therefore, only if the evidence shows that each, acting through its human agents, deliberately did these acts, that is, with the corporation "knowing" that they were being done for it. Inquiry along this line brings us face-to-face with the everyday problem of imputing knowledge to a corporation. As these defendants here are the first to acknowledge, several things afford no insulation from corporate knowledge. Thus, no contention is made that "knowledge" can be acquired only through supervisory or executive personnel. On the contrary, while status of the actor in the corporate hierarchy might well have decisive significance in determining the question we later discuss concerning the intention to benefit the corporation, the corporation may be criminally bound by the acts of subordinate, even menial, employees. Likewise, no contention is, or can at this late date, be made that mere violation of instructions would shield the corporation from criminal responsibility for actions which its agents have taken for it.

The purpose to benefit the corporation is decisive in terms of equating the agent's action with that of the corporation. For it is an elementary principle of agency that an act of a servant is not within the scope of employment if it is done with no intention to perform it as a part of or incident to a service on account of which he is employed.

We agree that benefit is evidential in determining the purpose and motive for which the agent does the act in question. If it is done with a view of furthering the master's business, or doing something for the master, then the expectation or hope of a benefit, whether direct or indirect, makes the act that of the principal. The act is no less the principal's if from such intended conduct either no benefit accrues, a benefit is undiscernible, or, for that matter, the result turns out to be adverse.

On the facts of this record, only the most hypercritical, artificial view would find any benefit intended by the actions of Morgan, Hart or Purcell.

For these corporations to be found guilty of violating the Connally Hot Oil Act we may assume that it is not necessary to prove that through imputation each corporation consciously knew that the acts being done were in violation of the law. But to subject these corporations to criminal accountability it was necessary on accepted principles of imputation for each to know that these acts of Morgan, Hart and Purcell were being done. Under a statute requiring that there be "a specific wrongful intent," and the "presence of culpable intent as a necessary element of the offense . . ." the corporation does not acquire that knowledge or possess the requisite "state of mind essential for responsibility," through the activities of unfaithful servants whose conduct was undertaken to advance the interests of parties other than their corporate employer.

Consequently, the Court ought to have entered a judgment of acquittal on these counts, and the judgments must be reversed and here rendered.

For a corporation to be criminally liable under federal law for crimes committed by its agent, the agent must have acted with the purpose to benefit the corporation if the crime in question requires proof of a specific intent to violate the law. However, if the actions also benefit the employees, the corporation still can be held criminally responsible. Suppose that employees of one company agree to fix prices with another company. Even if the employees intended to benefit themselves, since they also intended to benefit the company, the company can be prosecuted under the antitrust laws.

Many states do not follow the federal rule. They follow the rule proposed in the Model Penal Code that a corporation will not be liable for a felony unless "the commission of the offense was authorized, requested, commanded, performed, or recklessly tolerated by the board of directors or by a high managerial agent acting on behalf of the corporation" Model Penal Code Section 2.07(1)(c).

SUMMARY

Society imposes prison sentences and fines on persons engaging in illegal activities or crimes. More serious crimes are called felonies, while less serious crimes generally are referred to as misdemeanors.

In the typical felony case, the government must, after informing the defendant of the crime he or she is accused of having committed, convince a judge, or a grand jury in some cases, that a crime was committed and that evidence indicates the accused committed the crime. The defendant is then bound over for trial.

The United States Constitution protects persons accused of a violation of the law. The Constitution, in the Bill of Rights, places important restraints on the manner in which the legal system may operate. The Fourth Amendment protects the public, including businesses, from unreasonable searches and seizures. A judge must generally issue a search warrant before a lawful search can be made. The Fifth Amendment prohibits the government from compelling a person to be a witness against himself or herself. Business records, while possibly harmful if released to the government, must be turned over to the prosecutor if the government requests them. The Sixth Amendment guarantees everyone a right to the assistance of a defense attorney. This is true even if a person can not afford a lawyer.

Violent crime is a matter of grave concern to everyone, yet nonviolent, white-collar crime does extensive damage to the economic system. A number of different types of activity fall into this category, for example, bank fraud, insurance fraud, and consumer fraud. Many state and federal statutes make certain types of nonviolent activities criminal.

In the past, the government concentrated its enforcement efforts on violent crimes. Today, more and more emphasis is being devoted by government officials to white-collar crime. There appears to be a trend to deal more harshly with such crimes than in the past.

REVIEW QUESTIONS

1. Define the following terms:
   a. Civil case
   b. Criminal case
   c. Felony
   d. Misdemeanor
   e. Bill of Rights
   f. Search warrant

2. What is the significant point of the *Park* case?

3. What process do the police follow before conducting a search of a business or home?

4. Why does the Supreme Court require the government to provide a person accused of a crime an attorney if he or she cannot afford one?

5. Discuss the stages in the criminal prosecution of a felony.

6. If the police violate the Fifth Amendment in obtaining a confession, why do the courts refuse to admit such a confession?

7. Couch turned her financial records over to her accountant for the purpose of preparing her income tax records. The Internal Revenue Service now wishes to obtain those records. Couch asserts that requiring these records to be turned over to the IRS would violate her Fifth Amendment privilege against compulsory self-incrimination. Must Couch's accountant turn the records over to the IRS?

8. The Food and Drug Administration inspected the warehouse of Chaney Brothers Food Corporation. Its secretary-treasurer, Starr, was charged with violating the Food, Drug, and Cosmetic Act by allowing contamination of food stored in the warehouse. Starr was convicted at trial. The warehouse in question had been infected by mice. Mr. Starr, following an investigation by the FDA, knew of the condition and took some corrective measures, but on the next inspection, the FDA again found mice. May Starr lawfully be convicted of a crime?

9. Scalon Corporation sold products to Greenmass Corporation. In the course of the transactions, Scalon sent a number of letters to Greenmass with fraudulent representations. Greenmass brought a civil suit against Scalon for treble damages caused by Scalon's acts. Scalon made two arguments in this suit: suit may not be commenced against him because he had never been convicted of mail fraud, and suit may not be brought against him under the RICO Act because he is a respectable businessman. Is Scalon right?

10. A steamship company ordered its crew not to discharge refuse from the ship while it was in port. A crew member tossed a pail of garbage overboard—just as a harbor-patrol boat was passing under the stern of the ship. The Navigable Rivers and Harbors Act prohibits pollution of the harbor. In light of the effort of the company to prohibit pollution, is the company criminally liable?

11. Operators of hotels in Portland entered into a group boycott against certain suppliers that refused to make contributions to a local association. This is a per se violation of the Sherman Act. The president of the Hilton Hotels testified that it is contrary to the policy of the corporation for the manager of one of its hotels to condition purchases upon payment of a contribution to a local association by a supplier. The hotel's purchasing agent was told several times not to take part in the boycott. Even so, the purchasing agent (who did not personally like the supplier's representative) threatened a supplier with loss of the hotel's business unless the supplier paid the association assessment. Can Hilton Hotel Corporation be held criminally liable in light of its instructions to the purchasing agent?

12. Officers of several corporations were charged with having engaged in a combination and conspiracy in unreasonable restraint of trade and commerce in the transportation of household goods. They argued that they cannot be prosecuted for acts done by them as representatives of their corporations in their capacity as corporate officers. Is this argument correct?

13. Rappoport found Small Business Administration financing in exchange for contingent fees of ten percent of the loans sought. He advised his clients not to disclose this information on their loan applications since the law prohibits such fees. Is it possible to convict Rappoport in light of the fact that his clients were the persons violating the law?

14. Charles Louderman, who operated a business

that attempted to locate debtors who have "skipped-out" on unpaid bills, used various devices to locate such people. Among other things, he called telephone company offices and/or United States post office branches, representing himself as telephone or postal employees. He would then request confidential internal information concerning telephone customers or post-office-box holders. Does Louderman's behavior constitute fraud?

CHAPTER 17

Ethics and Business:
Extra-Legal Controls
on Business and Business
Decision Making

What Is Corporate Social Responsibility?
Why Should a Corporation Seek to Act Ethically?
An Analytical Framework for Corporate Social Responsibility

The legal system regulates corporate behavior by providing a means for injured parties to seek damages from corporations that cause their injuries. It imposes legal duties on certain members of corporations in their dealings with others. Yet there is a regulatory force beyond the law. This force is called business ethics or corporate social responsibility. The concept that a business firm should act like a good citizen is a major factor in the nonlegal regulation of business behavior. But what attributes define a "good citizen"? How do business managers know if their decisions are consistent with good corporate citizenship?

This chapter is about corporate social responsibility as an analytical, decision-making process. It will suggest that corporate social responsibility is made up of a number of factors that produce a course of ethical corporate conduct. These factors may be divided into two groups: first, an appreciation for the rules of law and of society; and second, an appreciation of the various attributes of the corporation's environment. However, be aware that the suggested decision-making process is not a precise method for finding the "right" course of corporate conduct. It is but one means of assessing the consequences of corporate decision making from an ethical perspective.

The study of ethics is the study of what is right or good. It is a branch of philosophy useful in determining conduct in any given instance. Philosophers study problems of ethics that arise in many fields—medicine, law, engineering, and business. For example, is it right to permit terminally ill persons to commit suicide? Is it right for an attorney to withhold information of a client's wrongdoing? Is it right for an engineer to design nuclear weapons?

These questions are extremely difficult, for there are no specific answers. A study of corporate social responsibility will not provide an absolute ethical yardstick by which to measure all business conduct. What should be gained from a study of business ethics, however, is an appreciation for the problems facing business and a way in which to analyze those problems in order to seek the socially responsible decision.

WHAT IS CORPORATE SOCIAL RESPONSIBILITY?

Corporate social responsibility is an elusive term that has been defined in many ways. However, none of them provides guidance to business managers as they attempt to make socially responsible decisions. Consider a first definition of corporate social responsibility: earning a profit in one's business while inflicting the least possible harm to society. This definition is very broad, raising more questions than it answers. From a corporate viewpoint, how would a manager determine "social" injuries?

Definitions of the Term

For example, do social injuries occur to employees who are furloughed in recessionary times? Or would social injuries occur to shareholders if the firm refused to reduce its workforce in a recession, thereby jeopardizing its financial position? Should noncorporate members of the community who are affected by corporate decisions be included in its sphere of responsibility? (For example, worker layoffs may hurt the business of a local movie theater.) Should there be an ordering of the groups that may be injured by a corporate decision? Even though such social injuries may occur, apparently a value must be attached to them in order to balance them against corporate dollars otherwise lost. This seems simple, but how are social injuries to be so weighted? Placing a numerical value on the social injury to an unemployed worker is a vague approximation at best. As H. L. Mencken wrote: "Explanations exist; they have existed for all time; There is always a well-known solution to every human problem—neat, plausible, and wrong."[1]

In summary, the first definition of corporate social responsibility is overly broad, too vague and, therefore, not useful. In trying to describe what the firm should do—balance profits against social injury—the definition fails to tell us how to strike that balance or how to measure social injury.

By contrast, a second definition is a very narrow characterization of corporate social responsibility: Corporate social responsibility involves voluntary activity undertaken for nonbusiness reasons; the marginal return of the corporate expenditures for socially responsible activity being less than an alternative business-related expenditure of the same funds. This definition ignores any responsible corporate decision-making process except one based solely on altruistic reasons, which results in economic loss to the corporation. But suppose that ABC, Inc., gave one thousand dollars to the community ballet company. If the contribution garners a great deal of "free" publicity for the corporation and contributes to the quality of life in the community, thereby making it more attractive to employees, the return from that contribution may be much greater than any alternative business use of the funds (such as purchasing advertising or offering bonuses to key employees). This contribution could not be considered socially responsible, given a definition based on pure altruism, because market mechanisms would have yielded such a decision anyway. In this case, good citizenship was good business. However, if ABC had given the money anonymously, thereby gaining no publicity for its act, then it may be assumed that any return to the corporation would be less than the marginal return of alternative uses of the money. In this example, the contribution would be considered socially responsible according to our definition. However, it is not clear why, when a corporation benefits from a community-oriented decision, the activity should *not* be labeled socially responsible.

In any event, this characterization of the term also provides little guidance to the business manager. The definition suggests that such conduct must be in addition to obeying the laws and using corporate resources in an economically efficient manner. It requires that socially responsible conduct "harm" the corporation by imposing a negative effect on its total return. There seems little practical reason for this narrow definition of corporate social responsibility, since the business manager can make decisions that benefit not only the corporation, but also the community.

A third definition of corporate social responsibility maintains: Should the corporation function in a manner that raises criticism, then the company has not acted in accordance with community values and, therefore, is not a responsible firm. It is frequently used by those who seek to make a political issue of certain corporate behavior. For example, if ABC does business in South Africa or supports Planned Parenthood or manufactures electronic components for nuclear weapons, then some persons and communities might hold that ABC is not acting in a socially responsible manner. This concept of corporate social responsibility is the one most often encountered. Newspaper articles and television commentaries focus on such issues as being "tests" of the responsible nature of corporate behavior. The only value of such a characterization is that it clearly labels the speaker's position on social or political issues. It provides no guidance to the manager, nor is it a useful way to understand the concept.

Should a Simple Definition of the Term Be Sought?

The existence of broad, narrow, and sometimes cynical definitions of the term *corporate social responsibility* highlights the confusion this idea causes. Corporate social responsibility has a nice ring to it—like patriotism or justice—but it may seem that the term has no real meaning. If this is the case, why study corporate social responsibility and how could it ever affect corporate behavior? In short, a determination of social responsibility seems impossible in that it becomes merely a question of personal opinion.

This belief is quite common but erroneous. It assumes that there are many different equally valid moral principles or opinions and no way to choose among them. Yet there is surprising agreement on some basic principles with which to analyze any situation. Societies throughout history, even when differing in customs and practices, have been in basic agreement concerning a number of ethical or moral principles. Such principles include respect for human life, the importance of being honest, the need for cooperation, and the desirability of being helpful.

However, there have been different practices among some societies with regard to the moral principles. These differences were based on the varied circumstances of the cultures rather than rejection of the principle itself. In some nomadic tribes, enfeebled, elderly members would be left behind to die as the tribe moved on. The tribe did not condone the killing of its members, but it was incapable of supporting those who could not fend for themselves. The circumstance of the society yielded the practice, not the rejection of the principle that life should be respected.

Thus, ethical analysis of business problems will yield a course of conduct for the business manager to follow that will be consistent with basic ethical principles. Note, however, that this "course of conduct" will not somehow magically appear. Disagreements about ethical analysis abound so that an expectation of finding an answer if one looks hard enough will not be forthcoming. However, by this time such a lack of readily available answers should be understandable. The nature of law and legal analysis discussed throughout this text provides the same dilemma. Consider the majority and dissenting opinions in some of the cases. Even with legal theory there are different conclusions about the proper outcome. Nonetheless, the business manager cannot ignore the law as it affects business decisions on the grounds that not all people can agree as to the outcome of legal analysis on a certain course of

TYLENOL POISONINGS AND SOCIALLY RESPONSIBLE BUSINESS DECISION MAKING

In 1982, seven people in the Chicago area died after taking cyanide-laced Tylenol capsules. Investigators found that someone unknown (and never found) had tampered with the capsules. Tylenol is made by Johnson & Johnson, and accounted for approximately fifteen percent of the corporation's $468 million in net earnings the previous year. It held an approximately thirty-five percent share of the $1.2 billion painkiller market.

Immediately consumers throughout the country stopped using Tylenol in both capsule and tablet form. The price of Johnson & Johnson stock dropped eighteen percent in one week. Tylenol users stated that they would never again use the product. Should the product continue to be sold?

A variety of responses to this crisis was considered. Food and Drug Administration officials urged that no mass re-

call be undertaken, fearing that such an action would increase the national panic over the Chicago deaths. The FBI argued that a recall, which would be very expensive, would encourage terrorist groups to use similar tactics as means to attack major corporations.

Nonetheless, corporate officials decided to recall the thirty-one million boxes of Tylenol capsules in stores throughout the country at a cost of fifty million dollars. The corporation cooperated fully with the investigation, and its CEO appeared on television programs to discuss the incident. Within ten weeks, the product was again on the market, this time in triple-seal tamper-resistant packaging. Eighty million Tylenol coupons worth $2.50 were provided to consumers. Within a year, Tylenol had regained most of its lost market share and customer confidence.

conduct. Similarly, managers should not forego ethical analysis even though clear "right" decisions will not always be apparent.

The application of ethical principles may well produce disagreement. However, deciding on an appropriate corporate course of conduct is not impossible. Corporations who operate in areas where the law is uncertain must still make decisions based on legal analysis even though later events may prove that decision wrong. Thus, where differences occur about the proper ethical mode of conduct, a consensus can be found in order to formulate the socially responsible business decision.

Arriving at a consensus requires an informed analysis of the proposed activity, the surrounding circumstances, and the applicable ethical principles. In a corporate context, one must look to the effect of the exercise of corporate power on various groups in society and then determine to which groups the corporation owes a duty in the exercise of that power.

What follows is a rejection of any single definition for corporate social responsibility. Instead, one should view the concept as a decision-making process with a number of factors to be weighed. Additionally, no final decision should be considered a litmus test of corporate responsiveness. Instead, the process of decision making should be considered crucial. Do not expect a single, straightforward answer to problems of social responsibility by any definition or approach.

WHY SHOULD A CORPORATION SEEK TO ACT ETHICALLY?

Before embarking on a discussion of the ethical decision-making process, a preliminary problem must be addressed. Namely, why should a business seek to act in an ethical manner? A common naive belief is that such inquiries are "soft" or otherworldly. Perhaps ethical thinking is appropriate for the clergy or professors, the argument goes, but in the "real world," such decision-making techniques are fruitless and perhaps harmful to the organization. In this real world, the race is won by the strong, the swift, and the cunning. Nice guys finish last.

Although there are complexities when a corporation adopts socially responsible decision making, there is little doubt that the role of American business has been reevaluated, and that its behavior is affected by these nonlegally mandated goals. In the early history of American corporations, the organizations were chartered with a business purpose as well as a public purpose in mind. These early corporations were akin to public utilities in that their businesses included such public interest activities as the operation of canals and turnpikes. In such organizations, public benefits and profits to the membership mixed naturally.

As the Industrial Revolution became firmly established, the corporate form was used more for traditional, purely private business purposes. The attitude regarding the corporation's responsibility to the public changed too. A quotation from a late-nineteenth-century case captures this attitude: "The law does not say that there are to be no cakes and ale, but there are to be no cakes and ale except such as required for the benefit of the company. It is not charity sitting at the board of directors, because as it seems to me, charity has no business to sit at the board of directors."[2]

Today, of course, a corporation deciding to act ethically or in a socially responsible manner is acting for a valid purpose. The attitude that a corporation's decisions should take into account the interests of the community is firmly established. However, except for certain statutory regulations (for example, the antipollution laws), there is no legal requirement for such behavior. The corporation, except for following its legal duties, is under no compulsion to consider the effect of alternative courses of action on its surrounding environment. Doing so is a part of corporate social responsibility—responsibility beyond that imposed by the legal system.

Two arguments support corporate social responsibility. First, remember that corporations are merely groups of people that the law categorizes in a certain way. Corporate behavior is therefore the decisions and actions of certain individuals in that group. The more cultivated and civilized individuals recognize that responsible behavior goes beyond what is mandated by law. They do not change somehow by making decisions on behalf of a corporation instead of individually.

Corporate decisions, therefore, are governed by the same standards of civilized behavior that govern individual decisions. Society expects voluntary personal restraint and respect for others, even in absence of law. The corporate fictitious personality does not remove this expectation from its activities. Thus, a nebulous, unwritten compact exists to make life in an organized society tolerable. No legal rule prohibits a person from laughing at the handicapped. However, the compact condemns such behavior as boorish and crude. Such a person may not have legal sanctions imposed, but will lose respect and credibility. The person may be shunned by others. Similarly, corporations that violate the compact risk losing the intangible image of respectability they seek to create.

Thus, if civilization is to exist, people must voluntarily choose to act in a socially responsible manner. The corporation is under the same mandate. By being a part of society, the corporation cannot legitimately ignore the unwritten duties.

A second reason why socially responsible decision making should be used is that it is the corporation's best interest. First, it is a good business practice. Society expects corporations to be good citizens and supportive members of the communities in which they operate. By recognizing this expectation, the corporation is responding to the demand of the market. Long-term profitability is influenced not merely by economic forces, but also by social and political forces.

Second, corporate responsibility is good public relations. It shows the corporation in a favorable light, and like advertisements or an advertising campaign, exposes the public to the firm (or its products). Finally, corporate social responsibility is an alternative to additional government regulation. Consider the regulatory chapters in this text such as antitrust, consumer law, labor relations, and environmental law. These chapters reflect the movement in regulation from voluntary good citizenship to mandated good citizenship through legislation and accompanying administrative regulation. Thus, social responsibility is not only a part of society's expectations, but is also in the long-term interest of the firm. The following case provides a practical example of a corporation acting with questionable ethics and the response of a court to that activity. Something is amiss when corporate employees comb through the trash of a competitor, trying to secure shreds of secret information. Note the court's comment about a lack of ethical concern by management. Note also the large jury award that was upheld.

Tennant Company v. Advance Machine Company
Minnesota Court of Appeals
355 N.W.2d 720 (1984)

Tennant and Advance are competitors in manufacturing and marketing floor cleaning equipment. From fall 1978 through spring 1979, certain Advance employees rummaged through the trash in a dumpster behind Tennant's Western regional sales offices in California. The raids uncovered some confidential sales information that George McIntosh, an Advance employee, forwarded to other Advance salesmen and to company officers. McIntosh, who reported directly to Jerry Rau, Advance's vice-president for industrial sales, sent Rau memos summarizing information stolen from the Tennant documents.

Rau testified that when he learned of the clandestine activity, he handled it very lightly because he did not consider it a terrible thing. He considered it a joke. Jerry Pond, president of Advance, learned about this activity from Rau early in 1979. Pond also handled it in a very light fashion until this lawsuit was commenced in early 1980. Then he discharged McIntosh. When asked whether he thought raiding the dumpster and rifling through a competitor's trash was unethical, Pond equivocated by saying that he did not have enough information to make a judgment on those practices.

The jury determined that Advance engaged in unlawful business practices, and that Tennant was entitled to one hundred thousand dollars compensatory damages and four hundred thousand dollars punitive damages.

Parker, Judge

California law imposes punitive damages to deter employment of unfit persons for important positions. It reflects certain policy judgments about corporations, primarily that top management sets the company's ethical tone. Accountability of the principal is necessary to enforce corporate responsibility: If we allow the master to be careless of his servants' torts we lose hold upon the most valuable check in the conduct of social life. In this case the president of Advance, who personally hired the individuals responsible for illegal activity, was indifferent to the ethics of their behavior.

Anything which convincingly shows the intention of the principal to adopt or approve the act in question is sufficient to establish ratification and therefore liability. It may also be shown by implication. Where an agent is authorized to do an act, and he transcends his authority, it is the duty of the principal to repudiate the act as soon as he is fully informed of what has been thus done in his name, else he will be bound by the act as having ratified it by implication. Both the president and vice president of Advance, Pond and Rau, were aware of McIntosh's activities early in 1979. Rau had discussed the matter directly with McIntosh. He also received memos containing the illegal information. The obviously sensitive nature of the material would have caused suspicions about their source. Pond had been informed by Rau and received the same memos when Rau was recovering from his heart attack.

Advance officers took no action against McIntosh until nearly one year after the fact. The failure to discharge or even reprimand an agent for illegal activity is evidence of the principal's approval. Pond never repudiated the act by informing Tennant of its occurrence. In fact, he was equivocal about the ethics of the activity.

While there was no direct evidence of ratifi-cation, the jury nonetheless had ample circum-stancial evidence to sift through.

AN ANALYTICAL FRAMEWORK FOR CORPORATE SOCIAL RESPONSIBILITY

In his book *Where the Law Ends*, Professor Christopher D. Stone suggested that social responsibility contains two major components: first, an emphasis on following rules of law and unwritten rules of society; second, an emphasis on a thinking process. The balance of this chapter will present a framework for understanding these two components. The framework will contain a number of factors that may be useful to a manager seeking to make socially responsible decisions. It will not provide final answers. However, it should result in a better understanding of ethical business conduct.

Corporate social responsibility first involves an emphasis on following the law and rules of society. The initial inquiry in any social responsibility analysis should, therefore, be whether the corporation has obeyed the law. For example, a corporation that dumps toxic waste into a stream in violation of federal antipollution regulations is not acting responsibly. One might hesitate to say that obeying the pollution regulations automatically makes a corporation responsible. However, it is clear that a decision to violate the law shows irresponsibility.

Emphasis on Obeying Rules

Rules of law reflect the values of a society. Although they cannot require a corporation to be "good," they can limit behavior that society considers to be wrong or irresponsible. However, merely obeying the commands of the legal system will not alone yield corporate social responsibility. Often, important behavioral controls exist outside the commands of the legal system. As in following the legal rules, a corporation that violates "unwritten rules" may be considered irresponsible.

Unwritten rules are general norms of civilized human conduct. They permit society to function without an overburdensome legal system. However, if groups begin to act outside these general norms, the law will be used to regulate their behavior. For example, before the enactment of environmental laws, some corpora-tions dumped their waste products in rivers adjoining their factories. There were no legal rules forbidding that type of waste disposal. However, as rivers became polluted and fish began to die, communities became alarmed. General norms of civilized behavior required that those who produced waste refrain from leaving it for others. Polluting rivers, though not illegal, violated unwritten rules.

However, following laws and unwritten social rules will not alone provide socially responsible conduct. In fact, just the opposite might occur. Obeying rules and customs may instead yield irresponsible conduct. In the case of *State of Israel* v. *Adolph Eichmann* (in Chapter 4), Adolph Eichmann was charged with being respon-sible for millions of deaths in the concentration camps and gas chambers of Nazi Germany. Eichmann was in charge of the human extermination programs of the Nazis during World War II. Eichmann and many others followed the rules of their government. Yet they did not act responsibly—in fact, had they *disobeyed* the rules they would have been acting responsibly. In another example, many businesses throughout the United States (before the enactment of antidiscrimination legislation) openly discriminated against black people and women. Certain jobs were not available to them. Rates of pay were less than for white male workers. In many communities, such discrimination was an accepted social practice. However, conforming to such rules was not responsible behavior. Therefore, some other element must enter the picture in defining corporate social responsibility.

Emphasis on a Thinking Process

Corporate social responsibility also involves a thinking process, beyond mere obedience of laws or social rules. Two factors compose this thinking process: first, thorough reflection or examination of the problem as opposed to an immediate, instinctive reaction to it; second, consideration of various alternatives available and how they might affect the corporate environment (this factor requires a familiarity with the external corporate environment and the groups in a responsibility relationship with the corporation).

Reflection

A thorough examination of a business problem requires not only reflection on the actions that might be taken, but also consideration of the available alternatives and an awareness of their implications. These alternatives need to be carefully considered in relation to the goals of the corporation and with respect to the way each might affect the firm, the recipients, and the community.

Simple reflection, however, will not necessarily yield a socially responsible decision. A methodology or thinking process needs to be followed. For any problem, no multiple-choice will be apparent, with one "right" choice waiting to be selected. Instead, creative thinking about the types of alternatives available to solve the problem will be required.

The reflection process really takes place in two steps. First, the manager needs to devise alternatives based on the areas of responsibility, to be discussed. Then, one alternative needs to be selected. The selection should be based on the alternative that is best for the most people within the corporation's sphere of responsibility. Of course, quantitative comparison will not be possible. Estimates, rules of thumb, and the like will provide the standards for comparison. The key is to identify the possible effects of various solutions and to then make the decision that provides the most benefit. Admittedly, this will be an imprecise task; but the active interest in searching for the good should, overall, yield ethical corporate conduct.

Effect on Surrounding Environment: Identifying Areas of Responsibility

In weighing alternatives, the manager must understand that all corporate activities affect the surrounding environment, since corporations do not exist in a vacuum. They are organizations of people and capital. Corporate decisions can have unlimited effects. However, no corporation is responsible for *all* the implications of its decisions. No manager could possibly act in a socially responsible manner if the corporation's responsibilities extended far beyond its sphere of control. To determine whether a particular corporate decision is socially responsible, the definition of *external environment* must be limited. Otherwise, virtually no decision could ever be considered socially responsible. The following discussion will provide an analytical method for determining to whom the corporation owes its responsibility.

The key to this inquiry is to understand not only the environment in which the corporation exists, but also to whom the corporation is responsible for the consequences of its actions. This process is aided by dividing the relevant corporate environment into four areas: first, the corporation as an institution; second, the people who make up the corporate organization, such as employees and shareholders; third, the customers of the corporation, or the ultimate consumers of its products or services; and fourth, the community or area where the corporation operates or where its business has an economic influence.

The Corporation As an Entity. The corporation should be concerned that its decision does not jeopardize its existence. Managerial decisions that cause harm to a corporation harm its employees, shareholders, customers, and the communities that rely upon its continued existence. Therefore, profit making and the decisions that account for it are not socially irresponsible. Decisions that yield higher profits are not necessarily wrong or insensitive. The corporation as an institution can justifiably make decisions that ensure its continued existence. This includes the notion that the corporation's decisions be within its competence. For example, a decision by an automobile manufacturing corporation to assist hungry people would not require the purchase and operation of a farm. Such a decision would be outside the competence of the corporation, and the inefficiencies caused by its choice could result in more social harm than any small benefits it might produce. Furthermore, such an investment would not be consistent with any profit-making goal of the firm.

Members of Organization. The corporate environment also consists of its members, primarily its employees and shareholders. Corporate decision making must take into account the effect of various alternatives on these internal groups. As members of the corporate organization, they may be greatly affected by various decisions and, therefore, are within the sphere of the corporation's responsibility.

The following case is a shareholder challenge to certain corporate spending decisions. The shareholders are arguing that the corporation wrongfully spent funds that would have been better used for a direct business purpose—perhaps as dividends. The shareholders were affected by the decisions, but was the effect negative? The expenditures did enhance the community, through college scholarships. Could these be characterized as long-term "investments" creating intangible benefits for the corporation and, therefore, for its members?

A. P. Smith Mfg. Co. v. Barlow

Superior Court of New Jersey
97 A.2d 186 (1953)

Stein , Judge

The question calling for decision is whether a New Jersey corporation may lawfully in 1951 donate from its funds for the general maintenance of an educational institution like Princeton University.

The plaintiff-stockholders claim that this is a wrongful use of corporate funds.

It is from the millions of young men and women who are the products of higher American education that industry has picked, and will have need to pick, its scientists and its business executives. It is the youth of today which also furnishes tomorrow's leaders in economics and in government, thereby erecting a strong breastwork against any onslaught from hostile forces which would change our way of life either in respect of private enterprise or democratic self-government. The proofs before me are abundant that Princeton emphasizes by precept and indoctrination the principles which are very vital to the preservation of our own democratic system of business and government. I cannot conceive of any greater benefit to corporations in this country than to build, and continue to build, respect for and adherence to a system of free enterprise and democratic government, the serious impairment of either of which may well spell the destruction of all corporate enterprise. It is no answer to say that a company is not so benefited unless such need is immediate. A long-range view must be taken of the matter. A small company today might be under no imperative requirement to engage the services of a research chemist or other scientist, but its growth in a few years may be such that it must have available

an ample pool from which it may obtain the needed service. It must also be remembered that industry cannot function efficiently or enjoy development and expansion unless it has at all times the advantage of enlightened leadership and direction. The value of that kind of service depends in great measure upon the training, ideologies and character of the personnel available. All of these considerations must lead the reflecting mind to the conclusion that nothing conducive to public welfare, other than perhaps public safety, is more important than the preservation of the privately supported institutions of learning which embrace in their enrollment about half the college-attending youth of the country.

I am strongly persuaded by the evidence that the only hope for the survival of the privately supported American college and university lies in the willingness of corporate wealth to furnish in moderation some support to institutions which are so essential to public welfare and therefore, of necessity, to corporate welfare. What promotes the general good inescapably advances the corporate weal. I hold that corporate contributions to Princeton and institutions rendering the like public service are, if held within reasonable limitations, a matter of direct benefit to the giving corporations, and this without regard to the extent or sweep of the donors' business.

Customers or Consumers of Corporate Products and Services. A third group in the corporate environment is the customers or the ultimate consumers of its products or services. This element involves not only the typical business-related decision of, for example, making a quality product, but also concern for the health and safety of the users of the corporation's output. A corporation without customers will quickly cease to exist. Furthermore, the legal system, through its consumer legislation and through product liability and warranty litigation, enforces the need for corporations to perceive their actions as they affect their customers, although they are not members of the corporate organization. Socially responsible decision making requires that their interests be considered as a part of the corporate environment. The following case is an example of erroneous corporate decision making, which resulted in the placing of an unsafe product on the market. Examine the implications of that unfortunate decision, especially the legal system's concern with it.

Toole v. Richardson-Merrell, Inc.

California Court of Appeal
60 Cal. Rptr. 398 (1967)

Salsman, Justice

Appellant Richardson-Merrell, Inc., appeals from a judgment on a jury's verdict awarding respondent Toole $175,000 general damages and $500,000 punitive damages for injuries suffered as a result of the use of a drug manufactured and marketed by appellant and prescribed for respondent's use by his physician.

Respondent, 43 years of age, developed cataracts in both eyes as a result of taking the drug triparanol, manufactured and sold by appellant under the trade name of "MER/29". He developed a condition known as ichthyosis, characterized by dry, flaky, red and inflamed skin. He also suffered hair loss over his entire body. His sight is now distorted, peripheral vision is reduced, his eyes have lost their ability to adjust for distances, are painfully sensitive to light and he is required to wear corrective glasses. There was also evidence that he is now more apt to suffer detached retinas which could lead to blindness. He has an emotional overlay of fear that the drug may have some other long-term ill effect that may manifest itself later in life.

Appellant's Toxicology Department began animal testing of MER/29 in 1957. In the first six-week test, all female rats on a high dosage died. All were found to have suffered abnormal blood changes.

A second rat study was begun, using a reduced dosage of MER/29. This test also produced abnormal blood changes in the rats.

In March 1959 a test of MER/29 in monkeys was completed. Again, abnormal blood changes were found. But Dr. Van Maanen ordered Mrs. Beulah Jordan, the laboratory technician, to falsify a chart of this test by recording false body weights for the monkeys, by extending their records beyond dates after which the monkeys had been killed, and by adding data for an imaginary monkey that had never been in the test group at all. Mrs. Jordan protested but was told: "He (Van Maanen) is higher up. You do as he tells you and be quiet."

Knox Smith had prepared a brochure reflecting Merrell's test results of MER/29 on rats. This literature was intended for use of medical doctors clinically testing the drug on human beings. This brochure was revised and the revision eliminated all reference in it to the abnormal blood findings previously recited. Dr. McMaster, of the Medical Science Division, who was in charge of medical research on MER/29, had knowledge of the deletions, and consented to them.

On July 21, 1959 appellant filed a drug application with the FDA seeking permission to place MER/29 on the market. The application contained many false statements, among them these:

(1) It was reported that only four out of eight rats had died during a certain study, whereas in truth all had died.

(2) Wholly fictitious body and organ weights and also blood tests were reported for dead rats as if they had continued to live and to take MER/29.

(3) None of the abnormal blood changes encountered in experiments was disclosed.

(4) False data was related for a monkey being tested with the drug, and also data was stated for a monkey that was never part of the test group.

(5) The falsified chart, prepared by Mrs. Jordan under protest was included in the application.

The FDA informed appellant that its new drug application was incomplete. Dr. Murray, appellant's liaison officer, replied to the FDA and specifically informed it that there had been no blood changes in appellant's tests of MER/29 on rats or monkeys, and that a 16-month study in monkeys had adequately demonstrated the safety of

MER/29. These statements concerning absence of blood changes in animals were of course untrue.

In January 1960 appellant completed another study on the effect of MER/29 in rats. Nine out of ten rats in this study developed eye opacities. Appellant's report to the FDA of the results of this study was false or misleading because it reported that eight out of twenty rats had developed mild inflammation of the eye, but did not disclose the eye opacities seen in the test animals.

In February 1960 appellant reported to the FDA the results of its further tests of MER/29 in dogs. One dog in the test group developed eye opacities and blindness, but again this information was eliminated from the report to the FDA. In the same month, appellant completed a long-term test of the drug used in rats. Of 36 test rats in this group, 25 developed eye opacities. The results of this test were also withheld from the FDA.

In April 1960 the FDA granted appellant's application to market MER/29.

MER/29 was introduced to the market by the greatest promotional and advertising effort ever made by appellant in support of a product. There was testimony that doctors had never before seen so much promotion of a single drug. Doctors were bombarded with sales promotion, and subjected to brainwashing sessions with detailmen (salesmen). One advertising brochure stated that MER/29 was ". . . virtually nontoxic and remarkably free from side effects even in prolonged clinical use."

Appellant's drug salesmen were told that MER/29 was a "proven drug. There is no longer any valid question as to its safety or lack of significant side effects."

In April 1961 appellant began a long-term study of MER/29 in rats and dogs. By June opacities had begun to develop in the eyes of the rats, and by August, 35 out of 46 rats in the experiment had developed eye opacities. Despite these findings, and a field report that a doctor using MER/29 had suffered a change of eyesight, promotion of the drug continued unabated. Appellant gave no report to the FDA or warning to the medical profession in general concerning these developments.

In April 1962 FDA officials made an unannounced visit to appellant's laboratories and took all of appellant's records relating to its animal experiments. After the records were seized, President Getman drafted a letter to the FDA requesting withdrawal of MER/29 from the market.

MER/29 was administered to approximately 400,000 persons during its relatively short market life. In its first year at large it contributed $7,000,000 to appellant's gross sales. 490 cases of cataracts caused by use of the drug were reported. The majority of those on the drug maintained its use for less than three months. There was evidence that a very high percentage of those taking the drug would have developed cataracts if the drug had remained on the market and they had continued its use.

The judgment is affirmed.

The Community. The final group that should be considered as part of the corporate decision-making environment is the community in which the corporation does business. Of all the corporate environmental factors, this one is least closely tied to the traditional operation of a business. Concerns about how management decisions affect the vitality of the corporate organization, its employees, shareholders, and the marketplace arise in most business decision making. As already noted, these elements are also a part of a socially responsible corporation's thinking process. This final element involves consideration of the effect of the corporation's decisions upon those who are not connected with the organization. However, this community does not include the entire world. The community factor is limited to those areas in which the corporation does business, has offices or operations, or has other significant economic influences. In so characterizing this factor, business managers will be able to recognize and consider the direct community consequences of their decisions. They should be able to more readily recognize (through community and social pressure) the concerns of those outside the traditional corporate spheres of responsibility.

One instance in which the interests of the surrounding community were considered carefully by management in making a decision was the decision not to install lights in the Chicago Cubs home baseball park, Wrigley Field, discussed in Chapter 11 (see *Shlensky* v. *Wrigley et al.*, pp. 298–299). Note that traditional corporate interests (the long-term effect of night baseball on the team's attendance) and the interests of the community were important factors in the decision.

SUMMARY

Corporate social responsibility is an important factor in regulating corporate power. It is the result of a deliberate decision-making process. As long as difficult decisions must be made, as long as resources are limited, the effects of corporate decisions (both positive and negative) will be felt. However, there is no neat definition with which to characterize corporate decisions as responsible or not. Instead, an inquiry should focus on the corporate decision-making process and the effects of that decision on various components of the corporation's environment.

In a sense, corporate social responsibility requires an analysis of the traditional constituents of the business firm as well as the outside community. However, to determine the extent of the corporation's community responsibility, two inquiries must be made. First, the effect of the exercise of corporate power must be noted. Second, groups who are within the corporate sphere of influence must be identified. It is to these groups that the corporation owes its responsibility. Once a group of possible alternatives to a problem has been identified, the solution that benefits the most people within the corporation's spheres of responsibility should be selected.

The discussion of corporate social responsibility is illustrative of a major influence on corporate behavior, other than that exercised by the legal system. It is, therefore, an important component of the regulatory environment of business.

REVIEW QUESTIONS

1. Analyze the following case using the suggested corporate social responsibility decision-making process as discussed in this chapter.

    XYZ, Inc., operates a hospital. The hospital is a profit-making business. The relevant legal rule, in this case, concerns the duty to rescue. Under the common law, which is applicable here, a person has no obligation to rescue another person in distress. For example, if A notices that B is drowning, A has no legal duty to rescue B even if what would be required of A (tossing B a life preserver) would not endanger or inconvenience A. Additionally, assume that for-profit hospitals have no legal duty to treat anyone who seeks assistance.

    Margaret O'Neill awoke at 5:00 A.M. and saw her husband standing at the window, rubbing his arms and chest. His mouth was open and he was trying to get as much air as he possibly could. He was perspiring, his face was white, as contrasted with his normally ruddy complexion, and he complained of severe pains in his chest and arms. With Mrs. O'Neill's assistance, John O'Neill dressed and walked to

XYZ's hospital, which was three blocks away. The O'Neills did not own an automobile, and no taxis were available at that time.

The hospital maintained an emergency room. When the O'Neills arrived, they were directed to the nurse in charge. Mrs. O'Neill told the nurse that her husband was very ill. She explained the symptoms she observed and stated that she thought he was having a heart attack. She requested the services of a doctor. At that point, John O'Neill mentioned that they were members of the Hospital Insurance Plan (HIP). Thereupon, the nurse, following corporate policy, stated that the XYZ Hospital had no connection with that insurance plan and did not, therefore, care for HIP patients. She did allow Mr. O'Neill to telephone an HIP doctor, who informed Mr. O'Neill that HIP services would be available at 8:00 A.M.

Mrs. O'Neill asked the nurse to have a doctor examine her husband anyway, since it was an emergency. The nurse refused. Thereafter, the O'Neills left the hospital and returned home. They walked, pausing occasionally to permit John O'Neill to catch his breath. After they arrived at their apartment, and as Mrs. O'Neill was helping her husband to undress, he fell to the floor and died before any medical attention could be obtained.

2. General Motors Corporation (GM) has its headquarters in Detroit, Michigan. GM, like other major American automobile concerns, has a number of factories in the Detroit area that produce a large number of cars. In the spring of 1980, General Motors notified the city of Detroit that it would close one of its major Detroit plants within three years. Detroit, like many other old Northern industrial communities, had for some time experienced deteriorating economic conditions.

General Motors' decision to close the plant would inevitably worsen the economic problems: over six thousand jobs would be lost directly, as well as millions of dollars in tax revenue, and the effect on other businesses would make the loss even more costly to the city. GM,

therefore, offered to build the replacement facility in Detroit if a suitable site could be found. Otherwise, the plant would be built in another part of the country.

A number of sites were considered by the city, but none was suitable, except a 465-acre tract that included an area known as Poletown. Poletown was an ethnic neighborhood consisting primarily of Polish-American families. The city of Detroit condemned the 465-acre tract, including the Poletown area, so that it could be cleared, converted into an industrial park, and then conveyed to General Motors. The condemnation action affected approximately three thousand people, sixteen churches, and one hundred businesses. The area was not a slum.

Was General Motors' decision to build in the Detroit area on the Poletown site a socially responsible one, given the loss of Poletown?

3. Dunes Park is an ecologically sensitive area. It consists of fifty acres of lakefront property. The land is sandy and large sand hills dot the area. A few shrubs and trees grow in the sandy soil and tend to provide a uniquely landscaped area. It is a very popular area. Dunes Park is not protected under any federal environmental legislation. However, it is a state park, having been dedicated in 1920. During the past ten years, various environmental groups have attempted to have the federal government take over the park and bring it under its control. However, there is no interest on behalf of the federal government to do so. The standard response given to the groups was that "there are a number of other dune areas under federal environmental protection and there is no reason to add another."

Last year the state's budgetary problems became virtually insurmountable. While searching for new sources of revenue, the state received a report from a university geologist that predicted that Dunes Park contained large quantities of natural gas. However, the report also noted that current natural gas-drilling technology, if used, would severely strain the environmental capacity of the park. In fact, there was a great danger that the ecological makeup of the park would be destroyed. On the basis of this information, the state decided to offer natural gas-drilling permits to various corporations with the expectation that a discovery would lead to improved financial conditions for the state.

You are an executive with XYZ, Inc., an energy development firm. You are contacted by the state concerning a possible bid for drilling rights in Dunes Park. You are aware of the university geologist's report, which confirms a number of internal exploration reports. In fact, internal reports project that huge reserves of natural gas may be found beneath the park. During the past five years, the natural gas reserves of XYZ have been greatly depleted. New discoveries have not kept pace with the removal of gas from existing fields. As a result, the stock price of XYZ has been decreasing. Industry analysis paints a grim picture for energy firms that fail to replace the resources they use. One of the firms so pictured is XYZ. Environmental groups are expected to vigorously protest any move to explore for gas in Dunes Park. This may well result in unfavorable publicity for the firm that does the exploring.

On the basis of the socially responsible decision-making process discussed in the chapter, should XYZ seek to drill for gas in the park? Justify whatever decision you make.

4. XYZ, Inc. manufactures automobiles. The industry is very competitive and the corporation has lost twenty percent of its market share over the last ten years. Furthermore, its current share is being threatened by lower priced cars being produced overseas and imported to the American market. Therefore, XYZ has become very cost conscious. Labor, materials, and design features for the cars must be proven to be cost effective.

You are the senior project manager for the production of the new low-priced car being produced by XYZ. The car is scheduled to begin being sold in about eighteen months. Currently, the goal is to be able to produce a quality small car to effectively compete with the imports. Already the corporation is advertising its determination to "drive the imports from the highways." Your responsibility is to make absolutely sure that the car will be profitable when sold at the intended five-thousand-dollar range. Additionally, the car must also be a high-quality product.

Company engineers recommend that the gasoline tank system be redesigned for the car. The current design made the tank somewhat vulnerable to puncture (and explosion) during rear-end collision tests that were conducted. In order to meet their suggested specifications, an additional fifteen million dollars would need to be invested in the car. Doing so will make the five-thousand-dollar price impossible to meet. Furthermore, company actuaries estimate that the current design would produce ten million dollars in damage awards that the corporation would have to pay as a result of exploding gasoline tanks. This figure is already factored into overall costs that go toward computing the five-thousand-dollar sales price.

What decision should you make? Justify your decision. Would it be different if the design change would not affect the five-thousand-dollar price? Would your decision be different if you and members of your family would be driving the car?

NOTES

[1] H. L. Mencken, *Selected Prejudices* (New York: Octagon, 1926), p. 67.
[2] *Hutton v. West Cork Ry.*, 23 Ch. Div. 654, 673, (C.A. 1883).

PART V

Regulation of Business Activity

CHAPTER 18

 Products
Liability

Products Liability

In the torts chapter, we discussed the theories of recovery injured parties have relied upon when they have sustained an injury due to the actions of another party. This chapter is devoted to the very serious problem of products that cause injuries to people. Very often, even when the seller exercises the very highest level of care with respect to its products, those products sometimes injure people.

As a society we have several options. One is to take no action whatsoever when products injure people. A second possibility is to allow people who have been injured to sue the person or company responsible for their injuries. A third approach is for the government to pass laws that are designed to make certain unsafe products are kept off the market. In this chapter, we discuss the second approach to the problem.

As you will note, the law in this area actually comes in part from tort law and in part from contract law. The law evolved over a period of years and slowly permitted more and more people to recover from an ever larger pool of defendants. This tendency to increase the pool of defendants liable to injured parties seems to still be taking place, causing grave concern to people in business.

PRODUCTS LIABILITY

Many products pose a significant risk of harm. Sometimes the danger associated with a product results from a poorly thought-out design. In other cases, the manufacturer fails to exercise sufficient care in the assembly or inspection of its products. In the course of transporting the product to a retailer, the product may be damaged due to improper packaging or handling. Retailers sometimes improperly handle products or fail to adequately prepare them for marketing. Consumers frequently mishandle or misuse products because of ignorance or an indifference to the dangers created by many products. The failure to warn consumers quite often contributes to the high number of accidents.

The government, through the activities of such agencies as the Consumer Product Safety Commission, tries to keep unsafe products out of the marketplace. It regulates design and warnings for many products. Business also strives to keep unsafe products from reaching the public. In spite of all the effort by business and government, a certain number of dangerous products reach the public. In many instances, these products maim or kill people.

Products liability is actually a label that encompasses several theories of recovery—most importantly, negligence, strict liability, and warranties. Each theory may be used by a plaintiff injured as a result of a mishap involving a product. If possible, all three theories will be asserted to further the chances of recovery.

Over the past few decades, there has been an increasing trend in the direction of consumer protection. All too often an innocent person has been injured by a product through no fault of his own. Society is faced with the question of whether a person who is injured by a dangerous product should bear the loss caused by the product or whether this loss should be sustained by the manufacturer, distributor, or seller of a product—parties arguably better able to insure against potential losses. The scales clearly appear to be tipping in favor of the consumer.

Making the manufacturer or those in the distributive chain pay for losses sustained by an innocent person may be viewed as a matter of allocating the risk of loss to the entity in the position to correct the product's dangerous qualities. Various portions of the manufacturing process may be the cause of an injury: design, production, assembling, packaging, or warranty representations. In light of the fact that experts are available at the time of trial to explain defects in a product, it seems only reasonable for those in the position of marketing a product to take advantage of experts *prior* to marketing to make the product safe.

Privity of Contract

Historically, many injured people found it difficult if not impossible to recover any compensation for their injuries. The major doctrine that prevented people from recovering was the requirement that the plaintiff in a personal injury suit be in **privity of contract** with the defendant—that is, there must have been a direct contractual relationship between the injured party and the defendant. In many cases, the injured person had purchased the goods from a retailer. Thus the buyer was in privity of contract only with the retailer and not with anyone else in the distributive chain. As a practical matter, plaintiffs generally prefer to institute suit against well-heeled defendants, especially if the plaintiffs have sustained very serious injuries. It is pointless to receive a large judgment against a defendant who has very little money. For this reason, the average plaintiff would prefer filing suit against a manufacturer as opposed to a retailer, or worse yet, against a private individual. Now that is possible.

Suppose that Tom purchased a new automobile manufactured by Acme Corporation. Acme, in turn, purchased component parts from various suppliers. One of its suppliers delivered a defective wheel to Acme, which Acme used on the vehicle sold to Tom. Tom, of course, purchased the vehicle from an automobile dealer in his hometown, not directly from Acme. While driving the car, the wheel collapsed. At one time the only person Tom could bring suit against was the retail dealer from whom he purchased the automobile. A major departure from the requirement of privity of contract occurred in 1916 in *MacPherson* v. *Buick Motor Co.*, which follows. The New York Court of Appeals abandoned this requirement in negligence suits. As time passed, other courts followed the lead set by New York. More recently, the courts have abandoned the requirement of privity of contract in most products liability suits. Thus, today, in most states, Tom could bring suit against the manufacturer, the distributor, or the retailer.

MacPherson v. Buick Motor Co.

Court of Appeals of New York
111 N.E. 1050 (1916)

Defendant, Buick Motor Co., a manufacturer of automobiles, sold an automobile to a retail dealer who in turn resold the car to the plaintiff, MacPherson. While MacPherson was operating the car, the wheel suddenly collapsed, throwing him out and injuring him. One of the wheels had been made out of defective wood, and its spokes had crumbled into fragments. Defendant had not made the wheels but had bought them from another manufacturer. There was evidence, however, that its defects could have been discovered by reasonable inspection, and inspection had been omitted. The charge in this case was one, not of fraud, but of negligence. The question to be determined was whether Buick owed a duty of care and vigilance to anyone but its immediate purchaser—the retail automobile dealer. The court ruled for the plaintiff.

Cardozo, Justice

The foundations of this branch of the law, at least in this state, were laid in *Thomas* v. *Winchester*. A poison was falsely labeled. The sale was made to a druggist, who in turn sold to a customer. The customer recovered damages from the seller who affixed the label. "The defendant's negligence," it was said, "put human life in imminent danger." A poison, falsely labeled, is likely to injure anyone who gets it. Because the danger is to be foreseen, there is a duty to avoid the injury.

We hold, then, that the principle of *Thomas* v. *Winchester* is not limited to poisons, explosives, and things of like nature, to things which in their normal operation are implements of destruction. If the nature of a thing is such that it is reasonably certain to place life and limb in peril when negligently made, it is then a thing of danger. Its nature gives warning of the consequences to be expected.

If to the element of danger there is added knowledge that the thing will be used by persons other than the purchaser, and used without new tests, then, irrespective of contract, the manufacturer of this thing is under a duty to make it carefully. That is as far as we are required to go for the decision in this case.

From his survey of the decisions, there thus emerges a definition of the duty of a manufacturer which enables us to measure this defendant's liability. Beyond all question, the nature of an automobile gives warning of probable danger if its construction is defective. This automobile was designed to go 50 miles an hour. Unless its wheels were sound and strong, injury was almost certain. The defendant knew the danger. It knew also that the car would be used by persons other than the buyer.

There is nothing anomalous in a rule which imposes upon A., who has contracted with B., a duty to C. and D. and others according as he knows or does not know that the subject-matter of the contract is intended for their use. Subtle distinctions are drawn by the defendant between things inherently dangerous and things imminently dangerous, but the case does not turn upon these verbal niceties. If danger was to be expected as reasonably certain, there was a duty of vigilance, and this is true whether you call the danger inherent or imminent.

We think the defendant was not absolved from a duty of inspection because it bought the wheels from a reputable manufacturer. It was not merely a dealer in automobiles. It was a manufacturer of automobiles. It was responsible for the finished product. It was not at liberty to put the finished product on the market without subjecting the component parts to ordinary and simple tests. Under the charge of the trial judge nothing more was required of it. The obligation to inspect must vary with the nature of the thing to be inspected. The more probable the danger the greater the need of caution.

Courts across the United States followed the decision of Judge Cardozo. Today, plaintiffs who wish to bring suit based upon negligence need not prove a direct contractual relationship with the defendant. As time passed, courts across the United States eventually abandoned this requirement in warranty cases as well.

Negligence

Manufacturers. The law relating to torts varies from state to state. Efforts have been made to encourage uniformity in the law. One such effort, the work of scholars examining the state of the law in the field of torts, resulted in a number of recommendations as to rules states should adopt in this area. It is called the **Restatement (Second) of Torts.** Many judges have followed the provisions in the *Restatement* in deciding the proper rule of law to adopt for their states.

In Section 395, the *Restatement (Second) of Torts* sets forth a standard by which the courts may judge the actions of a manufacturer of a product. It states:

> A manufacturer who fails to exercise reasonable care in the manufacture of a chattel which, unless carefully made, he should recognize as involving an unreasonable risk of causing physical harm to those who use it for a purpose for which the manufacturer should expect it to be used and to those whom he should expect to be endangered by its probable use, is subject to liability for physical harm caused to them by its lawful use in a manner and for a purpose for which it is supplied.

A manufacturer can be held liable for physical injuries to a person caused by a defective product because of poor design, improper construction, or assembly of the product. In Section 398, the *Restatement (Second) of Torts* announces a standard for design of products.

> A manufacturer of a chattel made under a plan or design which makes it dangerous for the uses for which it is manufactured is subject to liability to others whom he should expect to use the chattel or to be endangered by its probable use for physical harm caused by his failure to exercise reasonable care in the adoption of a safe plan or design.

This means that a manufacturer must exercise due care in the design of all products. Putting a product on the market that later is determined to be unsafe for normal use may result in liability for physical injuries caused to people by the product.

The manufacturer generally must exercise due care to make certain the product he places on the market is safe. This means the manufacturer must conduct reasonable tests and exercise reasonable care in inspecting a product to discover latent defects before putting it on the market.

It is not sufficient for a manufacturer merely to inspect and test a product. The manufacturer also sometimes has a duty to warn the public of the dangerous propensities of a product. In Section 388, the *Restatement (Second) of Torts* suggests the following standard with respect to a duty to warn:

> One who supplies directly or through a third person a chattel for another to use is subject to liability to those whom the supplier should expect to use the chattel with the consent of the other or to be endangered by its probable use, for physical harm caused by the use of the chattel in the manner for which and by a person for whose use it is supplied, if the supplier
>
> a. knows or has reason to know that the chattel is or is likely to be dangerous for the use for which it is supplied, and
> b. has no reason to believe that those for whose use the chattel is supplied will realize its dangerous condition, and
> c. fails to exercise reasonable care to inform them of its dangerous condition or of the facts which make it likely to be dangerous.

Numerous cases have arisen with respect to the issue of duty to warn. All too often people coming into contact with certain products do not realize the dangers associated with using them. An excellent illustration of this point can be found in the case *Outlaw* v. *Firestone Tire and Rubber Co.*, which appears later in this chapter. It deals with the dangers associated with filling an automobile tire with air, a task most people think is relatively risk free.

Not only must sellers warn people of the dangers associated with proper uses of a product, sellers must also warn the public of foreseeable dangers associated with the misuse of their products. A very common example of this situation is when a young child comes into contact with a product that he or she fails to understand is dangerous. Suppose an infant is crawling on a kitchen floor and opens a cabinet. The child reaches in and pulls out a bottle of drain cleaner. Such a product is not made for drinking, nonetheless, it is foreseeable that an infant could consume it. Because such a misuse is foreseeable, a manufacturer must warn of the product's capacity to injure persons if they swallow it. Such a warning hopefully will cause people to keep the product out of the reach of infants.

Even if a manufacturer places a warning on its products, other questions concerning the warning can arise. For example, was the warning adequate? Was the warning clear and intelligible? Was it written in a language people coming into contact with the product could read? Another problem concerns who should receive the warning. Is it sufficient to warn physicians of the dangers of a drug and not the consuming public? In another case, *Griggs* v. *Firestone Tire and Rubber Co.*, the court held that Firestone had failed to give a proper warning even though a warning appeared in literature supplied by Firestone to purchasers of its products. As a warning did not appear directly on the product itself, the court ruled that Firestone had not exercised reasonable care in warning the public.

The *Restatement* requires a manufacturer to use reasonable care in every step of the manufacturing process—design, construction, testing, labeling, and packaging— if it realizes the product poses an unreasonable risk of causing physical harm to users of the product. The manufacturer owes this duty to exercise reasonable care to any person who uses or is endangered by the use of its product. This provision dispenses with the defense of the lack of privity of contract, that is, the necessity of establishing a direct contractual relationship between buyer and seller. If a manufacturer fails to exercise such care, it will be liable for physical harm caused by the product.

Retailers. Retailers also owe a duty of due care to the public. Some states require the retailer to inform purchasers of any defect in products that could be discovered by an inspection of the product. Other states do not require the retailer to take such steps to warn purchasers. In general, recovery from a retailer under negligence theory is difficult. Retailers quite often deal in packaged containers that they know very little about. Courts take this into consideration when evaluating the obligations of retailers.

The chief problem with negligence is the difficulty for the plaintiff in establishing the defendant failed to exercise due care. This creates a very substantial burden of proof for the plaintiff in many cases. Furthermore, the defendant may be able to establish to the satisfaction of a court that it did in fact exercise a reasonable amount of care in manufacturing, assembling, testing, and packaging the product. In this situation, because the defendant acted reasonably, the plaintiff receives nothing. Certain theories of recovery discussed later in this chapter permit the plaintiff to recover even if the manufacturer exercised all care possible. That being the case, pursuing a case under negligence in many instances makes very little sense.

Warranty

Because of the problems with respect to negligence, injured parties began to attempt to bring suit under other theories of recovery. The next theory of recovery to gain popular acceptance by the courts was warranty. Unlike negligence, which is a tort theory of recovery, warranty theory is contractual in nature.

Today, courts across the United States permit a person injured by a product to recover if the injured party is able to show that there was a breach of warranty by the defendant and that the injury was sustained as a result of the breach of warranty.

Sellers may create warranties by express agreement. Other warranties arise automatically by operation of law whenever a seller enters into a contract.

Express Warranty. An express warranty may be created in one of three ways: (1) by a promise made by the seller to the buyer that relates to the goods, (2) by a specific description of the goods made by the seller, or (3) by the seller's sample or model.

For example, a tire manufacturer who states that its tires will not blow out during the life of the tread creates an express warranty. Suppose the manufacturer made such a statement and the tire on a driver's car exploded. If the explosion caused his car to run off the road into a tree, would he have a cause of action against the tire manufacturer for his injuries? Yes. The manufacturer breached its warranty when the tire exploded. It would be liable for the resulting injuries to the driver.

The following case deals with an express warranty created by an advertisement.

Drayton v. Jiffee Chemical Corp.
United States District Court
395 F. Supp. 1081 (1975)

This suit arose out of a severe facial disfigurement incurred by a child, Terri Drayton. On December 21, 1968, Terri and her parents were living in a boarding house in Cleveland, Ohio. Terri's father was attempting to clear a clogged sink in the bathroom. He was using a bottle of "liquid-plumr" that he had borrowed from the landlady, Mrs. Sorrell. At the trial, Terri's father testified that he had entered the bathroom alone and poured half a bottle of liquid-plumr into the drain. He then placed a towel over the open drain and stepped back from the sink. At that moment, Terri grabbed his leg and screamed. When he looked down at the child it appeared that she had been doused with the drain cleaner. He testified that he was unaware of the child's presence in the bathroom until he heard her scream.

Battisti, Chief Judge

Plaintiffs contend that defendant's use of such a highly caustic concentration of sodium hydroxide in liquid-plumr rendered such product unsafe, unmerchantable, and unfit for the use intended—that of a common, household drain cleaner. Besides breaching such implied warranties of merchantability and fitness for the use intended, plaintiffs also argue that the defendant breached its express warranty, contained in its advertising, that liquid-plumr was "safe" for ordinary household use.

At trial there was introduced into evidence a copy of a letter from The Code Authority, National Association of Broadcasters to Mr. Harold F. Bull, president of the Bull Advertising Agency, which had as one of its accounts the Jiffee Chemical Corporation. The letter requested documentation in support of Jiffee's claim that liquid-plumr is "safe." Also introduced into evidence was Mr. Bull's letter in response wherein he stated that as of March 28, 1967 all references to the word "safe" were being deleted from Jiffee's advertisements for liquid-plumr. Such advertising, however, continued beyond the point in time when Mrs. Sorrell purchased the bottle of liquid-plumr that was used on the night of the accident. Mrs. Sorrell testified that she bought the drain cleaner before Terri was born (1966) and that she had seen the product advertised on television and that it was represented to be "safe" and capable of "fast action." It is clear that Mrs. Sorrell relied, at least in part, on such representations in making her choice of which product to purchase. Under those circumstances Mrs. Sorrell would have a viable cause of action against Jiffee for breach of express warranty:

"Under modern merchandising practices, where the manufacturer of a product in his advertising makes representations as to the quality and merit of his product aimed directly at the ultimate consumer and urges the latter to purchase the product from a retailer, and such ultimate consumer does so in reliance on and pursuant to the inducements of the manufacturer and suffers harm in the use of such product by reason of deleterious ingredients therein, such ultimate consumer may maintain an action for damages immediately against the manufacturer on the basis of express warranty, notwithstanding that there is no direct contractual relationship between them." *Rogers v. Toni Home Permanent Co.*, 167 Ohio St 244, 147 NE2d 612 (1958).

Such cause of action would also be vested in Terri Drayton as "one whose presence at the [scene of the accident] was foreseeable and whose safety it was the duty of the manufacturer to protect by producing a chattel that when used as intended would not endanger the safety of those lawfully at the place of its use."

Defendant is therefore liable to plaintiff for breach of warranty.

Implied Warranty of Merchantability. Warranties may be created by operation of law. Here the seller neither says nor writes down any warranties, but the law creates a warranty anyway. One such type of warranty is the implied warranty of merchantability. Only a merchant seller creates such a warranty. The foremost question in deciding whether goods are merchantable or not is whether the goods are fit for the ordinary purposes for which such goods are used. If the buyer orders a furnace for his or her home, the buyer expects a certain level of performance from the heater even though the seller said nothing regarding its performance. Suppose the buyer turned the heater on after its installation and the heater exploded. Obviously, a heater that explodes on its first use fails to comply with the implied warranty of merchantability. The buyer may bring suit for any injuries caused by the defective heater.

Implied Warranty of Fitness for a Particular Purpose. This warranty also is created by operation of law. If at the time of contracting, the seller has reason to know any particular purpose for which the goods are required and that the buyer is relying on the seller's skill or judgment to select or furnish suitable goods, there is an implied warranty that the goods shall be fit for such purpose. Suppose a consumer purchased a gas range installed by the seller. If the seller used a defective brass tube to connect the range to the gas pipe, and the defective pipe caused an explosion, the seller is liable to the purchaser. The seller knew the buyer was relying upon it to furnish a suitable tube. Its failure to do so breaches the implied warranty of fitness for a particular purpose.

Hurley v. Larry's Water Ski School
United States Court of Appeals, Eleventh Circuit
762 F.2d 925 (1985)

Cornelius Hurley severely injured his right leg during a skiing lesson. The ski school program was designed to teach beginners to ski. Larry's Water Ski School provided all the necessary ski equipment. Hurley testified that after several lessons he was attempting to get up on the skis when suddenly he felt the rope give way on his right-hand side. This caused him to lose his balance and fall into the water. Either just before or during the fall, the wooden tow handle that he was holding snapped and struck his leg. He suffered a four-inch cut which required immediate stitching and additional medical treatment when infection set it.

On appeal, Hurley contends that the trial court erred in granting the Larry's motion for a directed verdict on the breach of implied warranty count of Hurley's complaint.

Vance, Circuit Judge

Hurley filed this diversity suit alleging that his injury was caused by the faulty and negligent assembly of the tow handle and tow rope used by Larry's in towing its skiers. Hurley's complaint sought relief under breach of implied warranty.

Larry's asserted that the tow handle had broken in this case only because Hurley continued to hold onto it after he had fallen in spite of several warnings not to do so. Weisberg, who was driving the boat at the time of the accident, testified that he felt a pull against the boat when Hurley fell. He said this was unusual because the boat normally accelerates when a skier falls since the skier releases the rope immediately. He explained that when a skier continues to hold onto the rope after falling it creates a "drag" against the boat. He believed that the pull against the boat which he felt was caused by Hurley's failure to release the handle immediately upon falling.

Hurley correctly points out that Larry's may be liable under a breach of implied warranty even if it were not the manufacturer, assembler or seller of the tow rope and handle in question. The Florida courts have extended products liability law to hold lessors and bailors for hire liable for breach of implied warranty in the same manner that manufacturers, assemblers and sellers may be. Florida's decision to extend these types of liability to leases and bailments stemmed from its perception of the need to extend the same protection to consumers who rent and lease as had already been afforded to consumers who buy.

We cannot accept the proposition that Hurley had a lease or bailment agreement for the skiing equipment. By definition, both a lease and a bailment require that at some point the lessee or bailee have possession and control over the leased or bailed property. Hurley is unable to point to any moment in time at which he maintained undisputed possession and control over the tow handle and rope in question, which were at all times connected to the boat.

We agree that the implied warranty of fitness is applicable to this situation. At the heart of the *Johnson Equipment* opinion is the Florida Supreme Court's desire to protect all consumers—whether they be buyers, lessees or bailees—from defective products. The same concerns which the court expressed for lessees and bailees are present in the instant case. Hurley, who had never skied before, was relying totally on Larry's to provide him with proper instruction and with equipment fit for the purpose of learning to ski.

Larry's has freely acknowledged from the beginning that it solicited Hurley to enter into a contractual agreement for skiing lessons. If the contract for lessons had not included free use of the equipment and Larry's had furnished the equipment to Hurley under a separate rental agreement or for an additional fee, Hurley would unquestionably have had a cause of action against Larry's. Larry's conduct in supplying the equipment under the contract for lessons is precisely the same. Larry's stated in its brief and reiterated at oral argument before this court that it was implicit in the agreement that the fee for the ski lessons included the use of a boat, skis and a tow line. Equally implicit in that agreement, we believe, was an implied warranty that the equipment supplied by Larry's was fit for the purpose of teaching an individual to ski. While we have been unable to find a Florida case directly on point, our holding is based on our understanding of the Florida Supreme Court's reasoning in *Johnson Equipment* and the subsequent application of that case by the Florida district courts of appeals.

We conclude that the district court erred in directing a verdict on the breach of implied warranty count. In so doing, we express no opinion on the merits of Hurley's breach of warranty claim. We find only that it should have been presented to the jury.

Breach of Warranty As a Basis for a Products Liability Suit. If a seller creates an express warranty or an implied warranty exists and the seller breaches this warranty, a person injured as a result of the breach of warranty may bring suit to recover for his or her injuries if the plaintiff also establishes the express or implied warranty was part of the basis of the bargain between the parties.

Even today, in somes states a plaintiff will be unable to recover if he or she is unable to establish a direct contractual relationship with the defendant.

Proceeding on a personal injury suit based on a warranty theory of recovery creates a number of other hurdles for plaintiffs to overcome. In some cases, the defendant may be able to successfully demonstrate it disclaimed all warranties. A defendant who makes no warranties obviously cannot be liable for breach of an express warranty. Even though the implied warranties arise by operation of law, and not by express warranty, sellers may exclude the operation of these warranties. The power to disclaim warranties gives sellers the opportunity to limit their liability under this theory of recovery. Furthermore, in the case of the implied warranty of merchantability, the plaintiff must establish the defendant is a merchant. If the defendant is not a merchant, the implied warranty of merchantability does not arise. Finally, if a plaintiff wishes to institute suit based on breach of warranty, it must notify the defendant of the breach. If requisite notice of breach of warranty is not given at the appropriate time, however, the plaintiff may not use breach of warranty as a basis for recovery.

Misrepresentation

Another theory of recovery in the products liability field developed even more recently than negligence or warranty. This theory of recovery, referred to generally as *misrepresentation,* permits the injured party to recover in certain instances when the defendant has misrepresented the product and the misrepresentation causes the injury. Untrue statements in radio or television broadcasts, in newspapers, magazines, billboards, posters, or pamphlets may lead to liability for personal injuries if the statement misleads the public.

During the last decade, an increasing number of plaintiffs have chosen to establish their case on the basis of **innocent misrepresentation.** Liability arises under innocent misrepresentation even though the seller never intended to mislead the public. The *Restatement (Second) of Torts* suggests that a plaintiff be permitted to collect for any physical injuries he or she sustained, if the harm in question resulted from a misrepresentation of the character or quality of the product sold, even though the misrepresentation was an innocent one, and not made fraudulently or negligently, and the plaintiff demonstrates that he or she relied upon the misrepresentation in purchasing or using the product. The absence of privity of contract is not a defense.

In the following case, the court adopts innocent misrepresentation as a theory of recovery. Note that the facts in this case clearly indicate that Klages had been misled by General Ordnance's statements. As a result of his reliance on the statements in question, he sustained an injury for which the court permitted him to recover.

WARRANTIES AND COMPUTER SOFTWARE

James A. Cummings, Inc., was a construction firm. It purchased Lotus Development Corporation's business program, "Symphony" and used it to prepare a bid for constructing an office building complex. As the bid was being prepared, an employee noticed that it did not include $254,000 in general costs. The preparer then inserted this figure at the top of the column of figures used to calculate the bid. The number appeared on the preparer's computer screen but was never added to the bid amount by the computer program. Cummings did not know this until after the miscalculated bid was accepted.

Cummings filed suit against Lotus seeking $254,000 in consequential damages, contending that their Symphony software did not perform properly, thereby causing the loss. However, Lotus' software package provides a written limited warranty under which the company will only replace a defective disc. Furthermore, these limited warranties are a part of a licensing agreement common to software purchases under which the buyer does not own the product. Instead, the buyer simply purchases a license to use the software maker's product.

This issue of software maker liability may be viewed from two perspectives. The companies contend that no maker represents that its software is flawless, since there are too many ways a computer program can go wrong. The problems that arise, they contend, are with users who blindly rely on computer output for their major decisions without adequate controls. Furthermore, some small software companies are concerned that potential liability for consequential damages arising from flawed software might stifle innovation and cause some to go out of business because of a costly lawsuit or increased liability insurance premiums. On the other hand, software companies are selling a very sophisticated product that they intend their customers to rely on. Software is sold to business as a major time-saving device that can be used for complex operations. Thus, should not the maker be liable if the software does not perform according to specifications?

Klages v. General Ordnance Equipment Corporation

Superior Court of Pennsylvania

367 A.2d 304 (1976)

Plaintiff, John R. Klages, was employed as a night auditor at Conley's Motel. After once being held up by armed robbers, plaintiff purchased the defendant's mace weapon for protection. He sued for injuries sustained while using the mace weapon. The lower court ruled in his favor and the superior court affirmed the lower court decision.

Hoffman, Judge

The instant case presents a question of first impression in Pennsylvania: Is the *Restatement (Second)* *of Torts* Section 402B the law of this Commonwealth?

The facts are not in dispute. The appellee, John R. Klages, was employed as a night auditor at Conley's Motel on Route 8, Hampton Township. He worked from eleven o'clock at night until seven o'clock in the morning, five days a week. On March 30, 1968, at approximately one-thirty in the morning, two individuals entered the motel and announced "This is a stickup. Open the safe."

The next day Klages and a fellow employee, Bob McVay, decided that they needed something to protect themselves against the possibility of future holdups. After reading an article concerning the effects of mace, McVay suggested that they investigate the possibility of using mace for their protection. McVay secured four leaflets describing certain mace weapons from the Markl Supply Company. The leaflets were distributed to retail outlets by the appellant manufacturer, General Ordnance Equipment Corporation. The literature indicated that three different types of mace weapons were available. Two of the weapons were too large for Klages' and McVay's purposes, but the third, the MK-II, was easily concealable and otherwise appeared to meet their requirements. The literature contained, in pertinent part, the following description of the mace's effectiveness: "Rapidly vaporizes on face of assailant effecting instantaneous incapacitation. . . . It will instantly stop and subdue entire groups . . . instantly stop assailants in their tracks . . . an attacker is subdued—instantly, for a period of 15 to 20 minutes. . . . Time Magazine stated the Chemical Mace is 'for police the first, if not the final answer to a nationwide need—a weapon that disables as effectively as a gun and yet does no permanent injury. . . . The effectiveness is the result of a unique incapacitating formulation (patent pending), projected in a shotgun-like pattern of heavy liquid droplets that, upon contact with the face, cause extreme tearing, and a stunned, winded condition, often accompanied by dizziness and apathy." After reading and discussing the literature with their employer, McVay purchased an MK-II mace weapon from Markl Supply Company.

At approximately 1:40 A.M., on the morning of September 22, 1968, while the appellee was on duty, two unknown individuals entered the motel office and requested a room. After the appellee had placed a registration form in front of one of the men and had turned to secure a room key, the individuals announced a stickup. One of the intruders took out a gun and directed the appellee to open the safe. Klages, planning to use the mace before the intruder used the gun, moved from the counter to the cash register where the mace was kept. Using the cash register as a shield, Klages squirted the mace, hitting the intruder "right beside the nose." Klages immediately ducked below the register, but the intruder followed him down and shot him in the head. The intruders immediately departed and Klages called the police. The bullet wound caused complete loss of sight in the appellee's right eye.

The appellee, Klages, commenced separate actions against the Markl Supply Company and the General Ordnance Equipment Corporation. The Markl Supply Company also joined the General Ordnance Corporation as an additional defendant in each of its cases. On October 26, 1973, the cases were consolidated for trial. A jury trial commenced on March 4, 1974, and the jury returned a verdict in the amount of $42,000.00, in favor of Klages against the appellant, General Ordnance Equipment Corporation, and a verdict in favor of the Markl Supply Company. This appeal followed.

The appellant raises as grounds for reversal the argument the lower court erred in charging the jury on misrepresentation of a material fact under section 402B of the *Restatement (Second) of Torts.*

Section 402B of the *Restatement (Second) of Torts* provides as follows: "One engaged in the business of selling chattel who, by advertising, labels, or otherwise, makes to the public a misrepresentation of a material fact concerning the character or quality of a chattel sold by him is subject to liability for physical harm to a consumer of the chattel caused by justifiable reliance upon the misrepresentation, even though (a) it is not made fraudulently or negligently, and (b) the consumer has not bought the chattel from or entered into any contractual relation with the seller."

Having adopted Section 402B of the *Restatement (Second) of Torts* as the law of this Commonwealth, we must determine whether the appellant misrepresented "a material fact concerning the character or quality of a chattel sold by him. . . ."

The comments to Section 402B are helpful in this regard. First, Comment f states that "[t]he fact misrepresented must be a material one, upon which the consumer may be expected to rely in making his purchase. . . ." Comment g states that section 402B "does not apply to statements of opinion, and in particular it does not apply to the kind of loose general praise of wares sold which, on the part of the seller, is considered to be 'sales talk', and is commonly called 'puffing'—as, for example, a statement that an automobile is the best on the market for the price. . . . In addition, the fact misrepresented must be a material one, of importance to the normal purchaser by which the ultimate buyer may justifiably be expected to be influenced in buying the chattel."

The facts and circumstances surrounding the purchase of a product are helpful in determining whether the repesentation is of a material fact. In this case, the appellant sold a product designed as a tool to deter violence. Its sole anticipated use was to protect the purchaser from harm under extremely dangerous circumstances and the appellee specifically purchased the product with these explicit purposes in mind. Specific representations about the effectiveness of the weapon under such dangerous circumstances are clearly material. The mace weapons were described as effecting an instantaneous, immediate, complete incapacitation of an assailant. This is not "loose, general praise"; rather it is specific data on the capability of a product.

Strict Liability

As the years passed, plaintiffs became weary of the difficult problems of proof associated with negligence and the various defenses to warranty cases. In many cases, people who sustained injuries as a result of a defective product found themselves unable to recover, not because they were not injured, but because of some technical rule of law. As more and more people sustained injuries, the mood in the courts and the legislatures gradually began to shift from protecting business to protecting consumers. People began to argue that the manufacturer is in the best position to shoulder any loss caused by its products. A manufacturer has the power to produce better and safer products. The public is powerless to control the quality of products on the marketplace. Lawyers argued that by placing more responsibility on corporations to produce safe products, corporations would be encouraged to take more care in the design, manufacture, testing, and inspection of products.

In some instances, neither the manufacturer nor the consumer really is at fault. Sometimes a bad product reaches the marketplace even though the manufacturer takes every step possible to keep this from occurring. When this happens, who ought to bear the loss—the injured party or the manufacturer? Lawyers increasingly began to accept the idea that a manufacturer is in the best position to insure against any possible loss caused by its products. If one of two innocent persons must bear the loss caused by a defective product, let the manufacturer purchase insurance and bear the loss.

This idea gained popularity following Judge Traynor's famous comments in *Escola* v. *Coca Cola Bottling Co. of Fresno*. A waitress in a restaurant was injured when a bottle of Coca Cola exploded in her hand. Neither she nor anyone else was able to explain why this accident occurred. In ruling in her favor, Judge Traynor wrote:

I believe the manufacturer's negligence should no longer be singled out as the basis of a plaintiff's right to recover in cases like the present one. In my opinion it should now be recognized that a manufacturer incurs an absolute liability when an article he has placed on the market, knowing that it is to be used without inspection, proves to have a defect that causes injury to human beings. . . . Even if there is no negligence, however, public policy demands that responsibility be fixed wherever it will most effectively reduce the hazards to life and health inherent in defective products that reach the market.

The *Restatement (Second) of Torts* adopted such a rule, which now appears in Section 402A. It reads as follows:

1. One who sells any product in a defective condition unreasonably dangerous to the user or consumer or to his property, is subject to liability for physical harm thereby caused to the ultimate user or consumer, or to his property, if (a) the seller is engaged in the business of selling such a product, and (b) it is expected to and does reach the consumer or user without substantial change in the condition in which it is sold.

2. The rule stated in subsection (1) applies although (a) the seller has exercised all possible care in the preparation and sale of his product, and (b) the user or consumer has not bought the product from or entered into any contractual relation with the seller.

The *Restatement* adopts a rule that is almost one of absolute liability on the part of the seller. It makes the seller liable even if it exercised "all possible care in the preparation and sale" of the product. In a negligence case, evidence of this type would absolve the defendant of any liability. Under **strict liability** in tort, it is irrelevant whether the seller acted negligently. As long as the plaintiff is able to establish the other elements, he or she recovers even if there is no evidence of negligence on the part of the defendant.

The *Restatement* also eliminates the need to establish a direct contractual relationship between the plaintiff and the defendant; that is, it eliminates the absence of privity of contract as a defense in a strict liability case. This permits an injured party to sue anyone in the distributive chain: manufacturers, distributors, or retail sellers. Any user or consumer is permitted to bring suit. Further, many states permit bystanders to bring suit. Suppose a person on a skateboard lost control because a roller came off the skateboard. If the person on the skateboard crashed into John, John would be an innocent bystander injured by the failure of the skateboard. Many states permit a person in John's position to bring suit against the manufacturer of the skateboard, the distributor, or the retail seller.

Plaintiffs must establish that the product in question was expected to and in fact did reach the consumer without substantial change in the condition in which it was sold. In the case of packaged goods, such a requirement creates few difficulties for the plaintiff. Suppose Mrs. Jones purchases some hair dye to change the color of her hair. If the formula of the dye causes users to lose their hair, and Mrs. Jones's hair falls out, she may sue the seller for damages. As the dye comes in a package, she will have no problems proving the product was in the same condition as when it was sold. But suppose Mrs. Jones was injured instead in her two-year-old car when the brakes failed. If she brings suit against the manufacturer, will she be able to prove the brakes were in the same condition as when the vehicle was sold to her? Obviously, this creates a substantial burden of proof. Many people may have touched the brakes. These people might have somehow tampered with the brakes and caused them to fail; in that case, the manufacturer would not be liable.

This provision applies only to persons regularly engaged in selling a particular product. If a person purchases an automobile from a local automobile dealer, clearly the dealer is in the business of selling automobiles. The dealer could be liable. But suppose the buyer purchased the automobile from a next-door neighbor. The neighbor, as he or she is not regularly engaged in selling automobiles, would have no liability.

A company must provide adequate instructions and warnings with its products. Suppose a company sold paint with the following warning: "Keep away from heat and open flame. Use with adequate ventilation." Does this fully inform users of the product of all dangers inherent in using the product? What if flammable vapors could accumulate in a closed area? Does this warning adequately alert potential users to this danger? A product that is otherwise safe may be rendered unreasonably dangerous by the failure of the seller to provide adequate warnings of the dangerous characteristics of its products. Such a warning might be inadequate if it failed to clearly warn users of all dangers in using the product.

The following case deals with a failure of the manufacturer to warn users of the danger of putting air in a tire.

Outlaw v. Firestone Tire and Rubber
United States Court of Appeals, Eleventh Circuit
770 F.2d 1012 (1985)

On July 28, 1981, Jay Outlaw was pumping air in a low tire. He pumped air into the tire and the gauge still registered 25 psi of tire pressure. He heard a "pop" within the tire and checked the pressure one more time. The gauge registered between 35 and 45 psi. He began to release air from the tire and the tire exploded, injuring his right eye and ear.

Outlaw sued Firestone based on the Alabama Extended Manufacturer's Liability Doctrine (AEMLD). In order to recover under AEMLD, there must be proof that a manufacturer was at fault in placing a product on the market that was in an unreasonably unsafe or dangerous condition. The trial court granted a directed verdict for the defendant, Firestone.

Henderson, Circuit Judge

Outlaw does not claim that the tire was defectively designed or manufactured. Rather, he contends that Firestone failed to give adequate warning that a tire operated at low pressure for an extended period of time would melt down and explode. Alabama law recognizes that a failure to warn can provide the basis for AEMLD liability. "When a seller knows or should know that its product is imminently or inherently dangerous when used in its customary manner, the seller is under a duty to use due care to acquaint the user with the danger."

In granting the defendant's motion for a directed verdict, the district court found that Outlaw had failed to establish a prima facie case. Although the reason for the directed verdict is not totally clear from the record, it was apparently based on (1) Outlaw's failure to establish a duty to warn and (2) his failure to show that the lack of warning caused his injuries.

As stated earlier, Alabama law imposes a duty to warn of inherent and imminent dangers in a product when used in its usual manner. Whether there is a duty to warn, and if so, the adequacy of the warning are usually questions for the jury. The issue may be withdrawn from the jury only if the risk is so remote that reasonable persons could not agree on the existence of a duty to warn. After a careful review of the evidence, we find that reasonable persons could find a duty to warn of the risk of a tire explosion under these conditions. As such, the jury was entitled to decide whether there existed such a duty.

Our conclusions are supported largely by the testimony of Bronaugh, Outlaw's expert witness. The explosion was caused when heat, produced by the continuous contact of the deflated tire with the surface of the highway, created temperatures hot enough to melt the sidewall. Bronaugh knew of other instances in which the same sequence of events had led to the same result. This evidence would be sufficient for a jury to infer knowledge of this danger by the tire industry generally. Bronaugh also knew that Firestone was aware of this particular risk with truck tires. The product was being put to its intended use by the plaintiff who had no knowledge of the dangerous circumstances although the manufacturer knew or should have known of the hazard.

From this testimony, we find that a jury could determine that the tire posed a nonobvious risk of serious injury when used in its intended manner. The jury also could conclude that Firestone was aware of this risk. From this, the jury would be authorized to find that Firestone had a duty to warn of the risk. At this juncture of the case it was error to direct a verdict in favor of the defendant.

Because genuine issues of fact remain, the judgment of the district court granting a directed verdict in favor of Firestone is reversed and the case is remanded for a new trial.

The law of products liability has for a long time required manufacturers to warn consumers of dangers associated with their products. The following case discusses the question of whether the states can require manufacturers to disclose more information than is already required by federal law.

Cipollone v. Liggett Group, Inc.
Third Circuit Court of Appeals
789 F.2d 181 (1986)

Mrs. Cipollone developed lung cancer allegedly as a result of smoking cigarettes manufactured and sold by Liggett. She began smoking in 1942 and died in October 1984. Suit was filed on August 1, 1983. Her husband continued the prosecution of the case following her death.

Liggett contended that the Federal Cigarette Labeling and Advertising Act preempted her claims. Several of the claims involved the failure to provide an adequate warning of the dangers of the cigarettes sold by the defendant. The Cipollones made a motion to strike the preemption defenses. The district court granted the Cipollones' motion to strike the defenses. The defendant appealed to the Third Circuit, which reversed the decision of the district court.

Hunter, Circuit Judge:

The Federal Cigarette Labeling and Advertising Act, originally enacted in 1965, was a response to a growing awareness among members of federal as well as state government that cigarette smoking posed a significant health threat to Americans. The original Act required the following warning label on cigarette packages: "Caution: Cigarette Smoking May Be Hazardous to Your Health." The warnings have been changed several times after that time.

The Act contains a preemption provision, which provides that

(a) No statement relating to smoking and health, other than the statement required by section 1333 of this title, shall be required on any cigarette package.

(b) No requirement or prohibition based on smoking and health shall be imposed under State law with respect to the advertising or promotion of any cigarettes the packages of which are labeled in conformity with the provisions of this chapter.

We turn to examining whether congressional intent to preempt the Cipollones' claims may be inferred under the two general principles of implied preemption.

Under the principles of implied preemption, we must first determine whether Congress intended to occupy the field relating to cigarettes and health to the exclusion of state law product liability actions such as the Cipollones. Our examination of the Act leads us to agree with the district court's statements that "Congress . . . intended to occupy a field" and "indicated this intent as clearly as it knew how." Not only did Congress use sweeping language in describing the preemptive effect of the Act, but it expressed its desire to establish "a comprehensive Federal program" in order to avoid "diverse, nonuniform, and confusing cigarette labeling and advertising regu-

lations with respect to any relationship between smoking and health."

In determining the scope of this field, we observe that the Cipollones' tort action concerns rights and remedies traditionally defined solely by state law. We therefore must adopt a restrained view in evaluating whether Congress intended to supersede entirely private rights of action such as those at issue here. In light of this constraint, we cannot say that the scheme created by the Act is "so pervasive" or the federal interest involved "so dominant" as to eradicate all of the Cipollones' claims. Nor are we persuaded that the object of the Act and the character of obligations imposed by it reveal a purpose to exert exclusive control over every aspect of the relationship between cigarettes and health. Thus, we look to the extent to which the Cipollones' state law claims "actually conflict" with the Act to ascertain whether they are preempted.

The test enunciated by this court for addressing a potential conflict between state and federal law requires us to examine first the purposes of the federal law and second the effect of the operation of the state law on these purposes. The preemption provision, read together with the statement of the Act's purposes, makes clear Congress's determination that this balance would be upset by either a requirement of a warning other than that prescribed by the Act or a requirement or prohibition based on smoking and health with respect to the advertising or promotion of cigarettes.

We conclude that claims relating to smoking and health that result in liability for noncompliance with warning, advertisement and promotion obligations other than those prescribed in the Act have the effect of tipping the Act's balance of purposes and therefore actually conflict with the Act.

We hold that the Act preempts those state law damage actions relating to smoking and health that challenge either the adequacy of the warning on cigarette packages or the propriety of a party's actions with respect to the advertising and promotion of cigarettes. We further hold that where the success of a state law damage claim necessarily depends on the assertion that a party bore the duty to provide a warning to consumers in addition to the warning Congress has required on cig-

arette packages, such claims are preempted as conflicting with the Act.

At this stage of the litigation it is not necessary for us to identify which of the Cipollones' claims are preempted by the Act. We reverse the district court to the extent that it granted the Cipollones' motion to strike appellants' preemption defenses. We will also remand the case for further proceedings consistent with this opinion.

The requirement that gives the courts the greatest problem is the requirement that the product be in a "defective condition unreasonably dangerous to the user or consumer or to his property." The states have adopted various positions regarding the terminology "defective condition unreasonably dangerous." Some states have greatly modified these concepts.

For example, not every court has found that the marketing of handguns is not an unreasonably dangerous activity. Courts that are willing to hold sellers of handguns liable are attempting to stretch strict liability law to its limits. The following case also represents a willingness by a court to give a very broad interpretation to the term **unreasonably dangerous.**

Fraust v. Swift and Company
United States District Court, W.D. Pennsylvania
610 F. Supp. 711 (1985)

A products liability action was brought against Swift and Company, a peanut butter manufacturer, by Judith Fraust, the mother of Isaac Fraust, a sixteen-month-old child who choked while eating peanut butter spread on bread. The child subsequently died of severe brain damage. Swift claimed that as a matter of law its product should be declared to be not unreasonably dangerous.

The plaintiff's theory is that the peanut butter supplied by the defendant was unsafe for its intended use because it lacked a warning that it should not be fed to children under four years of age. Fraust contends that peanut butter is dangerous to children under four years of age because of its texture and consistency and the immature eating and swallowing abilities of children of that age.

Teitelbaum, Chief Judge

Liability cannot be imposed on the seller for failure to warn of a danger associated with its product if the danger was or should have been known to the

user. The issue of necessity of warnings must also be considered in light of any contradictory promotional activities on the part of the seller. The

Court cannot say as a matter of law that Isaac's mother knew or should have known of the danger associated with feeding a peanut butter sandwich to him.

As its second argument, defendant contends that because plaintiffs do not allege that the peanut butter was not in the condition expected by the ordinary consumer it was not unreasonably dangerous as a matter of law. Although at first this argument appears different from defendant's first argument, it is really a variant of the same argument.

Comment (i) to section 402A of the Restatement (2nd) of Torts differentiates "those products which are by their very nature unsafe but not defective from those which can truly be called defective. Comment (i) states:

> Good whiskey is not unreasonably dangerous merely because it will make some people drunk, and is especially dangerous to alcoholics; but bad whiskey, containing a dangerous amount of fuel oil, is unreasonably dangerous. Good tobacco is not unreasonably dangerous merely because the effects of smoking may be harmful; but tobacco containing something like marijuana may be unreasonably dangerous. Good butter is not unreasonably dangerous merely because, if such be the case, it deposits cholesterol in the arteries and leads to heart attacks; but bad butter, contaminated with poisonous fish oil, is unreasonably dangerous.

Defendant argues that similarly good peanut butter is not unreasonably dangerous because a young child may choke on it. Defendant then prematurely ends its analysis. However, comment (j) goes on to explain why good whiskey and good butter; and by inference, good tobacco; although "unsafe" are not defective, even without a warning of their dangers.

> . . . a seller is not required to warn with respect to products, or ingredients in them, which are only dangerous, or potentially so, when consumed in excessive quantity, or over a long period of time, when the danger, or potentiality of danger, is generally known and recognized. Again the dangers of alcoholic beverages are an example, as are also those of foods containing such substances as saturated fats, which may over a period of time have a deleterious effect upon the human heart.

That is, because these "unsafe" products present known dangers no warning is required. Therefore, although "unsafe", they are not defective.

Again the Court cannot say as a matter of law that the danger of a sixteen month old choking on a peanut butter sandwich is generally known and recognized so that admittedly good peanut butter, without warning of such a danger, is not unreasonably dangerous.

Generally, the courts have not been willing to permit people to recover mere mental injuries. There is a trend, however, for more and more courts to permit recovery for their emotional injuries—a point discussed in the following case.

Sease v. Taylor's Pets, Inc.
Court of Appeals of Oregon
700 P.2d 1054 (1985)

The defendants appeal judgments of twenty thousand dollars for plaintiffs Nora Thayer, Paula Hill, and Bradford Hill in a product liability action. On June 21, 1979, Janice Sease bought a pet skunk from defendant, Perfected Pets, Inc., a pet shop in Portland, Oregon. It had purchased the skunk from defendant Taylor's Pets,

Inc. Nine or ten days after Janice bought the skunk, it began to attack and bite people, lose fur, and develop sores on its body. It bit Paula Hill. Although it did not bite Nora Thayer, she handled it, fed it, and came in contact with its saliva. The skunk did not bite Brad Hill either, but he came in contact with its saliva when he had open cuts and scratches on his arms. The skunk also bit Janice Sease.

The skunk died, and Janice took it to a veterinarian for an autopsy. The veterinarian told her the skunk was rabid. A doctor from the Oregon State Health Division ordered rabies treatments for Nora and Paula and others whom the skunk had bitten or who had been exposed to its saliva. Brad's physician concluded that because of his history of allergies, the rabies injections could cause anaphylactic shock and death and advised against them. Brad did not take the injections. Both Paula and Nora were aware that their lives were in danger even after taking the treatments. None of the plaintiffs contracted rabies.

Newman, Judge

As to the right to recover for emotional distress in a strict products liability action, ORS 30.920 provides:

"One who sells or leases any product in a defective condition unreasonably dangerous to the user or consumer or to his property is subject to liability for *physical harm* or damage to property caused by that condition. . . ." ORS 30.920(1). (Emphasis supplied.)

Defendants concede that Nora, whom the rabid skunk bit, and Paula, who was also in contact with the skunk's saliva, did suffer "physical harm," because they received the rabies injections. Defendants argue, however, that Brad did not suffer physical harm, because he did not take the injections and did not suffer illness or death from contact with the skunk's saliva. They argue that the evidence shows only that he suffered anxiety because he knew that he might develop rabies. They assert that the court should have directed a verdict against Brad and should have granted a judgment notwithstanding the verdict, because he suffered no "physical harm." We agree.

Although we reject the Illinois rule that a live animal is not a product, we find helpful two cases from Illinois bearing on the recovery of damages for emotional distress in an action for strict products liability. In *Woodill v. Parke Davis & Co.*, the plaintiffs sought damages based on strict products liability for injuries to their son, and for their emotional distress because of his injuries, which they alleged resulted from the administration of a prescription drug to the mother while she was pregnant. The Appellate Court affirmed the dismissal of the count for plaintiffs' emotional distress, stating:

"[W]e do not believe that strict liability should be extended to include recovery for emotional distress and mental anguish to the parents of a minor who had suffered injury. First, because section 402A of the Restatement expressly limits recovery to physical harm. That section is entitled 'Special Liability of Seller of Product for *Physical Harm* to User or Consumer' (emphasis added), and it provides that '[o]ne who sells any product in a defective condition unreasonably dangerous to user or consumer or to his property is subject to liability for *physical harm* thereby caused to the ultimate user or consumer. . . .' (emphasis added). Given the limitation underlined above in section 402A, we conclude that the Restatement did not intend a strict liability action for mental anguish or emotional distress. Furthermore, at present, Illinois recognizes no such action. Case law here allows a cause of action only for severe emotional distress caused by intentional conduct."

In *Mink v. University of Chicago*, the court relied on section 402A as stating the law of Illinois.

It held that women who had been subjected to an increased risk of cancer by administration of DES without their knowledge had failed to state a claim for strict products liability:

"[O]ne of the essential elements in a claim for strict liability is physical injury to the plaintiff. The closest the complaint comes to alleging physical injury is the allegation of a 'risk' of cancer. The mere fact of a risk without any accompanying physical injury is insufficient to state a claim for strict products liability. Likewise, the plaintiffs may not rely on injury to their children to state a claim for relief for themselves, even though they allege mental anxiety and emotional distress as a consequence of the injury to their children."

Here, Brad's exposure to and contact with the rabid skunk increased the risk that he would suffer physical harm. He did not, however, suffer physical harm. Accordingly, we reverse the judgment for Brad Hill.

In other cases the courts have permitted plaintiffs to recover even though they did not sustain a physical injury. The Sease case represents the traditional view followed by courts with respect to this issue.

SUMMARY

Over the last hundred years or so, the courts and the legislatures have expanded the theories of liability in the products liability field. They have gradually made it easier and easier for an injured person to recover for any injuries he or she has sustained as a result of coming into contact with a product. At one time, it was virtually impossible for a person injured by a product to sue at all unless he or she actually purchased the product in queston. Furthermore, the injured person could sue only

MARKET SHARE LIABILITY

Abbott Laboratories, as well as a number of other drug companies, many years ago manufactured the synthetic drug, DES. DES was administered to mothers who were pregnant for the purposes of preventing miscarriages. At the time of the administration of the drug it was unknown, but it was later discovered, that the drug might cause cancerous vaginal and cervical growths in the daughters exposed to it before birth. In recent years, a number of women have in fact developed cancer. They want to recover but are unable to prove which company manufactured the drug that injured them.

In the seminal case, *Sindell* v. *Abbott Laboratories*, 607 P.2d 924 (California Supreme Court, 1980), the court decided that each manufacturer's liability would approximate its responsibility for the injuries caused by its own products. This has since been referred to as market share liability. A number of courts, but not all courts, have adopted this as a theory of recovery when the plaintiff is unable to identify which company manufactured the product. In the states that have adopted this theory of recovery, it is much easier for an injured party to establish a case, and thus the possibility of recovering for injuries is much higher than in states that have not adopted this theory of recovery.

the business that actually sold the product. This made it extremely difficult to sue anyone other than retail sellers. Today, it is possible to sue virtually anyone in the distributive chain. Furthermore, a person does not have to be the purchaser of a product in order to sue.

For many years plaintiffs had to establish their cases by relying upon negligence as a theory of recovery. This was not a totally satisfactory theory of recovery from the plaintiff's standpoint because he or she needed to establish that the defendant was in fact negligent. As time passed, some people began to bring their suits based upon breach of warranty as a theory of recovery. More recently, the courts and state legislatures have permitted injured parties to sue based upon the concept of strict liability in tort or misrepresentation. If a plaintiff can prove that he or she was personally injured as a result of a misrepresentation by the defendant of the character or quality of its product, the plaintiff may recover damages based on misrepresentation. A business that sells a product in a defective condition unreasonably dangerous to people can be sued for any personal injuries caused by the defective product. This is true even if the seller exercised all possible care in the preparation and sale of the product.

Suits by consumers have encouraged sellers to take more care in making certain that their products are safe.

REVIEW QUESTIONS

1. Define the following terms:
   a. Privity of contract
   b. Innocent misrepresentation
   c. Strict liability

2. List the theories under which a manufacturer or seller of personal property may have liability to one injured by a product and explain each theory.

3. Plaintiff was riding as a passenger in the front seat of a 1956 model Ford automobile owned and operated by Clarence Dailey. Plaintiff had dropped a lighted cigarette, and as he was attempting to retrieve it from the floor of the vehicle, with his head down, the brakes of the automobile were applied suddenly and with great force, throwing the plaintiff forward and causing his face to come into contact with the dashboard. (Dailey, the driver, had applied the brakes to avoid a collision with another automobile that had pulled out in front of his car.) Immediately following the plaintiff's contact with the dashboard, he realized that his right eye had been seriously injured.

The Ford automobile was equipped with an ash tray, which was located in the center of the dashboard. This tray was found on the floor of the vehicle after plaintiff was injured. After taking plaintiff to the hospital, Dailey examined the ash tray and for the first time discovered a "jagged" edge on the top right-hand front corner. This sharp edge is the defect upon which plaintiff predicates his case. Is the defendant, Ford Motor Company, which designed and manufactured the automobile containing the allegedly defective ash tray, liable?

4. Defendants manufacture and sell the Golfing Gizmo, a training device designed to aid unskilled golfers to improve their games. In 1966, Louise Hauter purchased a Gizmo and gave it to Fred Hauter, her thirteen-and-a-half-year-old son, as a Christmas present. On July 14, 1967, Fred was seriously injured while using defendant's product when the ball flew back and struck him sharply on the forehead.

The label on the shipping carton and the cover of the instruction booklet urged players to "drive ball with full power" and further stated: "Completely Safe Ball Will Not Hit Player." This is the statement that plaintiffs sued upon, alleging false representation. Should plaintiffs recover based on a misrepresentation theory of recovery?

5. This was a suit by decedent's (i.e., deceased's) family, alleging that the manufacturer of a bulldozer was liable in negligence and strict liability in tort for the defective design of the machine. When decedent was struck, the bulldozer was in the process of reversing to position itself to move forward to spread and tamp down fill; decedent was behind the bulldozer directing dump trucks in depositing fill that was to be spread and tamped by the bulldozer at the later time. Before backing up, the operator of the bulldozer, who had not observed decedent for about five minutes, looked to the rear to ascertain if it was clear, but he did not see decedent, who was standing thirty to forty feet behind the vehicle. The operator testified that there was a substantial blind spot to the rear of the bulldozer because of its design. The bulldozer had no rearview mirrors and no audible or visible backup warning signal. Is the manufacturer liable for its failure to include these design features?

6. Martin applied Ben-Gay to his chest because he was suffering from a cold. When he attempted to light a cigarette, the match head fell off and struck his chest. This caused the Ben-Gay to catch on fire. Martin was severely burned. Nowhere on the package did the company warn that Ben-Gay was flammable. Is the company liable to Martin for his injuries?

7. When Ford produced the 1966 Ford Fairlane, it used a flange-mounted gasoline tank rather than a strap-mounted tank. The top of the flange-mounted tank served as the floor of the trunk. The only shield separating the trunk compartment from the passenger compartment was a fiberboard panel and the rear seat padding. Neither of these materials signifi-

cantly limits the passage of fire. The cost of placing a shield between the passenger compartment and the fuel containing system would only be one dollar plus one-half hour of labor time. Buehler was involved in a rear end collision in which he was seriously injured. Had such a shield been in place, it would have substantially reduced the risk of injury to Buehler by having provided him additional time to escape from the accident. Should Ford be held liable to Buehler under the strict liability in tort theory of recovery?

8. Floyd Roysdon claimed that he suffered from severe peripheral vascular disease as a result of many years of smoking cigarettes manufactured by R. J. Reynolds Tobacco Company. He argued that the cigarettes are defective and unreasonably dangerous to the health of users and that the warnings on cigarette packages and in their advertising are inadequate to fully apprise users of the medical risks involved in smoking. Should Roysdon prevail on either argument?

9. Selectone is the manufacturer of mobile pagers, which it had promoted as being suitable for use by police agencies. Hollenbeck, a police officer, used his Selectone mobile pager to obtain assistance during an arrest. The pager failed to activate, and Hollenbeck was severely injured by the family of the person he was attempting to arrest. Hollenbeck brought suit based upon misrepresentation as a theory of recovery. Selectone argued that the assault by the family members was an intervening criminal act that broke the causal connection between the product and the injury. Is Selectone correct?

10. Lamb was eating an oven roasted chicken that her daughter had prepared. She accidentally swallowed the pop-up thermometer inserted in the chicken which indicated when the chicken was properly cooked. Lamb brought suit based on the theory that the thermometer was dangerous because it could be inadvertently

ingested, that the arrow-like points at its ends made it prone to being caught in the intestine if swallowed, and that the defendant had neither tested the thermometer for safety nor issued warnings concerning the danger of ingestion. Will the plaintiff prevail?

11. Woodworth was copiloting a Learjet. He was killed when a loon flew through the jet's windshield. Woodworth's family alleged that the windshield should have been designed to resist bird impact. Learjet argued that windshield should not have to withstand the impact of the 11.5-pound loon. Who should win?

12. Maybelline is the manufacturer of cosmetic products. Walker was applying Maybelline mascara and accidentally scratched the cornea of her left eye with the applicator brush. Walker eventually became blind in her eye as a result of an infection due to the defendant's mascara.

Maybelline knew that scratching of the eye surface with a mascara brush posed a danger of infection by the bacteria present in the mascara. Maybelline placed the following warning on the back side of the card that went with the mascara: "Note: In case of eye irritations or infections or scratches do not use this or any eye cosmetic. Consult a physician at once." Does this constitute an adequate warning by Maybelline?

13. Cox brought a products liability suit. He alleged that he developed asbestosis as a result of exposure to Eagle-Picher's asbestos products. At trial, Cox was permitted to show that having asbestosis increased his risk of contracting lung cancer. He sought damages for present emotional distress caused by his fear of developing cancer and damages for the risk of developing cancer in the future. Will he be able to recover on either of these theories?

CHAPTER 19

Consumer Law

The Consumer As Buyer
The Consumer As Borrower

Freedom of contract is a basic principle of American business and the common law. Parties are said to bargain over various terms for the purchase of a product or the borrowing of funds. The resulting agreement reflects their individual needs and choices. The courts would enforce that contract, based on freedom of contract theory, with few exceptions.

As noted in Chapter 8 on contracts, recent trends in society have emphasized concerns over contract fairness. The freedom to bargain may be illusory if one of the parties to the contract had little power to bargain or was confronted with a transaction of such complexity that it could not be understood. As a result, numerous legislative and regulatory changes in basic contract law occurred that were aimed at alleviating this problem.

One of the major changes, the subject of this chapter, is the protections afforded to certain parties to the contract by virtue of their status. That is, if a party to a contract is a consumer, different contract rules apply.

Compare General Motors' borrowing fifteen million dollars from Citibank for research and development with Joe Smith who borrows fifteen hundred dollars in order to take a vacation. In the GM example, both corporations would have negotiated the terms of the loan. Each would have a team of attorneys to provide advice and draft clauses for the loan agreement. Each corporation is sophisticated in business dealings and is powerful enough to protect its own interests. However, in the Smith loan, little negotiation will take place. Smith can accept the terms and sign the preprinted contract or he can look elsewhere. Furthermore, Smith most likely will not fully understand many of the provisions in the loan agreement. The difference in the creation of the contract in the two examples illustrates the purpose of the consumer laws. Those laws are aimed at providing certain protections that ordinarily might be points of negotiation for a more powerful party (like GM, for example). As a result, many of the terms and disclosures in the Smith contract are required by consumer legislation. The disparity in bargaining power is lessened somewhat by the imposition of various consumer protection rules.

Thus, an initial question in contract matters is whether a consumer is involved. If so, various regulatory provisions apply that are aimed at general contract fairness. A **consumer** is defined as a person who buys (or borrows) for personal, family, or household purposes. The focus of the definition is the use that person intends to make of the product or funds obtained under the contract. In the example just mentioned, Joe Smith is a consumer because the funds are for a personal use, a vacation. Similarly, if he planned to use the funds to purchase a pool table for his den or a new furnace for his house, the law would also consider Smith a consumer. However, if the funds were to be used to purchase new carpeting in Smith's office, the consumer protection laws would not apply. Smith would be using the money for a business purpose and would fall outside the scope of the protection of the statutes.

The consumer laws are paternalistic. They provide protection for certain buyers or borrowers who are deemed unable to protect themselves. However, note that Joe Smith would not be protected by consumer legislation if his purpose was to carpet his business office. Even though Smith would not magically gain any new insights or bargaining power in that transaction, he is considered able to fend for himself in the marketplace without the help of consumer laws. Or, if not, as a businessman he can spread his losses among all those who deal with him. Neither assumption is necessarily accurate.

This chapter will examine some of the more prominent statutes in several areas of consumer protection, first focusing on the consumer as a buyer and then on the consumer as a borrower.

THE CONSUMER AS BUYER

Deceptive and Unfair Trade Practices

The marketing and sales efforts of a large company often generate considerable public comment. These facets of a company's operations are the most visible to the general public—few persons escape hearing or seeing advertising every day. Other operations within a company, such as accounting, never come to the attention of the average American consumer. For this reason, unfair and deceptive sales practices of any company very likely will not escape the attention of the general public or government regulators.

As is noted in Chapters 13, 14, and 15 on antitrust law, the Federal Trade Commission was created to help strengthen the enforcement of the antitrust laws and to help further fair competition. The FTC interpreted its mission to also encompass the protection of consumers. In 1938, with the passage of the Wheeler-Lea amendment to the Federal Trade Commission Act, the Congress expanded the language of the original act from "unfair methods of competition" to also include "unfair and deceptive acts." Congress wanted the FTC to protect not only competition, but consumers as well, by prohibiting unfair and deceptive practices by business.

Over the years, the FTC has vigorously enforced this rather vague language prohibiting unfair and deceptive acts. The FTC prohibits the use of deceptive price advertising. For example, advertisers must exercise great caution when advertising a free product. Suppose Burger Company used the following promotion: "Buy one burger, get the second burger free." The day before, Burger Company had doubled the price of its burgers. Such a course of action clearly is deceptive. Likewise, the FTC has found television advertising that fails to disclose the use of mockups in place of the real object to be deceptive. In a case involving a television commercial that stated a given brand of shaving cream could shave sandpaper, the FTC found the advertising to be deceptive. The advertiser failed to disclose to viewers that what appeared on television to be sandpaper covered with shaving cream was in fact merely sand on glass covered with shaving cream.

In order to correct the false impression left by deceptive advertising, the FTC developed the corrective advertising remedy. This remedy requires a company to place advertisements that attempt to correct the false impression created by earlier deceptive advertising.

Not only does the Federal Trade Commission Act prohibit unfair and deceptive acts, but many states also prohibit such practices by statute. In addition, competitors may seek to have deceptive advertising curtailed. The following case concerns a provision in the Trademark Act that prohibits false and misleading advertising. Note that although the inaccurate statements did not concern the product, the advertising still created a false impression that the court found violated the act.

Vidal Sassoon, Inc. v. Bristol-Myers Company
United States Court of Appeals, Second Circuit
661 F.2d 272 (1981)

In the spring of 1980, appellant Bristol-Myers Co. (Bristol), a pharmaceutical manufacturer, decided to wage an aggressive, new advertising campaign on behalf of its shampoo product, Body on Tap, so named because of its high beer content. Accordingly, Bristol began in June to broadcast on national television a commercial starring the high-fashion model, Cristina Ferrare. The commercial depicts a turbaned Miss Ferrare, apparently fresh from shampooing her hair, holding a bottle of Body on Tap. She claims: "[I]n shampoo tests with over nine hundred women like me, Body on Tap got higher ratings than Prell for body. Higher than Flex for conditioning. Higher than Sassoon for strong, healthy looking hair." As is well known to the consuming public, Prell, Flex, and Sassoon are shampoo competitors of Body on Tap. The "Ferrare-900 Women" commercial, although the prototype, was only the first in a series developed for a complex sales campaign. Bristol played variations on the same theme in newspaper advertisements and in brochures which it intended to mail to over ten million households.

The shampoo tests mentioned in all the advertisements were conducted for Bristol in 1978 and 1980 by an independent market research firm. It is undisputed that nine hundred women did not, after trying both shampoos, make product-to-product comparisons between Body on Tap and Sassoon, or, for that matter, between Body on Tap and any of the other shampoos mentioned in the advertisements. Rather, groups of approximately two hundred women, in what the advertising trade terms *blind monadic testing,* each tested one shampoo and rated it on a qualitative scale (outstanding, excellent, very good, good, fair, or poor) with respect to twenty-seven attributes, such as body and conditioning. Thus, no woman tried more than one shampoo. The data for an attribute of a particular shampoo were combined by category of qualitative rating, so that a percentage figure for each qualitative rating could be derived. The "outstanding" and "excellent" ratings were then added, and the lower four ratings were discarded. Following this procedure, thirty-six percent of the women who tested Body on Tap found it "outstanding" or "excellent" with relation to "strong, healthy looking hair," whereas only twenty-four percent of the separate group of women who tested Sassoon gave it such ratings. These results are the basis of Bristol's advertising claim that the women preferred Body on Tap to Sassoon. When the "very good" and "good" ratings are combined with the "outstanding" and "excellent" ratings, however, there is only a statistically insignificant difference of one percent between the ratings of the two shampoos respecting "strong, healthy looking hair."

That nine hundred "women like" Cristina Ferrare had tried the shampoos might suggest, at the very least, that nine hundred adult women participated in the test. In actuality, approximately one-third of the "women" were age thirteen to eighteen. This fact is noteworthy in light of the testimony of Alfred Lowman, the advertising executive who created the Ferrare-900 Women campaign, that the commercial was designed to attract a larger portion of the adult women's shampoo market to Body on Tap. Sassoon had always fared well among adult women, whereas Body on Tap had appealed disproportionately to teenagers. Bristol's marketing studies have revealed that the advertisements were successful in increasing usage and awareness of Body on Tap among adult women.

In September 1980, Sassoon commenced this action, claiming that the several Ferrare-900 Women advertisements violated the prohibition of § 43(a) of the Lanham Trademark Act against false and misleading advertising. Sassoon charged that Bristol had made false and misleading representations since, (a) only about two hundred women, not "over nine hundred women," tested each shampoo; (b) the women tested only one shampoo without making product-to-product comparisons; (c) only two-thirds of the test participants were adult women; (d) the advertisements failed to portray the test results accurately, because Bristol used only the top two qualitative rating categories.

Kaufman, Circuit Judge

Whether or not the statements made in the advertisements are literally true, § 43(a) of the Lanham Act encompasses more than blatant falsehoods. It embraces "innuendo, indirect intimations, and ambiguous suggestions" evidenced by the consuming public's misapprehension of the hard facts underlying an advertisement.

Bristol asserts that the misrepresentations alleged by Sassoon are only misstatements concerning the test results and the manner in which the tests were conducted, not the "inherent quality" of Body on Tap. Misleading statements regarding consumer test methodology, Bristol argues, do not fall within § 43(a). We agree that Bristol has not in so many words falsely described the quality of Body on Tap. It has not, to give a hypothetical example, baldly stated that the shampoo smells like roses when it in fact does not. The inaccuracies alleged concern the number and age of the women in the tests, how the comparisons were made, and how the results were tabulated. However, we are persuaded that § 43(a) does prohibit the misrepresentations alleged here.

One of the principal purposes of the 1946 revisions of the Lanham Act was "[t]o modernize the trade-mark statutes so that they will conform to legitimate present-day business practice." We are therefore reluctant to accord the language of § 43(a) a cramped construction, lest rapid advances in advertising and marketing methods outpace technical revisions in statutory language and finally defeat the clear purpose of Congress in protecting the consumer. The language of § 43(a) is indeed very broad: "Any person who shall . . . use in connection with any goods or services . . . any false description or representation . . . shall be liable."

In a case like this, where many of the qualities of a product (such as "body") are not susceptible to objective measurement, it is difficult to see how the manufacturer can advertise its product's "quality" more effectively than through the dissemination of the results of consumer preference studies. In such instances, the medium of the consumer

test truly becomes the message of inherent superiority. We do not hold that every misrepresentation concerning consumer test results or methodology can result in liability pursuant to § 43(a). But where depictions of consumer test results or methodology are so significantly misleading that the reasonably intelligent consumer would be deceived about the product's inherent quality or characteristics, an action under § 43(a) may lie.

One of the most delicate tasks a court faces is the application of the legislative mandate of a prior generation to novel circumstances created by a culture grown more complex. In the instant case, we must determine whether statutory language derived from a 1920 prohibition against false advertising embraces misrepresentations regarding the results and methods of tests purporting to reflect consumer preferences for one named brand over another, a relatively new development in the burgeoning advertising and marketing fields. The district court preliminarily enjoined the dissemination of the shampoo advertisements at issue. Because we believe that the Lanham Trademark Act addresses the misrepresentations alleged here, relating to a consumer preference test, we affirm the court's order.

Studies in the late 1960s concluded that written warranties on consumer products were often unfair. They were difficult to understand, and consumers were confused concerning the amount of protection the warranties provided. Sometimes the warranties were so limited in scope that they provided less protection than if no warranty had been given at all. Nonetheless, these written warranties were advertised as providing protection or guarantees for buyers. The Magnuson-Moss Warranty-Federal Trade Commission Improvement Act created special rules relating to written warranties on consumer products. The act defines a consumer product as "any tangible personal property which is distributed in commerce and which is normally used for personal, family or household purposes." For example, if John Doe purchases a stereo for his home, any written warranty relating to this purchase must comply with the Magnuson-Moss Act.

Federal Warranty Act

The purpose of the act was to provide purchasers of consumer products knowledge of the terms of a written warranty before purchase in language comprehensible to the average consumer. Oral warranties are not covered by the act. The act does not require sellers to provide a written warranty, and a seller who wishes to avoid the provisions of this act may simply not provide one with its products. The act also does not prevent a seller from limiting the duration of an express warranty.

A DEFECTIVE TRANSMISSION AND THE MAGNUSON-MOSS WARRANTY ACT

In 1977, Arlie Skelton purchased a new Oldsmobile Delta 88. When the transmission did not seem to work properly, he returned to the dealer who told him the transmission was fine and to keep driving the car. When the transmission broke, after the warranty expired, Skelton went to a mechanic who charged him five hundred dollars but could not assure Skelton that the transmission would last for another six months. The mechanic explained that the transmission in Skelton's car was too small. It was designed for small General Motors' cars, such as the Chevrolet Chevette, rather than the full-size models, such as Skelton's Delta 88.

Skelton attempted to resolve this problem, without success, through the dealer, where he had purchased eight or nine other cars, and through representatives of General Motors. Finally, in 1979, he filed a lawsuit against GM under the Magnuson-Moss Warranty Act. This suit evolved into a class action with thousands of plaintiffs having the same complaint against GM and is considered one of the largest suits ever filed under the Magnuson-Moss consumer protection statute.

In February 1987, the suit was settled with General Motors agreeing to place $19.5 million in an escrow account to be used to reimburse car owners for transmission repairs. The lawsuit contended that as many as 4.7 million cars could be involved. General Motors also agreed to contact present or former car owners about the defective transmissions and the settlement.

When a written warranty is given on a consumer product that costs more than ten dollars, the warranty must be clearly and conspicuously designated a **full warranty** or a **limited warranty.** Congress wished to make it easy for purchasers to differentiate between the types of warranties offered by companies. If a product has a written full warranty, it must provide at least the following:

1. Any defects, malfunctions, or inability to conform to the terms of a written warranty must be corrected by the warrantor without charge and within a reasonable length of time.

2. The warrantor cannot limit the period within which implied warranties will be effective with respect to the consumer product.

3. The warrantor cannot limit or exclude consequential damages in a consumer product unless noted conspicuously on the face of the warranty.

4. The warrantor must allow the consumer to choose between a refund of the purchase price or replacement of the defective product or part whenever a reasonable number of attempts to remedy the defect or malfunction have occurred.

A limited warranty is any warranty that does not give the consumer these guarantees. Such a product warranty must be conspicuously labeled as limited.

The act excuses a seller if it demonstrates that the defect, malfunction, or failure of the product resulted from consumer misuse.

Buyers seem most vulnerable to sales pitches at home because they do not expect to be purchasing products in this setting. Some sellers would exert enormous pressure on consumers at home in order to convince them to buy. Frequently, the consumer regrets the purchase.

A Federal Trade Commission rule regulates door-to-door sales. It states that contracts used by such companies must conspicuously disclose that the buyer has a right to cancel the contract any time before midnight of the third business day after the contract date. The product purchased must cost twenty-five dollars or more for the rule to apply. The rule does not cover sales of real estate, insurance, or securities, or sales for emergency home repairs.

If a person elects to cancel a contract within the three-day period, the merchant must within ten days cancel the order and return any papers signed by the buyer, refund any money paid, inform the buyer whether any product left will be picked up, and return any trade-in. Within twenty days, the merchant must either pick up the items left with the buyer or pay any shipping expenses necessary for the buyer to ship the goods back if the buyer agrees to ship them back.

While the rule applies to door-to-door sales, the scope of the rule is broader than one might think. It not only applies to sales made at a person's home, but to any sale made at some place other than the seller's normal place of business. In other words, the rule is also designed to cover sales made by companies using party plans. Suppose Melinda's neighbor, Alice, invites Melinda to her home for a party with some other neighbors. At the party, Alice demonstrates and sells some dishware to the women. This transaction is a door-to-door sale even though it took place at Alice's home rather than Melinda's.

THE CONSUMER AS BORROWER

In today's economic environment, borrowing money has become common for both consumers and business. The average consumer finances the purchase of a home, a car, clothing, and many other items.

People desiring to finance the purchase of products have a variety of sources from which to acquire credit. A borrower may go to a bank or credit union to finance the purchase of an automobile. A person who lacks an established credit record may choose to borrow money from a finance company. Many stores provide financing for the purchase of products. For more high-priced purchases, the retailer may sell the instrument signed by the debtor to a finance company or bank. Alternatively, the buyer may use a credit card.

A credit card purchase is an example of **open-end credit**. Under an open-end credit plan, the consumer is permitted to make periodic charges up to a certain credit limit, and may pay the balance owing either in full or in installments. The finance charge is computed on the basis of the outstanding balance on the account at the time of billing.

On the other hand, if a person borrows one thousand dollars from the bank and agrees to repay it in twelve months, this type of credit plan is called **closed-end**

credit. In such a situation, a specific sum is borrowed, which will be repaid over a particular period of time, with a certain number of payments to be made at certain designated times.

Truth in Lending

In 1969, Congress passed the Consumer Credit Protection Act, one section of which is commonly referred to as the **Truth-in-Lending Act.** The purpose of the act was to enable consumers to make meaningful comparisons between the rates charged by different lenders. Before this time, lenders expressed the amount charged for the use of money in different manners, which made a comparison of rates difficult. The Truth-in-Lending Act acts as a full disclosure mechanism for consumer borrowers. The theory of the act was that if the borrower had information about various loan offers, comparisons could be made and lenders would have to compete on terms and conditions of the consumer loans. However, in practice, accomplishing that goal proved illusive.

Creditors had difficulty complying with the act. In 1980, one study noted that eighty percent of the banks were in violation. The problem was in the act's complexity and numerous judicial and administrative interpretations. Between 1969 and 1980, over fifteen hundred administrative regulations and interpretations were issued. Furthermore, most litigation involved very technical violations of the act. Note that the act provided for attorney fees and statutory damages irrespective of actual damages that were incurred by the debtor. Often these technical violations were raised as defenses by debtors sued for nonpayment. For example, in one case, a bank-creditor sued a debtor for nonpayment of a $750 loan. The debtor counter-claimed with both federal and state truth-in-lending contentions. Both were based on the same disclosure error. The court found that the error did occur and awarded statutory damages to the debtor under both acts, totaling approximately four thousand dollars.

By the late 1970s, it was clear that the act needed revision. Congress, in 1980, passed the Truth-in-Lending Simplification and Reform Act. Its purpose was to reduce the number of required disclosures and make compliance easier. Model forms were provided, that if used, would guarantee compliance.

Two very important figures must be provided to borrowers—the finance charge and the annual percentage rate (APR). These figures make the comparison of borrowing costs relatively simple. The finance charge is the total dollar amount the borrower pays to use credit. It includes interest costs and such other costs as service charges and appraisal fees. The annual percentage rate is the percentage cost of the credit on a yearly basis.

If a person goes to the bank and desires to borrow $1,000 for one year, the bank must tell the customer the finance charge, for example, $150, and APR, for example, 15 percent. If another lender agrees to loan the same $1,000 for one year for a finance charge of $125 at an APR of 12.5 percent, obviously the borrower would save money by patronizing the second lender.

Lost or Stolen Credit Cards. People have only a limited liability in the event unauthorized charges appear on their credit cards. The most one can be liable for as a result of unauthorized credit card use is fifty dollars on each card. This applies only to charges made before the loss or theft of the card is reported to the credit card company. The following case illustrates the issue of determining when the use of a credit card was unauthorized. Note that if the consumer protection legislation does not apply, the court applies general contract principles.

Walker Bank & Trust Company v. Gloria Harlan
Utah Supreme Court
672 F.2d 73 (1983)

In July 1979, Gloria Harlan, who was prior to that time a VISA cardholder at the bank, requested that her husband, John Harlan, be added to the account as an authorized user. The bank honored this request and issued a card to Mr. Harlan. Shortly thereafter, at some point between July and the end of 1979, the Harlans separated and defendant (Mrs.) Harlan informed the bank by letter that she either wanted the account closed or wanted the bank to deny further extensions of credit to her husband.

Notwithstanding the explicit requirement in the account agreement that all outstanding credit cards be returned to the bank in order to close the account, defendant Harlan did not tender either her card or her husband's at the time she made the request. As to her card, she informed the bank that she could not return it because it had been destroyed in the bank's automated teller machine. Notwithstanding, however, she returned the card to the bank three months later.

In the interim period, that is, after defendant's correspondence with the bank regarding the exclusion of her husband from her account and prior to the relinquishment of her card, several charges were made (purportedly by Mr. Harlan) on the account for which the bank now seeks recovery. The bank has sued only Mrs. Harlan, as owner of the account.

Hall, Chief Justice

Defendant's sole contention on appeal is that the Federal Truth in Lending Act (hereinafter "TILA") limits her liability, for the unauthorized use of the credit card by her husband, to a maximum of $50.

The Bank's position is that unauthorized use within the meaning of the Act is precisely what the statutory definition says it is, to wit: "[U]se by a person who does not have actual, implied, or apparent authority," and that notification to the card issuer has no bearing whatsoever on whether the use is unauthorized, so as to entitle a cardholder to the statutory limitation of liability. We agree with this position.

The liability of the cardholder for unauthorized charges is limited to $50 regardless of any notification to the card issuer. Notification, if given

prior to the unauthorized charges, serves only to eliminate the $50 liability and not, as defendants argue, to render a use unauthorized. Unless and until the unauthorized nature of the use has been established, the notification provision, as well as the statute itself, is irrelevant and ineffectual.

At the defendant's request her husband was issued a card bearing the husband's own name and signature. The card was, therefore, a representation to the merchants (third parties) to whom they were presented that defendant's husband was authorized to make charges upon the defendant's account. This apparent authority conferred upon defendant's husband by reason of the credit card thus precluded the application of the TILA.

We hold that liability for defendant's husband's use of the card is governed by the contract with the Bank. The contractual agreement between the defendant and the Bank provided clearly and unequivocally that all cards issued upon the account be returned to the Bank in order to terminate defendant's liability. Accordingly, defendant's refusal to relinquish either her card or her husband's, at the time she notified the Bank that she no longer accepted liability for her husband's charges, justified the Bank's disregard of that notification and refusal to terminate defendant's liability at that time.

Durham, Justice (dissenting)

The result of the majority opinion runs counter to the purpose of TILA. Under present circumstances, I acknowledge that the burden or risk of liability should initially fall on the cardholder because use of the credit card by a spouse is, and remains, authorized until notice is given to the card issuer that the authority to use the credit card is revoked. However, once the cardholder notified the card issuer of the revocation of that authority, it is clear that the card issuer is in the best position to protect itself, the cardholder and third parties. The card issuer can protect both itself and the card issuer by refusing to pay any charges on the account, and it can protect third parties by listing the credit card in the regional warning bulletins. The issuer need only terminate the existing account, transfer all existing charges to a new number, and issue a new card to the cardholder.

The majority opinion ignores the impracticality of imposing the burden on a cardholder of obtaining a credit card from an estranged spouse in order to return it to the Bank. It is unrealistic to think that estranged spouses will be cooperative. Moreover, it is extremely unwise to arm one spouse with a weapon which permits virtually unlimited spending at the expense of the other. As is illustrated by the facts of this case, where the whereabouts of the unauthorized spouse are unknown, the cardholder may be powerless to acquire possession of her card and return it to the Bank, which, according to the majority opinion, is the only way to limit liability. One result of the majority opinion will surely be to encourage the "theft" by divorcing spouses of credit cards they were authorized to use during the marriage and the liberal use of those cards at the other spouse's expense.

Fair Credit Reporting Act

Lenders, insurance companies, and the like may subscribe to consumer reporting services that provide information on applicants they are evaluating. For example, a person seeking a loan to purchase a sailboat will most likely have a credit report forwarded by a credit bureau to the bank. The report will provide a record of the credit activity of the consumer and will assist the bank in determining whether that person is a good credit risk.

However, errors may arise in consumer credit reports. Assume that the person seeking the loan is turned down because the report noted that bills were never paid to Smith's Department Store and Jones's Used Cars. The person, however, had never dealt with either business, but was being denied credit because of misinformation on the credit report. Congress passed the Fair Credit Reporting Act to protect consumers from unfair and inaccurate credit reports.

A consumer who has been denied credit because of an adverse credit rating has the following rights: (1) the right to receive the name and address of the agency that keeps the consumer's report; (2) the right to review at least a summary of the information held by the credit bureau; (3) the right to demand any important error be investigated and corrected if the bureau finds an error in the report; and (4) if the person disagrees with the findings of the bureau, the right to prepare a short statement, which must be included in the record in the future.

Millstone v. O'Hanlon Reports, Inc.
United States District Court (E.D.Mo.)
383 F.Supp. 269 (1974)

James Millstone, an assistant managing editor of the *St. Louis Post-Dispatch,* moved to St. Louis in 1971. He applied for auto insurance with Norman Kastner, who placed a policy with Firemen's Fund Insurance Company. The policy took effect November 25, 1971. The company notified Millstone a personal investigation would be made. Based on the information in the report, Firemen's Fund canceled the policy. The report in question was made by the defendant, O'Hanlon Reports, Inc. The court in this case ruled that Millstone was entitled to damages for injury arising out of a breach of the Fair Credit Reporting Act.

Wangelin, District Judge

On December 22, 1971, Millstone went to the office of O'Hanlon Reports where he spoke to William O'Connell, the Office Manager. Millstone was told that he was entitled to know what was in his report but that O'Hanlon was entitled to reasonable notice of ten (10) days before giving the information. When Millstone protested, O'Connell called the New York Home Office of O'Hanlon and allowed Millstone to speak to a Kenneth Mitchell. Mitchell told Millstone that the information would be available as soon as possible but that he could not give disclosure immediately because the Millstone file was en route from St. Louis to New York through the mails. After Millstone left the office, O'Connell then mailed the file to New York.

On December 28, 1971, Millstone received the disclosure of the information in its file from O'Connell at the O'Hanlon offices. O'Connell read the disclosure from a single sheet of paper which had been prepared by David Slayback, the Vice President of O'Hanlon. The disclosure sheet stated in part that:

"The file shows that you are very much disliked by your neighbors at that location [Millstone's Washing-ton residence], and were considered to be a 'hippy type.' The file indicates that you participated in many demonstrations in Washington, D.C., and that you also housed out-of-town demonstrators during demonstrations. The file indicates that these demonstrators slept on floors, in the basement and wherever else there was room on their property. The file shows that you were strongly suspected of being a drug user by neighbors but they could not positively substantiate these suspicions. You are shown to have had shoulder length hair and a beard on one occasion while living in Washington, D.C. The file indicates that there were rumors in the neighborhood that you had been evicted by neighbors from three previous residences in Washington, D.C. prior to living at the 48th Street, N. W. location."

. . . After protesting virtually all the information contained in the disclosure, Millstone asked O'Connell to explain certain facts contained therein. O'Connell told Millstone that he had no further information and could not answer the questions.

Slayback ordered the Manager of his Silver Springs office, the office which had conducted the original investigation of Millstone, to re-investigate the information.

On or about January 12, 1972, O'Connell notified Millstone that the re-investigation was completed and at a meeting between the two read to Millstone both the first and second disclosure sheets along with a cover letter written by Mr. Slayback to the Firemen's Fund Insurance Company. The thrust of these documents was to correct the previous allegations that Millstone was a: "drug user," "hippy type" and the statements about the "peace demonstrators staying at the Millstone residence."

In each conversation and meeting with O'Hanlon's agents, Millstone requested to see his file but was flatly denied access to it. After O'Connell mailed the file to the New York office of the defendant it remained there.

The original report on Millstone was prepared by Alexander Mayes, an employee of defendant in defendant's Silver Springs office. Mayes contacted four neighbors of the Millstones on the block where they last lived while residing in Washington, D. C.

Of the four persons contacted, one refused to speak to Mayes, two others told him that they knew of trouble in the neighborhood but knew nothing first hand and wished not to become involved. All the data recovered in Mayes' report was gleaned from a discussion with one neighbor identified as one McMillan, now deceased. Mayes gathered the data in a period of less than one-half hour. Mayes worked on a commission basis and received approximately one-third of the fee charged by the defendant, which amounted approximately to $1.85 in the Millstone investigation. . . .

The actions of O'Hanlon's agent Mayes are so wanton as to be certainly a willful non-compliance with the standard of care imposed by the Act. These actions by defendant's agent Mayes are so heinous and reprehensible as to justify the harsh damages imposed by the Act.

. . . To say that O'Hanlon was parsimonious in its disclosures in this case would be an exercise in understatement. The whole thrust of defendant O'Hanlon's actions was an attempt to withhold from Millstone the information that was rightfully due him under the law. The evidence in the case at bar as a whole is so overwhelming and persuasive as to leave no other conclusion that O'Hanlon was in willful violation of various previously discussed portions of the Fair Credit Reporting Act. . . .

**Equal Credit
Opportunity Act**

The Equal Credit Opportunity Act (ECOA) makes it illegal for creditors to discourage applicants from applying for a loan, refuse a loan to a qualified person, or lend money on terms different from those granted to similar persons because of the applicant's sex, race, marital status, national origin, religion, age, or because they receive public assistance income. The act initially was aimed at sex and marital status discrimination. Studies in the early 1970s indicated that women had a far more difficult time securing credit than did men. For example, single women were less likely to obtain credit than single men. Those that did receive credit, upon marriage would need to reapply for credit in the husband's name. Newly married men were not required to reapply. Furthermore, creditors were often unwilling to count a wife's income when a married couple sought credit.

Thus, the Equal Credit Opportunity Act attempted to remove barriers to the credit markets that existed for certain people for reasons unrelated to financial status. Since credit is an important aspect of society, Congress acted to make it available to anyone who is creditworthy on a nondiscriminatory basis.

Although the act addressed a widespread problem, only a relatively few cases have arisen under it. Some reasons have been advanced for the lack of development under the act. First, most overt types of credit discrimination have been eliminated. Credit institutions, for example, as a matter of policy stopped discounting the wife's income in a marital loan application. In addition, compliance with the act has been furthered by industry educational efforts and forms provided by the Federal Reserve Board (the agency responsible for ECOA matters). Finally, the more complex forms of discrimination are more difficult to find and far more difficult to prove.

Nonetheless, some cases do illustrate the type of discriminatory treatment that violate the act. Note that discrimination is prohibited in any aspect of the credit transaction.

United States v. American Future Systems, Inc.
United States Court of Appeals, Third Circuit
743 F.2d 169 (1984)

American Future Systems, Inc. sells china, cookware, crystal, and tableware and extends credit to its customers. Since its incorporation, AFS's sales on a credit basis have amounted to over ninety-five percent of its total sales.

AFS alleges that it has two separate marketing programs. One program comprises only single white females who are upperclasspersons (sophomores, juniors, and seniors) in a four-year college or nursing school. The district court found this to be the preferred program. The other program comprises minorities, males, and married people attending college or vocational school. The district court found this to be the nonpreferred program.

The applicants for the preferred credit program for single white females are treated as preferred sales targets, regardless of age, prior credit histories, or any other normal indicia of creditworthiness. They receive immediate credit. Sales to this group are always made on an immediate-shipment basis unless there is a specific request for a delay in shipment.

Unlike the preferred credit program, the nonpreferred credit program withholds the shipment of goods to its credit applicants until the applicant makes three successive monthly payments. If nonpreferred applicants fail to make three consecutive monthly payments, AFS retains the payments made and retains the good earmarked for shipment.

Both programs are designed to meet the "special social need" for credit shared by eighteen- to twenty-one-year-olds. The distinction between the two programs—based on race, sex, and marital status—is not, however, a matter of differential "social need." Rather it stems from a marketing judgment made by AFS. AFS does not inform potential credit applicants that they are participants in an alleged special purpose credit program. As the district court noted, "[a]ll applicants between 18 and 21 are carefully led to believe that they are being treated the same as all other applicants."

Potential credit applicants who fall into the nonpreferred category because of their race, sex, or marital status are therefore unable to decline credit offered through an alleged special purpose credit program. Moreover, these same nonpreferred credit applicants are not told that they are being rejected for the credit terms extended to other persons identically situated, except for the characteristics of race, sex, marital status, or year in school.

Higginbotham, Jr., Circuit Judge

The Equal Credit Opportunity Act (ECOA) proscribes discrimination in the extension of credit. The ECOA does provide, however, for special purpose credit programs responsive to special social needs of a class of persons.

AFS readily admits that it treats participants in its two credit programs, members of the class of persons between the ages of 18 and 21, differently on the basis of race, sex and marital status. Thus the specific issue before us is whether the ECOA permits such differential treatment where the district court expressly found that each person in the group of individuals between the ages of 18 and 21 shares the same credit disability. That is, once the social need is defined only as extending credit to a particular age group can a creditor use factors such as race, sex and marital status in setting up special purpose credit programs designed to address that social need when such factors are not related to the need? Although special program participants may be required to share one or more of those characteristics ordinarily considered prohibited bases, we believe they may be required to share only those factors inextricably tied to the need being addressed.

In this case, AFS identified one broad class of persons excluded from the customary credit market: the 18 to 21 year old age group. The district court found that each person in this age group irrespective of race, sex or marital status shared the same credit disability. In our view, where each person in the class shares the same special need but does not receive the same credit terms solely because of the individual's sex, race or marital status the program in question violates the ECOA. . . .

There is a particular irony in AFS's approach where it singles out white women as a "disadvantaged" group and gives them a special advantage that it unhesitatingly denies to black and other minority women. Certainly we recognize that this country has a tragic history in gender discrimination in that women have not been and still today are often not, treated as equals.

Despite all of the disadvantages that women have had, historically and at present, the significant disadvantages suffered by white women have been far less than those disadvantages black women, Native American women (Indians), Hispanic and other minority American women have had to endure for centuries. Yet, the paradox of AFS's plan is that it perpetuates the past disparities between white and minority women and rather than helping all women it aids only white women and slams the door of equal credit opportunity in the faces of minority women.

Fair Debt Collection Practices Act

Since litigation is often a time-consuming and uneconomic way to proceed against delinquent debtors, some creditors become rather aggressive in trying to collect the unpaid account. If the loan was secured by collateral, for example an automobile loan, the creditor may simply repossess the property. However, if the loan was not backed by collateral, the only nonlitigation remedy for the creditor is to convince the debtor to continue repaying the debt.

Aggressive creditor collection practices may at times cross the line and be considered harassment. When that occurs, the debtor may have a claim for damages against the creditor.

Unscrupulous debt collection practices led to the passage of the Fair Debt Collection Practices Act. When Congress held hearings before the passage of this act, it determined that debt collection practices contributed to a number of personal bankruptcies, to marital instability, to the loss of jobs, and to the invasion of individual privacy.

The act is designed to protect consumers from unfair and abusive collection practices. Thus, the term **debt,** in the act, is restricted to obligations arising out of a transaction in which the property, services, insurance, or money received is used primarily for person, family, or household purposes.

Whether a person or entity is protected by this act is for the most part determined by the definition of the term **debt collector.** The act defines the term to cover the activities of all third-party debt collectors—that is, anyone other than the creditor who regularly collects debts for others.

At one time, the courts regarded such secondary pressure as a violation of the or abuse any person. This expressly includes the use or threat of use of violence, obscene or profane language, publication of a list of consumers who allegedly refuse to pay debts, and telephoning a person repeatedly and continuously with the intent to annoy, abuse, or harass a person.

False and misleading representations used to collect a debt have also been prohibited. For example, a debt collector cannot imply that nonpayment of a debt will result in property or wages being seized, unless the action threatened is lawful and the debt collector intends to take such action. A person may not be imprisoned for failing to pay a debt. Thus, threatening to file criminal charges because a person fails to pay a debt would be unlawful. On the other hand, a civil action may be instituted if a person refused to pay a debt. If the creditor prevails in such a suit, it may be possible to seize and sell certain assets of the debtor. However, merely threatening to file such a civil suit is unlawful unless the person making such a threat actually intends to take such action.

Communicating with the debtor may in certain instances violate the act. Communicating with the consumer at any unusual time or place or at a time or place that should be known to be inconvenient to the consumer is unlawful. The act specifies that the convenient time for communicating with a consumer is after 8:00 A.M. and before 9:00 P.M. Normally, if the debt collector knows a consumer is represented by an attorney, all communications should be solely with the attorney and not with the debtor. The debt collector also may not communicate with the consumer at work if the debt collector knows or has reason to know the employer prohibits such communication.

Bankruptcy

Bankruptcy is a safety valve. It provides an orderly mechanism for salvaging the financial affairs of those who have acquired overly burdensome debts. Although a system of credit depends on enforceable legal obligations to repay money, at times debtors through misfortune or poor planning may acquire more obligations than they can bear. In those circumstances, bankruptcy law is available to mitigate the otherwise harsh effects.

Providing a system of relief for debtors as a part of a credit system is not a recent phenomenon nor is it uniquely American. Bankruptcy originated under Roman law and has been available in England for over three hundred years. In fact, the Bible refers to periodic relief from debts: "At the end of every seven years thou shalt make a release. And this is the manner of the release: every creditor shall release that which he has lent unto his neighbor and his brother; because the Lord's release hath been proclaimed." Deut. 15:1–2.

The Constitution grants Congress the power to enact bankruptcy laws. Thus, bankruptcy is a federal law, and the same law is applicable throughout the country. States are prohibited from regulating bankruptcies, although they are free to regulate other debtor-creditor relationships.

The bankruptcy code was revised by Congress in 1978 (with amendments in 1984). Prior to that time, the basic provisions were enacted in 1898. Although the first congressional efforts in enacting bankruptcy legislation occurred in 1800, bankruptcy legislation did not always exist. No bankruptcy law was in effect at various intervals for over half the time since the Constitution was ratified.

Bankruptcy provisions can provide relief for vastly different types of debtors, from large corporations (W. T. Grant, Johns Manville) to small business owners to consumers. Once a bankruptcy proceeding has begun, all other creditor actions against the debtor must stop (e.g., repossessing property, filing a lawsuit for non-payment for a loan). Thereafter, any creditor actions must take place pursuant to bankruptcy law.

Two general types of relief are available. First, under Chapter 7, the debtor's assets will be liquidated and the proceeds distributed to general creditors. Note that some assets are exempt from this process. The bankruptcy law provides a list and also permits states to create their own exemptions. Thereafter, the debtor will be discharged from any legal obligation to pay the debts. Creditors who hold a lien or interest in some property of the debtor (for example, a bank holding a mortgage on a home) may simply enforce their lien against the property, thereby keeping that property from being used to pay general creditor claims. Of course, the debtor may decide to reaffirm the debt with the lienholding creditor and thereafter retain the property.

Since most consumer bankrupts have little property either not covered by an exemption or encumbered by a creditor lien, relief under Chapter 7 of the Bankruptcy Act will essentially provide them with a fresh start without loss of assets. However, a person who receives a discharge under Chapter 7 is unable to seek another for six years.

The second general type of debtor relief provided by the bankruptcy law is to restructure the debtor's financial affairs. Rather than liquidating the debtor's assets to pay creditor claims, this process provides that the debtor formulate a plan under which a certain portion of creditor obligations will be paid. This plan, once approved by the court, is carried out under court supervision and protection of the debtor from other creditor action. When this plan has been completed, the debtor is discharged from further liability to those creditors. For individuals, this type of relief is in Chapter 13 of the Bankruptcy Act. Business reorganizations are subject to Chapter 11 of the act.

Thus, the bankruptcy laws can be seen as having two major purposes. They provide debtors with a fresh start so that they may seek new opportunities without being burdened by the pressure and hardship of preexisting debts. Risk taking and entrepreneurship is thereby enhanced since bankruptcy does limit the ultimate risk of failure. Those who do fail are given a new start. Without bankruptcy protection for debtors, productive risk taking behavior would be more costly and perhaps, as a result, not taken.

Implicit in this discussion is the fact that the bankruptcy laws are also designed to protect creditors. They provide for a fair distribution of debtor property among similarly situated creditors. Thus, a creditor need not fear that another creditor will strip a nearly insolvent debtor of most assets and thereby gain a windfall. The law contains provisions whereby those assets will be returned and divided equitably among all creditors.

SUMMARY

Consumer law illustrates a recent trend in the law of contracts. Principles of contract freedom have been modified by concerns over contract fairness. Consumers, those who enter transactions for personal, family, or household purposes, are given certain statutory protections to remedy their lack of bargaining power or marketplace sophistication.

Innumerable statutes and regulations protect consumers from unfair business practices. Deceptive and unfair practices have been violations of the Federal Trade Commission Act for many years. The FTC has attempted to cut down on the use of deceptive advertising by sellers. In particular, it has developed a rule prohibiting bait and switch advertising.

In the 1960s and 1970s, Congress and the state legislatures passed statutes and regulations outlawing particular types of business practices. Written warranties on consumer products costing more than ten dollars must be labeled full or limited, and must be disclosed prior to purchase. Credit has been extensively regulated. The law today requires credit terms be presented in a simple, comparable manner. It provides an easier resolution of disputes dealing with credit payments. Debt collectors must act with caution to avoid harassing or abusing debtors.

In virtually every area in which business deals with consumers, business must apprise itself of federal and state statutes and regulations. Consumer law limits the ability of business to set its own contract terms when dealing with certain persons.

REVIEW QUESTIONS

1. Define the following terms:
   a. Consumer
   b. Truth-in-Lending Act
   c. Bankruptcy

2. ABC, Inc., manufactures and sells turbine engines that are used for power generating plants. The engines cost five hundred thousand dollars each and are fifteen feet high. All customers of ABC are major corporations or public utilities. Should ABC be concerned with consumer regulation? If not, develop a scenario that would give rise to such a concern.

3. XYZ, Inc., sells small television sets that are used primarily in households. Smith purchases such a television so he can watch the early morning news while getting ready for work. The corporation gave Smith a written warranty when he purchased the television. The warranty was five pages long, written in very fine print in technical legal language. The warranty is labeled a "full warranty." It provided that implied warranties will be recognized for three months after the date of purchase. Furthermore, it provided that the buyer will be liable for any defects except problems with the pic-

ture tube. Can XYZ expect to have problems with this written warranty? Explain.

4. Sally Jenkins purchased an automobile for her private use from Joe's Used Cars. She agreed to pay Joe in equal installments for the car over the next two years. Although Joe told Jenkins that the installment payments included an interest charge, the amount of interest to be paid was never disclosed. Furthermore, the interest rate was also not disclosed. Can Joe's Used Cars expect to have problems with this loan transaction? Explain.

5. Discuss the relationship of consumer regulation with the principle of freedom of contract.

6. Continental Baking Company advertised Profile bread as being effective for weight reduction. The FTC charged Continental with false, misleading, and deceptive advertising. It alleged the bread was not low-calorie, but simply sliced very thinly. If the FTC proves its case, may the FTC compel any special form of advertising by Continental in the future?

7. The Firestone Tire and Rubber Company was charged with unfair and deceptive advertising practices in violation of the Federal Trade Commission Act. The charge was in relation to two particular ads, one called the "Safe Tire" ad, and the other the "Stop 25% Quicker" ad. The "Safe Tire" ad naturally had safety as its dominant theme and contained the following statement: "Every new Firestone design goes through rugged tests of safety far exceeding any driving condition you'll encounter." The other ad made claims that a specific tire stopped "25% quicker" than "regular" tires. Do you see any problems with the ads?

8. When Jill Student enrolled in the university her parents gave her a credit card. They arranged with the Charge-it Credit Card Company for a card to be issued in her name on their account. After Jill began to receive low grades, her parents decided to take away her credit card. She refused to relinquish it. They telephoned Charge-it to cancel their credit account. Charge-it informed them to send in all the outstanding cards on their account. This procedure for cancelation was provided in the credit card contract. No cards were submitted to the company for three months. In the meantime, Jill charged two thousand dollars' worth of merchandise. Her parents have been sued for that amount by Charge-it. They contend that they should, at most, be liable for fifty dollars. Discuss.

9. Mary Jones and Tom Smith were accountants, employed by the same firm. Their positions and salaries were identical. Both were unmarried, with approximately the same monthly expenses. They also had a similar credit history. On July 5, each visits Loan Company to borrow five thousand dollars. Smith is given a one-page information sheet to fill out. Jones must prepare a ten-page questionnaire as well as provide three personal references. Upon completion of the documents, Smith is immediately granted the loan. Jones must meet with officers of Loan Company for a personal interview. Note that the financial information on both Smith and Jones's information sheets was virtually the same. Jones was granted the loan, but was to pay interest at three percent higher than market rates. When Jones learned about Smith's different experience with the same company, she became angry. Does Jones have a claim against Loan Company? Discuss.

10. Discuss the functions of bankruptcy law in the legal environment of business.

CHAPTER 20

Labor-Management Relations: The Regulation of Management

Historical Background
General Explanation of Collective Bargaining
Unfair Labor Practices by Employers

For many years, unions struggled to obtain recognition by employers. The unions often met with frustration and hostility. On some occasions, this hostility erupted into virtual open warfare between the companies and the employees. A major piece of legislation drafted in the 1930s, the Wagner Act, sought to cool the fires between labor and management. Congress hoped to institute a period of labor peace.

The first part of this chapter will present an overview of the conditions that led to the unionization of many industries in America. The text will then address the specific laws passed by Congress to promote collective bargaining and explain the nature and function of the chief federal agency in this area, the National Labor Relations Board (NLRB). One of the board's important functions is the conduct of representation elections in which the employees are permitted to vote for or against unionization. The text next discusses the way the government handles these representation elections.

Managers need to be aware of the types of activities they must avoid when dealing with unions. Certain types of activities will result in the filing of unfair labor practice charges against their corporations. The activities that were outlawed by the Wagner Act will be given considerable attention in the latter part of this chapter.

In the next chapter we will discuss improper activities by unions under the federal labor laws.

HISTORICAL BACKGROUND

Before the 1930s, the courts strove for but failed to formulate a workable labor relations policy. In a typical case early in the nineteenth century, *Commonwealth* v. *Pullis*, a Pennsylvania court ruled that any joint employee action violated the criminal laws of Pennsylvania. The court imprisoned workers because they joined together for purposes of gaining better working conditions. In the mid-nineteenth century, the courts began to reject the application of the criminal laws to union activities.

In the early nineteenth century, many employees tried to form unions on a city-by-city basis. Union activities tended to be localized, rather than statewide or nationwide. These unions sought a number of goals, such as a ten-hour working day, an end to child labor, and improved working conditions. When the Civil War broke out in 1861, it stimulated industrial activity. During the war, a railroad system was built stretching out to the Midwest. By the end of the Civil War, a large number of local unions operated in the Northern states, and a few national unions had begun to take root. Several unions attempted to consolidate their organizing efforts on a nationwide basis.

Early Union Goals

Early union leaders often advocated a major restructuring of the United States economic system. The leaders in these movements argued the manufacturers in the United States ought to be required to treat their employees in a more decent, humane manner. One such union, the National Labor Union of Baltimore, worked for many years to encourage workers to form cooperatives in which the workers would own the company they worked for. The National Labor Union envisioned happy workers producing goods in worker-owned plants.

Very little came of these efforts to restructure the economic system. Over time, the unions in America turned from grandiose plans to alter the conduct of business to more immediately attainable goals, such as higher wages.

Injunctions

In spite of a groundswell in favor of unions throughout the United States, the courts failed to reflect their increasing acceptance by the general public. Initially, the courts stifled the growth of union membership by sentencing union members to prison. The courts eventually turned to the use of civil sanctions, and in particular favored the **injunction.** An injunction is a court order requiring the person or group against which it is issued to refrain from a particular activity. A judge quite often issued a temporary **ex parte** injunction restraining a union from engaging in certain activities. In other words, on the basis of a motion by the employer and without hearing evidence presented by the union, the judge temporarily restrained certain types of union activity pending a formal trial on the merits of the case. Injunctions were vaguely worded. The only safe way to avoid violating the injunction was to cease acting collectively. Quite often, such temporary relief broke the union. The injunction became very unpopular with unions, and the unions in turn became disenchanted with the courts.

Violence

The use of injunctions exacerbated the unfriendly relationship between unions and management. Companies in the 1890s opposed unions with force. The unions met force with force, and violence erupted throughout the United States. Workers of the

Amalgamated Association of Iron and Steel Workers and the management of the Carnegie Steel Company fought a heated battle in 1892. Carnegie brought in Pinkerton detectives to fight the strikers. The strike culminated in the deaths of ten people and the injury of numerous others. In 1894, the American Railway Union led a strike against the Pullman Palace Parlor Car Company. Twenty-five people died and sixty were injured in this strike. All of this violence merely increased the hostility of the company owners to the union movement.

The unions fought companies in the streets and in the halls of Congress and the state legislatures in the early twentieth century. At the state level, they succeeded in enacting legislation regulating the employment of women and children. Most states passed workmen's compensation laws. In 1913, the Congress created a separate Department of Labor. In 1914, Congress passed the Clayton Antitrust Act, which attempted to limit the issuance of injunctions by federal courts in labor disputes. The act failed to stop the courts from enjoining strikes and picketing because the courts failed to interpret and apply the act in such a manner as to limit the use of injunctions.

Legislative Successes

Railway Labor Act. In the 1920s, the unions intensified their efforts to unionize industry. In 1926, Congress passed the Railway Labor Act, which regulated labor relations in the railroad industry. The act heralded the beginning of public acceptance of unions. The Railway Labor Act gave railroad employees the right to organize and join unions without employer interference and the right to bargain collectively. The act was based on the premise that peaceful labor-management relations are best promoted through collective bargaining between employers and unions.

Norris-LaGuardia Act. In 1932, Congress passed the Norris-LaGuardia Act, which drastically limited the power of the federal courts to issue injunctions against strikes, picketing, and boycotts. It outlawed the "yellow dog" contract (such contracts prohibited workers, as a condition of employment, from joining a union). It also limited the liability of unions and union members for unlawful acts committed by union officers, agents, or members.

Wagner Act. Congress tried in 1933 to guarantee the right of employees to organize and to bargain collectively through the passage of the National Industrial Recovery Act. The Supreme Court ruled the act unconstitutional in 1935 in *Schechter Poultry Co. v. United States*. Congress responded by enacting the Wagner Act that same year. The Wagner Act guaranteed employees "the right to self-organization, to form, join, or assist labor organizations to bargain collectively through representatives of their own choosing, and to engage in concerted activities for the purpose of collective bargaining or other mutual aid or protection." The act created the National Labor Relations Board (NLRB) and outlawed a number of practices by employers, which we will examine in depth later in this chapter. In *NLRB v. Jones and Laughlin Steel Corp.*, the Supreme Court upheld the constitutionality of the Wagner Act.

Congress continued to pass legislation favorable to labor throughout the 1930s. In order to assure workers of a minimum wage and to set maximum hours of work, it passed the Fair Labor Standards Act in 1938. Earlier, in 1935, it had attempted to secure some income for the elderly through the adoption of the Social Security Act.

Growth of Unions

The Norris-LaGuardia Act and the Wagner Act served as the impetus for the growth of the labor movement. In 1937, 7.25 million workers belonged to unions. The unions succeeded in organizing much of the heavy industry in the United States, such as automobile, rubber, and steel plants. Union membership continued to grow for many decades, aided by this favorable regulatory environment.

Shift in the Law in Favor of Management

Taft-Hartley Act. The mood in Congress turned against the unions in the 1940s, and the tide turned in favor of management. Many people thought organized labor had become too strong in relation to the power of the companies. To offset this imbalance in bargaining power, Congress passed the Labor Management Relations Act (Taft-Hartley) in 1947. The act outlawed a number of practices by unions. (We will discuss this act in the next chapter.)

Landrum-Griffin Act. Congress continued to strengthen the rules regulating the behavior of unions with the passage of the Landrum-Griffin Act in 1959. Congress outlawed certain activities by labor and management. Landrum-Griffin requires a large amount of information disclosure by unions. It closes loopholes in the protection against secondary boycotts and limited organizational and jurisdictional picketing. Congress hoped the Landrum-Griffin Act would serve as a bill of rights for union members. (This act is also dealt with in the next chapter.)

Over the years, the mood of Congress shifted back and forth on the issue of labor relations. The goal of Congress in the 1940s and 1950s was to equalize the bargaining power between management and labor in order to promote peaceful collective bargaining.

We will now examine the manner in which the labor laws are structured at the federal level to enable management and labor to achieve their goals through the collective bargaining process.

GENERAL EXPLANATION OF COLLECTIVE BARGAINING

Organization of the National Labor Relations Board

The National Labor Relations Board (NLRB) has two structural divisions, the office of the general counsel, and the board.

The general counsel's office has the responsibility for the day-to-day operations of the agency, both in Washington and in the regional offices. All regional offices work under the auspices of the general counsel, which administers the operations of the field offices. Much of the work of the agencies is done by the regional offices, which look into complaints brought within their respective regions, file charges, and prosecute complaints. The regional offices also conduct representation elections. The general counsel's office also is responsible for filing petitions to enforce board orders, if necessary, and for the prosecution of any appeals.

The board is composed of five members, each of whom serves for five years. Each board member has a staff of attorneys. Cases are initially taken before an administrative law judge. These judges are controlled by the board.

The agency has two major functions, the conduct of representation elections, and the resolution of unfair labor practices charges.

The Investigation. Any person may file a charge with the National Labor Relations Board. After someone files, a board agent (a field examiner or field attorney) makes an investigation, unless the charge is clearly defective on its face. The investigation normally takes several weeks. The agent makes the initial contact with the charging party within forty-eight to seventy-two hours. The agent takes affidavits (sworn statements) to support the charge. While field examiners are not attorneys, they conduct most of the investigation of the charges. The attorneys rely heavily on the material gathered by the agent. This investigation is critical to the success of a case because the board must learn all the facts of a case.

General
Procedure before
the NLRB

In the event the agent determines the case is meritorious, he or she may try to settle the case. Otherwise, the agent takes it to a board attorney. The board agent and his or her supervisor meet with the associate regional director, or chief attorney, or regional director, or the entire group in an important case. The agent presents the case to the group, and they decide whether to proceed. If they find the case has merit, they contact the parties and give them seventy-two hours to settle the case before a complaint is issued.

Dismissal and Withdrawal. In the event a charging party (the party that made the original charge) withdraws his or her charge, such a withdrawal of charges does not prevent the charge from being refiled later.

The charging party may receive a letter formally dismissing the case. This ends the case unless the charging party appeals the case to the general counsel in Washington. The office of appeals determines if the regional office erred in dismissing the charges. If it concludes the charges should not have been dismissed, the regional office refiles the charges against the defendant.

Time Limits. A person who thinks the labor relations law has been violated must act quickly. There is a six-month statute of limitation for filing a charge. The reason for requiring all charges to be filed within six months after the alleged violation is that evidence gets stale quickly. Investigations become more difficult as time passes. Because the board needs witnesses, a field agent needs to contact the witnesses quickly, as their recollection of the event diminishes rapidly. Quite often, the charging party and the witnesses are unsophisticated. They lack the ability to communicate. This poses additional problems for the field agent in obtaining evidence of a violation. Furthermore, as they usually are employees at the plant where the violation occurred, they may be inhibited, fearing reprisals by the employer if they cooperate with the board agents.

Assuming the investigation convinces the regional director of a violation, a formal pleading is issued setting forth the jurisdiction of the board, the alleged violation, and a date for a hearing. The defendant, as with other cases, must answer the pleading within ten days or risk a default judgment. (In a default judgment, the judge enters a verdict against the party who fails to appear.)

Settlement. In the event the parties settle a case without a hearing, a **formal** or **informal settlement** may be used. If a party fails to obey an informal settlement, the agency must issue a complaint and conduct a hearing. If the parties enter into a formal settlement, the board may petition a court for enforcement without first going through a hearing.

Trial and Appeal. Not every case gets settled. Sometimes the agency must try the case before an administrative law judge. Unlike a federal district judge or federal court of appeals judge, an administrative law judge hears only cases arising in his or her agency. The federal rules of evidence apply at such a hearing. An attorney representing the general counsel prosecutes the case for the complaining party. As in other trials, there are opening statements, examination and cross examination of witnesses, and introduction of any other evidence relevant to the case. Even if the charging party wishes to drop the case, the agency may compel him or her to proceed in the event a significant public issue is involved. There is no jury in an administrative proceeding, just the administrative law judge. This judge reads the attorneys' briefs, hears the evidence, and makes findings of fact and conclusions of law.

In the event a party wishes to appeal the decision of an administrative law judge, he or she must file an exception to the hearing within twenty days after the judge renders an opinion. The matter is then appealed from the regional office to the National Labor Relations Board in Washington. The board considers the case on the basis of the record prepared by the parties at the administrative hearing, and it examines the briefs of the attorneys. The board then renders a decision.

A party that believes the board erred in its decision may appeal the decision to the appropriate federal court of appeals. To some extent, a party that loses a case before the board may select the court that will hear the appeal. If the defendant files first, the board must file a cross petition for enforcement in the court in which the petition for review is filed.

Scope of the National Labor Relations Act

Power to Regulate. Congress possesses the power to regulate labor relations. The Constitution grants Congress the power to regulate commerce among the states. A labor dispute must come within the ambit of interstate activities to be covered by the labor laws.

While Congress gave the board a broad grant of power to deal with disputes between employers and employees, not every group of employees is covered by the National Labor Relations Act. For example, federal and state employees are excluded from the coverage of the act, as are railroad and airline workers.

Federal Preemption. In general, the parties must first go to the NLRB to settle their dispute before going to court. The board determines whether the dispute in question is covered by federal law. If the activities are protected or prohibited by federal law, state law yields to the federal law.

The federal law is said to have **preempted** the field; that is, the federal government in such a case has the *exclusive* right to regulate in this area. The Constitution, in the supremacy clause, declares that acts passed by Congress are the supreme law of the land. This means that if a state and a federal act conflict, the federal act controls the disposition of a case. The board has several options if the federal and the state law cover the same area but do not conflict. In some cases, it takes charge of the case and disposes of it. If the board declines to act, then a state may act if the board first had defined the legal issues in the case.

A regional office of the NLRB determines the composition of the bargaining units and conducts representation elections. The goal of the board is to provide conditions in which the workers may exercise a free, uncoerced choice in any election.

The Conduct of Representation Elections

Support for Election. Before a union files a petition with the board calling for an election, the board must first obtain some evidence of support from the workers. A union often starts with an employee in the plant to spearhead the organizing effort—when possible an intelligent, respected worker with a good record.

The unions prefer to line up the support of a *majority* of the employees in the bargaining unit for tactical reasons. However, in order to call for an election, the union needs to demonstrate the *support of thirty percent* or more of the workers. The union requests employees to sign a card and date it. These cards constitute proof of support by the employees for an election.

The union's efforts to organize the workers often are hampered by a number of factors. Among other things, the employer need not provide a list of the names and addresses of the employees during the election campaign until seven days before the election. Without a list of the people in the workforce, the unions must work harder to obtain employee support for an election.

Pre-Election Activities. In the event an unfair labor practice occurs during the election campaign, the NLRB can set aside the election. It also may put aside an election if acts by either management or labor prevent the workers from exercising a free, uncoerced choice. The board considers only conduct after the date of the filing of a petition for an election. After an election, the complaining party must immediately file an objection to any improper conduct during the election campaign if it wishes to protect the outcome of the election.

During the period after the filing of a petition for an election, but before the election, an employer must exercise great caution in talking to the employees. While Section 8(c) of the Taft-Hartley Act guaranteed employers the right of free speech, an employer still must not threaten or coerce its employees. An employer also must refrain from talking to the employees in a group within twenty-four hours of the election.

Unions also must exercise restraint in their pre-election activities.

In order to prevail if an election takes place, the union must receive the vote of a majority of the employees who *actually* vote—not a majority of the employees qualified to vote.

Voting. When voting takes place, both sides often place observers to challenge persons attempting to vote. For example, a union might wish to challenge a supervisor who tries to vote. The ballot in question is set aside, marked, and put in a special envelope. Normally, those challenged votes are examined only if they would make a difference in the outcome of the election. If this vote is critical, the regional director must rule on the validity of the challenge.

The Bargaining Unit

One complex issue is that of defining the appropriate unit in which to conduct an election. The board tries to find a cohesive unit of employees whose interests are basically the same. Section 9(a) of the National Labor Relations Act makes the union designated by a majority of the employees in an appropriate unit the exclusive representative of all employees in that unit "for purposes of collective bargaining in respect to rates of pay, wages, hours of employment, or other conditions of employment." But which unit of employees is appropriate? The *board* makes this determination. Needless to say, the makeup of a unit may be critical to the outcome of an election.

A court has very limited review powers in examining the designation of a bargaining unit.

In order to be included in the bargaining unit, a person must be an employee. The act in Section 2(3) defines an employee as "any employee . . . but shall not include any individual employed as an agricultural laborer, or in the domestic service of any family or person at his home, or any individual employed by his parents or spouse, or any individual having the status of an independent contractor, or any individual employed as a supervisor." Certain people do not come within the scope of the definition of employee and therefore may not be included in any bargaining unit designated by the NLRB.

The National Labor Relations Board excludes from bargaining units any confidential employee who falls within the board's labor-nexus test. Under this test, all employees who may have access to confidential business information are not automatically excluded. Only those employees who assist and act in a confidential capacity to persons who exercise managerial functions in the field of labor relations are excluded from the bargaining unit under the labor-nexus test. This test was upheld by the United States Supreme Court in *NLRB* v. *Hendricks County*.

Establishing Representative Status through Unfair Labor Practice Proceedings

A union becomes the representative of the employees in the designated bargaining unit in one of three ways: (1) by a voluntary agreement entered into with the company after the union demonstrates majority support by the employees, (2) by winning an election conducted by the NLRB, or (3) through an unfair labor practice proceeding.

Voluntary Recognition. The easiest way for a union to obtain recognition is to demonstrate union support by presenting the employer with authorization cards. The employer may voluntarily recognize the union when it presents cards signed by a majority of the employees.

An Election. Alternatively, the union might seek an election conducted by the NLRB. This normally is quicker than bringing an unfair labor practice charge.

Unfair Labor Practice Charges. The circumstances may be such that a free election appears impossible because the employer has tainted the atmosphere by violating some rights of the employees. In this case, a union may choose to bring a Section

8(a)(5) charge rather than calling for an election. Section 8(a)(5) makes it an unfair labor practice for an employer to refuse to bargain collectively with the representatives of his employees.

When an employer commits an unfair labor practice, many employees feel coerced or frightened. They may feel unable to exercise their own free will and judgment. In this situation, an election would be of minimal value. The union would surely lose, not because the employees opposed the union, but because they feared reprisals if they voted in favor of the union. In this case, the board—assuming the union can demonstrate a majority of the employees signed authorization cards—may certify the union as the bargaining representative for the employees without calling for an election.

The Court in the following case approved the use of single-purpose cards. A union organizer using such cards may tell the employee he or she is signing the employee up for purposes of representation, but the card will probably be used to request an election. The case also discusses the question of recognition of a union through an unfair labor practice proceeding when the employer is guilty of an unfair labor practice.

NLRB v. Gissel Packing Co.
United States Supreme Court
395 U.S. 576 (1969)

The unions here waged organizational campaigns, obtained authorization cards from a majority of employees in the appropriate bargaining units, and demanded recognition by the employers. The employers refused to bargain on the ground that the cards were inherently unreliable and carried out vigorous antiunion campaigns.

In one instance the union did not seek a representation election but filed unfair labor practice charges against the employer. In a second, an election sought by the union was not held because of unfair labor practice charges filed by the union as a result of the employer's antiunion campaign. In the third, an election petitioned by the union and won by the employer was set aside by the NLRB because of the employer's pre-election unfair labor practices.

In each instance, the NLRB found that the union had obtained valid authorization cards from a majority of the employees in the bargaining unit and was thus entitled to represent the employees for bargaining purposes, and that the employer's refusal to bargain, in violation of Section 8(a)(5) of the National Labor Relations Act, was motivated, not by a good faith doubt of the union's majority status, but by a desire to gain time to dissipate that status. The NLRB ordered the employers to stop their unfair labor practices, offer reinstatement and back pay to employees discriminatorily discharged, and bargain with the unions on request.

The Court of Appeals for the Fourth Circuit upheld the NLRB's findings as to violations of Sections 8(a)(1) and (3) but declined to enforce the orders to bargain. The court held that the cards were so inherently unreliable that their use gave the employer an automatic, good faith claim that such a dispute existed, for which an election was necessary. The Supreme Court reversed.

Chief Justice Warren

The first issue facing us is whether a union can establish a bargaining obligation by means other than a Board election and whether the validity of alternate routes to majority status, such as cards, was affected by the 1947 Taft-Hartley amendments. A union is not limited to a Board election, however, for, in addition to section 9, the present Act provides in section 8(a)(5) that "[i]t shall be an unfair labor practice for an employer . . . to refuse to bargain collectively with the representatives of his employees, subject to the provisions of section 9(a)." Since section 9(a), in both the Wagner Act and the present Act, refers to the representative as the one "designated or selected" by a majority of the employees without specifying precisely how that representative is to be chosen, it was early recognized that an employer had a duty to bargain whenever the union representative presented "convincing evidence of majority support." It was recognized that a union did not have to be certified as the winner of a Board election to invoke a bargaining obligation; it could establish majority status by other means under the unfair labor practice provision of section 8(a)(5)—by showing convincing support, for instance, by a union-called strike or strike vote, or, as here, by possession of cards signed by a majority of the employees authorizing the union to represent them for collective bargaining purposes. We agree with the Board's assertion here that there is no suggestion that Congress intended to relieve any employer of his section 8(a)(5) bargaining obligation where, without good faith, he engaged in unfair labor practices disruptive of the Board's election machinery. An employer can insist on a secret ballot election, unless, in the words of the Board, he engages "in contemporaneous unfair labor practices likely to destroy the union's majority and seriously impede the election."

In short, we hold that the 1947 amendments did not restrict an employer's duty to bargain under section 8(a)(5) solely to those unions whose representative status is certified after a Board election.

We next consider the question whether authorization cards are such inherently unreliable indicators of employee desires that, whatever the validity of other alternate routes to representative status, the cards themselves may never be used to determine a union's majority and to support an order to bargain. The employers urge us to rule out completely the use of cards in the bargaining arena. They argue that we should establish stricter controls over the solicitation of the cards by union representatives.

The objections to the use of cards voiced by the employers and the Fourth Circuit boil down to two contentions. First, that, as contrasted with the election procedure, the cards cannot accurately reflect an employee's wishes, either because an employer has not had a chance to present his views and thus a chance to insure that the employee choice was an informed one, or because the choice was the result of group pressures and not individual decision made in the privacy of a voting booth. The board itself has recognized, and continues to do so here, that secret elections are generally the most satisfactory—indeed the preferred—method of ascertaining whether a union has majority support. The acknowledged superiority of the election process, however, does not mean that cards are thereby rendered totally invalid, for where an employer engages in conduct disruptive of the election process, cards may be the most effective—perhaps the only—way of assuring employee choice. As for misrepresentation, in any specific case of alleged irregularity in the solicitation of the cards, the proper course is to apply the Board's customary standards and rule that there was no majority if the standards were not satisfied. It does not follow that because there are some instances of irregularity, the cards can never be used; otherwise, an employer could put off his bargaining obligation indefinitely through continuing interference with elections.

The employers' second complaint, that the cards are too often obtained through misrepresentation and coercion, must be rejected also, where the cards involved state their purpose clearly and unambiguously on their face.

Remaining before us is the propriety of a bargaining order as a remedy for a section 8(a)(5) refusal to bargain where an employer has committed independent unfair labor practices which have made the holding of a fair election unlikely or which have in fact undermined a union's ma-

jority and caused an election to be set aside. We see no reason now to withdraw this authority from the Board. If the board could enter only a cease-and-desist order and direct an election or a rerun, it would in effect be rewarding the employer and allowing him "to profit from [his] own wrongful refusal to bargain," while at the same time severely curtailing the employees' right freely to determine whether they desire a representative. The employer could continue to delay or disrupt the election processes and put off indefinitely his obligation to bargain; and any election held under these circumstances would not be likely to demonstrate the employees' true, undistorted desires.

In a later case, *Linden Lumber* v. *NLRB* (1974), the employer did not commit an unfair labor practice before the union request for recognition. The Supreme Court ruled "unless an employer has engaged in an unfair labor practice that impairs the electoral process, a union with authorization cards purporting to represent a majority of the employees, which is refused recognition, has the burden of taking the next step in invoking the Board's election procedures." In other words, if the employer did *not* commit an unfair labor practice before the union's request for recognition, the union *must call for an election*.

TERMINATION OF CONTRACT

In September of 1983, Continental Air Lines, a major air carrier, filed a petition to reorganize. In a very innovative move, Continental rejected the contracts it had with various unions with whom Continental had previously entered into collective bargaining agreements.

It was in fact possible for Continental to reject all executory contracts, including labor relations contracts, at the time it took this action. In 1984 Congress modestly reformed the law pertaining to this issue. Prior to filing an application for rejection of a collective bargaining agreement, the company must propose to the authorized representative of the

union any modifications of the contract that are necessary to permit a reorganization of the company. It must also supply any relevant information required to evaluate the proposal. Thereafter, a court should only permit a rejection of a collective bargaining agreement if it finds that the union has refused to accept the proposal without good cause, and the balance of the equities clearly favors rejection of the agreement.

A collective bargaining agreement may not, therefore, be unilaterally terminated or altered without first complying with these procedures.

UNFAIR LABOR PRACTICES BY EMPLOYERS

Employer Interference with Employee Rights

Section 8(a) of the Wagner Act declared it an unfair labor practice for an employer "to interfere with, restrain, or coerce employees in the exercise of the rights guaranteed in section 7." Section 7 reads as follows:

> Employees shall have the right to self-organization, to form, join or assist labor organizations, to bargain collectively through representatives of their own choosing, and to engage in other concerted activities for the purpose of collective bargaining or other mutual aid or protection, and shall also have the right to refrain from any or all of such activities except to the extent such right may be affected by an agreement requiring membership in a labor organization as a condition of employment.

Organizing Efforts on Employer's Property

To what extent may an employer limit the ability of unions to speak and distribute literature on the company property? Is such an attempt an unfair labor practice under Section 8(a)?

Once again, the law must resolve a conflict between the property rights of an employer and the rights of other persons, in this case unions. A union obviously wishes to come into the plant to speak with the workers in order to get its message across to them. An employer often wishes to limit this contact in the hope the employees will not gain an interest in unionizing.

An employer might go further than merely trying to keep the union and the workers apart. For example, the company could threaten to fire anyone engaged in union activities. Such threats stifle discussion and promote fear. Remarks of this character are calculated to intimidate the employees and violate Section 8(a).

With respect to organizational activities on an employer's premises, the property rights of the company must be weighed against the union's need for access to convey its message to the employees.

As indicated in Section 8(a), the employer must not interfere with rights guaranteed to the employees in Section 7. To prove a violation, the board need not demonstrate any particular person was coerced, but merely that an employer's actions had a natural tendency to restrain or coerce employees in the exercise of their rights.

Nonemployee Distribution of Literature. In *NLRB* v. *Babcock & Wilcox Co.*, the Court examined Babcock's nondistribution-of-literature rule. The rule prohibited nonemployees from distributing literature on the company parking lot. The union argued that contact with employees was practically impossible except on company property. Ninety percent of the workers drove to the plant. This argument failed to persuade the Court, which ruled that Babcock & Wilcox had no obligation to permit distribution of union literature by nonemployees. It did suggest that if no other means of communication with the employees exists, then the board might be justified in ordering a company to permit contacts on company property. In the *Babcock* case, the Court found it was possible to reach the employees without entering company property.

What if the employees worked at a lumber camp and lived on the premises? Or suppose they lived and worked at a resort. In these situations, perhaps no reasonable alternatives for contact exists. The Court probably would require the company to let the union distribute literature on the company property.

Employee Conversations. Bear in mind that the *Babcock* case involved *nonemployee* distribution of literature, as opposed to distribution of literature by an employee. An employee has a legitimate reason for being on company property, but a nonemployee does not. This suggests an employee may be able to distribute literature or talk to workers at times and places not accessible to nonemployees.

Normally, an employee may speak with other employees during nonworking hours in *working or nonworking areas* unless a nonsolicitation rule is necessary to maintain discipline. Companies may prohibit such solicitation during working hours. The rationale for such a rule is fairly clear. In many cases, speaking with employees distracts them from their jobs.

Employee Distribution of Literature. What about the distribution of literature by employees? In general, employers may prohibit the distribution of literature in a working area but not in a nonworking area unless the company demonstrates special circumstances. Any such rule against distribution of literature must be nondiscriminatory; that is, the rule must apply to everyone who wishes to distribute literature. A company that prohibits the distribution of literature in working areas must apply the rule to the Red Cross, the Salvation Army, or any other organization that wishes to distribute literature as well as to unions. The basic problem with any literature is the litter it creates. When employees receive handbills, they often throw the material on the floor and create a hazard to others working in that area.

In some instances, determining whether a union activity is solicitation or distribution is difficult. For example, what if an employee handed out union cards while he spoke with other employees? The board found this activity to be solicitation, although it possesses the characteristics of distribution. In other cases, the facts suggest that an activity possibly amounts to solicitation. What if an employee wears a union button while on the job? The cases vary, but *generally* an employee is permitted to wear a union button at all times. A case decided against an employee involved a button reading "Ma Bell is a cheap mother." The employee lost because the button created a disturbance.

In Summation. The following rules apply to solicitation and distribution of literature by employees: (1) an employee may be restricted from distributing literature in working areas, in working or nonworking times; (2) a rule forbidding the distribution of literature in nonworking areas during nonworking times is presumptively invalid; and (3) a rule against solicitation during nonworking times is presumptively invalid even if confined to working areas.

No-Distribution Rule. Suppose an employer posted a lawful no-distribution-of-literature rule. Is it an unfair labor practice for an employer to violate its own rule by distributing antiunion literature, while refusing to permit the union to do the same thing? The Supreme Court ruled in favor of the company in a case dealing with this point, *NLRB* v. *United Steel Workers*. The Court stated that if an alternative means of communication exists, the union must make an attempt to communicate by that means before challenging the company no-distribution rule.

While the company prevailed in that case, many other grounds exist for challenging the actions of an employer as an interference with the rights of employees.

Determining Union Support. Speaking with employees after the union asserts support by a majority of the workers presents an employer with a dilemma. Should the company question the employees to determine the depth of employee support for the union? In *Blue Flash Express, Inc.,* the manager of the company interrogated each employee separately in his office to determine if the employee supported the union. Every employee denied such support. The employer refused to recognize the union. The NLRB ruled for the employer in this instance in light of the absence of evidence of threats or hostility toward union activity. This ruling does not, however, create a carte blanche to interrogate employees. Employers must act with caution. Most courts require some *coercion* on the part of an employer along with the questioning in order to establish an unfair labor practice.

Another alternative open to an employer who wishes to determine the depth of union support is to poll the employees. Once again, this must be done with great caution, or the employer runs the risk of violating Section 8(a).

Threats and Benefits	Because the NLRB wishes to conduct an election in an atmosphere conducive to the free exercise of an employee's beliefs, coercive tactics by an employer violate that act.

But threats of reprisal are not the only form of coercion. An employee's right to exercise his free will may be influenced by promises of benefits. In these cases, the board examines (1) the timing and impact of the benefits, (2) whether the employer places conditions on the granting of benefits, and (3) whether any valid reasons exist for the conferring of benefits other than the election. Conferring benefits puts the employer in an awkward position when he or she grants them before an election. Custom is crucial in these cases. An employer who regularly grants increases each year around October 1, probably may grant one at that time even if an election is scheduled. The following case discusses the issue of granting benefits.

NLRB v. Exchange Parts Co.
United States Supreme Court
375 U.S. 405 (1964)

A representation election to unionize Exchange Parts' employees was to be held. Shortly before the election respondent, Exchange Parts, sent its employees a letter denouncing the union and listing all previous benefits granted by the company to the employees. The list also announced new benefits for the employees, including a birthday holiday, longer vacations, and increased wages for holiday work. The union lost the election. The NLRB held that the letter violated Section 8(a)(1) of the National Labor Relations Act. The court of appeals would not enforce the NLRB's order and the NLRB appealed. The Supreme Court ruled in favor of the NLRB.

Justice Harlan

This case presents a question concerning the limitations which section 8(a)(1) of the National Labor Relations Act places on the right of an employer to confer economic benefits on his employees shortly before a representation election. The precise issue is whether that section prohibits the conferral of such benefits, without more, where the employer's purpose is to affect the outcome of the election. For reasons given in this opinion, we conclude that the judgment below must be reversed.

Section 8(a)(1) makes it an unfair labor practice for an employer "to interfere with, restrain, or coerce employees in the exercise of the rights guaranteed in section 7." We think the Court of Appeals was mistaken in concluding that the conferral of employee benefits while a representation election is pending, for the purpose of inducing employees to vote against the union, does not "interfere with" the protected right to organize.

The broad purpose of section 8(a)(1) is to establish "the right of employees to organize for mutual aid without employer interference." We have no doubt that it prohibits not only intrusive threats and promises but also conduct immediately favorable to employees which is undertaken with the express purpose of impinging upon their freedom of choice for or against unionization and is reasonably calculated to have that effect. The danger inherent in well-timed increases in benefits is the suggestion of a fist inside the velvet glove. Employees are not likely to miss the inference that the source of benefits now conferred is also the source from which future benefits must flow and which may dry up if it is not obliged. The danger may be diminished if, as in this case, the benefits are conferred permanently and unconditionally. But the absence of conditions or threats pertaining to the particular benefits conferred would be of controlling significance only if it could be presumed that no question of additional benefits or renegotiation of existing benefits would arise in the future; and, of course, no such presumption is tenable.

Another prohibited activity, employer domination or support of a union, is covered in Section 8(a)(2) of the Wagner Act. At one time, employers who foresaw unionization as inevitable often attempted to subvert the employees' effort to organize by forming their own unions—without informing the employees of the company support for the union. In this manner, companies assured themselves of weak unions, favorably disposed to their goals and easier to deal with than a powerful independent union. Ostensibly, the company union represented the employees. In fact, the union operated as an arm of the company.

Domination or Support of a Union

While the law today forbids company domination of a union, the factual situations may make it difficult to distinguish employer domination from employer cooperation with a union. The Wagner Act requires cooperation but forbids domination.

The courts view as improper any assistance or support of a union to such an extent that the union must be regarded as the employer's own creation and subject to its control. What if a company permitted a union to use the company printing equipment—does this constitute cooperation or support of a union? Too much activity of this nature looks like company support. An employer must remain neutral in order to avoid running afoul of Section 8(a)(2).

Recognition of Union. The prohibition of employer domination or support of a union appears in the act to allow unions to organize without any hindrance by companies. What if a company agrees to bargain with a union that in fact represents less than a majority of the employees? Does this recognition of the union violate Section 8(a)(2)? The Supreme Court has ruled that the recognition of a union in this situation provides encouragement to join a union, and thus deprives the employees of their freedom of choice. A company must not recognize a union that represents less than a majority of the employees.

The wise course of action for an employer confronted by a union that demands recognition is to carefully review the cards signed by the employees calling for an election or to insist upon an election conducted by the NLRB. Before an employer bargains with a union, the union must represent a *majority* of the employees.

Discrimination to Encourage or Discourage Union Membership	It is also an unfair labor practice for an employer "by discrimination in regard to hiring or tenure of employment or any term or condition of employment to encourage or discourage membership in any labor organization" (Wagner Act, Section 8[a][3]). Generally, the *motive* of an employer is critical.

Discharging Employees. For the government to establish an unfair labor practice when a company discharges an employee, it must demonstrate that (1) the company had a deep-seated hostility toward unions, (2) the person involved in the charges was active in the union, (3) the employer knew that the employee was active in the union, (4) prior treatment by the company of other employees was not as harsh, and (5) the employer did not have just cause for his or her actions. In the event an employer wrongfully discharged an employee in violation of Section 8(a)(3), the board has the power to order reinstatement of the employee with back pay if it determines the employee was fired in order to discourage union activity. On the other hand, an employee discharged for a legitimate reason, such as missing work, may not be reinstated.

What if an employee violates a rule in the plant? May the employer safely fire him or her? As indicated, an employer must not discriminate in the employment of workers on the basis of union membership. If it treats a union member more harshly for an offense than other nonunion members, the company runs the risk of violating this part of the act. When the board examines the case, it looks at the past practices in the plant, the severity of the violation, the type of disciplinary actions imposed in the past, and other factors.

The following case involves an attempt by an employer to punish its employees for engaging in union activities.

Sure-Tan, Inc. v. NLRB
United States Supreme Court
104 S.Ct. 2803 (1984)

A small employer, Sure-Tan, was organized by a union. The union won an election conducted by the NLRB in 1976. After receiving notice the union would be certified as the bargaining representative of the employees, the president of Sure-Tan, Surak, sent a letter to the Immigration and Naturalization Service (INS) asking that it check the status of a number of his employees as soon as possible. The president knew these employees were Mexican nationals present illegally in the United States without visas or immigration papers authorizing them to work. The INS agents discovered five illegal aliens. These people soon left the country. The NLRB brought unfair labor charges against Sure-Tan. It alleged Sure-Tan had violated Section 8(a)(3) by requesting the INS to investigate these employees solely because they supported the union and with full knowledge that the employees in question had no papers or work permits. The Supreme Court ruled Sure-Tan had violated section 8(a)(3).

Justice O'Connor

We first consider the predicate question whether the NLRA should apply to unfair labor practices committed against undocumented aliens. The Board has consistently held that undocumented aliens are "employees" within the meaning of § 2(3) of the Act. That provision broadly provides that "[t]he term 'employee' shall include any employee," subject only to certain specifically enumerated exceptions. Since undocumented aliens are not among the few groups of workers expressly exempted by Congress, they plainly come within the broad statutory definition of "employee."

Counterintuitive though it may be, we do not find any conflict between application of the NLRA to undocumented aliens and the mandate of the Immigration and Nationality Act (INA). Since the employment relationship between an employer and an undocumented alien is not illegal under the INA, there is no reason to conclude that application of the NLRA to employment practices affecting such aliens would necessarily conflict with the terms of the INA.

Accepting the premise that the provisions of the NLRA are applicable to undocumented alien employees, we must now address the more difficult issue whether, under the circumstances of this case, petitioners committed an unfair labor practice by reporting their undocumented alien employees to the INS in retaliation for participating in union activities. Section 8(a)(3) makes it an unfair labor practice for an employer "by discrimination in regard to hire or tenure of employment or any term or condition of employment to encourage or discourage membership in any labor organization."

The Board, with the approval of lower courts, has long held that an employer violates this provision not only when, for the purpose of discouraging union activity, it directly dismisses an employee, but also when it purposefully creates working conditions so intolerable that the employee has no option but to resign—a so-called "constructive discharge."

Petitioners do not dispute that the antiunion animus element of this test was, as expressed by the lower court, "flagrantly met." Petitioners contend, however, that their conduct in reporting the undocumented alien workers did not force the workers' departure from the country; instead, they argue, it was the employees' status as illegal aliens that was the actual "proximate cause" of their departure.

This argument is unavailing. According to testimony by an INS agent, petitioners' letter was the sole cause of the investigation during which the employees were taken into custody. And there can be little doubt that Surak foresaw precisely this result when, having known about the employees' illegal status for some months, he notified the INS only after the Union's electoral victory was assured.

It is only when the evidence establishes that the reporting of the presence of an illegal alien employee is in retaliation for the employee's protected union activity that the Board finds a violation of § 8(a)(3). Absent this specific finding of anti-union animus, it would not be an unfair labor practice to report or discharge an undocumented alien employee.

Encouraging Union Membership. While an employer violates the act by discouraging union membership, it also violates the act by discrimination that encourages union membership. A company must strive to remain neutral in order to let the employees freely and voluntarily decide in favor of or against union affiliation.

Closing a Plant. What if a company operates several plants and decides to close a plant that voted in favor of a union? Does this violate Section 8(a)(3)? The following case discusses this point.

Textile Workers Union v. Darlington
United States Supreme Court
380 U.S. 263 (1965)

An organizational campaign by petitioner-union at Darlington, although strongly resisted by the company, including threats to close the mill, was successful. Shortly thereafter the company was liquidated, the plant closed, and the equipment sold. The NLRB found that the closing showed a deep-seated hostility toward unions and that it violated Section 8(a)(3) of the National Labor Relations Act. The court of appeals held that the employer had the right to terminate all or part of its business regardless of antiunion motives. The Supreme Court reversed.

Justice Harlan

We consider first the argument that an employer may not go completely out of business without running afoul of the Labor Relations Act if such action is prompted by a desire to avoid unionization.

The AFL-CIO suggests in its amicus brief that Darlington's action was similar to a discriminatory lockout, which is prohibited "'because designed to frustrate organizational efforts, to destroy or undermine bargaining representation, or to evade the duty to bargain.'" One of the purposes of the Labor Relations Act is to prohibit the discriminatory use of economic weapons in an effort to obtain future benefits. The discriminatory lockout designed to destroy a union, like a "runaway shop," is a lever which has been used to discourage collective employee activities in the future. But a complete liquidation of a business yields no such future benefit for the employer, if the termination is bona fide. It may be motivated more by spite against the union than by business reasons, but it is not the type of discrimination which is prohibited by the Act. The personal satisfaction that such an employer may derive from standing on his beliefs and the mere possibility that other employers will follow his example are surely too remote to be considered dangers at which the labor statutes were aimed. Although employees may be prohibited from engaging in a strike under certain conditions, no one would consider it a violation of the Act for the same employees to quit their employment en masse, even if motivated by a desire to ruin the employer. The very permanence of such action would negate any further economic benefit to the employees. The employer's right to go out of business is no different.

We hold here only that when an employer closes his entire business, even if the liquidation is motivated by vindictiveness toward the union, such action is not an unfair labor practice.

While we thus agree with the Court of Appeals that viewing Darlington as an independent employer the liquidation of its business was not an unfair labor practice, we cannot accept the lower court's view that the same conclusion necessarily follows if Darlington is regarded as an integral part of the Deering Milliken enterprise.

The closing of an entire business, even though discriminatory, ends the employer-employee relationship; the force of such a closing is entirely spent as to that business when termination of the enterprise takes place. On the other hand, a dis-

criminatory partial closing may have repercussions on what remains of the business, affording employer leverage for discouraging the free exercise of section 7 rights among remaining employees of much the same kind as that found to exist in the "runaway shop" and "temporary closing" cases. By analogy to those cases involving a continuing enterprise we are constrained to hold, in disagreement with the Court of Appeals, that a partial closing is an unfair labor practice under section 8(a)(3) if motivated by a purpose to chill unionism in any of the remaining plants of the single employer and if the employer may reasonably have foreseen that such closing would likely have that effect.

While we have spoken in terms of a "partial closing" in the context of the Board's finding that Darlington was part of a larger single enterprise controlled by the Milliken family, we do not mean to suggest that an organizational integration of plants or corporations is a necessary prerequisite to the establishment of such a violation of section 8(a)(3). If the persons exercising control over a plant that is being closed for antiunion reasons (1) have an interest in another business, whether or not affiliated with or engaged in the same line of commercial activity as the closed plant, of sufficient substantiality to give promise of their reaping a benefit from the discouragement of unionization in that business; (2) act to close their plant with the purpose of producing such a result; and (3) occupy a relationship to the other business which makes it realistically foreseeable that its employees will fear that such business will also be closed down if they persist in organizational activities, we think that an unfair labor practice has been made out.

Lockouts. While a plant closing might constitute discrimination in regard to the hiring and tenure of employees in order to encourage or discourage union membership, a **lockout** could also result in legal problems for the company. (In a lockout, the employer refuses to permit the employees to work.)

A lockout is unlawful if it is used to oppose unionization or to force the employees to choose the union the employer prefers.

Sometimes a lockout is legal. A single employer economic lockout is legal when used to avoid unusual economic losses or operational difficulties that would result from a threatened strike.

A union may negotiate with a multiemployer group (more than one company in the bargaining unit) but choose to strike only one member of the association. The United Auto Workers usually operates in this fashion. It bargains with all the automobile companies at once, but if a strike occurs, only one company gets closed down. Rather than continuing to operate, the other automobile companies might stage a lockout. The Supreme Court has ruled that a lockout is legal under these circumstances.

Discrimination against Employees Who File Charges

In order to increase the cooperative spirit among the employees, Section 8(a)(4) makes it an unfair labor practice for an employer to "discharge or otherwise discriminate against an employee because he has filed charges or given testimony under this Act." Many employees might refuse to cooperate with the NLRB field agent if they believed their employers could fire them. This provision restricts the employer from taking any vindictive actions against the employees for either filing charges with the NLRB or giving testimony. The phrase *giving testimony* has been construed by the Supreme Court to also cover the process of collecting information before the filing of formal charges. Any employee who cooperates with the board field agents or participates in a trial is protected by this provision.

Bargaining in Good Faith

The Wagner Act, Section 8(a)(5), makes it an unfair labor practice for an employer "to refuse to bargain collectively with the representatives of his employees." This provision escorts the parties to the door of the bargaining room. It prohibits fictitious negotiation and a de facto refusal to recognize and bargain with the union.

The Taft-Hartley Act added some additional guidance on this point in Section 8(d):

> For the purposes of this section, to bargain collectively is the performance of the mutual obligation of the employer and the representative of the employees to meet at reasonable times and confer in good faith with respect to wages, hours, and other terms and conditions of employment, or the negotiation of an agreement, or any question arising thereunder, and the execution of a written contract incorporating any agreement reached if requested by either party, but such obligation does not compel either party to agree to a proposal or require the making of a concession.

The Taft-Hartley thus specified that the parties must *meet and confer,* but it does not compel the parties to arrive at an agreement or to make concessions. Congress added this language to the National Labor Relations Act because it felt the board was going too far in requiring the parties to agree to specific terms. Section 8(d) was a response to the zealous enforcement of this provision by the board. Even so, in examining Section 8(a)(5) claims, the board still examines the substance of the parties' discussion. It is not blinded by empty talk.

A tension exists between the right to not agree to any specific points, as set forth in Taft-Hartley, and the obligation to make a serious effort to resolve the differences between the parties, but some fairly clear rules exist as to one's obligation to bargain.

Both the company and the union must bargain collectively if the union has been certified by the board. The obligation to bargain collectively means the union and the company must "meet at reasonable times and confer in good faith with respect to wages, hours and other terms and conditions of employment . . . but such obligation does not compel either party to agree to a proposal or require the making of a concession."

Mandatory Subjects of Bargaining. In general, the parties may insist to the point of impasse on *mandatory* subjects of bargaining. They may not insist to the point of impasse on nonmandatory (voluntary) subjects; that is, if a union goes on strike over a nonmandatory issue, the workers are not protected. The employer may fire the employees in this situation. Examples of mandatory subjects on which the parties must bargain are wages, merit increases, pensions, disciplinary rules, seniority, nonstrike provisions, and contracting work out. An example of a nonmandatory issue would be a request by the union that the employer change its negotiator.

A unilateral change by an employer on a mandatory subject of bargaining is a violation of the act. For example, if an employer changed its sick leave policy during the negotiation sessions, without first offering this to the union, the company has violated Section 8(a)(5). However, an employer may give its employees something it offered the union at the bargaining table, if the union rejected the offer, and the parties *reached an impasse* in their negotiations. In this situation, an employer could unilaterally grant the employees the benefit the union rejected. This is true even though negotiations continue after the expiration of the old contract. Either party may decline to negotiate after a true impasse is reached. Determining when the parties have reached an impasse poses problems for the negotiators. Both the union and the company must make certain an impasse has been reached before a refusal to negotiate further, or they run the risk of being guilty of a failure to bargain in good faith.

The following case discusses whether the price charged for food in the company plant was a mandatory subject for bargaining.

Ford Motor Co. v. NLRB
United States Supreme Court
441 U.S. 488 (1979)

When Ford notified the union that cafeteria and vending machine prices in its in-plant facilities would be increased, the union requested bargaining over both prices and services. These requests were refused by Ford, which took the position that food prices and services were not terms or conditions of employment subject to mandatory bargaining. The union filed an unfair labor practice charge with the NLRB, alleging Ford had refused to bargain in good faith. The board held for the union, and the court of appeals enforced the board's order against Ford. The court was particularly influenced by the lack of reasonable eating alternatives for the employees. Ford appealed to the Supreme Court. The Supreme Court affirmed.

Justice White

The principal question in this case is whether prices for in-plant cafeteria and vending machine food and beverages are "terms and conditions of employment" subject to mandatory collective bargaining under sections 8(a)(5) and 8(d) of the National Labor Relations Act.

The Board has consistently held that in-plant food prices are among those terms and conditions of employment defined in section 8(d) and about which the employer and union must bargain under sections 8(a)(5) and 8(b)(3).

Section 8(a)(5) of the National Labor Relations Act, as originally enacted, declared it an unfair practice for the employer to refuse to bargain collectively. Although the Act did not purport to define the subjects of collective bargaining, section 9(a) made the union selected by a majority in a bargaining unit the exclusive representative of the employees for bargaining about "rates of pay, wages, hours of employment, or other conditions of employment." Under these provisions, the Board was left with the task of identifying on a case-by-case basis those "other conditions of employment" over which management was required to bargain.

We conclude that the Board's consistent view that in-plant food prices and services are mandatory bargaining subjects is not an unreasonable or unprincipled construction of the statute and that it should be accepted and enforced.

The availability of food during working hours and the conditions under which it is to be consumed are matters of deep concern to workers, and one need not strain to consider them to be among those "conditions" of employment that should be subject to the mutual duty to bargain. The terms and conditions under which food is available on the job are plainly germane to the "working environment." Furthermore, the company is not in the business of selling food to its employees, and the establishment of in-plant food prices is not among those "managerial decisions, which lie at the core of entrepreneurial control." The Board is in no sense attempting to permit the Union to usurp managerial decision making; nor is it seeking to regulate an area from which Congress intended to exclude it.

Including within section 8(d) the prices of in-plant-supplied food and beverages would also serve the ends of the National Labor Relations Act. National labor policy contemplates that areas of common dispute between employers and employees be funneled into collective bargaining. The assumption is that this is preferable to allowing recurring disputes to fester outside the negotiation process until strikes or other forms of economic warfare occur.

We affirm, therefore, the Court of Appeals' judgment upholding the Board's determination in this case that in-plant food services and prices are "terms and conditions of employment" subject to mandatory bargaining under sections 8(a)(5) and 8(d) of the National Labor Relations Act.

Information. In general, a company must furnish any information to the union that probably or potentially is relevant to the collective bargaining between the parties. The employer must make this material promptly available to the union in a manner or form that is not burdensome to the bargaining process. The company must also substantiate any claim that it is unable to pay higher wages. An employer need only provide information that is reasonably responsive to the request by the union. Generally, the employer has the defenses that the material requested is too burdensome, is privileged, or is a trade secret, or that the union waived the right to seek this information in the collective bargaining agreement in clear and explicit language.

Good Faith Bargaining. Much of the negotiation process between the company and the union takes place on a give and take basis. Presumably, the company devises a range of wages and benefits it will offer, and the union sets up a scale of wages and benefits it hopes to receive. If the parties fail to agree, a strike may occur. What if, rather than secretly holding back the best offer, a company puts the best offer on the table at the beginning of the bargaining sessions and then communicates the information to the employees? The following case discusses this strategy.

NLRB v. General Electric Co.
Second Circuit Court of Appeals
418 F.2d 736 2nd Cir. (1969) Cert. Den. 397 U.S. 965 (1970)

After a crippling strike in 1946, GE changed its bargaining tactics. It made its best offer to the union at the very beginning of negotiations, and then it heavily publicized the offer to employees. The NLRB found three specific unfair labor practices and an overall failure to bargain in good faith, a violation of Section 8(a) of the National Labor Relations Act. The court of appeals was petitioned to enforce the NLRB's order against GE.

Kaufman, Judge

In addition to the three specific unfair labor practices, G.E. is also charged with an overall failure to bargain in good faith.

The Board chose to find an overall failure of good faith bargaining in G.E.'s conduct. Specifically, the Board found that G.E.'s bargaining stance and conduct, considered as a whole, were designed to derogate the Union in the eyes of its members and the public at large. This plan had two major facets: first, a take-it-or-leave-it approach ("firm, fair offer") to negotiations in general which emphasized both the powerlessness and uselessness of the Union to its members, and second, a communications program that pictured the Company as the true defender of the employees' interests, further denigrating the Union, and sharply curbing the Company's ability to change its own position.

Given the effects of take-it-or-leave-it proposals on the Union, the Board could appropriately infer the presence of anti-Union animus, and in conjunction with other similar conduct could rea-sonably discern a pattern of illegal activity designed primarily to subvert the Union.

G.E. argues forcefully that it made so many concessions in the course of negotiations—concessions which, under section 8(d), it was not obliged to make—that its good faith and the absence of a take-it-or-leave-it attitude were conclusively proven, despite any contrary indicia on which the Trial Examiner and the Board rely.

The Company's stand, however, would be utterly inexplicable without the background of its publicity program. Only when viewed in that context does it become meaningful. We have already indicated that one of the central tenets of "the Boulware approach" is that the "product" or "firm, fair offer" must be marketed vigorously to the "consumers" or employees, to convince them that the Company, and not the Union, is their true representative. G.E., the Trial Examiner found, chose to rely "entirely" on its communications program to the virtual exclusion of genuine negotiations, which it sought to evade by any means possible. Bypassing the national negotiators in favor of direct settlement dealings with employees and local officials forms another consistent thread in this pattern. The aim, in a word, was to deal with the Union through the employees, rather than with the employees through the Union.

The Company's refusal to withhold publicizing its offer until the Union had had an opportunity to propose suggested modifications is indicative of this attitude. The command of the Boulware approach was clear: employees and the general public must be barraged with communications that emphasized the generosity of the offer, and restated the firmness of G.E.'s position.

In order to avoid any misunderstanding of our holding, some additional discussion is in order. We do not today hold that an employer may not communicate with his employees during negotiations. Nor are we deciding that the "best offer first" bargaining technique is forbidden. Moreover, we do not require an employer to engage in "auction bargaining," or compel him to make concessions, "minor" or otherwise.

We hold that an employer may not so combine "take-it-or-leave-it" bargaining methods with a widely publicized stance of unbending firmness that he is himself unable to alter a position once taken. Such conduct, we find, constitutes a refusal to bargain "in fact." It also constitutes, as the facts of this action demonstrate, an absence of subjective good faith, for it implies that the Company can deliberately bargain and communicate as though the Union did not exist, in clear derogation of the Union's status as exclusive representative of its members under section 9(a).

The petition for review is denied, and the petition for enforcement of the Board's order is granted.

Surface Bargaining. In some situations, an employer may go through the motions of meeting and talking with the union, but nothing meaningful occurs. This is called **surface bargaining.** The board must review such negotiations step by step to determine if the party went to the bargaining table with the intent to frustrate the other side. The parties must negotiate with the view of reaching an agreement. In order to determine if mere surface bargaining is taking place, the board must look at a number of factors. Did one of the parties come into the bargaining sessions with an inflexible attitude, as in the GE case? Did the employer and the union make meaningful counter-proposals in crucial areas? For example, did the company refuse to discuss economic terms until all noneconomic issues were covered? Did the parties meet at appropriate times and places, or did one of the parties try to delay the bargaining? What if an employer insisted on meeting at twelve different locations over the period of a year? This probably amounts to a failure to bargain in good faith. Did the bargaining representatives have authority to bind the parties? A union may refuse to agree until its members ratify a contract, but a company must send representatives with the power to bind the company. Did one of the parties withdraw concessions made earlier at the bargaining table? Did a party impose unfair conditions on the bargaining process, for example, refusing to bargain with the union until it withdrew an unfair labor practice charge? Did the employer make unilateral changes in the working conditions without first offering these to the union? This shows the employer is going to the bargaining table with an intent to disparage the union. Conduct away from the bargaining table is significant in determining the attitude at the bargaining table. The board considers all these factors in determining whether a party actually was bargaining in good faith or was merely trying to give the appearance of bargaining.

Some other examples of a failure to bargain in good faith are the refusal to sign a written agreement after the negotiators agree upon the terms orally, an attack on the composition of the bargaining unit, or the insistence the other side pick new negotiators.

If a Contract Exists. Before entering into negotiations, the parties have several obligations. Assuming there is in effect a collective-bargaining contract covering the employees, Section 8(d) of the Taft-Hartley Act requires that no party may terminate or modify the contract unless the party desiring the termination or modification (1) serves written notice upon the other party to the contract of the proposed termination or modification *sixty days prior* to the expiration of the contract; (2) offers to negotiate; (3) notifies the Federal Mediation and Conciliation Service and appropriate state agencies within thirty days after such notice of existence of a dispute; and (4) continues to comply with all terms of the existing contract for the sixty-day period or until the contract expires, whichever occurs later. Once the parties comply with these requirements, they may begin negotiations on a new contract.

Duration of Duty to Bargain

If There Is No Contract. If there is no collective-bargaining agreement in force, but a union won the representation election, the parties must negotiate. No other election may take place for *twelve months* following a valid election. In the event an employer voluntarily recognized the union, rather than insisting upon an election, the time period for negotiations is a *reasonable time*. Once this reasonable time runs out, in the case of voluntary negotiations, or after one year, in the case of an elected union, if the parties still have not concluded a bargaining agreement, another election for a union could occur.

Intervention by Other Unions. If the parties enter into a contract, even if the union does not represent a majority of the employees, the contract is a bar to another election. In order to call for a new union, a petition for an election must be filed *sixty to ninety days before* the expiration of the collective-bargaining agreement or after the agreement expires. During these periods, another union may intervene and attempt to persuade the employees to support it rather than the union currently certified by the board.

The First Amendment of the Constitution prohibits Congress from passing laws that restrict the right of free speech. Although the Constitution guarantees the right of free speech, employers for many years ran into trouble when they exercised it. Quite often, the NLRB construed a statement by an employer before an election as an unfair labor practice. In response to the decisions of the NLRB, Congress passed Section 8(c) of the Taft-Hartley Act. This provision reads as follows: "The expressing of any views, argument or opinion, or the dissemination thereof, whether in written, printed, graphic or visual form, shall not constitute and be evidence of an unfair labor practice under any of the provisions of this act, if such expression contains no threat of reprisal or force or promise of benefit."

Employer's Free Speech

Section 8(c) permits the employer to communicate his general views as to unionization as long as he does not make any threats or promises. The employer is free only to state what he feels will be the economic consequences of unionization, which are outside of his control and do not constitute reprisals.

The NLRB has taken the position that conduct that creates an atmosphere that renders free choice improbable sometimes may warrant invalidating an election even though the conduct does not rise to the level of an unfair labor practice. Some employer statements, which may not constitute a threat of reprisal under Section 8(c), may so cloud the atmosphere as to warrant the board's setting aside an election.

SUMMARY

In the late 1800s and early 1900s, relations between management and labor were very poor. Workers tried to improve working conditions through collective action, while most companies tried to thwart the workers' organizing efforts. This led to a period of social unrest and violence. The workers finally turned to Congress to obtain just treatment in the workplace. Congress responded by passing a series of acts, the most important of which, the Wagner Act, gave employees the right to organize and bargain collectively.

The Wagner Act created the National Labor Relations Board whose function is to conduct representation elections and process labor disputes. (Much of this work is done by the board's local offices.) Persons who disagree with the decisions of the regional offices may appeal their cases to the board itself, and from there, to the courts.

Much of the board's time is devoted to conducting representation elections. An employer may voluntarily recognize a union that represents a majority of the employees, but elections are customarily held to determine if a majority of the employees favor unionization. An employer must act carefully after a representation petition has been filed. Employers may not threaten workers or promise them benefits in order to influence the outcome of a representation election. A company that commits a serious unfair labor practice after the filing of a petition runs the risk that the board will certify the union as the bargaining representative of the employees solely on the basis of authorization cards signed by the employees.

Prior to asking the board for a representation election, the union will attempt to organize the workers. The circumstances under which union representatives may speak with workers and distribute union literature in the workplace are governed by the labor law. Generally, employee-representatives have greater right to speak with workers and distribute literature than nonemployees would have.

The labor laws place a number of obligations on management. Certain types of activities are treated as unfair labor practices. An employer may not discriminate against workers to encourage or discourage union membership. An employer may not discriminate against workers who file charges under the Wagner Act. Once the board recognizes a union as the bargaining representative of a designated group of employees, it is unfair labor practice for the employer to refuse to bargain in good faith with the union. The union and the employer must meet and confer with one another. They are not required to arrive at an agreement or to make concessions; however, certain subjects must be considered at the bargaining table.

It should finally be noted that the labor law guarantees employers a right of free speech.

REVIEW QUESTIONS

1. Define the following terms:
   a. Injunction
   b. Preemption
   c. Lockout
   d. Surface bargaining

2. Why did Congress pass the Norris-LaGuardia Act?

3. Describe the handling of a charge before the National Labor Relations Board.

4. Steel Corporation learns from the board that a union has filed a petition to conduct a representation election. One week before the election, Steel Corporation grants the employees two extra paid vacation days and increases everyone's salary by twenty-five cents per hour if the employees vote against the union. Does this violate the labor law?

5. Alfred owns a chemical company with one plant. The employees vote to unionize. Alfred announces his displeasure with the vote and closes the plant. Has he violated the labor law?

6. Darling Toys produced most of its toys during the spring and summer because most of its toys were sold at Christmas. The company engaged in collective bargaining and reached an impasse with the union. The company feared the employees intended to strike during the spring, so it locked them out starting on December 25. Is this legal?

7. Is it legal for a company to make its best offer immediately to the union, then inform the employees of its actions?

8. A union obtained thirteen signed authorization cards from a plant with thirty employees and demanded recognition as the bargaining agent for the company's production and maintenance employees. The employer refused to recognize the union, and the union filed unfair labor practice charges with the NLRB. How should the NLRB rule on the charge? Has the union done enough to obtain recognition?

9. During contract negotiations, an employer unilaterally implemented a new system of automatic wage increases, changes in sick-leave benefits, and merit increases, even though these matters were subjects of pending contract negotiation. Was this a violation of the duty to bargain collectively?

10. A nonprofit general hospital had a rule prohibiting solicitation by its employees in any area of the hospital that was accessible to the public—including lobbies, gift shops, cafeterias, main floor entrances, corridors, sitting rooms, and public restrooms. Is this rule valid? What part(s) may be enforceable?

11. Metropolitan Edison Company had a collective bargaining agreement with the International Brotherhood of Electrical Workers. The agreement had a no-strike clause that prohibited strikes during the term of the agreement. Despite the no-strike clause, union members participated in an unlawful work stoppage. Another union set up an informational picket line in front of the construction site. The Electrical Workers refused to cross the picket line. Metropolitan Edison asked the union president to cross the picket line, but he refused to do so. The company suspended the workers for ten days, but suspended the president for twenty-five days. Did the company violate the labor laws?

12. Mary Weatherman was secretary to the general manager of the Hendricks County Rural Electric Membership Corporation. She was discharged after she wrote a letter in support of another worker who had lost his arm in the

course of employment. She filed an unfair labor practice charge with the National Labor Relations Board. Hendricks's main defense was that Weatherman was not protected by the act because as a confidential employee she was excluded from the act's definition of an employee in Section 2(3). Weatherman did not act in a confidential capacity with respect to labor relations matters. Is Hendricks correct?

13. Employees of Eastex sought to distribute a union newsletter in nonworking areas of Eastex's property during nonworking times. The company refused to permit the newsletter to be distributed. The newsletter urged support for the union. It also discussed a right-to-work statute and the federal minimum wage. Did Eastex commit an unfair labor practice?

CHAPTER 21

Labor-Management Relations: The Regulation of Union Activity

Bargaining
Duty of Fair Representation
Unfair Labor Practices
Protected Concerted Activities
The Right to Strike
Picketing
Secondary Pressure

In the preceding chapter, we dealt with the historical forces that resulted in the creation of the present extensive body of federal regulatory law in the area of labor relations. In particular, we covered the manner in which the National Labor Relations Board regulates employers and employees, and certain types of activities by employers that are unfair labor practices.

In this chapter, we will focus on some of the major types of union activities. In the first section, we will deal briefly with some issues unions and management bargain over. We will then discuss the duty of a union to fairly represent *all* persons in the bargaining unit.

After examining very briefly a few unfair labor practices, we will focus in depth on three important areas—strikes, picketing, and secondary activities. We will conclude with a brief discussion of the goals of the labor movement.

BARGAINING

Must Meet and Confer

As with employers, the National Labor Relations Act creates certain obligations for unions with respect to bargaining with an employer. It is an unfair labor practice for a union certified by the board as the representative of the employees to refuse to bargain collectively with the employer (Section 8[b][3]).

Both the company and the union must bargain collectively if the union has been certified by the board. The obligation to bargain collectively means the union and the company must "meet at reasonable times and confer in good faith with respect to wages, hours, and other terms and conditions of employment . . . but such obligation does not compel either party to agree to a proposal or require the making of a concession" (Section 8[d]).

One of the issues unions typically are quite concerned over and may wish to discuss with employers when they bargain is whether employees will be required to join a union as a condition of employment.

Union Security

Closed Shop. If a union signs a contract to bargain collectively, it may wish to include in the collective bargaining agreement provisions that help it survive. At one time, unions sought **closed shop** agreements from employers. A clause such as "The employer hereby agrees to employ only members in good standing of the union" is a closed shop clause. Such a clause in contracts today is illegal. With such a clause, before a person could be eligible to work, he or she would have to first be a member of a union. Such a clause gave unions great power over the pool of available workers because the union had power to control its own membership. The closed shop is illegal because it discriminates in the hiring or tenure of employees so as to encourage union membership.

Union Shop. The act recognizes the **union shop** as a valid agreement. With a union shop clause, employees must join a union within a certain period after they begin to work for the employer. Section 8(a)(3) permits a company and a union to agree that employees must join a union after thirty days of employment. (Section 8[f] lowers the number of days to seven in the case of construction industry jobs.)

Section 8(b)(2) makes it clear that a union may not request the company to discharge an employee for any reason other than failure to pay the initiation fee or dues. This means that union employees could not be discharged from the company because, for example, they failed to attend a union meeting.

While the union shop agreement forces the employees to join a union after so many days, an employee still is in a stronger position than he would be if the company signed a closed shop agreement. With the closed shop, the union determines which employees are eligible for hiring. Furthermore, a union possesses more power to control which employees continue to work under a closed shop, because the union could force the discharge of an employee if he or she failed to comply with a union rule or regulation. The Taft-Hartley Act protects a worker from losing his or her job because of a failure to comply with the union's rules. Only the failure to pay the dues and initiation fees exposes the employee to the possible loss of his or her job.

Agency Shop. An **agency shop** agreement requires the employees to pay union dues and initiation fees, but does not require an employee to join a union as a condition to gaining employment. Some religious groups refuse to join unions. The agency shop permits these people to work without joining a union. At the same time, it forces them to pay for the services rendered to them by the union. The Taft-Hartley Act permits the agency shop as well as the union shop.

Right to Work. Both the union shop and the agency shop may be outlawed by state law. Section 14(b) of the Taft-Hartley Act permits each state to adopt a law giving workers in the state the "right to work." These state laws are designed to outlaw the use of agreements that require membership in a labor organization as a condition of employment. A number of the states have adopted right-to-work legislation.

In addition to meeting and confering with employers over such issues as whether employees must join a union, unions must negotiate wages and terms and conditions of employment for the workers in the unit the union represents. They must try to fairly represent everyone in the bargaining unit—both in negotiating and in enforcing the bargain eventually struck with the employer.

DUTY OF FAIR REPRESENTATION

The union must represent all the members in the unit that it was certified by the board to represent—not just the people who voted in favor of unionization. It is the representative of all the people in the bargaining unit. This is true even in right-to-work states that prohibit the use of the union or agency shop.

The duty of fair representation began as a court doctrine. The courts ruled the union must fairly represent *all* people in the bargaining unit. Even so, a union violates its obligation of fair representation only if it acts in an arbitrary, discriminatory, or bad faith manner. A union needs wide discretion in how it handles various matters brought to its attention. Over time, the board came to the conclusion that a union violates Section 8(b)(1) when it fails to fairly represent all the people in the bargaining unit. If a company permits a union to unfairly represent the employees, the company violates Section 8(a)(1).

A union must investigate cases in a fair and impartial manner. It must represent an employee even if he is not a member of the union.

UNFAIR LABOR PRACTICES

While it is certainly improper for a union to fail to represent a worker in the bargaining unit, this is not the only activity that may run a union afoul of the National Labor Relations Act. A number of practices by unions were made unfair by the Taft-Hartley Act. A few of them will be briefly noted here.

A union must not restrain or coerce the employees in the exercise of their right to engage in concerted activities (Section 8[b][1]). Forcing employees to vote for a union in a representation election would be an example of a violation of this provision.

While unions may charge their members initiation fees or dues, and the failure to pay such fees may result in an employee's expulsion from the union and dismissal from his or her job, a union may not charge excessive or discriminatory fees (Section 8[b][5]).

The Taft-Hartley Act made it an unfair labor practice for a union to require an employer to pay for work not performed, otherwise known as **featherbedding.** There has been very little activity recently concerning featherbedding.

PROTECTED CONCERTED ACTIVITIES

The Wagner Act guarantees workers "the right to self-organization, to form, join, or assist labor organizations, to bargain collectively through representatives of their own choosing, and to engage in other concerted activities for the purpose of collective bargaining or other mutual aid or protection, and . . . the right to refrain from any and all of such activities except to the extent that such right may be affected by an agreement requiring membership in a labor organization as a condition of employment."

Not only does the act give employees the right to engage in concerted activities, it also gives them the right to refrain from such activities. The following case deals with this provision.

Pattern Makers' League of North America v. NLRB
United States Supreme Court
105 S.Ct. 3064 (1985)

The Pattern Makers' League of North American AFL-CIO (the league), a labor union, fined ten of its members who, in violation of the league's constitution, resigned during a strike and returned to work. The National Labor Relations Board ruled that the league had committed an unfair labor practice by fining the employees. The Supreme Court upheld the board's decision in this case.

Justice Powell

Section 7 of the Act grants employees the right to "refrain from any or all [concerted] . . . activities. . . ." This general right is implemented by § 8(b)(1)(A). The latter section provides that a union commits an unfair labor practice if it "restrain[s] or coerce[s] employees in the exercise" of their § 7 rights. When employee members of a union refuse to support a strike (whether or not a rule prohibits returning to work during a strike), they are refraining from "concerted activity." Therefore, imposing fines on these employees for returning to work "restrain[s]" the exercise of their

§ 7 rights. Indeed, if the terms "refrain" and "restrain or coerce" are interpreted literally, fining employees to enforce compliance with any union rule or policy would violate the Act.

Despite this language from the Act, the Court in *NLRB v. Allis-Chalmers* held that § 8(b)(1)(A) does not prohibit labor organizations from fining current members. In *NLRB v. Textile Workers* and *Machinists & Aerospace Workers v. NLRB,* the Court found as a corollary that unions may not fine former members who have resigned lawfully. Neither *Textile Workers* nor *Machinists,* however, involved a provision like League Law 13, restricting the members' right to resign. We decide today whether a union is precluded from fining employees who have attempted to resign when resignations are prohibited by the union's constitution.

The Court's reasoning in *Allis-Chalmers* supports the Board's conclusion that petitioners in this case violated § 8(b)(1)(A). In *Allis-Chalmers*, the Court held that imposing court-enforceable fines against current union members does not "restrain or coerce" the workers in the exercise of their § 7 rights. In so concluding, the Court relied on the legislative history of the Taft-Hartley Act. It noted that the sponsor of § 8(b)(1)(A) never intended for that provision " 'to interfere with the internal affairs or organization of unions' " (statement of Sen. Ball), and that other proponents of the measure likewise disclaimed an intent to interfere with unions' "internal affairs." From the legislative history, the Court reasoned that Congress did not intend to prohibit unions from fining present members, as this was an internal matter.

The Congressional purpose to preserve unions' control over their own "internal affairs" does not suggest an intent to authorize restrictions on the right to resign. Traditionally, union members were free to resign and escape union discipline. The Board has found union restrictions on the right to resign to be inconsistent with the policy of voluntary unionism implicit in § 8(a)(3). We believe that the inconsistency between union restrictions on the right to resign and the policy of voluntary unionism supports the Board's conclusion that League Law 13 is invalid.

Therefore, the Board was justified in concluding that by restricting the right of employees to resign, League Law 13 impairs the policy of voluntary unionism.

To what extent may employees engage in concerted activities? They may act together without the assistance of a union. Washington Aluminum asked its employees to work on a bitterly cold day, and the employees, finally unable to tolerate the cold, left the job without first receiving the permission of their foreman. Washington Aluminum fired them for walking off the job. Such joint action by the employees constitutes a concerted activity protected by the Wagner Act. The company violated the employees' rights to engage in concerted activity by firing them.

While the act protects collective actions by employees, the employees lose the protection afforded by the Wagner Act if they use unprotected means (such as violence and destruction of property) or if the objective of the employees violates the labor law (as would a strike to compel an employer to commit an unfair labor practice).

Are the actions of a single employee, acting *pursuant to* rights guaranteed to employees in a collective bargaining agreement, concerted activity protected by Section 7? This issue is discussed in the following case, *City Disposal Systems*.

NLRB v. City Disposal Systems, Inc.
United States Supreme Court
104 S.Ct. 1505 (1984)

James Brown was an employee of City Disposal, which hauls garbage for the city of Detroit. The employees of City Disposal are represented by the Teamsters Union.

Brown was ordered by his manager to drive truck number 244. He refused, explaining that "There's something wrong with that truck. . . . Something was wrong with the brakes." Brown did not explicitly refer to the collective bargaining agreement in his discussion with his manager. However, the collective bargaining agreement, in article XXI provided: "The Employer shall not require employees to take out on the streets any vehicle that is not in safe operating condition. . . . It shall not be a violation of the agreement where employees refuse to operate such equipment unless such refusal is unjustified." Brown filed an unfair labor practice charge with the NLRB, challenging his discharge. The board found that Brown's refusal to drive the truck was based on his honest and reasonable belief the brakes on the truck were faulty. The board ruled for Brown as did the United States Supreme Court.

Justice Brennan

The NLRB's decision in this case applied the Board's longstanding "*Interboro* doctrine," under which an individual's assertion of a right grounded in a collective-bargaining agreement is recognized as "concerted activit[y]" and therefore accorded the protection of § 7. The Board has relied on two justifications for the doctrine: First, the assertion of a right contained in a collective-bargaining agreement is an extension of the concerted action that produced the agreement, and second, the assertion of such a right affects the rights of all employees covered by the collective-bargaining agreement. What is not self-evident from the language of the Act, and what we must elucidate, is the precise manner in which particular actions of an individual employee must be linked to the actions of fellow employees in order to permit it to be said that the individual is engaged in concerted activity.

Although one could interpret the phrase, "to engage in concerted activities," to refer to a situation in which two or more employees are working together at the same time and the same place toward a common goal, the language of § 7 does not confine itself to such a narrow meaning. In fact, § 7 itself defines both joining and assisting labor organizations—activities in which a single employee can engage—as concerted activities.

It is evident that, in enacting § 7 of the NLRA, Congress sought generally to equalize the bargain-ing power of the employee with that of his employer by allowing employees to band together in confronting an employer regarding the terms and conditions of their employment. There is no indication that Congress intended to limit this protection to situations in which an employee's activity and that of his fellow employees combine with one another in any particular way. Nor, more specifically, does it appear that Congress intended to have this general protection withdrawn in situations in which a single employee, acting alone, participates in an integral aspect of a collective process.

Respondent argues that Brown's action was not concerted because he did not explicitly refer to the collective-bargaining agreement as a basis for his refusal to drive the truck. The Board, however, has never held that an employee must make such an explicit reference for his actions to be covered by the *Interboro* doctrine, and we find that position reasonable. As long as the nature of the employee's complaint is reasonably clear to the person to whom it is communicated, and the complaint does, in fact, refer to a reasonably perceived violation of the collective-bargaining agreement, the complaining employee is engaged in the process of enforcing that agreement.

The NLRB's *Interboro* doctrine recognizes as concerted activity an individual employee's reasonable and honest invocation of a right provided for in his collective-bargaining agreement. We conclude that the doctrine constitutes a reasonable interpretation of the Act. Accordingly, we accept the Board's conclusion that James Brown was engaged in concerted activity when he refused to drive truck No. 244.

THE RIGHT TO STRIKE

A concerted activity of great importance to workers is the right to strike. Employees utilize the right to strike as a means of protecting their rights and of obtaining benefits. When employees strike, they act together to obtain what the workers believe will serve their collective interests. Clearly, when employees exercise the right to strike they are engaging in a concerted activity for the purpose of mutual aid or protection.

There are two important types of strikes. If employees go out on strike to obtain better wages or working conditions, they are engaging in an **economic strike**. A strike in protest over an unfair labor practice allegedly committed by an employer is called an **unfair labor practice strike**.

Injunctions. While Section 7 and Section 13 of the National Labor Relations Act reflect the view that employees have a right to strike, this right is a qualified one. A court, because the right to strike is protected, generally may not enjoin a strike. (The Norris-LaGuardia Act generally prohibits federal courts from enjoining such strikes. This area of law has been preempted by federal law.) In some circumstances, when the means and ends of a strike are unlawful, an employer may obtain an injunction. For example, if a company's employees engage in violence, a state court,

Situations When Employees May Not Strike

ECONOMIC STRIKES

On August 17, 1985, the meat packers began a strike at the main plant of George A. Hormel & Company. During the course of this strike there were more than 200 arrests as well as assorted acts of violence. Union members were upset when Hormel hired replacements for the 1400 workers out on strike.

The strike finally ended on September 12, 1986, with the signing of a new contract. The new contract restored wage cuts instituted in 1984.

The contract signed by the union did not guarantee the strikers their jobs back. There was no immediate rehiring of the 800 workers who stayed out on strike for the whole year. However, the company agreed to let the strikers return on the basis of seniority as openings arose.

This illustrates the fact that there is a great risk to workers who go out on an economic strike. These employees did not immediately get their jobs back, which undoubtedly was a severe economic hardship for these employees and their families.

in spite of Norris-LaGuardia, may enjoin violence by strikers. Furthermore, strikers who block access to a plant may be enjoined. If workers engage in a strike, and the collective bargaining agreement contains a no-strike clause, both federal and state courts may enjoin the strike. If a union gives notice of an intent to terminate or modify a collective bargaining agreement, it may not strike for sixty days after the union serves written notice upon the company. If employees strike during this period, they may be fired. Finally, in the event of a national emergency, the Taft-Hartley Act gives the federal courts the right to enjoin a strike for eighty days if the strike threatens the national health and safety. After the eighty-day period elapses, the strike may resume. Not only may employees be prevented from striking in these cases, but they also may be enjoined for engaging in a jurisdictional dispute.

Jurisdictional Disputes. Section 8(b)(4) deals with the problem of **jurisdictional disputes.** The act makes it an unfair labor practice to engage in or encourage a strike or refusal to handle goods, or to threaten or coerce any person, where the object is "forcing or requiring any employer to assign particular work to employees in a particular labor organization or in a particular trade, craft or class rather than to employees in another labor organization or in another trade, craft or class, unless such employer is failing to conform to an order or certification of the Board determining the bargaining representative for employees performing such work."

Congress included this provision in the labor laws in 1947 to counteract the many work stoppages in industry arising out of controversies between unions as to which union was entitled to perform certain work. The Wagner Act failed to set up any machinery to deal with such disputes between unions. Essentially, the Taft-Hartley Act prohibits a union from striking to force an employer to assign work to a certain group of workers unless the employer is failing to comply with a board order. It is the board's duty to consider the merits of a dispute when requested to do so, and to make an award of work to one union or the other. The courts require the board to make such an assignment of work because the board possesses experience with such problems.

National Emergency Disputes

While the National Labor Relations Act goes to great lengths to protect the right to strike, in some cases employees may not strike. One such instance is when a strike threatens to cripple the economy of the entire nation. Some strikes not only cripple an individual company, but also threaten the safety and well-being of the entire nation. The Taft-Hartley Act set up a system for dealing with severe strikes without impairing the system of collective bargaining created by the Wagner Act.

Process Followed

The president of the United States may order an eighty-day postponement of a strike, a threatened strike, or a lockout affecting an entire industry when the president determines such a strike or lockout would impair the national health or safety. The president may appoint a board of inquiry to examine the issues involved in the dispute and to make a written report to him. This board is for fact finding only; Congress did not want the government setting the terms for wages and working conditions. On receipt of the report from the board, the president may direct the attorney general to file a petition to enjoin the strike or lockout. If the court finds that the threatened or actual strike or lockout (1) affects an entire industry or a substantial part thereof, and (2) if permitted to occur or to continue, will imperil the national health or safety, the court may issue an injunction.

Whenever a court issues such an injunction, it is the duty of the parties to make every effort to adjust and settle their differences with the assistance of the **Federal Mediation and Conciliation Service.**

Federal Mediation and Conciliation Service

The Taft-Hartley Act created this service whose function is to assist parties to labor disputes in industries affecting commerce to settle such disputes through conciliation and mediation. The service may offer its services whenever a dispute threatens to cause a substantial interruption of commerce. The service does not mediate disputes that have only a minor effect on interstate commerce.

Neither party, in a national emergency dispute, is under any duty to accept any proposal of settlement made by the Federal Mediation and Conciliation Service. However, if the service fails to convince the parties to settle the dispute at the end of sixty days, the board of inquiry will issue another report to the president. The president makes this report available to the public. Fifteen days after the publication of the report, the National Labor Relations Board takes a secret ballot of the employees of each employer involved in the dispute on the question of whether they wish to accept the final offer of settlement made by their employer. This vote permits the employees, rather than the union leaders, to determine whether the offer should be accepted. The NLRB has five days to report the result of the election to the attorney general. The attorney general, if the workers reject the company's final offer, must discharge the injunction. The president then makes a report to Congress of the proceeding. At this point, the strike or lockout could resume.

Not only may strikes in certain instances be enjoined, but the employer may replace the workers who go out on strike. Whether the employees who strike may be reinstated depends upon the nature of the strike.

Reinstatement of Employees Following a Strike

In examining this question, strikes for *economic* benefits are distinguished from *unfair labor practice* strikes. A worker has an absolute right to strike if it is in protest over an unfair labor practice by an employer. If an employer fires an unfair labor practice striker, the employer may be compelled to reinstate the employee. But if an employee engages in an economic strike, the employer may hire a *permanent* replacement.

In *Mastro Plastics Corp.* v. *NLRB*, an employer was faced with a struggle between three unions. The union holding a collective bargaining agreement with Mastro served notice it intended to renegotiate its contract. This started the sixty-day period running. The employer, who supported another union, precipitated a strike by committing an unfair labor practice. He fired the strikers, contending they violated Section 8(d) by striking during the sixty-day period. Furthermore, the collective bargaining agreement contained a no-strike clause. The Supreme Court construed the no-strike clause in this case as covering only economic strikes, not unfair labor practice strikes. The contract did not say the employees gave up the right to *any* strike. The Court also construed Section 8(d) as applying only to economic strikes. The Court stated the sixty-day cooling-off period is to encourage peaceful, reflective discussion of economic questions and not to render the union defenseless in the event of unfair labor practices by an employer that might destroy the union.

In the following case, the Court discusses the question of rehiring workers following an economic strike.

NLRB v. Mackay Radio & Telegraph Co.

United States Supreme Court
304 U.S. 333 (1938)

Negotiations between Mackay and the union regarding wages and employment terms failed, so employees in one of Mackay's offices went on strike. After the strike ended, Mackay required strikers who were prominent in organizing the strike to fill out applications for reinstatement and did not allow them to return to work, although it did reinstate the rest of the striking employees. The NLRB held that Mackay committed an unfair labor practice by violating its employees' rights guaranteed by Section 7 of the National Labor Relations Act. The court of appeals refused to uphold the NLRB's ruling, and the board appealed. The Supreme Court ruled for the NLRB.

Justice Roberts

It is contended that the Board lacked jurisdiction because respondent was at no time guilty of any unfair labor practice. Section 8 of the Act denominates as such practice action by an employer to interfere with, restrain, or coerce employees in the exercise of their rights to organize, to form, join or assist labor organizations, and to engage in concerted activities for the purpose of collective bargaining or other mutual aid or protection, or "by discrimination in regard to . . . tenure of employment or any term or condition of employment to encourage or discourage membership in any labor organization. . . ." The claim put forward is that the unfair labor practice indulged by the respondent was discrimination in reinstating striking employees by keeping out certain of them for the sole reason that they had been active in the union. As we have said, the strikers retained, under the Act, the status of employees. Any such discrimination in putting them back to work is therefore, prohibited by Section 8.

The Board's findings as to discrimination are supported by evidence. There was evidence, which the Board credited, that several of the five men in question were told that their union activities made them undesirable to their employer. The Board found, and we cannot say that its finding is unsupported, that, in excluding five who were active union men, the respondent's officials discriminated against them on account of their union activities and that the excuse given was an afterthought and not the true reason for the discrimination against them.

As we have said, the respondent was not bound to displace men hired to take the strikers' places in order to provide positions for them. It might have refused reinstatement on the ground of skill or ability, but the Board found that it did not do so. It might have resorted to any one of a number of methods of determining which of its striking employees would have to wait because five men had taken permanent positions during the strike, but it is found that the action taken by the respondent, was with the purpose to discrim- inate against those most active in the union. There is evidence to support these findings.

Economic Strikes. An employer may not punish his or her employees for engaging in a protected activity. A company may not discharge employees as a reprisal. However, an employer may hire other people in order to keep the business running. If an employer hires replacements following an economic strike, he or she still must rehire the strikers on a nondiscriminatory basis as vacancies appear. The former employees are entitled to reinstatement unless in the meantime they have acquired regular and substantially similar employment.

Unfair Labor Practice Strikes. On the other hand, if employees strike because the employer committed an unfair labor practice, when the strike ends, they have an *absolute* right to return even if this means replacing the workers the employer hired during the strike. An economic strike may be converted to an unfair labor practice strike if the employer commits an unfair labor practice during the strike. Those replacements hired before the unfair labor practice may not be bumped, but those hired after the violation will be replaced by the strikers.

Employees place a high value on the right to strike. It gives them some leverage to attempt to force the employer to meet their demands. Of course, in some instances, a strike is of little value—for example, when a plant has not yet been organized by a union. In this situation, the employees must resort to some other form of concerted activity.

PICKETING

A very important type of concerted activity that the law permits employees to engage in for mutual aid or protection is picketing. The United States Constitution protects picketing—it is a form of that free speech which was guaranteed to everyone in the First Amendment.

Constitutional Protections

The Supreme Court has dealt with a number of cases involving picketing—for example, *Food Employees Local 590* v. *Logan Valley Plaza, Inc.* (1968). Wise Markets located a store in the Logan Valley shopping center. After it opened for business, a union picketed the Wise store next to the parcel pickup door. Signs carried by the men stated Wise employed nonunion labor. The pickets worked for other grocery companies and hoped to organize the Wise employees. Ten days after the picketing commenced, Wise obtained a restraining order enjoining the pickets from trespassing on the parking lot. This confined the pickets to a grass strip 350 feet from the Wise store. The union appealed the granting of the injunction against its picketing to the Supreme Court. It argued the injunction violated the First Amendment rights of its members. The shopping center argued it was located on private property; that it, a private company, banned the activities, and therefore the state took no part in the banning of this form of speech.

State action is critical in such a case as this, because the First Amendment prohibits Congress and the states from curtailing free speech. The First Amendment says nothing that prevents private parties from restricting free speech.

The Supreme Court rejected the argument of the Logan Valley shopping center owners. It characterized the actions of the shopping center as state action because the picketing took place on the sidewalks of the shopping center. Streets and sidewalks are places where First Amendment rights traditionally have been exercised. The justices reasoned that a shopping center has the same characteristics as public property if the owners open the center to the public. The argument that a private corporation, not the government, owned the streets and sidewalks, failed to influence the Supreme Court's characterization of the banning of speech in this case as state action.

The Court held the use of an injunction against the picketing to be improper, as it violated the First Amendment's guarantee of free speech. It ruled the center must have had a more specific reason to ban picketing (if, for example, the means used by the picketers had been illegal—had involved violence, perhaps).

The following case overrules the *Logan Valley Plaza* case. As you read this case, ask yourself if the Court has been influenced by any factors other than precedents. It was decided after a major change in the composition of the Court. Between 1968 and 1976, President Nixon replaced four members of the Court. President Ford also added a member to the Court. The political climate changed between 1968 and 1976, as did the composition of the Court.

Hudgens v. NLRB
United States Supreme Court
424 U.S. 507 (1976)

Striking warehouse employees, who were members of a union, started to picket their employer's retail store, which was located in a privately owned shopping center. They departed when the owner of the center threatened to arrest them for trespassing. The union filed an unfair labor practice charge with the NLRB against the owner, alleging interference with employees' rights under Section 7 of the National Labor Relations Act. The board concluded that the shopping center owner had committed an unfair labor practice, and the court of appeals affirmed. The owner appealed. The Supreme Court reversed.

Justice Stewart

In the present posture of the case the most basic question is whether the respective rights and liabilities of the parties are to be decided under the criteria of the National Labor Relations Act alone, under a First Amendment standard, or under some combination of the two. It is to that question, accordingly, that we now turn.

It is, of course, a commonplace that the constitutional guarantee of free speech is a guarantee only against abridgment by government, federal or state. Thus, while statutory or common law may in some situations extend protection or provide redress against a private corporation or person who seeks to abridge the free expression of others, no such protection or redress is provided by the Constitution itself.

If a large self-contained shopping center is the functional equivalent of a municipality, as *Logan Valley* held, then the First and Fourteenth Amendments would not permit control of speech within such a center to depend upon the speech's content. For while a municipality may constitutionally impose reasonable time, place, and manner regulations on the use of its streets and sidewalks for First Amendment purposes, and may even forbid altogether such use of some of its facilities, what a municipality may not do under the First and Fourteenth Amendments is to discriminate in the regulation of expression on the basis of the content of that expression. Above all else, the First Amendment means that government has no power to restrict expression because of its message, its ideas, its subject matter, or its content. It conversely follows, therefore, that if the respondents in the *Lloyd* case did not have a First Amendment right to enter that shopping center to distribute handbills concerning Vietnam, then the pickets in the present case did not have a First Amendment right to enter this shopping center for the purpose of advertising their strike against the Butler Shoe Co.

We conclude, in short, that under the present state of the law the constitutional guarantee of free expression has no part to play in a case such as this.

From what has been said it follows that the rights and liabilities of the parties in this case are dependent exclusively upon the National Labor Relations Act. Under the Act the task of the Board, subject to review by the courts, is to resolve conflicts between Section 7 rights and private property rights, and to seek a proper accommodation between the two. What is "a proper accommodation" in any situation may largely depend upon the content and the context of the Section 7 rights being asserted. The task of the Board and the reviewing courts under the Act, therefore, stands in conspicuous contrast to the duty of a court in applying the standards of the First Amendment,

which requires "above all else" that expression must not be restricted by government "because of its message, its ideas, its subject matter, or its content."

In the *Central Hardware* case, and earlier in the case of *N.L.R.B. v. Babcock & Wilcox Co.* the Court considered the nature of the Board's task in this area under the Act. Accommodation between employees' Section 7 rights and employers' property rights, the Court said in *Babcock & Wilcox,* "must be obtained with as little destruction of one as is consistent with the maintenance of the other."

Both *Central Hardware* and *Babcock & Wilcox* involved organizational activity carried on by nonemployees on the employers' property. The context of the Section 7 activity in the present case was different in several respects which may or may not be relevant in striking the proper balance. First, it involved lawful economic strike activity rather than organizational activity. Second, the Section 7 activity here was carried on by Butler's employees (albeit not employees of its shopping center store), not by outsiders. Third, the property interests impinged upon in this case were not those of the employer against whom the Section 7 activity was directed, but of another.

The *Babcock & Wilcox* opinion established the basic objective under the Act: accommodation of Section 7 rights and private property rights "with as little destruction of one as is consistent with the maintenance of the other." The locus of that accommodation, however, may fall at differing points along the spectrum depending on the nature and strength of the respective Section 7 rights and private property rights asserted in any given context. In each generic situation, the primary responsibility for making this accommodation must rest with the Board.

For the reasons stated in this opinion, the judgment is vacated and the case is remanded to the Court of Appeals with directions to remand to the National Labor Relations Board, so that the case may be there considered under the statutory criteria of the National Labor Relations Act alone.

Violence As a Ground for an Injunction

Both the United States Constitution and the National Labor Relations Act protect picketing. Picketing may not be banned outright. The basic approach of most state courts to picketing is that peaceful, noncoercive picketing for lawful purposes is legal. What if the picketing becomes violent? Should a state court enjoin all forms of picketing in the future? Once pickets become violent, a court might consider a prohibition of peaceful picketing as appropriate in order to punish the pickets, or because it suspects violence will recur, or because the previous violence gives any future peaceful picketing a coercive effect.

Today, the state courts, because of the preemption doctrine, may enjoin future acts of violence by the pickets but may *not* enjoin future *peaceful picketing*.

In the event picketing is not violent, it is generally lawful. There have been some restrictions, however, placed on the right to picket, which are discussed in the next section.

Organizational and Recognition Picketing

The existence and growth of the labor movement depends upon the ability to organize and picket. The picket line is more than free speech. It may involve coercive behavior. Many people will refuse to cross a picket line because they find the pickets intimidating. For this reason, some limitations were placed on picketing in the Landrum-Griffin Act.

The Landrum-Griffin Act creates rules to address the problem of recognition and organizational picketing. It covers picketing or threatened picketing by a union *not currently recognized* by an employer or certified by the NLRB, the object of which is to *gain recognition* by the employer or to *organize* the employees.

There is thus a technical distinction between organizational and recognition picketing. **Organizational picketing** is directed at the employees; that is, it is designed to convince the employees to sign up with the union. **Recognition picketing** is directed at the employer; it is used to convince the employer to recognize the union.

A union may picket an employer for recognitional or organizational purposes—but only under certain circumstances. It may not picket an employer for these purposes if the employer has already recognized another union or if a valid representation election has taken place within the last twelve months. Additionally, a union may not picket for these purposes for more than thirty days without filing a petition for an election.

When a union files a petition for an election, the board conducts an election. The picketing may continue until the time of the election once the union files a petition—even if the time runs beyond thirty days. Once the election takes place, if the union continues to picket, it violates the act.

While the Landrum-Griffin Act places these restrictions on picketing, it does not prevent **informational picketing** *or other publicity* for the purpose of advising the public that an employer does not have a union contract—unless an effect of such picketing is to induce employees of other companies in the course of employment not to pick up, deliver, or transport any goods, or not to perform any services.

Quite often picketing has characteristics both of a desire to inform and of a wish to be recognized or to organize the employees. If the *immediate purpose* of the picketing is to gain recognition or to organize, the picketing may not go beyond thirty days without the filing of a petition for an election. On the other hand, if the object of the picketing is *informational*, the union may picket beyond the thirty-day limit so long as it does not induce employees of other companies not to pick up, deliver, or transport any goods, or not to perform any services. This is true even if an attorney could argue that the union also intends to seek recognition or intends to organize the employees at some point in the future.

We have seen that employees may picket and strike in order to protect their rights. The next section discusses a more complex issue—secondary pressure. In many cases, if union activity results in pressure on an employer, other than the employer with whom the union has a dispute, it is unlawful.

SECONDARY PRESSURE

The law in the area of **secondary pressure** is complex. Section 8(b)(4) of the Taft-Hartley Act as amended by the Landrum-Griffin Act states the law relating to secondary activity. What does a court mean when it uses the term *secondary pressure?*

The courts, in using this phrase, are speaking of a boycott of an employer other than the employer with whom the employees have a dispute.

The term **boycott** is taken from a man's name, that of Captain Boycott. Captain Boycott evicted his tenants. The tenants banded together to urge people in the community not to deal with the captain. The term *boycott* now describes a concerted effort to stop people from doing business with someone.

Suppose that the employees of a meat packer wished to put pressure on the packer. The employees could stage a strike at the meat packer's plant, or they might urge *customers* shopping at a retail grocery store not to buy the products of the meat packer. The **primary pressure** in this situation would be against the packer. Primary pressure is pressure put on an employer by the employees of that company. If the employees exert pressure on the grocery store, urging consumers not to buy the products of the meat packer, they are exerting secondary pressure.

There are three parties to any case involving a secondary boycott: employer A, the union of employer A, and employer B. The union working for employer A puts pressure on employer B by striking, picketing, and so on. Quite frequently, employer B is a customer or supplier of employer A. In this fashion, the union exerts pressure indirectly against the ultimate target—employer A.

Why would a union attempt to exert pressure on an employer in this roundabout fashion? Perhaps employer A is not unionized, thus making actions such as picketing against it ineffective, or perhaps, though the union represents the employees of employer A, a strike against employer A would be futile. The ultimate objective of such secondary pressure is to force employer B to stop doing business with employer A. This puts pressure on employer A to settle the dispute with the union.

At one time, the courts regarded such secondary pressure as a violation of the antitrust laws—a conspiracy in restraint of trade. The Norris-LaGuardia Act prohibited the classification of such secondary activity as a violation of the antitrust laws.

Over time, the pro-labor mood in Congress shifted, and in 1947 Congress passed the Taft-Hartley Act. Congress concluded that secondary pressure should not be permitted, because it is unfair to subject employer B to this type of economic pressure. In such a situation, there is no manner in which employer B may settle the dispute.

The Taft-Hartley Act

It is an innocent neutral. Congress also wanted to confine disputes to employer A to keep commerce from being disrupted. Section 8(b)(4) now covers secondary activity.

Primary Activity. In the statute, Congress used complicated language. It did not use the terms *boycott* or *secondary*. Even so, it is clear that when a union's activity is primary, it does not fall under the ban of the act.

Suppose agents of a union picketed a mill although they were not certified or recognized as representatives of the employees. The union hoped to secure recognition of the union as the collective bargaining representative of the mill employees. A driver from another company arrived at the mill to pick up supplies. The union men asked the driver to turn away. The conduct of the union was lawful primary activity.

Generally, when pickets are at a plant gate and employees of other companies refuse to cross the picket line, the effect is secondary but **legal**. Section 8(b)(4)(B) states that primary strikes and primary picketing are legal in this situation.

Common Situs Problems

The problem of several unions working at the same location poses significant problems for both employers and unions. If a union strikes one employer, employees of the other unions working at the same location may walk off the job. This is referred to as the **common situs** problem. As an example of this problem, suppose a shipping company and a union had a dispute. The company put a ship in a dock to change crews. The union picketed the dock, although its dispute was with the owner of the ship, and the employees of the dock refused to work on the ship. In this case, a court must balance the right of a union to picket against the right of a secondary employer (the owner of the dock) not to be picketed. Such picketing complies with the law. Under carefully controlled circumstances, the union may picket at the location of the secondary employer (in this case, at the dock).

Construction Site. Suppose instead the dispute is at a construction site. Many employees from different unions and employers often work at a construction site. Should a strike against one of the employers be allowed to shut the whole project down?

In *NLRB* v. *Denver Building & Construction Trades Council,* a contractor awarded a subcontract to a firm that employed nonunion labor. A picket was placed at the site of the construction, and all union members walked off the job, including employees of other companies working at the site. The Supreme Court found this to be an illegal secondary boycott in violation of Section 8(b)(4), as the whole purpose or object of the picketing was to *force* the general contractor to stop doing business with the nonunion subcontractor.

In *Building & Construction Trades Council of New Orleans,* an employer at a construction site created a gate to be used exclusively by employees of subcontractors and their suppliers. A union that had a dispute with the general contractor placed pickets at the gate used by the subcontractors. The employees of the subcontractor refused to cross the picket lines. The board found picketing at the subcontractor's gate to be a violation of Section 8(b)(4). It hoped through this ruling to minimize the impact of such activities on secondary employers.

This case suggests that in a construction case, where the contractor sets up a reserve gate to be used exclusively by the employer with whom a union has a dispute, the union may not picket any gate other than the reserve gate.

Manufacturers. The Supreme Court has created another rule that applies to the use of special entrances by independent contractors at a manufacturing plant. The following case discusses the use of reserve gates in this situation.

Local 761, International Union of Electrical, Radio, and Machine Workers v. NLRB

United States Supreme Court
366 U.S. 667 (1961)

A manufacturer operated a plant in a large area to which a drainage ditch made ingress and egress impossible except over five roadways across culverts, which were called gates. Four of these gates were used by its own employees, but they were forbidden to use the fifth, which was reserved for the exclusive use of employees of independent contractors. Petitioner union, which represented most of the manufacturer's employees at the plant, called a strike and picketed all gates, including that reserved for the exclusive use of employees of independent contractors. NLRB held that the picketing at that gate was intended to involve those employees of neutral employers in a dispute with the manufacturer and that it violated Section 8(b)(4)(A). The court of appeals sustained this finding and granted enforcement of the board's order. The union appealed. The Supreme Court reversed.

Justice Frankfurter

Section 8(b)(4)(A) of the National Labor Relations Act provides that it shall be an unfair labor practice for a labor organization

". . . to engage in, or to induce or encourage the employees of any employer to engage in, a strike or a concerted refusal in the course of their employment to use, manufacture, process, transport, or otherwise handle or work on any goods, articles, materials, or commodities or to perform any services, where an object thereof is: (A) forcing or requiring . . . any employer or other person . . . to cease doing business with any other person. . . ."

This provision could not be literally construed; otherwise it would ban most strikes historically considered to be lawful, so-called primary activity.

The impact of the section was directed toward what is known as the secondary boycott whose sanctions bear, not upon the employer who alone is a party to the dispute, but upon some third party who has no concern in it.

The objectives of any picketing include a desire to influence others from withholding from the employer their services or trade. Picketing which induces secondary employees to respect a picket line is not the equivalent of picketing which has an object of inducing those employees to engage in concerted conduct against their employer in order to force him to refuse to deal with the struck employer.

The question is whether the Board may make unlawful picketing at a gate utilized exclusively by employees of independent contractors who work on the struck employer's premises. The effect of such a holding would not bar the union from picketing at all gates used by the employees, suppliers, and customers of the struck employer. Of course an employer may not, by removing all his employees from the situs of the strike, bar the union from publicizing its cause.

The union claims that, if the Board's ruling is upheld, employers will be free to erect separate gates for deliveries, customers, and replacement workers which will be immunized from picketing. This fear is baseless. The key to the problem is found in the type of work that is being performed by those who use the separate gate. It is significant that the Board has since applied its rationale, first stated in the present case, only to situations where the independent workers were performing tasks unconnected to the normal operations of the struck employer—usually construction work on his buildings. In such situations, the indicated limitations on picketing activity respect the balance of competing interests that Congress has required the Board to enforce. On the other hand, if a separate gate were devised for regular plant deliv-eries, the barring of picketing at that location would make a clear invasion on traditional primary activity of appealing to neutral employees whose tasks aid the employer's everyday operations.

The legal path by which the Board and the Court of Appeals reached their decisions did not take into account that if Gate 3-A was in fact used by employees of independent contractors who performed conventional maintenance work necessary to the normal operations of General Electric, the use of the gate would have been a mingled one outside the bar of section 8(b)(4)(A). In short, such mixed use of this portion of the struck employer's premises would not bar picketing rights of the striking employees. While the record shows some such mingled use, it sheds no light on its extent. It may well turn out to be that the instances of these maintenance tasks were so insubstantial as to be treated by the Board as de minimis. We cannot here guess at the quantitative aspect of this problem. It calls for Board determination. For determination of the questions thus raised, the case must be remanded by the Court of Appeals to the Board.

This case suggests a second rule for union activity at manufacturing plants, as opposed to construction sites. In construction type cases, if the employer sets up a reserve gate to be used exclusively by the subcontractors it has a dispute with, the union may picket *only* that gate.

In the manufacturing cases, where the employer uses several entrances, the NLRB must examine the type of work being performed by the independent contractors who use the gate. If the work performed by the independent contractor normally would be performed by employees of the manufacturer, then this gate may be picketed. However, if the independent contractor performs work unconnected with the everyday operations of the manufacturer, the union may not picket the reserve gate.

Ally Doctrine

May a union place pickets in front of a business that does work for the company with whom the union has its primary dispute? This involves the **ally doctrine**.

In *NLRB* v. *Business Machine & Office Appliance Mechanics Conference Board, IUE, Local 459*, the court discussed the ally doctrine. Royal sent its customers to repair shops not owned by Royal when a dispute erupted between Royal and its employees. Royal agreed to reimburse the people for their expenses. Royal's union set up picket lines at the repair shops. The owners of these shops *knew* they were performing work normally performed by the strikers. The court ruled the union's actions were lawful.

The rationale for this decision lies in the fact that an employer must remain neutral. If a strike occurs at the primary employer's premises and the employer farms out work normally performed by the striking workers, the second employer becomes entangled in the dispute and may be picketed. The second employer may eliminate the pickets by refusing to do work for the primary employer.

For the ally doctrine to apply, the picketing must be against work that but for the strike would have been done by the primary employer. The second employer must knowingly accept the work realizing that it normally is performed by the strikers. The second employer need not be directly paid by the primary employer.

Publicity. Merely handing out leaflets to encourage people not to purchase a product usually poses no problems under Section 8(b)(4). The act contains a proviso permitting *publicity, other than picketing,* for the purpose of truthfully advising the public that a product or products produced by an employer with whom the labor organization has a primary dispute are being distributed by another employer. This right to advise is subject to several limitations. It must not have the effect of inducing any employee of secondary employers to refuse to pick up, deliver, or transport any goods, or not to perform any services at the establishment of the employer engaged in such distribution. The proviso ensures the right to free speech guaranteed to every person under the Constitution. The union's aim here must not be to induce the employees of the secondary employer not to work. The union must solely intend to exercise its *right to inform* the public of its dispute with the primary employer.

Picketing. Suppose a union places members outside a candy manufacturer with whom it has a dispute. If the union members hand out leaflets concerning their dispute with the candy company, this is clearly lawful primary activity. Secondary activity becomes a problem if a union places people around an establishment with which the union has no dispute but which carries goods manufactured by a company with which the union has a dispute. If a union that worked for a candy company places pickets outside retail stores carrying the candy, the union is engaging in secondary activity.

Not only unions picket businesses. A union may try to enlist public support for its strike against an employer.

In *NLRB* v. *Fruit and Vegetable Packers & Warehousemen* (the *Tree Fruits* case), the Court dealt with the problem of picketing by consumers. The packers commenced a strike in Washington State over apples. The union organized a consumer boycott of Washington State apples. It placed pickets in front of retail stores urging customers not to purchase these apples. The union tried to make clear its desire merely to discourage people from buying apples and not to discourage customers from patronizing the retail stores. No deliveries or pickups were stopped. Customers were not interfered with. The Supreme Court held the union may picket and urge people not to buy the apples. However, had the union requested the customers to not trade at all with the secondary employer (the retail grocery store), this would have violated Section 8(b)(4). Whether the grocery store experienced a drop in business or not, the Court sanctioned picketing to urge customers not to purchase the apples. The

Consumer Boycotts

union's activities in this case were closely confined to the primary dispute—the strike against the apple producer. Note in this case that the product was clearly identifiable—apples. Retail grocery stores sell many products in addition to apples. When the pickets asked people not to purchase apples, little chance of a misunderstanding existed. What if a union decided to picket a company with only a single product, such as gasoline? The Court implied that a union may not boycott a store that sells only one product. (See the *Retail Store Employees Union, Local 1001* case, which follows, on this point.)

Generally, if the union asks consumers not to buy a particular product, no unfair labor practice has been committed. Asking customers not to patronize the secondary employer is unlawful.

In the following case, on secondary picketing, the Supreme Court ruled the attempted consumer boycott violated the Taft-Hartley Act.

NLRB v. Retail Store Employees Union, Local 1001
United States Supreme Court
447 U.S. 607 (1980)

Safeco Title Insurance Co. does business with several title companies that derive over ninety percent of their gross incomes from the sale of Safeco insurance policies. When contract negotiations between Safeco and respondent union, the bargaining representative for certain Safeco employees, reached an impasse, the employees went on strike. The union picketed each of the title companies, urging customers to support the strike by canceling their Safeco policies. Safeco and one of the title companies filed complaints with the NLRB charging that the union had engaged in an unfair labor practice by picketing in order to promote a secondary boycott against the title companies. The board agreed and ordered the union to cease picketing. The board held that the union's secondary picketing violated Section 8(b)(4)(ii)(B) of the National Labor Relations Act. The court of appeals reversed, holding that the union's activity was lawful product picketing. The NLRB appealed. The Supreme Court reversed.

Justice Powell

Section 8(b)(4)(ii)(B) of the National Labor Relations Act makes it "an unfair labor practice for a labor organization . . . to threaten, coerce, or restrain" a person not party to a labor dispute "where . . . an object thereof is . . . forcing or requiring [him] to cease using, selling, handling, transporting, or otherwise dealing in the products of any other producer . . . or to cease doing business with any other person. . . ."

In *Tree Fruits*, the Court held that Section 8(b)(4)(ii)(B) does not prohibit all peaceful picketing at secondary sites. There, a union striking certain Washington fruit packers picketed large supermarkets in order to persuade consumers not to buy Washington apples. Concerned that a broad ban against such picketing might run afoul of the First Amendment, the Court found the statute directed to an isolated evil. The evil was the use of secondary picketing to persuade the customers of the secondary employer to cease trading with him in order to force him to cease dealing with, or to put pressure upon the primary employer. Congress intended to protect secondary parties from pressures that might embroil them in the labor disputes of others, but not to shield them from business losses caused by a campaign that successfully persuades consumers to boycott the primary employer's goods. Thus, the Court drew a distinction between picketing "to shut off all trade with the secondary employer unless he aids the union in its dispute with the primary employer" and picketing that "only persuades his customers not to buy the struck product." The picketing in that case, which "merely follow[ed] the struck product," did not, " 'threaten, coerce, or restrain' " the secondary party within the meaning of Section 8(b)(4)(ii)(B).

Although *Tree Fruits* suggested that secondary picketing against a struck product and secondary picketing against a neutral party were "poles apart," the courts soon discovered that product picketing could have the same effect as an illegal secondary boycott.

There is a critical difference between the picketing in this case and the picketing at issue in *Tree Fruits*. The product picketed in *Tree Fruits* was but one item among the many that made up the retailer's trade. If the appeal against such a product succeeds, the Court observed, it simply induces the neutral retailer to reduce his orders for the product or "to drop the item as a poor seller." The decline in sales attributable to consumer rejection of the struck product puts pressure upon the primary employer, and the marginal injury to the neutral retailer is purely incidental to the product boycott. The neutral therefore has little reason

to become involved in the labor dispute. In this case, on the other hand, the title companies sell only the primary employer's product and perform the services associated with it. Secondary picketing against consumption of the primary product leaves responsive consumers no realistic option other than to boycott the title companies altogether. If the appeal succeeds, each company stops buying the struck product, not because of a falling demand, but in response to pressure designed to inflict injury on its business generally. Thus, the union does more than merely follow the struck product; it creates a separate dispute with the secondary-employer.

As long as secondary picketing only discourages consumption of a struck product, incidental injury to the neutral is a natural consequence of an effective primary boycott. But the Union's secondary appeal against the central product sold by the title companies in this case is reasonably calculated to induce customers not to patronize the neutral parties at all. Product picketing that reasonably can be expected to threaten neutral parties with ruin or substantial loss simply does not square with the language or the purpose of Section 8(b)(4)(ii)(B). Since successful secondary picketing would put the title companies to a choice between their survival and the severance of their ties with Safeco, the picketing plainly violates the statutory ban on the coercion of neutrals with the object of forcing or requiring them to cease dealing in the primary product or to cease doing business with the primary employer.

Accordingly, the judgment of the Court of Appeals is reversed, and the case is remanded with directions to enforce the National Labor Relations Board's order.

What if, rather than objecting to the product handled by the other employer, the employees of the primary employer wish to influence the political affairs of the country? Such activities would be an illegal secondary boycott because the Court has ruled that there is no exemption in the act for political boycotts.

Secondary Pressure—Hot Cargo Agreements

Section 8(e) of the Landrum-Griffin Act makes it an unfair labor practice for a union *or* an employer "to enter into any contract or agreement, express or implied, whereby such employer ceases or refrains or agrees to cease or refrain from handling, using, selling, transporting or otherwise dealing in any of the products of any other employer, or to cease doing business with any other person, and any contract or agreement entered into . . . containing such an agreement shall be . . . void." This provision outlaws **hot cargo** provisions in labor contracts—a clause in a contract that states that workers will not be required to handle nonunion material. Such clauses are designed to protect a worker who refuses to work with nonunion material. A hot cargo clause might read as follows: "The union reserves the right to refuse to accept the freight from, or to make pickups from or deliveries to, establishments where picket lines, strikes, walkouts, or lockouts exist."

Construction and Garments. Section 8(e) does not apply to work done at a construction site or in the garment industry. For example, it still is *legal* to include a clause in a labor contract that states that work done at a construction site must be performed by union workers.

Secondary Pressure—Work Preservation Clause

A **work preservation clause** might read as follows: "It shall not be a violation of this agreement, nor shall it be cause for discipline, if an employee refuses to handle or work on prefabricated, factory precut doors or other wood products."

In *National Woodwork Manufacturers Ass'n. v. NLRB,* the Supreme Court dealt with a bargaining agreement with a clause prohibiting the members of the union from handling prefabricated doors. The contractor substituted fitted doors, and the union ordered its members not to hang them. The Supreme Court held it was *not* an illegal secondary boycott by one local to refuse to handle the prefabricated doors in order to protect the work customarily done by members of a sister local for the same employer.

Collective activity by employees of the primary employer, the object of which is to affect labor policies at the **primary employer,** and not to affect other employers, is protected primary activity. Section 8(e) does not prohibit agreements made for primary purposes, including the purpose of preserving for the contracting employees work they traditionally have done.

For this reason, the touchstone is whether an agreement or its maintenance is addressed to the labor relations of the contracting employer with his or her own employees, or is calculated to satisfy union objectives elsewhere.

Damages

In the event a union violates the rights of a company by engaging in unlawful secondary activity, the union may be liable to the company for damages caused by the illegal activity. Punitive damages are not available. In the event a union engages in such illegal secondary activity, an employer may file an unfair labor practices charge with the NLRB. It also may file a separate damages suit in federal court.

We have now examined the extent to which unions may engage in certain types of activities. Employees have considerable leeway in engaging in such collective activities as strikes and picketing, but they must be careful not to place pressure on an employer with whom they do not have a dispute.

SUMMARY

A union may not enter into a contract with an employer that requires people to become union members before they are eligible to work. However, an employee may be required to join a union after thirty days of employment unless a state has outlawed such a contractual agreement.

The Taft-Hartley Act made a number of union practices a violation of the labor laws. A union must fairly represent all the members in the unit that it was certified by the board to represent. It may not coerce employees in the exercise of their right to engage in concerted activities or charge its members excessive or discriminatory fees.

One of the most important rights guaranteed to unions by the labor laws is the right to strike. Only under very limited circumstances can an injunction be issued against a strike, such as when a strike threatens to cripple the economy of the entire nation. If employees do engage in an economic strike, they may be permanently replaced. However, when workers go out on an unfair-labor-practice strike, they have an absolute right to reinstatement.

Another important right guaranteed to labor by the labor laws is the right to picket. The law places some restrictions, however, on the exercise of this right. For example, a union may not picket an employer to obtain recognition if the board has certified another union as the bargaining representative of the employees.

The law also places restrictions on the right of unions to exert secondary pressure in order to obtain concessions for the workers of the primary employer. Secondary pressure is a significant problem in the construction and manufacturing businesses.

Generally, a union may picket to inform the public of its dispute with the primary employer. In most cases a union may urge the public not to purchase products produced by the primary employer.

Unions may also enter into contracts with companies to try to preserve work for the employees they represent.

REVIEW QUESTIONS

1. Define the following terms:
   a. Organizational picketing
   b. Recognition picketing
   c. Secondary pressure
   d. Ally doctrine
   e. Hot cargo
   f. Work preservation clause
   g. Jurisdictional disputes
   h. Featherbedding
   i. Closed shop
   j. Union shop
   k. Agency shop
   l. Federal Mediation and Conciliation Service

2. Under what circumstances must an employer rehire strikers—if ever?

3. May the employees of Company X form a picket line in front of the plant if it has the effect of discouraging other persons from doing business with X?

4. Under what circumstances may an employee who is discharged from the union be fired at the union's request?

5. E Company changed its method of computation of pay to employees from a piece-rate basis to an hourly rate. As a result, the wages of the employees were significantly reduced. Five employees responded to the changes with a work slowdown and were subsequently fired for unsatisfactory production. Is the employ-

ees' action protected by Section 7 of the National Labor Relations Act as a concerted activity? Was their discharge an unfair labor practice?

6. The union was a council of local building and construction unions. It asked a particular construction company about its wage rates and was told that the company operated an open shop and that its wage rates were lower than those negotiated in the area by local unions. The union protested these "substandard wages" and picketed the company for thirty days, interfering with deliveries. The union was not the certified representative of the company's employees. Was the picketing illegal?

7. The union called a strike and picketed all entrances of the company's plant, including an entrance to a railroad-owned track adjacent to the plant, hoping to induce railroad employees not to make pickups and deliveries at the plant. The picketing became violent. Did the union violate Section 8(b)(4) of the National Labor Relations Act, or was this protected as primary picketing?

8. The union, while on strike against Dow Chemical Co., picketed six gas stations that sold gasoline refined by Dow. The union asked consumers to boycott only Dow-refined gasoline. The sales of this gas represented most of each gas station's gross revenues. The gas stations were neutral parties to the dispute and the picketing was peaceful. Was the picketing lawful?

9. A typographical union insisted that newspaper publishers pay printers for reproducing advertisements that had been already furnished by the advertiser. The publisher charged the union with an unfair labor practice in violation of Section 8(b)(6) regarding featherbedding. How should the NLRB rule?

10. Several employees were discharged by their employer for alleged dishonesty. Their union did not investigate the employees' claims of wrongful discharge, and the employees sued the union and the employer, alleging that the falsity of the charges could easily have been discovered. Did the union breach its duty of fair representation?

11. The International Longshoremen's Association bargained for rules that required marine shipping companies to permit longshoremen to load and unload cargo containers at the pier. Traditionally, longshoremen employed by shipping companies loaded and unloaded cargo into and out of oceangoing vessels at the pier. The advent of containerization profoundly transformed this practice by eliminating the need for cargo handling at intermediate stages. The rules apply only to containers that would otherwise be loaded or unloaded within the local port area, defined for convenience as anywhere within a fifty-mile radius of the port. The effect of the rules is that eighty percent of the containers pass over the pier intact. In analyzing whether the union was guilty of unlawful secondary activity, the National Labor Relations Board focused on the effect of these rules on certain truckers and warehouses. Was the board correct in finding the union was guilty of engaging in unlawful secondary activity? Does it make any difference that the rules preserve work that was made utterly useless by containerization?

12. DeBartolo owned a shopping center in Tampa, Florida. Wilson Company, a department store, agreed to lease land in the center. Wilson hired a general building contractor, High, to build a department store in the shopping center. Neither DeBartolo nor any of the tenants in the shopping center had any right to control the actions of the building contractor, High. A union that had a wage dispute with High passed out handbills urging consumers not to patronize any of the stores in the shopping center until DeBartolo agreed that any construction at the shopping center would be done by contractors who paid fair wages. DeBartolo

claimed the union's actions were an unfair labor practice. Is he correct?

13. Larry Shepard owned a dump truck and operated it in the San Diego area. Contractors in San Diego hired dump truck operators on a day-to-day basis. Brokers supplied dump trucks to contractors, and then referred hauling jobs to individual owners such as Shepard. Shepard was not a member of any union before August 1978. In 1977, the Teamsters entered into an agreement with the contractors. The effect of the agreement was to enlist the aid of the contractors to insure only brokers who had signed the agreement received subcontracts, and that only union truck operators performed hauling services for the contractors. Shepard challenged this agreement. Will he win?

14. The Postal Service discharged Bowen as a result of a fight with another employee. He filed a grievance with the union. The national office, for no apparent reason, refused to take the matter to arbitration. Bowen sued the union and the Postal Service. The trial court found that Bowen had been discharged without just cause. Has the union breached its duty of fair representation? Should the union have to pay any damages to Bowen?

15. The president of the International Longshoremen's Association on January 9, 1980, ordered ILA members to stop handling cargoes arriving from or destined for the Soviet Union. He did this to protest the Russian invasion of Afghanistan. Allied Inernational imports Russian wood products. As a result of the boycott, Allied's shipments were completely disrupted. Allied challenged the union's actions as a secondary boycott in violation of the Taft-Hartley Act. Is this an illegal secondary boycott?

CHAPTER 22

Employment Discrimination

Historical Background
Title VII: Civil Rights Act of 1964
What Is Discrimination?
Permitted Discrimination: The Bona Fide Occupational Qualification
Developments in Equal Employment Law

The equal employment opportunity laws reflect the influence of historical and social movements. In Chapter 1 of this text, a discussion of race relations and law concluded with a brief mention of the Civil Rights Act of 1964. One of the major provisions of that statute is Title VII, which prohibits discrimination in employment because of race, color, sex, national origin, or religion.

This chapter will provide an overview of the major aspects of Title VII of the Civil Rights Act of 1964. Note, that this is not the only source of discrimination in employment law. Other federal statutes, such as the Equal Pay Act, also play a role. Additionally, executive orders, administrative regulations, and state law concern employment discrimination. However, none of the other sources of law has had as great an effect on business as has Title VII. Thus, a more focused study of that provision will provide the background for further study in employment law or will provide an appreciation for additional developments that are sure to be proposed in this area.

HISTORICAL BACKGROUND

The demise of slavery did not mean that black people were accepted into the mainstream of American life. Jim Crow laws created a dual society, one black and one white. Private attitudes reinforced the legal segregation, and many employers refused to hire black workers or placed them in low-level jobs. The civil rights movement and the national concern with racial segregation led to the Civil Rights

Act, proposed during the Kennedy administration. However, women too were treated differently based on certain stereotypes. But in the early 1960s, suggestions that women should be permitted to become police officers, construction workers, or business executives were considered too radical. In fact, the Civil Rights Act, as proposed, did not forbid discrimination based on sex. During the debate in the House of Representatives, a representative opposed to the act introduced an amendment to forbid sex discrimination as a tactic for defeating the act. The amendment passed with segregationist and women's group support. Discrimination based on sex reflected society's view of the traditional roles of men and women: Men were strong, aggressive, and worked to support their families; women were nurturing and cared for their families at home. Some of this attitude can be traced to the progressive movement at the turn of the century. The industrial revolution led to the employment of women in factories. Long hours, low pay, and poor working conditions for the women workers led reformers to seek protective legislation that would outlaw certain practices. The United States Supreme Court in *Muller* v. *Oregon* (1908) upheld an Oregon statute that prohibited women from working in factories longer than ten hours per day. By 1920, most states had enacted various types of protective legislation.

The attitudes of society toward women consisted of more than simply a concern that women not be exploited in the workplace. As the following case notes, based solely on their sex, women were commonly thought to be ill-equipped to do certain work.

Bradwell v. The State of Illinois
United States Supreme Court
83 U.S. 130 (1872)

Mrs. Myra Bradwell made application to the judges of the Supreme Court of Illinois for a license to practice law. The practice of law without a license was forbidden by an Illinois statute. Mrs. Bradwell's application for the license was refused. After the announcement of this decision, Mrs. Bradwell filed an appeal maintaining that she had a right to admission under the Fourteenth Amendment of the United States Constitution.

The decision of the Supreme Court was to deny her appeal on the now overruled grounds that the Fourteenth Amendment does not apply to the laws of a state. Justice Bradley (joined by two other justices) filed the following concurring opinion.

Justice Bradley

The civil law, as well as nature herself, has always recognized a wide difference in the respective spheres and destinies of man and woman. Man is, or should be, woman's protector and defender. The natural and proper timidity and delicacy which belongs to the female sex evidently unfits it for many of the occupations of civil life. The constitution of the family organization, which is founded in the divine ordinance, as well as in the nature of things, indicates the domestic sphere as that which properly belongs to the domain and functions of womanhood. The harmony, not to say identity, of interests and views which belong, or should belong, to the family institution is repugnant to the idea of a woman adopting a distinct and independent career from that of her husband. So firmly fixed was this sentiment in the founders of the common law that it became a maxim of that system of jurisprudence that a woman had no legal existence separate from her husband, who was regarded as her head and representative in the social state; and, notwithstanding some recent modifications of this civil status, many of the special rules of law flowing from and dependent upon this cardinal principle still exist in full force in most States. One of these is, that a married woman is incapable, without her husband's consent, of making contracts which shall be binding on her or him. This very incapacity was one circumstance which the Supreme Court of Illinois deemed important in rendering a married woman incompetent fully to perform the duties and trusts that belong to the office of an attorney and counselor.

It is true that many women are unmarried and not affected by any of the duties, complications, and incapacities arising out of the married state, but these are exceptions to the general rule. The paramount destiny and mission of women are to fulfill the noble and benign offices of wife and mother. This is the law of the Creator. And the rules of civil society must be adapted to the general constitution of things, and cannot be based upon exceptional cases.

It is the prerogative of the legislator to prescribe regulations founded on nature, reason, and experience for the due admission of qualified persons to professions and callings demanding special skill and confidence. This fairly belongs to the police power of the State; and, in my opinion, in view of the peculiar characteristics, destiny, and mission of women, it is within the province of the legislature to ordain what offices, positions, and callings shall be filled and discharged by men, and shall receive the benefit of those energies and responsibilities, and that decision and firmness which are presumed to predominate in the sterner sex.

The civil rights movement raised questions about the morality of discrimination in all areas of American life, including the workplace. Two fundamental principles clashed in this movement: first, that all people should be treated as individuals, based on their character and merit; and second, that all people should be free to associate with whomever they choose. The Civil Rights Act of 1964 was a balance of those principles. In some circumstances, employment, for example, certain individual characteristics (race, sex) may not be used to distinguish between employees. However, for any non-Title VII reason, employers are generally free to act. Throughout the material that follows, consider the arguments that related to each principle and note the balance in the outcome.

TITLE VII: CIVIL RIGHTS ACT OF 1964

Title VII of the Civil Rights Act of 1964 prohibits discrimination in any aspect of employment because of race, color, sex, religion, or national origin. Note that other types of discrimination may be prohibited by law beyond that covered in this chapter. For example, age (between forty and seventy) and handicap (for federal contractors) are other personal characteristics that in some circumstances may not influence employment decisions.

Two major policy goals are contained in Title VII. First, the decision to eliminate

EQUAL OPPORTUNITY AND JAPANESE BUSINESS

At a meeting of his Liberal Democratic Party on September 22, 1986, Japan's Prime Minister Yasuhiro Nakasone raised deep concerns about the racial attitudes in his economically powerful country. *Time* quoted Nakasone: "So high is the level of education in our country that Japan's is an intelligent society. Our average score is much higher than those of countries like the United States. There are many blacks, Puerto Ricans and Mexicans in America. In consequence the average score over there is exceedingly low." He issued an apology five days later.

Immediate outrage was expressed by American minority leaders who were offended by Nakasone's remarks linking race and intelligence. A full page advertisement was placed in the *New York Times* and *Washington Post* responding to Nakasone's slur. Andrew Young, mayor of Atlanta, noted that no Japanese auto franchise is held by any of the 250 black car dealers in the United States, Japanese companies did not advertise through black-owned media, and no Japanese company deposits funds with black-controlled banks.

Only about two percent of Japan's population are minorities, with Koreans being the largest group. They are descendants of forced laborers brought to Japan from Korea during World War II. Numerous opportunities are unavailable to them, including citizenship. Blacks are regularly portrayed as caricatures in films and publications. This attitude toward non-Japanese is consistent with a major theme in Japanese social and political theory: that they are a unique, homogeneous race with a superior culture. Thus, things foreign remain outside the community.

race, color, sex, religion, and national origin from being used as employment criterion was designed to limit social conflict by providing the opportunity for all workers to compete without regard to certain personal characteristics. In addition, nondiscriminatory employment practices were considered a means of entry for black people, especially, into the economic mainstream of the country. At the time of the passage of the act, dramatic economic inequality existed between black and white people.

Note, however, that these policy goals have raised conflicts about the extent of equal employment opportunity laws. Should employment practices be designed in a "color-blind" (or sex-neutral, etc.) manner, or should those practices be designed to hasten the economic integration of historically disadvantaged groups? This conflict will be illustrated by some of the materials that follow.

The **Equal Employment Opportunity Commission (EEOC)** is the federal administrative agency charged with enforcing Title VII. The EEOC has the power to investigate allegations of employment discrimination and file charges against businesses, unions, or employment agencies. Additionally, the EEOC, in its fact finding role, may hear evidence from employee and employer and attempt to reach a resolution of the complaint. Finally, the agency also promulgates regulations that provide guidance to businesses concerned with the agency's attitude toward certain employment practices.

The Equal Employment Opportunity Commission was created by the Civil

The Equal Employment Opportunity Commission

Rights Act of 1964. Its powers were strengthened in 1972 by the Equal Employment Opportunity Act, which gave the commission authority to file suit on behalf of aggrieved parties.

Persons who believe they have been discriminated against in an employment situation because of race, color, religion, sex, or national origin have 180 days after the discriminatory act to file a complaint with the EEOC. The district office that receives the complaint must refer it to any existing state or local fair employment practices agency. The state or local agency has sixty days to act on a charge. If no fair employment practices agency exists, the EEOC assumes immediate responsibility for processing the charge. If the state or local agency fails to process the charge within sixty days, the EEOC assumes responsibility for processing the charge on the sixty-first day. That date is the official filing date.

The EEOC, within ten days of the official filing date, will notify the parties being charged with a violation. It will then investigate the charges. If the investigation reveals that the discrimination may have occurred, the EEOC reports its findings to the parties. Thereafter, an attempt to resolve the matter through conciliation takes place. If the parties reach an agreement, the case is concluded. If no agreement is reached, the EEOC may file suit in federal district court.

However, if the EEOC investigation concludes that no discrimination occurred, it will inform the persons that filed the charges of their private right to sue. A suit must be filed within sixty days of the receipt of this notice. If the EEOC has failed to act within 180 days from the official filing date of the charge, the complaining person may request a right-to-sue letter.

WHAT IS DISCRIMINATION?

Discriminate means to choose or differentiate. A generation ago, to indicate that someone was "discriminating" was to compliment that person. The choices referred to by that word usually involved high-quality taste in music, literature, and lifestyle. Today, however, the choices suggested by the word "discriminate" are far from complimentary. However, the idea behind the use of the word remains the same. Instead of differentiating between a fine Bordeaux wine and iced tea, the word means distinguishing between people based upon innate characteristics.

Thus, the antidiscrimination provisions of Title VII may be considered to prohibit certain bases for choice in employment decisions. Race, color, sex, religion, and national origin may not be used in making those decisions. Any other factors can be used; whether or not they are wise is a decision left to the employer. For example, assume George and Sam are vying for a special training program offered by ABC, Inc. The employer may select the worker with the best job record or, who through past performance, has shown the most aptitude for that program. Or, perhaps, ABC will make the choice based on whether or not one of the workers likes tomatoes. None of these criteria for choosing between George or Sam would violate Title VII, since they do not involve any of the prohibited decision-making rationales. Title VII, therefore, does not eliminate employer discretion in distinguishing between employees, even if the means to make the distinction is foolish (enjoying tomatoes). The only concern is that race, color, sex, national origin, or religion do not play a part in the decision.

Thus, the initial inquiry in an employment discrimination problem is whether the basis for the employer's decision was prohibited by Title VII. Unless the employee can show that the choice was based on race, color, sex, religion, or national origin, no violation of the act will arise. The following case illustrates that although an employer's action may be unfair, it may not violate Title VII.

Ulane v. Eastern Airlines, Inc.
United States Court of Appeals, Seventh Circuit
742 F.2d 1081 (1984)

Plaintiff, as Kenneth Ulane, was hired in 1968, as a pilot for defendant, Eastern Air Lines, Inc., but was fired as Karen Frances Ulane in 1981. Ulane filed a timely charge of sex discrimination with the Equal Employment Opportunity Commission, which subsequently issued a right-to-sue letter. This suit followed.

Ulane became a licensed pilot in 1964, serving in the United States Army from that time until 1968 with a record of combat missions in Vietnam for which he received the Air Medal with eight clusters. Upon discharge in 1968, Ulane began flying for Eastern. With Eastern, Ulane progressed from second to first officer, and also served as a flight instructor, logging over eight thousand flight hours.

Ulane was diagnosed as a transsexual in 1979. She explains that although embodied as a male, from early childhood she felt like a female. Ulane first sought psychiatric and medical assistance in 1968 while in the military. Later, Ulane began taking female hormones as part of her treatment, and eventually developed breasts from the hormones. In 1980, she underwent "sex reassignment surgery." After the surgery, Illinois issued a revised birth certificate indicating Ulane was female, and the FAA certified her for flight status as a female. Ulane's own physician explained, however, that the operation would not create a biological female in the sense that Ulane would not "have a uterus and ovaries and be able to bear babies." Ulane's chromosomes, all concede, are unaffected by the hormones and surgery. Ulane, however, claims that the lack of change in her chromosomes is irrelevant. Eastern was not aware of Ulane's transsexuality, her hormone treatments, or her psychiatric counseling until she attempted to return to work after her reassignment surgery. Eastern knew Ulane only as one of its male pilots.

Wood, Jr., Circuit Judge

The district judge first found that Eastern discharged Ulane because she was a transsexual and that Title VII prohibits discrimination on this basis. While we do not condone discrimination in any form, we are constrained to hold that Title VII does not protect transsexuals, and that the district court's order on this count therefore must be reversed.

The district judge based this holding on his finding that "sex is not a cut-and-dried matter of chromosomes," but is in part a psychological question—a question of self-perception; and in part a social matter—a question of how society perceives the individual. The district judge further supported his broad view of Title VII's coverage by recognizing Title VII as a remedial statute to be liberally construed. He concluded that it is reasonable to hold that the statutory word "sex" literally and scientifically applies to transsexuals even if it does not apply to homosexuals or transvestites. We must disagree.

Even though Title VII is a remedial statute, and even though some may define "sex" in such a way as to mean an individual's "sexual identity," our responsibility is to interpret this congressional legislation and determine what Congress intended when it decided to outlaw discrimination based on sex.

While we recognize distinctions among homosexuals, transvestites, and transsexuals, we believe that the same reasons for holding that the first two groups do not enjoy Title VII coverage apply with equal force to deny protection for transsexuals.

The phrase in Title VII prohibiting discrimination based on sex, in its plain meaning, implies that it is unlawful to discriminate against women because they are women and against men because they are men. The words of Title VII do not outlaw discrimination against a person who has a sexual identity disorder, i.e., a person born with a male body who believes himself to be female, or a person born with a female body who believes herself to be male; a prohibition against discrimination based on an individual's sexual identity disorder or discontent with the sex into which they were born.

When Congress enacted the Civil Rights Act of 1964 it was primarily concerned with race discrimination. This sex amendment was the gambit of a congressman seeking to scuttle adoption of the Civil Rights Act. The ploy failed and sex discrimination was abruptly added to the statute's prohibition against race discrimination.

The total lack of legislative history supporting the sex amendment coupled with the circumstances of the amendment's adoption clearly indicates that Congress never considered nor intended that this 1964 legislation apply to anything other than the traditional concept of sex.

Members of Congress have, moreover, on a number of occasions, attempted to amend Title VII to prohibit discrimination based upon "affectational or sexual orientation." Each of these attempts has failed.

In our view, to include transsexuals within the reach of Title VII far exceeds mere statutory interpretation. Congress had a narrow view of sex in mind when it passed the Civil Rights Act, and it has rejected subsequent attempts to broaden the scope of its original interpretation. For us to now hold that Title VII protects transsexuals would take us out of the realm of interpreting and reviewing and into the realm of legislating. This we must not and will not do.

If Congress believes that transsexuals should enjoy the protection of Title VII, it may so provide. Until that time, however, we decline on behalf of the Congress to judicially expand the definition of sex as used in Title VII beyond its common and traditional interpretation.

Outlawing certain employment practices does not necessarily change attitudes. Nor will the effects of long-time discrimination become irrelevant. Barriers to equal employment opportunities proved far more complex than the enactment of a statute could remedy. The concerns that led to the passage of Title VII remained to create complex questions concerning the application of equal employment opportunity laws. To illustrate, what follows are four theories or categories of employment discrimination that have arisen under Title VII.

Disparate Treatment

The most evident employment practice that violates the act has been labeled "disparate treatment." The term means that a person is treated differently from others based upon the prohibited categories of Title VII. For example, if in the preceding example, George is rejected for the training program because he is a Methodist, then the act is violated on the basis of disparate treatment. Religion is one of the categories in Title VII that may not be used to make employment decisions. Similarly, if an employer disciplines Spanish-surnamed workers more harshly than others for the same rule infraction, a violation occurs based on disparate treatment. Discrimination based on national origin is prohibited.

The following case is a recent example of disparate treatment on the basis of sex. Note that Title VII applies to all aspects of employment, including promotion and evaluation.

Hopkins v. Price Waterhouse
Federal District Court, District of Columbia
618 F. Supp. 1109 (1985)

Price Waterhouse is a partnership that specializes in providing auditing, tax, and management consulting services primarily to private corporations and government agencies. At the time this action was filed, Price Waterhouse had 662 partners operating in ninety offices scattered across the nation.

In 1982, the plaintiff was proposed for partnership by her branch office, which specializes in designing and implementing consulting and management projects for government agencies. Plaintiff was the only woman among eighty-eight candidates for partnership that year. Indeed, as of July, 1984 only seven of the 662 partners at Price Waterhouse were women.

Plaintiff had had a successful career as a senior manager and had played a significant role in developing business for the firm. She had no difficulty dealing with clients, and her clients appear to have been very pleased with her work. None of the other partnership candidates at Price Waterhouse that year had a comparable record in terms of successfully securing major contracts for the partnership.

Comments submitted to the admissions committee indicated that plaintiff had problems with her "interpersonal skills"; specifically, she had trouble in dealing with staff members. Supporters and opponents of her candidacy indicated that she was sometimes overly aggressive, unduly harsh, difficult to work with, and impatient with staff. She sometimes used profanity and appeared to be insensitive to others. The plaintiff's partnership nomination was held for further consideration in the next year. The following year she was not proposed for partnership at all.

After the decision not to repropose, the plaintiff was advised that it was very unlikely that she would be admitted to partnership. Rather than waiting to try again or accepting an offer to remain as a senior manager, she resigned from Price Waterhouse in January 1984. The plaintiff then filed this suit alleging sex discrimination in violation of Title VII.

From the outset, Price Waterhouse has conceded that plaintiff was qualified to be considered for partnership and probably would have been admitted but for the complaints about her interpersonal skills. The only dispute between the parties is whether Price Waterhouse's concerns about the plaintiff's interpersonal skills present a legitimate, nondiscriminatory reason to deny partnership or constitute a pretext to disguise sex discrimination.

Gesell, District Judge

The interpersonal skills of prospective partners was properly an important part of Price Waterhouse's written partnership evaluation criteria. Inability to get along with staff or peers is a legitimate, nondiscriminatory reason for refusing to admit a candidate to partnership.

Contemporaneous records of counseling sessions and evaluations conducted well before the plaintiff was proposed for partnership indicate that partners found her too assertive, overly critical of others, impatient with her staff, and counseled her to soften her image. At the time, plaintiff indicated that she agreed with many of these criticisms. Even partners who strongly supported her partnership candidacy acknowledged these deficiencies, although in more muted tones, when emphasizing the high quality of her work and her value to the firm. Staff members who testified on the plaintiff's behalf indicated that she was an effective manager but her hard-driving style might be regarded as "controversial" and it required "diplomacy, patience and guts" to work with her. Plaintiff's conduct provided ample justification for the complaints that formed the basis of the Policy Board's decision.

In the course of this trial, Price Waterhouse has been very forthcoming in providing information on its partnership selection process. The evidence as a whole indicates that over the years the firm has consistently placed a high premium on candidates' ability to deal with subordinates and peers on an interpersonal basis and to promote cordial relations within a firm which is necessarily dependent on team effort. Despite the fact that the negative comments of short form evaluators are often in sharp contrast to the glowing reports of partners who have had extensive contact with the candidate, such comments are treated as serious reservations and given great weight.

Thus, while plaintiff argues that her accomplishments in generating business, management and client satisfaction were so far above average that she would have been admitted despite any interpersonal skills problems if Price Waterhouse had honestly balanced all her qualifications, Price Waterhouse responds by pointing out that she received very few "yes" votes and more "no" votes than all but two of the 88 candidates that year. These no votes and negative comments effectively placed the plaintiff toward the bottom of the candidate pool. Regardless of its wisdom, the firm's practice of giving "no" votes great weight treated male and female candidates in the same way. The issue in a case of alleged failure to hire or promote is not the objective superiority or inferiority of the plaintiff's qualifications, but rather whether the defendant's selection criteria—be they wise or foolish—are nondiscriminatory. The Court finds that the firm's emphasis on negative comments did not, by itself, result in any discriminatory disparate treatment.

Plaintiff's final argument begins with the allegation that the male partners who criticized her interpersonal skills applied a double standard. She claims that she was not evaluated as a manager, but as a woman manager, based on a sexual stereotype that prompts males to regard assertive behavior in women as being more offensive and intolerable than comparable behavior in men because some men do not regard it as appropriate "feminine" behavior.

Some comments on other women partnership candidates in prior years support the inference that the partnership evaluation process at Price Waterhouse was affected by sexual stereotyping. Candidates were viewed favorably if partners believed they maintained their femininity while becoming effective professional managers. To be identified as a "women's liber" was regarded as negative comment. Nothing was done to discourage sexually biased evaluations. One partner repeatedly commented that he could not consider any woman seriously as a partnership candidate and believed that women were not even capable of functioning as senior managers—yet the firm took no action to discourage his comments and recorded his vote in the overall summary of the evaluations. Besides the plaintiff, the Admissions Committee rejected at least two other women candidates because partners believed that they were curt, brusque and abrasive, acted like "'Ma Barker'" or tried to be "'one of the boys.'" Comments suggesting that sex stereotypes may have influenced the partners' evaluations of interpersonal skills were not frequent, but they appear as part of the regular fodder of the partnership evaluations. Despite the fact that the comments on women candidates suggested that the male evaluators may have been influenced by a sex bias, the Policy Board never addressed the problem. The firm never took any steps in its partnership policy statement or in the evaluation forms submitted to partners to articulate a policy against discrimination or to discourage sexual bias. The Admissions Committee never attempted to investigate whether any of the negative comments concerning the plaintiff were based on a discriminatory double standard.

Whenever a promotion system relies on highly subjective evaluations of candidates by individuals or panels dominated by members of a different sex, there is ground for concern that such high level subjectivity subjects the ultimate promotion decision to the intolerable occurrence of conscious or unconscious prejudice. Such procedures "must be closely scrutinized because of their capacity for masking unlawful bias." An employer who treats a woman with an assertive personality in a different manner than if she had been a man is guilty of sex discrimination. A female cannot be excluded from a partnership dominated by males if a sexual bias plays a part in the decision and the employer is aware that such bias played a part in the exclusion decision.

Title VII does not bar a partnership from considering subjective evaluations of interpersonal skills as significant criteria in the partnership selection process. Subjective evaluations in high-level, professional jobs have received particular deference in Title VII cases. However, while partnerships must be given freedom to evaluate the qualifications of employees who seek to become partners, they are not free to inject stereotyped assumptions about women into the selection process. Neither a partnership nor any other employer can remain indifferent to indications that its evaluation system is subject to sex bias, as Price Waterhouse did in plaintiff's case. Price Waterhouse's failure to take the steps necessary to alert partners to the possibility that their judgments may be biased, to discourage stereotyping, and to investigate and discard, where appropriate, comments that suggest a double standard constitutes a violation of Title VII in this instance.

Title VII may be violated even though the employer has not used any of the prohibited factors in any employment-related decision. All employment policies or practices are then considered to be neutral on their face, meaning that there has been no disparate treatment. However, the effect of the application of those policies might be as if direct discrimination had been practiced. The next two theories of discrimination apply to such situations.

Neutral Practices or Policies That Discriminate

Policies or Practices That Have a Disparate Effect on a Protected Group. The application of some employment standards may have the effect of discriminating against members of a group protected by Title VII, as if the employer had used one of the prohibited factors. For example, assume that ABC, Inc., is interviewing applicants for an entry-level management trainee position. One of the factors used to distinguish between candidates is height. No job candidate under six feet tall would be considered. At first glance, although the requirement seems silly, it appears that there is no violation of Title VII. The factors of disparate treatment do not include size. However, on further reflection, that "neutral" standard would have a discriminatory effect on women. Far fewer females than males would be able to meet the height standard; thus, the standard has a disparate effect based on sex.

No intent to exclude women from the management trainee jobs needs to be established. The key is that the standard used served as a substitute for direct sex discrimination. However, simply because a neutral job evaluation standard has a disparate effect on one of the Title VII categories does not automatically result in a violation of Title VII. If the employer can show that the standard was related to the job in question, then the standard can be used. However, the courts will closely scrutinize any such job requirement. In the management trainee example, height would have nothing to do with the job. Therefore, the use of that standard would be impermissible sex discrimination. As Justice Burger noted in the case that follows: "What Congress has commanded is that any tests used must measure the person for the job and not the person in the abstract."

Griggs v. Duke Power Co.
United States Supreme Court
401 U.S. 424 (1971)

The plaintiffs are black employees of the defendant generating plant. The plaintiffs brought this action to challenge, under Title VII of the Civil Rights Act of 1964, the defendant's requirements of a high school diploma or the passing of intelligence tests as a condition of employment in or transfer to jobs at the plant. These requirements were not directed at or intended to measure ability to learn to perform a particular job. Further, the requirements operated to disqualify black applicants at a substantially higher rate than white applicants. The jobs in question formerly had been filled only by white employees as part of a long-standing practice of giving preference to whites.

Chief Justice Burger

The objective of Congress in the enactment of Title VII is plain from the language of the statute. It was to achieve equality of employment opportunities and remove barriers that have operated in the past to favor an identifiable group of white employees over other employees. Under the Act, practices, procedures, or tests neutral on their face, and even neutral in terms of intent, cannot be maintained if they operate to "freeze" the status quo of prior discriminatory employment practices.

The Court of Appeals' opinion, and the partial dissent, agreed that, on the record in the present case, "whites register far better on the Company's

alternative requirements" than Negroes. This consequence would appear to be directly traceable to race. Basic intelligence must have the means of articulation to manifest itself fairly in a testing process. Because they are Negroes, petitioners have long received inferior education in segregated schools and this Court expressly recognized these differences in *Gaston County v. United States.* There, because of the inferior education received by Negroes in North Carolina, this court barred the institution of a literacy test for voter registration on the ground that the test would abridge the right to vote indirectly on account of race. Congress did not intend by Title VII, however, to guarantee a job to every person regardless of qualifications. In short, the Act does not command that any person be hired simply because he was formerly the subject of discrimination, or because he is a member of a minority group. Discriminatory preference for any group, minority or majority, is precisely and only what Congress has proscribed. What is required by Congress is the removal of artificial, arbitrary, and unnecessary barriers to employment when the barriers operate invidiously to discriminate on the basis of racial or other impermissible classification.

The Act proscribes not only overt discrimination but also practices that are fair in form, but discriminatory in operation. The touchstone is business necessity. If an employment practice which operates to exclude Negroes cannot be shown to be related to job performance, the practice is prohibited.

On the record before us, neither the high school completion requirement nor the general intelligence test is shown to bear a demonstrable relationship to successful performance of the jobs for which it was used. Both were adopted, as the Court of Appeals noted, without meaningful study of their relationship to job-performance ability. Rather, a vice president of the Company testified, the requirements were instituted on the Company's judgment that they generally would improve the overall quality of the work force.

The Court of Appeals held that the Company had adopted the diploma and test requirements without any "intention to discriminate against Negro employees." We do not suggest that either the District Court or the Court of Appeals erred in examining the employer's intent; but good intent or absence of discriminatory intent does not redeem employment procedures or testing mechanisms that operate as "built-in headwinds" for minority groups and are unrelated to measuring job capability.

Nothing in the Act precludes the use of testing or measuring procedures; obviously they are useful. What Congress has forbidden is giving these devices and mechanisms controlling force unless they are demonstrably a reasonable measure of job performance. Congress has not commanded that the less qualified be preferred over the better qualified simply because of minority origins. Far from disparaging job qualifications as such, Congress has made such qualifications the controlling factor, so that race, religion, nationality, and sex become irrelevant. What Congress has commanded is that any tests used must measure the person for the job and not the person in the abstract.

Thus, employers need to exercise care in the factors they use to make employment decisions. Those factors must relate to the tasks being sought, and the factors must also be predictive of success in the performance of the job. One example may be a typing skills test given to all applicants for word processing jobs at ABC, Inc. The typing test, assuming it was properly designed, is directly related to the job. ABC is not required to hire people who cannot type even if the effect of such a test would be to exclude, for example, most Catholics from the job.

Policies or Practices That Perpetuate the Effects of Past Discrimination. Some "neutral" employment decision factors may mirror the discriminatory conditions that existed prior to the passage of the Civil Rights Act of 1964; that is, in some way the factors are related to pre-1964 employment practices that were made illegal by Title VII. For example, in one case, a local union restricted its membership to white workers prior to 1964. Thereafter, no such restriction was legally permissible. A new regulation was adopted requiring all new members to be either related to a current union member or be recommended by a current member. Such a regulation was held to violate Title VII. It carried forward the effects of past discrimination against black workers. Few blacks could meet the new "neutral" requirements for union membership because black people were excluded from membership in the union before the new requirements were adopted.

Another case will further illustrate this category or theory of employment discrimination. Prior to the enactment of the Civil Rights Act of 1964, an employer assigned white workers to one type of job and black workers to another. The employer also had a rule, for valid business reasons, that prohibited the transfer of workers between those types of jobs. After 1964, white and black workers were not assigned to separate job categories, but the no-transfer rule remained. Even in absence of an intent to discriminate, the court held that the no-transfer rule violated Title VII. Black workers in one type of job were forever assigned to it because of the rule, even though the initial hiring decision was based on racial discrimination. The effects of the prior discriminatory hiring policy were carried on by the application of the no-transfer rule.

Two major issues have been litigated under this discrimination theory. One involved seniority systems that were started prior to 1964 and were based on discriminatory hiring practices by employers. The other issue involved wage rates set by the market where jobs that were traditionally limited to women (e.g., nurses, secretaries) are paid less than comparable jobs held by men.

Seniority Systems. Seniority systems are a means to protect workers from arbitrary and subjective treatment by employers. For example, during a layoff, the application of seniority would require the last hired workers to be the first laid off. This criterion is viewed as unbiased and is common throughout the unionized workplace. Since seniority is based on time in job, employment discrimination that kept certain workers from being hired is carried forward through seniority. If a factory before 1964 refused to hire black workers, then blacks hired after Title VII was enacted may have less seniority than if a nondiscriminatory hiring policy had always existed. During an economic decline, those black workers would be the first to be laid off because of their relatively low seniority.

The Civil Rights Act of 1964 contained a provision designed to protect bona fide seniority systems from the terms of Title VII. Those systems were deemed by Congress to be an important part of workplace harmony, and thus employment decisions based on a bona fide seniority system were not in violation of Title VII. However, questions arose concerning whether a seniority system that reflected pre-act employment discrimination could be considered "bona fide."

Teamsters v. United States
United States Supreme Court
431 U.S. 324 (1977)

The United States brought suit alleging that the Teamsters Union and T.I.M.E.-D.C., Inc., had engaged in a pattern or practice of discrimination against blacks and Spanish-surnamed persons. Bargaining-unit seniority determined the order in which employees were permitted to bid for jobs, were laid off, or were recalled from layoff. A line driver's seniority took into account only the length of time he had been a line driver at a particular terminal. When transferring to a line driver's job, all employees forfeited all seniority accumulated in a previous position. Before the passage of the 1964 Civil Rights Act, blacks and Spanish-surnamed persons had been denied an equal opportunity to become line drivers. The government contended the employees should receive retroactive seniority dating to the time the employee was hired, as the seniority system locked in past discrimination. The union and company argued retroactive seniority could not be granted because of pre-act discrimination, in light of the fact that the company granted seniority based on a bona fide seniority plan. The lower courts ruled for the government. The Supreme Court reversed.

Justice Stewart

Because the company discriminated both before and after the enactment of Title VII, the seniority system is said to have operated to perpetuate the effects of both pre- and post-Act discrimination. Post-Act discriminatees, however, may obtain full "make whole" relief, including retroactive seniority, without attacking the legality of the seniority system as applied to them. Retroactive seniority may be awarded as relief from an employer's discriminatory hiring and assignment policies even if the seniority system agreement itself makes no provision for such relief. Here the government has proved that the company engaged in a post-Act pattern of discriminatory hiring, assignment, transfer, and promotion policies. Any Negro or Spanish-surnamed American injured by those policies may receive all appropriate relief as a direct remedy for this discrimination.

What remains for review is the judgment that the seniority system unlawfully perpetuated the effects of pre-Act discrimination. We must decide, in short, whether Section 703(h) validates otherwise bona fide seniority systems that afford no constructive seniority to victims discriminated against prior to the effective date of Title VII, and it is to that issue that we now turn.

Throughout the initial consideration of H.R. 7152, later enacted as the Civil Rights Act of 1964, critics of the bill charged that it would destroy existing seniority rights. The consistent response of Title VII's congressional proponents and of the

Justice Department was that seniority rights would not be affected even where the employer had discriminated prior to the Act.

In sum, the unmistakable purpose of Section 703(h) was to make clear that the routine application of a bona fide seniority system would not be unlawful under Title VII. As the legislative history shows, this was the intended result even where the employer's pre-Act discrimination resulted in whites having greater seniority rights than Negroes. Although a seniority system inevitably tends to perpetuate the effects of pre-Act discrimination in such cases, the congressional judgment was that Title VII should not outlaw the use of existing seniority lists and thereby destroy or water down the vested seniority rights of employees simply because their employer had engaged in discrimination prior to the passage of the Act.

To be sure, Section 703(h) does not immunize all seniority systems. It refers only to "bona fide" systems, and a proviso requires that any differences in treatment not be "the result of an intention to discriminate because of race . . . or national origin. . . ." But our reading of the legislative history compels us to reject the Government's broad argument that no seniority system that tends to perpetuate pre-Act discrimination can be "bona fide." We hold that an otherwise neutral, legitimate seniority system does not become unlawful under Title VII simply because it may perpetuate pre-Act discrimination. Congress did not intend to make it illegal for employees with vested seniority rights to continue to exercise those rights, even at the expense of pre-Act discriminatees.

Because the seniority system was protected by Section 703(h), the union's conduct in agreeing to the maintaining the system did not violate Title VII. On remand, the District Court's injunction against the union must be vacated.

Comparable Worth. The first governmental use of **comparable worth** appeared in 1942, when the National War Labor Board issued General Order Number 16 allowing employers to adjust pay to equalize male and female wage rates. However, when Congress adopted the Equal Pay Act in 1963, the issue of comparable worth was considered and rejected in favor of requiring equal pay for equal work.

The current theory of comparable worth developed in response to the belief that, because of a variety of factors, women are underpaid in comparison with men. Comparable worth is a principle of wage determination involving the evaluation of the worth or value of an employee's job and the relative value of that job compared to all others within the company. Those who espouse the comparable worth doctrine argue that employees who perform work of comparable value to their employer should receive equal pay, even though the jobs being compared are not the same.

Proponents of comparable worth argue that market-based wage rates perpetrate past, pre-1964 discrimination against women, when many high-paying jobs were closed to women. Typical jobs that were available, such as secretary or nurse, attracted primarily women and were relatively low paying. The low pay, proponents argue, resulted from the fact that these jobs were considered women's work. Today, those jobs remain relatively low paying.

Opponents of the theory dispute that the value of jobs can be measured independently of the workings of the market. Another layer of bureaucracy would be needed to assess and compare the worth of dissimilar work with their results being highly subjective and questionable. Although women as a group are paid less than men, the comparable worth theory is seen as unfit to address that problem.

One question, however, is whether a wage system that was begun when sex discrimination was practiced can be applied if it carries forward discriminatory pay inequities. Does the use of market wages instead of comparable worth theory violate Title VII?

American Federation of State, County, and Municipal Employees v. State of Washington

United States Court of Appeals, Ninth Circuit
770 F.2d 1401 (1985)

In 1974, the state commissioned a study to determine whether a wage disparity existed between employees in jobs held predominately by women and jobs held predominately by men. The study examined sixty-two classifications in which at least seventy percent of the employees were men. It found a wage disparity of about twenty percent, to the disadvantage of employees in jobs held mostly by women, for jobs considered of comparable worth. The state of Washington conducted similar studies in 1976 and 1980, and in 1983, the state enacted legislation providing for a compensation scheme based on comparable worth. The scheme is to take effect over a ten-year period.

In 1982, AFSCME brought this action in the district court, seeking immediate implementation of a system of compensation based on comparable worth. The district court found the state discriminated on the basis of sex in violation of Title VII of the Civil Rights Act of 1964, by compensating employees in jobs where females predominate at lower rates than employees in jobs where males predominate, if these jobs, though dissimilar, were identified by certain studies to be of comparable worth. The state appealed. The court of appeals held that a violation of Title VII was not established.

Kennedy, Circuit Judge

AFSCME alleges sex-based wage discrimination throughout the state system, but its explanation and proof of the violation is, in essence, Washington's failure as early as 1979 to adopt and implement at once a comparable worth compensation program. The comparable worth theory, as developed in a case before us, postulates that sex-based wage discrimination exists if employees in job classifications occupied primarily by women are paid less than employees in job classifications filled primarily by men, if the jobs are of equal value to the employer, though otherwise dissimilar. . . .

AFSCME contends discriminatory motive may be inferred from the study, which finds the State's practice of setting salaries in reliance on market rates creates a sex-biased wage disparity for jobs deemed of comparable worth. AFSCME argues from the study that the market reflects a historical pattern of lower wages to employees in positions staffed predominately by women; and it contends the State of Washington perpetuates that disparity, in violation of Title VII, by using market rates in the compensation system. The inference of discriminatory motive which AFSCME seeks to draw from the State's participation in the market system fails, as the State did not create the market disparity and considerations in setting salaries.

Neither law nor logic deems the free market system a suspect enterprise. Economic reality is that the value of a particular job to an employer is but one factor influencing the rate of compensation for that job. Other considerations may include the availability of workers willing to do the job and the effectiveness of collective bargaining in a particular industry. We recognize that employers may be constrained by market forces to set salaries under prevailing wage rates for different job classifications. We find nothing in the language of Title VII or its legislative history to indicate Congress intended to abrogate fundamental economic principles such as the laws of supply and demand or to prevent employers from competing in the labor market.

While the Washington legislature may have the discretion to enact a comparable worth plan if it chooses to do so, Title VII does not obligate it to eliminate an economic inequality which it did not create.

The final theory of discrimination that arises under Title VII only involves discrimination based upon religion. In 1972, the Civil Rights Act was amended to impose an additional requirement on employers whose policies have the effect of discrimi-

Reasonable Accommodation

nating against a person because of religion. The employer was placed under a duty to reasonably accommodate an employee's religious beliefs unless doing so would cause undue hardship.

Most of the cases that have arisen under this theory have involved workers whose beliefs forbade Saturday work. Like the case following, those cases have not required the employer to go to extraordinary lengths to accommodate those workers. However, the courts do note any reasonable attempts that have been made in such cases.

Trans World Airlines v. Hardison
United States Supreme Court
431 U.S. 324 (1977)

The following case arises from a dispute between Trans World Airlines and an employee, Hardison. Hardison started to work at the overhaul base on June 5, 1967. In the spring of 1968, he began to study religion under the Worldwide Church of God. One of its tenets is that people must not work from sunset on Friday until sunset on Saturday. Hardison informed the manager of his religious beliefs. TWA found Hardison a job that permitted him to observe his religious beliefs. Hardison then bid for and received another job in another building. The two buildings had separate seniority lists. Hardison lacked enough seniority to qualify for a schedule that permitted work at a time he desired. TWA tried to accommodate his religious beliefs, but was unable to do so because of the seniority list. Hardison refused to report for work on Saturdays. TWA fired him. He then brought charges of religious discrimination against TWA. The trial court ruled for TWA. The Eighth Circuit Court of Appeals ruled for Hardison. The Supreme Court ruled for TWA.

Justice White

It might be inferred from the Court of Appeals' opinion and from the brief of the EEOC in this Court that TWA's efforts to accommodate were no more than negligible. The findings of the District Court, supported by the record, are to the contrary. In summarizing its more detailed findings, the District Court observed:

"TWA established as a matter of fact that it did take appropriate action to accommodate as required by Title VII. It held several meetings with plaintiff at which it attempted to find a solution to plaintiff's problems. It did accommodate plaintiff's observance of his special religious holidays. It authorized the union steward to search for someone who would swap shifts, which apparently was normal procedure."

It is also true that TWA itself attempted without success to find Hardison another job. The District Court's view was that TWA had done all that could reasonably be expected within the bounds of the seniority system.

As will become apparent, the seniority system represents a neutral way of minimizing the number of occasions when an employee must work on a day that he would prefer to have off. Additionally, recognizing that weekend work schedules are the least popular, the company made further accommodation by reducing its work force to a bare minimum on those days.

Hardison and the EEOC insist that the statutory obligation to accommodate religious needs takes precedence over both the collective-bargaining contract and the seniority rights of TWA's other employees. We agree that neither a collective-bargaining contract nor a seniority system may be employed to violate the statute, but we do not believe that the duty to accommodate requires TWA to take steps inconsistent with the otherwise valid agreement. Collective bargaining, aimed at effecting workable and enforceable agreements between management and labor, lies at the core of our national labor policy, and seniority provisions are universally included in the contracts. Without a clear and express indication from Congress, we cannot agree with Hardison and the EEOC that an agreed-upon seniority system must give way when necessary to accommodate religious observances. To require TWA to bear more than a de minimus cost in order to give Hardison Saturdays off is an undue hardship. Like abandonment of the seniority system, to require TWA to bear additional costs when no such costs are incurred to give other employees the days off that they want would involve unequal treatment of employees on the basis of their religion. By suggesting that TWA should incur certain costs in order to give Hardison Saturdays off the Court of Appeals would in effect require TWA to finance an additional Saturday off and then to choose the employee who will enjoy it on the basis of his religious beliefs. While incurring extra costs to secure a replacement for Hardison might remove the necessity of compelling another employee to work involuntarily in Hardison's place, it would not change the fact that the privilege of having Saturdays off would be allocated according to religious beliefs.

PERMITTED DISCRIMINATION: THE BONA FIDE OCCUPATIONAL QUALIFICATION

In certain circumstances, the Civil Rights Act permits disparate treatment in employment; that is, one of the Title VII categories may be used to distinguish between job applicants. The circumstance when the otherwise prohibited category may be used is when the characteristic is a **bona fide occupational qualification (BFOQ)**. Note however, that the BFOQ analysis does not apply to discrimination based on race or color. Its applicability is limited to employment decisions made on the basis of religion, sex, or national origin.

A bona fide occupational qualification arises when religion, sex, or national origin is a requirement that is reasonably necessary to operate the business. For example, a gym could hire only women to work in the women's locker room. Although a person of either sex could adequately perform the job of locker room attendant, the circumstances of the job create a business necessity that sex be used as a means to distinguish between job applicants.

Courts have narrowly construed the BFOQ exception to Title VII's discrimination prohibition. The employer has a heavy burden to establish a business necessity for a job qualification concerning sex, religion, or national origin. Three elements must be established before a BFOQ will be found.

First, there must be a connection between the classification (sex, religion, national origin) and job performance. Women, for example, were frequently denied certain job opportunities based on stereotyped or romantic notions. Thus, under the assumption that women were not aggressive, sales jobs were assigned to men. However, there is no link between the sex of a sales representative and the job of selling. Personal characteristics other than the sex of the applicant are central to that job.

Second, the classification must be necessary for the successful performance of the job. However, this necessity test is not to be based on customer or fellow employee preferences. For example, even if customers prefer female sales representatives, requiring that sales representative applicants be women will not generally be found to be necessary for the successful performance of the job. Instead, the classification itself must be somehow intertwined with the job. Hiring women for wet nurse positions or actors and actresses for certain roles needed to assure authenticity in a play are examples.

Finally, the job performance affected by the classification must be the "essense" of the employer's business. For example, in the case that follows, the "essense" of the airline's business is safe air transport. The tasks that women attendants may perform better than men (those requiring agility) are tangential to the safety aspect of the business. Thus, refusing to hire men flight attendants cannot be justified because the agility feature of the job is an insignificant part of the airline's business.

As suggested by this discussion, very few bona fide occupational qualifications will be found. Title VII was designed to remove stereotyping and replace it with measuring the individual for the job. The following case is an example of a claimed BFOQ that was not allowed.

Diaz v. Pan American World Airways, Inc.
United States Court of Appeals, Fifth Circuit
442 F.2d 385 (1971)

Celio Diaz applied for a job as flight cabin attendant with Pan American Airlines in 1967. He was rejected because Pan Am had an admitted policy of restricting its hiring for that position to females. Thus, both parties stipulated that the primary issue for the district court was whether, for the job of flight cabin attendant, being a female is a "bona fide occupational qualification reasonably necessary to the normal operation" of Pan American's business.

Having reviewed the evidence submitted by Pan American regarding its own experience with both female and male cabin attendants it had hired over the years, the trial court found that Pan Am's current hiring policy was the result of a pragmatic process "representing a judgment made upon adequate evidence acquired through Pan Am's considerable experience, and designed to yield under Pan Am's current operating conditions better average performance for its passengers than would a policy of mixed male and female hiring." The performance of female attendants was better in the sense that they were superior in such nonmechanical aspects of the job as "providing reassurance to anxious passengers, giving courteous personalized service and, in general, making flights as pleasurable as possible within the limitations imposed by aircraft operations."

The trial court also found that Pan Am's passengers overwhelmingly preferred to be served by female stewardesses. Moreover, on the basis of the expert testimony of a psychiatrist, the court found that an airplane cabin represents a unique environment in which an air carrier is required to take account of the special psychological needs of its passengers. These psychological needs are better attended to by females. This is not to say that there are no males who would not have the necessary qualities to perform these nonmechanical functions, but the trial court found that the actualities of the hiring process would make it more difficult to find these few males.

In what appears to be a summation of the difficulties which the trial court found would follow from admitting males to this job, the court said "that to eliminate the female sex qualification would simply eliminate the best available tool for screening out applicants likely to be unsatisfactory and thus reduce the average level of performance."

Tuttle, Circuit Judge

This appeal presents the important question of whether Pan American Airlines' refusal to hire appellant and his class of males solely on the basis of their sex violates Title VII of the 1964 Civil Rights Act. Because we feel that being a female is not a "bona fide occupational qualification" for the job of flight cabin attendant, appellee's refusal to hire appellant's class solely because of their sex, does constitute a violation of the Act.

We begin with the proposition that the use of the word "necessary" in section 703(e) requires that we apply a business necessity test, not a business convenience test. That is to say, discrimination based on sex is valid only when the essence of the business operation would be undermined by not hiring members of one sex exclusively.

The primary function of an airline is to transport passengers safely from one point to another. While a pleasant environment, enhanced by the obvious cosmetic effect that female stewardesses provide as well as, according to the finding of the trial court, their apparent ability to perform the non-mechanical functions of the job in a more effective manner than most men, may all be important, they are tangential to the essence of the business involved. No one has suggested that having male stewards will so seriously affect the operation of an airline as to jeopardize or even minimize its ability to provide safe transportation from one place to another.

We do not mean to imply, of course, that Pan Am cannot take into consideration the ability of individuals to perform the non-mechanical functions of the job. What we hold is that because of non-mechanical aspects of the job of flight cabin attendant are not "reasonably necessary to the normal operation" of Pan Am's business, Pan Am cannot exclude all males simply because most males may not perform adequately.

Before sex discrimination can be practiced, it must not only be shown that it is impracticable to find the men that possess the abilities that most women possess, but that the abilities are necessary to the business, not merely tangential.

Similarly, we do not feel that the fact that Pan Am's passengers prefer female stewardesses should alter our judgment. A BFOQ ought not be based on "the refusal to hire an individual because of the preferences of co-workers, the employer, clients or customers."

While we recognize that the public's expectation of finding one sex in a particular role may cause some initial difficulty, it would be totally anomalous if we were to allow the preferences and prejudices of the customers to determine whether the sex discrimination was valid. Indeed, it was, to a large extent, these very prejudices the Act was meant to overcome. Thus, we feel that customer preference may be taken into account only when it is based on the company's inability to perform the primary function or service it offers. The judgment is reversed.

DEVELOPMENTS IN EQUAL EMPLOYMENT LAW

Affirmative Action Plans

The issue of **affirmative action plans** illustrates a conflict between goals of Title VII. On the one hand, employees are to be free of job-related decisions based on their race, color, sex, religion, or national origin. Those decisions are to be based on neutral standards. However, victims of historical discriminatory practices are to be moved into the mainstream of economic life in America. Elimination of the gap in earnings between black and white workers as an effect of discrimination was an aim of the Civil Rights Act.

Minority workers have argued that simply removing the barriers to equal opportunity in employment is not enough. The lasting economic effects of long-term discrimination can be overcome only if they are given a fair share of the available positions. Affirmative action is needed to provide employment advantages to certain people to remedy the ingrained inequalities of long-term discrimination.

Critics of affirmative action focus on the color-blind or neutral standard goal of Title VII. By allowing preferences to be given to certain groups, the discrimination that the act meant to eliminate remains. Primarily white, male workers are made the new victims of discrimination. The real culprits, the decision makers, were doing the same thing under affirmative action that they did before the Civil Rights Act— using a person's race or sex as a means of assigning the benefits or burdens of society.

In 1979 the United States Supreme Court upheld a union-management voluntary affirmative action plan that was aimed at ending racial imbalance in Kaiser Aluminum Corporation's craft workforce. However, affirmative action as a legal issue was not settled by that case, *United Steelworkers* v. *Weber.* Cases and disputes continue to arise. The difficulty is in reconciling the dual goals of Title VII.

Johnson v. Transportation Agency, Santa Clara County

United States Supreme Court

55 U.S.L.W. 4379 (1987)

In December 1978, the Santa Clara County Transit District Board of Supervisors, adopted an Affirmative Action Plan (Plan) for the County Transportation Agency. In reviewing the composition of its work force, the Agency noted in its Plan that women were represented in numbers far less than their proportion of the county labor force in both the Agency as a whole and in five of seven job categories. The Agency stated that its Plan was intended to achieve a statistically measurable yearly improvement in hiring, training, and promoting women throughout the Agency in all major job classifications where they are underrepresented. Its long-term goal was to attain a work force whose composition reflected the proportion of women in the area labor force. The Agency's Plan set aside no specific number of positions for women, but authorized the consideration of sex as a factor when evaluating qualified candidates for jobs in which members of such groups were poorly represented.

On December 12, 1979, the Agency announced a vacancy for the promotional position of road dispatcher. Nine of the applicants, including Diane Joyce and Paul

Johnson, were deemed qualified for the job and were interviewed by a two-person board. Seven of the applicants scored above 70 on this interview, which meant that they were certified as eligible for selection. Johnson was tied for second with a score of 75, while Joyce ranked next with a score of 73. A second interview was conducted by three Agency supervisors, who ultimately recommended that Paul Johnson be promoted. Prior to the second interview, Joyce had contacted the County's Affirmative Action Office because she feared that her application might not receive disinterested review. Joyce testified that she had disagreements with two of the three members of the second interview panel. The Office in turn contacted the Agency's Affirmative Action Coordinator, whom the Agency's Plan makes responsible for keeping the agency director informed. At the time, the Agency employed no women in any Skilled Craft position and had never employed a woman as a road dispatcher. The Coordinator recommended to the Director of the Agency, James Graebner, that Diane Joyce be promoted. After deliberation, Graebner concluded that the promotion should be given to Joyce. Paul Johnson filed a complaint with the EEOC alleging that he had been denied promotion on the basis of sex in violation of Title VII.

Justice Brennan

The first issue is whether consideration of the sex of applicants for skilled craft jobs was justified by the existence of a "manifest imbalance" that reflected underrepresentation of women in "traditionally segregated job categories." The requirement that the "manifest imbalance" relate to a "traditionally segregated job category" provides assurance both that sex will be taken into account in a manner consistent with Title VII's purpose of eliminating the effects of employment discrimination and that the interests of those employees not benefitting from the plan will not be unduly infringed.

It is clear that the decision to hire Joyce was made pursuant to an Agency plan that acknowledged the limited opportunities that have existed in the past for women to find employment in certain job classifications where women have not been traditionally employed in significant numbers. The Plan sought to remedy these imbalances through hiring, training, and promoting women throughout the Agency in all major job classifications where they are underrepresented.

As an initial matter, the Agency adopted as a bench mark for measuring progress in eliminating underrepresentation the long-term goal of a work force that mirrored in its major job classifications the percentage of women in the area labor market. Even as it did so, however, the Agency acknowledged that such a figure could not by itself necessarily justify taking into account the sex of applicants for positions in all job categories. The Plan stressed that such goals should not be construed as 'quotas' that must be met, but as reasonable aspirations in correcting the imbalance in the Agency's work force. These goals were to take into account factors such as turnover, layoffs, lateral transfers, new job openings, retirements and availability of women in the area work force who possess the desired qualifications or potential for placement. The Plan specifically directed that, in establishing such goals, the Agency work with the County Planning Department and other sources in attempting to compile data on the percentage of women in the local labor force that were actually working in the job classifications comprising the Agency work force.

Had the Plan simply calculated imbalances in all categories according to the proportion of women in the area labor pool, and then directed that hiring be governed solely by those figures, its validity fairly could be called into question. This is because analysis of a more specialized labor pool normally is necessary in determining under-representation in some positions. If a plan failed to take distinctions in qualifications into account in providing guidance for actual employment decisions, it would dictate mere blind hiring by the numbers. The Agency's Plan emphatically did not authorize such blind hiring. It expressly directed that numerous factors be taken into account in making hiring decisions, including specifically the qualifications of female applicants for particular jobs. Thus, the Agency's management nevertheless had been clearly instructed that they were not to hire solely by reference to statistics.

Given the obvious imbalance in the Skilled Craft category, and given the Agency's commitment to eliminating such imbalances, it was plainly not unreasonable for the Agency to determine that it was appropriate to consider as one factor the sex of Ms. Joyce in making its decision. The promotion of Joyce thus satisfies the first requirement since it was undertaken to further an affirmative action plan designed to eliminate Agency work force imbalances in traditionally segregated job categories.

We next consider whether the Agency Plan unnecessarily trammeled the rights of male employees or created an absolute bar to their advancement. The Plan sets aside no positions for women. Rather, the Plan merely authorizes that consideration be given to affirmative action concerns when evaluating qualified applicants. As the Agency Director testified, the sex of Joyce was but one of numerous factors he took into account in arriving at his decision. The Agency Plan requires women to compete with all other qualified applicants. No persons are automatically excluded from consideration; all are able to have their qualifications weighed against those of other applicants.

Seven of the applicants were classified as qualified and eligible, and the Agency Director was authorized to promote any of the seven. Thus, denial of the promotion unsettled no legitimate firmly rooted expectation on the part of the petitioner Paul Johnson. Furthermore, while the petitioner in this case was denied a promotion, he retained his employment with the Agency, at the same salary and with the same seniority, and remained eligible for other promotions.

In this case, substantial evidence shows that the Agency has sought to take a moderate, gradual approach to eliminating the imbalance in its work force, one which establishes realistic guidance for employment decisions, and which visits minimal intrusion on the legitimate expectations of other employees. Given this fact, as well as the Agency's express commitment to "attain" a balanced work force, there is ample assurance that the Agency does not seek to use its Plan to maintain a permanent sexual balance.

We therefore hold that the Agency appropriately took into account as one factor the sex of Diane Joyce in determining that she should be promoted to the road dispatcher position. The decision to do so was made pursuant to an affirmative action plan that represents a moderate, flexible, case-by-case approach to effecting a gradual improvement in the representation of women in the Agency's work force. Such a plan is fully consistent with Title VII, for it embodies the contribution that voluntary employer action can make in eliminating the vestiges of discrimination in the workplace.

Sexual Harassment

Sexual harassment is one of the major issues in employment law today. As more women have entered the workplace, concern has arisen about unwanted advances or demands for sexual favors as a condition of employment. Such conduct violates Title VII of the Civil Rights Act of 1964.

The Equal Employment Opportunity Commission has promulgated guidelines in this area. The EEOC defines sexual harassment as follows:

Harassment on the basis of sex is a violation of Sec. 703 of Title VII. Unwelcome sexual advances, requests for sexual favors, and other verbal or physical conduct of a sexual nature constitute sexual harassment when (1) submission to such conduct is made either explicitly or implicitly a term or condition of an individual's employment, (2) submission to or rejections of such conduct by an individual is used as the basis for employment decisions affecting such individual, or (3) such conduct has the purpose or effect of unreasonably interfering with an individual's work performance or creating an intimidating, hostile or offensive working environment.

Sexual harassment is an abuse of power. Often the cases involve a supervisor exploiting his authority by preying on women employees under his control. The victim is forced to choose between tolerating or submitting to the employer's demands or risking disciplinary action. However, a violation might also occur if the workplace environment becomes intolerable because of activities of fellow employees. Jokes, slurs, comments, leers, and the like may so burden the workplace that working there becomes insufferable.

Note that although most sexual harassment cases have a woman victim, the principles also apply to men. In a case from Wisconsin, a jury awarded damages to a male employee who was demoted because he rejected a female supervisor's sexual advances.

Cases involving sexual harassment often name the employer as a defendant. Some courts held that an employer's liability for sexual harassment on the job went beyond traditional agency principles. In order to encourage the employer to insure that those practices were eliminated, a standard of absolute liability was adopted. The following case, from the United States Supreme Court, rejects the theory that employers are absolutely liable for sexual harassment in the workplace.

Meritor Savings Bank v. Vinson
United States Supreme Court
54 U.S.L.W. 4703 (1986)

In 1974, respondent Mechelle Vinson met Sidney Taylor, a vice-president of what is now petitioner Meritor Savings Bank and manager of one of its branch offices. When respondent asked whether she might obtain employment at the bank, Taylor gave her an application, which she completed and returned the next day; later that same day Taylor called her to say that she had been hired. With Taylor as her supervisor, respondent started as a teller-trainee, and thereafter was promoted to teller, head teller, and assistant branch manager. She worked at the same branch for four years, and it is undisputed that her advancement there was based on merit alone. In September 1978, respondent notified Taylor that she was taking sick leave for an indefinite period. On November 1, 1978, the bank discharged her for excessive use of that leave.

Respondent brought this action against Taylor and the bank, claiming that during her four years at the bank she had "constantly been subjected to sexual harassment" by Taylor in violation of Title VII. Respondent testified that during her probationary period as a teller-trainee, Taylor treated her in a fatherly way and made no sexual advances. Shortly thereafter, however, he invited her out to dinner and, during the course of the meal, suggested that they go to a motel to have sexual relations. At first she refused, but out of what she described as fear of losing her job, she eventually agreed. According to respondent, Taylor thereafter made repeated demands upon her for sexual favors, usually at the branch, both during and after business hours. She estimated that over the next several years she had intercourse with him some forty or fifty times. In addition, respondent testified that Taylor fondled her in front of other employees, followed her into the women's restroom when she went there alone, exposed himself to her, and even forcibly raped her on several occasions. These activities ceased after 1977, respondent stated, when she started going with a steady boyfriend. Finally, respondent testified that because she was afraid of Taylor she never reported his harassment to any of his supervisors and never attempted to use the bank's complaint procedure.

Taylor denied respondent's allegations of sexual activity, testifying that he never fondled her, never made suggestive remarks to her, never engaged in sexual intercourse with her, and never asked her to do so. He contended instead that respondent made her accusations in response to a business-related dispute. The bank also denied respondent's allegations and asserted that any sexual harassment by Taylor was unknown to the bank and engaged in without its consent or approval.

Although it concluded that respondent had not proved a violation of Title VII, the district court nevertheless went on to address the bank's liability. After noting the bank's express policy against discrimination and finding that neither respondent nor any other employee had ever lodged a complaint about sexual harassment by Taylor, the court ultimately concluded that "the bank was without notice and cannot be held liable for the alleged actions of Taylor.

The court of appeals for the District of Columbia Circuit reversed.

Justice Rehnquist

This case presents important questions concerning claims of workplace "sexual harassment" brought under Title VII of the Civil Rights Act of 1964.

Title VII of the Civil Rights Act of 1964 makes it "an unlawful employment practice for an employer . . . to discriminate against any individual with respect to his compensation, terms, conditions, or privileges of employment, because of such individual's race, color, religion, sex, or national origin." Without question, when a supervisor sexually harasses a subordinate because of the subordinate's sex, that supervisor "discriminate[s]" on the basis of sex. Petitioner apparently does not challenge this proposition. It contends instead that in prohibiting discrimination with re-

spect to "compensation, terms, conditions, or privileges" of employment, Congress was concerned with what petitioner describes as "tangible loss" of "an economic character," not "purely psychological aspects of the workplace environment."

We reject petitioner's view. First, the language of Title VII is not limited to "economic" or "tangible" discrimination. The phrase "terms, conditions, or privileges of employment" evinces a congressional intent "to strike at the entire spectrum of disparate treatment of men and women" in employment. Second, the EEOC guidelines fully support the view that harassment leading to non-economic injury can violate Title VII. The EEOC drew upon a substantial body of judicial decisions and EEOC precedent holding that Title VII affords employees the right to work in an environment free from discriminatory intimidation, ridicule, and insult.

Since the guidelines were issued, courts have uniformly held, and we agree, that a plaintiff may establish a violation of Title VII by proving that discrimination based on sex has created a hostile or abusive work environment.

For sexual harassment to be actionable, it must be sufficiently severe or pervasive "to alter the conditions of [the victim's] employment and create an abusive working environment." Respondent's allegations in this case—which include not only pervasive harassment but also criminal conduct of the most serious nature—are plainly sufficient to state a claim for "hostile environment" sexual harassment.

The District Court's conclusion that no actionable harassment occurred might have rested on its earlier "finding" that "[i]f [respondent] and Taylor did engage in an intimate or sexual relationship . . . that relationship was a voluntary one." But the fact that sex-related conduct was "voluntary," in the sense that the complainant was not forced to participate against her will, is not a defense to a sexual harassment suit brought under Title VII. The gravamen of any sexual harassment claim is that the alleged sexual advances were "unwelcome." The correct inquiry is whether respondent by her conduct indicated that the alleged sexual advances were unwelcome, not whether her actual participation in sexual intercourse was voluntary.

Although the District Court concluded that respondent had not proved a violation of Title VII, it nevertheless went on to consider the question of the bank's liability. Finding that "the bank was without notice" of Taylor's alleged conduct, and that notice to Taylor was not the equivalent of notice to the bank, the court concluded that the bank therefore could not be held liable for Taylor's alleged actions. The Court of Appeals took the opposite view, holding that an employer is strictly liable for a hostile environment created by a supervisor's sexual advances, even though the employer neither knew nor reasonably could have known of the alleged misconduct. The court held that a supervisor, whether or not he possesses the authority to hire, fire, or promote, is necessarily an "agent" of his employer for all Title VII purposes, since "even the appearance" of such authority may enable him to impose himself on his subordinates.

The EEOC, in its brief as amicus curiae, contends that courts formulating employer liability rules should draw from traditional agency principles. Examination of those principles has led the EEOC to the view that where a supervisor exercises the authority actually delegated to him by his employer, by making or threatening to make decisions affecting the employment status of his subordinates, such actions are properly imputed to the employer whose delegation of authority empowered the supervisor to undertake them. Thus, the courts have consistently held employers liable for the discriminatory discharges of employees by supervisory personnel, whether or not the employer knew, should have known, or approved of the supervisor's actions.

This debate over the appropriate standard for employer liability has a rather abstract quality about it given the state of the record in this case. We do not know at this stage, whether Taylor made any sexual advances toward respondent at all, let alone whether those advances were unwelcome, whether they were sufficiently pervasive to constitute a condition of employment, or whether they were "so pervasive and so long continuing . . . that the employer must have become conscious of [them]."

We therefore decline the parties' invitation to issue a definitive rule on employer liability, but we do agree with the EEOC that Congress wanted courts to look to agency principles for guidance in this area. While such common-law principles may not be transferable in all their particulars to Title VII, Congress' decision to define "employer" to include any "agent" of an employer, surely evinces an intent to place some limits on the acts of employees for which employers under Title VII are to be held responsible. For this reason, we hold that the Court of Appeals erred in concluding that employers are always automatically liable for sexual harassment by their supervisors. For the same reason, absence of notice to an employer does not necessarily insulate that employer from liability.

Finally, we reject petitioner's view that the mere existence of a grievance procedure and a policy against discrimination, coupled with respondent's failure to invoke that procedure, must insulate petitioner from liability. While those facts are plainly relevant, the situation before us demonstrates why they are not necessarily dispositive. Petitioner's general nondiscrimination policy did not address sexual harassment in particular, and thus did not alert employees to their employer's interest in correcting that form of discrimination. Moreover, the bank's grievance procedure apparently required an employee to complain first to her supervisor, in this case Taylor. Since Taylor was the alleged perpetrator, it is not altogether surprising that respondent failed to invoke the procedure and report her grievance to him. Petitioner's contention that respondent's failure should insulate it from liability might be substantially stronger if its procedures were better calculated to encourage victims of harassment to come forward.

Accordingly, the judgment of the Court of Appeals reversing the judgment of the District Court is affirmed.

SUMMARY   For many years, a large segment of society struggled to overcome unfair treatment. Although the Supreme Court outlawed racial segregation in *Brown* v. *Board of Education,* the decision failed to address the problem of discrimination in the workplace. While the civil rights movement took a giant stride forward as a result of *Brown,* many people still dealt with discrimination on a day-to-day basis—particularly in getting and keeping a good job.

Title VII of the Civil Rights Act of 1964 prohibited employment discrimination based on race, color, religion, sex, or national origin. Needless to say, passing legislation failed to stop discrimination. Consequently, litigation continues to arise over unfair employment practices.

Four theories of Title VII discrimination have been advanced. They involve both direct and indirect forms of discrimination. Note that even benign employment practices may have the effect of discriminating and therefore violate the act.

Two major issues continue to arise under Title VII. The first is affirmative action, which involves the conflict between the policies of individual treatment and economic gains for the disadvantaged that are contained in the act. The second issue is sexual harassment. Sexual harassment involves an abuse of power in which employees are victimized based on their sex.

REVIEW QUESTIONS

1. Define these terms:
   a. Equal Employment Opportunity Commission
   b. Bona fide occupational qualification
   c. Affirmative action plans
   d. Sexual harassment
   e. Comparable worth

2. Why should employers be held liable for sexually harassing actions of their employees?

3. The Southern Pacific Co. refused to hire Ann Rosenfeld as an agent telegrapher. It argued that because of the arduous nature of the work, women were physically unsuited for the jobs.

At times, the job requires work in excess of ten hours a day and eighty hours a week. It requires heavy physical effort, such as lifting objects weighing more than twenty-five pounds. May the company refuse to hire Ann Rosenfeld for this position?

4. Mary Tomkins, an employee of Public Service Electric and Gas Co., progressed to positions of increasing responsibility. On October 30, 1973, Mary's supervisor asked her to go to lunch to discuss his upcoming evaluation of her. At lunch, he indicated his desire to have sexual relations with her. He stated this would be necessary if they were to have a satisfactory working relationship. Tomkins alleged that PSE&G knew or should have known that such incidents would occur. She was subsequently demoted and subjected to pressure from other employees. In 1975, she was fired. Does she have a case?

5. Fernandez was a female employee of Wynn Oil Company. When she lost a promotion to a male employee, she alleged sex discrimination in violation of Title VII of the Civil Rights Act of 1964. Wynn alleged that Fernandez lacked the qualifications necessary for the job. She lacked proficiency in the English language, had difficulty with articulation, had no secondary education, a drinking problem, and erratic work habits. Alternatively, Wynn argued the male sex was a bona fide occupational qualification for a job performed in foreign countries where women are barred from business. Who should prevail?

6. Donnell, a black employee of General Motors, sought entrance into two skilled trades training programs established by GM. GM required a high school degree. Donnell asserted such a requirement violated Title VII because it operated to disqualify more blacks than whites and was not justified as a business necessity. Only .3 percent of black employees were in skilled trades, while 3.2 percent of the white

employees were in skilled trade positions. Did the educational requirement violate Title VII?

7. Rawlinson was a twenty-two-year-old female applying as a prison guard trainee at an Alabama penitentiary. She was rejected because she failed to meet the 120-pound weight requirement of an Alabama statute, which also established a height minimum of five feet two inches. Only men were allowed to be prison guards where there was close contact with prisoners. Rawlinson asserted this practice violated Title VII. The Alabama statute would exclude 33.2 percent of the women in the United States between the ages of eighteen and seventy-nine while excluding only 1.28 percent of the men in the same age group. Does this statute violate Title VII?

8. Female matrons who worked at the Washington County jail in Oregon brought suit against the county, maintaining that although their jobs were comparable (not equal) in skill, effort, responsibility, and working conditions to the male-held guard jobs, the women were paid less money. The matrons argued that part of the pay disparity could only be explained by sex discrimination. Do the matrons have a case?

9. Discuss the historical background of Title VII of the Civil Rights Act of 1964.

10. Jenkins works in an accounting firm. Recently he has become active in the gay rights movement and has acknowledged his homosexuality. Soon thereafter Jenkins is fired because the accounting firm is concerned that its clients will object to a known homosexual working on their behalf. Does Jenkins have a claim under Title VII?

11. Smith belongs to a conservative Baptist church. He is considered a religious fundamentalist. Smith works for ABC Corporation as a sales representative and is being consid-

ered, along with twelve other candidates, for a promotion to a sales management position. The candidates are evaluated by their corporate supervisors and a committee of three vice-presidents that interviews each candidate. Each candidate is rated from one to ten by the evaluators. The candidate with the highest score is given the promotion. One of the evaluators gives Smith the lowest possible score; he rated very high with the others. This evaluator disagrees with the political positions of certain prominent fundamentalist ministers. He is concerned that Smith will use his management position as a forum for his religious beliefs and create discord in the company even though Smith had never done so before. ABC knew about this evaluator's views, but did nothing. Would Smith have a claim against ABC under Title VII? Explain.

12. XYZ Corporation had a policy not to hire any black workers until they were sued in 1971 under Title VII of the Civil Rights Act. Thereafter, the corporation eliminated the policy. However, it instituted a new policy that required all new employees to be recommended by at least two current or retired XYZ employees. Would this rule raise problems for the corporation under Title VII?

13. Mary Jones is an athletic trainer. She has studied, taught, and worked for a number of years in the specialty of athletic injuries. She has one of the finest backgrounds for this type of work in the country. Jones applies to be an assistant trainer with a National Football League team. Each NFL team has four assistant trainers. Usually only one assistant trainer is present at each game; the assistant trainers work out a game rotation schedule.

Because of her religion, Jones informs the team that she will not be able to work for them on Sundays. Because of this, the team refuses to consider her application. Does Jones have a claim under Title VII?

14. Discuss the concept of affirmative action as it relates to the goals of Title VII of the Civil Rights Act of 1964. What problems and benefits can be noted for those affected by affirmative action plans?

CHAPTER 23

Environmental Law

What Is the Environment?
Legal Control of Environmental Pollution

Few areas of government activity have had as great an effect on all aspects of business as environmental regulation. Nonetheless, environmental regulation is rather new and still evolving as more pollution problems are discovered. Although the federal environmental statutes and the activities of the Environmental Protection Agency (EPA) are more widely known, state and local governments also act to protect the environment.

This chapter will present environmental law in three sections, beginning with a general discussion of the environment and pollution. Thereafter, a discussion of state and local efforts will be undertaken. Note the inherent conflict between the geographical jurisdiction of those levels of government and the nature of pollution. Finally, the chapter will focus on federal regulation. This discussion will not provide a specific statute-by-statute commentary on the various types of pollution regulated by law. Instead, the basic approach of federal regulation will be defined, and major issues will be noted to illustrate the effect of this body of law on business. Recognize that traditional business concerns such as economics, cost, and the availability of technology may not outweigh social concerns for a clean environment.

WHAT IS THE ENVIRONMENT?

The environment consists of all the physical elements of the world except human beings. A study of environmental laws, therefore, is a study of the regulation of human conduct in relation to air, water, land, plant and animal life, and natural resources. Environmental law acts to protect the environment in order to preserve it for people to use and enjoy.

Three major benefits or functions of the environment may be noted. First, the environment provides a place for life. Clean air and pure water are essentials to human life and health. The land is also essential in that it provides minerals and

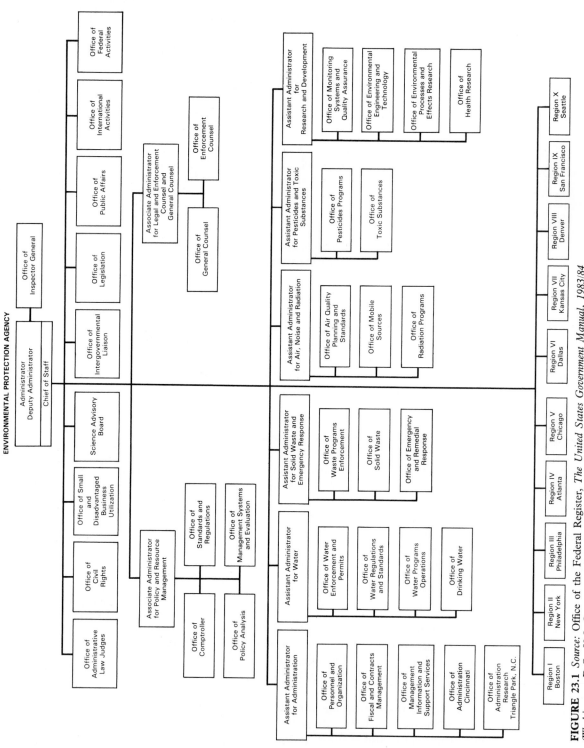

FIGURE 23.1 *Source:* Office of the Federal Register, *The United States Government Manual, 1983/84* (Washington, D.C.: U.S. Government Printing Office, 1983).

animal and plant life for food and shelter. Environmental regulation, therefore, reflects a concern of the legal system for the survival of human life.

A second important function of the environment is to provide resources needed for the production of goods. Clothing, houses, office buildings, books, televisions, automobiles, and countless other products are derived from the environment. Environmental law seeks to preserve and manage our resources. Waste management regulation and controls on the use of pesticides are examples of such laws.

A final function of the environment is to symbolize or personify certain intangible qualities that are important to people. These qualities include the majesty of a range of snow-capped mountains, the tranquility of a pine forest, and the timelessness of the sea crashing into a rocky coastline. Environmental law seeks to preserve these qualities of nature. National parks, wildlife refuges, and other controls on land use are examples of the law protecting the intangible qualities of the environment.

The environment, therefore, provides a broad range of benefits. Not surprisingly, the environmental statutes that encompass those benefits and the various policies of those statutes may at times create conflict. One commentator identified four goals promoted by the environmental statutes: first, to protect the environment; second, to provide recreational opportunities (e.g., national parks); third, to avoid social dislocation that would result from excessive environmental controls; and fourth, to promote economic growth.

Thus, understanding the nature of the environment is the first step in the study of environmental law. Although providing a clean environment is a major facet of the laws, the importance of economic growth and development is not to be ignored. The first task of the business manager, therefore, is to appreciate the breadth and complexity of the topic.

What Is Pollution? Pollution is more extensive than emitting particles into the air or dumping waste into a river. Pollution may be defined as the human-caused diminished capacity of the environment to perform its functions. This may involve dumping noxious chemicals into a groundwater supply, thereby making the water unsafe to drink. It may involve harvesting trees or planting crops in such a manner as to deplete the soil or encourage erosion. It may involve a mine that leaves a scar on the earth where rolling hills once existed. All these activities adversely affect one of the primary functions of the environment. All may be considered polluting and all are monitored by environmental laws.

Pollution

Concern over damage to the environment emerged during the 1960s. Some writers trace its origins to Rachel Carson's book, *Silent Spring*, which chronicled the harmful effect pesticides had on the environment. In addition, studies were published that predicted the death of all life in certain lakes and rivers. One river in Ohio, the Cuyahoga, was so polluted that it caught fire. Weather forecasts began to include reports on air quality as well as temperature and precipitation.

However, pollution is not a modern phenomena. In the late thirteenth century, smog was already a problem in London because soft coal was used for fuel. With the development of cannons in the fourteenth century came deforestation in some areas of Europe, caused by the newly created demand for potash, sulfur, iron ore, and charcoal.

THE ENVIRONMENTAL PROBLEM OF ACID RAIN

The interaction of certain pollutants, like sulphur dioxide and oxide of nitrogen, with the atmosphere can cause acid rain hundreds of miles from the source of that pollution. Acid rain refers to a high acid level pollution that is destroying forests and lakes. Until recently, the focus of the acid rain problem has been Eastern Canada and the Northeastern part of the United States. For example, Midwestern industries are suspected for emissions that have harmed forests and lakes in the Adirondack and Green Mountains. Now, the problem has been found in wilderness areas of the Rocky Mountains, the pine forests of the Southeast, and Southwestern deserts.

Trout populations in Rocky Mountain lakes decreased during both 1983 and 1984, while the acidity of the water increased to seventy times the average following the spring snow melt in those years. Pine tree girths in forestland of Georgia and North and South Carolina are smaller than in the early 1970s. The salamander population is decreasing in the mountains of Arizona and New Mexico. Salamanders are affected by increased acidity.

Current environmental regulations are ineffective in controlling this pollution that may have originated in a distant state or a foreign country. For example, environmentalists found that the acid levels of snow in Wyoming and Idaho dropped significantly during work stoppages at ore smelters in Arizona and New Mexico. Concerns are also being expressed about emissions from a new copper smelter in Nacozari, Mexico, about sixty miles from the Arizona border.

The Reagan administration is reluctant to impose new clean air regulations aimed at acid rain. Scientists have not yet determined the exact cause of acid rain, although environmentalists point to certain industry emissions. Furthermore, the estimated cost to industry of such controls could be twenty billion dollars. Executives from Phelps Dodge, for example, indicated that the cost of additional pollution control devices at its Douglas, Arizona, copper installation might force its closing.

The regulation of acid rain is still in dispute.

Causes of Pollution. Although pollution is not new, its extent and its consequences became very serious in the 1960s because of the convergence of four factors. One was high population densities. An old saying had been that a river cleansed itself every ten miles. This aphorism may have been true decades ago. A community of five thousand may have been able to dispose of its untreated sewage in a passing river without environmental harm. The river could naturally dispose of that level of waste. But as the community grew to thirty-five thousand, the dumping of the untreated sewage began to pollute. The river could no longer handle the increased waste. Larger numbers of people concentrated in smaller areas strained the capacity of the environment.

Not only did the community increase in population, but its members consumed more resources than their predecessors, a second factor in the ecology crisis. Modern appliances created a greater demand for electricity. Families that may have had one automobile began to acquire two or more. As personal income increased, people were able to afford more products and luxuries. Pollution occurs at each stage of the production cycle. It occurs in the making of the product, during its distribution, and in its consumption. As demand for products increased, so did the demands on the environment to supply the resources.

Business practices made up another major factor of the pollution problem. Factories that were built to meet increased demand spewed added particles into the air and dumped more waste into the water. New types of products and manufacturing processes created more deadly forms of pollutants. Disposable products (for example, beverage containers, cigarette lighters, pens) replaced reusable or returnable products. Nonbiodegradable plastic containers began to replace paper products.

A final factor in the ecology crisis was that the legal and economic systems did not discourage the use of the environment as a dumping ground. The firm that refused to use a river as a sewer would need to make additional expenditures in order to purify its wastes. Competitors who continued to pollute would have those funds available for alternative productive uses. Since the legal system did not prevent such dumping, the economic system, in a sense, rewarded those who chose the "free" method of waste disposal.

None of these factors was alone the culprit, but coming together they caused a crisis in the ability of the environment to fulfill its important functions. During the late 1960s and early 1970s, concern for the environment led the different levels of government to seek legal solutions to the problems of pollution.

LEGAL CONTROL OF ENVIRONMENTAL POLLUTION

Local Regulation. Local regulation of pollution occurs in a variety of ways. Zoning and land-use planning are frequently used to control property development—one of the goals being to reduce the risk of further pollution. For example, a few years ago, Tiburon, California, a small and wealthy suburban community, enacted an open-space zoning ordinance. The purpose of the ordinance was to limit the density of new housing. The community believed that overbuilding would lead to traffic congestion, environmental hazards, and destruction of scenic beauty. The ordinance was therefore a preventive measure. Instead of limiting its concern to the removal of environmental problems, the community sought to limit the occurrence of those problems. Thus, although federal environmental law did not affect density of housing, developers in Tiburon had their building decisions influenced by the local environmental open-space ordinance.

State and Local
Environmental
Regulation

Local governments have a variety of other tools to regulate the environment. Ordinances designed to limit the size of outdoor advertising signs and billboards work to preserve the aesthetic features of the local area. Antilitter ordinances and city offices, such as the parks and recreation department, work to eliminate wastes being dumped in the city. Some local governments require that public works projects be preceded by an analysis of the effect on the local environment.

The following case is an example of local (and state) regulation of noise pollution. Both the state of Illinois and the city of Chicago used their lawmaking powers to regulate certain noisy business activities in residential neighborhoods. The "incidental" effect of the regulation was to prevent the Chicago Cubs from playing night baseball games at Wrigley Field.

Chicago National League Ball Club v. Thompson
Supreme Court of Illinois
483 N.E.2d 1245 (1985)

The Chicago National League Ball Club, Inc., is a corporation which owns and operates the Chicago Cubs, the major league baseball team, and the Cubs' home ball park, Wrigley Field. On December 19, 1984, the Cubs challenged the constitutionality of a section of the Illinois Environmental Protection Act, since night baseball games at Wrigley Field would violate the nighttime-noise-emission regulations of the Pollution Control Board. All parties are agreed that the ordinance would have the effect of prohibiting night games at Wrigley Field. Wrigley Field is located on the north side of Chicago in the Lake View area. It is the only park in the major leagues that, because it does not have lights, does not have night games.

The area surrounding Wrigley Field is predominately residential, with some light industry to the south and west of the ball park. Most of the buildings in the area are multi-unit dwellings, which gives Lake View a highly concentrated population. There are no expressways in close proximity to Wrigley Field to accommodate the influx of spectators on days when games are played at the field, and there are few off-street parking facilities in the area. In general, only the neighborhood streets are available for parking.

Ward, Justice

It is clear that the legislature has broad discretion to determine not only what the public interest and welfare require, but to determine the measures needed to secure such interest. Here the legislature amended Section 25 of the Environmental Protection Act to establish guidelines for protecting the interests, including property interests, of residents who live near stadia from intolerable noise from nighttime sporting events. . . .

The declared purpose of Title VI of the Environmental Protection Act is "to prevent noise which creates a public nuisance." Forming a background to the legislation we consider here, Section 25 directs the Pollution Control Board to categorize the types and sources of noise emissions that unreasonably interfere with the enjoyment of life, or with any lawful business, or activity, and shall prescribe for each such category the maximum permissible limits on such noise emissions. The purpose of this amendment to the Act was to protect, within the comprehensive regulatory scheme, the property and other rights of residents who live near stadia by making the nighttime use of the stadia subject to the regulations of the Pollution Control Board.

Only stadia in cities with more than one million inhabitants are subject to the regulations. Chicago is the only city in our State that has a population of more than one million. Considering the terms of this statute, there is a rationally founded difference between a less populous city and a city with a greater population. It might be reasonably anticipated that in a typical urban setting more people would be affected in the larger city by the noise from spectators in a stadium for a nighttime event. The problems attending a densely populated area would be exacerbated: limited areas for parking would become overburdened; neighborhood streets would become busier and thus potentially more dangerous to residents of the area and their children; and thoroughfares to and from the area would become more congested. Too, a rational basis may be found in the concern that there would be less open space in an area with a highly concentrated population that could serve as a buffer zone against the noise generated.

The same considerations serve as a proper basis for the distinction made by the legislature between nighttime and daytime sporting events.

The General Assembly well might have concluded that the evening hours are traditionally spent in restful and quieter pursuits and should be protected by closer regulation. More residents would be at home during the evening hours, and there are variations in traffic patterns and in police patrol deployment between night and day hours which might have served as reasonable considerations by the legislature in enacting the statute.

Simply, the Cubs have failed to meet the burden of showing the unconstitutionality of the legislative actions.

The preceding case shows an example of local government pollution control. However, the power of local government is not unlimited. Zoning and other ordinances are limited to the local community that enacts them. Pollution problems may exist outside its boundaries or enter the community by air or water. Furthermore, there are both federal and state constitutional limits on a local community's power. For example, one community in California was concerned about noise pollution caused by the taking off and landing of airplanes at night. Therefore, the community enacted an ordinance restricting the nighttime use of its airport. However, the federal government has exclusive control of air traffic. Upon legal challenge, the ordinance fell, since the community was found to be unable to regulate an area from which the federal government excluded them.

State Regulation. State governments regulate pollution through legislation, administrative agency actions, and their judicial systems. A number of states have adopted a process in which written analyses must be prepared when any major state activity has an effect on the environment. This is a process similar to that adopted by some cities. Both city and state environmental analyses were patterned after the environmental impact statement requirements placed on the federal government by the National Environmental Policy Act of 1969. Some states have extended this requirement to private projects. In addition, laws have been enacted protecting ecologically sensitive areas (for example, shore and coastal regions). State agencies oversee parklands, wildlife, and soil and water conservation programs. These activities, too, regulate the use of the environment and may affect business decisions.

Legal rules involving contracts, torts, and property are primarily governed by state law. These legal rules are a part of the common law. Two common law doctrines that have been used to regulate pollution are the doctrines of trespass and nuisance. **Trespass** is an unauthorized, intentional entry upon the land of another. It may occur if someone walks across another's land or if one causes particles to enter the airspace above another person's land. For example, if Mary dumped trash on a field owned by Sam, Sam would have a common law trespass claim against Mary. **Nuisance** has been defined as an act that annoys or disturbs the enjoyment of a landowner's property. Acts that make the use of property physically uncomfortable, endanger the health, or revolt the senses are considered a nuisance. For example, Tom decides to burn some leaves. The smoke, fumes, and ash drift next door, polluting the air around Sally's home. Sally would have a nuisance claim against Tom. The residue from his burning lessens her ability to enjoy her property. In addition she would have a trespass claim, for the waste matter from Tom's burning invades her property—through its airspace.

A court in rendering a decision in either type of dispute may award monetary damages to the property owner to compensate for the nuisance or trespass injury. The court may also enter an injunction prohibiting further pollution.

Common law pollution remedies have a limited effect on regulating the environment. Litigation is time-consuming and costly. Even if a case is filed, the doctrines tend to break down when the polluting party is not an individual. For example, assume a large corporation, rather than Tom, had been burning its trash. The corporation has resources not only to defend the claim at trial, but also to appeal it through the judicial system. Sally may be unable to afford to compete. Furthermore, a monetary damage award to Sally will not stop the pollution unless it is worthwhile to the firm to choose an alternative means of trash disposal. She will have money as compensation, but will still have pollution. The remedy of an injunction—ordering the corporation to stop polluting—may have social effects far beyond the case. The company may be forced to close its plant or move its operations elsewhere. This cost often outweighs the benefit of permanently halting the nuisance.

The following case is an example of the common law approach to controlling pollution. Note the inherent limitations involved in judge-ordered environmental remedies.

Boomer v. Atlantic Cement Co.

Court of Appeals of New York
257 N.E.2d 870 (1970)

Bergan, Judge

Defendant operates a large cement plant near Albany. These are actions for injunction and damages by neighboring landowners alleging injury to property from dirt, smoke and vibration emanating from the plant. A nuisance has been found after trial, temporary damages have been allowed; but an injunction has been denied.

The public concern with air pollution arising from many sources in industry and in transportation is currently accorded ever wider recognition accompanied by a growing sense of responsibility in State and Federal Governments to control it. Cement plants are obvious sources of air pollution in the neighborhoods where they operate.

But there is now before the court private litigation in which individual property owners have sought specific relief from a single plant operation. The threshold question raised by the division of view on this appeal is whether the court should resolve the litigation between the parties now before it as equitably as seems possible; or whether, seeking promotion of the general public welfare, it should channel private litigation into broad public objectives.

It seems apparent that the amelioration of air pollution will depend on technical research in great depth; on a carefully balanced consideration of the economic impact of close regulation; and of the actual effect on public health. It is likely to require massive public expenditure and to demand more than any local community can accomplish and to depend on regional and interstate controls.

A court should not try to do this on its own as a by-product of private litigation and it seems manifest that the judicial establishment is neither equipped in the limited nature of any judgment it can pronounce nor prepared to lay down and implement an effective policy for the elimination of air pollution. This is an area beyond the circumference of one private lawsuit. It is a direct responsibility for government and should not thus be undertaken as an incident to solving a dispute between property owners and a single cement plant—one of many—in the Hudson River valley.

The rule in New York has been that a nuisance will be enjoined although marked disparity be shown in economic consequence between the effect of the injunction and the effect of the nuisance.

But to follow the rule literally would be to close down the plant at once. This court is fully

agreed to avoid that immediately drastic remedy; the difference in view is how best to avoid it.

To grant the injunction unless defendant pays plaintiffs permanent damages as may be fixed by the court seems to do justice between the contending parties. All of the attributions of economic loss to the properties on which plaintiffs' complaints are based will have been redressed.

The nuisance complained of by these plaintiffs may have other public or private consequences, but these particular parties are the only ones who have sought remedies and the judgment proposed will fully redress them.

It seems fair to both sides to grant permanent damages to plaintiffs which will terminate this private litigation. The theory of damage is the "servitude on land" of plaintiffs imposed by defendant's nuisance.

The judgment, by allowance of permanent damages imposing a servitude on land, which is the basis of the actions, would preclude future recovery by plaintiffs or their grantees.

Jasen, Judge (dissenting)

It has long been the rule in this State that a nuisance which results in substantial continuing damage to neighbors must be enjoined. To now change the rule to permit the cement company to continue polluting the air indefinitely upon the payment of permanent damages is, in my opinion, compounding the magnitude of a very serious problem in our State and Nation today.

I see grave dangers in overruling our long-established rule of granting an injunction where a nuisance results in substantial continuing damage. In permitting the injunction to become inoperative upon payment of permanent damages, the major-

ity is, in effect, licensing a continuing wrong. It is the same as saying to the cement company, you may continue to do harm to your neighbors so long as you pay a fee for it. Furthermore, once such permanent damages are assessed and paid, the incentive to alleviate the wrong would be eliminated, thereby continuing air pollution of an area without abatement.

In a day when there is a growing concern for clean air, highly developed industry should not expect acquiescence by the courts, but should, instead, plan its operations to eliminate contamination of our air and damage to its neighbors.

Federal environmental law may be divided into two categories. One is a full disclosure of the environmental effects of major federal activity. The second category consists of a number of statutes (and accompanying administrative regulations) aimed at limiting pollution. Together these approaches have resulted in over $215 billion being spent on compliance by business in the decade ending in 1983. It has also resulted in tremendous strides being made in reducing the amount of environmental damage.

Federal Regulation of the Environment

NEPA. The National Environmental Policy Act of 1969 (**NEPA**) was enacted as a full disclosure statute. It recognized that the environmental consequences of major federal activity must be considered. Furthermore, this weighing must occur at the beginning of the project planning stage. The purpose of the act was stated by Congress in Section 2:

> The purposes of the Act are: To declare a national policy which will encourage productive and enjoyable harmony between man and his environment; to promote efforts which will prevent or eliminate damage to the environment and biosphere and stimulate the health and welfare of man; to enrich the understanding of the ecological systems and national resources important to the Nation; and to establish a Council on Environmental Quality.

NEPA requires an environmentally related decision-making technique. If federal activity has a major effect on the environment, then a detailed report, called an **environmental impact statement,** must be prepared. This report analyzes the effect of the project on the human environment. If the activity *might* have an effect on the environment, then the environment must be considered along with the other factors involved in the planning.

The act is significant in that it clearly recognizes federal government responsibility for the quality of the human environment. However, it is not a means for eliminating causes or sources of pollution. Nor does it provide a legal right to a clean and unpolluted environment. The following case is an example of the application of NEPA. Note that if the federal activity is challenged in court because none or an inadequate environmental impact statement has been prepared, a court may order the project stopped until a statement has been properly prepared. NEPA does not require an analysis of all effects of federal activities. It is aimed at the protection of the environment.

Breckinridge v. Rumsfeld
United States Court of Appeals, Sixth Circuit
537 F.2d 864 (1976)

On November 22, 1974, the secretary of defense announced 111 actions involving realignment of units and the closing of particular bases. One of the actions affected the Lexington-Bluegrass Army Depot (LBAD) to the extent that 18 military and 2,630 civilian jobs would be eliminated in the Lexington area. The army prepared an environmental assessment, which concluded that because there was to be no significant effect on the human environment, a formal environmental impact statement was not required. Additionally, a nongovernmental research institution, Batelle Columbus Laboratories, studied the possible socioeconomic impact of the action and concluded that the Lexington area would suffer only minimal short-term unemployment as a result of the partial closing.

The question presented on this appeal involves the breadth to be given to the term *human environment* as used in the National Environmental Policy Act (NEPA).

Specifically, does action by the United States Army that reduces jobs and transfers personnel from the Lexington-Bluegrass Army Depot (LBAD) to depots in California and Pennsylvania constitute "a major Federal action significantly affecting the quality of the human environment"?

Phillips, Chief Judge

In the present case there is no long term impact, no permanent commitment of a national resource and no degradation of a traditional environmental asset, but rather short term personal inconveniences and short term economic disruptions. We conclude that such a situation does not fall within the purview of the Act.

The contention that NEPA goes beyond what might be stated to be the "physical environment" is not in dispute. Environmental impact statements have been mandated in such diverse instances as construction of a federal jail in the back of the United States Court House in Manhattan.

Although factors other than the physical environment have been considered, this has been done only when there existed a primary impact on the physical environment.

In discussion of NEPA on the floor of the Senate, Senator Jackson provided insight into the breadth of the statute:

What is involved in a congressional declaration that we do not intend, as a government or as a people, to initiate actions which endanger the continued existence or the health of mankind: That we will not intentionally initiate actions which will do irreparable damage to the air, land, and water which support life on earth.

An environmental policy is a policy for people. Its primary concern is with man and his future. The basic principle of the policy is that we must strive in all that we do, to achieve a standard of excellence in man's relationships to his physical surroundings.

To extend the meaning of NEPA to apply to the factual situation involved in this case would distort the congressional intent.

NEPA is not a national employment act. Environmental goals and policies were never intended to reach social problems such as those presented here.

Direct Statutory Control of Pollution. In addition to NEPA, there is another type of federal environmental law. This is a series of statutes that address certain environmental problems such as air pollution, water pollution, toxic waste disposal, use of insecticides and pesticides, and strip mining.

These direct controls of pollution involve efforts by Congress, which enacts the statute, and an administrative agency (usually the Environmental Protection Agency), which promulgates regulations to carry out the policies of that statute. For example, the policy behind the Clean Air Act and its amendments was to limit the emission of certain pollutants into the air. The Environmental Protection Agency (EPA) was given the authority to set and enforce these limits. As a result, automobiles needed to be redesigned in order to meet pollution standards for exhaust emissions. Factories and power plants needed to have devices installed to cleanse the smoke they emitted of pollutants.

However, these direct controls of pollution through statute and administrative activity raised problems, which may be divided into two categories: first, the ability of the EPA (or other governmental agency) to determine the "correct" level of pollution; second, the effect such an approach has on a business.

Some contend that it is extremely difficult for the EPA to determine the correct level of pollution. Any controls imposed on business to reduce the level of pollutants use resources that could have been used for the production of additional goods and services. Therefore, there is a trade-off between the tolerable levels of pollution and the costs of compliance. What is "tolerable" for various pollutants has caused great controversy. Furthermore, some argue that if a desirable level of pollution is determined, the allocation of permissible polluting would not be done efficiently. That is, assuming that there are numerous sources of a certain pollutant being emitted into the air, how should permissible levels of pollution be allocated between polluters? For example, it may be more efficient to allow plant X to emit a higher proportion of pollutants than plant Y, with the total amount of particles being within the level set by the government. Efficiency suggests that plant X should be governed by a different emission standard than plant Y.

Although this distinction has not been made, an EPA definition of pollution source has been extended to cover plantwide pollution. The definition has been called the "bubble concept" and provides that as long as the entire plant does not increase its pollution, the replacement or modification of any individual piece of equipment is exempt from meeting emissions requirements.

Chevron v. Natural Resources Defense Council, Inc.
United States Supreme Court
81 L.Ed.2d 694 (1984)

In the Clean Air Act Amendments of 1977, Congress enacted certain requirements applicable to states that had not achieved the national air quality standards established by the Environmental Protection Agency (EPA) pursuant to earlier legislation. The amended Clean Air Act required these "nonattainment" states to establish a permit program regulating "new or modified major stationary sources" of air pollution. Generally, a permit may not be issued for a new or modified major stationary source unless several stringent conditions are met. The EPA regulation promulgated to implement this permit requirement allows a state to adopt a plantwide definition of the term "stationary source." Under this definition, an existing plant that contains several pollution-emitting devices may install or modify one piece of equipment without meeting the permit conditions if the alteration will not increase the total emissions from the plant. The question presented by this case is whether EPA's decision to allow states to treat all of the pollution-emitting devices within the same industrial grouping as though they were encased within a single "bubble" is based on a reasonable construction of the statutory term "stationary source."

Justice Stevens

When a court reviews an agency's construction of the statute which it administers, it is confronted with two questions. First, always, is the question whether Congress has directly spoken to the precise question at issue. If the intent of Congress is clear, that is the end of the matter; for the court, as well as the agency must give effect to the unambiguously expressed intent of Congress. If, however, the court determines Congress has not directly addressed the precise question at issue, the court does not simply impose its own construction on the statute, as would be necessary in the absence of an administrative interpretation. Rather, if the statute is silent or ambiguous with respect to the specific issue, the question for the court is whether the agency's answer is based on a permissible construction of the statute. . . .

In light of these well-settled principles it is clear that the Court of Appeals misconceived the nature of its role in reviewing the regulations at issue. Once it determined, after its own examination of the legislation, that Congress did not actually have an intent regarding the applicability of the bubble concept to the permit program, the question before it was not whether in its view the concept is "inappropriate" in the general context of a program designed to improve air quality, but whether the Administrator's view that it is appropriate in the context of this particular program is a reasonable one. Based on the examination of the legislation and its history we agree with the Court of Appeals that Congress did not have a specific intention on the applicability of the bubble concept in these cases, and conclude that the EPA's use of that concept here is a reasonable policy choice for the agency to make.

The 1977 Amendments contain no specific reference to the "bubble concept." Nor do they contain a specific definition of the term "stationary source." The legislative history of the portion of the 1977 Amendments dealing with nonattainment areas does not contain any specific comment on the "bubble concept" or the question whether a plantwide definition of a stationary source is permissible under the permit program. It does, however, plainly disclose that in the permit program Congress sought to accommodate the conflict between the economic interest in permitting capital improvements to continue and the environmental interest in improving air quality.

Our review of the EPA's varying interpretations of the word "source"—both before and after the 1977 Amendments—convinces us that the agency primarily responsible for administering this important legislation has consistently interpreted it flexibly—not in a sterile textual vacuum, but in the context of implementing policy decisions in a technical and complex arena. The fact that the agency has from time to time changed its interpretation of the term "source" does not, as repondents argue, lead us to conclude that no deference should be accorded the agency's interpretation of the statute. An initial agency interpretation is not instantly carved in stone. On the contrary, the agency, to engage in informed rulemaking, must consider varying interpretations and the wisdom of its policy on a continuing basis. Moreover, the fact that the agency has adopted different definitions in different contexts adds force to the argument that the definition itself is flexible, particularly since Congress has never indicated any disapproval of a flexible reading of the statute.

In this case, the Administrator's interpretation represents a reasonable accommodation of manifestly competing interests and is entitled to deference: the regulatory scheme is technical and complex, the agency considered the matter in a detailed and reasoned fashion, and the decision involves reconciling conflicting policies. When a challenge to an agency construction of a statutory provision, fairly conceptualized, really centers on the wisdom of the agency's policy, rather than whether it is a reasonable choice within a gap left open by Congress, the challenge must fail.

We hold that the EPA's definition of the term "source" is a permissible construction of the statute which seeks to accommodate progress in reducing air pollution with economic growth.

A second group of problems raised by federal efforts to control environmental pollution directly involves business. The first problem is the imposition of unrealistic pollution standards. This raises an issue of cost-benefit analysis. A second problem is the inflexible nature of set standards. Extensive regulation potentially strains a firm's ability to meet the standards—some standards may even require that new technology be developed to meet them.

Cost-Benefit Analysis and Pollution Standards. An environmental regulation often sets a precise numerical limit on the amount of permissible pollution. It may establish the number of particles a factory can emit from its smokestack or the amount of waste that may be dumped into a nearby river. It may also reflect a concern over the exposure of workers to certain chemicals.

Often questions are raised concerning the relationship of the standard to the benefit it affords society, as well as the cost it imposes on business. For example, assume a regulation limits the amount of pollution in the air to 100 parts per million. A factory currently emits 500 particles. A two-million-dollar expenditure will lower the emission to 125 particles. However, in order to reach the 100-particle standard, an additional two million dollars will have to be spent. To remove 25 additional particles, twice the sum of money will be needed. The question posed by business is whether the cost of removing the "last" 25 particles is worth the benefits it will produce.

Cost-benefit analysis is an economic tool used to determine the efficient allocation of funds. The business decision to allocate money to a certain project will be made if the expected benefits from that expenditure exceed the costs. Therefore, businesses argue that the administrative agency that sets a pollution standard should employ a similar technique. The agency should determine industry cost of compliance with a proposed standard and the amount of benefit the standard is expected to produce. The costs and benefits should be weighed and the standard issued only if it is determined that its benefits outweigh its costs.

The use of cost-benefit analysis in environmental regulation raises questions because of the difficulty of measuring quality-of-life cost and benefits. Antipollution standards are not always limited to what could be achieved given present technology. Standards may require industry to create new technology in order to be in compliance. The costs of such a standard are highly speculative, since it may be an estimate of technology development.

Assigning a dollar value to the benefits to be gained from the standard is even more difficult. Often the benefits associated with cleaner air or water have no dollar value. Longer life expectancy, less disease, and fewer foul smells are quality-of-life benefits that are not readily measured in terms of dollars.

However, cost-benefit analyses based on similar intangibles are made every day. Automobiles are not banned or made impregnable even though it is predictable that thousands of people will be injured or die in accidents each year. The highway speed limit, with some exceptions for interstates, is fifty-five miles per hour, even though lives would be saved if it was set and enforced at thirty miles per hour. Trade-offs are accepted, even though a precise measure of the costs and benefits of automobiles, accidents, and speed limits are impossible. Instead, an approximation is made. Similarly, businesses contend, the costs and benefits of environmental regulation must be considered before their implementation.

The *Cotton Dust* case, which follows, is an example of this argument by business. It involves an issue of particle pollution in the workplace and a regulation setting forth a precise standard limiting those particles. The agency that created the regulation was the Occupational Safety and Health Administration (OSHA). The case is from the United States Supreme Court. By the time the case reached the Court, it appeared that OSHA was ready to agree with business criticism concerning that regulation. The reason for this apparent change of position was that the Reagan administration took office at about that time. In fact, President Reagan was inaugurated the day before oral arguments were held. The new administration filed a motion with the Supreme Court requesting a return of the case to OSHA for further consideration. Reagan campaigned on an antiregulation platform, and it was expected that if the Court approved the request, OSHA would decide that it had the discretion to use cost-benefit analysis in promulgating this type of regulation.

The Supreme Court denied OSHA's motion. It rejected the claim that the agency could use cost-benefit analysis at its discretion. As a further note, in February 1981, President Reagan issued an executive order that required agency regulations to be issued only if the costs of compliance were less than the potential benefits to society.

American Textile Manufacturer's Institute v. Donovan
United States Supreme Court
452 U.S. 490 (1981)

Congress enacted the Occupational Safety and Health Act of 1970 to assure so far as possible every working man and woman in the nation safe and healthful working conditions. The act authorizes the secretary of labor to establish, after notice and opportunity to comment, mandatory nationwide standards governing health and safety in the workplace. In 1978, the secretary, acting through the Occupational Safety and Health Administration (OSHA), promulgated a standard limiting occupational exposure to cotton dust, an airborne particle byproduct of the preparation and manufacture of cotton products, exposure to which induces a constellation of respiratory effects known as byssinosis. This disease was one of the expressly recognized health hazards that led to passage of the act.

Petitioners in these consolidated cases, representing the interests of the cotton industry, challenge the validity of the cotton dust standard. They contend that the act requires OSHA to demonstrate that its standard reflects a reasonable relationship between the costs and benefits associated with the standard. Respondents counter that Congress balanced the costs and benefits in the act itself, and that the act should therefore be construed not to require OSHA to do so. They interpret the act as mandating that OSHA enact the most protective standard possible to eliminate a significant risk of material health impairment, subject to the constraints of economic and technological feasibility.

Justice Brennan

Estimates indicate that at least 35,000 employed and retired cotton mill workers, or 1 in 12 such workers, suffer from the most disabling form of byssinosis. One study found that over 25 percent of a sample of active cotton-preparation and yarn-manufacturing workers suffer at least some form of the disease at a dust exposure level common prior to adoption of the current Standard.

The Cotton Dust Standard promulgated by OSHA establishes mandatory PEL's over an 8-hour period of 100 ug/m^3 for yarn manufacturing, 750 ug/m^3 for slashing and weaving operations, and 500 ug/m^3 for all other processes in the cotton industry.

OSHA chose an implementation strategy for the Standard that depended primarily on a mix of engineering controls, such as installation of ventilation systems, and work practice controls, such as special floorsweeping procedures. Full compliance with the PEL's is required within four years, except to the extent that employers can establish that the engineering and work practice controls are infeasible.

On the basis of the evidence in the record as a whole, the Secretary determined that exposure to cotton dust represents a significant health hazard to employees, and that the prevalence of byssinosis should be significantly reduced by the adoption of the standards. In assessing the health risks from cotton dust and the risk reduction obtained from lowered exposure, OSHA relied particularly on data showing a strong linear relationship between the prevalence of byssinosis and the concentration of lint-free respirable cotton dust.

In promulgating the Cotton Dust Standard, OSHA interpreted the Act to require adoption of the most stringent standard to protect against material health impairment, bounded only by technological and economic feasibility. OSHA therefore rejected the industry's alternative proposals.

The starting point of our analysis is the language of the statute itself. The Act provides:

> The Secretary, in promulgating standards dealing with toxic materials or harmful physical agents under this subsection, shall set the standard which most adequately assures, to the extent feasible, on the basis of the best available evidence, that no employee will suffer material impairment of health or functional capacity even if such employee has regular exposure to the hazard dealt with by such standard for the period of his working life.

The plain meaning of the word "feasible" supports respondents' interpretation of the statute. In effect then Congress itself defined the basic relationship between costs and benefits, by placing the "benefit" of worker health above all other considerations save those making attainment of this "benefit" unachievable. Any standard based on a balancing of costs and benefits by the Secretary that strikes a different balance than that struck by Congress would be inconsistent with the command set forth in the Act. Thus, cost-benefit analysis by OSHA is not required by the statute because feasibility analysis is.

When Congress has intended that an agency engage in cost-benefit analysis, it has clearly indicated such intent on the face of the statute. One early example is the Flood Control Act of 1936. A more recent example is the Outer Continental Shelf Lands Act Amendments of 1978.

The legislative history of the Act, while concededly not crystal clear, provides general support for respondents' interpretation of the Act. The congressional reports and debates certainly confirm that Congress meant "feasible" and nothing else in using that term. Congress was concerned that the Act might be thought to require achievement of absolute safety, an impossible standard, and therefore insisted that health and safety goals be capable of economic and technological accomplishment. Perhaps most telling is the absence of any indication whatsoever that Congress intended OSHA to conduct its own cost-benefit analysis before promulgating a toxic material or harmful physical agent standard. The legislative history demonstrates conclusively that Congress was fully aware that the Act would impose real and substantial costs of compliance on industry, and believed that such costs were part of the cost of doing business.

After estimating the cost of compliance with the Cotton Dust Standard, OSHA analyzed whether it was "economically feasible" for the cotton industry to bear this cost. OSHA concluded that it was, finding that "although some marginal employers may shut down rather than comply, the industry as a whole will not be threatened by the capital requirements of the regulation." In reaching this conclusion on the Standard's economic impact, OSHA made specific findings with respect to employment, energy consumption, capital financing availability, and profitability. To support its findings, the agency relied primarily on a comprehensive investigation of the Standard's economic impact.

Even if OSHA's estimate was understated, we are fortified in observing that the study found that a standard more than four times as costly was nevertheless economically feasible.

When Congress passed the Occupational Safety and Health Act in 1970, it chose to place preeminent value on assuring employees a safe and healthful working environment, limited only by the feasibility of achieving such an environment. We must measure the validity of the Secretary's actions against the requirements of that Act.

Accordingly, the judgment of the Court of Appeals is affirmed.

Economic and Technological Infeasibility. Federal environmental regulation is a creation of Congress. As noted in the *Cotton Dust* case, important balances of various interests are made by Congress during the course of the enactment of the applicable environmental law. An important issue for businesses is that some environmental regulation is set beyond the limits of current technology or the financial ability of a firm to comply. Two acts that raise this issue are the Clean Air Act and the Water Pollution Control Act. These acts have had a great effect on business. One writer estimated that two-thirds of the funds business has spent in complying with environmental regulations have been required by these acts. At times the standards were set beyond the technological or economic limits of an industry. One commentator noted that Congress may have viewed a corporation's survival instinct as the strongest motivator in encouraging compliance with the antipollution standards. Therefore, infeasibility claims have caused much concern in the business world.

The following cases are examples of corporations seeking judicial relief from air or water pollution regulations based upon claims of **technological infeasibility** or economic infeasibility. Note that the request for relief on those grounds was denied by the Supreme Court in each instance. However, note too that the Court did not foreclose all consideration of the issue.

Union Electric Co. v. Environmental Protection Agency
United States Supreme Court
427 U.S. 246 (1976)

Petitioner is an electric utility supplying power in the St. Louis metropolitan area, a large part of Missouri, and parts of Illinois and Iowa. It alleges that it cannot continue to operate if forced to comply with the sulfur dioxide restrictions contained in the Missouri implementation plan of the Clean Air Act which was approved by the administrator. Specifically, petitioner alleges that since the administrator's approval of the plan, low-sulfur coal has become too scarce and expensive to obtain; reliable and satisfactory sulfur dioxide removal equipment that would enable it to comply with the plan's requirements simply has not been devised; the installation of the unsatisfactory equipment that is available would cost over $500 million, a sum impossible to obtain by bonds that are contingent on approval by regulatory bodies and public acceptance; and, even if the financing could be obtained, the carrying, operating, and maintenance costs of over $120 million a year would be prohibitive. Petitioner further alleges that recent evidence has disclosed that sulfur dioxide in the ambient air is not the hazard to public health that it was once thought to be, and that compliance with the sulfur regulation in the Missouri plan is not necessary to the attainment of national primary and secondary ambient air standards in the St. Louis area.

Justice Marshall

After the Administrator of the Environmental Protection Agency (EPA) approves a state implementation plan under the Clean Air Act, the plan may be challenged in a court of appeals within 30 days, or after 30 days have run if newly discovered or available information justifies subsequent review. We must decide whether the operator of a regulated emission source, in a petition for review of an EPA-approved state plan filed after the original 30-day appeal period, can raise the claim that it is economically or technologically infeasible to comply with the plan.

The Clean Air Amendments reflect congressional dissatisfaction with the progress of existing air pollution programs and a determination to take a stick to the States, in order to guarantee the prompt attainment and maintenance of specified air quality standards. The heart of the Amendments is the requirement that each State formulate, subject to EPA approval, an implementation plan designed to achieve national primary ambient air quality standards—those necessary to protect the public health—as expeditiously as practicable but . . . in no case later than three years from the date of approval of such plan. Each State is given wide discretion in formulating its plan.

After the promulgation of the national standards, the State of Missouri formulated its implementation plan and submitted it for approval.

We reject at the outset petitioner's suggestion that a claim of economic or technological infeasibility may be considered upon a petition for review based on new information and filed more than 30 days after approval of an implementation plan even if such a claim could not be considered by the Administrator in approving a plan or by a court in reviewing a plan challenged within the original 30-day appeal period.

Since a reviewing court—regardless of when the petition for review is filed—may consider claims of economic and technological infeasibility only if the Administrator may consider such claims in approving or rejecting a state implementation plan, we must address ourselves to the scope of the Administrator's responsibility. After surveying the relevant provisions of the Clean Air Amendments of 1970 and their legislative history, we agree that Congress intended claims of economic and technological infeasibility to be wholly foreign to the Administrator's consideration of a state implementation plan.

As we have previously recognized, the 1970 Amendments to the Clean Air Act were a drastic remedy to what was perceived as a serious and otherwise uncheckable problem of air pollution. The Amendments place the primary responsibility for formulating pollution control strategies on the States, but nonetheless subject the States to strict minimum compliance requirements. These requirements are of a "technology-forcing character," and are expressly designed to force regulated sources to develop pollution control devices that might at the time appear to be economically or technologically infeasible.

This approach is apparent on the face of the Act. The provision sets out eight criteria that an implementation plan must satisfy, and provides that if these criteria are met and if the plan was adopted after reasonable notice and hearing, the Administrator shall approve the proposed state plan. The mandatory "shall" makes it quite clear that the Administrator is not to be concerned with factors other than those specified and none of the eight factors appears to permit consideration of technological or economic infeasibility.

If a State makes the legislative determination that it desires a particular air quality by a certain date and that it is willing to force technology to attain it—or lose a certain industry if attainment is not possible—such a determination is fully consistent with the structure and purpose of the Amendments, and they provide no basis for the EPA Administrator to object to the determination on the ground of infeasibility.

In sum, we have concluded that claims of economic or technological infeasibility may not be considered by the Administrator in evaluating a state requirement that a primary ambient air quality standard be met in the mandatory three years.

Our conclusion is bolstered by recognition that the Amendments do allow claims of technological and economic infeasibility to be raised in situations where consideration of such claims will not substantially interfere with the primary congressional purpose of prompt attainment of the national air quality standards. Thus, we do not hold that claims of infeasibility are never of relevance in the formulation of an implementation plan or that sources unable to comply with emission limitations must inevitably be shut down.

Perhaps the most important forum for consideration of claims of economic and technological infeasibility is before the state agency formulating the implementation plan. So long as the national standards are met, the State may select whatever mix of control devices it desires and industries with particular economic or technological problems may seek special treatment in the plan itself.

Environmental Protection Agency v. National Crushed Stone Assn.

United States Supreme Court
449 U.S. 64 (1980)

In April and July 1977, the Environmental Protection Agency (EPA), acting under the Federal Water Pollution Control Act, promulgated pollution discharge limitations for the coal-mining industry and for that portion of the mineral mining and processing industry comprising the crushed-stone, construction-sand, and gravel categories. Although the act does not expressly authorize or require variances from the 1977 limitation, each set of regulations contained a variance provision. Respondents sought review of the regulations in various courts of appeals, challenging both the substantive standards and the variance clause.

To obtain a variance from the 1977 uniform discharge limitations, a discharger must demonstrate that the factors relating to the equipment or facilities involved, the process applied, or other such factors relating to such discharger are fundamentally different from the factors considered in the establishment of the guidelines. Although a greater-than-normal cost of implementation will be considered in acting on a request for a variance, economic ability to meet the costs will not be considered. A variance, therefore, will not be granted on the basis of the applicant's economic inability to meet the costs of implementing the uniform standard.

Justice White

The basic structure of the Act, translates Congress' broad goal of eliminating the discharge of pollutants into the navigable waters into specific requirements that must be met by individual point sources. A "point source" is defined as any discernible, confined and discrete conveyance from which pollutants are or may be discharged.

The two factors listed in the Act—"maximum use of technology within the economic capability of the owner or operator" and "reasonable further progress toward the elimination of the discharge of pollutants"—parallel the general definition of BAT (best available technology) standards as limitations that "require application of the best available technology economically achievable for such category or class, which will result in reasonable further progress toward eliminating the discharge of all pollutants." A variance, thus, creates for a particular point source a BAT standard that represents for it the same sort of economic and technological commitment as the general BAT standard creates for the class. As with the general BAT standard, the variance assumes that the 1977 BPT (best practicable technology) standard has been met by the point source and that the modification represents a commitment of the maximum resources economically possible to the ultimate goal of eliminating all polluting discharges. No one who can afford the best available technology can secure a variance.

There is no similar connection between the Act and the considerations underlying the establishment of the 1977 BPT limitations. First, requirement of "reasonable further progress" must have reference to some prior standard. BPT serves as the prior standard with respect to BAT. There is, however, no comparable, prior standard with respect to BPT limitations. Second, BPT limitations do not require an industrial category to commit the maximum economic resources possible to pollution control, even if affordable. Those point sources already using a satisfactory pollution control technology need take no additional steps at all. The variance factor, the "maximum use of technology within the economic capability of the

owner or operator," would therefore be inapposite in the BPT context. It would not have the same effect there that it has with respect to BAT's, i.e., it would not apply the general requirements to an individual point source.

More importantly, to allow a variance based on the maximum technology affordable by the point source, even if that technology fails to meet BPT effluent limitations, would undercut the purpose and function of BPT limitations. Rather than the 1987 requirement of the best measures economically and technologically feasible, the statutory provisions for 1977 contemplate regulations prohibiting discharges from any point source in excess of the effluent produced by the best practicable technology currently available in the industry.

To put the matter another way, the Administrator is directed to consider the benefits of effluent reductions as compared to the costs of pollution control in determining BPT limitations. Thus, every BPT limitation represents a conclusion by the Administrator that the costs imposed on the industry are worth the benefits in pollution reduction that will be gained by meeting those limits. To grant a variance because a particular owner or operator cannot meet the normal costs of the technological requirements imposed on him, and not because there has been a recalculation of the benefits compared to the costs, would be inconsistent with this legislative scheme and would allow a level of pollution inconsistent with the judgment of the Administrator.

Because the 1977 limitations were intended to reduce the total pollution produced by an industry, requiring compliance with BPT standards necessarily imposed additional costs on the segment of the industry with the least effective technology. If the statutory goal is to be achieved, these costs must be borne or the point source eliminated. In our view, requiring variances from otherwise valid regulations where dischargers cannot afford normal costs of compliance would undermine the purpose and the intended operative effect of the 1977 regulations.

Congress did not respond to this foreseen economic impact by making room for variances based on economic impact. In fact, this possibility was specifically considered and rejected. Instead of economic variances, Congress specifically added two other provisions to address the problem of economic hardship.

First, provision was made for low-cost loans to small businesses to help them meet the cost of technological improvements.

Second, an employee protection provision was added, giving EPA authority to investigate any plant's claim that it must cut back production or close down because of pollution control regulations. This provision had two purposes: to allow EPA constantly to monitor the economic effect on industry of pollution control rules and to undercut economic threats by industry that would create pressure to relax effluent limitation rules.

As we see it, Congress anticipated that the 1977 regulations would cause economic hardship and plant closings: The question is not what a court thinks is generally appropriate to the regulatory process; it is what Congress intended for these regulations.

We conclude, therefore, that the Court of Appeals erred in not accepting EPA's interpretation of the Act. EPA is not required by the Act to consider economic capability in granting variances from its uniform BPT regulations.

SUMMARY

Legal regulation of the environment occurs at all levels of government. Business managers, therefore, must appreciate the wide range of controls that exist when their activities affect the environment. Although state and local activities may regulate pollution, they are limited in what they can accomplish. Federal regulation, on the other hand, is broad and has been the dominant source of environmental laws.

Two aspects of federal environmental regulation should be emphasized: first, the full disclosure policy of NEPA through the environmental impact statement. This law requires that harmful environmental effects of public projects be revealed and considered before work on the projects begin. The second important aspect of federal environmental regulation is its direct control of certain pollution problems. Federal statutes regulate such areas as water pollution, air pollution, and toxic substances. The main issues that have arisen under environmental regulation should be noted: first, cost-benefit analysis as a tool for imposing specific regulations; and second, the effect of burdensome regulations, economically or technologically, on business.

REVIEW QUESTIONS

1. Define the following terms:
   a. Pollution
   b. Nuisance
   c. NEPA
   d. Environmental impact statement
   e. Technological infeasibility

2. Discuss the functions of the environment and give an example of each function.

3. What is pollution and why did it become a major problem in the 1960s?

4. Jack owned a farm. A stream of pure water flowed through it. One of the main reasons Jack purchased the farm was to enjoy the benefits the stream provided. Jack diverted water from the stream to use in his house. He also built a small dam across the stream to create a pond. The water was therefore being used for household purposes as well as landscaping. Soon after Jack purchased the farm, XYZ, Inc., began dumping wastes into the stream. The corporation's plant was located upstream from Jack's farm. The stream became pol-

luted, and Jack could no longer use its water for household purposes. In addition, the pollution discolored the water and caused it to smell. Discuss common law claims Jack may have against XYZ.

5. What practical problems may exist for Jack in seeking remedies for the pollution problem under common law?

6. Discuss the two general methods by which the federal government regulates the environment.

7. Discuss business problems arising from federal efforts to control environmental pollution through regulation.

8. You are project manager for ABC Corporation. Your job involves coordinating all aspects of new factory construction that the corporation undertakes. One of the major concerns you have is satisfying the EPA concerning possible pollution that may be emitted once the factory is operating. Currently, ABC is constructing a factory in California. You have worked closely with the EPA and anticipate no problems with them. Is your concern about environmental regulation at an end?

9. Because of deficit concerns, the IRS decides to close its regional offices in four cities. As a result, numerous workers will lose their jobs and, at least in the short term, the economy of those cities will be adversely affected. Jones files a claim against the IRS contending that its decision violates the National Environmental Policy Act since the human environment is adversely affected by job loss. Discuss.

10. Discuss the "bubble concept," noting particularly its effect on corporate decision making.

11. The Army Corps of Engineers is planning to dam a river in order to create a large reservoir. The reservoir will replace farmland and woodland that currently surrounds the dam site. Discuss how this project is regulated by the federal environmental laws. Limit your discussion to materials contained in the chapter.

PART VI

International Regulation of Business Activity

CHAPTER 24

The International
Legal Environment
of Business

Problems Associated with Selling Goods in an International Environment
Activities by American Companies Overseas
Legal Disputes with Foreign States
Developing a Sales Organization Abroad
Extraterritorial Application of U.S. Laws

Competition, product markets, and supply sources are now international in scope and even domestically-oriented firms are fundamentally affected by international economic pressures. Thus, an awareness of the basic laws associated with international business transactions has become increasingly important.

In no other area of business are legal considerations so central to the success of an enterprise. American multinational businesses must deal with three sets of laws—international, American, and the domestic law of the foreign country in which the firm operates. We focus here on international commercial law and American law. While the domestic legal codes of countries around the world are important, they are too many and too diverse to be considered in this chapter.

But what is international commercial law? Is it just a consensus on legal norms, or the laws of the United Nations, or both? International commercial law is the product of consensus among trading nations that culminated in various unilateral, bilateral, and multilateral governmental accords and voluntary nongovernmental agreements. Thus, there are numerous international agreements, a few of which we will review, that regulate international commerce.

PROBLEMS ASSOCIATED WITH SELLING GOODS IN AN INTERNATIONAL ENVIRONMENT

Documentary Credits

One of the most important agreements in international commerce is the International Chamber of Commerce's (ICC) Uniform Customs and Practice for Documentary Credits. Issued in 1933 and revised periodically, it establishes a foundation for standardizing worldwide transactions. It is the product of nongovernmental action and is based on business practice. As of 1974, banks in 156 countries adhered to its provisions.

A **documentary credit** is a conditional bank payment instrument. The buyer requests his bank to pay the seller or the seller's bank at sight (upon seeing), or at some future date, a stated amount upon receipt of the required documents, assuming the individual documents list the prescribed information (i.e., are "correct" documents) and arrive within the prescribed time. The terms of the documentary credit in regard to the documents, their content, and the time limit must be exact and followed to the letter; otherwise the buyer can refuse shipment. The documentary credit and the underlying sales contract exist separately. Thus, the buyer's bank reviews the presented documents and not the original sales contract before paying the stated sum. As long as the seller delivers the correct documents within the stipulated time, the buyer's bank must pay the seller or the seller's bank.

All documentary credits must indicate which documents are to be presented in order for the seller to be paid. Typically, a transport document listing the goods, the companies involved, and other details is agreed upon. The mode of transport and the transport document must be in agreement. For example, if the credit indicates air transportation, an air waybill must be employed. If ocean transportation is specified, a marine bill of lading is a necessity.

In addition to the transport document, other documents are usually involved. The insurance certificate must cover the risks specified in the credit and be consistent with the other documents. The certificate of inspection verifies that the goods comply with the manufacturer's and the buyer's specifications. The certificate of origin certifies that the goods were produced in a certain country. All the documents must be dated and issued in accordance with the time constraints of the credit, which usually coincide with the date of shipment.

There are several possible configurations for documentary credits. Credits can be revocable or irrevocable, and should be so stated. In the absence of such a statement, credits are considered revocable. Revocable credits allow the buyer to withdraw the letter of credit at any time before the buyer's bank, or in some cases the seller's bank, receives correct documents from the seller.

Furthermore, credits can be advised or confirmed. If a credit is advised, the buyer's bank requests the seller's bank to advise the seller of the credit and review the documents without the seller's bank incurring any liability. In the case of a confirmed credit, the buyer's bank requests the seller's bank to confirm the credit to the seller. The seller's bank reviews the documents with full liability. Thus, in a confirmed credit the seller has two banks and the buyer, of course, who are liable to the seller for the stated sum upon delivery of correct documents. Revocable credits are not confirmed. All credits must indicate the mode of payment. There are a few special credits (such as revolving, red clause, transferable, and back-to-back), but a description of each goes beyond the scope of this book.

An example will help us better understand the cycle of documentary credits. Assume an American liquor importer wishes to special order one hundred thousand kegs of Wetzlarer Brau from Sabine AG in Wetzlar, West Germany, for a client who is celebrating his graduation. Since the importer has never dealt with Sabine before, he desires the security of a documentary credit. Sabine in turn requests that the letter of credit be irrevocable and confirmed for its own protection. Thus, the buyer, the American importer, requests his bank, Americanbank, to establish an irrevocable, confirmed documentary letter of credit for the seller, Sabine. Americanbank telexes its partner bank, Germanbank, that the buyer wishes to open the letter of credit. Germanbank, which is also Sabine's local bank, informs Sabine that the buyer has established the letter of credit and confirms it to Sabine.

To fulfill the terms of the credit, Sabine must deliver the transportation document, an air waybill, and an insurance certificate that states that the beer is insured against spoilage. In addition, the buyer stipulates a certificate of origin. It must state that the beer comes from Wetzlar, West Germany. Further, Sabine must submit a certificate of inspection, which assures the buyer that he is receiving the one and only Wetzlarer Brau. The credit requires that the one hundred thousand kegs be shipped by air two days before graduation. Upon delivery of correct documents, Germanbank will pay Sabine at sight.

A week before graduation, Sabine delivers the prescribed documents. All are predated two days before graduation. Germanbank, however, refuses payment because the air waybill states that one hundred thousand barrels instead of one hundred thousand kegs are being shipped. Sabine then requests the air carrier to change the air waybill, after which Sabine resubmits the documents. Germanbank reviews the documents again and determines that it now has correct documents. Thus, Germanbank must pay Sabine regardless of further events. Germanbank in turn sends the documents to Americanbank and requests payment. After examining the documents, Americanbank pays Germanbank and informs the American importer that Sabine submitted correct documents. (Note that the bank's legal department does not usually review the documents. The review is performed by the bank's staff.) Thus, the American importer owes Americanbank and must pay its debt to obtain the documents so that he can claim the shipment from the carrier.

Documentary credits offer both the buyer and seller a great deal of convenience and security. They need only deal with their local bank. The banks provide advice and assistance throughout the process. The buyer is assured that he will not make payment until the exact goods arrive, and the seller is certain that the goods will not be delivered to the buyer until payment is received. Thus, in a world in which buyer and seller often do not know one another, documentary credits provide the perfect vehicle for international trade.

The following case deals with a situation in which the court declined to force the bank to pay an irrevocable letter of credit.

Sztejn v. J. Henry Schroder Banking Corporation
Supreme Court, Special Term, New York County
31 N.Y.S.2d 631 (1941)

Chester Charles Sztejn contracted with Transea Traders, Ltd., a corporation located in Lucknow, India, for the purchase of a quantity of bristles. To pay for the bristles, he contracted with J. Henry Schroder for the issuance of an irrevocable letter of credit to Transea. The letter of credit was delivered to Transea. Transea placed fifty cases of material on board a steamship and received a bill of lading and invoices. The documents described the bristles called for by the letter of credit. Sztejn asserted that in fact the cases were loaded with worthless cow hair. Transea drew a draft under the letter of credit to the order of the Chartered Bank of India and delivered the draft and the fraudulent documents to the bank for collection. The bank presented the draft along with the documents to Schroder for payment.

Sztejn argued that because Schroder had been notified of the seller's fraud before it made payment to the seller, the letter of credit and drafts should be declared null and void. The court ruled for Sztejn.

Shientag, Justice

It is well established that a letter of credit is independent of the primary contract of sale between the buyer and the seller. The issuing bank agrees to pay upon presentation of documents, not goods. This rule is necessary to preserve the efficiency of the letter of credit as an instrument for the financing of trade. One of the chief purposes of the letter of credit is to furnish the seller with a ready means of obtaining prompt payment for his merchandise. It would be a most unfortunate interference with business transactions if a bank before honoring drafts drawn upon it was obliged or even allowed to go behind the documents, at the request of the buyer and enter into controversies between the buyer and the seller regarding the quality of the merchandise shipped. If the buyer and the seller intended the bank to do this they could have so provided in the letter of credit itself, and in the absence of such a provision, the court will not demand or even permit the bank to delay paying drafts which are proper in form. Of course, the application of this doctrine presupposes that the documents accompanying the draft are genuine and conform in terms to the requirements of the letter of credit.

This is not a controversy between the buyer and seller concerning a mere breach of warranty regarding the quality of the merchandise; on the present motion, it must be assumed that the seller has intentionally failed to ship any goods ordered by the buyer. In such a situation, where the seller's fraud has been called to the bank's attention before the drafts and documents have been presented for payment, the principle of the independence of the bank's obligation under the letter of credit should not be extended to protect the unscrupulous seller. It is true that even though the documents are forged or fraudulent, if the issuing bank has already paid the draft before receiving notice of the seller's fraud, it will be protected if it exercised reasonable diligence before making such payment. However, in the instant action Schroder has received notice of Transea's active fraud before it accepted or paid the draft. The Chartered Bank, which under the allegations of the complaint stands in no better position than Transea, should not be heard to complain because Schroder is not forced to pay the draft accompanied by documents covering a transaction which it has reason to believe is fraudulent.

The first real progress toward a global agreement on tariffs and trade came at the end of the Second World War. In 1947, the United States and twenty-two other nations completed negotiations on the General Agreement on Tariffs and Trade (**GATT**); today some ninety countries are members of the organization. The signators agreed to trade with all other signators on the same terms. The ultimate goal of the GATT is to reduce tariffs and nontariff trade barriers. The GATT has evolved into a complex framework for regulating trade, as it monitors the flow of thousands of products.

General Agreement on Tariffs and Trade (GATT)

Generalized System of Tariff Preferences for Developing Countries. An exception to the GATT principles of reciprocity and nondiscrimination is the Generalized System of Tariff Preferences for Developing Countries (GSP). As the title implies, less developed countries (LDC)s face lower tariffs than developed nations exporting the same items. The GSP concept is aimed at helping LDCs diversify their economic structure by progressing from the development of primary sectors (agriculture) to the intermediate and manufacturing sectors.

The GATT established four safeguards to protect countries against unforeseen adverse consequences of trade: antidumping duties, countervailing duties, the escape clause, and the market disruption clause.

Dumping is defined as selling products or services in a foreign market at less than their fair value. To rectify the situation, offsetting duties may be imposed, regardless of the source of the goods, if the domestic industry is harmed.

Dumping

Countervailing duties are special duties that offset a foreign subsidy. Basically, there are two types of subsidies, domestic and export. In most countries, the tax code is the source of a great many domestic subsidies. For example, many countries allow tax deductions for interest payments and have generous depreciation schedules. The list is almost infinite and, in many countries, quite diverse. This makes it exceedingly difficult to monitor abuses that lead to an unfair competitive advantage. Export subsidies are usually in the form of government payments; these are easier to detect.

Countervailing Duties

The GATT provision on the **escape clause** was adopted from previous U.S. laws in this area. It allows countries to raise tariffs on certain items if there is a serious threat to the domestic industry as a consequence of earlier tariff reductions. Other trade restrictions may also be implemented.

Escape Clause

Market Disruption Clause. Market disruption, a special escape clause, is applicable to communist countries. In contrast to the conventional escape clause, the imported good need only be a significant cause of injury rather than a substantial cause of injury. This may be easier to prove. The president is empowered to take immediate action. The whole process is faster than with the traditional escape clause.

Tariffs

Periodically, the signators convene for rounds of negotiations. One of the more notable ones was the Kennedy round, during which substantial reductions in tariffs were achieved. In fact, by the time the Tokyo round began in 1979, the signators determined that tariffs were no longer the major problem. More elusive nontariff trade barriers (NTBs) had taken their place.

There are two types of import duties, specific and ad valorem. These tariffs are applied differently. Specific duties are assessed in units of money per quantity of good. For example, a duty on gold might be one dollar per ounce. Ad valorem duties are calculated by multiplying a certain percentage times the value of the good. For example, if a good has a value of one hundred dollars and the duty on the good is ten percent, the duty would be ten dollars.

It is frequently very important how an item being imported into the United States is classified. Products may be classified in various ways. Importers are likely to argue the goods in question should be classified in the manner that will result in the lowest possible duty, as is illustrated by the following case.

James S. Baker (Imports) v. United States
United States Customs Court, Second Division
November 19, 1968

In this case, the plaintiffs argued that two importations of lawn rakes manufactured in Japan should not be classified as "rakes, other" under the United States Tariff Schedules. This classification was subject to an assessment of duty at the rate of 15 per centum ad valorem. They argued that the rakes in question should be classified as "agricultural or horticultural tools" instead, and thus subject only to a duty at the rate of 7.5 per centum ad valorem. The question for the court was whether or not a lawn rake should be classified as an "agricultural or horticultural tool" or as "rakes, other." The court ruled on behalf of the importer that the rakes in question were "horticultural tools."

Rao, Chief Judge

The pertinent statutory provisions read as follows:

Tariff Schedules of the United States, schedule 6, part 3, subpart E:

Drainage tools, scoops, shovels, spades, picks, mattocks, hoes, rakes and forks . . . all the foregoing which are hand tools, and metal parts thereof . . .

Hoes and rakes, and parts thereof:

648.55 Agricultural or horticultural tools, and parts thereof	7.5 % ad val.
648.57 Other	15.0 % ad val.

We deem it appropriate to resort to legislative history and other available data to determine the intent of Congress with respect to this language.

It is defendant's contention that the term "horticultural" does not embrace those tools used on the lawn, as the caring for and growing of a lawn is not a horticultural pursuit. With this we cannot agree.

In reaching our decision we must determine what Congress has intended by including "horticultural" hoes and rakes in item 648.55.

The following definition of the word "horticulture" is pertinent to the resolution of the issue:

The *Random House Dictionary of the English Language*, unabridged edition, 1966:

1. The cultivation of a garden, orchard, or nursery; the cultivation of flowers, fruits, vegetables, or ornamental plants.
2. The science and art of cultivating such plants.

The common meaning of the term as cited above is undisputed. However, defendant argues that under this definition the care and propagation of a lawn is excluded as not being a horticultural pursuit.

We can find no basis for excluding the care of a lawn from being a horticultural activity. In its treatment of horticulture, the *Encyclopaedia Britannica*, volume 11, page 775, 1947 edition, discusses horticulture and the home. It describes the lawn as "one of the first considerations, since it serves as the floor covering of the living room, so to speak, and is the setting for the buildings and ornamental plantings."

Clearly, the treatment of the lawn in this work leaves us with no doubt that the caring of a lawn may properly be considered a horticultural pursuit. Nor do we believe that Congress intended to exclude lawn rakes from the provision for horticultural tools, as it was set forth in item 648.55.

In view of the foregoing considerations, we hold that the lawn rakes here in issue are horticultural tools within the meaning of item 648.55 of the Tariff Schedules of the United States, and are subjected to duty at the rate of 7.5 per centum ad valorem. The claim in the protest to that effect is sustained.

Judgment will be entered accordingly.

Nontariff Trade Barriers

As mentioned earlier, nontariff trade barriers (NTBs) replaced tariffs as the main obstacle to free trade. The following are some examples of NTBs. A **quota** is probably the most familiar. It stipulates that only a certain amount of a good will be allowed to enter the country during a given period. By paying a special duty, an importer might be able to import an additional amount above the amount specified by the quota. Product standards rank second to quotas in terms of frequency of use. They often serve to make certification of products more expensive. For example, France required the importers of video recorders to ship their goods to an interior point in France for testing. This caused large time delays and increased costs. To deal with such problems, the Tokyo round produced the Standards Code. The goal of the code is for foreigners to be treated like domestics when product standards are certified. A GATT committee on technical barriers to trade settles disputes.

Domestic content laws, increasingly used by LDCs, require that a certain percentage of a good's value be produced in the domestic economy. Japan manufactures certain products in the United States due to the possibility of such legislation. *Voluntary restraint agreements* are informal, nonbinding constraints on the foreign producer. For example, Japan has agreed to limit its car exports to this country. This also tends to encourage the foreign producer to manufacture or assemble products in the domestic economy.

Direct investment restrictions often require that a certain portion of a business be domestically owned. In the past, Canada required that businesses be at least partially

Canadian. Certain industries are closed to foreigners. For example, entry into the airline industry in the United States is restricted to U.S. nationals.

ACTIVITIES BY AMERICAN COMPANIES OVERSEAS

Contractual Problems

Choice of Law Clause. Often in international contracts, the parties insert a **choice of law clause.** By inserting such a clause, the parties determine the governing law of the contract. English law or the law of the state of New York is usually stipulated. New York State law rather than American law is specified because the laws of the fifty states differ.

Common law countries, such as the United States and Great Britain, will usually respect the right of the parties to choose the governing law of the contract. If the clause stipulates English law, American courts will normally apply English law and vice versa. Civil law countries, for example Germany and France, show less respect for the parties' right to contract and may only uphold a choice of law clause if the contract or the parties bear some connection to the chosen law. Certain Latin American countries, also civil law countries, ignore choice of law clauses completely and apply their own laws to contracts that are performed in their countries.

Choice of Forum Clause. A **choice of forum** clause determines the location of the court or arbitration proceeding. An agreement that stipulates arbitration in London or New York implicitly means that English or New York courts will have jurisdiction in proceedings to compel arbitration or enforce arbitral awards. The United States Supreme Court ruled in *The Bremen* v. *Zapata* (1972) that "the forum clause should control absent a strong showing that it should be set aside. . . ." Thus, the more reasonable a choice of forum clause is, the more likely it is that the courts will uphold the clause in the United States.

Antiboycott Laws

The United States Export Administration Act of 1979 and Tax Reform Act of 1976 preclude the participation of American companies in secondary boycotts. These regulations are enforced by the Department of Commerce and the Internal Revenue Service, respectively. The antiboycott provisions were originally enacted to protect Israel against boycotts instituted by Middle Eastern nations, but they apply to all nonauthorized boycotts. For example, an American company or its subsidiary cannot enter into any agreement in which it must agree not to do business with a boycotted country.

Arbitration

An arbitration agreement is usually a clause in a contract that specifies that all disputes concerning the contract will be settled by means of arbitration. Usually, arbitration is preferred to litigation because it circumvents several problems associated with litigation, such as a tremendous backlog of cases may be before the court causing long delays.

Ideally, an arbitration clause should include exclusive remedies for all issues so that litigation is completely avoided. In addition, all parties should relinquish the right to pursue the matter in the courts. A single arbitrator is generally best. If one party is domiciled in a common law country and the other in a civil law country, the right to engage in discovery should be included, since civil law codes do not always allow for discovery. The location of the proceeding is extremely important, for local law may determine the applicable procedure and substantive law. An arbitral body, such as the American Arbitration Association, United Nations Committee on International Trade Law, or the International Chamber of Commerce, should be stipulated. "Ad hoc" arbitration is also a possiblity. In this case, the arbitration is administered according to the exact specifications of the parties without regard to any institutional framework.

The International Chamber of Commerce is the oldest international arbitral institution and has established rules and procedures for the arbitration process.

Courts worldwide will usually enforce the orders of arbitrators and judgment awards, even though the arbitration agreement prevents the courts from judging the merits.

For the parties to obtain the maximum benefit from arbitration, they must construct an arbitration agreement in advance and with great attention to detail, for this will reduce conflicts and expedite the arbitration process.

The following is a recent United States Supreme Court case dealing with the enforceability of agreements to arbitrate.

Mitsubishi Motors Corporation v. Soler Chrysler-Plymouth, Inc.

United States Supreme Court
105 S.Ct. 3346 (1985)

Mitsubishi entered into a contract with Soler Chrysler-Plymouth. The contract required arbitration by the Japan Commercial Arbitration Association of all disputes arising with respect to the contract. A dispute arose between the parties, and Mitsubishi brought suit in federal court under the federal Arbitral Act and the Convention on the Recognition and Enforcement of Foreign Arbitral Awards seeking an order to compel arbitration. Soler counter-claimed that Mitsubishi had violated the Sherman Act. The court of appeals ruled that Soler could not be forced to arbitrate its antitrust claim. The United States Supreme Court reversed.

Justice Blackmun

As in *Scherk* v. *Alberto-Culver Co.,* we conclude that concerns of international comity, respect for the capacities of foreign and transnational tribunals, and sensitivity to the need of the international commercial system for predictability in the resolution of disputes require that we enforce the parties' agreement, even assuming that a contrary result would be forthcoming in a domestic context.

Even before *Scherk,* this Court had recognized

the utility of forum-selection clauses in international transactions. *Scherk* establishes a strong presumption in favor of enforcement of freely negotiated contractual choice-of-forum provisions. Here, as in *Scherk,* that presumption is reinforced by the emphatic federal policy in favor of arbitral dispute resolution. And at least since this Nation's accession in 1970 to the Convention, and the implementation of the Convention in the same year by amendment of the federal Arbitration Act, that federal policy applies with special force in the field of international commerce.

There is no reason to assume at the outset of the dispute that international arbitration will not provide an adequate mechanism. To be sure, the international arbitral tribunal owes no prior allegiance to the legal norms of particular states; hence, it has no direct obligation to vindicate their statutory dictates. The tribunal, however, is bound to effectuate the intentions of the parties. Where the parties have agreed that the arbitral body is to decide a defined set of claims which includes, as in these cases, those arising from the application of American antitrust law, the tribunal therefore should be bound to decide that dispute in accord with the national law giving rise to the claim.

Having permitted the arbitration to go forward, the national courts of the United States will have the opportunity at the award enforcement stage to ensure that the legitimate interest in the enforcement of the antitrust laws has been addressed. The Convention reserves to each signatory country the right to refuse enforcement of an award where the recognition or enforcement of the award would be contrary to the public policy of that country. While the efficacy of the arbitral process requires that substantive review at the award-enforcement stage remain minimal, it would not require intrusive inquiry to ascertain that the tribunal took cognizance of the antitrust claims and actually decided them.

Accordingly, we require this representative of the American business community to honor its bargain, by holding this agreement to arbitrate enforceable . . . in accord with the explicit provisions of the Arbitration Act.

Joint Ventures

Joint venture is a descriptive term rather than a legal one. Often joint ventures take the form of a corporation in which each partner has a proportionate interest. They can carry out one-time projects, engage in an ongoing enterprise, or undertake extremely risky, large-scale projects. A master contract between two or more parties determines the rights and responsibilities of the participants.

Joint ventures exist because the partners possess unique characteristics which complement and augment each other. They have become more popular in LDCs due to capital shortages. The foreign partner usually brings the necessary technology and human capital (management). The host countries provide inexpensive labor, raw materials, and relief from taxes. Control is usually a major consideration. Mexico, for example, requires fifty-one percent domestic ownership. Having domestic partners offers some protection against expropriation and might allow the enterprise to qualify for participation in local government export programs. Repatriation (return to the home country) of profits is a key consideration for both the investor and the LDC. LDCs try to keep profits in the domestic economy. Brazil indirectly requires reinvestment of a portion of profits in Brazil through special taxes and foreign exchange rationing.

LEGAL DISPUTES WITH FOREIGN STATES

Sovereign Immunity Doctrine

Jurisdiction in cases involving governments and their agents is complicated by the Sovereign Immunity and Act of State Doctrines. Originally, the **Sovereign Immunity Doctrine** offered foreign lands complete immunity from lawsuits. The Foreign Sovereign Immunities Act (FSIA) distinguishes between governmental acts and private or commercial acts, the former being generally immune from lawsuits.

There are several instances in which a foreign land is within the jurisdiction of U.S. courts. If the sovereign grants an explicit or implied waiver of immunity or engages in commercial activities in the United States or in commercial activities that have a direct impact on the United States, U.S. courts have jurisdiction. For example, an arbitration clause that requires arbitration in the United States constitutes a waiver. Examples of commerce are the issuance of debt or purchase of military hardware in the United States.

Where property rights are taken in violation of international law and the property, or property exchanged therefor, is present in the United States in connection with a commercial activity in the United States, or if such property is owned or operated by an agency or instrumentality of the foreign state which is engaged in a commercial activity in the United States, American courts can sit in judgment. For example, a state-owned airline that employs confiscated aircraft for passenger transport to the United States could be sued in U.S. courts.

Obtaining a favorable judgment does not mean that the plaintiff can readily satisfy his claim. A foreign state is generally immune from attachments and execution (court ordered payment of the judgment). The FSIA actually affords the foreign state more protection from execution than from suit, which may render litigation useless.

The **Act of State Doctrine** was originally based on *Underhill* v. *Hernandez* (1897), in which the Supreme Court stated that "Every sovereign state is bound to respect the independence of every other sovereign state, and the courts of one country will not sit in judgment on the acts of the government of another done within its own territory." The doctrine strikes a balance between the three branches of government. It represents the desire of the Supreme Court to defer to the executive branch in the conduct of foreign policy. The Court recognizes that its actions may interfere with presidential efforts to resolve certain disputes. For example, a foreign state might agree to a negotiated settlement through the State Department, whereas a court order would be counterproductive. The Congress has incorporated these thoughts into legislation.

Act of State Doctrine

The Act of State Doctrine no longer grants blanket immunity to foreign governments. A court must analyze the effect of the governmental action on the foreign investor and determine whether the act was in the public interest as opposed to an act which might be committed by a private person. If a governmental act was in the public interest, the Act of State Doctrine is a valid defense to suit. For example, if a country nationalizes foreign firms in the oil industry and it was in the public interest, U.S. courts do not have jurisdiction to review the action of the foreign country.

The Court established the commercial exception to the Act of State Doctrine in *Alfred Dunhill of London, Inc.* v. *Republic of Cuba* (1976). Here the Court held that "in their commercial capacities, foreign governments do not exercise powers peculiar to sovereigns. . . . The concept of an Act of State should not be extended to include the repudiation of a purely commercial obligation owed by a foreign sovereign or by one of its commercial instrumentalities." For example, if the Federal Republic of Germany sold bonds in the United States and subsequently defaulted on the bonds, it could not avail itself of the Act of State Doctrine to prevent lawsuits.

A difficult question remains. When is a commercial act so bestowed with sovereign power—thus in the public interest—and beyond the jurisdiction of U.S. courts? If the foreign state views a particular action as being a national security issue regardless of the commercial activity, or an examination by the courts represents a potential embarrassment to the executive branch, the Act of State Doctrine will usually be a defense to suit.

In the following case, the Court considered the expropriation of property by the Cuban government.

Banco Nacional De Cuba v. Sabbatino
Supreme Court of the United States
376 U.S. 398 (1964)

An American Commodity broker, Farr, Whitlock, had contracted with a Cuban corporation to buy Cuban sugar. Thereafter, in retaliation for an American reduction in the import quota for Cuban sugar, the Cuban government nationalized many American companies, including the sugar seller. Farr, Whitlock entered into a new agreement to buy the sugar from the Cuban government. After obtaining the documents necessary to get the sugar, Farr, Whitlock paid the original seller, rather than the Cuban government. The Cuban government brought suit to recover the money in question. Farr, Whitlock defended on the ground that title to the sugar never passed to Cuba because it unlawfully expropriated the sugar. The Supreme Court held the Act of State doctrine merited a decision for Cuba in this case.

Justice Harlan

We do not believe that this doctrine is compelled either by the inherent nature of sovereign authority . . . or by some principle of international law.

The act of state doctrine does, however, have "constitutional" underpinnings. It arises out of the basic relationships between branches of government in a system of separation of powers. It concerns the competency of dissimilar institutions to make and implement particular kinds of decisions in the area of international relations. The doctrine as formulated in past decisions expresses the strong sense of the Judicial Branch that its engagement in the task of passing on the validity of foreign acts of state may hinder rather than further this country's pursuit of goals both for itself and for the community of nations as a whole in the international sphere. Therefore, rather than laying down or reaffirming an inflexible and all-encompassing rule in this case, we decide only that the Judicial Branch will not examine the validity of a taking of property within its own territory by a

foreign sovereign government, extant and recognized by this country at the time of suit, in the absence of a treaty or other unambiguous agreement regarding controlling legal principles, even if the complaint alleges that the taking violates customary international law.

Following an expropriation of any significance, the Executive engages in diplomacy aimed to assure that United States citizens who are harmed are compensated fairly. Representing all claimants of this country, it will often be able, either by bilateral or multilateral talks, by submission to the United Nations, or by the employment of economic and political sanctions, to achieve some degree of general redress. Judicial determinations of invalidity of title can, on the other hand, have only an occasional impact, since they depend on the fortuitous circumstance of the property in question being brought into this country. Such decisions would, if the acts involved were declared invalid, often be likely to give offense to the expropriating country; since the concept of territorial sovereignty is so deep seated, any state may resent the refusal of the courts of another sovereign to accord validity to acts within its territorial borders. Piecemeal dispositions of this sort involving the probability of affront to another state could seriously interfere with negotiations being carried on by the Executive Branch and might prevent or render less favorable the terms of an agreement that could otherwise be reached. Relations with third countries which have engaged in similar expropriations would not be immune from effect.

However offensive to the public policy of this country and its constituent States an expropriation of this kind may be, we conclude that both the national interest and progress toward the goal of establishing the rule of law among nations are best served by maintaining intact the act of state doctrine in this realm of its application.

The Sabbatino Amendment was enacted in response to the failure of the Supreme Court in the *Sabbatino* case to find a violation of international law exception to the Act of State Doctrine. The amendment states:

> No court in the United States shall decline on the ground of the federal act of state doctrine to make a determination on the merits . . . in a case in which a claim of title or other right [to property] is asserted by any party including a foreign state (or a party claiming through such state) based upon (or traced through) a confiscation or other taking by an act of state in violation of international law. . . .

The courts have construed the Sabbatino Amendment very narrowly for the most part, applying it only to cases that fit exactly within the language of the act.

Expropriation can be broken down into two separate issues: the right to take property and the right to compensation. While the right to take property is anchored in both domestic and international law, there is no international agreement as to what constitutes adequate compensation or when it should be paid. U.S. courts have not specified what "fair" compensation is, but they nevertheless recognize the right to compensation.

Expropriation

Disputes with foreign nations often involve not only financial considerations, but political ones as well. Suits may create tensions with foreign countries. It is possible for the president to settle claims of U.S. nationals against foreign governments in order to minimize tensions between the nations. The following case illustrates this point.

Settlement of Disputes

Chas. T. Main Int'l. v. Khuzestan Water and Power Authority
United States Court of Appeals, First Circuit
651 F.2d 800 (1981)

The plaintiff, an engineering firm, brought an action to recover payment for services rendered in connection with Iranian electrification projects. After the Iranian hostage release agreement, the plaintiff brought a second action against the United States, seeking a declaration that the executive agreement with Iran and the implementing executive orders and regulations were in excess of the president's authority. This appeal represents a consolidation of these cases.

Campbell, Circuit Judge

On January 19, 1981, Iran released the hostages pursuant to an agreement with the United States, embodied in two Declarations of the Government of the Democratic and Popular Republic of Algeria. The agreement states that it is "the purpose of both parties . . . to terminate all litigation as between the Government of each party and the nationals of the other, and to bring about the settlement and termination of all such claims through binding arbitration." In furtherance of this goal, the agreement calls for the establishment of an Iran-United States Claims Tribunal (Tribunal), which will, with certain exceptions, arbitrate any such claims not settled within six months of the date of agreement; awards of the Tribunal will be "final and binding" and "enforceable . . . in the courts of any nation in accordance with its laws."

On January 19, 1981, President Carter issued a series of executive orders implementing the terms of the agreement with Iran. In pertinent part, these orders revoked all licenses permitting persons to exercise "any right, power or privilege" with regard to Iranian funds, securities or deposits, "nullified" all non-Iranian interests in such assets acquired subsequent to the November 14, 1979, blocking order, and required those holding blocked Iranian assets to transfer them to the Federal Reserve Bank of New York, "to be held or transferred as directed by the Secretary of the Treasury." On February 24, 1981, President Reagan "ratified" the January 19 orders; he also ordered "suspended" all "claims which may be presented to the (Tribunal)" and provided that they "shall have no legal effect in any action not pending in any court of the United States."

International agreements settling claims by nationals of one state against the government of another are established international practice reflecting traditional international theory. In numerous instances, dating back to the earliest days of this country's history, the President, often acting without the advice or consent of the Senate, has agreed to extinguish claims of United States nationals against foreign governments, in return for lump sum payments or the establishment of arbitration procedures.

It is not difficult to understand why it has become generally accepted that the President possess power, at least in times of crisis in our international relations, to settle the claims of United States nationals against a foreign government. The matter becomes particularly clear if, as Justice Jackson maintained in his *Youngstown* concurrence, "any actual test" of the President's constitutional powers, especially in the foreign relations field, "is likely to depend on the imperatives of events and contemporary imponderables rather than on abstract theories of law." This case well illustrates the imperative need to preserve a presidential flexibility sufficient to diffuse an international crisis, in order to prevent the crisis from escalating or even leading to war. As the Supreme Court has consistently recognized, it is the President who is charged with responsibility as the United States representative and negotiator in the international arena. The authority to remove impediments to the peaceful resolution of international disputes is an authority necessary to meet the responsibilities of presidential office, and in the words of the Supreme Court, a "modest implied" attribute of presidential power.

We need not and do not hold that the executive possesses plenary power to settle claims, even as against foreign governmental entities. It may be that much of this area is within that "zone of twilight in which (the President) and Congress may have concurrent authority." The sheer magnitude of such a power, considered against the background of the diversity and complexity of modern international trade, cautions against any broader construction of authority than is necessary. Here, however, the President has acted to resolve what was indisputably a major crisis in the foreign relations of this country. His settlement of the claims of Main and others was not an isolated event but a necessary incident to the resolution of a dispute between our nation and another. Whatever may be the reach of the executive power under circumstances that implicate less squarely the conduct of foreign relations, the executive power extends so far as to permit the accord reached here.

We hold, therefore, that the President had authority to settle Main's claims against the Iranian defendants, by providing for their submission to binding arbitration. This being the case, we need not decide whether the President went too far in purporting to "order" the "suspension" of litigation relating to the claims. The claims having been settled, they are no longer cognizable in the courts, except insofar as permitted by the settlement's terms.

DEVELOPING A SALES ORGANIZATION ABROAD

Foreign Agents and Distributors

American firms that wish to market their products in other countries have several options from which to choose. In terms of direct American involvement, a branch office or production facility ranks at the top of the list. Traveling American sales representatives rank second, followed by foreign distributors, American distributors, and foreign agents in that order. To avoid foreign income and employment taxes, American companies use foreign agents and distributors, thereby circumventing a "permanent establishment" in the foreign country. If the agent is an individual as opposed to a corporation, the firm must exercise caution, for the agent can be viewed as an employee. Thus, the company would have a "permanent establishment" and be liable for income and employment taxes.

International laws tend to give more protection to an agent than to a distributor based on the assumption that a company possesses more bargaining power relative to the agent. Companies usually register agents, establish a commission schedule and payment timetable. European laws provide for longer termination notices and more severance pay in the form of lost commissions than American law. To protect the company, the agency agreement should include a nonexclusive agency clause, be short term, provide for no automatic extension, specify causes for termination and the specific required notice period.

Sale of Data, Patents, and Know-How Abroad— Licensing

Firms that do not want to enter foreign markets, but nonetheless do not want to forego the additional income from their special technology or know-how, can license the use of their processes. Thus, such a firm eliminates the potential risk of establishing a production facility abroad and marketing the output there. The licensee benefits from the arrangement if it thereby has a monopoly or a real competitive advantage in the domestic market.

Licensing becomes more complicated when the export of the technology or know-how involved is restricted by the U.S. government. The rules are very complex and apply to all transactions—not just licensing. Antitrust issues are also involved in licensing arrangements. Both topics are addressed in the following section.

EXTRATERRITORIAL APPLICATION OF U.S. LAWS

Antitrust

United States antitrust laws affect many of the previously discussed topics, such as joint ventures, distributorship agreements, and licensing arrangements. The two major aims of U.S. antitrust law in the international arena are: (1) to protect American consumers by assuring that they benefit from competition between foreign and domestic firms; and (2) to assure that U.S. export and investment opportunities are not restricted. Basically, the same laws and standards that apply in the United States will apply to international transactions.

There is one important exemption to U.S. antitrust laws. The Webb-Pomerene Act permits the formation of collective export associations of American producers, provided that the association does not (1) artificially or intentionally restrain U.S. domestic trade or affect U.S. domestic prices, or (2) restrain the export trade of any U.S. competitor of the association. The Webb-Pomerene Act applies solely to the export of "goods, wares or merchandise" and, therefore, does not explicitly extend to service and licensing transactions. An association must be limited to domestic firms.

There has been an international response to the extraterritorial application of U.S. antitrust laws. In 1980, the United Kingdom enacted the Protection of Trading Interests Act to prevent the payment of antitrust awards by British firms and provide a forum for recovering treble damages paid by British firms to U.S. plaintiffs. The act allows the United Kingdom to prevent (1) compliance with U.S. antitrust laws, and (2) enforcement of U.S. judgments. The clawback provision of the act allows the British firm to recover any punitive damages.

Foreign Corrupt Practices Act

In 1977, Congress passed the Foreign Corrupt Practices Act (FCPA) in an attempt to curb questionable payments made by businesses to foreign officials. In passing this act, congressmen and senators voiced concern over the fact that information being supplied to the Securities and Exchange Commission and to corporate shareholders contained false information. Corporations were not disclosing information relating to payoffs made in foreign countries; therefore, the financial information supplied to the public by these corporations was not totally accurate. Members of Congress also worried that bribery of foreigners by U.S. corporations might adversely affect our relations with other countries.

The Foreign Corrupt Practices Act makes it illegal to use an instrument of interstate commerce to further the offer, payment, or promise to pay or authorization to pay corrupt payments to (1) foreign officials; (2) foreign political party officials or a foreign political party or a candidate for political office in a foreign country; or (3) any person whom the person paying knows or has reason to know will offer, promise, or give money or anything of value to a foreign official, political party, or political candidate.

FCPA does not prohibit all foreign political campaign contributions, only those motivated by a desire to obtain favorable business treatment.

A payment is corrupt if its purpose is to obtain some form of action or inaction by the person in question in order for a business to retain or obtain business or to direct business to another person. If the person acting for the business knows or should know the payment violates the act, the person and the business may be held liable.

Two types of foreign payments were excluded from the act: (1) grease payments and (2) extortion payments. Grease payments are made to ministerial or clerical workers to get them to perform their jobs. For example, if a clerk is required to give a business a permit, but is rather slow, a business might make a payment to encourage him to do his job. In such an instance, a business really is not getting anything that it is not entitled to anyway. An extortion payment might be, for example, a payment given to a person who threatened to kill employees of a corporation unless the corporation paid off the extortionist. On the other hand, paying an official who demands money before he will grant a business contract to the corporation is a violation of the act.

For violations of the antibribery provisions of this act, businesses may be fined as much as one million dollars. Penalties of as much as ten thousand dollars per violation and/or a sentence of up to five years in prison may be imposed on individual violators. Any fine imposed may *not* be paid, directly or indirectly, by the corporation on whose behalf the individual was acting.

The Foreign Corrupt Practices Act, in addition to its antibribery provisions, also has provisions relating to accounting controls. These provisions are designed to force a business to adopt controls in order to allow it to prepare financial statements that accurately reflect the existence and movement of assets. Furthermore, these provisions are designed to further the goal of corporate accountability. The Securities and Exchange Commission has promulgated rules to help implement the accounting standards.

Businesses that are issuers of registered securities and issuers that must file reports with the Securities and Exchange Commission must make and keep books, records, and accounts which, in reasonable detail, accurately and fairly reflect the transactions and dispositions of the assets of the issuer. Thus, while all companies are obliged to comply with the antibribery provisions, only companies subject to the federal securities law must comply with the accounting rules.

Secondly, such businesses must devise and maintain a system of internal accounting controls sufficient to provide reasonable assurances that the following goals will be achieved: (1) that any transactions are executed in accordance with management's orders; (2) that the system of controls used to record transactions permits the preparation of financial statements in conformity with generally accepted accounting principles or other appropriate criteria and permits the business to maintain accountability for assets; (3) that access to assets will be permitted only according to management's orders; and (4) that recorded and existing assets will be compared at reasonable intervals and appropriate action will be taken with respect to any differences.

It is possible to be prosecuted for a violation of these accounting rules. A willful violation of the Securities Exchange Act is punishable by imprisonment up to five years and/or a fine not exceeding ten thousand dollars.

Export Controls

Export controls impede the free flow of goods, but unlike nontariff trade barriers, they may have more of a political flavor. The Export Administration Act of 1979 permits export controls for national security reasons, foreign policy considerations, or short supply situations. Under the Export Administration Regulations (EAR), which are administered by the Department of Commerce, permits or licenses are required for sensitive items with Eastern European or Soviet destinations. Exports to countries that support terrorism are also closely scrutinized.

SUMMARY

A number of issues are of interest to executives who are engaged in international trade. Many businesses are engaged in importing and exporting. In such a situation, sellers are concerned about whether they will ever be paid, and buyers are concerned about whether they will receive the goods they ordered. In order to overcome these problems, parties in international transactions frequently use documentary credits.

One of the goals of governments around the world for many years has been the elimination of barriers to free trade. To help achieve this goal, a number of nations have entered into an agreement called the General Agreement on Tariffs and Trade or GATT.

American companies operating abroad encounter various problems. In order to protect themselves in the event of a suit, they generally use certain clauses in their contracts, such as choice of law and choice of forum clauses. One clause that is frequently utilized is an arbitration clause. Companies often prefer arbitration of disputes to litigation.

When a business tries to sue a foreign government, it generally will have to overcome the Sovereign Immunity Doctrine and the Act of State Doctrine.

Rather than simply exporting or importing goods, a company may choose to develop a sales organization abroad. Companies frequently license foreign businesses to exploit their patents or manufacturing processes.

Three final issues discussed in this chapter were the extraterritorial application of U.S. antitrust laws, a subject of great concern to other countries, the U.S. Foreign Corrupt Practices Act, and export controls.

REVIEW QUESTIONS

1. Define the following terms:
   a. Documentary credit
   b. Dumping
   c. Countervailing duties
   d. Escape clause
   e. Domestic content laws
   f. Choice of law clause
   g. Choice of forum clause

2. Why would a seller use a documentary letter of credit? What is an irrevocable credit? What is the difference between advised and confirmed credits?

3. Why might arbitration be preferred to litigation?

4. If a court determines that a foreign state has engaged in commercial activity, does this mean a plaintiff will always be able to collect damages?

5. What is the difference between the Act of State Doctrine and the Foreign Sovereign Immunities Act?

6. How does the doctrine of separation of powers relate to the Act of State doctrine?

7. What possible alternatives are open to a business firm that wishes to make money in foreign countries?

8. An American business wishes to sell products to a purchaser in France. Because the French purchaser is located in Europe, the American business knows practically nothing about the creditworthiness of the French company. If the American business decides to sell goods, how should it protect itself to make certain it is paid?

9. Cambridge Sporting Goods Company entered into a contract to purchase boxing gloves from Duke Sports, a Pakistani Corporation. Duke agreed to manufacture twenty-eight thousand pairs of boxing gloves for forty-two thousand dollars. Cambridge opened an irrevocable letter of credit with its bank in New York, Manufacturers Hanover Trust Company. The seller perpetrated a fraud upon Cambridge by shipping worthless fragments of boxing gloves. Can the defense of fraud be asserted against United Bank Limited (Duke's bank) when it requests payment of the letter of credit?

10. Nigeria contracted to purchase huge quantities of Portland cement. It overbought and was unable to accept delivery of the cement because its harbors became clogged with ships waiting to unload. It repudiated its contracts. When sued in the United States, it asserted the doctrine of sovereign immunity as defense. Will Nigeria prevail on this defense?

11. Allied Bank made loans to three Costa Rican banks. The Costa Rican banks executed promissory notes for the amounts in question to Allied. Several years later, the Costa Rican government issued a law preventing any institution in Costa Rica from paying any external debt. Allied brought suit in the United States against these Costa Rican banks. The banks raised as defenses the doctrine of sovereign immunity and the Act of State Doctrine. Will the Costa Rican banks prevail on any of these arguments?

The Constitution of the United States of America

Preamble

We the People of the United States, in Order to form a more perfect Union, establish Justice, insure domestic Tranquility, provide for the common defence, promote the general Welfare, and secure the Blessings of Liberty to ourselves and our Posterity, do ordain and establish this Constitution for the United States of America.

Article I

SECTION 1. All legislative Powers herein granted shall be vested in a Congress of the United States, which shall consist of a Senate and House of Representatives.

SECTION 2. [1] The House of Representatives shall be composed of Members chosen every second Year by the People of the several States, and Electors in each State shall have the Qualifications requisite for Electors of the most numerous Branch of the State Legislature.

[2] No Person shall be a Representative who shall not have attained to the Age of twenty five Years, and been seven Years a Citizen of the United States, and who shall not, when elected, be an Inhabitant of that State in which he shall be chosen.

[3] [Representatives and direct Taxes shall be apportioned among the several States which may be included within this Union, according to their respective Numbers, which shall be determined by adding to the whole Number of free Persons, including those bound to Service for a Term of Years, and excluding Indians not taxed, three fifths of all other Persons.] The actual Enumeration shall be made within three Years after the first Meeting of the Congress of the United States, and within every subsequent Term of ten Years, in such Manner as they shall by Law direct. The Number of Representatives shall not exceed one for every thirty Thousand, but each State shall have at Least one Representative; and until such enumeration shall be made, the State of New Hampshire shall be entitled to chuse three, Massachusetts eight, Rhode Island and Providence Plantations one, Connecticut five, New York six, New Jersey four, Pennsylvania eight, Delaware one, Maryland six, Virginia ten, North Carolina five, South Carolina five, and Georgia three.

The clause of this paragraph inclosed in brackets was amended, as to the mode of apportionment of representatives among the several states, by the Fourteenth Amendment, § 2, and as to taxes on incomes without apportionment, by the Sixteenth Amendment.

[4] When vacancies happen in the Representation from any State, the Executive Authority thereof shall issue Writs of Election to fill such Vacancies.

[5] The House of Representatives shall chuse their Speaker and other Officers; and shall have the sole Power of Impeachment.

SECTION 3. [1] The Senate of the United States shall be composed of two Senators from each State, [chosen by the Legislature thereof,] for six Years; and each Senator shall have one Vote.

This paragraph and the clause of following paragraph inclosed in brackets were superseded by the Seventeenth Amendment.

[2] Immediately after they shall be assembled in Consequence of the first Election, they shall be divided as equally as may be into three Classes. The Seats of the Senators of the first Class shall be vacated at the Expiration of the Second Year, of the second Class at the Expiration of the fourth Year, and of the third Class at the Expiration of the sixth Year, so that one third may be chosen every second Year; [and if Vacancies happen by Resignation, or otherwise, during the Recess of the Legislature of any State, the Executive thereof may make temporary Appointments until the next Meeting of the Legislature, which shall then fill such Vacancies.]

[3] No Person shall be a Senator who shall not have attained to the Age of thirty Years, and been nine Years a Citizen of the United States, and who shall not, when elected, be an Inhabitant of that State for which he shall be chosen.

[4] The Vice President of the United States shall be President of the Senate, but shall have no Vote, unless they be equally divided.

[5] The Senate shall chuse their other Officers, and also a President pro tempore, in the Absence of the Vice President, or when he shall exercise the Office of President of the United States.

[6] The Senate shall have the sole Power to try all Impeachments. When sitting for that Purpose, they shall be on Oath or Affirmation. When the President of the United States is tried, the Chief Justice shall preside: And no Person shall be convicted without the Concurrence of two thirds of the Members present.

[7] Judgment in Cases of Impeachment shall not extend further than to removal from Office, and disqualification to hold and enjoy an Office of honor, Trust, or Profit under the United States: but the Party convicted shall nevertheless be liable and subject to Indictment, Trial, Judgment, and Punishment, according to Law.

SECTION 4. [1] The Times, Places and Manner of holding Elections for Senators and Representatives, shall be prescribed in each State by the Legislature thereof; but the Congress may at any time by Law make or alter such Regulations, except as to the Places of chusing Senators.

[2] The Congress shall assemble at least once in every Year, and such Meeting shall [be on the first Monday in December,] unless they shall by Law appoint a different Day.

The part included in brackets was changed by Section 2 of the Twentieth Amendment.

SECTION 5. [1] Each House shall be the Judge of the Elections, Returns, and Qualifications of its own Members, and a Majority of each shall constitute a Quorum to do Business; but a smaller Number may adjourn from day to day, and may be authorized to compel the Attendance of absent Members, in such Manner, and under such Penalties as each House may provide.

[2] Each House may determine the Rules of its Proceedings, punish its Members for disorderly Behavior, and, with the Concurrence of two thirds, expel a Member.

[3] Each House shall keep a Journal of its Proceedings, and from time to time publish the same, excepting such Parts as may in their Judgment require Secrecy; and the Yeas and Nays of the Members of either House on any question shall, at the Desire of one fifth of those Present, be entered on the Journal.

[4] Neither House, during the Session of Congress, shall, without the Consent of the other, adjourn for more than three days, nor to any other Place than that in which the two Houses shall be sitting.

SECTION 6. [1] The Senators and Representatives shall receive a Compensation for their Services, to be ascertained by Law, and paid out of the Treasury of the United States. They shall in all Cases, except Treason, Felony and Breach of the Peace, be privileged from Arrest during their Attendance at the Session of their respective Houses, and in going to and returning from the same; and for any Speech or Debate in either House, they shall not be questioned in any other Place.

[2] No Senator or Representative shall, during the Time for which he was elected, be appointed to any civil Office under the Authority of the United States, which shall have been created, or the Emoluments whereof shall have been increased during such time; and no Person holding any Office under the United States, shall be a Member of either House during his Continuance in Office.

SECTION 7. [1] All Bills for raising Revenue shall originate in the House of Representatives; but the Senate may propose or concur with Amendments as on other Bills.

[2] Every Bill which shall have passed the House of Representatives and the Senate, shall, before it become a Law, be presented to the President of the United States; If he approve he shall sign it, but if not he shall return it, with his Objections to the House in which it shall have originated, who shall enter the Objections at large on their Journal, and proceed to reconsider it. If after such Reconsideration two thirds of that House shall agree to pass the Bill, it shall be sent together with the Objections, to the other House, by which it shall likewise be reconsidered, and if approved by two thirds of that House, it shall become a Law. But in all such Cases the Votes of both Houses shall be determined by Yeas and Nays, and the Names of the Persons voting for and against the Bill shall be entered on the Journal of each House respectively. If any Bill shall not be returned by the President within ten Days (Sundays excepted) after it shall have been presented to him, the Same shall be a Law, in like Manner as if he had signed it, unless the Congress by their Adjournment prevent its Return in which Case it shall not be a Law.

[3] Every Order, Resolution, or Vote, to Which the Concurrence of the Senate and House of Representatives may be necessary (except on a question of Adjournment) shall be presented to the President of the United States; and before the Same shall take Effect, shall be approved by him, or being disapproved by him, shall be repassed by two thirds of the Senate and House of Representatives, according to the Rules and Limitations prescribed in the Case of a Bill.

SECTION 8. [1] The Congress shall have Power To lay and collect Taxes, Duties, Imposts and Excises, to pay the Debts and provide for the common Defence and general Welfare of the United States; but all Duties, Imposts and Excises shall be uniform throughout the United States;

[2] To borrow money on the credit of the United States;

[3] To regulate Commerce with foreign Nations, and among the several States, and with the Indian Tribes;

[4] To establish an uniform Rule of Naturalization, and uniform Laws on the subject of Bankruptcies throughout the United States;

[5] To coin Money, regulate the Value thereof, and of foreign Coin, and fix the Standard of Weights and Measures;

[6] To provide for the Punishment of counterfeiting the Securities and current Coin of the United States;

[7] To Establish Post Offices and Post Roads;

[8] To promote the Progress of Science and useful Arts, by securing for limited Times to Authors and Inventors the exclusive Right to their respective Writings and Discoveries;

[9] To constitute Tribunals inferior to the Supreme Court;

[10] To define and punish Piracies and Felonies committed on the high Seas, and Offenses against the Law of Nations;

[11] To declare War, grant Letters of Marque and Reprisal, and make Rules concerning Captures on Land and Water;

[12] To raise and support Armies, but no Appropriation of Money to that Use shall be for a longer Term than two Years;

[13] To provide and maintain a Navy;

[14] To make Rules for the Government and Regulation of the land and naval Forces;

[15] To provide for calling forth the Militia to execute the Laws of the Union, suppress Insurrections and repel Invasions;

[16] To provide for organizing, arming, and disciplining, the Militia, and for governing such Part of them as may be employed in the Service of the United States, reserving to the States respectively, the Appointment of the Officers, and the Authority of training the Militia according to the discipline prescribed by Congress;

[17] To exercise exclusive Legislation in all Cases whatsoever, over such District (not exceeding ten Miles square) as may, by Cession of particular States, and the Acceptance of Congress, become the Seat of the Government of the United States, and to exercise like Authority over all Places purchased by the Consent of the Legislature of the State in which the Same shall be, for the Erection of Forts, Magazines, Arsenals, dock-Yards, and other needful Buildings;—And

[18] To make all Laws which shall be necessary and proper for carrying into Execution the foregoing Powers, and all other Powers vested by this Constitution in the Government of the United States, or in any Department or Officer thereof.

SECTION 9. [1] The Migration or Importation of Such Persons as any of the States now existing shall think proper to admit, shall not be prohibited by the Congress prior to the Year one thousand eight hundred and eight, but a Tax or duty may be imposed on such Importation, not exceeding ten dollars for each Person.

[2] The privilege of the Writ of Habeas Corpus shall not be suspended, unless when in Cases of Rebellion or Invasion the public Safety may require it.

[3] No Bill of Attainder or *ex post facto* Law shall be passed.

[4] No Capitation, or other direct, Tax shall be laid, unless in Proportion to the Census or Enumeration herein before directed to be taken.

See also the Sixteenth Amendment.

[5] No Tax or Duty shall be laid on Articles exported from any State.

[6] No Preference shall be given by any Regulation of Commerce or Revenue to the Ports of one State over those of another: nor shall Vessels bound to, or from, one State be obliged to enter, clear, or pay Duties in another.

[7] No money shall be drawn from the Treasury, but in Consequence of Appropriations made by Law; and a regular Statement and Account of the Receipts and Expenditures of all public Money shall be published from time to time.

[8] No Title of Nobility shall be granted by the United States: And no Person holding any Office of Profit or Trust under them, shall, without the Consent of the Congress, accept of any present, Emolument, Office, or Title, of any kind whatever, from any King, Prince, or foreign State.

SECTION 10. [1] No State shall enter into any Treaty, Alliance, or Confederation; grant Letters of Marque and Reprisal; coin Money; emit Bills of Credit; make any Thing but gold and silver Coin a Tender in Payment of Debts; pass any Bill of Attainder, *ex post facto* Law, or Law impairing the Obligation of Contracts, or grant any Title of Nobility.

[2] No State shall, without the Consent of the Congress, lay any Imposts or Duties on Imports or Exports, except what may be absolutely necessary for executing it's inspection Laws: and the net Produce of all Duties and Imposts, laid by any State on Imports or Exports, shall be for the Use of the Treasury of the United States; and all such Laws shall be subject to the Revision and controul of the Congress.

[3] No State shall, without the Consent of Congress, lay any Duty of Tonnage, keep Troops, or Ships of War in time of Peace, enter into any Agreement or Compact with another State, or with a foreign Power, or engage in War, unless actually invaded, or in such imminent Danger as will not admit of delay.

Article II

SECTION 1. [1] The executive Power shall be vested in a President of the United States of America. He shall hold his Office during the Term of four Years, and, together with the Vice President, chosen for the same Term, be elected, as follows:

[2] Each State shall appoint, in such Manner as the Legislature thereof may direct, a Number of Electors, equal to the whole Number of Senators and Representatives to which the State may be entitled in the Congress; but no Senator or Representative or Person holding an Office of Trust or Profit under the United States, shall be appointed an Elector.

[3] [The Electors shall meet in their respective States, and vote by Ballot for two Persons, of whom one at least shall not be an Inhabitant of the same State with themselves. And they shall make a List of all the Persons voted for, and of the Number of Votes for each; which List they shall sign and certify, and transmit sealed to the Seat of the Government of the United States, directed to the President of the Senate. The President of the Senate shall, in the Presence of the Senate and House of Representatives, open all the Certificates, and the Votes shall then be counted. The Person having the greatest Number of Votes shall be the President, if such Number be a Majority of the whole Number of Electors appointed; and if there be more than one who have such Majority, and have an equal Number of Votes, then the House of Representatives shall immediately chuse by Ballot one of them for President; and if no Person have a Majority, then from the five highest on the List the said House shall in like Manner chuse the President. But in chusing the President, the Votes shall be taken by States the Representation from each State having one Vote; A quorum for this Purpose shall consist of a Member or Members from two thirds of the States, and a Majority of all the States shall be necessary to a Choice. In every Case, after the Choice of the President, the Person having the greatest Number of Votes of the Electors shall be the Vice President. But if there should remain two or more who have equal Votes, the Senate shall chuse from them by Ballot the Vice President.]

This paragraph, inclosed in brackets, was superseded by the Twelfth Amendment.

[4] The Congress may determine the Time of chusing the Electors, and the Day on which they shall give their Votes; which Day shall be the same throughout the United States.

[5] No person except a natural born Citizen, or a Citizen of the United States, at the time of the Adoption of this Constitution, shall be eligible to the Office of President; neither shall any Person be eligible to that Office who shall not have attained to the Age of thirty five Years, and been fourteen Years a Resident within the United States.

[6] In case of the removal of the President from Office, or of his Death, Resignation or Inability to discharge the Powers and Duties of the said Office, the Same shall devolve on the Vice President, and the Congress may by Law provide for the Case of Removal, Death, Resignation or Inability, both of the President and Vice President, declaring what Officer shall then act as President and such Officer shall act accordingly, until the Disability be removed, or a President shall be elected.

[7] The President shall, at stated Times, receive for his Services, a Compensation, which shall neither be increased nor diminished during the Period for which he shall have been elected, and he shall not receive within that Period any other Emolument from the United States, or any of them.

[8] Before he enter on the Execution of his Office, he shall take the following Oath or Affirmation: "I do solemnly swear (or affirm) that I will faithfully execute the Office of President of the United States, and will to the best of my Ability, preserve, protect and defend the Constitution of the United States."

SECTION 2. [1] The President shall be Commander in Chief of the Army and Navy of the United States, and of the militia of the several States, when called into the actual Service of the United States; he may require the Opinion, in writing, of the principal Officer in each of the Executive Departments, upon any Subject relating to the Duties of their respective Offices, and he shall have Power to grant Reprieves and Pardons for Offenses against the United States, except in Cases of Impeachment.

[2] He shall have Power, by and with the Advice and Consent of the Senate to make Treaties, provided two thirds of the Senators present concur; and he shall nominate, and by and with the Advice and Consent of the Senate, shall appoint Ambassadors, other public Ministers and Consuls, Judges of the supreme Court, and all other Officers of the United States, whose Appointments are not herein otherwise provided for, and which shall be established by Law; but the Congress may by Law vest the Appointment of such inferior Officers, as they think proper, in the President alone, in the Courts of Law, or in the Heads of Departments.

[3] The President shall have Power to fill up all Vacancies that may happen during the Recess of the Senate, by granting Commissions which shall expire at the End of their next Session.

SECTION 3. He shall from time to time give to the Congress Information of the State of the Union, and recommend to their Consideration such Measures as he shall judge necessary and expedient; he may, on extraordinary Occasions, convene both Houses, or either of them, and in Case of Disagreement between them, with Respect to the Time of Adjournment, he may adjourn them to such Time as he shall think proper; he shall take Care that the Laws be faithfully executed, and shall Commission all the Officers of the United States.

SECTION 4. The President, Vice President and all civil Officers of the United States, shall be removed from Office on Impeachment for, and Conviction of, Treason, Bribery, or other high Crimes and Misdemeanors.

Article III

SECTION 1. The judicial Power of the United States, shall be vested in one supreme Court, and in such inferior Courts as the Congress may from time to time ordain and establish. The Judges, both of the supreme and inferior Courts, shall hold their Offices during good Behaviour, and shall, at stated Times, receive for their Services a Compensation, which shall not be diminished during their Continuance in Office.

SECTION 2. [1] The judicial Power shall extend to all Cases, in Law and Equity, arising under this Constitution, the Laws of the United States, and Treaties made, or which shall be made, under their Authority;—to all Cases affecting Ambassadors, other public Ministers and Consuls;—to all Cases of admiralty and maritime Jurisdiction;—to Controversies to which the United States shall be a Party;—to Controversies between two or more States;—between a State and Citizens of another State;*—between Citizens of different States;—between Citizens of the same State claiming Lands under the Grants of different States, and between a State, or the Citizens thereof, and foreign States, Citizens or Subjects.

[2] In all Cases affecting Ambassadors, other public Ministers and Consuls, and those in which a State shall be a Party, the supreme Court shall have original Jurisdiction. In all the other Cases before mentioned, the supreme Court shall have appellate Jurisdiction, both as to Law and Fact, with such Exceptions, and under such Regulations as the Congress shall make.

[3] The Trial of all Crimes, except in Cases of Im-

*This clause has been affected by the Eleventh amendment.

peachment, shall be by Jury; and such Trial shall be held in the State where the said Crimes shall have been committed; but when not committed within any State, the Trial shall be at such Place or Places as the Congress may by Law have directed.

SECTION 3. [1] Treason against the United States, shall consist only in levying War against them, or, in adhering to their Enemies, giving them Aid and Comfort. No Person shall be convicted of Treason unless on the Testimony of two Witnesses to the same overt Act, or on Confession in open Court.

[2] The Congress shall have Power to declare the Punishment of Treason, but no Attainder of Treason shall work Corruption of Blood, or Forefeiture except during the Life of the Person attainted.

Article IV

SECTION 1. Full Faith and Credit shall be given in each State to the public Acts, Records, and judicial Proceedings of every other State. And the Congress may by general Laws prescribe the Manner in which such Acts, Records and Proceedings shall be proved, and the Effect thereof.

SECTION 2. [1] The Citizens of each State shall be entitled to all Privileges and Immunities of Citizens in the several States.

[2] A Person charged in any State with Treason, Felony, or other Crime, who shall flee from Justice, and be found in another State, shall on demand of the executive Authority of the State from which he fled, be delivered up, to be removed to the State having Jurisdiction of the Crime.

[3] [No Person held to Service or Labour in one State, under the Laws thereof, escaping into another, shall, in Consequence of any Law or Regulation therein, be discharged from such Service or Labour, but shall be delivered up on Claim of the Party to whom such Service or Labour may be due.]

This paragraph has been superseded by the Thirteenth Amendment.

SECTION 3. [1] New States may be admitted by the Congress into this Union; but no new State shall be formed or erected within the Jurisdiction of any other State; nor any State be formed by the Junction of two or more States, or Parts of States, without the Consent of the Legislatures of the States concerned as well as of the Congress.

[2] The Congress shall have Power to dispose of and make all needful Rules and Regulations respecting the Territory or other Property belonging to the United States; and nothing in this Constitution shall be so construed as to Prejudice any Claims of the United States, or of any particular State.

SECTION 4. The United States shall guarantee to every State in this Union a Republican Form of Government, and shall protect each of them against Invasion; and on Application of the Legislature, or of the Executive (when the Legislature cannot be convened) against domestic Violence.

Article V

The Congress, whenever two thirds of both Houses shall deem it necessary, shall propose Amendments to this Constitution, or, on the Application of the Legislatures of two thirds of the several States, shall call a Convention for proposing Amendments, which, in either Case, shall be valid to all Intents and Purposes, as part of this Constitution, when ratified by the Legislatures of three fourths of the several States, or by Conventions in three fourths thereof, as the one or the other Mode of Ratification may be proposed by the Congress; Provided that no Amendment which may be made prior to the Year One thousand eight hundred and eight shall in any Manner affect the first and fourth Clauses in the Ninth Section of the first Article; and that no State, without its Consent, shall be deprived of its equal Suffrage in the Senate.

Article VI

[1] All Debts contracted and Engagements entered into, before the Adoption of this Constitution shall be as valid against the United States under this Constitution, as under the Confederation.

[2] This Constitution, and the Laws of the United States which shall be made in Pursuance thereof; and all Treaties made, or which shall be made, under the Authority of the United States, shall be the supreme Law of the Land; and the Judges in every State shall be bound thereby, any Thing in the Constitution or Laws of any State to the Contrary notwithstanding.

[3] The Senators and Representatives before mentioned, and the Members of the several State Legislatures, and all executive and judicial Officers, both of the United States and of the several States, shall be bound by Oath or Affirmation, to support this Constitution; but no religious Test shall ever be required as a Qualification to any Office or public Trust under the United States.

Article VII

The Ratification of the Conventions of nine States shall be sufficient for the Establishment of this Constitution between the States so ratifying the Same.

Done in Convention by the Unanimous Consent of the States present the Seventeenth Day of September in the Year of Our Lord one thousand seven hundred and Eighty seven and of the Independence of the United States of America the Twelfth. IN WITNESS whereof We have hereto subscribed our Names,

                         Go. Washington—Presidt.
                         and deputy from Virginia

New Hampshire

John Langdon   Nicholas Gilman

Massachusetts

Nathaniel Gorham   Rufus King

Connecticut

Wm. Saml. Johnson   Roger Sherman

New York

Alexander Hamilton

New Jersey

Wil: Livingston   Wm. Paterson
David Brearley   Jona: Dayton

Pennsylvania

B. Franklin   Thos. FitzSimons
Thomas Mifflin   Jared Ingersoll
Robt. Morris   James Wilson
Geo. Clymer   Gouv Morris

Delaware

Geo: Read   Richard Bassett
Gunning Bedford Jun   Jaco: Broom
John Dickinson

Maryland

James McHenry   Danl. Carroll
Dan of St Thos. Jenifer

Virginia

John Blair   James Madison, Jr.

North Carolina

Wm. Blount   Hu Williamson
Richd. Dobbs Spaight

South Carolina

J. Rutledge   Charles Pinckney
Charles Cotesworth Pinckney   Pierce Butler

Georgia

William Few   Abr Baldwin
                Attest   William Jackson
                                Secretary

Amendments to the Constitution of the United States

AMENDMENT I [1791]

Congress shall make no law respecting an establishment of religion, or prohibiting the free exercise thereof; or abridging the freedom of speech, or of the press; or the right of the people peaceably to assemble, and to petition the Government for a redress of grievances.

AMENDMENT II [1791]

A well regulated Militia being necessary to the security of a free State, the right of the people to keep and bear Arms, shall not be infringed.

AMENDMENT III [1791]

No Soldier shall, in time of peace be quartered in any house, without the consent of the Owner, nor in time of war, but in a manner to be prescribed by law.

AMENDMENT IV [1791]

The right of the people to be secure in their persons, houses, papers, and effects, against unreasonable searches and seizures, shall not be violated, and no Warrants shall issue, but upon probable cause, supported by Oath or affirmation, and particularly describing the place to be searched, and the persons or things to be seized.

AMENDMENT V [1791]

No person shall be held to answer for a capital, or otherwise infamous crime, unless on a presentment or indictment of a Grand Jury, except in cases arising in the land or naval forces, or in the Militia, when in actual service in time of War or public danger; nor shall any person be subject for the same offence to be twice put in jeopardy of life or limb, nor shall be compelled in any criminal case to be a witness against himself, nor be deprived of life, liberty, or property, without due process of law; nor shall private property be taken for public use, without just compensation.

AMENDMENT VI [1791]

In all criminal prosecutions, the accused shall enjoy the right to a speedy and public trial, by an impartial jury of the State and district wherein the crime shall have been committed; which district shall have been previously ascertained by law, and to be informed of the nature and cause of the accusation; to be confronted with the witnesses against him; to have compulsory process for obtaining Witnesses in his favor, and to have the Assistance of Counsel for his defence.

AMENDMENT VII [1791]

In Suits at common law, where the value in controversy shall exceed twenty dollars, the right of trial by jury shall be preserved, and no fact tried by jury shall be otherwise reexamined in any Court of the United States, than according to the rules of the common law.

AMENDMENT VIII [1791]

Excessive bail shall not be required, nor excessive fines imposed, nor cruel and unusual punishments inflicted.

AMENDMENT IX [1791]

The enumeration in the Constitution, of certain rights, shall not be construed to deny or disparage others retained by the people.

AMENDMENT X [1791]

The powers not delegated to the United States by the Constitution, nor prohibited by it to the States, are reserved to the States respectively, or to the people.

AMENDMENT XI [1798]

The Judicial power of the United States shall not be construed to extend to any suit in law or equity, commenced or prosecuted against one of the United States by Citizens of another State, or by Citizens or Subjects of any Foreign State.

AMENDMENT XII [1804]

The electors shall meet in their respective states and vote by ballot for President and Vice-President, one of whom, at least, shall not be an inhabitant of the same state with themselves; they shall name in their ballots the person voted for as President, and in distinct ballots the person voted for as Vice-President, and they shall make distinct lists of all persons voted for as President, and of all persons voted for as Vice-President, and of the number of votes for each, which lists they shall sign and certify, and transmit sealed to the seat of the government of the United States, directed to the President of the Senate;—The President of the Senate shall, in the presence of the Senate and House of Representatives, open all the certificates and the votes shall then be counted;—The person having the greatest number of votes for President, shall be the President, if such number be a majority of the whole number of Electors appointed; and if no person have such majority, then from the persons having the highest numbers not exceeding three on the list of those voted for as President, the House of Representatives shall choose immediately, by ballot, the President. But in choosing the President, the votes shall be taken by states, the representation from each state having one vote; a quorum for this purpose shall consist of a member or members from two-thirds of the states, and a majority of all the states shall be necessary to a choice. [And if the House of Representatives shall not choose a President whenever the right of choice shall devolve upon them before the fourth day of March next following, then the Vice-President shall act as President, as in the case of the death or other constitutional disability of the President.] The person having the greatest number of votes as Vice-President, shall be the Vice-President, if such number be a majority of the whole number of electors appointed, and if no person have a majority, then from the two highest numbers on the list, the Senate shall choose the Vice-President; a quorum for the purpose shall consist of two-thirds of the whole number of Senators, and a majority of the whole number shall be necessary to a choice. But no person constitutionally ineligible to the office of President shall be eligible to that of Vice-President of the United States.

The part included in brackets has been superseded by section 3 of the Twentieth Amendment.

AMENDMENT XIII [1865]

SECTION 1. Neither slavery nor involuntary servitude, except as a punishment for crime whereof the party shall have been duly convicted, shall exist within the United States, or any place subject to their jurisdiction.

SECTION 2. Congress shall have power to enforce this article by appropriate legislation.

AMENDMENT XIV [1868]

SECTION 1. All persons born or naturalized in the United States, and subject to the jurisdiction thereof, are citizens of the United States and of the State wherein they reside. No State shall make or enforce any law which shall abridge the privileges or immunities of citizens of the United States; nor shall any State deprive any person of life, liberty, or property, without due process of law; nor deny to any person within its jurisdiction the equal protection of the laws.

SECTION 2. Representatives shall be apportioned among the several States according to their respective numbers, counting the whole number of persons in each State, excluding Indians not taxed. But when the right to vote at any election for the choice of electors for President and Vice President of the United States, Representatives in Congress, the Executive and Judicial officers of a State, or the members of the Legislature thereof, is denied to any of the male inhabitants of such State, being twenty-one years of age, and citizens of the United States, or in any way abridged, except for participation in rebellion, or other crime, the basis of representation therein shall be reduced in the proportion which the number of such male citizens shall bear to the whole number of male citizens twenty-one years of age in such State.

SECTION 3. No person shall be a Senator or Representative in Congress, or elector of President and Vice President, or hold any office, civil or military, under the United States, or under any State, who, having previously taken an oath, as a member of Congress, or as an officer of the United States, or as a member of any State legislature, or as an executive or judicial officer of any State, to support the Constitution of the United States, shall have engaged in insurrection or rebellion against the same, or given aid or comfort to the enemies thereof. But Congress may by a vote of two-thirds of each House, remove such disability.

SECTION 4. The validity of the public debt of the United States, authorized by law, including debts incurred for payment of pensions and bounties for services in suppressing insurrection or rebellion, shall not be questioned. But neither the United States nor any State shall assume or pay any debt or obligation incurred in aid of insurrection or rebellion against the United States, or any claim for the loss or emancipation of any slave; but all such debts, obligations and claims shall be held illegal and void.

SECTION 5. The Congress shall have power to enforce, by appropriate legislation, the provisions of this article.

AMENDMENT XV [1870]

SECTION 1. The right of citizens of the United States to vote shall not be denied or abridged by the United States or by any State on account of race, color, or previous condition of servitude.

SECTION 2. The Congress shall have power to enforce this article by appropriate legislation.

AMENDMENT XVI [1913]

The Congress shall have power to lay and collect taxes on incomes, from whatever source derived, without apportionment among the several States, and without regard to any census or enumeration.

AMENDMENT XVII [1913]

The Senate of the United States shall be composed of two Senators from each State, elected by the people thereof, for six years; and each Senator shall have one vote. The electors in each State shall have the qualifications requisite for electors of the most numerous branch of the State legislatures.

When vacancies happen in the representation of any State in the Senate, the executive authority of such State shall issue writs of election to fill such vacancies: *Provided*, That the legislature of any State may empower the executive thereof to make temporary appointments until the people fill the vacancies by election as the legislature may direct.

This amendment shall not be so construed as to affect the election or term of any Senator chosen before it becomes valid as part of the Constitution.

AMENDMENT XVIII [1919]

SECTION 1. [After one year from the ratification of this Article the manufacture, sale, or transportation of intoxicating liquors within, the importation thereof into, or the exportation thereof from the United States and all territory subject to the jurisdiction thereof for beverage purposes is hereby prohibited].

SECTION 2. [The Congress and the several States shall have concurrent power to enforce this article by appropriate legislation].

SECTION 3. [This article shall be inoperative unless it shall have been ratified as an amendment to the Constitution by the legislatures of the several States, as provided in the Constitution, within seven years from the date of the submission hereof to the States by the Congress].

The eighteenth amendment was repealed by the twenty-first amendment to the Constitution of the United States.

AMENDMENT XIX [1920]

The right of citizens of the United States to vote shall not be denied or abridged by the United States or by any State on account of sex.

Congress shall have power to enforce this Article by appropriate legislation.

AMENDMENT XX [1933]

SECTION 1. The terms of the President and Vice President shall end at noon on the 20th day of January, and the terms of Senators and Representatives at noon on the 3d day of January, of the years in which such terms would have ended if this article had not been ratified; and the terms of their successors shall then begin.

SECTION 2. The Congress shall assemble at least once in every year, and such meeting shall begin at noon on the 3d day of January, unless they shall by law appoint a different day.

SECTION 3. If, at the time fixed for the beginning of the term of the President, the President-elect shall have died, the Vice President-elect shall become President. If the President shall not have been chosen before the time fixed for the beginning of his term, or if the President-elect shall have failed to qualify, then the Vice President-elect shall act as President until a President shall have qualified; and the Congress may by law provide for the case wherein neither a President-elect nor a Vice President-elect shall have qualified, declaring who shall then act as President, or the manner in which one who is to act shall be selected, and such a person shall act accordingly until a President or Vice President shall have qualified.

SECTION 4. The Congress may by law provide for the case of the death of any of the persons from whom the House of Representatives may choose a President whenever the right of choice shall have devolved upon them, and for the case of the death of any of the persons from whom the Senate may choose a Vice President whenever the right of choice shall have devolved upon them.

SECTION 5. Sections 1 and 2 shall take effect on the 15th day of October following the ratification of this article.

SECTION 6. This article shall be inoperative unless it shall have been ratified as an amendment to the Constitution by the legislatures of three-fourths of the several States within seven years from the date of its submission.

AMENDMENT XXI [1933]

SECTION 1. The eighteenth article of amendment to the Constitution of the United States is hereby repealed.

SECTION 2. The transportation or importation into any State, Territory, or possession of the United States for delivery or use therein of intoxicating liquors, in violation of the laws thereof, is hereby prohibited.

SECTION 3. This article shall be inoperative unless it shall have been ratified as an amendment to the Constitution by conventions in the several States, as provided in the Constitution, within seven years from the date of the submission hereof to the States by the Congress.

AMENDMENT XXII [1951]

SECTION 1. No person shall be elected to the office of the President more than twice, and no person who has held the office of President, or acted as President, for more than two years of a term to which some other person was elected President shall be elected to the office of President more than once. But this Article shall not apply to any person holding the office of President when this Article was proposed by the Congress, and shall not prevent any person who may be holding the office of President, or acting as President, during the term within which this Article becomes operative from holding the office of President or acting as President during the remainder of such term.

SECTION 2. This Article shall be inoperative unless it shall have been ratified as an amendment to the constitution by the legislatures of three-fourths of the several States within seven years from the date of its submission to the States by the Congress.

AMENDMENT XXIII [1961]

SECTION 1. The District constituting the seat of Government of the United States shall appoint in such a manner as the Congress may direct:

A number of electors of President and Vice President equal to the whole number of Senators and Representatives in Congress to which the District would be entitled if it were a State, but in no event more than the least populous state; they shall be in addition to those appointed by the States, but they shall be considered, for the purposes of the election of President and Vice

President, to be electors appointed by a State; and they shall meet in the District and perform such duties as provided by the twelfth article of amendment.

SECTION 2. The Congress shall have power to enforce this article by appropriate legislation.

AMENDMENT XXIV [1964]

SECTION 1. The right of citizens of the United States to vote in any primary or other election for President or Vice President, for electors for President or Vice President, or for Senator or Representative in Congress, shall not be denied or abridged by the United States or any State by reason of failure to pay any poll tax or other tax.

SECTION 2. The Congress shall have power to enforce this article by appropriate legislation.

AMENDMENT XXV [1967]

SECTION 1. In case of the removal of the President from office or of his death or resignation, the Vice President shall become President.

SECTION 2. Whenever there is a vacancy in the office of the Vice President, the President shall nominate a Vice President who shall take office upon confirmation by a majority vote of both Houses of Congress.

SECTION 3. Whenever the President transmits to the President pro tempore of the Senate and the Speaker of the House of Representatives his written declaration that he is unable to discharge the powers and duties of his office, and until he transmits to them a written declaration to the contrary, such powers and duties shall be discharged by the Vice President as Acting President.

SECTION 4. Whenever the Vice President and a majority of either the principal officers of the executive departments or of such other body as Congress may by law provide, transmit to the President pro tempore of the Senate and the Speaker of the House of Representatives their written declaration that the President is unable to discharge the powers and duties of his office, the Vice President shall immediately assume the powers and duties of the office as Acting President.

Thereafter, when the President transmits to the President pro tempore of the Senate and the Speaker of the House of Representatives his written declaration that no inability exists, he shall resume the powers and duties of his office unless the Vice President and a majority of either the principal officers of the executive department or of such other body as Congress may by law provide, transmit within four days to the President pro tempore of the Senate and the Speaker of the House of Representatives their written declaration that the President is unable to discharge the powers and duties of his office. Thereupon Congress shall decide the issue, assembling within forty-eight hours for that purpose if not in session. If the Congress, within twenty-one days after receipt of the latter written declaration, or, if Congress is not in session, within twenty-one days after Congress is required to assemble, determines by two-thirds vote of both Houses that the President is unable to discharge the powers and duties of his office, the Vice President shall continue to discharge the same as Acting President; otherwise, the President shall resume the powers and duties of his office.

AMENDMENT XXVI [1971]

SECTION 1. The right of citizens of the United States, who are eighteen years of age or older, to vote shall not be denied or abridged by the United States or by any State on account of age.

SECTION 2. The Congress shall have power to enforce this article by appropriate legislation.

Warranty Provisions of the Uniform Commercial Code and Unconscionability

Section 2-302. Unconscionable Contract or Clause.

(1) If the court as a matter of law finds the contract or any clause of the contract to have been unconscionable at the time it was made the court may refuse to enforce the contract, or it may enforce the remainder of the contract without the unconscionable clause, or it may so limit the application of any unconscionable clause as to avoid any unconscionable result.

(2) When it is claimed or appears to the court that the contract or any clause thereof may be unconscionable the parties shall be afforded a reasonable opportunity to present evidence as to its commercial setting, purpose and effect to aid the court in making the determination.

Section 2-313. Express Warranties by Affirmation, Promise, Description, Sample.

(1) Express warranties by the seller are created as follows:

(a) Any affirmation of fact or promise made by the seller to the buyer which relates to the goods and becomes part of the basis of the bargain creates an express warranty that the goods shall conform to the affirmation or promise.

(b) Any description of the goods which is made part of the basis of the bargain creates an express warranty that the goods shall conform to the description.

(c) Any sample or model which is made part of the basis of the bargain creates an express warranty that the whole of the goods shall conform to the sample or model.

(2) It is not necessary to the creation of an express warranty that the seller use formal words such as "warrant" or "guarantee" or that he have a specific intention to make a warranty, but an affirmation merely of the value of the goods or a statement purporting to be merely the seller's opinion or commendation of the goods does not create a warranty.

Section 2-314. Implied Warranty: Merchantability; Usage of Trade.

(1) Unless excluded or modified (Section 2-316), a warranty that the goods shall be merchantable is implied in a contract for their sale if the seller is a merchant with respect to goods of that kind. Under this section the serving for value of food or drink to be consumed either on the premises or elsewhere is a sale.

(2) Goods to be merchantable must be at least such as

(a) pass without objection in the trade under the contract description; and

(b) in the case of fungible goods, are of fair average quality within the description; and

(c) are fit for the ordinary purposes for which such goods are used; and

(d) run, within the variations permitted by the

agreement, of even kind, quality and quantity within each unit and among all units involved; and

(e) are adequately contained, packaged, and labeled as the agreement may require; and

(f) conform to the promises or affirmations of fact made on the container or label if any.

(3) Unless excluded or modified (Section 2-316) other implied warranties may arise from course of dealing or usage of trade.

Section 2-315. Implied Warranty: Fitness for Particular Purpose.

Where the seller at the time of contracting has reason to know any particular purpose for which the goods are required and that the buyer is relying on the seller's skill or judgment to select or furnish suitable goods, there is unless excluded or modified under the next section an implied warranty that the goods shall be fit for such purpose.

Secton 2-316. Exclusion or Modification of Warranties.

(1) Words or conduct relevant to the creation of an express warranty and words or conduct tending to negate or limit warranty shall be construed wherever reasonable as consistent with each other; but subject to the provisions of this Article on parol or extrinsic evidence (Section 2-202) negation or limitation is inoperative to the extent that such construction is unreasonable.

(2) Subject to subsection (3), to exclude or modify the implied warranty of merchantability or any part of it the language must mention merchantability and in case of a writing must be conspicuous, and to exclude or modify any implied warranty of fitness the exclusion must be by a writing and conspicuous. Language to exclude all implied warranties of fitness is sufficient if it states, for example, that "There are no warranties which extend beyond the description on the face hereof."

(3) Notwithstanding subsection (2)

(a) unless the circumstances indicate otherwise, all implied warranties are excluded by expressions like "as is," "with all faults" or other language which in common understanding calls the buyer's attention to the exclusion of warranties and makes plain that there is no implied warranty; and

(b) when the buyer before entering into the contract has examined the goods or the sample or model as fully as he desired or has refused to examine the goods there is no implied warranty with regard to defects which an examination ought in the circumstances to have revealed to him; and

(c) an implied warranty can also be excluded or modified by course of dealing or course of performance or usage of trade.

(4) Remedies for breach of warranty can be limited in accordance with the provisions of the Article on liquidation or limitation of damages and on contractual modification of remedy (Section 2-718 and 2-719).

Section 2-317. Cumulation and Conflict of Warranties Express or Implied.

Warranties whether express or implied shall be construed as consistent with each other and as cumulative, but if such construction is unreasonable the intention of the parties shall determine which warranty is dominant. In ascertaining that intention that following rules apply:

(a) Exact or technical specifications displace an inconsistent sample or model or general language of description.

(b) A sample from an existing bulk displaces inconsistent general language of description.

(c) Express warranties displace inconsistent implied warranties other than an implied warranty of fitness for a particular purpose.

Section 2-318. Third Party Beneficiaries of Warranties Express or Implied.

Alternative A

A seller's warranty whether express or implied extends to any natural person who is in the family or household of his buyer or who is a guest in his home if it is reasonable to expect that such person may use, consume or be affected by the goods and who is injured in person by breach of the warranty. A seller may not exclude or limit the operation of this section.

APPENDIX C

Restatement of Torts, Second (excerpts)

Section 402 A. Special Liability of Seller of Product for Physical Harm to User or Consumer.

(1) One who sells any product in a defective condition unreasonably dangerous to the consumer or to his property is subject to liability for physical harm thereby caused to the ultimate user or consumer, or to his property, if

(a) the seller is engaged in the business of selling such a product, and

(b) it is expected to and does reach the user or consumer without substantial change in the condition in which it is sold.

(2) The rule stated in Subsection (1) applies although

(a) the seller has exercised all possible care in the preparation and sale of his product, and

(b) the user or consumer has not bought the product from or entered into any contractual relation with the seller.

Section 402 B. Misrepresentation by Seller of Chattels to Consumer.

One engaged in the business of selling chattels who, by advertising, labels, or otherwise, makes to the public a misrepresentation of a material fact concerning the character or quality of a chattel sold by him is subject to liability for physical harm to a consumer of the chattel caused by justifiable reliance upon the misrepresentation, even though

(a) it is not made fraudulently or negligently, and

(b) the consumer has not bought the chattel from or entered into any contractual relations with the seller.

APPENDIX D

National Labor Relations Act (excerpts)

Rights of Employees

SECTION 7. Employees shall have the right to self-organization, to form, join or assist labor organizations, to bargain collectively through representatives of their own choosing, and to engage in other concerted activities for the purpose of collective bargaining or other mutual aid or protection, and shall also have the right to refrain from any or all of such activities except to the extent that such right may be affected by an agreement requiring membership in a labor organization as a condition of employment as authorized in section 8(a)(3).

Unfair Labor Practices

SECTION 8. (a) It shall be an unfair labor practice for an employer—

(1) to interfere with, restrain, or coerce employees in the exercise of the rights guaranteed in section 7;

(2) to dominate or interfere with the formation or administration of any labor organization or contribute financial or other support to it: Provided, That subject to rules and regulations made and published by the Board pursuant to section 6, an employer shall not be prohibited from permitting employees to confer with him during working hours without loss of time or pay;

(3) by discrimination in regard to hire or tenure of employment or any term or condition of employment to encourage or discourage membership in any labor organization: Provided, That nothing in this Act, or in any other statute of the United States, shall preclude an employer from making an agreement with a labor organization (not established, maintained, or assisted by any action defined in section 8(a) of his Act as an unfair labor practice) to require as a condition of employment membership therein on or after the thirtieth day following the beginning of such employment or the effective date of such agreement, whichever is the later (i) if such labor organization is the representative of the employees as provided in section 9(a), in the appropriate collective-bargaining unit covered by such agreement when made, and (ii) unless following an election held as provided in section 9(e) within one year preceding the effective date of such agreement, the Board shall have certified that at least a majority of the employees eligible to vote in such election have voted to rescind the authority of such labor organization to make such an agreement: Provided further, That no employer shall justify any discrimination against an employee for nonmembership in a labor organization (A) if he has reasonable grounds for believing that such membership was not available to the employee on the same terms and conditions generally applicable to other members, or (B) if he had reasonable grounds for believing that membership was denied or terminated for reasons other than the failure of the employee to tender the periodic dues and the initiation fees uniformly required as a condition of acquiring or retaining membership;

(4) to discharge or otherwise discriminate against an employee because he has filed charges or given testimony under this Act;

(5) to refuse to bargain collectively with the representatives of his employees, subject to the provisions of section 9(a).

(b) It shall be an unfair labor practice for a labor organization or its agents—

(1) to restrain or coerce (A) employees in the exercise of the rights guaranteed in section 7: Provided, That this paragraph shall not impair the right of a labor organization to prescribe its own rules with respect to the acquisition or retention of membership therein; or (B) an employer in the selection of his representatives for the purposes of collective bargaining or the adjustment of grievances;

(2) to cause or attempt to cause an employer to discriminate against an employee in violation of subsection (a)(3) or to discriminate against an employee with respect to whom membership in such organization has been denied or terminated on some ground other than his failure to tender the periodic dues and the initiation fees uniformly required as a condition of acquiring or retaining membership;

(3) to refuse to bargain collectively with an employer, provided it is the representative of his employees subject to the provisions of section 9(a);

(4) (i) to engage in, or to induce or encourage [the employees of any employer] an individual employed by any person engaged in commerce or in an industry affecting commerce to engage in, a strike or a refusal in the course of his employment to use, manufacture, process, transport, or otherwise handle or work on any goods, articles, materials, or commodities or to perform any services; or (ii) to threaten, coerce, or restrain any person engaged in commerce or in an industry affecting commerce, where in either case an object thereof is—

(A) forcing or requiring any employer or self-employed person to join any labor or employer organization or to enter into any agreement which is prohibited by section 8(e);

(B) forcing or requiring any person to cease using, selling, handling, transporting, or otherwise dealing in the products of any other producer, processor, or manufacturer, or to cease doing business with any other person, or forcing or requiring any other employer to recognize or bargain with a labor organization as the representative of his employees unless such labor organization has been certified as the representative of such employees under the provisions of section 9: Provided, That nothing contained in this clause (B) shall be construed to make unlawful, where not otherwise unlawful, any primary strike or primary picketing;

(C) forcing or requiring any employer to recognize or bargain with a particular labor organization as the representative of his employees if another labor organization has been certified as the representative of such employees under the provisions of section 9;

(D) forcing or requiring any employer to assign particular work to employees in a particular labor organization or in a particular trade, craft, or class rather than to employees in another labor organization or in another trade, craft, or class, unless such employer is failing to conform to an order or certification of the Board determining the bargaining representative for employees performing such work:

Provided, That nothing contained in this subsection (b) shall be construed to make unlawful a refusal by any person to enter upon the premises of any employer (other than his own employer), if the employees of such employer are engaged in a strike ratified or approved by a representative of such employees whom such employer is required to recognize under this Act: Provided further, That for the purposes of this paragraph (4) only, nothing contained in such paragraph shall be construed to prohibit publicity, other than picketing, for the purpose of truthfully advising the public, including consumers and members of a labor organization, that a product or products are produced by an employer with whom the labor organization has a primary dispute and are distributed by another employer, as long as such publicity does not have an effect of inducing any individual employed by any person other than the primary employer in the course of his employment to refuse to pick up, deliver, or transport any goods, or not to perform any services, at the establishment of the employer engaged in such distribution:

(5) to require of employees covered by an agreement authorized under subsection (a)(3) the payment, as a condition precedent to becoming a member of such organization, of a fee in an amount which the Board finds excessive or discriminatory under all the circumstances. In making such a finding, the Board shall consider, among other relevant factors, the practices and customs of labor organizations in the particular industry, and the wages currently paid to the employees affected;

(6) to cause or attempt to cause an employer to pay or deliver or agree to pay or deliver any money or other thing of value, in the nature of an exaction, for services which are not performed or not to be performed; and

(7) to picket or cause to be picketed, or threaten to picket or cause to be picketed, any employer where an

object thereof is forcing or requiring an employer to recognize or bargain with a labor organization as the representative of his employees, or forcing or requiring the employees of an employer to accept or select such labor organization as their collective bargaining representative, unless such labor organization is currently certified as the representative of such employees:

(A) where the employer has lawfully recognized in accordance with this Act any other labor organization and a question concerning representation may not appropriately be raised under section 9(c) of this Act;

(B) when within the preceding twelve months a valid election under section 9(c) of this Act has been conducted, or

(C) where such picketing has been conducted within a petition under section 9(c) being filed within a reasonable period of time not to exceed thirty days from the commencement of such picketing: Provided, That when such a petition has been filed the Board shall forthwith, without regard to the provisions of section 9(c)(1) or the absence of a showing of a substantial interest on the part of the labor organization, direct an election in such unit as the Board finds to be appropriate and shall certify the results thereof: Provided further, That nothing in this subparagraph (C) shall be construed to prohibit any picketing or other publicity for the purpose of truthfully advising the public (including consumers) that an employer does not employ members of, or have a contract with, a labor organization, unless an effect of such picketing is to induce any individual employed by any other person in the course of his employment, not to pick up, deliver or transport any goods or not to perform any services.

Nothing in this paragraph (7) shall be construed to permit any act which would otherwise be an unfair labor practice under this section 8(b).

(c) the expressing of any views, argument, or opinion, or the dissemination thereof, whether in written, printed, graphic, or visual form, shall not constitute or be evidence of an unfair labor practice under any of the provisions of this Act, if such expression contains no threat of reprisal or force or promise of benefit.

(d) For the purposes of this section, to bargain collectively is the performance of the mutual obligation of the employer and the representative of the employees to meet at reasonable times and confer in good faith with respect to wages, hours, and other terms and conditions of employment, or the negotiation of an agreement, or any question arising thereunder, and the execution of a written contract incorporating any agreement reached if requested by either party, but such obligation does not compel either party to agree to a proposal or require the making of a concession: Provided, That where there is in effect a collective-bargaining contract covering employees in an industry affecting commerce, the duty to bargain collectively shall also mean that no party to such contract shall terminate or modify such contract, unless the party desiring such termination or modification—

(1) serves a written notice upon the other party to the contract of the proposed termination or modification sixty days prior to the expiration date thereof, or in the event such contract contains no expiration date, sixty days prior to the time it is proposed to make such termination or modification;

(2) offers to meet and confer with the other party for the purpose of negotiating a new contract containing the proposed modifications;

(3) notifies the Federal Mediation and Conciliation Service within thirty days after such notice of the existence of a dispute, and simultaneously therewith notifies any State or Territorial agency established to mediate and conciliate disputes within the States or Territory where the dispute occurred, provided no agreement has been reached by that time; and

(4) continues in full force and effect, without resorting to strike or lock-out, all the terms and conditions of the existing contract for a period of sixty days after such notice is given or until the expiration date of such contract, whichever occurs later:

The duties imposed upon employers, employees, and labor organizations by paragraphs (2), (3), and (4) shall become inapplicable upon an intervening certification of the Board, under which the labor organization or individual, which is a party to the contract, has been superseded as or ceased to be the representative of the employees subject to the provisions of section 9(a), and the duties so imposed shall not be construed as requiring either party to discuss or agree to any modification of the terms and conditions contained in a contract for a fixed period, if such modification is to become effective before such terms and conditions can be reopened under the provisions of the contract. Any employee who engages in a strike within any notice periods specified in this subsection, or who engages in any strike within the appropriate period specified in subsection (g) of this section, shall lose his status as an employee of the employer engaged in the particular labor dispute, for the purposes of section 8, 9, and 10 of this Act, but such loss of status for such employee shall terminate if and when he is reemployed by such employer. Whenever the collective bargaining involves employees of a health care institution, the provisions of this section 8(d) shall be modified as follows:

(A) The notice of section 8(d)(1) shall be ninety days; the notice of section 8(d)(3) shall be sixty days; and the contract period of section 8(d)(4) shall be ninety days.

(B) Where the bargaining is for an initial agreement following certification or recognition, at least thirty days' notice of the existence of a dispute shall be given by the labor organization to the agencies set forth in section 8(d)(3).

(C) After notice is given to the Federal Mediation and Conciliation Service under either clause (A) or (B) of this sentence, the Service shall promptly communicate with the parties and use its best efforts, by mediation and conciliation, to bring them to agreement. The parties shall participate fully and promptly in such meetings as may be undertaken by the Service for the purpose of aiding in a settlement of the dispute.

(e) It shall be an unfair labor practice for any labor organization and any employer to enter into any contract or agreement, express or implied, whereby such employer ceases or refrains or agrees to cease or refrain from handling, using, selling, transporting, or otherwise dealing in any of the products of any other employer, or to cease doing business with any other person, and any contract or agreement entered into heretofore or hereafter containing such an agreement shall be to such extent unenforceable and void: Provided, That nothing in this subsection (e) shall apply to an agreement between a labor organization and an employer in the construction industry relating to the contracting or subcontracting of work to be done at the site of the construction, alteration, painting, or repair of a building, structure, or other work: Provided further, That for the purposes of this subsection (e) and section 8(b)(4)(B) the terms "any employer," "any person engaged in commerce or any industry affecting other producer, processor, or manufacturer," "any other employer," or "any other person" shall not include persons in the relation of a jobber, manufacturer, contractor, or subcontractor working on the goods or premises of the jobber or manufacturer or performing parts of an integrated process of production in the apparel and clothing industry: Provided further, That nothing in this Act shall prohibit the enforcement of any agreement which is within the foregoing exception.

(f) It shall not be an unfair labor practice under subsections (a) and (b) of this section for an employer engaged primarily in the building and construction industry to make an agreement covering employees engaged (or who, upon their employment, will be engaged) in the building and construction industry with a labor organization of which building and construction employees are members (not established, maintained, or assisted by any action defined in section 8(a) of this Act as an unfair labor practice) because (1) the majority status of such labor organizations has not been established under the provisions of section 9 of this Act prior to the making of such agreement, or (2) such agreement requires as a condition of employment, membership in such labor organization after the seventh day following the beginning of such employment or the effective date of the agreement, whichever is later, or (3) such agreement requires the employer to notify such labor organization of opportunities for employment with such employer, or gives such labor organization an opportunity to refer qualified applicants for such employment, or (4) such agreement specifies minimum training or experience qualifications for employment or provides for priority in opportunities for employment based upon length of service with such employer, in the industry or in the particular geographical area: Provided, That nothing in this subsection shall set aside the final proviso to section 8(a)(3) of this Act: Provided further, That any agreement which would be invalid, but for clause (1) of this subsection shall not be a bar to a petition filed pursuant to section 9(c) or 9(e).

(g) A labor organization before engaging in any strike, picketing, or other concerted refusal to work at any health care institution shall, not less than ten days prior to such action, notify the institution in writing and the Federal Mediation and Conciliation Service of that intention, except that in the case of bargaining for an initial agreement following certification or recognition the notice required by this subsection shall not be given until the expiration of the period specified in clause (b) of the last sentence of section 8(d) of this Act. The notice shall state the date and time that such action will commence. The notice, once given, may be extended by the written agreement of both parties.

Representatives and Elections

SECTION 9. (a) Representatives designated or selected for the purposes of collective bargaining by the majority of the employees in a unit appropriate for such purposes, shall be the exclusive representatives of all the employees in such unit for the purposes of collective bargaining in respect to rates of pay, wages, hours of employment, or other conditions of employment: Provided, That any individual employee or a group of employees shall have the right at any time to present grievances to their employer and to have such grievances adjusted, without the intervention of the bargaining representative, as long as the adjustment is not inconsistent with the terms of a collective-bargaining contract or agreement then in effect: Provided further, That the bargaining representative has been given opportunity to be present at such adjustment.

(b) The Board shall decide in each case whether, in order to assure to employees the fullest freedom in exercising the rights guaranteed by this Act, the unit appropriate for the purposes of collective bargaining shall be the employer unit, craft unit, plant unit, or subdivision thereof: Provided, That the Board shall not (1) decide that any unit is appropriate for such purposes if such unit included both professional employees and employees who are not professional employees unless a majority of such professional employees vote for inclusion in such unit; or (2) decide that any craft unit is inappropriate for such purposes on the ground that a different unit has been established by a prior Board determination, unless a majority of the employees in the proposed craft unit vote against separate representation or (3) decide that any unit is appropriate for such purposes if it includes, together with other employees, any individual employed as a guard to enforce against employees and other persons rules to protect property of the employer or to protect the safety of persons on the employer's premises; but no later organization shall be certified as the representative of employees in a bargaining unit of guards if such organization admits to membership, or is affiliated directly or indirectly with an organization which admits to membership, employees other than guards.

(c)(1) Whenever a petition shall have been filed, in accordance with such regulations as may be prescribed by the Board—

(A) by an employee or group of employees or an individual or labor organization acting in their behalf alleging that a substantial number of employees (i) wish to be represented for collective bargaining and that their employer declines to recognize their representative as the representative defined in section 9(a), or (ii) assert that the individual or labor organization, which has been certified or is being currently recognized by their employer as the bargaining representative, is no longer a representative as defined in section 9(a); or

(B) by an employer, alleging that one or more individuals or labor organizations have presented to him a claim to be recognized as the representative defined in section 9(a);

the Board shall investigate such petition and if it has reasonable cause to believe that a question of representation affecting commerce exists shall provide for an appropriate hearing upon due notice. Such hearing may be conducted by an officer or employee of the regional office, who shall not make any recommendations with respect thereto. If the Board finds upon the record of such hearing that such a question of representation exists, it shall direct an election by secret ballot and shall certify the results thereof.

(2) In determining whether or not a question of representation affecting commerce exists, the same regulations and rules of decision shall apply irrespective of the identity of the persons filing the petition or the kind of relief sought and in no case shall the Board deny a labor organization a place on the ballot by reason of an order with respect to such labor organization or its predecessor not issued in conformity with section 10(c).

(3) No election shall be directed in any bargaining unit or any subdivision within which, in the preceding twelve-month period, a valid election shall have been held. Employees engaged in an economic strike who are not entitled to reinstatement shall be eligible to vote under such regulations as the Board shall find are consistent with the purposes and provisions of this Act in any election conducted within twelve months after the commencement of the strike. In any election where none of the choices on the ballot receives a majority, a run-off shall be conducted, the ballot providing for a selection between the two choices receiving the largest and second largest number of valid votes cast in the election.

(4) Nothing in this section shall be construed to prohibit the waiving of hearings by stipulation for the purpose of a consent election in conformity with regulations and rules of decision of the Board.

(5) In determining whether a unit is appropriate for the purposes specified in subsection (b) the extent to which the employees have organized shall not be controlling.

(d) Whenever an order of the Board made pursuant to section 10(c) is based in whole or in part upon facts certified following an investigation pursuant to subsection (c) of this section and there is a petition for the enforcement or review of such order, such certification and the record of such investigation shall be included in the transcript of the entire record required to be filed under section 10(e) or 10(f), and thereupon the decree of the court enforcing, modifying, or setting aside in whole or in part the order of the Board shall be made and entered upon the pleadings, testimony, and proceedings set forth in such transcript.

(e)(1) Upon the filing with the Board, by 30 per centum or more of the employees in a bargaining unit covered by an agreement between their employer and a labor organization made pursuant to section 8(a)(3), of a petition alleging they desire that such authority be rescinded, the Board shall take a secret ballot of the employees in such unit, and shall certify the results thereof to such labor organization and to the employer.

(2) No election shall be directed in any bargaining unit or any subdivision within which, in the preceding twelve-month period, a valid election shall have been held.

APPENDIX E

The Sherman Act (excerpts)

1. Every contract, combination in the form of trust or otherwise, or conspiracy, in restraint of trade or commerce among the several States, or with foreign nations, is declared to be illegal. Every person who shall make any contract or engage in any combination or conspiracy declared by section 1 to 7 of this title to be illegal shall be deemed guilty of a felony, and, on conviction thereof, shall be punished by fine not exceeding one million dollars if a corporation, or if any other person, one hundred thousand dollars, or by imprisonment not exceeding three years, or both said punishments, in the discretion of the court.

2. Every person who shall monopolize, or attempt to monopolize, or combine or conspire with any other person or persons, to monopolize any part of the trade or commerce among the several States, or with foreign nations, shall be deemed guilty of a felony, and, on conviction thereof, shall be punished by fine not exceeding one million dollars if a corporation, or if any other person, one hundred thousand dollars, or by imprisonment not exceeding three years, or by both said punishments, in the discretion of the court.

APPENDIX F

Clayton Act (excerpts)

An act to supplement existing laws against unlawful restraints and monopolies, and for other purposes.

SECTION 2. (a) That it shall be unlawful for any person engaged in commerce, in the course of such commerce, either directly or indirectly, to discriminate in price between different purchasers of commodities of like grade and quality, where either or any of the purchases involved in such discrimination are in commerce, where such commodities are sold for use, consumption, or resale within the United States or any Territory thereof or the District of Columbia or any insular possession or other place under the jurisdiction of the United States, and where the effect of such discrimination may be substantially to lessen competition or tend to create a monopoly in any line of commerce, or to injure, destroy, or prevent competition with any person who either grants or knowingly receives the benefit of such discrimination, or with customers of either of them; Provided, That nothing herein contained shall prevent differentials which make only due allowance for differences in the cost of manufacture, sale, or delivery resulting from the differing methods or quantities in which such commodities are to such purchasers sold or delivered: Provided, however, That the Federal Trade Commission may, after due investigation and hearing to all interested parties, fix and establish quantity limits, and revise the same as it finds necessary, as to particular commodities or classes of commodities, where it finds that available purchasers in greater quantities are so few as to render differentials on account thereof unjustly discriminatory or promotive of monopoly in any line of commerce; and the foregoing shall then not be construed to permit differentials based on differences in quantities greater than those so fixed and established: And provided further, That nothing herein contained shall prevent persons engaged in selling goods, wares, or merchandise in commerce from selecting their own customers in bona fide transactions and not in restraint of trade: And provided further, That nothing herein contained shall prevent price changes from time to time where in response to changing conditions affecting the market for or the marketability of the goods concerned, such as but not limited to actual or imminent deterioration of perishable goods, obsolescence of seasonal goods, distress sales under court process, or sales in good faith in discontinuance of business in the goods concerned.

(b) Upon proof being made, at any hearing on a complaint under this section, that there has been discrimination in price or services or facilities furnished, the burden of rebutting the prima facie case thus made by showing justification shall be upon the person charged with a violation of this section, and unless justification shall be affirmatively shown, the Commission is authorized to issue an order terminating the discrimination: Provided, however, That nothing herein contained shall prevent a seller rebutting the prima facie case thus made by showing that his lower price or the furnishing of services or facilities to any purchaser or purchasers was made in good faith to meet an equally low price of a competitor, or the services or facilities furnished by a competitor.

(c) That it shall be unlawful for any person engaged in commerce, in the course of such commerce, to pay or grant, or to receive or accept, anything of value as a commission, brokerage, or other compensation, or any allowance or discount in lieu hereof, except for services rendered in connection with the sale or purchase of goods, wares, or merchandise, either to the other party to such transaction or to an agent, representative, or other intermediary therein where such intermediary is acting in fact for or in behalf, or is subject to the direct or indirect control, of any party to such transaction other than the person by whom such compensation is so granted or paid.

(d) That it shall be unlawful for any person engaged in commerce to pay or contract for the payment of anything of value to or for the benefit of a customer of such person in the course of such commerce as compensation or consideration for any services or facilities furnished by or through such customer in connection with the processing, handling, sale, or offering for sale of any products or commodities manufactured, sold, or offered for sale by such person, unless such payment or consideration is available on proportionally equal terms to all other customers competing in the distribution of such products or commodities.

(e) That it shall be unlawful for any person to discriminate in favor of one purchaser against another purchaser or purchasers of a commodity bought for resale, with or without processing, by contracting to furnish or furnishing, or by contributing to the furnishing of, any services or facilities connected with the processing, handling, sale, or offering for sale of such commodity so purchased upon terms not accorded to all purchasers on proportionally equal terms.

(f) That it shall be unlawful for any person engaged in commerce, in the course of such commerce, knowingly to induce or receive a discrimination in price which is prohibited by this section.

SECTION 4. That any person who shall be injured in his business or property by reason of anything forbidden in the antitrust laws may sue therefor in any district court of the United States in the district in which the defendant resides or is found, or has an agent, without respect to the amount in controversy, and shall recover threefold the damages by him sustained, and the cost of suit, including a reasonable attorney's fee.

SECTION 4A. Whenever the United States is hereafter injured in its business or property by reason of anything forbidden in the antitrust laws it may sue therefor in the United States district court for the district in which the defendant resides or is found or has an agent, without respect to the amount in controversy, and shall recover actual damages by it sustained and the cost of suit.

SECTION 4B. Any action to enforce any cause of action under sections 4 or 4A shall be forever barred unless commenced within four years after the cause of action accrued. No cause of action barred under existing law on the effective date of this act shall be revived by this Act.

SECTION 4C. (a)(1) Any attorney general of a State may bring a civil action in the name of such State, as parens patriae on behalf of natural persons residing in such State, in any district court of the United States having jurisdiction of the defendant, to secure monetary relief as provided in this section for injury sustained by such natural persons to their property by reason of any violation of the Sherman Act. The court shall exclude from the amount of monetary relief awarded in such action any amount of monetary relief (A) which duplicates amounts which have been awarded for the same injury, or (B) which is properly allocable to (i) natural persons who have excluded their claims pursuant to subsection (b)(2) of this section, and (ii) any business entity.

(2) The court shall award the State as monetary relief threefold the total damage sustained as described in paragraph (1) of this subsection, and the cost of suit, including a reasonable attorney's fee.

(b)(1) In any action brought under subsection (a)(1) of this section, the State attorney general shall, at such times, in such manner, and with such content as the court may direct, cause notice thereof to be given by publication. If the court finds that notice given solely by publication would deny due process of law to any person or persons, the court may direct further notice to such person or persons according to the circumstances of the case.

(2) Any person on whose behalf an action is brought under subsection (a)(1) may elect to exclude from adjudication the portion of the State claim for monetary relief attributable to him by filing notice of such election with the court within such time as specified in the notice given pursuant to paragraph (1) of this subsection.

(3) The final judgment in an action under subsection (a)(1) shall be res judicata as to any claim under section 4 of this Act by any person on behalf of whom such action was brought and who fails to give such notice within the period specified in the notice given pursuant to paragraph (1) of this subsection.

(c) An action under subsection (a)(1) shall not be dismissed or compromised without the approval of the court, and notice of any proposed dismissal or compromise shall be given in such manner as the court directs.

(d) In any action under subsection (a)—

(1) the amount of the plaintiffs' attorney's fee, if any, shall be determined by the court; and

(2) the court may, in its discretion, award a reason-

able attorney's fee to a prevailing defendant upon a finding that the State attorney general has acted in bad faith, vexatiously, wantonly, or for oppressive reasons.

SECTION 6. That the labor of a human being is not a commodity or article of commerce. Nothing contained in the antitrust laws shall be construed to forbid the existence and operation of labor, agricultural, or horticultural organizations, instituted for the purposes of mutual help, and not having capital stock or conducted for profit, or to forbid or restrain individual members of such organizations from lawfully carrying out the legitimate objects thereof; nor shall such organizations, or the members thereof, be held or construed to be illegal combinations or conspiracies in restraint of trade, under the antitrust laws.

Glossary

Act of State Doctrine The doctrine that states that a court in one country will not sit in judgment on the acts of another government done within its own territory.

Actual Authority Authority for an agent to act that is granted either expressly or by implication by the principal.

Administrative Rule Making Administrative agency function to promulgate rules and regulations having the same force and effect as laws passed by a legislature.

Adversary System Theory that all the facts will be uncovered and the truth will come out if each side in a dispute presents its case in the best possible light.

Advisory Opinion Advice given by the courts to other branches of government concerning the law or the constitutionality of a proposed law.

Affirmative Action Plans Plans designed to ensure that all persons have an opportunity to work at a given company.

Agency Adjudication The function of an administrative agency to hear complaints, similar to a judicial function.

Agency Shop A contract with a union that does not require employees to join the union but does require them to pay union dues and initiation fees.

Agent A person who has the power to act on behalf of a principal.

Ally Doctrine The doctrine that permits unions to picket secondary employers doing the work of a primary employer.

Amicus Curiae Brief A brief filed in a case by someone who is not a party to that case. Amicus curiae means "a friend of the court."

Answer The response filed in court by the defendant to the plaintiff's petition. It states the defendant's response to each of the plaintiff's allegations.

Apparent Authority A doctrine covering agents and contracts with third parties by which authority exists in the absence of actual authority.

Appellant Party in a case who petitions a court of appeals to review the decision of a lower court.

Appellate Court A court that reviews the rulings of a trial court when the losing party in a trial case is dissatisfied with the verdict.

Appellee The party in a case against whom an appeal is filed.

Attorney-Client Privilege A privilege by which a client's confidential discussions with an attorney remain confidential.

Bench Trial A trial that is heard only by a judge and not by a jury.

Bill of Rights The first ten amendments to the Constitution.

Blind Trust A legal and business relationship in which one person holds in trust and invests the property of another. The person whose property is being held is precluded from knowing the assets in the trust or the investments made on his behalf.

Blue Sky Laws State laws attempting to regulate the securities industry.

Bona Fide Occupational Qualification (BFOQ) A job qualification that arises when religion, sex, or national origin is a requirement that is reasonably necessary to operate the business.

Boycott A concerted effort by someone or some group to encourage people to stop doing business with someone.

Brandeis Brief A brief making use of social science studies to supplement more traditional legal arguments. First used by Louis D. Brandeis.

Brief Written argument to the court concerning points the parties want the court to consider.

Burden of Proof The duty of a party to substantiate an allegation or issue to avoid dismissal of that issue early in the trial or in order to convince the trier of facts as to the truth of the claim and therefore win at trial.

Cause of Action A legal claim or complaint for which a party may seek redress in a court.

Caveat Emptor Literally, let the buyer beware. A doctrine in which the buyer of a product assumed any risks associated with the purchase or use of the product.

Certiorari A procedure of appellate practice whereby a higher court is given the opportunity to review a decision by a lower court.

Challenge for Cause The right of an attorney to ask that a person be disqualified from serving on a jury because of the person's bias or prejudice.

Choice of Forum Clause A contractual provision that specifies where a dispute arising under a contract will be tried.

Choice of Law Clause A contractual provision that specifies the law of the country or state that will be applied in the event of a contract dispute.

Civil Case Case in which the plaintiff institutes suit against the defendant for some civil wrong.

Civil Litigation All the trial work of our judicial system that does not involve the violation of a criminal statute.

Civil War Amendments The Thirteenth, Fourteenth, and Fifteenth Amendments to the Constitution.

Class Action A lawsuit or legal action brought on behalf of a large number of people with similar claims.

Closed-End Credit A credit plan in which a person borrows a fixed amount that is to be paid back over a designated period of time.

Closed Shop An agreement, now illegal, by an employer to hire only members of a union.

Closing Argument The point during a trial, after the conclusion of the presentation of evidence, when the attorneys present their final arguments concerning a case to the judge or jury.

Colgate Doctrine A doctrine by which a manufacturer may unilaterally announce that it will not deal with customers who fail to abide by the price it sets for a product.

Commerce Clause A provision in the U.S. Constitution created to protect interstate commerce from discriminatory state action.

Commercial Speech Doctrine The doctrine that states commercial speech is protected by the United States Constitution.

Common Law The body of law formulated and created by judicial decision.

Common Law Copyright The property right in a written item as recognized by common law.

Common Situs A location where employees from several employers work at the same place.

Comparable Worth The concept that employers should pay workers the same wage rate if their jobs are of comparable worth, or equal value, to the employer.

Comparative Negligence A tort law doctrine under which the plaintiff's negligence may be factored to reduce the verdict.

Concurring Opinion An opinion, written by an appellate court justice, that agrees with the appellate court's decision but disagrees with the reasoning of the court.

Conglomerate Merger A business combination or merger in which there are no economic relationships between the acquiring and the acquired firm.

Consumer A person who buys or borrows for personal, family, or household use.

Contract An agreement, obligation, or legal tie whereby a party binds himself or herself, expressly or impliedly, to pay a sum of money or to perform or omit to do a certain act or thing.

Contract of Adhesion A contract heavily weighted to favor the party that possesses significantly more bargaining power.

Corporation A business organizational form that is considered to be a legal being. It may have perpetual life, and it insulates its owners (shareholders) from personal liability.

Counterclaim A claim presented by a defendant against the plaintiff. Answers often contain counterclaims against the plaintiff.

Countervailing Duties Special duties used to offset a foreign subsidy.

Criminal Case Case in which a prosecutor representing the state or federal government brings suit against the defendant for an alleged violation of law.

Criminal Law Branch or division of law that defines crimes, treats their nature, and provides for their punishment.

Cross Examination The point when an attorney for the opposing party asks questions of a witness who is testifying.

Custom A nation's present habits and an important aspect of its system of laws.

Debt A financial obligation owed by one person or business to another.

Debt Collector A person or business that tries to collect from persons or businesses who fail to pay a debt.

Defendant The party in a case against whom criminal charges have been filed (in criminal law) or against whom a legal claim has been filed (in a civil suit).

Deposition The process of questioning under oath, prior to trial, the witnesses and parties to a lawsuit.

Dicta Portions of a judge's opinion that are not the ruling in the case.

Direct Examination The point when an attorney calls a witness to testify and asks the witness questions.

Discovery A process before a trial begins through which

opposing counsel can learn the case to be presented by the other side.

Dissenting Opinion An opinion, written by an appellate court justice, that disagrees with the outcome of the case being decided.

Diversity of Citizenship A situation when all the plaintiffs are from states other than the state of residence of any of the defendants.

Documentary Credit An instrument in which a bank agrees to pay another party if certain conditions in the instrument have been complied with by the presenting party.

Due Diligence Defense A doctrine arising under the 1933 Act in which those liable (other than the issuer) for material omissions or misstatements in the registration statement can be exonerated.

Due Process A constitutional principle which requires that government actions not be arbitrary or capricious. Its concern is with establishing fundamental procedural fairness in our system of government.

Dumping Selling products or services in a foreign market at less than their fair value.

Economic Strike A strike solely to force an employer to grant the employees better wages or working conditions.

Ejusdem Generis Doctrine A method of interpretation in which a general phrase is inserted after a series of specific words in a statute. The general phrase shall be interpreted to include words of the same kind as those used in the preceding series.

Eminent domain The right of the government to take property from a private owner for public use. Just compensation must be paid to those private owners.

Enabling Act A congressional statute that calls into existence a federal administrative agency.

Environment Impact Statement An analysis of the effect of major federal activity on the environment as required by the National Environmental Policy Act.

Equal Employment Opportunity Commission (EEOC) Federal administrative agency charged with the enforcement of Title VII of the Civil Rights Act of 1964.

Equal Protection Clause The clause in the United States Constitution that requires equal treatment of people.

Escape Clause A provision in GATT that permits countries to raise tariffs if there is a serious threat to domestic industry as a consequence of earlier trade reductions.

Executive Order An order issued by the president of the United States or governor of a state.

Executive Privilege Doctrine under which the president is able to keep certain communications from being disclosed in court.

Ex Parte An application by one party to a case made to a judge without first giving notice of the application to the other party.

Expropriation The seizure of foreign owned property by a government.

Featherbedding A union requirement, now illegal, that an employer pay for work not performed.

Federal Mediation and Conciliation Service An agency created by the Taft-Hartley Act to assist parties to labor disputes in industries affecting commerce to settle such disputes through conciliation and mediation.

Federal Register The official public notice organ of the federal administrative agencies.

Felony Generic term to distinguish certain crimes such as murder, robbery, and larceny from minor offenses known as misdemeanors. The distinction lies in the extent of punishment provided.

Fiduciary Duty The duty of a person who is vested with power over another's property to act with good faith, diligence, and loyalty with regard to that property.

Fixture Personal property that is so attached to or used with real property that it is considered to be a part of real property.

Formal Settlement An agreement to resolve a case entered into after a complaint is filed against a party.

Fraud A deliberate misrepresentation or nondisclosure of a material fact made with the intent that the other party will rely upon it, and in fact the party to whom the statement is made does rely upon it to his or her detriment.

Full Warranty The Magnuson-Moss Act requires certain consumer products to be labeled as having either a full or limited warranty. Products with a full warranty must meet certain requirements specified in the act.

GATT General Agreement on Tariffs and Trade. A trade agreement between many of the world's countries.

General Verdict A decision for one of the parties to a case without any special findings of fact.

Grand Jury A proceeding to determine whether there exists probable cause to initiate a criminal proceeding.

History A nation's past and an important aspect of its system of law.

Horizontal Merger The acquisition of one company by another company producing the same product or similar product and selling it in the same geographic market.

Hot Cargo A clause, now illegal, stating that workers are not required to handle nonunion material.

Hung Jury When a jury is unable to arrive at a verdict.

Illusory Promise A promise in which the obligation to

perform is entirely optional on the part of one of the parties.

Implied Agency Rule In contract law, if the offer does not state that the acceptance will not be effective until it is received, the moment an acceptance is sent by an authorized means a contract is effective.

Indictment A finding by a grand jury that reasonable grounds exist to believe that a crime has been committed. It is not a final determination or conviction.

Informal Settlement An agreement to resolve a case entered into before a complaint has been filed against a party.

Informational Picketing Picketing designed to advise the public that an employer does not have a union contract with its employees.

Injunction An order by a court that prohibits or restrains a party from doing a particular act.

Innocent Misrepresentation Unintended misrepresentation of a product that causes injury to a person.

Insider Trading Trading in securities by someone who has information on those securities not available to the general investing public and who has a duty not to use the information for personal benefit. Under the 1934 Act, certain people who buy or sell securities having secret material information are liable both civilly and criminally.

Intentional Tort A tort in which the aim of a certain act is to cause injury.

Interrogatories Written questions submitted to a person concerning a case that must be answered under oath.

Investigative Consumer Report A report gathered by a company about a person's credit history. The Fair Credit Reporting Act calls this an investigative consumer report.

Investment Contracts Type of security that includes a large number of unusual schemes.

Judgment on the Pleadings A motion at the close of the pleading stage made by any party to a suit which alleges the other party is not entitled to prevail at trial.

Judicial Immunity The inability of a dissatisfied litigant to sue the judge.

Judicial Review The power of a court to review a statute and declare it void if it violates various constitutional guarantees.

Jurisdiction The power or authority of a court to hear a particular legal dispute.

Jurisdictional Dispute A dispute between unions as to which union is entitled to perform certain work.

Justiciable A dispute that may properly be decided by a court.

Legal Lawful.

Legislative History A body of documentation created at the time a statute was drafted. A judge will consult the documents, consisting of reports, studies, speeches, etc., to determine the legislature's purpose in enacting the statute.

Limited Liability The characteristic of a corporation by which no individual member of the corporation is liable for claims made against it.

Limited Partnership Business organization with characteristics of both a corporation and a partnership; often used for a tax shelter.

Limited Warranty The Magnuson-Moss Act requires certain consumer products to be labeled as having either a full or limited warranty. Limited warranties are those that do not comply with the act's requirement for a full warranty.

Lockout An employer's refusal to allow employees to work.

Long-Arm Statutes Statutes that permit a plaintiff to obtain service of a summons and petition beyond the physical borders of a state.

Mediation A proceeding used to try to resolve disputes. The mediator tries to help the parties to a dispute work out their differences.

Minitrial An informal procedure used by parties in which a simplified version of the case is presented to a neutral party for a decision. The decision in the minitrial is not binding on the parties.

Misdemeanor Misconduct or offense inferior to a felony.

Missouri Plan A method of appointing judges whereby a panel recommends suitable candidates for the judiciary and voters are periodically questioned in the voting booth whether to retain the judge or not.

Mitigation of Damages The obligation of the injured party in a breach of contract to keep losses or damages as small as possible.

Monopoly The power to fix prices or exclude competition, coupled with policies designed to use or preserve that power.

Motion A request to the court for an order or rule in favor of the party making the motion.

Motion for a Directed Verdict A motion by which the moving party states that the other side has failed to prove all the facts necessary to establish a case.

Motion for a Judgment Notwithstanding the Verdict Motion in which, at the conclusion of a trial, after the verdict is announced, the defeated party asks the judge to set the verdict aside because it was not supported by the evidence or the law.

Motion for Summary Judgment A motion which states that there is no genuine issue of material fact remaining to be decided in the case, therefore the judge should grant the motion and decide who should prevail in the case.

Motion to Dismiss A motion made by the defendant which alleges that even if everything in the plaintiff's petition is assumed to be true, the plaintiff still is not entitled to a remedy, and therefore the plaintiff's petition should be dismissed.

Natural Law An overriding sense of justice or fairness that is fundamental to the law.

Negligence A lapse in an acceptable pattern of conduct that creates an unreasonable risk of injury.

NEPA The National Environmental Policy Act of 1969, the purposes of which are to encourage harmony between man and the environment and to eliminate environmental damage.

NLRB (The National Labor Relations Board) A national public agency created by statute to enforce the provisions of the National Labor Relations Act—not a tribunal for the enforcement of private rights through administrative remedies. An agency of the United States, an entity apart from its members, having legal capacity to sue in the federal courts to carry out its statutory functions.

Nolo Contendere An admission of every essential element of the offense stated in the charge. It is tantamount to an admission of guilt for the purpose of the case, but it is only a confession and does not dispose of the case or constitute a conviction or determination of guilt.

Nuisance An act that annoys or disturbs the enjoyment of property by its owner.

Offer A manifestation by a person of a desire to enter into a contract.

Offeree The person to whom an offer is made.

Offeror The person who makes an offer.

Oligopoly An industry composed of several large firms, each possessing a major part of trade in a given market.

Open-End Credit A credit plan that permits a person to keep charging on an account until he reaches a certain amount. The account can be paid off in full or in installments.

Opening Statement The statement made by the attorney in a case prior to the actual presentation of evidence. It generally provides an overview of what evidence will be presented and what the attorneys have to prove.

Option Contract A special contract that provides that a certain offer will remain open to a certain offeree upon the offeree providing some consideration.

Organizational Picketing Picketing designed to convince employees to sign up with the union.

Parens Patriae Suit brought by the attorney general of a state on behalf of persons living in that state.

Parol Evidence Rule A rule of evidence that prevents the introduction of oral testimony in a court proceeding which adds to, alters, or varies the terms of a written agreement.

Per Se The rule that a court need not inquire into the reasonableness of a case before determining that it is a violation of the antitrust laws, if an anticompetitive business activity is blatant in its intent and pernicious in its effect.

Peremptory Challenge The right of an attorney to strike certain prospective jurors from the jury panel. This is exercised by the attorneys after the conclusion of the voir dire.

Petition A document filed with a court by the plaintiff asking the court to grant the plaintiff some type of relief. The petition states paragraph by paragraph the nature of the claims the plaintiff has against the defendant and the relief requested of the court.

Petit Jury A jury that hears evidence presented by witnesses at trial, and based upon instructions given to them by the judge, renders a decision in a case.

Piercing the Corporate Veil Doctrine in corporate law under which a court will ignore the limited liability protection of the corporate form and hold those members behind it personally liable.

Plain Meaning Doctrine A method of statutory interpretation in which the court looks solely at the ordinary and usual meaning of the words of the statute to determine what the statute says.

Plaintiff The party in a civil suit who commences the action.

Pleadings The documents filed by the respective parties to a lawsuit that state their contentions. The first pleading is the petition, filed by the plaintiff, to which the defendant is required to file an answer.

Pollution The human-caused diminished capacity of the environment to perform its function.

Precedent A previously decided case that serves as authority for a court's decision in a current dispute.

Preemption The doctrine that deprives a state of the power to pass legislation dealing with the same matters as covered in federal legislation.

Prescription Doctrine that confers a property right on a person who uses another's land without permission and without interruption for twenty years (usually).

Pretrial Conference A conference held by a judge prior to trial concerning an upcoming trial. The purpose is to try to narrow the issues of the case and to attempt to encourage a settlement of the case.

Preventive Law A lawyer's advice to a client on a variety of legal matters in order to minimize the possibility of future legal problems for the client.

Primary Employer The employer for whom employees who are engaged in collective activity work.

Primary Line Competitive Injury Price discrimination by which a national firm attempts to put a local competitive firm out of business by lowering its prices only in the region where the local firms sell its products.

Primary Pressure Direct pressure put on an employer by its own employees.

Principal In agency law, the employer or person for whom an agent acts.

Privity of Contract A direct relationship between the parties to a contract.

Probate Process in law by which a will is proven and its terms given effect.

Promise Voluntary commitment by a person to another person to perform in some manner or refrain from some action in the future.

Promissory Estoppel The doctrine that makes certain contracts binding although they are not supported by consideration.

Property A relationship between the holder of rights and all others recognized and enforced by government.

Prospectus A summary of the information contained in a registration statement. It is provided to all offerees of the initial issuance of the securities.

Proximate Cause A term of art in tort law that refers to a policy that limits to scope of a tortfeasor's liability. The act that is the dominant cause or is in a close relation to an injury is said to be the proximate cause of that injury.

Public Use The only reason that entitles government to exercise its right of eminent domain.

Punitive Damage Damage that is awarded by a court in order to punish a party that has violated the law.

Quota A limit on the importation of a certain type of good imposed by a country.

Ratification The acceptance by the principal of the benefits of a contract entered into by an agent in absence of an authority. The principal is thereafter bound by that contract.

Reasonable Person Used in tort law as a test for actionable conduct. A reasonable person acts with ordinary care and prudence.

Recognition Picketing Picketing used to convince the employer to recognize the union.

Recusal A situation in which a judge declines to hear a case because he fears that a personal bias may effect its outcome.

Registration Statement Under the 1933 Act, a company

issuing new nonexempt securities must file a full disclosure statement with the SEC. This statement is called a registration statement.

Res Ipsa Loquitur A doctrine in the law of torts which presumes that the defendant was the negligent cause of an accident. Rather than requiring the plaintiff to prove that the defendant was negligent, the doctrine shifts the burden to the defendant to prove that he or she was not negligent.

Restatement of Contracts An analysis of contract law based on existing judicial decisions.

Restatement (Second) of Torts A scholarly work that discusses the law of torts as it exists across the United States. It also includes suggestions for changes the scholars think ought to be adopted by the states with respect to the law of torts.

Restraint of Trade In antitrust law, business combinations or practices that seek to stiffle competition and obstruct the market from its natural operation.

Restrictive Covenant In a contract, an agreement by one of the parties to the contract not to engage in certain behavior in a designated area for a designated period of time at the conclusion of the contractual relationship.

Retail Price Maintenance Scheme in which a single manufacturer and a retail seller or distributor agree to set the price at which a commodity may be sold.

RICO The Racketeer Influenced Corrupt Organization Act.

Rights Powers of free action that a person has and that are recognized by law.

Rule Making A process by which administrative agencies promulgate regulations.

Rule of Reason Court decision stating that only unreasonable restraints of trade and unreasonable attempts to monopolize violate the Sherman Act.

Search Warrant Written order by a court that gives the police the right to search certain premises or property for items that may be used, if found, as evidence in a criminal trial.

Secondary Line Competitive Injury A price discrimination that causes injury to certain buyers.

Secondary Pressure A boycott of an employer other than the employer with whom the employees have a dispute.

Secondary Pressure Action Action taken against a customer or supplier of an employer in order to pressure the employer to settle a labor dispute in favor of the employees.

Securities Stocks, bonds, and other investment contracts.

Securities and Exchange Commission (SEC) Federal

commission responsible for administering federal securities laws.

Separate but Equal The constitutional doctrine put forth in *Plessy* v. *Ferguson* (1896) that the equal protection clause was not violated if segregated facilities were equivalent.

Separation of Powers The principle by which each of the three branches of government—executive, legislative, and judicial—has different functions so that no one of them becomes too powerful.

Sexual Harassment Unwelcome sexual advances, requests for sexual favors, and other verbal or physical conduct of a sexual nature.

Sovereign Immunity Doctrine The doctrine under which governments are immune from suit when engaging in governmental acts.

Special Verdict A verdict in a case where a jury makes specific findings concerning the facts presented at trial.

Stare Decisis A doctrine of judicial decision making that governs the application of precedent to a current dispute. The doctrine provides for stability in the legal system by having current disputes controlled by decisions in past cases.

Statute of Limitations A statute which specifies that a certain type of case must be filed within a certain designated period of time after the cause of action arises.

Strict Liability The standard of culpability to which a seller will be held for breach of an implied warranty that is imposed as a matter of public policy on a product he sells. Such liability is "strict liability" because it attaches even though the seller has exercised all possible care in the preparation and sale of his or her product.

Summary Judgment A decision by a court in a case without holding a trial. It occurs on motion of a party that since the facts of the case are not in dispute, the court should make a ruling based upon the law.

Summary Trial A trial in which a summary of the case is presented to a judge or jury. Decisions in such cases may or may not be binding on the parties depending upon the agreement between the parties.

Summons A document issued by a court which is served on the defendant, notifies him that suit has been instituted by the plaintiff, and requires the defendant to answer the plaintiff's petition in a certain designated period of time.

Surface Bargaining A situation in which the employer goes through the outward motions of bargaining but is really not willing to negotiate.

Technological Infeasibility The inability of industry to comply with environmental regulations because existing technology is inadequate.

Tort A body of law covering civil wrongs other than breaches of contract.

Trespass The unauthorized, intentional entry upon the land of another.

Trial Court The first step in resolving disputes in the judicial system. Evidence is given and a verdict is rendered.

True Bill A grand jury's endorsement of an indictment that it finds supported by the evidence presented to them.

Trust An obligation arising out of confidence reposed in a person, for the benefit of another, to apply property faithfully and according to such confidence.

Truth-in-Lending Act Act passed by Congress in 1969 in order to make meaningful comparisons between the rates charged by different lenders.

Ultra Vires Limitation of agency power by which no act outside the power granted may be performed. Such acts would be voidable.

Unconscionablity A lack of meaningful choice in a contractual relationship coupled with a contract term that is so one-sided as to be oppressive.

Unfair Labor Practice Strike A strike in response to an unfair labor practice committed by an employer.

Uniform Commercial Code A model code that deals with sale of goods, commercial paper, secured transactions, and other commercial activities.

Union Shop An agreement that employees must join a union within a certain period after they begin to work for an employer.

Unreasonably Dangerous More dangerous than would be contemplated by an ordinary consumer.

Vertical Merger A merger between or joining of two firms that have a buyer-seller relationship. That is, one produces a product that is then sold to the other.

Voir Dire The period in a trial when the attorneys question prospective jurors concerning their qualifications to sit as jurors in the case.

Workmen's Compensation State system of insurance whereby employees injured on the job would receive damages from a fund made up of employers' premiums.

Work Preservation Clause An agreement designed to preserve work for certain employees.

Zoning Local government ordinances regarding use of land.

Index

About the Authors

Douglas Whitman is a Professor at the School of Business Administration of the University of Kansas and a member of the Kansas and Missouri bars. He received his B.A. from Knox College, his M.B.A. from the University of Kansas, J.D. from the University of Missouri, and LL.M. from the University of Missouri at Kansas City. He has served twice as a staff editor for the *American Business Law Journal*. He is a past president of the Midwest Business Law Association. He has written articles on advertising law and products liability and has published in such journals as the *Indiana Law Review; St. John's Law Review; Southwestern Law Journal* (at Southern Methodist Law School); *The University of California Davis Law Review; The University of Pittsburgh Law Review; The Journal of Products Liability;* and *American Business Law Journal*. His articles have also been reprinted in *The Advertising Law Anthology, The Personal Injury Desk Book, The Corporate Counsel's Annual,* and by The American Trial Lawyer's Association. He has also written a number of articles for the Advertising Compliance Service. He is also a coauthor of *Modern Business Law, Law and Business,* and *Commercial Law*. Professor Whitman also is a consultant on business law matters.

John William Gergacz is a Professor at the School of Business Administration of the University of Kansas and a member of the Illinois and Indiana bars. He was appointed as School of Business Alumni Faculty Scholar at the University of Kansas from 1984–1986. Gergacz received his B.S. from the School of Business, Indiana University, Bloomington, Indiana, and his J.D. from the School of Law, Indiana University, Bloomington, Indiana. He is currently editor-in-chief of the *Corporate Information and Privacy Reporter* and served as staff editor for the *American Business Law Journal*. He has written numerous scholarly articles in such journals as *The Business Lawyer, Boston College Environmental Affairs Law Review, New Mexico Law Review, Wake Forest Law Review, Real Estate Law Journal,* and the *American Business Law Journal*. Professor Gergacz is an authority on attorney-corporate client privilege and has published a treatise on the topic, *Attorney-Corporate Client Privilege*.